Lascu

International Marketing

4e

Dana-Nicoleta Lascu

University of Richmond

▓ **Textbook Media Press**

- Replacing Oligarch Textbooks since 2004
- The Quality You Expect at Uniquely Affordable Prices
- Made in the USA by Independent Publishers

Supplements

For the Instructor:

Instructor Manual
Test Bank
PowerPoint Slides

Textbook Options

Online Book
Online Book + PDF Chapters
Online Book + Paperback
Online Book + i-Phone App

©2013 TEXTBOOK MEDIA PRESS

For more information, contact

Textbook Media Press
1808 Dayton Avenue
Saint Paul, MN 55104

Or you can visit our Internet site at

http://www.textbookmedia.com

or write

info@textbookmedia.com

For permission to use material from this text

or product, submit a request online at

info@textbookmedia.com

International Marketing, 4e

Dana-Nicoleta Lascu

ISBN: 1-930789-39-4

Textbook Media Press is a Minnesota-based educational publisher. We deliver textbooks and supplements with the quality instructors expect, while providing students
with unique media options at uniquely affordable prices.
All our publications are 100% made in the U.S.A.

Dedication

This book is dedicated to my parents, Lucia and Damian Lascu,
with deep appreciation for their courage to cross the Iron Curtain,
and to Ofra Haza and Umm Kulthoum,
the divas of music who inspired the world to unite through song.

—Dana-Nicoleta Lascu

Brief Table of Contents

Detailed Table of Contents

Preface

International Marketing, fourth edition, has been thoroughly revised to reflect current international issues and developments in international marketing. The revised edition has new case studies that offer insights into marketing in countries that have received little attention to date, such as Mongolia and Cuba, and fully revised cases that offer current company examples and overviews of industry developments. Each chapter has at least one case study. In addition to the International Marketing Illustration boxes addressing specific nuances of conducting business and marketing products internationally, this edition offers brief versions of company illustrations for the topics covered.

International Marketing reflects the author's teaching philosophy: creating vivid, memorable examples that help students retain international marketing theory and facts. The author shares her own perspectives as a product of different cultures who has experienced and observed marketing on five continents, both as an expatriate and as a local, in a free-market system and under a repressive, anticonsumerist command economy. These experiences are further supplemented with material collected in the author's recent research and other fieldwork and with materials obtained from various international sources: newspapers and magazines (*The Financial Times, Le Monde, The Economist, Wall Street Journal Europe and Asia, Frankfurter Allgemeine, Süddeutsche Zeitung, Die Zeit, L'Express, Le Point, Jeune Afrique, Far Eastern Economic Review,* and local and international fashion magazines), government and nongovernmental organizations' publications (World Bank, United Nations Development Program, among others), as well as publications aimed at expatriates *(Delegates' World, Le Monde Diplomatique).*

The text adopts strategic, applications-oriented approaches to country- and region-specific environments. These are also illustrated, in the text and in the case studies, with interviews conducted with international and local marketing managers and with marketing theorists who hold different international marketing philosophies.

ANCILLARY MATERIALS

Textbook Media is pleased to offer a competitive suite of supplemental materials for instructors using its textbooks. These ancillaries include a Test Bank, PowerPoint Slides, and an Instructor's Manual. This text comes with a test bank created by the author, and it includes questions in a wide range of difficulty levels for each chapter. All Textbook Media test banks offer not only the correct answer for each question but also a rationale or explanation for the correct answer and a reference-the location in the chapter where materials addressing the question content can be found. The Test Item Files are available in computerized Test Banks that use Diploma Software from Wimba (part of Blackboard, Inc.) The software allows the instructor to eas-ily create customized or multiple versions of a test and includes the option of editing or adding to the ex-isting question bank.

A full set of PowerPoint Slides, written by the author, is available for this text. This is designed to provide instructors with comprehensive visual aids for each chapter in the book. These slides include outlines of each chapter, highlighting important terms, concepts, and discussion points.

The Instructor's Manual for this book has also been written by the author and offers suggested syllabi for 10- and 14-week terms; lecture outlines and notes; in-class and take-home assignments; recommendations for multimedia resources such as films and Web sites; and long and short essay questions and their answers, appropriate for use on tests.

Acknowledgements

The author expresses her deep gratitude for the immense support received in the process of developing this textbook. I would especially like to thank Tom Doran and Ed Laube for their unrelenting support and creativity and for their exacting oversight of this project for almost a decade. The author also expresses thanks to Andrew Gross at Cleveland State University, to Al Rosenbloom at Dominican University, and to Bonita Kolb at Lycoming College for their valuable and continued formal and informal feedback.

My gratitude also goes to my family, to Bram, Michael, and Daniel Opstelten, and to my parents, Lucia and Damian Lascu for the formidable international experiences that this book is based on and for creating and facilitating the foundations for this text.

About the Author

Dana-Nicoleta Lascu is Professor of Marketing and Chair of the Marketing Department at the University of Richmond. She has a Ph.D. in marketing from the University of South Carolina, a master's in international management from Thunderbird, and a B.A. in English and French from the University of Arizona. She was a Fulbright Distinguished Chair in International Business at the Johannes Kepler University of Linz, Austria. She has published in *International Marketing Review, International Business Review, European Journal of Marketing, Journal of Business Research, Journal of Business Ethics, Journal of Euromarketing, Journal of East-West Business*, and *Multinational Business Review,* among others, and is the author of *Principles of Marketing 4e*. Dr. Lascu has consulted with companies such as Ford Motor Company, Stihl, IDV North America, Yellow Book International and others, and was a simultaneous and consecutive translator in English, French, and Romanian in Romania and Rwanda. She also worked as an international training coordinator in the United States, teaching managerial skills to civil servants from developing countries.

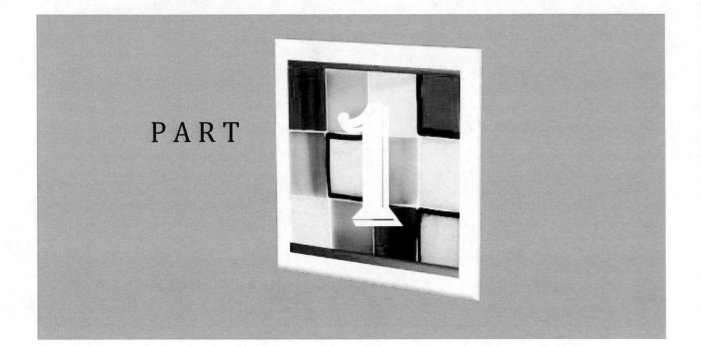

PART 1

Introduction to International Marketing

Chapter 1: Scope, Concepts and Drivers of International Marketing

Learning Objectives

After studying this chapter, you should be able to:

• Define international marketing and identify the different levels of international involvement.

• Describe the different company orientations and philosophies toward international marketing.

• Identify environmental and firm-specific drivers that direct firms toward international markets.

• Identify obstacles preventing firms from engaging in successful international ventures.

FedEx

When assessing its growth opportunities, FedEx states: "International, sky is the limit." In spite of its slogan, however, FedEx has traditionally pursued markets only in industrialized countries. In many low-income countries (in sub-Saharan Africa, for example), its competitor, DHL, was the first to enter the market, securing business from the national government to the expatriate community, and to local and international businesses operating there. When FedEx decided that these markets had potential, it had to spend large amounts of money to promote its services in these middle- and low-income countries to be able gain access there.

Coca-Cola

For many decades, Coca-Cola ignored Central and Eastern Europe because the market was not especially attractive. These regions had government restrictions on the repatriation of profits—for consumer products, such as Coke, these restrictions were the highest. The distribution was problematic and it did not appear to warrant the required high investment. Moreover, consumers in these countries could barely afford to purchase a Coke.

Pepsi, on the other hand, decided that middle- and low-income countries were worth the investment. In Central and Eastern Europe, it set up strategic alliances with government agencies in the late 1960s, at a time when Coca-Cola did not consider the Communist countries in Europe as attractive investment venues. As a first mover into this market—that is, the first significant company to move into a new market—Pepsi was able to secure exclusive access to distributors and retailers, and effectively blocked Coca-Cola's access for many years. In the 1990s, when these markets opened their doors to foreign investment, Coca-Cola had to spend huge amounts of money to overtake Pepsi's lead in these markets. Eventually, it was successful, advertising itself as the product of the post-Communist generation.

This chapter introduces the different internationalization philosophies of international firms and explores the motivations for going international, addressing the environmental and firm-specific drivers of international expansion. It also provides an overview of the challenges and obstacles encountered in international expansion.

Figure 1-1: *Coca Cola is present everywhere in Tallinn, Estonia.*

1-1 The Importance of International Marketing

The United States constitutes one of the most important target markets in the world, consuming a high percentage of worldwide products and services. Over time, however, even as foreign investment in the United States continues to increase (it totaled $234 billion in 2011 – a 14% jump over 2010) [1], it has become evident that this target market is losing its dominant position: the percentage of consumers is getting smaller—currently, less than 25 percent of the total world market. For U.S. companies to achieve their full potential and to effectively compete with foreign companies in the same league, it is crucial that they expand into international markets to take advantage of global market opportunities, to keep pace with competition, and to maximize the potential of their product mix.

Throughout history, companies have achieved worldwide dominance in spite of the smaller size and limited market of their home country. It should be noted, however, that an international presence was essential for their success. Take, for example, successful global companies from the Netherlands, a small country in Western Europe, that are giants of industry worldwide. Among them are Philips, a leading electronics manufacturer; Royal Ahold, a large retailer; Royal Dutch/Shell, a major Dutch-British oil company; and Unilever, a leading consumer products company, the latter in joint Dutch and British ownership. Japan, a comparatively small industrialized country in East Asia, boasts a number of firms that are industry leaders. Among them are Mitsui and Mitsubishi (electronics, banking, import-export, among others), Dentsu (advertising), Sony and Panasonic (electronics), and Ito Yokado (retail).

International companies such as General Motors, Mitsubishi, Microsoft, and Exxon earn profits greater than the gross domestic product of many low-income countries, and their total market value is several times the size of their profits. Even successful small businesses can attribute their survival and success to international markets. Also, companies may find that, with products in the late stage of their life cycle, emerging markets in middle- and low-income countries can offer them a new life. Consider the case of Avon.

Avon in China

China may be the most difficult place to be an Avon Lady. The sign-up process takes many weeks, and candidates must take a written test on China's sales regulations and attend a related class. Then they have to abide by many regulations, including a cap on sales commission. But being an Avon Lady is at least an option now. China lifted its ban on direct sales in 2005, after being required to liberalize its retail industry.

In spite of these restrictions, however, Avon has been doing reasonably well in China until recently, reporting double-digit increases in sales for the company, as it changed gears to focus primarily on store sales – until recently. In 2012, Avon was accused of breaching the U.S. Foreign Corrupt Practices Act, promoting their business interests by bribing Chinese government officials. And its reputation suffered subsequently, when Coty, the fragrance company, reneged on a buyout offer. Despite these challenges, Avon penetrated markets in large and small cities in even the most remote areas in China. In Figure 1-2, an Avon store in Lhasa, Tibet, has a prominent central location and a local clientele vying for Western beauty products.[2]

Figure 1-2: *Avon display at 13,000 feet in Lhasa, Tibet.*

To achieve their potential, companies must constantly monitor the international environment for opportunities. For the past two decades, privatization in countries previously dominated by government monopolies has made it possible for multinationals to compete for local energy, airline, railway, and telecommunications industries. In the future, postal services might constitute the new competitive territory of international companies. Already, in many markets, post offices are enterprising competitors to established private sector firms, increasingly and effectively competing not only for mailing services, but also for banking services.

1-2 Levels of International Marketing Involvement

All companies are affected by elements of the international marketing environment. In terms of international marketing involvement, however, companies have different degrees of commitment. A company engaging in **domestic marketing** has the least commitment to international marketing. This company focuses solely on domestic consumers and on the home-country environment. The home-country environment, however, is affected by developments in the international environment; furthermore, the local company is directly affected by local competition, which could come from global companies.

At the next level, **export marketing,** a firm could be involved in exporting indirectly, the company takes orders from international clients, or directly, the company actively seeks international clients. For both export marketers and domestic marketers, the international market constitutes an extension of the domestic market and is not given special consideration. Such firms have an ethnocentric philosophy to internationalization, as will be shown in Section 1-3a, "Ethnocentric Orientation."

International marketing activities require a substantial focus on international consumers in a particular country or countries. (When more countries are involved, international marketing is often referred to as **multinational marketing.**) International marketing is thus defined as the processes involved in the creation, production, distribution, promotion, and pricing of products, services, ideas, and experiences for international markets. The international company is present in different countries with sales offices and subsidiaries or is an active partner in strategic alliances with local companies. It is important to note that, in this case, international activities are not coordinated across the different countries or across different regions. An international company, according to this definition, has a polycentric, or regiocentric, philosophy to internationalization, as will be seen in Sections 1-3b, "Polycentric Orientation," and 1-3c, "Regiocentric Orientation."

Global marketing involves marketing activities across different countries without focusing primarily on national or regional segmentation. Global marketing is possible due to the emergence of global consumer segments with similar preferences (see Figures 1-3a and 1-3b) and due to efficient global allocation of company talent and resources. A company engaging in global marketing has a geocentric philosophy to internationalization.

It should be noted, however, that the terms defined in the preceding paragraphs are often used interchangeably by nonbusiness and business alike—even by international managers. *International, global,* and *multinational* are used to refer to any company crossing borders, without particular reference to the global strategy used. The descriptions of the levels of international marketing involvement should primarily guide one to understand when distinctions are made. A superior approach to distinguishing between companies' international orientation and philosophy is the ethnocentric, polycentric, regiocentric, and geocentric (EPRG) framework.

domestic marketing
Marketing that is focused solely on domestic consumers and on the home-country environment.

export marketing
Involvement in international marketing limited to the exporting function; although the firm actively seeks international clients, it considers the international market an extension of the domestic market and does not give it special consideration.

international marketing
The processes involved in the creation, production, distribution, and pricing of products, services, ideas, and experiences for international markets; these processes require a substantial focus on international consumers in a particular country or countries.

multinational marketing
Marketing in different countries without coordinating across operations.

global marketing
International marketing activities that do not have a country or region focus and that are possibly due to the emergence of global consumer segments and efficient global allocation of company talent and resources.

1-3a

1-3b

Figure 1-3: *Consumers North America and Europe have a strong preferences for pastries – croissants, danishes, brioches, you name it. Thus they are similar in preferences. Where they differ is in their tolerance for high prices: in Berlin upscale stores (1-3a), such pastries are €1.50, or about $1.85, whereas in similar stores in Helsinki (1-3b), they cost about €4.60, or about $5.60.*

1-3 The Ethnocentric, Polycentric, Regiocentric, and Geocentric Framework and International Marketing Concepts

Management's orientation toward the internationalization of the firm's operations affects each of the functional areas of the firm and, as such, has a direct effect on the marketing functions within the firm. Management's philosophy on international involvement affects decisions such as the firm's response to global threats and opportunities and related resource allocation. Companies' philosophies on international involvement can be described, on the basis of the EPRG framework, as ethnocentric, polycentric, regiocentric, and geocentric.[3]

1-3a Ethnocentric Orientation

Eli Lilly is an ethnocentric firm.[4] Top management at Eli Lilly places most of the emphasis on product research and development in an effort to bring to the marketplace high-performance pharmaceutical products. Firms with an **ethnocentric orientation** are guided by a *domestic market extension concept*. In general, top management of firms with an ethnocentric orientation consider that domestic strategies, techniques, and personnel are superior to foreign ones and therefore provide the most effective framework for the company's overseas involvement. Consequently, international operations and customers are considered secondary to domestic operations and customers.[5] Ethnocentric firms are likely to be highly centralized and consider that the purpose of their international operations is to identify markets that could absorb surplus domestic production. Alternatively, international operations could represent a cash cow that generates revenue and necessitates only minimal

> **ethnocentric orientation**
> Company strategies consistent with the belief that domestic strategies, techniques, and personnel are superior to foreign ones and therefore provide the most effective framework for the company's overseas involvement; companies adopting this perspective view international operations and customers as secondary to domestic operations and customers.

attention and investment. As a result, plans for international markets are developed primarily in-house by an international division and are similar to those for the domestic market.[6] Firms in the tobacco industry,[7] as well as firms at the forefront of technology, tend to have an ethnocentric marketing orientation.

It should be mentioned that, often, ethnocentric firms approach globalization by internationalizing at the level of the function, rather than the firm. For example, the marketing department may have a geocentric strategy even if top management has an ethnocentric orientation.[8]

In many cases, U.S. firms sell American brands along with their related U.S. lifestyles and traditions—for example, cigarettes, blue jeans, and entertainment. Hollywood movies are one example in the entertainment category. Another example is Disney, where an ethnocentric marketing approach worked well in some markets, but not in others. Ethnocentric marketing was, traditionally, all that Disney was about: the mouse, princes and princesses, Cinderella and her castle, rides . . . the works. And, along with those things, Main Street U.S.A., Frontierland, Adventureland, Tomorrowland—in other words, America and its present, past, and future in a cute package of several fun-packed acres. It was a formula that worked well in the United States and in Japan at Tokyo Disney Resort. Exporting the concept to France and Hong Kong seemed like a good idea. However, the company quickly found that an ethnocentric approach to the marketing of its entertainment parks in these two markets would not be an easy task. In Europe, consumers were unhappy with the U.S. themes resonating exclusively throughout the park such that Disneyland Resort Paris had to reinvent the offering and adapt it to local preferences, creating entertainment based on European fairy tales, serving food that would appeal to European consumers, and creating a more lax approach to the dress code for the park's French staff. In 2012, Disneyland Resort Paris celebrated its twentieth anniversary with parades and special events, attesting to the fact that the European public embraced the transformed American icon.

At the Hong Kong Disneyland, which opened in 2005, attendance fell short of expectations, with visitors complaining of mistreatment and the number of attractions as well as size of the park being considered insufficient. Shortly after opening, during the Chinese New Year, the park had to close due to ticketing problems, and ticket holders forced their way in by storming through gates and climbing over fences. However, even though Chinese authorities were at first reluctant to entertain the possibility of Disney opening yet another park in Shanghai,[9] the park is scheduled to open its doors in 2015.

1-3b Polycentric Orientation

Firms with a **polycentric orientation** are guided by a *multidomestic market concept.* Managers of polycentric firms are very much aware of the importance of individual international markets to the success of their business and are likely to establish individual businesses, typically wholly owned subsidiaries or marketing subsidiaries, in each of the countries where they operate. The assumption the company makes is that each market is unique and needs to be addressed individually. Consequently, the company is fully decentralized and engages in minimal coordination with the headquarters.

polycentric orientation
Company strategies predicated on the assumption that each country's market is unique and should be addressed individually, with a country-specific marketing mix.

Each subsidiary has its own marketing plans and objectives and operates autonomously as an independent profit center on an individual country basis to achieve its goals; all marketing activities are performed in each country independently of the company headquarters.[10] To address local consumer needs, marketing research is conducted independently in each overseas market, and products are fully adapted to meet these needs. Alternatively, separate product lines are developed to meet the needs of the individual markets.

In the process of developing individual strategies for each market, the company does not coordinate activities across the different countries and cannot benefit from economies of scale that such coordination would allow. Furthermore, numerous functions are duplicated, and, ultimately, final product costs are higher to the end consumer. For decades, Ford used a polycentric strategy in meeting the needs of budget-conscious consumers by developing a Ford Escort automobile for the United Kingdom that looked different from the one sold in the United States or Southeast Asia.[10] Currently, the Ford automobile addressing the needs of the budget-conscious consumer, the Ford Focus, looks identical in each market: Ford has adopted a geocentric approach to product development.

1-3c Regiocentric Orientation

Firms with a regiocentric or a geocentric orientation are guided by a *global marketing concept.* Companies adopting a **regiocentric orientation** view world regions as distinct markets that share economic, political, and cultural traits such that they would be viable candidates for a regionwide marketing approach. A regiocentric orientation is now possible due to the success of regional economic and political integration that allows for implementing a uniform marketing strategy in the entire region. Member countries of the European Union, for example, are candidates for Pan-European marketing strategies, whereas signatory countries of the North American Free Trade Agreement (NAFTA) lend themselves to a successful marketing strategy aimed at the North American market. PepsiCo appears to have a regiocentric orientation. Its divisions are organized on the basis of location, with regional offices coordinating all local marketing activities. For example, Pepsi's South-Eastern European operations are coordinated by its Turkey-based PepsiCo subsidiary, which devises the company's regional objectives and oversees the implementation of the company's marketing strategy in the region.

1-3d Geocentric Orientation

Firms in which top management adopts a **geocentric orientation** perceive the entire world—without national and regional distinctions—as a potential market with identifiable, homogeneous segments that need to be addressed with tailored marketing strategies, regardless of geographic location or nationality. Coordinated management policies are designed to reflect the full integration among worldwide operations.

The objective of a geocentric company is most often to achieve a position as a low-cost manufacturer and marketer of its product line; such a firm achieves a strategic competitive advantage by developing manufacturing processes that add more value per unit cost to the final product than its rivals.[11] An example of a geocentric company is McDonald's (see Figure 1-4).

> **regiocentric orientation**
> Company strategies that view world regions as distinct markets that share economic, political, and cultural traits that will respond to a regionwide marketing approach.
>
> **geocentric orientation**
> Company strategies that are consistent with the belief that the entire world, without national and regional distinctions, constitutes a potential market with identifiable, homogeneous segments that need to be addressed differently.

Figure 1-4: *McDonald's restaurants pepper the landscape in China, even in the more remote districts of large cities.*

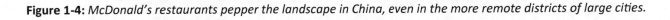

McDonald's

McDonald's has been successful as a result of its geocentric philosophy. The company uses local products to ultimately offer a similar service to consumers from Mexico City to Mumbay. In Europe, McDonald's uses Polish potatoes, which do not lend themselves to a thin, McDonald's-style cut French fry but are touted to be the best in the region. It also uses local beef from the European regions not affected or threatened by livestock disease. In India or Pakistan, for example, McDonald's serves lamb or vegetarian burgers. Throughout the world, it provides a uniform service that offers, in addition to the fast food it is known for, clean restrooms, air conditioning, and service with a smile—even in markets where a smile is a rare occurrence in a service encounter.

IBM

IBM has been going through massive reorganizations to keep abreast of the ever-changing international market. And, with Sam Palmisano's retiring as CEO at the end of 2011, more transformations followed to create a dynamic geocentric company. Under IBM's old system, a corporate customer with operations in several countries had to contract with small IBM offices in each country, and each IBM office had its own regulations. The IBM organization was, at the time, polycentric. The reorganization placed IBM's employees into 14 customer-focused groups, such as financial services, entertainment, and oil and gas, to be able to work with a central sales office to have IBM computers installed in the entire client organization. Organizing on the basis of function, rather than on country of operations, demonstrates a geocentric market orientation.

1-4 Drivers of International Expansion

Few companies operate in an isolated, country-specific environment, and even fewer can effectively avoid international involvement. Local firms manufacturing for local consumers are dependent on equipment, parts, and raw materials originating abroad. They sell to clients and final consumers who have had exposure to international trade practices and to international products. A complete isolation from international influence is possible only in a closed environment such as North Korea, where consumers are shielded from international influence.

Increasingly, companies cannot afford to avoid involvement in international marketing. Avoiding international expansion could mean losing market share to competitors and missing numerous opportunities created by changes in the international environment. Among reactive motivations for going international is the desire to remain competitive and maintain global market share relative to competitors. In addition, evading trade barriers and other government regulations in the home country can motivate a company to go international.

Firms should be proactive in their approach to internationalization. A proactive rationale for internationalization can be, among others, the search for new markets, new customers, increased market share and profits, tax advantages, or lower costs, as described in the next sections.

Drivers in the business environment and **firm-specific drivers,** addressed in Sections 1-4a, "Drivers in the Business Environment," and 1-4b, "Firm-Specific Drivers," as well as Table 1-1, help international companies benefit from such opportunities.

drivers in the business environment
Elements in the business environment, such as competition, technology, and labor costs, causing the firm to become involved internationally.

firm-specific drivers
Elements specific to the firm, such as product life cycle, causing the firm to become involved internationally.

Table 1-1	
Business Environment Drivers	**Firm-Specific Drivers**
Competition	Product life-cycle considerations
Regional economic and political integration	High new-product development costs
Technology	Standardization, economies of scale, and cheap labor
Improvements in the transportation and tele-communication infrastructure	Experience transfers
Economic growth	
Transition to a market economy	
Converging consumer needs	

1-4a Drivers in the Business Environment

Competition

Competitive pressure is often a driver of internationalization. Over time, service providers and client firms develop close relationships that last as long as the firms move together into new international markets. However, the relationship is in jeopardy when the service provider does not follow the client into the new market. McCann Erickson has been, for many years, the primary advertising agency for Coca-Cola and has followed the company into new markets, as illustrated in the following example.

McCann Erickson and Coca-Cola

McCann Erickson, a leading advertising agency, has followed for many years its longtime client Coca-Cola in most countries where the company was present around the globe: McCann Erickson had been handling the Coca-Cola account in 129 countries since 1942.[12] That sometimes meant McCann Erickson lost money in countries where its accounts are limited but where, nevertheless, it chose to be present to serve the advertising needs of Coke. If McCann Erickson chose not to serve its client in a market, Coca-Cola might resort to the services of a competitor, and on the basis of its experience with the competitor, Coca-Cola might replace McCann Erickson with the competing advertising firm.

However, in spite of efforts to serve their client firm, even the most dedicated service providers can be replaced. In 2007, Coca-Cola moved the management of its dedicated Red Lounge China marketing unit from McCann Erickson to Leo Burnett, a competing advertising agency, dealing McCann a significant blow. Coca-Cola executives decided that they needed to change the way they worked with agency partners. They placed Leo Burnett in charge of teams from different agencies because company executives felt that creating independence and tension among them and their agencies would lead to better ideas and better thinking. They will likely use this strategy in other markets as well, which does not bode well for McCann Erickson.[13]

As of 2012, Coca-Cola has been relying on Lowe Lintas, Weiden + Kennedy and McCann Erickson to produce its memorable advertising worldwide.

As a post-script to this story, Leo Burnett lost, also in 2007, some of the international accounts of its longtime client, McDonald's.

Regional Economic and Political Integration

In addition to cultural similarities—language and religion, for example—economic and political integration play an important part in facilitating international trade. Regional agreements such as NAFTA, the Southern Cone Common Market (MERCOSUR), and the politically and economically integrated European Union are examples of successful attempts at lowering or eliminating barriers among member countries and promoting trade within the perimeter of each common market. The benefits of integration extend to companies from nonmember states as well. Integration permits subsidiaries incorporated in the respective markets to benefit from free trade within the region and allows firms outside the integrated regions to conduct business within the common market without the impediments typically posed by crossing national borders—customs paperwork, separate tariffs for each country, and so on.

A company from the United States exporting products to multiple countries in the European Union, for example, will cross borders once. The company will do the customs paperwork and pay the required customs duties only once, instead of applying for an import license and paying customs duties in every country where it exports products. A subsidiary of a company from the United States incorporated in any country of the European Union is a corporate citizen of the European Union. Consequently, the subsidiary does not have to pay duties or foreign exchange costs when it crosses borders of European Union member states because all transactions are conducted in euros. See the following example of Ford Germany.

Ford Germany (www.ford.de)

Although Ford is a U.S. company, Ford Germany is a citizen of Germany and the European Union. As such, Ford Germany can freely ship its Ford Focus, Ford Ka, Ford Mondeo, Ford Fusion, Ford C-Max and S-Max, Ford Transit Euroline, the Ford Ranger, and its other models to dealers in the countries of the European Union without going through customs and engaging in related paperwork. Moreover, the company does not incur any foreign exchange cost because all the transactions take place in euros.

Technology

Technology has created opportunities for firms involved in international business. In terms of media development, consumers worldwide are exposed to programming originating in other countries. Programming from the United States in particular dominates the international airways: *Law & Order* is followed by audiences worldwide, CNN is popular with businesspeople around the world, and NBC eagerly exports its mix of late-night comedy and news magazines to the rest of the world. Advertising also crosses borders, exposing consumers to brands from other countries. The Internet has revolutionized the way many companies conduct business, offering businesses instant and unlimited international exposure—something that brick-and-mortar stores and traditional manufacturers have taken years to achieve. Such exposure offers tremendous opportunities to small businesses that do not normally have the advertising budget to communicate with the international market. For example, a Havasu-owned small business in Nevada, located two hours by car and another two on horseback from Las Vegas, can advertise weekend vacation opportunities to French businesspeople in the southern state of Languedoc-Roussillon planning to attend Las Vegas conferences or to French couples in the eastern state of Alsace looking for a unique honeymoon.

Improvements in the Transportation and Telecommunication Infrastructure

Closely linked to technology are the leaps in the area of transportation and, particularly, in the technology infrastructure. In 1982, a Mercedes-Benz service station in Bujumbura, Burundi (sub-Saharan East Africa), attempting to contact the company factory in Stuttgart, Germany, to order a part, would tie up an English- or German-speaking employee for most of the day for this purpose. The employee would book the telephone call with the operator early in the morning and would typically be contacted by the afternoon. The call would be facilitated by an operator in Brussels, Belgium (all calls to Burundi went via cable from Belgium to its former colonies in East Africa), who would link the factory to the service station. The quality of the connection would often be problematic, necessitating a second request for a telephone connection. An alternative would have been placing the request via telex (faxing was not an option at that time, nor was the use of e-mail).

Today, a telephone connection to Burundi would be handled via satellite, at a significantly lower cost than previously, and the communication would be crisp and clear. Video teleconferencing can take place using the telephone and projecting the image of the speaker on an overhead projector. Job interviews using Skype are used to hire Western employees in the United Arab Emirates, with the only challenge encountered in the process being the time that would be convenient to both parties, as 8 a.m. in the United States is 4 p.m. in the U.A.E.

Figure 1-5: *An infrastructure that can support high-speed train travel is characteristic of large European and Asian cities.*

Transportation has also greatly improved since the 1980s. The introduction of containers for international inter-modal (ship, truck, train) shipping greatly facilitates the transportation of physical goods. For passenger transport, efficient and rapid air travel has become more affordable, allowing for frequent interaction between expatriate or local employees and employees from the company headquarters. Alternatively, high-speed train travel on inter-city routes allows for rapid transportation in developed countries, such as Japan, and many countries in the European Union (see Figure 1-5). Emerging markets are also rapidly developing their transportation infrastructure; for example, in China, high-speed trains take merely a fraction of the time it used to take to travel between Shanghai to its Pudong Airport.

Economic Growth

Economic growth constitutes an important driver of internationalization. Economic development in general and increased buying power—attributed to the emergence of a strong middle class in large markets, such as those of Brazil and India, for example—have created great potential for international brands. Economic growth has also opened markets that were previously closed or that have limited international competition. A case in point is China, which now welcomes foreign direct investment and supports large-scale privatization of state-owned enterprises. Emerging economies in general are more open to free trade and no longer severely limit international firms operating in these markets.

Transition to a Market Economy

The transition of the former Eastern Bloc countries and formerly closed economies, such as those of China, Mongolia, and Vietnam, to a market economy has led to rapid economic development in these countries and has created important new markets for international brands. Another important outcome of the transition to a market economy has been the deregulation and privatization of former government monopolies; under the former Communist regimes, all industry was run by inefficient state enterprises. Opportunities exist for product manufacturers, such as Philip Morris, Whirlpool, Unilever, Procter & Gamble, Colgate-Palmolive, and others, to purchase or partner with local companies operating at a loss, producing low-quality goods and to turn them around into successful enterprises. Similarly, service providers, from Accenture to Pizza Hut, are entering these markets, engaging in the highest level of international commitment: foreign direct investment.

Currently, international companies, joint ventures between multinationals and local companies, private local businesses, as well as some remnants of the former system—for example, state-owned enterprises—compete for local consumers in these transition markets. At the same time, satellite television and the Internet expose these consumers to programming, information, and advertising for international brands, shaping consumer desires and brand preferences. Companies that have, initially, ignored these markets due to the obstacles they posed to international trade – for instance, limiting consumer goods companies access to hard currency and restricting the repatriation of profits – are now rapidly entering these newly-opened markets to take advantage of the many untapped opportunities. Investing in transition economies has generally proved to be a brilliant strategy for company growth. Most rewards are reaped by those companies investing in the larger transition economies, such as China. Take, for example, Yum! Brands, in the following example.

Yum! Brands

Yum! Brands, which owns a number of fast-food chains—Taco Bell, KFC, Long John Silver's, and Pizza Hut, among others—has not performed well in recent years in the United States. It grappled with an E. coli outbreak at Taco Bell on the East Coast of the United States and a rat infestation at a KFC/Taco Bell franchise store in New York City. However, the company continues to do well, primarily owing to its fast growth in China, where KFC is a dominant player (see Figure 1-6). China's division is expected to lead Yum!'s growth, as the company continues an aggressive strategy of opening restaurants around the world.[14]

Figure 1-6: *Yum! Brands is omnipresent in China and Taiwan.*

Converging Consumer Needs

Exposure to global brands in one's home country and, while traveling abroad, exposure to media advertising these brands, has created demand for many global products. Consumers worldwide are loyal to international brands such as Nike sneakers, Levi's jeans, Coca-Cola, Heineken beer, and Ralph Lauren shirts. Uniform consumer segments are emerging in high-income countries and low-income countries: Generation X consumers in the United States and in Southeast Asia are loyal to the same soft-drink brands, wear the same brands of clothing, listen to the same music, have the same teen idols, see the same television shows, and watch MTV for entertainment.

During their international travels, consumers purchase brands and services available in their home country, with which they are familiar. Most often, these offerings are successful international products and services. Alternatively, consumers traveling abroad bring with them product experiences and demand brands that may not be available in the home-country market. This would generate pull demand, whereby consumers request the product from the retailers, who subsequently convey the information up the distribution chain to wholesalers. The wholesalers would then order the product from manufacturers.

Converging consumer needs have created homogeneous segments of consumers that can be addressed similarly, regardless of their location. Figure 1-7 shows a bagel shop in Berlin. Bagels started with a Jewish baker in Vienna, who made a hard roll for the king of Poland, Jan Sobieski, in the shape of a riding stirrup-Bugel (commemorating the king's favorite pastime, riding) to thank him for protecting his countrymen from Turkish invaders. From there, the bagel made its way to Poland, Russia, and, eventually to Manhattan's Lower East Side. Surprise! The bagel made it back across the Atlantic, to Germany, where Salomon Bagels (www.salomon-bagels.de) at Berlin's trendy Potsdamer Platz is very popular. Here, the schmear (spread) consists of not just cream cheese and lox (salmon), but marmalade, hazelnut spread, honey, hummus, and Parmesan. Or one can have a pizza bagel with schinken (ham, oy!) or spinach.

Figure 1-7: *Bagels are back in Berlin, serving the needs of the city's cosmopolitan consumers.*

1-4b Firm-Specific Drivers

Product Life-Cycle Considerations

A main driver of international expansion is a firm's attempt to prolong the life cycle of its products and thus create higher profits for the company from a larger customer base. Products that are in late maturity, or even in the decline stage, can change their position on the global product life-cycle stage by going into markets where the product is in high demand. To illustrate this point, the cigarette industry is in either the late maturity stage or in the decline stage in many industrialized countries. By entering large emerging markets where cigarettes are in the growth stage and consumers have increasing purchasing power, such as China, India, and countries in Central and Eastern Europe, the cigarette industry is in fact prolonging its product's life cycle.

High New Product Development Costs

The concept of high costs for new product development is related to the product life cycle. Companies often spend long periods and significant amounts of money to develop new products. Nike, on the average, spends close to a year to develop, test, and manufacture new product designs that then last on the shelves in the United States for only six months. Despite the size and purchasing power of the U.S. market, it is unlikely that Nike would fully recover its product development costs and make a profit as well if it limited its sales to this country. This is especially true for companies at the forefront of technology (manufacturers of high-tech equipment and electronics, pharmaceutical firms, and others), which need to tap large markets for long periods to recoup costs and to make a profit as well. As a result, for these companies, going international is not a choice—it is a precondition for survival.

Standardization, Economies of Scale, and Cheap Labor

During the maturity stage of the product life cycle, the core product is likely to achieve a standard in a particular industry. Competitors—typically an oligopoly—respond to consumer needs by offering products whose components are interchangeable and which converge toward the brand experiencing the greatest consumer demand. To offer a historical illustration, standards were established in the personal computer industry, which converged on the IBM standard. Also, during the maturity stage, firms increasingly compete on price. Typically, they attempt to lower the product manufacturing costs by achieving economies of scale in production. In addition, firms with mature brands also move manufacturing operations and facilities abroad, to developing countries, in an attempt to take advantage of significantly lower labor costs.

Experience Transfers

International firms benefit from lessons they learn in the different parts of the world. Colgate-Palmolive, for example, developed its successful Axion dishwashing paste for its Latin American market after noting that women washed dishes by hand, dunking their hands in a small tub with a few slivers of soap. The same product was then offered to consumers in Central and Eastern Europe after noting that they washed dishes using a similar method—and the product was a hit. Service providers such as Pizza Hut found that they were more successful with consumers in general, but especially with younger generations of consumers in Central and Eastern Europe, if they played loud pop music in their restaurants. As a result, they started entering new markets by partnering with radio stations and discos.

Similar experience transfers have been helpful to retailers in the process of internationalization. The Tesco Extra hypermarket (superstore) in the city of Newcastle, United Kingdom, and the popular and busy Tesco hypermarket in the southern Czech Republic, in Cesky Budeovice, are based on a Tesco hypermarket first introduced by the same U.K. retailer in Hungary. Taking advantage of experience transfers, the company is able to go to different international markets and thus reduce its dependence on any one market.

1-5 Obstacles to Internationalization

Companies attempting to establish and maintain an international presence are likely to encounter **obstacles to internationalization** both from within the company and from outside. Such obstacles can be financial in nature; the company might not have the finances to expand beyond national frontiers. Others are psychological. Fear of an unknown international environment or of local business practices may keep the company from international engagement. These two types of barriers, however, could equally affect the company's local expansion efforts. Companies may not have the finances to expand beyond a small regional market, or they fear going into new markets where consumers may not be familiar with their products and hence may not respond to their marketing strategy.

There are obstacles that are typically encountered by firms in their process of internationalization—obstacles that they are unlikely to encounter in other expansion efforts. They are the self-reference criterion, government barriers, and international competition.

1-5a Self-Reference Criterion

Of crucial importance to international operations is the ability of the firm, and especially of its marketing strategy, to adapt to the local business environment to serve well the needs of local consumers and to address the requirements of local government, industry, and channels of distribution. An impediment to adaptation is the **self-reference criterion,** defined as individuals' conscious and unconscious reference to their own national culture and to home-country norms and values, as well as to their knowledge and experience, in the process of making decisions in the host country. At the company level, self-reference may lead the firm to fail to understand local consumers and their needs and to fail to understand the local business culture and deal effectively with local nationals.

Self-reference can lead to a breakdown in communication between parties from different cultures. For example, an employee of a large international company from the United States has been trained by career counselors in the United States that looking one's counterpart in the eyes conveys directness and honesty. When

> **obstacles to internationalization**
> Impediments that the firm may encounter in the process of internationalizing.
>
> **self-reference criterion**
> Individuals' conscious and unconscious reference to their own national culture, to homecountry norms and values, and to their knowledge and experience in the process of making decisions in the host country.

this individual conducts business in Japan using direct eye contact, he or she is likely to be perceived as abrasive, challenging the Japanese counterpart. Similarly, if an employee proceeds directly to transacting the business deal in Latin America or southern Europe instead of first interacting in a social setting to establish rapport, he or she would be perceived as arrogant, interested only in the bottom line, rather than in a long-term working relationship.

A first step to minimizing the effect of the self-reference criterion is selecting the appropriate personnel for international assignments. Such employees are sensitive to others and have experience working in different environments. Second, it is important to train expatriates to focus on and be sensitive to the local culture, rather than limit their personal interactions to own-country nationals or to expatriates from countries with cultures that are similar to their own. In fact, it is advisable that firms institute an organization-wide general orientation that instills and demonstrates sensitivity to international environments and openly rejects value judgments and national stereotyping.

1-5b Government Barriers

National governments, especially governments in low- and middle-income countries, keep a tight control over foreign investment. They scrutinize international marketers attempting to enter the market, permitting or denying access to international firms based on criteria that are deemed important for national industry and/or security considerations. Among formal methods used by national governments to restrict or impede entrance of international firms in the local market are tariffs and other barriers such as import quotas. Barriers may be imposed by restrictions in import license awards, by instituting foreign exchange restrictions, and by requiring a large percentage of local content for imported products, among others. Governments may decide to devalue the currency, change commercial laws, or radically change commercial regulations.

Member countries of the World Trade Organization or countries that are participants in regional economic and political integration agreements such as the North American Free Trade Agreement (NAFTA) and the European Union (EU), find it difficult to use tariffs as a means of restricting international expansion of companies in the countries' territories. Increasingly, they are using nontariff barriers, such as cumbersome procedures for import paperwork processing, delays in granting licenses, or preference given to local service providers and product manufacturing for all contracting work.

1-5c International Competition

Although competition can be a driver of internationalization, competitors can also erect barriers to new entrants in a market. Competitors' arsenals of barriers include the following: blocking channels of distribution, binding retailers into exclusive agreements, slashing prices temporarily to prevent product adoption, or engaging in an advertising blitz that could hurt a company's initial sales in a market and cause it to retrench. With heavy competition from new and lesser-known brands in Asia, Central and Eastern Europe, and North Africa and the Middle East, Marlboro created a strong defensive strategy for its cigarettes. It slashed prices by as much as a third and advertised heavily anywhere it was legal to do so, especially on billboards in the center of different capital cities and towns in the provinces.

As an example, sales of Marlboro in southeastern Europe were hurt by various local competitors and, in particular, by a successful regional brand, Assos, from Greece. Assos was rapidly gaining a leading position in a number of markets in the region when Marlboro went on the offensive with advertising blitzes and competitive prices, limiting Assos' market share to a point where the company was forced to abandon many of its markets. Marlboro effectively challenged the international expansion of many new European and Asian brands, as well as new brands from the United States. (It decimated, for instance, sales of new brands of U.S. cigarettes created specifically for the Russian market by small entrepreneurs.)

Summary

Define international marketing and identify the different levels of international involvement. Firms can elect to engage in different levels of international expansion. Domestic firms focus on the domestic market and ignore international possibilities. At the next level, firms can export their products overseas, taking advantage of international opportunities to increase their sales and profits. Firms involved in international marketing are serving international consumers and are present in different countries (but do not coordinate between-countries activities under a regional office or subsidiary) with sales offices, subsidiaries, or in partnership with local or other international firms. Global marketing involves coordination of all marketing activities within a particular region or worldwide.

Describe the different company orientations and philosophies toward international marketing. Depending on the type of industry or service and depending on the extent to which they have an international focus, companies adopt different orientations and philosophies toward internationalization. Ethnocentric companies consider domestic strategies, techniques, and personnel as superior to foreign ones. these strategies then provide the framework for the companies' overseas operations, which are secondary to domestic operations. Companies with a polycentric orientation focus on different international markets without coordinating between international activities. Companies with a regiocentric orientation coordinate their operations regionally, whereas companies with a geocentric orientation coordinate their marketing and management policies worldwide, fully integrating their operations and targeting uniform segments worldwide with similar strategies.

Identify environmental and firm-specific drivers that direct firms toward international markets. A number of elements in the business environment direct firms to explore international opportunities. One such element is competitive pressure, creating the need to serve clients regardless of market attractiveness and preventing them from switching to the service of a competitor. Opportunities in the environment, such as rapid economic growth and opening emerging markets, regional economic and political integration, and the removal of trade barriers, improvements in the transportation and telecommunication infrastructure, and advancement in technology also prompt international firms to pursue international markets. The advent of technology and media influence, economic prosperity, and consumer travel are creating uniform segments of consumers with similar preferences that international firms could serve effectively with standardized strategies. Firms facing decreasing sales attributed to a mature home market can extend the life cycle of their products by going international: Cigarette companies are in a late maturity stage in the United States but, most likely, they are in a late growth stage worldwide. During the maturity stage, as products start competing on price, companies benefit from going international to take advantage of cheaper and yet competent labor and new markets.

Identify obstacles preventing firms from engaging in successful international ventures. Obstacles to international marketing are the self-reference criterion—the conscious and unconscious reference to one's national culture and home-country norms and values, as well as to one's knowledge and experience, in the process of making decisions in the host country. Additional obstacles can be the local and national governments of the host country, which could impose entry barriers or prevent the companies from repatriating profits. Finally, competition can pose barriers to entry, diminishing the chance of success in attractive potential target markets.

Key Terms

drivers in the business environment

domestic marketing

ethnocentric orientation

export marketing

firm-specific drivers

geocentric orientation

global marketing

international marketing

multinational marketing

obstacles to internationalization

polycentric orientation

regiocentric orientation

self-reference criterion

Discussion Questions

1. Discuss the differences between firm internationalization philosophies.

2. Try to work backward from a company's webpage and attempt to identify its internationalization philosophy. Look at the Procter & Gamble (www.pg.com) webpages describing the company's international involvement and its international product mix. What orientation do you believe this company has and why?

3. What are the drivers in the international business environment that lead a firm to engage in international operations? What are some of the firm-specific drivers leading to internationalization?

4. What is the "self-reference criterion"?

5. How can governments and competitors prevent a firm from entering a particular market?

Chapter Quiz

True/False

1. International marketing involves marketing activities that have a substantial focus on international consumers in a particular country or countries.

Answer: True

Rationale: International marketing is marketing with an international focus; it refers to the processes involved in the creation, production, distribution, promotion, and pricing of products, services, ideas, and experiences for international markets.

Section 1-2, "Levels of International Marketing Involvement"

2. Firms involved in domestic marketing and export marketing are more likely to have an ethnocentric philosophy to internationalization.

Answer: True

Rationale: In general, these firms consider domestic strategies, techniques, and personnel to be superior o foreign ones.

Section 1-2, "Levels of International Marketing Involvement"

3. Nontariff barriers have been successful in restricting the international expansion of companies.

Answer: True

Rationale: Various nontariff barriers can impede internationalization by increasing the cost of foreign products.

Section 1-5b, "Government Barriers"

4. A regiocentric orientation calls for companies to focus on distinct markets and create country-specific marketing strategies.

Answer: False

Rationale: A regiocentric orientation involves creating programs for a world region with socio-cultural, political, or economic similarities.

Section 1-3c, "Regiocentric Orientation"

5. Reducing the cost of labor is a basic business-environment driver.

Answer: False

Rationale: Reducing the cost of labor is a firm-specific driver.

Section 1-4b, "Firm-Specific Driver"

Multiple Choice

1. International marketing obstacles include all the following EXCEPT

  a. the self-reference criterion.

  b. competition.

  c. new product development costs.

  d. government barriers.

Answer: c is correct.

Rationale: The self-reference criterion, competition, and government barriers constitute obstacles to international markets, whereas new product development costs are an incentive to go international.

Section 1-5, "Obstacles to Internationalization"

2. Similarities of teenagers in the United States, France, and Malaysia create opportunities for international firms. Their similarity is in fact a business-environment driver called

  a. economic growth.

  b. competition.

  c. converging consumer needs.

  d. regional economic and political integration.

Answer : c is correct.

Rationale: Teenagers in the United States belong to the broad global teenager segment, a market segment that shares many similar brand preferences.

Section 1-4a, "Drivers in the Business Environment"

3. Which internationalization philosophy best describes the Ford Focus strategy?

    a.   Geocentric orientation

    b.   Ethnocentric orientation

    c.   Polycentric orientation

    d.   Regiocentric orientation

Answer: a is correct.

Rationale: Ford Focus automobiles look identical in each market and appear to have a similar marketing mix.

Section 1-3b, "Polycentric Orientation"

4. CNN is known by businesspeople around the world mainly due to this driver.

    a.   Standardization

    b.   Competition

    c.   Technology

    d.   Economic growth

Answer: c is correct.

Rationale: Programming from the United States has penetrated most international markets. Technology makes it possible for CNN to broadcast its programs in key world markets.

Section 1-4a, "Drivers in the Business Environment"

5. The self-reference criterion is an obstacle to

    a.   government barriers.

    b.   internationalization.

    c.   a polycentric orientation.

    d.   standardization.

Answer b: is correct.

Rationale: The self-reference criterion is individuals' reference to their own national culture and to home-country norms and values, as well as their knowledge and experience, in the process of making decisions in the host country, and it could potentially prevent individuals from adapting to the local environment and from serving well the needs of local clients.

Section 1-5a, "Self-Reference Criterion"

Endnotes for Chapter 1`

1. Neil Shah, "Foreign Investment Surges: U.S. Attracts Billions of Dollars as Investors Seek Relief From Global Turmoil, *The Wall Street Journal*, June 15, 2012, pp. A3.

2. John McCary, "U.S. Still Luring Investors," *Wall Street Journal*, June 6, 2007, A5.

3. Howard Perlmutter, "The Tortuous Evolution of the Multinational Corporation," *Columbia Journal of World Business,* January–February 1969.

4. Thomas W. Malnight, "Globalization of an Ethnocentric Firm: An Evolutionary Perspective," *Strategic Management Journal,* Vol. 16, No. 2, February 1995, pp. 119–142.

5. David J. Lemak and Wiboon Arunthanes, "Global Business Strategy: A Contingency Approach," *Multinational Business Review,* Vol. 5, No. 1, Spring 1997, pp. 26–37.

6. Ibid.

7. Ibid.

8. Malnight, "Globalization of an Ethnocentric Firm," pp. 119–142.

9. Justine Lau, "Disneyland HK in Summer Push," *Financial Times*, July 13, 2006, 17.

10. Lemak and Arunthanes, "Global Business Strategy", pp. 26–37.

11. Ibid.

12. Hillary Chura, "Coke Brands IPG as Global Ad Strategist," *Advertising Age,* Vol. 71, No. 50, December 4, 2000, p. 50.

13. Atifa Hargrave-Silk, "Leo Burnett Takes Charge of Coca-Cola China," *Media*, January 26, 2007, 1.

14. *Forbes – Associated Press* online "Yum! Brands Stock Soars on Earnings," February 5, 2007.

Case 1-1

Alpaca Luxe: Marketing Opportunities in the Emerging Market of Mongolia

In the middle of a torrid Virginia summer, Gertrude Fowler, an artist on the Eastern Shore of Virginia, is reviewing the new designs of alpaca shawls made for her newest creative venture, Alpaca Luxe. With their signature fine stripes and vibrant colors, made from famously soft alpaca fiber from alpaca farms in the region, the scarves are both striking and luxurious. Alpaca Luxe works with a leading textile mill in North Carolina to make the scarves, which have been selling reasonably well in several high-end boutiques on the East Coast and in Chicago and Denver until the downturn in the economy. Her marketing team, led by John Gordon and Susan Spier, cautioned that the company's sales strategy was probably not going to be profitable in the long term and time was ripe for an expansion.

Gertrude set up a meeting to consult with John, Susan, and other marketing experts from various marketing service providers that Alpaca Luxe uses to research its target market and to design appropriate marketing strategies. At the meeting, John Gordon suggested a westward expansion – California, to him, seemed a reasonable prospect given Californians' preference for natural products and luxury offerings. Susan, who had previously worked in international marketing for a large multinational before moving to the Eastern Shore, suggested that they investigate the possibility of expanding into international markets. International expansion made sense to Gertrude, who thought that the scarves would appeal to consumers in European design capitals, such as Helsinki, Amsterdam, and Munich.

International expansion seemed to be the consensus for most of the participants in the meeting, and John and Susan were advised to evaluate such opportunities at the state government level and by contacting international trade representatives at the Department of Commerce. John and Susan quickly learned that contacting the Virginia Economic Development Partnership (VEDP), located just two hours away, in Richmond, Virginia, was a reasonable first step in exploring international expansion. Most states in the United States have similar organizations, whose charge is to aid companies in the state to explore international opportunities by identifying potential new markets, developing market entry strategies and locating possible distributors and representatives for products or services, at a very low cost to the exporter.

Approaching the Government

The meeting with the VDEP director produced mixed results. The Alpaca Luxe team described their offering in detail, emphasizing the luxury aspect of the scarves and their distinctiveness. The director offered specific insights into several European markets, which appeared to be saturated with well-known luxury brands and alpaca wool products from Bolivia and other countries in Central and South America.

Yes, Europeans responded well to design appeals and Gertrude's designs were certainly appealing. But Alpaca Luxe would be attempting to penetrate saturated markets, where consumer preferences were entrenched and where the new successful market entrants appealing to the luxury segment were primarily young designers with an attitude.

By chance, at the VDEP offices, the Alpaca Luxe team met a visiting delegation from the Mongolian Ministry of Commerce on a trade mission to promote Mongolia as a travel destination and to identify U.S. businesses interested in purchasing high quality Mongolian-sourced and processed cashmere. John and Susan initially qualified them as competitors, but, upon further discussions, they were intrigued: The luxury market in Mongolia was on the upswing and many of the leading brands have successfully entered the Mongolian market, achieving substantial market share and reaping high profits as first movers into the market. Mongolians, according to the team, appreciate European and U.S. brands, but, comparatively, there are many more European designers than designers from the United States present in Ulan Bator, the capital. True, Mongolians produce the finest quality cashmere, but Mongolian consumers would undoubtedly be interested in unique offerings, such as alpaca. Moreover, Mongolians are interested in unique designs, and the trade mission visitors deemed Gertrude Fowler's designs and strident colors as particularly appealing to the Mongolian consumer.

Before consulting with Gertrude, they decided to work with the marketing analysts at VDEP to probe further into expansion opportunities in Mongolia. They knew very little about the country and they had doubts that the market could sustain many luxury brands. However, the analysts provided interesting insights.

The Mongolian Market

After more than 200 years of oppressive Chinese rule, another 70 years as a Soviet satellite, which banned any reference to the proud history of Genghis Khan and his empire – the largest contiguous empire in history – Mongolia is ready to enter the world stage as a mineral-rich country taking huge leaps in its transition to a market economy.

According to the *Wall Street Journal*, Mongolia has immense reserves of coal, copper, gold, gas, and uranium, and an ongoing exploration of oil; Mongolia's current GDP of $7 billion a year had a yearly growth of a minimum of 20 percent in 2012, with the economy doubling every three to five years. On the other hand, it only has a population of 2.8 million, half of them living in Ulan Bator, while, in the rest of the country, many are nomads, living in yurts (ger, in Mongolian), and barely getting by. The capital is besieged by hundreds of thousands of people who are practically destitute, having lost all their cattle after a recent harsh winter. Mongolia also rates high on the Transparency International Corruption Perception Index, with Mongolians considering corruption to be one of the government's most serious problems.

Mongolia's market for luxury brands is thriving. In Ulan Bator's main square, Sukhbaatar Square, where once a bronze statue of Lenin reigned, there is an influx of luxury brands – Louis Vuitton, Armani, Zegna, Hugo Boss, Burberry, and others – elegantly displayed in the stores' lavish showrooms. And the luxury Mongolian consumer segment is responding enthusiastically. According to the *Wall Street Journal*, "Culturally, Mongolians like to show off. Mongolians are very proud of themselves—there is only one me. They think they deserve exclusivity."

Mongolia's primary luxury product is the best cashmere in the world; however, domestic producers are gradually put out of business, as the government levies high taxes on them, but does not tax Chinese exporters, who buy a large quantities of raw wool directly from herders, offering higher prices. The Chinese are also believed to mix the cashmere with wool, silk, or cotton, whereas Mongolian cashmere is pure and retains its cachet of a quality and exclusive product.

The Export Decision

John and Susan approached Gertrude and described to her at length their findings regarding the limitations of the European market and informed her about the insights obtained from the Mongolian Ministry of Commerce trade mission. Gertrude jumped at the idea of taking her beautiful scarves to Mongolia. She thought that the bright orange, fuschia, and purple designs would resonate well in Mongolia, with colors similar to those of traditional costumes. Plus, it would be a great opportunity for her to travel to Mongolia. She was in Tibet the previous year and found it fascinating. Although culturally very different, Mongolia would have a similar appeal, a sort of "last frontier" of authenticity, a country that is not cluttered with tourists and Western merchandise.

Gertrude was in favor of exploring the different types of distributors who could place the scarves on the luxury retailers' shelves. In fact, she herself might approach businesses in Sukhbaatar Square and persuade them to carry her scarves. She has had much success with a hands-on approach to marketing her Alpaca Luxe brand. She could try it in Mongolia.

Sources: Adapted from Maureen Orth, "The Luxury Frontier," *The Wall Street Journal*, http://online.wsj.com/article/SB10001424052702304186404576388153101917860.html, June 24, 2011; Virginia Exports: Virginia Economic Development Partnership, http://www.exportvirginia.org; company and characters are fictional.

Analysis Suggestions

1.   What are the environmental and firm-specific drivers that are driving Alpaca Luxe to explore international markets?

2.   Many companies use opportunistic approaches to internationalization – executives in charge of international expansion may have visited a particular country and felt that the company's products would do well. Or they might have friends who reside in the respective country who could potentially help them do business there. Aside from personal interests or connections, what are some of the drivers of internationalization that have prompted Alpaca Luxe to consider the Mongolian market for its international expansion?

Case 1-2

Zhang National Steel Company

Liu Hong, Director of International Accounts at the Zhang National Steel Company, has just been summoned by the company's chairman. Hong is expected to provide viable solutions for the company that will enable it to compete effectively in an increasingly saturated international steel market. China's steel production has been growing at breakneck pace in the past decade. Its rapid growth is posing serious threats to the industry, and Zhang National, one of the larger privatized steel companies, is part of the problem.

When Mao Zedong ordered an increase in the steel production as part of the Great Leap Forward, people left their fields, abandoned their work in agriculture, and fled to the large steel mills that produced millions of tons of useless substandard steel. Today, an enterprising China is taking another great leap, investing in industrial establishments, especially in the steel industry. The old, large steel mills have been privatized, becoming more efficient and producing high-quality steel, and investors are keen on banking on new and profitable steel mills.

According to industry reports, China produced 419 million metric tons of crude steel in 2006. This represents an increase of 314 percent from 101.2 million metric tons produced in 1996, when it became the largest steel producing country in the world for the first time. Today, China accounts for almost 34 percent of world steel production. With steel production growing at breakneck rates, in 2012, the Chinese crude steel capacity amounted to 840 tons, about 22% in excess of about 688 tons consumed. Adding to Zhang National Steel Company's woes, the Chinese government started imposing duties of 5 to 10 percent in 2007 on exports of more than 80 Chinese-made steel products, as well as other products containing steel, to trim its trade surplus.

Under these circumstances, Zhang National Steel Company would eventually have to cut its workforce by two thirds. Such a move would displace many workers and their dependent families and could very likely lead to political unrest in the region, as elsewhere in China. In fact, China's State Council, its cabinet, is starting to discourage investment in new steel mills by making such investments less attractive for investors. However, such efforts at the national level are countered by local officials whose goals are to increase local job opportunities and taxes. Locally, there is a strong push for establishing new steel mills, with local governments offering incentives for such investments.

Liu Hong gazed at the steel mill's dock on the Yangtze River. Many of China's steel mills are located on the banks of this river. River access facilitates barge access of ore imports, and the Yangtze is a magnet for competitors.

The steel Zhang National produces is used primarily to meet domestic demand and feed the building boom in China's large cities. Cement-and-steel structures line up the large avenues in Shanghai's Pudong district, and along many of Beijing's boulevards, massive structures line up against the hazy sky (see Figure 1-8).

Figure 1-8: *Steel and concrete dominate Beijing's landscape.*

However, China's economy has experienced a slow-down, and after the 2008 Olympics and the 2010 World's Fair, there is not as much incentive for the national government to push construction to showcase the new China to the world. The private investors in Zhang National Steel Company are starting to ask questions about the viability of the company in the near future.

In spite of the recently imposed export duties on Chinese steel, Liu Hong believes that going international is the best strategy for the company. Undoubtedly, going international will be a challenge in an environment that is fraught with unpredictability and protectionist measures. The world's largest steel consumer, the United States, is an important target market in Liu Hong's view, even though dozens of U.S. steel producers are going bankrupt because they cannot compete with imports that benefit from state subsidies. In an effort to protect the U.S. steel industry, the U.S. government has been threatening drastic steps that might challenge the entire world trade establishment, charging tariffs on steel imports. Furthermore, the European Union is contemplating measures to block a flood of steel imports from Asian countries—imports that normally would have had the United States as their destination. However, even though the United States and the European Union may raise some barriers to trade with China, Chinese steel will continue to remain more affordable than locally produced steel. Moreover, India's steel consumption is rapidly increasing, and with large revenues from outsourcing, India has the hard currency to purchase this commodity to meet local demand.

Liu Hong realizes that he must present a balanced perspective on going international. The challenge is convincing the chairman and the investors that going international is essential for Zhang National Steel Company.

Sources:

Adapted from Anjani Agrawal, Michel Nestour, Pierre Mangers, Angie Beifus, and Subhashish Sarkar, "Global steel – 2011 trends, 2012 outlook: Competing for growth in the steel sector," *Ernst & Young*, 2012; World Steel in Figures 2001–2006, International Iron and Steel Institute, June 15, 2007; www.worldsteel.org; "Another Leap by China, with Steel Leading Again," *The New York Times,* May 1, 2004, B1, B3; *Purchasing*, "Steel Output Increases 9% in 2006 to New High," February 15, 2007, 136, 2, B10; Andrew Batson, "China Adds Steel Duties to Curb Exports," *Wall Street Journal*, May 22, 2007, A2; company and characters are fictional.

Analysis Suggestions

1.   What arguments should Liu Hong offer the company chairman in favor of internationalization? What are the business environment internationalization drivers and the firm drivers that are likely to lead to the internationalization of the firm?

2.   What product life-cycle stage is the steel industry in worldwide? Should Zhang National Steel Company move its labor force overseas to China's neighboring countries? Why? Why not?

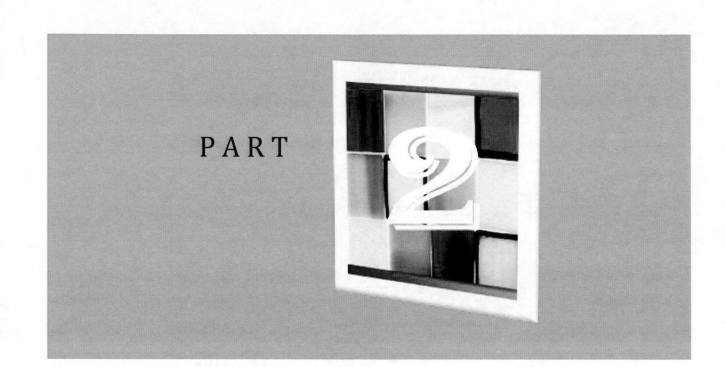

PART 2

The International Marketing
Environment

Chapter 2: An Overview of the International Marketing Environment

Learning Objectives

After studying this chapter, you should be able to:

- Provide an overview of the world economic environment and examine different perspectives on economic development.

- Address differences between countries of different levels of economic development and discuss the importance of emerging markets.

- Examine the indicators of political risk and address international firm approaches to political risk management.

- Describe how international law, home-country law, and host-country law affect international firm operations and address issues related to jurisdiction.

- Discuss different legal systems, intellectual property laws, and national laws with extra-territorial impact that affect international firms.

- Examine the natural and technological environments and the potential and limitations they present to international firms.

Kigali

Kigali is a city of contrasts: Internet cafés, dust, poverty, a luxurious German bakery-cum-grocery-cum-ice-cream store, persons with HIV estimated to constitute 50 percent of the local population, sporty foreigners, even better-dressed locals, and dust. The city center is busy with shops selling masks, nesting baskets, and trinkets to tourists, with many bars that stay open late, restaurants, and world-class hotels. Blue-hued Primus beer posters and red Coca-Cola billboards have replaced joyful cigarette ads previously plastered all over the city and framing the main road to the airport. Multinationals are vying for what might become a prosperous emerging market one day, as it was in the 1980s. The present and the future are topics of discussion. Bringing up the past is not appropriate, as indicated in tourist guidebooks and security briefings for nongovernmental organization staff.

Kigali is the capital city of Rwanda, where eight million people are jammed into a country smaller than Maryland, making it one of the world's most densely settled agrarian societies. In many places, nearly every patch of reddish earth is cultivated in a patchwork of fields that stretch up, and often over, Rwanda's countless hills. Just over a decade ago, Rwanda was the home of a 100-day ethnic slaughter in which most of the 800,000 victims were hacked to death with machetes or beaten to death with clubs. The Belgian colonists favored the Tutsi minority and used them to run the country, creating antagonism between the Hutu majority tribe and the Tutsis. Most of the killings happened as ethnic Hutu militias rampaged through steep hillside villages in search of Tutsis and those who sought to defend them.[1]

Today, the Tutsis are in charge again. Some Hutus are being tried for their crimes. Identity cards no longer list ethnic group information. Side-by-side, at the Nyabugogo market, Tutsis and Hutus sell clothing under the metal roofs, peddle their goods in the streets, and travel crowded in the matatus—open trucks that allow people to travel standing, as they weave from hill to hill. The heart of commerce in this land-locked country is bustling Kigali. But is this city—is the country—truly ready for business again?

Countries where multiple tribes have coexisted for decades without any conflict, where the president and his army have led effectively, spreading the wealth to the population and attracting in the country foreign direct investment, can still fall victim to a civil war, as in the case of Rwanda, discussed earlier. Multinational firms leave their assets open to plundering and promptly ship their expatriates to safety. This scenario is played out over and over in the world: Multinational companies in Chad, Rwanda, Burundi, the Congo, Sierra Leone, Haiti, Bosnia and Herzegovina, and Croatia have all experienced losses. Multinational companies are also victims of corporate terrorism, which is on the increase worldwide. The political environment poses many challenges to businesses.

The legal environment can be problematic as well. Some companies operate in environments where everything is forbidden unless expressly allowed. Other companies operate in environments where everything is perceived as allowed unless expressly forbidden. Companies operating in legally ambiguous environments face ethical and legal challenges from host-country national governments, para-national institutions, and the home-country government that they have to address effectively to be able to survive.

The natural environment of international marketing also poses challenges to businesses: Geology and the shortage of natural resources, coupled with a high population growth, can negatively affect market potential. Similarly, topography can affect access, and hydrology and climate can affect economic development. Phenomena such as a shortage of natural resources, the energy crisis, and the environmental quality crisis affect the business environment.

The technological environment of international marketing is rapidly opening international markets never before accessible to multinationals and is creating a viable future for small and medium enterprises that have never had such a broad exposure. The technological environment is also speeding the new-product development process and creating unprecedented distribution potential in industry.

This chapter focuses on elements in the environment of international marketing. We examine the effect of economic, political, legal, natural, and technological environments on the international marketing operations of firms.

2-1 The Economic Environment of International Marketing

2-1a The World Economy

It was common in the past to hear that, when the United States sneezed, the rest of the world would catch a cold. This remains true today, to a certain extent: When the United States experiences a downturn in the economy, reverberations echo throughout the world. However, there are many other economies that are just as influential. The Asian crisis of the late 1990s sent stock markets tumbling in the United States and in the rest of the world. In 2012, the Greek debt crisis sent the Dow Jones tumbling. In the Internet age, countries are becoming more and more connected by trade, capital markets, the flow of technology and ideas across national borders, and psychology. Rather than rising and falling separately, national economies increasingly respond to the same forces.[2] Interdependence has become the leading principle of globalization.

The rise in value of one currency and fall of another have repercussions. A weak dollar benefits workers in the United States, and U.S. business in general. More KFC fast food restaurants are opening in China than in the United States, and more than half of the automobiles that General Motors produces are sold internationally. A weak dollar makes American goods and services more competitive in foreign markets, keeps jobs at home, and decreases the trade deficit because America's workers keep more production at home and sell more goods abroad. However, if the dollar keeps falling, it can have adverse implications for foreign economies: Germany, for example, can suffer if the euro continues to appreciate relative to the dollar, slowing down demand for German-made goods.[3]

In sectoral examples, an excess of steel in the world markets, attributed to overproduction in Russia and China, led to restructuring of the industry elsewhere in the world, leaving only a few players in the world steel oligopoly. And underproduction of oil attributed to the control of the Organization for Petroleum Exporting Countries (OPEC) has historically led to inflation worldwide because the price of gas is leading to the increase in price of all other goods. On the positive side, the boom in technology stocks in 1999 led to much—albeit short-lived—prosperity in many industrialized countries. Technology continues to make a strong positive impact on the economies of countries that stress technical training and software design, such as India. Never in the history of mankind has there been such a degree of interdependence.

The international economy has indeed become one single unit. Major companies simply cannot afford a local, home-country focus. The market share game is played on a world scale. The one-world commercial future is becoming a reality in which large multinationals rule. The top 100 companies in the world control about 20 percent of foreign assets, and employ six million workers, and account for as much as seven percent of total world economic activity. Multinational companies account for two-thirds of world trade, and many have economic weight. More than half of the 100 largest economies in the world are now corporations, not nations. Mitsubishi is bigger than Indonesia, Ford is bigger than Turkey and Wal-Mart is bigger than Israel.[4] As a result, multinationals are able to break down barriers that have withstood armies, missionaries, crusaders, and politicians.[5]

2-1b The Economic Development Disparity

In the current economic environment, firms from high-income, industrialized countries and their representative governments dominate the world economy, allocating resources worldwide based on market potential, rather than on local population needs, creating a growing gap between the *have* countries and *have-not* countries. Low-income countries, on the other hand, control resources (raw materials, labor) that multinationals need and access to local consumers, and they frequently pose barriers to international business operations in an attempt to lessen the development gap. It is important, in this environment, to understand the existing dynamics between countries at different levels of economic and market development and the philosophies underlying those dynamics.

2-2 Perspectives on Economic Development

Marxist-Leninist development model
A development model attributed to Karl Marx and Vladimir Lenin that maps the development of society from an agrarian, traditional society to a society characterized by shared ownership of the means and outcomes of production and an equitable resource allocation; advancement from one stage to another is based on class struggle and transfer of ownership from one class to another and, ultimately, to the state.

Rostow modernization model
An economic development model attributed to Rostow, according to which each stage of economic advance is a function of productivity, economic exchange, technological improvements, and income.

traditional society
A stage in economic development defined by Rostow as one in which the economy is dominated by agriculture and relatively few exchange transactions occur.

transitional society
A stage in the economic development process described by Rostow as characterized by increased productivity in agriculture and by the emergence of modern manufacturing.

take-off
A stage in economic development described by Rostow as one in which economic growth becomes the norm and improvements in production lead to the emergence of leading sectors.

Two models of economic development have gained acceptance in the world: a Western model, best articulated by Rostow, and the **Marxist-Leninist development model**, which still constitutes a dominant development philosophy in many emerging markets in socialist countries with developed markets. It must be noted that the fall of communism in Europe and Asia have reduced considerably the areas dominated by the Marxist-Leninist (Maoist) philosophy on economic development.

2-2a The Rostow Modernization Model

According to the **Rostow modernization model,**[6] each stage is a function of productivity, economic exchange, technological improvements, and income. Economic growth requires advancing from one stage to another. The modernization stages are:

- Traditional society
- Transitional society
- Take-off
- The drive to maturity
- High mass consumption

Traditional Society

Countries in the **traditional society** stage are characterized by an economic structure that is dominated by agriculture. Minimal productivity occurs, and only a few exchange transactions take place. Economic change and technological improvements are not sufficient to sustain any growth in per capita output, which is low.

Transitional Society (Pre-Conditions for Take-Off)

The **transitional society** stage is characterized by increased productivity in agriculture, and modern manufacturing begins to emerge. In manufacturing, low productivity remains the norm. The preconditions for take-off are the following: Society engages in secular education, establishes banks and currency, has an emerging entrepreneurial class, and the concept of manufacturing emerges, with only few sectors developing at first. Overall, there is limited production and limited output. Assuming these preconditions are met, take-off is likely in 10 to 50 years.

Take-Off

During **take-off,** growth becomes the norm and improvements in production lead to the emergence of leading sectors. Income rises across the board, and a new class of established entrepreneurs emerges.

The Drive to Maturity

In the **drive-to-maturity stage,** modern technology is fully adopted in all economic activity, and new leading sectors emerge. The economy demonstrates the technological and entrepreneurial skill to produce anything it chooses to. The economy looks beyond the country's border for development.

High Mass Consumption

In the age of **high mass consumption,** leading sectors shift toward durable goods. A surge occurs in per capita income and increased allocation to social welfare programs. The masses can afford goods beyond food, clothing, and shelter.

> **drive-to-maturity stage**
> A stage in economic development, described by Rostow, as characterized by the technological and entrepreneurial skill to produce anything society chooses to produce.
>
> **high mass consumption**
> A stage in economic development, described by Rostow, as characterized by leading sectors shifting toward durable goods.

2-2b Alternative Models of Economic Development: The Marxist-Leninist (Maoist) Model

The Rostow model of economic development is, in fact, a Western perspective of development. Alternative models exist in spite of the global triumph of the market system and the entrenchment of a Rostow-type model in countries that have previously adopted alternative philosophies. One example is the Marxist-Leninist (Maoist) model, a competing alternative for developing nations seeking to avoid domination by advanced market capitalist economies. It endorses a collective orientation, one adopted by the more traditional developing countries, and competes with market-oriented capitalism, fueling anticolonial and anti-imperialist sentiments.[7] Socialist ideas of sharing wealth, leveling inequality, eliminating homelessness, and providing basic needs such as health care, food, education, and shelter to all citizens appeal to many in the poor, developing countries that were long suppressed and exploited by colonial and imperialist powers. At the heart of this philosophy are issues of equitable distribution of income, improvement in the welfare of the masses, and economic justice.[8]

The Marxist-Leninist model and its dialectic materialism theories approach economic development philosophy similarly to the Rostow model in the first stage. The subsequent stages are depicted as a class struggle ending in revolution, which is needed for advancement to the next stage. Advancement is a function of the control of means of production, production outcomes, resource allocation, and the development of a mindset devoid of materialist needs. The stages of this model are described next.

The Primitive Society

Countries in the **primitive society** stage are similar to those in traditional society. There is joint, tribal ownership of the means of production, which are minimal, primitive, and centered on agricultural tasks, for the use of all the members of the commune within the tribe. Much of the agriculture is slash-and-burn, with the tribes moving in the quest for new territory. All tribal members in this egalitarian society work for the common welfare of the tribe.

The Slavery-Based Society

The **slavery-based society** emerges as a result of tribes taking over other tribes and enslaving their population. Slaves are now property of the conquering tribe. Under Roman, Mesopotamian, and Egyptian rule, slaves toiled in agriculture and built infrastructures, such as access roads and irrigation systems. Tribal territory ownership is established as a first step toward establishing private property. Trading agricultural goods and tools between tribes becomes common.

Feudalism

Under the feudal society known as **feudalism,** feudal lords own armies, land, and the dwellers of the land. Land is primarily in the hands of the feudal family; production is still primarily agricultural. Guilds emerge as a production unit, manufactur-

> **primitive society**
> The first stage of economic and political development, characterized, according to Marxist-Leninist theory, by the joint tribal ownership of primitive means of production centered on agricultural tasks.
>
> **slavery-based society**
> A stage of economic and political development, which, according to Marxist-Leninist theory, emerges as a result of tribes' dominance over other tribes: Dominant tribes claim ownership of conquered tribes and their property.
>
> **feudalism**
> A stage in economic and political development, which, according to Marxist-Leninist theory, is characterized by the dominance of feudal lords, who own the land and its dwellers.

ing goods and training future manufacturers under apprenticeships. Trading is common and widespread, and exchange is now primarily based on gold as currency.

bourgeoisie
A dominant social class, which, according to Marxist-Leninist theory, establishes lucrative means of production and achieves high productivity at the expense of exploited workers.

capitalism
A stage of economic and political development, which, according to Marxist-Leninist theory, is characterized, in its early stages, by an emerging bourgeoisie, the shift of production from the agrarian sector to the industrial sector, and, in its later stages, by imperialism, where capital loses its national identity by crossing borders and establishing monopolies.

imperialism
A stage of economic and political development, in which, according to Marxist-Leninist theory, capital loses its national identity by crossing borders.

monopolistic capitalism
A stage of economic and political development, in which, according to Marxist-Leninist theory, multinational companies establish monopolies and expand internationally with the goal of subjugating developing countries

socialism
A transition stage of economic and political development, characterized, according to Marxist-Leninist theory, by the disappearance of private property and its replacement with collective, state property.

communism
A stage in economic and political development, which, according to Marxist-Leninist theory, is characterized by state and cooperative ownership of all means of production and property.

The Capitalist Society

The capitalist society is represented by two stages. The first stage is characterized by an emerging **bourgeoisie** (developed from the guild class) as a ruling class alongside the aristocracy (the former feudal family). The bourgeoisie creates lucrative means of production, and it achieves high productivity at the expense of exploited workers. Production shifts gradually from the agrarian sector to the industrial sector.

The second stage of **capitalism** is multinational **imperialism.** Imperialist capitalism is characterized by a capital that loses its national identity by crossing borders; in fact, the export of capital – international trade – is a central mechanism of imperialism. The international firm is a double parasite exploiting its own working class, as well as workers in less-developed countries. Multinational firms represent the modality for national domination of developing countries and for the domination and subjugation of workers and peasants worldwide. The creation of international monopolies **(monopolistic capitalism)** represents the most advanced stage of capitalist dominance.

The Socialist Society

The socialist society is also composed of two stages. The first, transitional stage, leads to the gradual disappearance of private property, which is replaced by collective, state property. Countries in this stage typically are formally known as People's Republics—as in People's Republic of China. China's ideological elite argues that this stage can take, potentially, hundreds of years, but, at the very least, 100 years. During this time, capitalist structures coexist with state-owned enterprises, leading to rapid economic development. In this way, China reconciles its communist ideology and aspirations with the capitalist enterprise that fuels China's double-digit economic growth.

Socialism in its more advanced stage takes the form of the multilaterally developed socialist society. Socialist Republics, as countries in this stage are referred to, are characterized by state ownership of all the means of production. The state also controls the modes of production, allocating resources to industry, agriculture, education, and health care on the basis of societal needs. The state has in place most mechanisms necessary for the transition to communism with some exceptions of remnants of capitalism, such as private property limited to one's personal home or personal automobile, and remaining individual philosophies that need to be erased at the next stage, such as individuals' desires for material possessions.

The Communist Society

No country has ever claimed to have reached the communist stage. Under **communism,** all means of production and private property are under state ownership and/or cooperative ownership. The state is in charge of allocation of resources to sectors as needed and to individuals (goods and services) according to their needs. Communism develops "the new man," who views work as a need and who will work according to his ability. According to socialist dogma, there is no need for private property, and there is no materialism in society under communism.

In the early stages of communism, Lenin argued that foreign capital is important in the development process as a source of advanced technology. His solution was a leasing system whereby foreign firms would participate in particular projects and regions in communist countries for a limited amount of time.[9] In practice, this concept was soon countered by the situation created by the Cold War and by Stalin's theory of two parallel markets (capitalist and socialist), which stressed internal integration among socialist countries for mutual economic development. According to this theory, capitalist markets were inherently weak, and socialist countries needed to isolate themselves from the capitalist world.[10]

The Rostow and Marxist-Leninist models are comparable, up to a point. In Figure 2-1, the models work in parallel up to the level of the drive-to-maturity stage in the Rostow model and the capitalist stage in the Marxist-Leninist model.

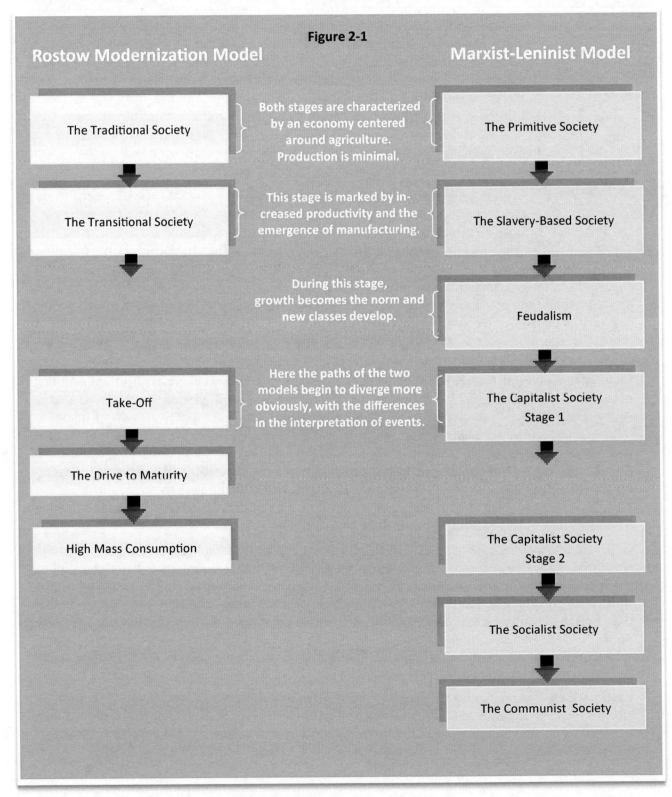

Figure 2-1

emerging markets (also middle-income countries)
Countries that are developing rapidly and have great economic potential; the World Bank characterizes them as middle-income countries, with a GNP per capita of US$766 to US$9,265.

high-income countries (developed countries)
Highly industrialized countries with well-developed industrial and service sectors and a GNI per capita of US$10,726 or more.

big emerging markets (BEMs)
Large markets characterized by rapid economic development and high potential; big emerging markets set the pace for the economy in their geographic region.

low-income countries
Countries that are primarily agrarian, and are often neglected or underserved by large multinationals, and have a GNI per capita of less than US$875.

2-3 Levels of Economic Development

There are many competing classifications of countries from an economic development perspective. Historically, the informal and frequently used classification in the Western world has referred to highly industrialized, developed countries as the First World, to socialist countries as the Second World, and to developing countries as the Third World. Of this classification, only the term "Third World" has been used widely, and it is still being used, even after the fall of communism. Another classification, advanced by the United Nations (www.un.org), provides for three groups: LLDCs (least-developed countries and the lowest-income countries); LDCs (less-developed countries and lower-income countries); and developed countries (DCs). Yet other classifications exist. For example, the term NIC (newly industrialized country) was initially used to describe the economies of Taiwan, Singapore, South Korea, and Hong Kong (known in the 1980s and 1990s as the *Asian Tigers*), whereas countries such as Brazil, Argentina, Chile, Peru, and the transitional economies of Central and Eastern Europe are described as **emerging markets**. For the purpose of this textbook, we will refer to three categories of countries, based on the classification used by the World Bank (www.worldbank.org):

- **High-income countries (developed countries in a pre-2007 classification)** These are highly industrialized countries with well-developed industrial and service sectors. In this category fall newly industrialized countries, as well as countries that have had a developed status for many years. Although these countries present great potential because they have consumers with the highest per capita income, they also present challenges to international firms because their markets are in the maturity stage, consumers have established preferences, and competition is intense. The World Bank refers to the countries in this category as high-income countries, with a Gross National Income (GNI) per capita of US$10,726 or more. GNI is an indicator of income developed by the World Bank that is the dollar value of the country's yearly income divided by its population – that is, the average income of the citizens.

- **Middle-income countries (countries with emerging markets in the previous classification)**—Among the countries in this category are countries in Latin America, such as Argentina, Brazil, Uruguay, Paraguay, Chile, Peru, and Bolivia, to name a few; countries in Asia, such as China, with its immense market and a substantial middle class; and the transition economies of Central and Eastern Europe, which are rapidly privatizing state-owned industries and adopting market reforms. Important in this category are **big emerging markets (BEMs),** the largest emerging markets, which present the greatest potential for international trade and expansion. The World Bank refers to the countries in this category as middle-income countries, with a GNI per capita of US$875 to US$10,725. The middle-income country category is further divided into two income groups, as follows:

- **Upper middle income countries**—These countries have rapidly developing economies, and especially in urban areas, they have an infrastructure that is on par with that of developed countries. Among them are countries in Latin America, such as Argentina, Chile, and Mexico. In this category are the transition economies of Central and Eastern Europe, new European Union member countries that have rapidly privatized state-owned industries and adopted market reforms, such as the Czech Republic, Estonia, Hungary, Latvia, Lithuania, and Poland. The Russian Federation is also in this category. According to the World Bank, countries considered upper middle income countries have a GNI per capita of US$3,466 to US$10,725.

- **Lower middle income countries**—This is a diverse group of countries that includes China, much of North Africa and the Middle East, and many of the former Soviet Socialist Republics, such as Armenia, Azerbaijan, Belarus, Georgia, Kazakhstan, Moldova, Turkmenistan, and the Ukraine. According to the World Bank, countries in this category have a GNI per capita of US$875 to US$3,465.

- **Low-income countries (developing countries, in the previous classification)**—Countries in this category are primarily agrarian, have low per capita income levels, and are located in different regions in Asia and in sub-Saharan Africa. Many low-income countries are often neglected or underserved by large multinationals and consequently present great potential as niche markets. But even the countries with the lowest per capita income have a stratum of society that can afford even the most expensive global brands. Furthermore, because they are the primary recipients of international development aid, they present important opportunities for firms operating in the areas of infrastructure development and industrial sector development and for related consultancies. The World Bank refers to the countries in this category as low-income countries, with a GNI per capita of less than US$875. It is important to note that these markets are grossly underserved by the international community and that consumer needs—even the most basic ones—in these markets are barely met by local administration. International Marketing Illustration 2-1 addresses challenges faced by consumers in low-income countries.

International Marketing Illustration 2-1
The Underserved Markets

In many low-income countries, children must walk miles to reach their schools. In Adaboya, Ghana, for example, children must walk three miles to attend school even though a school building is located in the village. The local school is in disrepair and cannot be used in the rainy season. An average poor child in Mali has to walk five miles to elementary school. In Portero Sula, El Salvador, villagers cannot obtain health services at the local clinic because there are no doctors or nurses on staff. In the Mutasa district of Zimbabwe, women report that they were hit by staff during delivery of their babies.

Even in markets where services are available, the quality of services and their delivery are low. Absenteeism of doctors in Bangladesh is about 74 percent. Teachers in Ethiopia are absent a large percentage of the time. Children may attend school, but there may not be any teaching activity. Plus, 1 billion people lack access to adequate water sources, and 2.5 billion lack access to adequate sanitation.

The World Bank and the rest of the international aid community are taking forceful action to ensure that communities take concerted action to improve service delivery to these markets. For example, in El Salvador, community-managed schools, where parents are involved in their children's education and visit the school regularly, have a lower rate of absenteeism. In Bangalore, India, and in Cambodia, consumers have successfully penalized the poor delivery of services and forced local politicians and service providers to act.

For developing country consumers, priorities are highest for meeting basic needs. From a marketing perspective, however, these consumers are not a priority for most multinationals, but, rather, an afterthought or a niche market at best. And yet, appropriate marketing strategies for these markets can, in the long run, serve the company well. The industrialized countries of the world account for only 15 percent of the total world population, and the greatest growth potential exists in the markets that are currently underserved.

There are many examples of successful marketing in low-income countries. For example, Grameen-Phone, a company in Bangladesh, markets cell phones to the country's 35,000 villages: women work as agents who lease phone time to other villagers, one call at a time. Colgate-Palmolive has increased its rural marketing budget for India many fold, using video vans that show infomercials about the benefits of toothpaste, and, currently, drawing half of its profits from rural areas. Head & Shoulders shampoo sells in India in small packets that cost 8 cents; women there shampoo their hair once a week, and they purchase shampoo as they need it. Amway, Gillette, and other multinationals sell their products in pillow-like packets that contain about an ounce of product, like shaving gel, dishwashing liquid, and toothpaste. These consumers also buy a single cigarette instead of a pack, one egg instead of a dozen. Today, there is hardly any shampoo brand in India that is not available in sachets.

Sources: Vijay Mahajan, Marcos V. Pratini De Moraes, and Jerry Wind, "The Invisible Global Market," *Marketing Management*, Winter 2000, pp. 9, 4, 30–35; *World Development Report 2004: Making Services Work for Poor People;* World Bank Group, http://econ.worldbank.org/wdr/wdr2004; Rasul Bailay, "Small Packets, Big Business," *Far Eastern Economic Review*, January 23, 2003, pp. 166, 3, 40–41.

The discrepancy between the countries in the three categories—high-income, middle-income, and low-income —is evident: With regard to the GNP distribution worldwide, high-income, highly industrialized countries account for close to 80 percent of the world's gross national product, whereas they account for less than 15 percent of the population.

To illustrate, the United Nations Development Program monitors human development worldwide and publishes its findings in the *Human Development Report*. The report compares countries based on adult illiteracy, access to a viable water source, children underweight for their age, and the percentage of the population living on less than $1 per day. Table 2-1 compares countries in the low-human-development category on those dimensions.

Table 2-1: An Illustration of Human Development in Select Low-Income Countries

Rank (of Total 175 Countries)	Country	Life Expectancy at Birth	Adult Literacy Rate (% age 15 or older)	Population without Adequate Water Access (%)	Children Under-weight for Age (% younger than age 5)	Population Living on $1 Per Day or Less (%)
166	Rwanda	55.4	70.7	35	17.2	76.8
167	Benin	56.1	41.7	25	17.6	n.a.
170	Cote d'Ivoire	55.4	55.3	20	28.4	23.8
171	Malawi	54.2	73.7	17	12.6	n.a.
184	Mozambique	50.2	55.1	55	16	60
185	Burundi	50.4	66.6	28	35.2	81.3
186	Niger	54.7	28.7	54	37.5	43.1

Source: Human Development Report, *United Nations Development Programme*, 2011, http://hdr.undp.org/en/reports/global/hdr2011/

2-3a The Importance of Emerging Markets

Countries with emerging markets present great potential to international firms. Their attractiveness lies primarily in their rate of economic growth—7 percent per year, in the past 20 years, compared with 2.3 percent for Western Europe and North America.[11] The following countries have been identified as emerging markets by *The Economist* in its regular reports on emerging markets:

- In Asia: China, India, Indonesia, Malaysia, the Philippines, Singapore, South Korea, Thailand
- In Africa and the Middle East: Israel, South Africa
- In Europe: The Czech Republic, Poland, Russia, Turkey
- In Latin America: Argentina, Brazil, Chile, Mexico, Venezuela

Other countries are likely prospects for the emerging market category on the basis of their economic policies and performance in the past 20 years. Among them are Slovenia, Slovakia, Croatia, Romania, Bulgaria, the Ukraine, Latvia, Estonia, Lithuania, and Belarus in Central and Eastern Europe and Colombia, Paraguay, Peru, and Uruguay in Latin America. These countries are rapidly privatizing their economies and adopting the economic reforms necessary to create a stable, growing economy.

Countries with emerging markets that are expected to have a successful economic future share a number of traits:[10]

- High political stability
- A sound currency
- A low level of inflation
- Privatization policies that reduce government deficit, create first-time share owners who vote for pro-business conservative policies, and diminish the power of trade unions
- Policies that facilitate repatriation of dividends and capital
- Policies that are in line with international accounting standards
- Open disclosure of directors' interests
- Policies that stress regular reporting of earnings and sales figures
- A sound and comprehensive system of corporate law
- A liquid and well-traded securities market reflecting fair prices
- A high savings rate
- Strong government support for internationalization
- A people characterized by integrity, a strong work ethic, and respect for the law

Of interest to multinationals are the big emerging markets (BEMs). These markets share all the traits of emerging markets and present the most potential because they are large, have large populations, and, consequently, set the pace for the economy in the region. Among these countries are China and India (both with populations exceeding 1 billion), South Korea, Argentina, Brazil, Mexico, South Africa, Poland, and Turkey. The big emerging markets are developing rapidly and making rapid strides toward industrialization. However, breakneck growth can be problematic, as in the case of India.

India

India has an economy with a double-digit growth coupled with an outsourcing industry that serves the world's multinationals. It also has hundreds of millions of consumers who demand class and comfort. However, this rapid development has created an overheated economy with an inflationary spiral. Food prices are quickly climbing so that the poor can barely afford it; housing prices are rising rapidly, especially in large cities; and factories are running behind in filling orders. Prices in India are rising twice as fast as in China—its rival for foreign investment and outsourcing—and considerably faster than in industrialized countries. In the fashionable neighborhoods of South Mumbai, home prices have increased by 60 percent a year in the recent years, and oil-rich investors are bidding against India's affluent business elite for these properties. A 2,000 square foot apartment with a cheap concrete floor and flimsy closets in the chic Malabar Hill neighborhood was selling for $1.5 million. The rising prices are rekindling nostalgia for the 1980s, when India was one of the most highly regulated economies.[12]

2-4 The Political Environment of International Marketing

Iran

Iran 1970, the period before the Islamic Revolution. The Iranian government focused on projects aimed at increasing industrial development. Iranians were generally satisfied with the increased socioeconomic facilities. In 1976, dissatisfied groups engaged in scattered demonstrations against the Shah's regime. The demonstrations increased in frequency and resulted in the occupation of state-owned, American, and Israeli facilities, finally resulting in the Shah's leaving the country. In 1979, the government and the banking industries were paralyzed.

1979–1984. After the 1979 revolution, the new government took hostile action against foreign multinationals, arresting expatriate staff and local staff related to the former regime and confiscating multinational companies, especially those from the United States and Israel. Business in general deteriorated due to the political intervention and the Iran-Iraq war.

1985. The Islamic regime consolidated and local businesses gained ground and stability.[13]

1997–2006. The European Union is Iran's largest trading partner; companies from the United States are banned from doing business with Iran. The U.S. government continues to threaten sanctions against non-U.S. companies doing business in Iran.

2007–Present. The International Atomic Energy Agency, the U.N.'s nuclear watchdog, faulted Iran for violating nuclear agreements by intensifying its efforts to create a nuclear-fuel cycle, while diminishing the IAEA's ability to monitor its activities.[14]

The preceding time line demonstrates the volatile nature of alliances in the present world market. The United States enjoyed a close rapport with the deposed Shah Reza Pahlavi, and U.S. businesses profited under his rule. The Islamic Revolution targeted the Shah's allies in particular. U.S. firms had all their assets confiscated, and their international executives were forced to repatriate. Today, the United States continues to ban the involvement of U.S. firms in Iran and to threaten sanctions on foreign firms with U.S. interests if they engage in operations in the country. Moreover, the relationship between the United States and Iran reached new levels of conflict in 2012, as Iran continued building its nuclear capabilities. This section illustrates the political uncertainties involved in international marketing and the legal challenges that firms face in their international operations.

Companies contemplating any international involvement must have an in-depth knowledge of the political environment in the countries where they do business. This is especially important for companies involved in foreign direct investment—companies that undertake the greatest level of risk in a foreign market. Whenever there are discussions of **political risk,** they typically involve the host country—the country where a company engages in business in accordance with the respective country's political and legal restrictions. It should be noted, however, that the international company is also affected by political developments in its home country, the country where the parent company is headquartered. A U.S.-based company planning to enter Cuba in the late 1990s, when the Clinton administration appeared to relax anti-Cuba restrictions, had many more prospects than it had thereafter, when subsequent administrations committed to enforcing the embargo.

political risk
The risk associated with actions of local, regional, and parastatal governing bodies affecting the international company, and with the overall economic and political stability within a particular country.

At the basis of international law lies the concept of sovereignty: Sovereignty is defined as a country's self-determination and independence from external interference in internal affairs and complete authority over all nationals living in the country and beyond its borders (individuals and corporations). All countries in the world are sovereign, and yet all must curtail their sovereignty to coexist in the world of nations and defend their national interests. By permitting international trade and by entering into international agreements, countries limit their sovereignty. When countries perceive that international firms, governments, or organizations have infringed on their right to self-determination, they can invoke national sovereignty and take actions that erect barriers to trade or even jeopardize the presence of international companies within their borders.

Ideally, a firm crossing borders will enter an environment that is politically stable and pro-trade. But this is often not the case: A company could find that the government with which it worked hard to establish a good working relationship collapsed overnight, and its replacement could have ties with a competitor—or it could be against foreign business altogether, as was the case of Iran during the Islamic Revolution, described in the preceding paragraphs. International companies doing business in Cuba and Eastern Europe experienced a similar fate after the communist takeover.

Similarly, the stable environment where a business has operated unfettered for decades could suddenly be at the center of a civil war that nobody had foreseen: In the case of Rwanda, formerly known as the Switzerland of Africa for its beauty and for its pro-business climate, many international businesses were forced to leave their inventory and buildings behind when the genocide began. In today's peaceful Venezuela and Russia, government leaders are threatening nationalization of various energy interests. In other examples, a protectionist measure of one government could launch a series of retaliations both by the government and by consumers: When the United States instituted measures against European protectionism by increasing duties on nonessential European exports (cheese, perfume, soap, accessories), it had not expected the retaliations of Europeans against icons of U.S. business, such as McDonald's and Coca-Cola. More recently, the United States have been faulted by Canada, the European Union, Australia, Brazil, Argentina, Nicaragua, Uruguay, Guatemala, and Thailand for exceeding the agricultural subsidies limit imposed under WTO rules, through direct payments, loan deficiency payments, and other programs for products such as wheat, soybeans, corn, and sugar. With appropriate political maneuvering, however, the United States averted the retaliation.[15]

2-4a Political Risk: An Overview

Evaluating Political Risk

A company has several resources at its disposal to evaluate country risk: The Department of State, the Department of Commerce, and other governmental and nongovernmental agencies provide data on country political risk that is current and continually updated to reflect new developments in each country around the world (see an example of country risk evaluation in Table 2-2). Some examples of useful publications providing periodic information on country risk are:

- Business periodicals such as *The Economist* and *The Wall Street Journal*.

- Commercial sources, such as *Country Reports,* the Economist Intelligence Unit, Ltd., Chase (particularly its guide for exporters), and RUNDT's World Business Intelligence. RUNDT's (S. J. Rundt & Associates, Inc.), for example, provides information on political developments, currency, and the regulatory environment; it provides insurance data and trade information, as well as a country risk rating on a scale from 1 to 10, and risk perception and collection experience for the previous four months.

Political Risk Signals

A number of country risk elements should be monitored on a regular basis to keep track of developments that might ultimately affect the international company. These elements are illustrated in Table 2-3.

Table 2-2 : Country Risk Score

Rank/Country	Risk Score (Max = 100)	Political Risk (Max = 100)	Economic Performance (Max = 100)
1 Norway	93.44	92.97	90.40
2 Luxembourg	91.03	93.67	81.00
3 Switzerland	89.59	87.23	82.50
15 United States	81.60	85.25	60.67
16 United Kingdom	80.04	81.91	59.80
25 Japan	74.66	76.79	53.80
38 Saudi Arabia	65.12	51.67	72.14
47 Hungary	59.67	59.42	47.55
56 India	56.96	49.66	57.00
57 Russia	56.83	44.30	61.56
93 Venezuela	42.47	32.16	47.67
98 Belarus	39.84	34.38	

Source: Adapted from "Country Risk," *Euromoney*, March 2011, p. 1.

Table 2-3: Country Risk Elements

Economic performance signal	United Kingdom unemployment is increasing due to higher immigration and falling levels of economic activity.
Political repression signal	Peaceful protest is not a right for Russians: violent clashes between riot police and pro-democracy demonstrators in Moscow and St. Petersburg are the norm.
Internal diversity and incongruent interests	Eastern European and Turkish migrants are flocking to the high-income countries of the European Union. They do not acculturate easily and create divergent interests in Old Europe.
Political instability and the instability of government policies	Taiwan's ruling party welcomes a closer relationship to China. However, the opposition, the DDP, endorses a separatist policy relative to China, limiting access to Taiwan's market. The two opposing parties occasionally have physical fights.

Economic Performance

A poor economic performance and forecast are likely to lead to greater levels of unrest in the country. Of particular concern are high inflationary rates and high unemployment rates, both of which could lead to political instability.

General business performance is also important. Commercial payment terms and collection experience indicate the availability of hard currency reserves and access to hard currency. Default on loans is likely to be a threat to companies contemplating entrance into the market. Finally, an increase in regulatory restrictions on investment, capital, or trade flows should be closely monitored.[16]

Political Repression

Repression of certain ethnic groups is a signal of potential political instability. The perceived repression of Muslims in France transformed the student riots in the last decade into quasi-ethnic uprisings. It did not help that the then secretary of the interior and president, Nicolas Sarkozy, adopted a strong stance against immigrant dissent, calling the rioters the "scum of the earth." The repression of gypsies and Muslims in Central and Eastern Europe continues to create flare-ups. Anti-Semitism is rampant in France, and the French government is unable to subdue the inflammatory rhetoric.

General repression by the elite—especially if the elite's position is not considered legitimate[17]—is always a signal of political instability. Personality cults in particular are problematic because they bring about widespread antipathy. Turkmenistan offered a relatively recent example. Its past leader, Saparmurad Niyazov, made himself president for life, calling himself the Father of the Turkmen and occupying virtually every high office of the state. His rule was symbolized by a revolving gold statue of himself and by grandiose marble-clad public buildings. At the same time, the country's education and health systems deteriorated greatly, and the regime piled up a record of human rights abuses. Niyazov died a natural death in December 2006 and was replaced by a dentist, Gurbanguly Berdymukhammedov, who kept in place most restrictions on civil society and the media. One of his first actions as president was to court the support of the political elite, continuing the patronage network, rewarding political loyalty with economic benefits. Like Mr. Niyazov, he balanced rival interests through regular personnel reshuffles, ensuring that no one faction gained the upper hand.[18]

Internal Diversity and Incongruent Interests

Even if no political repression exists within a country, ethnic diversity and incongruent interests lead to a history of distrust and conflict (open or simmering) in the population. There are numerous examples of repression and conflict due to diversity around the world—among the most obvious are Darfur in the Sudan and Eritrea in Ethiopia. The opening vignette also discusses the conflict between the Tutsis and the Hutus in Rwanda, a conflict that is equally alive in neighboring Burundi. Romania has a large minority of Hungarians who are actively advocating secession and annexation to Hungary of the region in Transylvania where Hungarians represent the dominant population. In more developed countries, substantial ethnic conflict still exists, not just between the established ethnicity. As in the case of Belgium, where the Flemish (Dutch) and Wallonians (French) often find themselves in opposition, but also between the new immigrants and long-established nationals, as in the case of Germany, where Turkish immigrants have been targets of hate crimes.

Political Stability and the Stability of Government Policies

Although presidents and governments change every few years, with a few exceptions, national government policies do not necessarily change radically, nor does the level of political risk. On average, Italy has had a new government for every year since World War II, and yet its commercial policies have remained unchanged. Germany has had pro-business conservatives at its helm, followed by a government with a more socialist bent, with no substantial impact on international business. Former communists have succeeded democratic presidents in Central and Eastern Europe without any substantial change in the countries' pro-business attitudes. Hong Kong has become an integral part of China, and to date, this has created more opportunities than threats for international Trade.

Yet political change can be a cause for concern for international firms. Companies that have operated in countries that have had decades of stability and prosperity under a one-party rule can be affected instantly by political turmoil. Although transition from a one-party rule can be peaceful, this is often the exception. In addition to a change in the ruling party, companies should look for other signals that announce political instability: Tamil separatists in Sri Lanka, political riots in Indonesia, Rwandan refugees in Uganda and the Congo—all spell trouble for the companies operating in the respective countries.

2-4b Nationalism

The expression of fierce nationalist sentiment, or **nationalism,** in a country where the company is operating could constitute a cause for concern to the international company. While the expression of nationalist feelings, such as pride in a country's history and accomplishments, is common in most countries, nationalist sentiment may signal attempts at separation from or isolation of a particular segment of society, which could lead to political instability in the country. This is the case of the Tamil separatist movement in Sri Lanka, which has led to economic chaos in the country. Particularly problematic for international business are expressions of antiforeigner sentiment and antiforeign business bias. Shared beliefs that engaging in international business represents selling one's country raise questions about the future trade environment in the respective country. In the United States in the 1980s, the "buy American" slogans echoing especially in the automobile and textile industries presented great concern to European and Asian business and private investors. Of special concern to international marketing managers is *consumer ethnocentrism*—the belief that buying foreign goods will put local companies out of business and is, consequently, morally wrong.[19] Countries where such beliefs dominate are more likely to erect barriers to international trade.

> **nationalism**
> An expression of fierce nationalist sentiment in a country where a company is operating, which poses an implicit threat to the company and its operations.

For example, Thailand experienced a military coup in September 2006, resulting in new rules in foreign investment that frightened foreign investors. The military-appointed cabinet initiated more stringent laws of foreign ownership, requiring investors to sell holdings that exceed 50 percent ownership in companies based in Thailand and to give up voting rights in excess of 50 percent. U.S. firms are protected from this rule by a treaty with Thailand that dates back to the Vietnam War, but European and Japanese companies were very much affected. The Foreign Business Act bans foreigners from owning majority shares in Thai businesses ranging from the media, rice farming, production of Buddha images, legal services, and construction.[20] It will be interesting to observe developments in Thailand's restrictions, particularly in light of the Association of Southeast Asian Nations plans, announced in 2011, to open the region to the free movement of capital and labor by 2015.

2-4c Political Risks and Risk Management in International Marketing

Nationalism and claims to national sovereignty can lead to protectionist measures on the part of the host-country government, whereas political instability can lead to the failure of the economy. All can harm the operations of the company in the respective country, from hurting sales and all prospects in the market to losing all company assets. In the following sections "Risks Related to Government Trade Policies," "Risks Related to Government Economic Policy," "Risks Related to Labor and Action Groups," and "Risks Related to Terrorism" are examples of risks a company can experience in international markets and examples of risk management for each category of risk.

Risks Related to Government Trade Policies

The host-country government can erect trade barriers, imposing tariffs and nontariff barriers on international business, such as exchange-rate controls, voluntary export restraints and different types of quotas and export/import license requirements. A company could also find itself falling victim to a trade war, in which the host country and home country reciprocally restrict the flow of goods. Or the company's home-country government can impose embargoes and sanctions on the host country, which could force the company to exit the market. All these risks are addressed at length in Chapter 3, International Trade: Institutional Barriers and Facilitators.

Risks Related to Government Economic Policy

Local governments can use taxes as a means to control foreign investment: During downturns in the economy, governments find that taxing foreign companies provides a source of valuable revenue. Under more extreme conditions, especially if accompanied by a radical change in the political leadership, change could potentially lead to the involuntary transfer of the firm's assets to local ownership. Companies face the following types of risks:

- Confiscation
- Expropriation
- Creeping expropriation
- Nationalization
- Domestication

Confiscation

Confiscation refers to the seizing of company assets and investors' assets without any compensation. In the 1940s and 1950s, most private companies operating in Central and Eastern Europe had their assets confiscated. More recently, all U.S. firms operating in Iran were confiscated after the Islamic Revolution of 1979, when Shah Reza Pahlavi was dethroned. The United States subsequently imposed an embargo on all trade with Iran in 1987, which prohibited the exportation or importation of all goods and services to and from Iran.

Expropriation

Expropriation involves some reimbursement for company assets, usually not at their market value. When Fidel Castro ascended to power in Cuba and a totalitarian regime was instituted, the assets of U.S. multinationals and U.S. citizens were seized. The Castro government offered payment that was deemed inappropriate, and as a result, the United States imposed an embargo on trade with Cuba that is currently still in effect. More recently, in 2012, South Africa's African National Congress decided to end the policy of buying land from willing white farmers, advocating for land grabs with partial compensation.

Creeping Expropriation

Creeping expropriation refers to a condition characterized as "difficult bureaucracies, unreliable judicial systems, shifting regulations, and corrupt operating environments."[21] Although not explicitly, government actions discourage foreign investment, especially investment in nonessential sectors. This strategy typically uses additional barriers that are imposed on international trade.

Nationalization

Nationalization involves a takeover by the local government with the aim of creating a government-run industry. International law regards nationalization as legitimate as long as it is in the public interest and it offers fair compensation to the international company and to its investors. In 1997, the Korean government decided to nationalize the automobile company Kia Motors by converting the state-run Korea Development Bank's debt into an equity stake in the company.[22] In the aftermath of the Asian crisis, governments began nationalizing ailing banks across the region. In Indonesia, the government controls nearly all the country's biggest banks and has taken over around 75 percent of all bank assets, whereas in Japan, as a result of nationalization, the government, instead of markets, now plays a larger role in determining the flow of capital.[23]

More recently, in 2012, the Argentine government announced plans to nationalize the YPF Argentine oil firm, or at least to reduce part of Spanish company

confiscation
The foreign government seizure of company assets and investors' assets without any compensation.

expropriation
The foreign government seizure of company assets with partial reimbursement, usually not at market value.

creeping expropriation
A situation characterized by bureaucratic red tape and corruption, an unreliable judicial system, and shifting regulations, where foreign government actions discourage foreign investment, especially investment in nonessential sectors.

nationalization
The takeover of company assets by a foreign government with the aim of creating a government-run industry.

Repson's majority stake in the Argentine oil company – an act reminiscent of former Argentine preside, Juan Perón's nationalizations in the 1940s, which lead to an economic downfall.

As mentioned earlier, Thailand now requires European and Japanese foreign investors to sell holdings such that they would ultimately own less than 50 percent of the company: The Foreign Business Act bans foreigners from owning majority shares in Thai businesses. [24]

In other examples, Venezuela's president Hugo Chavez nationalized companies in the telecommunications and electricity industries and attempted to gain more control over natural gas projects. His goal was to change Venezuela into a socialist state with strong state oversight. [25]

Domestication

Domestication occurs when the local government requires a gradual transfer of ownership and management to locals. This transfer is usually completed over time, through consecutive government decrees aimed at reducing the presence of multinationals in nonessential local sectors (such as the consumer goods sector).

Companies can protect themselves against political instability by understanding the structure of the government, the political parties, and the ideologies of the ruling party, as well as the competing ideologies of the opposition. As a first step, companies must make every attempt to be exemplary corporate citizens in every country where they operate. A solid reputation for product quality and community involvement can create a general environment that is favorable toward a company's local operations.

domestication
The process initiated by a foreign government leading to the gradual transfer of ownership and management to locals.

Overseas Private Investment Corporation (OPIC)
U.S. government corporation that provides loans, guarantees and insurance to U.S. corporations investing in countries that present high political risk.

A company also can minimize its risk by partnering with local companies, creating local expertise in product manufacturing and management, and using local suppliers. McDonald's, for example, frequently stresses the use of local ingredients in all its offerings. Similarly, companies that produce products deemed essential for local development, such as industrial products, high-technology products, or pharmaceutical products, are less vulnerable to changes in government policies than companies that manufacture goods that are considered nonessential, such as consumer goods.

Companies can obtain insurance coverage against nationalization from private insurance sources. For example, companies such as Global Risk Advisors insure against confiscation, expropriation, and nationalization, in addition to providing insurance against war risk; localized or subnational conflicts; kidnapping, ransom, and extortion; property terrorism; and currency inconvertibility; among others.[26] The U.S. government, through the **Overseas Private Investment Corporation,** or **OPIC** (http://www.opic.gov), also offers policies that insure companies against expropriation, nationalization, or confiscation by foreign governments. OPIC insures U.S. investments in emerging markets and developing countries against expropriation and political violence, such as revolution and war.

Risks Related to Labor and Action Groups

In many countries, labor unions are very powerful and can often influence national policies. For example, layoffs by foreign companies can bring about negative feelings that are likely to affect companies in the long term. Boycotts initiated by action groups can also negatively affect companies. Esso (Exxon) was the victim of a "Boycott Esso" campaign aimed at the United States' environmental policies. These actions are not usually sanctioned by the national government; they are, however, legal.

Companies have some control over the actions of labor and action groups. Although they cannot control market demand and derived demand for labor, companies can provide severance packages that are fair, as well as invest in the services of job placement businesses in an effort to seek placement for the employees who have been terminated. To avoid negative public sentiment, companies must be politically neutral and keep a distance from local politics. Too close an association with a governing regime could elicit a negative attitude toward the company and its products. Pepsi, unfairly, is perceived as the drink that greased the hands of the former communist elite in Central and Eastern Europe, whereas Coke is associated with the new, free society. It is important for a company to be perceived as a good citizen of the country where it operates, and as a company that has created opportunities for locals and that continues to serve their interests.

Risks Related to Terrorism

International terrorist attacks against multinational interests gained worldwide attention with the September 11, 2001, attack on the World Trade Center in New York City. In the years preceding this attack, terrorist attacks steadily increased in frequency. Organizations or businesses with a U.S. connection alone were hit 206 times in 2000, up from 169 in 1999; internationally, private-sector facilities were attacked 384 times, up from 276 in 1999, whereas only 17 government facilities and 13 military facilities were similarly hit around the globe. Terrorism was most lethal in Asia in the year 2000, with 281 of the 405 international victims perishing there. Africa had the second highest total, with 73 dead.[27] In 2003, the number of people killed by terrorism was 625 (with 725 killed the preceding year); and 208 terror incidents took place, resulting in the injury of 3,646 people.[28]

The events of September 2001 have exponentially altered the trend of those statistics. Experts evaluated these attacks as the culmination of a 20-year trend toward assaults aimed to kill many people in technically complex operations.[29] A blow to the financial nerve center of capitalism,[30] the September 11 events disrupted financial operations worldwide, displaced hundreds of businesses in the area and beyond, and for the first time ever, stopped all travel in U.S. airspace. An "attack on the world's . . . superpower, undertaken as a consequence of specific American alliances and actions,"[31] these actions are representative of **corporate terrorism** with the greatest of scopes. Today, the Economist Intelligence Unit in London estimates that businesses are the target of nearly 20 percent of international terrorist attacks.[32]

corporate terrorism
The use of violence or threat of violence aimed at corporations.

Companies have some control, however, in reducing their likelihood of becoming victims of terrorism by training employees in terrorism avoidance, such as briefing personnel on what to expect when entering high-risk areas and offering training for eluding roadblocks and avoiding hazardous encounters.[33] Companies can also purchase insurance against terrorist acts from private insurance companies. For example, Cigna International's International Specialty Products & Services offers insurance products that cover kidnapping, detention (kidnapping without asking for ransom), hijacking, evacuation, business interruption and extra expenses, product recall expenses, and expenses arising from child abduction, such as hiring private investigators or posting rewards for information.[34]

One year after the Arab Spring, in 2012, the global insurance broker Aon downgraded many of the countries in the Middle East on its terrorism and political risk index, due to the civil unrest, strikes, and protests in these countries. Corporations in these countries will have to pay higher risk premiums, as will companies in France, Italy, Spain, and Germany, among others as these countries have also been downgraded from low risk to medium risk.

2-5 The International Legal Environment

International marketing is affected by three types of law:

- **International Laws**—A body of rules and regulations that countries agree to abide by. International law addresses agreements among countries with regard to trade, protection of property, and other issues in the political and economic sphere. International law agreements, although not enforceable, can be appropriately addressed by international law bodies.

- **Host-Country Laws**—Laws of the different countries where the company operates. The legal system in the host country could differ substantially from that of the company's home country.

- **Home-Country Laws**—Laws of the company's home country. Home-country laws follow the company all over the world.

international laws
Rules and regulations that countries agree to abide by, addressing agreements among countries with regard to trade, protection of property, and other issues in the political and economic sphere.

host-country laws
Local laws; laws of the different countries where a company operates.

home-country laws
Laws of a company's home country that follow the international company all over the world.

U.S. companies must abide by all three types of law. For example, they must abide by international trade laws and agreements, such as WTO trade regulations; they must abide by host-country laws governing every aspect of the company's operations; and they must abide by home-country laws, such as antitrust regulations and corrupt practices regulations.

2-5a Legal Systems

Three legal systems are predominant: common law, code law, and Islamic law.

Common Law

Common law is based on prior court rulings (legal precedent). It has its roots in English common law, on which U.S. law is based. This system of law is shared by many of the countries formerly colonized by Great Britain.

Code (Civil) Law

Code law—or civil law—refers to comprehensive written laws that specify what constitutes legal behavior. Code law has its roots in Roman law. This system of law is shared by most of the countries in the world, including most of Europe, Latin America, China, Taiwan, Japan, and South Korea.

Formerly socialist countries have fully adopted civil law and are now struggling to ensure that it is properly implemented. Under the socialist system, countries of the former Soviet Union and the Eastern Bloc had a system of laws that allowed a large degree of flexibility in enforcement. All the nomenklatura, the high-ranking communist party officials and their offspring, were largely exempt from enforcement, with some exceptions. For the common person, however, activities deemed illegal, such as listening to Western radio stations or harboring a Western visitor, could place one in prison indefinitely. Selective enforcement persists even today along with corruption in some of the countries in this part of the world.

Islamic Law

Islamic law (sha'ria) is a system of law based on the interpretation of the Koran, Islam's holy book, and on interpretations of the practices and sayings of the prophet Muhammad. Islamic law establishes rules for business practices that can affect firms' operations. For example, it requires the sexes to be separate; in practice, this means that women cannot interact in any environment with men with whom they are not related. It also bans the consumption of products such as pork and alcohol, it does not allow banks to offer or charge interest. Islamic law requires Muslims to pray five times a day and to fast during the month of Ramadan.

All these factors have an impact on firms' local operations wherever Islamic law constitutes the basis of the legal system—in North Africa and the Middle East and in Pakistan and Malaysia, among others. For example, business activities must be organized daily around prayer time, with companies accommodating employees by stopping work and allowing for sufficient space for prayer. During Ramadan, business performance is generally limited and many international businesses rely on the foreign, non-Muslim, workforce to carry out their firms' operations during this month.

2-5b Jurisdiction

With different legal systems worldwide, and with international laws, home-country laws, and host-country laws that govern all aspects of doing business internationally, it is important to establish **jurisdiction** in international legal disputes. Normally, no automatic supranational jurisdiction is assigned to an international court, unless the dispute takes place between companies and/or countries in the European Union, in which case the jurisdiction lies with the European Court of Justice (www.europa.eu.int). Legal disputes that arise between governments are usually handled by the International Court of Justice (www.icj-cij.org) in the Hague, within the United Nations system. International commercial law is usually handled in the home or host country of the company, or even in a third country, depending on the

---

common law
Laws that are based on prior court rulings (legal precedents).

code law
Comprehensive written laws that specify what constitutes legal behavior.

Islamic law.
A system of law based on the interpretation of the Koran, Islam's holy book, and on interpretations of the practices and sayings of the prophet Muhammad.

jurisdiction
The country and legal body where a particular dispute should be adjudicated, according to the country's law, or according to the legal body's principles, respectively.

place of jurisdiction for the matter under litigation. Because jurisdiction is often difficult to determine, it is advisable that each contract specifies the venue for handling the dispute and the procedure involved.

The contract should also specify whether the dispute settlement process will involve procedures other than litigation, which is often too costly and leads to negative perceptions in the international business community of the companies involved. Such procedures may be as follows:

- **Mediation**—A nonbinding procedure that involves an independent third party. The disadvantage of mediation is that any decision of the mediator is nonbinding. The perspective of a neutral third party, however, could provide better insights into how the issue is perceived by the larger business community. Not accepting the terms of mediation could signal to firms outside the conflict that the firm in question may be at fault and might not be a reliable future partner.

- **Arbitration**—A procedure that involves an independent third party; the outcome of arbitration is a binding decision. Agreeing to arbitration does not necessarily mean that the companies found to be at fault will adhere to the decisions; if they do not, however, it is possible that their reputation in the international business community will suffer. Arbitration is often preferred to litigation. It is a much faster procedure that is likely to cost the company much less than a lawsuit.

2-5c Intellectual Property Rights Protection

Violation of **intellectual property rights** is the most significant threat to the competitiveness of companies involved in international business.[35] Intellectual property is the result of ideas and creativity transformed into products, services, and experiences that are protected for a specified period of time from unauthorized commercialization. Large multinationals with brand name products are the primary victims of intellectual property rights infringement and are leading the fight against violations. Losses attributed to the violation of intellectual property rights are estimated to be well over $60 billion a year, and its primary victims are the most innovative, fastest-growing industries such as software, pharmaceuticals, and entertainment (with high losses attributed to Internet piracy).[36]

Intellectual property protection takes on different forms:

- Protection of the rights of the inventor or of the firm employing the inventor to use and sell the invention for a specified period of time—this type of intellectual property is known as a **patent.** In many countries around the world, multinationals are racing to local patent offices to apply for patents to protect and enforce their technology. In Korea, for example, local memory chip and electronics firms are embroiled in patent disputes, fending off lawsuits initiated by multinational firms such as IBM, and the stakes are high: Losers will not only suffer financial setbacks in the form of paying royalties, but will also suffer the stigma of being labeled copycats.[37] This situation will ultimately be rectified by the WTO, which has instituted uniform patent rules that all members are expected to follow.

- Protection of the rights to an original work of art (literature, music, film, design, and other works), allowing the owner the right to reproduce, sell, perform, or film the work—this is known as **copyright.** National and international associations are actively fighting copyright infringement. In the United States, such an organization is the International Intellectual Property Alliance, or IIPA (www.iipa.com). The IIPA was formed in conjunction with the Association of American Publishers, the Business Software Alliance, the Interactive Digital Software Association, the Motion Picture Association of America, the National Music Publishers' Association, and the Recording Industry Association of America. In one example, the IIPA filed petitions with the Office of the U.S. Trade Representative to investigate copyright infringement in the CD markets in Brazil, Costa Rica, Guatemala, Russia, and Uruguay.[38]

mediation
Nonbinding procedure for conflict resolution involving an independent third party.

arbitration
Binding procedure for conflict resolution involving an independent third party; a faster and less costly procedure than a lawsuit.

intellectual property rights
Laws protecting the rights of the inventor or of the firm employing the inventor to use and sell an invention for a specified period of time.

patent
Protection of the rights of the inventor or of the firm employing the inventor to use and sell an invention for a specified period of time.

copyright
The rights to an original work of art (literature, music, film, design, and other works), enabling the owner to reproduce, sell, perform, or film the work.

• Protection of a brand name, mark, symbol, motto, or slogan that identifies a particular manufacturer's brand and distinguishes it from the competitors' brands in the same product category—this is known as **trademark.** Trademark infringement occurs at many levels, from directly copying the product, as in the case of counterfeit Rolex watches and Prada, Gucci and Fendi purses selling for $40 in the streets of New York City, Paris, Venice, and even at the entrance of the Vatican. These counterfeits are omnipresent in Asia and in many bazaars in emerging markets.

Brand name counterfeiting involves using the brand name, as in the case of the high quality Hermès Birkin bags selling in the backrooms of the Covered Bazaar in Istanbul, Turkey. The Birkin sells for about $10,000 at the Hermès store, although a special edition might go for as much as $150,000. At the Bazaar, a perfect copy allegedly made in Turkey, with quality leather, with a key chain appropriately displayed, and all the other details and sold with an Hermès protective bag, sells for about $150, whereas a copy of mediocre quality, allegedly made in China, sells for about $50.

Design copying, which is legal, involves using a popular design without the trademark. The popular Birkin bag is also a victim to design counterfeiting, with many store displays offering bags that look very similar to the Birkin, down to the emblematic orange color. Shirts with a crocodile or polo player that do not have the respective Izod and Ralph Lauren names, and Peugeot watches with designs that look just like the Rolex Oyster are among the many examples of design counterfeiting.

trademark
A brand name, mark, symbol, motto, or slogan that identifies a particular manufacturer's brand and distinguishes it from the competitors' brands in the same product category.

trade secrets
Intellectual property such as know-how, formulas, special blends, and other elements that are not registered, and are thus not protected by law.

• Protection of know-how, formulas, and special blends that are not registered, and thus not protected by law, but shared with licensees, franchisers, or other partners and are known as **trade secrets .**

Intellectual property violations are especially problematic in China, where all products, including automobiles, are at risk, as Marketing Illustration 2-2 shows.

International Marketing Illustration 2-2

Counterfeiting Chinese Style

There is a saying in Shanghai: "We can copy anything except your mother."

Soy sauce with carbonated water is sold as Pepsi, and mobile phones that look like Nokia's latest offering are within easy reach.

Figure 2-2: *Counterfeit luggage in Shanghai: Polo, Diesel, and so on. The copies look nothing like the authentic brands.*

International Marketing Illustration 2-2

Counterfeiting Chinese Style (continued).

Counterfeit cars first appeared in China in 1999: VW look-alikes were quickly followed by the Chery QQ, which appeared six months earlier than the Chevy Spark, the car it copied. Chery QQ was able to copy the Spark successfully because a Chinese firm somehow got hold of the blueprints. Cars bearing Honda's name ("Hongda" for motorcycles) are commonplace, and Nissan's bumpers have been under legal scrutiny.

Shuanghuan Automobile copied Audi's famous four-ring logo, then it copied the design of Honda's CR-V and called it the SR-V—and Shuanghuan is getting away with it. In 2007, it obtained an export license to export the CEO, an SUV that very much looks like the BMW X5, to Romania and Italy. Shuanghuan also launched an electric copy of Daimler's Smart car called the Dushi Mini in 2007, following in the tracks of Shandong Huoyun Electromobile, which launched its own version the year before. The Dushi Mini will be sold in Europe for less than half the price of the Smart car. The car has been temporarily withdrawn after Daimler threatened a lawsuit, but, after a redesign, Shandong Huoyun is ready to relaunch it. A third copy of the Smart car was also introduced by CMEC Suzhou, a maker of electric vehicles.

In other examples, Jiangling Motors' Landwind—which spectacularly failed European crash tests—is a copy of Opel's Frontera. Also, Great Wall, a producer of cars with names such as Sing, Wingle, and Sailor, copied the Toyota's Hilux and called it Deer. Great Wall is currently in litigation with Toyota for copying its Scion models and with Fiat for copying its new Panda.

Litigation with Chinese automobile manufacturers has proved useless. All legal action is stuck in legal machinations. Lawsuits have been thrown out on technical grounds, or because, according to the Chinese government, the foreign firm failed to properly register their designs. Foreign manufacturers, in turn, do not want to make waves, because that could prevent them from having access to China's fast-growing market. A question that still needs to be answered is, how can Chinese firms charge so little for their automobiles? Indeed, they do not spend much on research and development, but they have to purchase the materials at market prices. Moreover, most firms manufacture the cars in small volumes, so they do not gain any economies of scale. Selling the cars at half price suggests that something is fishy: either the Chinese firms do not know the costs or they are being subsidized.

Source: *The Economist*, "Business: The Sincerest Form of Flattery—Counterfeit Cars in China," April 7, 2007, p. 383 (8523), 76.

Factors Influencing Intellectual Property Rights Violations

The degree of intellectual property rights violation is influenced by a number of market factors,[39] such as:

- Lack of appropriate legislation (e.g., for software)
- Lax enforcement, especially for local firms
- Unavailability of the authentic products, or when available, their high price provides justification for both the violators and the respective governments to allow the practice

Such violations are also influenced by cultural factors, such as

- Values that perceive imitation as a high form of flattery
- A culture characterized by interpersonal distrust and feelings of not getting a fair deal
- A culture characterized by an emphasis on acquisition of material wealth at the expense of caring for others; in such a culture, the focus of acquisition is status brands consumed and/or displayed publicly, rather than privately
- Beliefs that technology is in the common domain and that use of others' intellectual property is appropriate

Involvement in regional trade agreements and other trade organizations is also sought to diminish the likelihood that a country would tolerate violation of intellectual property rights. In fact, intellectual property rights used to be largely a domestic issue, with individual countries deciding on their own levels of legal protection and enforcement. Today, countries that join the WTO must also sign on to the **Trade-**

Trade-Related Aspects of Intellectual Property Rights (TRIPS)
An international agreement, under the World Trade Organization, that sets out minimum standards for the legal protection of intellectual property.
(See www.wto.org.)

Related Aspects of Intellectual Property Rights (or **TRIPS**) agreement, an international agreement that sets out minimum standards for the legal protection of intellectual property.[40]

Multinationals seeking protection under TRIPS still depend on each country's patent office to grant those rights and on the country's judicial, customs, and police services to enforce them (in the European Union, companies need only apply for EU patents). TRIPS offers rules describing the protection provided, including extending intellectual property rights to include computer programs, integrated circuits, plant varieties, and pharmaceuticals. According to TRIPS, patents can be granted for any new technological process or product, and the protection lasts 20 years from the date of application.[41]

In addition to TRIPS, and working in conjunction with the WTO, international conventions have been gaining strength. Among these conventions are the Bern Convention for copyrighted works, under the auspices of the World Intellectual Property Organization;[42] the Paris Convention for the protection of industrial property; and the Madrid Arrangement, which established the Bureau for the International Registration of Trademarks.

Helping these organizations and conventions are national governments of primarily high-income countries, which are protecting their multinationals. In the United States, the Patent and Trademark Office has an annual budget of $1 billion; a staff of more than 3,000 highly trained scientists, engineers, and legal experts; more than 600 judges to preside over patent disputes; and a vast customs service to clamp down on counterfeiting.[43] To protect intellectual property rights in the Internet age, the U.S. government passed the Digital Millennium Copyright Act.

Some developing countries argue that intellectual property protection is yet another arm used to hold them in a position of economic disadvantage. According to this view, patents and copyrights impose great cost on low-income country consumers. For example, AIDS activists and the government in South Africa argued that patents were killing the country's millions of HIV-infected patients who could not afford the drugs. Mexican peasants were enraged that a U.S. company received the exclusive right to market enola beans in the United States because they have been growing the beans for generations, and the protection restricts their ability to export the beans north of the border.[44] Activists argue that intellectual property protection allows Western multinationals to set up monopolies, to drive out local competing brands, to divert research and development away from the needs of developing countries, and to drive up prices while preventing poor people from getting life-saving drugs, interfering with age-old farming practices, and allowing foreign "pirates" to raid local resources, such as medicinal plants, without getting permission or paying compensation.[45]

Finally, there are examples where companies, even though engaged in trademark litigation, continue to cooperate if it serves their interests. For example, Anheuser-Busch Companies and the Czech brewer Budejovicky Budvar have had a long-standing litigation over the Budweiser name. The Czech brewer has a long history in Europe, predating Anheuser-Busch's Budweiser. Budweiser is the German name of an individual living in the town of origin of the Czech Budweiser, and the Budweiser Budvar (see Figure 2-3) brand dates from the 1800s. However, even as the two companies continue their international legal fight over the Budweiser trademark – with over 40 lawsuits still in progress in 2012, – they agreed for Anheuser-Busch to distribute Budvar's Czechvar Premium Czech Lager, currently sold in 30 states in the United States. Through Anheuser-Busch, Budvar has access to 600 independent wholesalers.[46]

Figure 2-3: *The Budweiser Budvar brand is very popular in upscale German restaurants.*

2-5d Home-Country Legislation Affecting Multinational Firms Operating Overseas

Antitrust Laws

Antitrust laws of home and host countries are designed to prevent domestic anticompetitive activities, such as the creation of monopolies and cartels. The United States was among the first to impose its antitrust laws on firms in the United States and on U.S. firms operating abroad. Increasingly, governments of other countries are enacting and enforcing antitrust legislation that affects multinationals worldwide. In fact, antitrust enforcement in the United States often appears to be more lenient than in other developed countries. For example, the European Commission vetoed mergers between competitors after the United States gave these mergers a green light—as in the case of General Electric's failed takeover attempt of Honeywell and the MCI WorldCom and Sprint proposed merger.[47]

The United States allows certain types of collusion in the case of small and medium-sized firms that might not have the resources to embark on a successful export program. The U.S. Congress passed the Export Trading Company Act in the 1980s to encourage firms to join forces in exporting by exempting them from antitrust laws.

Corruption Laws

Corruption laws of home and host countries are designed to prevent multinational corporations from using unethical means to obtain competitive advantage in a particular market. The World Bank surveyed 3,600 companies in 69 countries and found that 40 percent of firms paid bribes. This figure in industrial countries was 15 percent, and in the former Soviet Union, it increased to 60 percent.[48] Similarly, the European Bank for Reconstruction and Development (EBRD), which encourages investments in the former Eastern Bloc, has called Eastern Europe's bribe-seeking a deterrent to foreign investment.[49]

The U.S. **Foreign Corrupt Practices Act (FCPA)** makes it illegal for companies and their representatives to bribe government officials and other politicians or candidates to political office. The Act also prohibits payment to third parties when the company has good reason to assume that part of that payment is being used for bribery purposes. U.S. multinational companies take such laws very seriously—some even address their commitment to reject bribery and other corruption in their mission statement (Caterpillar does so, for example)—even though forbidding these practices places U.S. firms at a disadvantage. In a number of high-profile cases, investigators found that illegal payments were made by firms operating in Canada, Colombia, Cook Islands, the Dominican Republic, Egypt, Germany, Iraq, Israel, Jamaica, Mexico, Niger, Nigeria, and Trinidad and Tobago. These payments ranged from $22,000 to $9.9 million and represented percentages of up to 20 percent of the business obtained. Seventeen companies have been charged under the FCPA, with fines ranging from $10,000 to $21.8 million.[50]

> **antitrust laws**
> Laws designed to prevent anticompetitive activities, such as the creation of monopolies and cartels.
>
> **corruption laws**
> Laws designed to prevent multinational corporations from using unethical means to obtain competitive advantage in a particular market.
>
> **Foreign Corrupt Practices Act (FCPA)**
> Legislation that makes it illegal for companies and their representatives to bribe government officials and other politicians or candidates to political office, either directly or through third parties.

The United States is not alone in the fight against bribery. The Organization for Economic Cooperation and Development (OECD), which consists of 30 primarily developed member countries (Australia, Austria, Belgium, Canada, the Czech Republic, Denmark, Finland, France, Germany, Greece, Hungary, Iceland, Ireland, Italy, Japan, South Korea, Luxembourg, Mexico, the Netherlands, New Zealand, Norway, Poland, Portugal, the Slovak Republic, Spain, Sweden, Switzerland, Turkey, United Kingdom, and the United States) adopted a Convention on Combating Bribery of Foreign Public Officials in International Business Transactions. Other signatories include nonmember countries Argentina, Brazil, Bulgaria, and Chile. The purpose of the Convention is to fight corruption in international business and to help level the competitive field for companies.[51]

2-6 The Natural Environment of International Marketing

The natural environment of international marketing addresses the relationship between natural resources worldwide and marketing. A country's geographic location determines how its key markets can be optimally accessed. Its climate determines its production and even its productivity capability. Geography facilitates or impedes relationships with other international markets. Southwestern China, for example, has been isolated from the mainland until very recently when train transportation became possible and airplane transportation became more affordable. To travel from Lhasa, Tibet, to the nearest city by road takes several days as the roads are very difficult, with many dangerous curves; this same distance takes less than two hours by airplane. Consequently, Western brands have only started to enter this market less than a decade ago and international tourism is barely present.

National boundaries determine access to the local market and the movement of goods, access to natural resources, and, overall, the potential for economic development. Landlocked countries have difficulty gaining access to low-cost water transportation. In Rwanda, a landlocked country, firms mostly bring their products to market by air, as access from Uganda and Congo is very problematic due to the instability in the two countries.

2-6a Geology and the Shortage of Natural Resources

A country's access to natural resources determines whether the country can be a viable trade partner in the international market. Its geology determines the natural resources available in the country and its potential for prosperity. For example, oil in North Africa and the Middle East has brought prosperity to countries where the climate is a challenge and whose terrain contains a large desert expanse. Countries in sub-Saharan Africa that have survived at subsistence level for centuries have found new prosperity from mining gold and diamonds. Botswana and the Central African Republic have attractive markets that are actively courted by multinationals. Mongolia is referred to as "minegolia" due to the substantial copper and uranium resources recently discovered there; as a result, the country is rapidly changing, with consumers demanding a high standard of living and Western brands.

A shortage of raw materials is slowly reverberating in most world markets, including the markets of industrialized countries. Prices of oil are steadily increasing, whereas access to oil sources is becoming more and more limited due to geologic and political factors. This shortage is translating to higher prices charged to consumers, which, in the long term, will lead to changes in consumption patterns. In the case of oil, it may mean that northern Europeans will no longer count on their southern European and North African vacations, which will, in turn, hurt tourism in southern Europe and North Africa. Consumers in the United States may have to trade in their gas-guzzling monster trucks and sports utility vehicles for fuel-efficient smaller and hybrid vehicles.

2-6b Topography and Access to Markets

Topography is important because it determines access to the market and affects distribution decisions. For example, Holland has a flat terrain, allowing for efficient transportation. Holland has also altered its topography to increase access by creating an effective network of man-made canals that cross the country in every direction allowing for easier access to markets (see Figure 2-4).

On the other hand, a mountainous terrain restricts access to markets. The Andes, for example, complicate access to local consumers, which can be accomplished only at high cost. High-income countries have devised sophisticated access to some of the more remote areas, such as the canyons in Utah and the peaks of the Alps. On the other hand, ac-

Figure 2-4: *Man-made canals in Holland allow for quick and inexpensive access to markets.*

cess remains especially problematic in lower-income countries, such as those of the Brahmaputra mountain chain – see Figure 2-5.

Figure 2-5: *Tibet was initially reached only by air or by road from the rest of mainland China. There is now a railway that facilitates access. Nevertheless, the Brahmaputra mountain chain presents a challenge to the movement of goods and access to markets in the surrounding countries.*

2-6c Hydrology and Economic Development

Hydrology determines access to local markets as well. Ocean access allows for the affordable shipping of goods to the local target market. Rivers and lakes offer access as well as potential for the development of agriculture and manufacturing. Historically, many communities were developed on river banks (see Figure 2-6). Hydroelectric power is essential for local development. In general, economic development is related to hydrology.

Figure 2-6: *Many communities are developed on river banks, to take advantage of access to markets.*

2-6d Climate

Climate is also an essential determinant of economic development. Arid lands, such as the desert lands of the Sahara, the Arabian Peninsula, or and the southwestern United States, are inhabitable only at a very high cost. In other areas, excessive rain and hurricane activity often lead to flooding and the destruction of the local infrastructure. On the other hand, a mild climate year round brings healthy crops of fruit, as well as tourists to the Amalfi Coast of Italy, the Cote d'Azur in France, and to the islands of Hawaii and the Caribbean.

2-6e Population and Human Capital

As mentioned earlier, one relevant aspect of the natural environment is the scarcity of natural resources, especially raw materials, in light of today's high population growth. High population growth in spite of limited natural resources has led to famine and precipitated conflict in Ethiopia, Somalia, Rwanda, and Burundi in sub-Saharan Africa. In these markets, the overall infrastructure is insufficient and cannot meet the basic needs of the population. The concentration of population in large cities of millions of inhabitants, such as Mexico City and Cairo, has taxed the infrastructure and impeded the optimal functioning of business.

Today, the world's population exceeds seven billion and is growing rapidly, especially in developing countries. Table 2-4 illustrates the high annual population growth in low- and middle-income countries, compared with that of high-income countries. The population growth rate is highest for the developing countries of South Asia and sub-Saharan Africa.

Table 2-4: Population Growth Trends				
	Population	Annual Growth (%)	Population Age Composition (%)	
	(2002)	(2002–2015)	(0–14)	(15–64)
Low-Middle Income	5,232.4	1.2	31.2	63.1
East Asia & Pacific	1,838.3	1.4	26.3	67.2
Europe/Central Asia	472.9	0.5	20.9	67.9
Latin America/Caribbean	524.9	1.3	30.9	63.6
Middle East/North Africa	305.8	2.6	35.3	60.7
South Asia	1,401.5	12.0	34.2	61.2
Sub-Saharan Africa	688.9	12.7	43.8	53.3
High Income Countries	966.2	0.7	18.3	67.3

Source: World Development Indicators, World Development Report 2004, World Bank Group, 2004, http://econ.worldbank.org/wdr/wdr2004/

Population growth determines the types of markets that multinational companies, as well as small and medium enterprises, can target. In high-income countries, marketers have mature markets—markets with a substantial population aged 65 and older. Population growth also has implications with regard to access to goods and services and to the environment.

The implications of population migration for international business are also considerable. Immigration from low- and middle-income countries to high-income countries has often resulted in strong anti-immigrant sentiment and instability of different degrees in countries known for their tolerance and openness to immigration, such as Belgium, Denmark, the Netherlands, France, and Sweden. Immigrants account for about 12 percent of Sweden's population of 9 million and, of those, 450,000 are Muslim. Immigrants in Sweden, as in much of Western Europe, often live in run-down immigrant neighborhoods, are less likely to learn Swedish, and more likely to go to all-immigrant schools and remain unemployed and poor. Countries that have, historically, encouraged immigration are now struggling to absorb their large immigrant populations. Most Western European countries have now passed laws restricting immigration.

The new immigrants are not fully aware of their rights or of their obligations to their adoptive country, creating difficulties for them. In Sweden, the minister of integration and gender equality, Nyamko Sabuni, an Afro-Swede, proposed banning the veil for girls younger than the age of 15, subjecting school-girls to compulsory medical examination to protect young women from the consequence of debilitating rituals, and proposed outlawing arranged marriage and the "honor culture" of some immigrant cultures, generating anger from immigrants and gaining support from most Swedes.[52]

The issues facing Sweden are not unusual. European media regularly addresses issues related to anti-immigrant sentiment. After France's 2006 student riots, anti-immigrant rhetoric from government officials no less, led to a process of national reflection and to the political change that toppled the conservative Sarkozy government and brought a left-leaning leadership into power in 2012.

One aspect of migration that has important economic consequences for the country affected is "brain drain," the migration of trained professionals. Historically, this migration has been mostly from developing to developed countries. The migration has created shortages of qualified medical personnel in many countries in South America and Eastern Europe, among others. More recently, open borders in the European Union have created a brain drain phenomenon for countries with high taxation and unemployment. For example, the brain drain from Germany, a country with a rapidly shrinking population, has become an issue of concern to business executives and government leaders. More professionals are leaving today than in the past years. A popular show on German television is *Goodbye Deutschland*. The show portrays emigrants to South Africa and Spain. About 150,000 Germans emigrate yearly, and only about 50,000 return. The emigrants who leave are doctors, lawyers, and scientists. France has many emigrants leaving for Britain. Adding to the burden of brain drain is the fact that Germany and France are less attractive to people pursuing jobs in medicine, academic research, and engineering. The reasons emigrants give for leaving are high taxes, chronic unemployment, a rigid labor market, a stifling bureaucracy, and the hierarchical structure of some professional environments such as academia and medicine. As a new employee, you have little time to pursue research and are under the thumb of your director.[53]

2-6f Environmental Quality

Concerns about the effects of the overall population growth and industry on the natural environment have led to the active regulation of business, especially in industrialized countries. For example, the European Union actively regulates the use of hormones in raising beef and the use of pesticides in agriculture. It continues to raise taxes on gasoline to reduce consumption and encourage the use of public transportation. It charges localities huge sums for refuse and actively encourages recycling at the individual and community level.

Worldwide, there is a concerted effort to reduce air and water pollution, to control the amount and disposal of nuclear waste, to reduce deforestation and land erosion, and to limit fishing and hunting activity to preserve a viable natural habitat. The effort to preserve environmental quality limits infrastructure development in protected areas and charges businesses to take responsibility of consumption by encouraging bottle reuse and recycling, by limiting packaging to its more basic forms, and by producing products that can be consumed with minimal harm to the environment. Outside the United States, Coca-Cola soft drinks and Heineken beer are sold in reusable glass bottles or in recyclable plastic bottles. Ford Motor Company competes in the international market by offering smaller automobiles with low gas consumption. And new, successful industries are emerging aimed at creating alternative energy sources and reducing the cost of electricity consumption. Windmills today populate not just the European landscape; they are increasingly present on the coast of California and on the East Coast of the United States.

Vehicular emissions are rising across the globe. Greenhouse gases are increasing even in countries where industry pollution is decreasing, due to increased car and truck use, and this is happening in spite of the popularity of environmentally friendly automobiles. Hybrid cars and ethanol buses do not compensate for the effect of the large number of vehicles on the road. High taxes on cars and gasoline, such as those imposed in Denmark, where a Czech-made Skoda automobile costs $34,000, compared with $18,000 in Italy or Sweden, scare voters away, making even environmentalist politicians reluctant to propose them. [54]

Yet, in spite of these challenges, the European Union remains the world's leader in the fight against climate change. The EU issued a challenge to the United States, China, and India to match Europe's environmental ambitions. The Kyoto Protocol – to the United Nations' Convention on Climate Change – required industrial nations to reduce the emission of global-warming gases by an average of 5 percent below 1990 levels by 2012; the EU, on the other hand, committed to reduce greenhouse gas emissions by 20 percent from 1990 levels by the year 2020. However, the EU also allows some of Europe's most polluting countries to limit their environmental goals. The former Eastern Bloc countries in the European Union, which rely heavily on cheap coal and oil for their energy needs, are reluctant to move to the more costly environmentally friendly alternatives. Consequently, the EU agreed to allow each of the 27 states to set their own targets to meet the renewable energy goals. Effectively, this means that these countries have less stringent targets compared with the other countries in the EU. [55]

The United States never signed the Protocol, and Canada renounced the Protocol in 2011. But also in 2011, the Durban Climate Talks ensured that the commitments of the Kyoto Protocol would be continued, leading to a global treaty on climate action in 2015.

Increasingly, environmental pollution is also attributed to developing countries, where cheap diesel generators from China are a preferred mode for providing electricity, powering home appliances and irrigation systems, allowing many in rural villages to grow crops and to connect to the world through Internet and television. In remote and roadless areas in India, China, Bangladesh, and Nepal, as many as half of the households have television sets and pay 40 cents every few days to the owner of the generator supplying the electricity for their bamboo hut. Diesel is cheap, owing to lavish government subsidies, making it difficult to introduce alternative renewable energy technologies. Efforts on the part of local government and international development organizations such as the United Nations Development Program to introduce expensive renewable energy have been successful for urban areas; however, the investment is not warranted in remote villages. China is offering a successful alternative: cheap roof-top water heaters that channel water through thin pipes crisscrossing a shiny surface. More than 5,000 small Chinese companies sell these water heaters to more than 30 million households. Today, China accounts for 60 percent of the market for solar water heaters. One such water heater costs $330, and it pays for itself in two years. [56]

Demand for cheap automobiles, costing less than $14,000, is huge, with many former motorcycle owners opting for an affordable automobile. Renault's Logan, manufactured in Romania, is a hit at less than $10,000. The car, sold in more than 50 countries, including India, Argentina, and Brazil, was launched in 2004. These developments carry with them bleak prospects for the environment, and governments of large emerging markets are attempting to stem the tide. In China, for example, the government imposes a graduated tax on vehicles based on their size: 9 percent for a 2.5-liter engine, compared with 3 percent for engines less than 1.5 liters.[57]

2-7 The Technological Environment

The technological environment is changing rapidly. New product development is proceeding at breakneck pace, with thousands of patents and trademarks registered worldwide on a daily basis. The technology revolution since the 1980s has radically changed the face of international marketing. Hub-and-spoke networks, warehouse management systems, and electronic data interchange (EDI) systems, which allow intermediaries worldwide to share standardized inventory information, all lower firms' inventory carrying costs, facilitating the flow of products and making it easier to achieve the goal of making the distribution channel more flexible and responsive to customer needs.[58]

The number of Internet users has more than doubled since the year 2000, and in 2012, the Internet was available to more than 1.3 billion people worldwide, with future growth expected especially from countries with large populations. With fewer than 20 percent of the world population having access to the Internet, there is plenty of room for expansion, and much of this growth will take place using wireless applications to access the Internet. [59]

The Internet allows for instant access to new international markets and creates potential for exchanges that have never been previously imagined. Multinational corporations, as well as small and medium size enterprises, benefit from the long reach of the Internet. The average amount of time each person spends on the Internet is 10 hours a month, visiting an average of 49 different sites, going online an average of 19 times per month.[60] Table 2-5 presents information on Internet usage relative to regional population statistics.

Table 2-5: Internet Usage and Population Statistics

World Regions	Population (2011 Est.)	Internet Users Dec. 31, 2000	Internet Users Latest Data	Penetration (% Popula-	Growth 2000-2011
Africa	1,037,524,058	4,514,400	139,875,242	13.5 %	2,988.4 %
Asia	3,879,740,877	114,304,000	1,016,799,076	26.2 %	789.6 %
Europe	816,426,346	105,096,093	500,723,686	61.3 %	376.4 %
Middle East	216,258,843	3,284,800	77,020,995	35.6 %	2,244.8 %
North America	347,394,870	108,096,800	273,067,546	78.6 %	152.6 %
Latin America / Carib.	597,283,165	18,068,919	235,819,740	39.5 %	1,205.1 %
Oceania / Australia	35,426,995	7,620,480	23,927,457	67.5 %	214.0 %
WORLD TOTAL	6,930,055,154	360,985,492	2,267,233,742	32.7 %	528.1 %

Source: www.internetworldstats.com/stats.htm: *Internet Usage and Population Statistics,* December 31, 2011.

The Internet has profoundly changed the lives of individuals, but it has also changed the way international business is conducted. Aside from the over 2 billion Internet users (see above statistics), and every day there are over 300 billion e-mails sent, over 3.5 million blog posts, and over 3.2 billion Google searches.[61]

Numerous companies in the United States have been successful selling to international clients through the Internet. Nevertheless, there are some pitfalls. For example, the company may need to make use of freight forwarders, who handle transportation, insurance, and export documentation but also substantially increase the cost to the buyer. Companies must also determine the appropriate payment mechanisms. Countries differ not only with regard to the currency they use for transactions, but also in their methods of payments. For example, Europeans tend to use the Eurocard, which is a debit card, for payments. Also, worldwide, there is a high rate of credit card theft, which increases the risks that sellers might face in the international market. Using the Internet to send Mother's Day flowers from the United States to one's mother-in-law in Holland is difficult, and using the telephone is not much easier because the local flower shops are reluctant to serve when it comes to accepting credit cards from unknown buyers. Nevertheless, transactions never before thought possible are today commonplace due to the advances in the past three decades.

Summary

Provide an overview of the world economic environment and examine different perspectives on economic development. Countries are becoming more and more interconnected by trade, and developments in one region have immediate repercussions in the rest of the world. There are divergent views on the economic development process. The Rostow model portrays economic development as a function of productivity, exchange, technology, and income. Alternative models portray development as a function of the control of the means of production, production outcomes, resource allocation, and the development of a mindset devoid of materialist needs, and may fuel anticolonial, anticapitalist sentiment, while advocating a collective societal orientation.

Address differences between countries of different levels of economic development and discuss the importance of emerging markets. Countries belong to different development categories. Developed countries are highly industrialized, have well-developed industrial and service sectors, and present great potential for new markets, with a GNP per capita of $9,266 or more; they also present a challenge because their markets are in the maturity stage, consumers have established preferences, and competition is intense. Countries with emerging markets are developing rapidly and have great potential, as they privatize state-owned industries and adopt market reforms; of these countries, big emerging markets present the greatest potential for international trade and expansion. These countries are middle-income countries, with a GNP per capita of US$766 to US$9,265. Developing countries are primarily agrarian, have a low GNP per capita (less than $755), and are located in different regions in Asia and in sub-Saharan Africa; they tend to be neglected or underserved by large multinationals and thus present great potential as niche markets.

Examine the indicators of political risk and address international firm approaches to political risk management. Several indicators signal political risk: economic performance, political repression, multiple groups with incongruent interests, rampant nationalism, and political instability. Some of the risks that companies can experience in foreign markets involve some level of dispossession, such as nationalization, expropriation, and confiscation; risks related to action groups and labor, as well as corporate terrorism, are on the rise. Firms can reduce risk by being good corporate citizens, by partnering with local firms, and by purchasing risk insurance.

Describe how international law, home-country law, and host-country law affect international firm operations and address issues related to jurisdiction. International companies are subject to multiple sets of laws: laws of the host country, laws of the home country—such as anticompetitiveness (antitrust) laws and corruption laws—and international laws, which could be laws of a regional governance body, such as the European Union, or laws of an international body, such as the World Trade Organization. Under this complex scenario, jurisdiction often becomes a problem. It is advisable that firms entering into agreements agree on jurisdiction and on the procedure needed for conflict resolution.

Discuss different legal systems, intellectual property laws, and national laws with extra-territorial impact that affect international firms. The three primary types of legal systems are common law, which is based on prior court rulings, with roots in English common law; code law, or civil law, which draws on comprehensive written laws that specify what constitutes legal behavior, with roots in Roman law; and Islamic law, a system of law based on the interpretation of Islam's holy book and the practices and sayings of the prophet Muhammad. One issue facing multinationals today is the violation of intellectual property rights, which constitutes a great threat to firms' competitiveness. Protection of patents, copyrights, trademarks, and trade secrets is difficult to enforce due to lax attitudes attributed to cultural values and to economic and political motivations of national governments. This type of protection might have better prospects now that more countries have become members of the World Trade Organization and are signatories of the TRIPS agreement.

Examine the natural and technological environments and the potential and limitations they present to international firms. Geography can offer opportunity for international business, or it can restrict access to the marketplace. Geography facilitates the relationship with other international markets, if those markets are located in the proximity of the home country or if the markets are located in the proximity of ports that allow easy access. Alternatively, geographical location that is remote from other international markets and that does not allow easy access impedes relationships. Geology determines the natural resources available in the country and its potential for prosperity, and climate and hydrology have a direct impact on a country's economic development. Population growth determines the types of markets that multinational companies, as well as small and medium enterprises, can target. In the high-income countries, marketers have a more mature market to contend with—markets with a substantial population aged 65 and older. Population growth also has implications with regard to the access to goods and services and to the environment. The environment is continually challenged by business interests; these challenges have led to extensive legislation aimed at limiting the negative impact of business on the environment. The technological environment is continally evolving, rapidly opening international markets never before accessible to multinationals and creating a viable future for small and medium enterprises that never had such a broad exposure. The technological environment is also speeding the new product development process and creating unprecedented distribution potential in industry.

Key Terms

antitrust laws
arbitration
big emerging markets (BEMs)
bourgeoisie
capitalism
code law
common law
communism
confiscation
copyright
corruption laws
creeping expropriation
domestication
drive to maturity stage

emerging markets
expropriation
feudalism
Foreign Corrupt Practices Act(FCPA)
high mass consumption
home-country laws
host-country laws
imperialism
intellectual property rights
international laws
Islamic law
jurisdiction
Marxist-Leninist development model
mediation
monopolistic capitalism
nationalism
nationalization

Overseas Private Investment Corporation (OPIC)
patent
political risk
primitive society
Rostow modernization model
slavery-based society
socialism
take-off
trade secrets
trademark
traditional society
Trade-Related Aspects of Intellectual Property Rights (TRIPS)
transitional society

Discussion Questions

1. Compare the Rostow and the Marxist-Leninist models of economic development. How do you explain the two models in light of developments over the past decade in Central and Eastern Europe? Why do developing countries continue to embrace the Marxist-Leninist model of economic development?

2. Describe indicators of political risk. Examine current events and identify some of the political risks that multinational companies face in the world today.

3. Discuss two home-country laws that affect U.S. businesses operating internationally.

4. What are some examples of violations of international property rights? Give some examples of counterfeiting.

Chapter Quiz

True/False

1. Crises in one region of the world are likely to influence economic performance worldwide.

Answer: True

Rationale: Interdependence has become the leading principle of globalization.

Section 2-1a, "The World Economy"

2. Low-income countries fully control national resources (raw materials, labor), control access to local consumers, and often pose barriers to international business operations.

Answer: True

Rationale: Low-income countries attempt to lessen the development gap by controlling these factors.

Section 2-1b, "The Economic Development Disparity"

3. In the Rostow model, advancement is a function of the control of means of production, production outcomes, resources allocation, and the development of a mind-set devoid of materialist needs.

Answer: False

Rationale: According to the Rostow model, each stage is a function of productivity, economic exchange, technological improvements, and income.

Section 2-2a, "The Rostow Modernization Model"

4. The key political risk signals are ethnic diversity and incongruent interests.

Answer: True

Rationale: Political repression in particular is indicative of political risk.

Section 2-4a, "Political Risk: An Overview"

5. Common law is defined as a body of written laws specifying what constitutes legal behavior.

Answer: False

Rationale: Code law is defined as a body of written laws specifying what constitutes legal behavior.

Section 2-5a, "Legal Systems"

6. The Foreign Corrupt Practices Act makes it legal for companies to bribe government officials and candidates to political office under certain circumstances.

Answer: False

Rationale: The Foreign Corrupt Practices Act does not permit companies to bribe government officials and candidates to political office, regardless of the common level of corruption in the respective business environment.

Section 2-5d, "Home-Country Legislation Affecting Multinational Firms Operating Overseas"

7. A country's geology can determine whether the country can be a viable trade partner in the international market.

Answer: True

Rationale: A country's access to natural resources determines whether the country can be a viable trade partner in the international market.

Section 2-6a, "Geology and the Shortage of Natural Resources"

Multiple Choice

1.The Rostow modernization model addresses all of the following EXCEPT

a. high mass consumption.

b. the drive- to- maturity.

c. transitional society.

d. the capitalist society.

Answer: d is correct.

Rationale: The capitalist society is not addressed in the Rostow model.

Section 2-2a, "The Rostow Modernization Model"

2.A stage in which modern technology is fully adopted in all economic activity and new leading sectors emerge is known as the _____ stage.

a. drive to maturity

b. high mass consumption

c. take-off

d. transitional society

Answer: a is correct.

Rationale: According to the Rostow model, the drive to maturity is facilitated by a focus on technology.

Section 2-2a, "The Rostow Modernization Model"

3.A stage in economic development characterized by leading sectors shifting toward durable goods is a

a.   transitional society.

b.   take-off.

c.   high mass consumption.

d.   drive to maturity.

Answer: c is correct.

Rationale: According to the Rostow model, the high mass consumption stage is characterized by a focus on the production of durable goods that would satisfy broad market segments.

Section 2-2a, "The Rostow Modernization Model"

4._____ countries are characterized by consumers with established preferences and intense competition.

a.   High-income

b.   Nationalized

c.   Emerging

d.   Low-income

Answer: a is correct.

Rationale: High-income countries have the highest per capita income. Consumers from developed countries have the means to purchase products and consequently have established preferences. Companies compete heavily for these consumers.

Section 2-3, "Levels of Economic Development"

5. _____ can impede the optimal functioning of business, tax the infrastructure, and lead to the scarcity of natural resources, especially raw materials.

a.   Economic development

b.   Population growth

c.   Technology

d.   All of the above

Answer: b is correct.

Rationale: High population growth in spite of limited natural resources has led to famine and precipitated conflict worldwide. High population growth has taxed the infrastructure and impeded the optimal functioning of business.

Section 2-6e, "Population"

Endnotes for Chapter 2

1.   Antiadvertising Agency, "Beer here!: The Poster and the Public Notice in Rural Rwanda," March 24, 2010,   http://antiadvertisingagency.com/%E2%80%9Cbeer-here%E2%80%9D-the-poster-and-the-public-notice-in-rural-rwanda. Craig Timberg, "In Rwanda, Suicides Haunt Search for Justice and Closure," *Washington Post Foreign Service,* Friday, February 17, 2006, A01.

2.   Michael J. Mandel, "In a One-World Economy, a Slump Sinks All Boats," *Business Week,* Industrial Technology Edition, No. 3738, June 25, 2001, pp. 38–39.

3.   Jeremy W. Peters, "Rising Exports: Putting Dent in Trade Gap," *Wall Street Journal*, May 14, 2007, A1, A16.

4.   Frances Maguire, "Multinationals: The New Master of the Universe," *The Banker*, January 1, 2006, p. 1.

5.   Russell W. Belk, "Hyperreality and Globalization: Culture in the Age of Ronald McDonald," *Journal of International Consumer Marketing,* Vol. 8, No. 3/4, 1996, pp. 23–37; and Leslie Sklair, "Competing Models of Globalization: Theoretical Frameworks and Research Agendas," working paper, London School of Economics and Political Science, University of London, London, United Kingdom.

6.   Walt W. Rostow, *The Stages of Economic Growth: A Non-Communist Manifesto,* London and New York: Cambridge University Press, 1960; "The Concept of a National Market and Its Economic Growth Implications," in *Marketing and Economic Development,* ed. P. D. Bennett, Chicago: American Marketing Association, 1965, pp. 11–20; and *The Stages of Economic Growth,* Second Edition, London: Cambridge University Press, 1971.

7.   Barkley Rosser, Jr., and Marina V. Rosser, "Islamic and Neo-Confucian Perspectives on the New Traditional Economy," *Eastern Economic Journal,* Vol. 24, No. 2, Spring 1998, pp. 217–227.

8.   Ali Farazmand, "Development and Comparative Public Administration: Past, Present, and Future," *Public Administration Quarterly,* Vol. 20, No. 3, Fall 1996, pp. 343–364.

9.   Rosser and Rosser, "Islamic and Neo-Confucian Perspectives," pp. 217–227.

10.   Roger Hayter and Sun Sheng Han, "Reflections on China's Open Policy Towards Foreign Direct Investment, *Regional Studies,* Vol. 32, No. 1, February 1998, pp. 1–16.

11.   Adapted from Robert Lloyd George, *The Handbook of Emerging Markets: A Country-By-Country Guide to the World's Fastest Growing Economies,* Chicago, IL: Probus Publications, 1994.

12. Keith Bradsher, "India Finds Its Economy on the Verge of Overheating," *New York Times*, February 10, 2007, B1, B9.

13.   Adapted from Amjad Hadjikhani, "Political Risk for Project-Selling Firms: Turbulence in Relationships between Business and Non-Business Actors," *Journal of Business & Industrial Marketing,* Vol. 13, No. 3, 1998, pp. 235–239.

14.   Jay Solomon, "Politics & Economics: New Sanctions Are Possible As U.N. Report Faults Iran," *Wall Street Journal*, May 24, 2007, A7.

15.   Courtney Tower, "Canada Wants WTO Panel in U.S. Farm Aid Case, *Journal of Commerce*, June 11, 2007, p. 1.

16.   Richard B. Loth, "How to Evaluate Country Risk," *Credit and Financial Management,* Vol. 88, No. 6, June 1986, p. 27.

17.   Ilan Alon and Matthew A. Martin, "A Normative Model of Macro Political Risk Assessment," *Multinational Business Review,* Vol. 6, No. 2, Fall 1998, pp. 10–19.

18.   *Economist.com*, "Turkmenistan's New Father," January 24, 2007, 1.

19.   Terence A. Shimp and Subhash Sharma, "Consumer Ethnocentrism: Construction and Validation of the CETSCALE," *Journal of Marketing Research,* Vol. 24, No. 3, August 1987, pp. 280–289.

20.   Thomas Fuller, "Thailand May Add Measures to Restrict Foreign Investment," *Wall Street Journal*, January 10, 2007, C11.

21.   Richard Karp, "Risk's Rewards," *Barron's,* Vol. 79, No. 16, April 1999, p. 16.

22.   Sohn Young-Ju, "Saving Kia," *Business Korea,* Vol. 15, No. 1, January 1998, p. 15.

23.   Henny Sender, "Reflation Is No Panacea," *Far Eastern Economic Review,* Vol. 161, No. 48, November 26, 1998, p. 93.

24.   Thomas Fuller, "Thailand May Add Measures to Restrict Foreign Investment," *Wall Street Journal*, January 10, 2007, C11.

25.   Simon Romero, "Chavez Begins New Term Vowing Socialism," *New York Times*, January 11, 2007, A14.

26.   Karp, "Risk's Rewards," p. 16.

27.   Michael Gips, "Businesses Bearing Brunt of Terrorism," *Security Management*, Vol. 45, No. 8, August 2001, p. 18.

28.   David S. Cloud, "Bush Team Says Data Were Wrong on Terror Deaths," *The Wall Street Journal*, June 23, 2004, B2.

29.   Joseph Kahn, "A Trend Toward Attacks That Emphasize Deaths," *The New York Times*, September 12, 2001, A18.

30.   Steve Lohr, "Financial District Vows to Rise from the Ashes," *The New York Times*, September 14, 2001, A6.

31.   Susan Sontag, "The Talk of the Town, Tuesday, and After," *The New Yorker*, September 24, 2001, p. 32.

32.   Ian McDonald, "Lyod's Tip: Businesses Should Assess Terror Risk," *Wall Street Journal*, May 10, 2007, C3.

33.   "Counter-Terrorism Driver Training May Thwart Executive Kidnapping," *Best's Review*, Vol. 98, No. 2, June 1997, p. 95.

34.   Ibid.

35.   Ilkka A. Ronkainen and Jose-Luis Guerrero-Cusumano, "Correlates of Intellectual Property Violation," *Multinational Business Review*, Vol. 9, No. 1, Spring 2001, pp. 59–65.

36.   Ibid.

37.   "Copycats Beware," *Business Korea*, Vol. 18, No. 3, March 2001, pp. 44–45.

38.   Heather R. Goldstein, David M. Lange, Andrew E. Roth, and James D. Lawrence, "International Intellectual Property Alliance Points USTR Toward Brazil, Costa Rica, Guatemala, Russia, Uruguay," *Intellectual Property & Technology Law Journal*, Vol. 12, No. 11, November 2000, p. 27.

39.   Ronkainen and Guerrero-Cusumano, "Correlates of Intellectual Property Violation," pp. 59–65.

40.   "Special: The Right to Good Ideas, Patents and the Poor," *The Economist*, Vol. 359, No. 8227, June 23, 2001, pp. 21–23.

41.   Ibid.

42.   Ronkainen and Guerrero-Cusumano, "Correlates of Intellectual Property Violation," pp. 59–65.

43.   "Special: The Right to Good Ideas, Patents and the Poor," *The Economist*, June 23, 2001, pp. 21–23.

44.   Ibid.

45.   Ibid.

46.   *New York Times*, "Cezch Republic: Busch-Budvar Thaw," January 9, 2007, C1.

47.   Edmund L. Andrews and Paul Meller, "EU Vetoes GE's Plan to Acquire Honeywell," *International Herald Tribune*, July 4, 2001, 1, 5.

48.   Aymo Brunetti, Gregory Kisunko, and Beatric Weder, "Institutional Obstacles to Doing Business: Region-by-Region Results from a Worldwide Survey of the Private Sector," *The World Bank Group Policy Research Working Papers*, 1997, http://wbln0018.worldbank.org/research/workpapers.nsf.

49.   Jack G. Kaikati, George M. Sullivan, John M. Virgo, T. R. Carr, and Katherine S. Virgo, "The Price of International Business Morality: Twenty Years Under the Foreign Corrupt Practices Act," *Journal of Business Ethics*, Vol. 26, No. 3, August 2000, pp. 213–222.

50.   Ibid.

51.   Organization for Economic Co-operation and Development (OECD), www.oecd.org.

52.   Sarah Lyall, "Sweden's Lightning Rod in a Storm over Assimilation," *New York Times*, January 13, 2007, A4.

53.   Mark Landler, "Germany Agonizes Over a Brain Drain." *New York Times*, February 6, 2007, A10.

54.   Elisabeth Rosenthal, "Car Boom Puts Europe on Road to a Smoggy Future," *New York Times*, January 7, 2007, Section 1, 3.

55.   Dan Bilefsky, "Europe Sets Ambitious Limits on Greenhouse Gases, and Challenges Others to Match It," *New York Times*, March 10, 2007, A5.

56.   Keith Bradsher, "India and China Explore Alternatives, but Too Often Diesel Generator Rules," *New York Times*, January 9, 2007, C1, C7.

57.   Joseph B. White, "For GM in China, Tiny Is Mighty; Wuling Venture Plans Expansion as Sales of Small Cars Surge," *Wall Street Journal*, April 20, 2007, A9.

58.   Sue Abdinnour-Helm, "Network Design in Supply Chain Management," *International Journal of Agile Management Systems,* Vol. 1, No. 2, 1999, pp. 99–106.

59.   www.budde.com.au/Reports/Contents/Global-Internet-Market-Statistics-2075.html?r=51

60.   Nielsen Netratings, http://www.nielsen-netratings.com.

61.   Worldometers, http://www.worldometers.info, accessed June 14, 2012.

62.   "What Exactly Does a Reinsurer Do?" *Jobs and Career,* Munich Re, www.munichre.com/index.html.

63.   "Finance and Economics: Premium Rates; Reinsurance," *The Economist,* February 9, 2002, p. 79.

64.   "Profit Through Pioneering Spirit," *History,* Munich Re, http://www.munichre.com/index.html, February 24, 2002, p. 1 (web).

65.   "Corporate Responsibility," *120 Years of Innovation,* Munich Re, http://www.munichre.com/index.html, February 24, 2002, p. 1 (web).

66.   Ibid.

67.   *Best's Review,* "2006 Top 35 Global Reinsurance Groups," August 2006,
pp. 107, 4, 40.

68.   "Reinsurer Munich Re Posts US $1.06B Loss, Keeps Damage Estimates from Attacks," *Canoe Money,* http://www.canoe.ca/MoneyEarnings/nov29_munichre-ap.html, November 29, 2001, pp. 1–2 (web); February 21, 2002.

69.   "Reinsurers Double Terrorist Claims," *CNN money,* http://money.cnn.com/2001/09/20/europe/insurance/index.htm, September 20, 2001, p. 1 (web); February 21, 2002.

70.   "Munich Re Posts $1.1B Loss," http://europe.cnn.com/.

71.   "After the Terrorist Attacks: US Rating Agencies Affirm Their Top Rating for Munich Re," *Munich American News,* http://www.marclife.com/news01/mr100501.htm, October 5, 2001, p. 1 (web); February 21, 2002.

72.   "Reinsurer Munich Re Posts US $1.06B Loss, Keeps Damage Estimate from Attacks," p. 2 (web).

73.   Meg Green, "Extreme Weather Patterns Pose Greater Insurance Risk," *Best's Review,* Vol. 104, No. 11, March 2004, p. 69.

74.   Green, "Extreme Weather Patterns," p. 69.

75.   Ulrike Dauer, "Munich Re Reports Net Profits as Write-Downs, Claims Decline," *The Wall Street Journal,* May 27, 2004, A6.

76.   Ivar Simensen, "Asbestos Pain Munich Re Faces Dollars 1 bn US Loss, *Financial Times*, March 14, 2007, 27.

77.   Deborah Orr, "Risk Buster," Forbes.com, http://www.forbes.com/, January 21, 2002, pp. 1–2 (web); February 21, 2002.

78.   "11th September 2001: The Attack on the World Trade Center in New York from an Insurance Point of View," www.munichre.com/index.html, accessed on
February 24, 2002.

79.   Rebecca Knight, "Report Shows Record Terrorism Insurance Levels," *Financial Times*, June 1, 2007, 26.

80.   "Topics: Worker's Compensation Insurance IT Risks Investment Strategies," January 2004, http://www.munichre.com/publications/302-04044_en.pdf.

81.   David Pilla, "Demand for Terror Coverage Continues to Fall in Germany," *Best's Review*, September 2005, 105, pp. 5, 14.

82.   Rebecca Knight, "Report Shows Record Terrorism Insurance Levels," *Financial Times*, June 1, 2007, 26.

83.   Mike Scott, "Experts Who Put a Premium on Expecting the Worst and Working Out What It Costs," *Financial Times*, April 2, 2007, 8.

84.   Stefan Hackl, "Environmental Liability: The State as Nature's Advocate," www.munichre.com

85.   www.munichre.com.

Case 2-1

Munich Re—Terrorism-Related Risk Management and Ecological Issues

Introduction

Munich Re (in German, Münchener Rückversicherungs-Gesellschaft) is one of the world's leading reinsurance companies. It has had its ups and downs, handling costly, massive catastrophes, but all the while, taking in profits for its innovative insurance products and maintaining its AAA rating. Its performance was so impressive that, by 2010, Warren Buffet decided it was worthy of investment – presently, he is its largest shareholder and owns more than 10 percent of the company.

As a reinsurance firm, Munich Re relies on insurance firms to minimize losses. It allows for costs attributed to insurance losses to be distributed among multiple companies. As such, the reinsurance industry makes it possible for insurance companies to take risks they otherwise would not take,[62] creating new opportunities for increased revenue and market share. The amount of risk assumed by reinsurers varies with the market. When the market is optimistic, reinsurers are more likely to assume greater risks; more capital is available, so the companies are capable of underwriting additional risk.[63]

Munich Re has been consistently rethinking its product mix and has actively pursued sustained insurance-product-related innovation in many facets of its activity. This case focuses primarily on two aspects of innovative risk management at Munich Re: terrorism risk management and ecological risk management.

Company Background

Munich Re was founded in 1880 by Carl Thieme, who, with a vision far ahead of his time, created the reinsurance business. He convinced investors of the insurance companies' need for reinsurance as a means for redistributing risk (and loss) among insurance firms, thus allowing them to take advantage of opportunities that otherwise they could not afford to consider.[64] Munich Re is headquartered in downtown Munich, Germany, where it covers a couple of square blocks with impressive older and contemporary architecture.

Inside the Munich Re complex, a Japanese garden offers an environment of meditation. Underground, all the buildings are connected with active corridors where color and light set a theatrical stage; here, a second "downtown"—the downtown of Munich Re employees—exists in parallel to the bustling street, Leopoldstrasse. The environment projects a strong spirit of innovation, the very theme of Munich Re's corporate culture.[65] In addition to its quest for product innovation, Munich Re was the first German company to introduce English working hours in the nineteenth century, requiring shorter days from its employees and granting them greater leisure time. The company is also among a few in Germany that provide benefits such as access to a holiday home in the Alps and an on-site daycare—the Munich Re Giants Childcare Center.[66]

The Munich Re Product

With a dependable brand, international presence, diversified product offering, and 42 offices around the world, Munich Re has attracted customers and investors alike, and today it remains the largest reinsurance company in the world. In the 2006 *Best Review* rankings, it recorded consolidated gross premiums of $26,482 million, followed by Swiss Re, with gross premiums of $23,151, and the Berkshire Hathaway Group, at $12,486.[67]

The company offers several different types of insurance services, such as Alternative Risk-Financing and Risk-Transfer Solutions (ART), Agricultural Insurance, Managed Care Services, and Life Insurance. ART, including Finite Risk Reinsurance and Integrated Risk Management, supplements conventional reinsurance as a means of maximizing risk retention and discovering additional financial resources. This is an area that Munich Re has pioneered and that is especially in great demand today, after the September 11, 2001, terrorist attacks. Finite Risk Reinsurance allows the company to undertake more risk by using innovative financing techniques, rather than simply by transferring risk from the insured to the insurer.

Integrated Risk Management merges insurance risks with the risks involved in financial markets—for example, in currency and interest rate fluctuation. The objective of Integrated Risk Management is to achieve both the reinsurer's goals of the lowest possible risk and the client's goals of highest possible security and support. Munich Re provides a number of other insurance services, covering all aspects of the economy. For example, Agricultural Insurance is a service that Munich Re has developed to protect commercial farmers in times of catastrophe and natural disaster. Its Managed Care Services, part of the Munich Re Health Division, are involved in evaluating each potential medical procedure that it insures to determine if, in fact, the procedure is essential. Finally, the company's Life Insurance services give the company access to final consumers—a different market than its traditional business-to-business market segments (its organizational consumers).

Insurance Losses at Munich Re

Munich Re, much like other reinsurance companies, has had numerous challenges, many dealing with medical advances and genetics decoding, and others with natural disasters. For example, Munich Re had to absorb the costs involved in the recall of Lipobay, a cholesterol-reducing drug that was linked to death among users; a large typhoon in Taiwan; and a chemical plant explosion in France.[68]

These losses were dwarfed by the September 11, 2001, terrorist attacks. Total damages for the reinsurance industry were more than $3 billion for the disaster.[69] Munich Re's claims totaled $1.84 billion.[70] Compared with competitors, Munich Re has handled the aftermath of September 11 well, and A.M. Best and Standard & Poor's concluded that their ratings of A++ and AAA/Stable, respectively, were still appropriate for Munich Re, based on the company's performance by the end of 2001.[71] The company's losses were offset by an increase in premium income by 20 percent; moreover, Munich Re found itself with less competition, as smaller reinsurers had incurred losses that caused them to leave the industry altogether.[72] In 2002, Munich Re experienced further losses, as natural catastrophes rose sharply due to heat waves, forest fires, severe floods in Asia and Europe, as well as tornadoes in the midwestern United States.[73] In 2003, more than 50,000 people were killed in natural catastrophes, such as more than 400 tornadoes in the Midwest of United States, California wildfires, Hurricane Isabel, and snow and ice storms. In Europe, the company lost more than $13 billion due to the heat waves.[74] In spite of these losses, the company quickly rebounded, after deciding to underwrite more profitable businesses, with a profit of 534 million euros (US$646.4 million) in 2003.[75]

In December 2006, Standard & Poor's rating was slightly lower, at AA/Stable. However, the company experienced additional losses in 2007, when high asbestos-related claims pushed Munich Re's operations into a $1 billion loss, resulting in earnings fall of 20 percent.[76]

Terrorism Risk Management

On September 11, 2001, apocalyptic images from the World Trade Center and the Pentagon inundated the media around the world. The events of 9/11 marked the beginning of new levels of vulnerability for businesses, national and local governments, airlines, and individuals. The insurance and reinsurance industries experienced the largest aggregate losses ever as a result of the attacks. Half a world away, Munich Re, suffered a loss of $1.84 billion as a result of the terrorist attacks on U.S. soil. Before September 11, 2001, terrorist attacks of this magnitude were inconceivable and were not considered in the calculations of premiums and the like. According to P. J. Crowley of the Insurance Institute of America, "There has never been a premium dollar collected to cover terrorism."[76] Reinsurance firms had to reconsider their stance on what coverage they would offer in the event of future terrorist attacks. Many insurance and reinsurance companies included clauses in their policies that exclude the coverage of losses from any type of terrorism. Munich Re "was hit by the claims from September 11 more than other members of the reinsurance industry and thus it had to make careful decisions concerning what to do about providing protection against terrorist claims."[77]

Reinsurance companies were not well prepared to handle a loss event of the magnitude of September 11. In 2001, the faltering state of markets worldwide depleted the reinsurance companies' capital. As a result, the reinsurance industry, and Munich Re in particular, were forced to explore the different ways in which it could alter the mix of products offered to insurance firms all over the world and their pricing strategies to most effectively operate in the present volatile environment. In an effort to adapt to the new, post-September 11 business environment and its new challenges, the insurance and reinsurance firms were forced to change their entire marketing mix. Munich Re underwent a complete overhaul of its marketing strategy.

Changing the Marketing Mix at Munich Re

No reinsurance company had ever considered terrorist actions of such magnitude when calculating Probable Maximum Loss (PML) for the properties insured. Insurance companies had to cover losses of more than 1,200 corporations housed in the World Trade Center complex, damage to the operating areas, loss of experienced employees, and destruction of business data and business income. More than 50 buildings were affected in addition to the World Trade Center, and 150,000 people were out of work permanently or temporarily.[78] These extreme circumstances led the reinsurance companies to change their marketing mix—especially the reinsurance product and its price.

According to Nicholas Roenneberg, senior executive manager, Corporate Underwriting—Global Clients division at Munich Re, if such a catastrophe were to happen, it did so at an opportune time for the company—when the company was renewing its policies for the year. At that point, the company placed all policy negotiations on hold so that it could reconfigure its marketing mix. For the short term, Munich Re determined that terrorism was no longer insurable, given the high risks especially in high property concentrations because in these environments, it was impossible to estimate the frequency of such attacks and their total impact, thus presenting a situation in which an important criterion of general risk insurability, assessibility, cannot be met. They were joined by most insurance companies, which decided to exclude terrorism risks from their commercial policies. However, the Terrorism Insurance Act, or Tria, signed into law by President George W. Bush in 2002, required insurers to offer cover for certain acts of terrorism that are "certified" by the U.S. government.[79]

In the long term, Munich Re decided to offer custom-insurance options for properties evaluated at more than 50 million euros (more than US$65 million), on a case-by-case basis. Ultimately, all types of insurance options were subject to negotiation. No terrorism exclusion, however, was imposed on life and personal accident insurance. In addition to insurance, Munich Re and most other insurers require some exclusions in property insurance and partner with local and state government to provide coverage.[80]

According to Christian Lahnstein, a specialist in genetic engineering law and liability law with Munich Re, the company studied at length the issue of government intervention and bailing out industries affected by disaster. It also studied issues related to the equity of distribution of funds from the government and charitable sources. The company used this information in decisions related to the company's marketing mix.

One issue currently under consideration at the company is related to the costs of corporate terrorism, which is driving up the price of directors' and officers' liability insurance. These are traditionally known as long-tail risks—risks that are not immediately apparent to the insurers and insurance buyers. Munich Re is among the first firms in the industry to offer coverage specifically for this type of risk.

Interestingly, German companies themselves do not feel compelled to purchase terrorism coverage, despite major attacks in the European Union—London and Madrid, among others. The German government provides terrorism coverage through Extremus, a government-backed insurer created in 2002; however, the insurer has little demand for coverage, even though there is little doubt about the continued presence of terrorists in the country. The reason is that the insurance is expensive, two to three times the cost of terrorism coverage under the U.S. Terrorism Risk Insurance Act.[81] However, in the United States, businesses are purchasing terrorism insurance at record levels: nearly two thirds of large businesses and 60 percent of mid-sized firms purchased the insurance.[82]

Environmental Risk Management

Every risk that global warming poses to the planet—higher sea levels, more frequent and intense storms, drought, flooding, heat waves, and winds, will come up in the balance sheet of an insurer. Munich Re has conducted extensive research on the issue and has the best climate scientists working for them. They are doing information and risk modeling to determine how much insurers should be paying for reinsurance. And, to respond to these risks, Munich Re developed innovative financial products, such as weather derivatives and mortality bonds.[83]

European environmental liability extended initially only to personal injury and property damage. However, in 2007, it also extended to statutory liability for damage to the environment. Munich Re immediately changed its coverage to environmental risks, as its traditional insurance did not adequately cover environmental risks. In the new European perspective, for instance, environmental consequences of fires and explosions are considered damage. For environmental damage, Munich Re requires risk assessment, underwriting, and damage remediation to be performed only by experienced scientists, engineers and specialist underwriters to ensure that the company remains profitable in the environmental sector.[84]

The basic principle of the EU environmental liability directive is that anyone who causes damage to the environment has to pay to have it cleaned up. This polluter-pays principle ensures that society as a whole no longer has to bear the costs of public law claims, as has so often been the case in the past. For example, land must be decontaminated until it no longer poses any significant risk to human health and the damaged protected species, natural habitats, or waters, must be restored to its original state. All remedial measures must compensate for the loss—to offer an example, damage to 100 valuable old trees could be compensated for by the planting of 1,000 new ones. It should be noted that the EU does not yet require mandatory insurance; however, it is likely that the directive will be amended to introduce mandatory insurance in all member states in the near future.[85]

Analysis Suggestions

1.   Address the political risk signals that bring about terrorist actions. How can companies reduce their likelihood of becoming victims of terrorism?

2.   Address the changes to the Munich Re marketing mix as a result of the September 11 terrorist attacks.

3.   How is Munich Re an innovator when it comes to the coverage of environmental risk?

Case 2-2

Doing Business in Cuba... One Day

As a small business operating in the Orlando area, Deco1 has been successful serving middle-class Hispanics' interior decorating needs. Its work has been featured in regional magazines illustrating its minimalist, yet colorful designs which appeal to the region's Hispanic population. One of the largest target markets is the Cuban American market in the region.

Deco1's owner, Terry Kaminer is born in Cuba, but came to the United States with her parents in the 1960s and Terry has been active in the Cuban community in the Orlando area. One of her dreams is one day to return "home" and to teach Cubans how to live simply with good, attractive design.

Cuba's highly centralized socialist economic system is still recovering from the loss of substantial Soviet subsidies, hurricanes, and a massive brain drain of its best and brightest. China is increasingly reluctant to underwrite Cuba's economy, and the country's infrastructure is in dire need of an upgrade.

In the past two years, Cuba has made strides in embracing a more market-oriented economy under its new leader, Raul Castro, the brother of Cuba's long-time leader, Fidel Castro, as head of the State. There is now a fledgling real estate market and individuals are able to buy and sell automobiles and homes. For the first time, small private businesses are allowed to hire employees and pay their workers' social security contributions - a total of 350,000 businesses licenses were granted for private enterprise. The government opened idle land to farmers and cooperatives, and it allows individuals to open lines of credit with no legal ceilings on how they can borrow.

At the same time, Cuba is instituting austerity measures, shrinking the buying power of the ration card that Cubans receive to purchase subsidized products, cutting unemployment benefits, and dismissing up to a million individuals working for the state. Cuba is currently in a difficult position: The United States refuses to change its strict policies, maintaining an economic, commercial, and financial blockade. As a result, Cuba is not a member of any international financial institution and the U.S. blockade made it impossible to obtain any additional lines of credit, which led Cuba to default on its payments to foreign creditors in 2008. Currently, Cuba earns hard currency by exporting nickel, sugar, and professional services (medical) and receives income from tourism and remittances from Cubans living abroad. With the hard currency, it imports everything, from food to manufactured goods and capital goods.

However, with all the difficulties Cuba continues to encounter and the insistence of the Cuban government on maintaining a Soviet-style economic and political system, Terry Kaminer's acquaintances in the Cuban-American community are preparing for a radical change and for open borders with the United States. Many are already looking at the possibility for investing in small businesses with the help of relatives living in Cuba. Terry is wondering about the prospects of Deco1 in Cuba. With the prospects of increasing tourism and prosperity, more Cubans will be interested in building new homes and interior design will be on their radar screen. And yet, what if the Cuban government insists on maintaining the status quo, enforcing the existing economic and political dictatorship?

Sources: Ted Piccone, "Cuba Is Changing Slowly but Surely," Brookings Institution, January 19, 2012, http://www.brookings.edu/research/reports/2012/01/19-cuba-picconeCTC, http://www.marxist.com/where-is-cuba-going-capitalism-or-socialism.htm; CNBC, "Inside Cuba Market Economy Takes Hold in Socialist State Under Raul," http://www.cnbc.com/id/46855968/Inside_Cuba_Market_Economy_Takes_Hold_in_Socialist_State; http://www.workers.org/2012/world/cuba_060, (accessed July 10, 2012).

Analysis Suggestions

1. Address Cuba's current situation in light of the different models of economic development discussed in the chapter. Is Cuba socialist? Capitalist?

2. Discuss the viability of Terry's small business in the new Cuba. Are Cubans going to turn to interior design businesses anytime soon?

Chapter 3: International Trade: Institutional Barriers and Facilitators

Learning Objectives

After studying this chapter, you should be able to:

• Identify different trade barriers imposed on international trade and arguments used by governments to erect and maintain these barriers.

• Provide an overview of key international organizations facilitating international trade directly or by promoting economic development.

• Identify government efforts involved in promoting economic development and trade.

• Describe other trade facilitators, such as foreign trade zones, offshore assembly plants, and special economic zones, and the Normal Trade Relations Status.

Businesses face numerous barriers when entering international markets. Barriers to entry can be imposed by the government, by local and international competition, by the local channel structure, and by logistics and other firms offering marketing support. Factors in the economic, political, financial, and legal environment also can create barriers for businesses attempting to expand internationally—as discussed in Chapter 2, "An Overview of the International Marketing Environment." Even protectionist tendencies within a regionally integrated area could impose barriers to entry. For example, one of the first nicknames that the European Union acquired in the late 1980s was "Fortress Europe," for its potential to restrict access of foreign companies to this large, integrated market. Fortunately, that has not been the case. This chapter focuses on government-initiated protectionist strategies, such as tariff and nontariff barriers.

The reduction in trade barriers constitutes a main concern of multinationals and their representative governments. In addition to participating in numerous regional treaties, governments have joined forces to create forums for discussion of trade issues and mechanisms for the reduction of trade restrictions. One such organization, the World Trade Organization (WTO), has had a significant positive impact on trade, reining in protectionist strategies of important players in the world of trade, such as China, and opening formerly closed markets to international companies. Nevertheless, despite its accomplishments, this organization has met substantial opposition from groups that perceive globalization as the promotion of large multinational companies' interests to the detriment of the individual, developing countries and of the environment. This chapter focuses on facilitators to international trade and addresses the opposition to trade expansion by environmentalists and developing countries. Chapter 4, "Regional Economic and Political Integration," addresses regional economic and political integration as yet another mechanism used to eliminate trade barriers.

Protection of local markets from foreign companies constitutes an important mandate for national and local governments alike. Many political careers have been built and defended on market protection rhetoric. "We will not sell our country" has been a slogan of countries resisting foreign economic and political dominance in the past. Today, it is a slogan used against multinationals that are rapidly expanding, taking over emerging markets, and bringing with them a consumption culture perceived to go against local culture and traditions. These multinationals also are seen as eliminating small local producers and service providers, bankrupting formerly productive factories, and replacing abundant local labor with more efficient advanced technology, increasing local unemployment and disrupting political stability.

protectionism
All actions by national and local governments aimed at protecting local markets from foreign competitors.

infant industry argument
Aims to protect an emerging national industry from powerful international competitors.

Some of the arguments for **protectionism** are indeed valid. The **infant industry argument** is aimed at protecting an emerging national industry from powerful international competitors, which could easily squeeze out a newcomer to the business merely with their brand name resonance and with pricing strategies that a new industry could not possibly sustain in the long term. The argument stressing the industrialization of developing countries also is valid for similar reasons. The national defense argument is regarded as justified in international trade forums and is widely accepted as a reasonable argument for protectionism.

There is also the argument for environmental protection and protection of natural resources and the need for maintaining standards for the benefit of all humankind. This line of arguments is also soundly reasoned. The problem with this defense of protectionism arises when the standards imposed are simply protectionist measures that unfairly require foreign competition to go through excessive and unwarranted bureaucratic exercise. It is particularly problematic when these requirements are imposed on international firms but not on local firms—or when they are imposed on local firms to a lesser degree.

It is believed that consumers pay the final price for the cost of protectionism. Arguments for protectionism ignore the economic advantages of free trade and the importance of adopting open market mechanisms for optimal long-term market performance. In fact, history has amply demonstrated that a government's right and authority to pick and choose winners among industries and firms could be corrupted and distorted by local influential firms, power-seeking politicians, and favor-seeking lobby groups.[1] Politicians favor trade barriers and vote for imposing them because such strategies appeal directly to the concerns of their constituencies regarding the possibility of losing their jobs. What these politicians do not consider is the subsequent retaliatory action of other governments that will negatively affect the domestic economy and the higher consumer prices attributed to the taxes imposed to subsidize the domestic industry and to the reduction in competition in the local market.[2]

3-1 Arguments for Protectionism

Sections 3-1a through 3-1f describe arguments most often advanced to justify the imposition of tariff and nontariff trade barriers.

3-1a Protection of Markets with Excess Productive Capacity

Markets that have excess productive capacity have committed significant resources to their production facilities. In the case of Central and Eastern Europe, for example, the standard for production during the central planning years under communism was represented by enormous factories employing hundreds of thousands of workers, sometimes each charged with minuscule tasks under an elaborate division-of-labor program. The goal of such programs was both to ensure productivity and a place of work to every individual, qualified or not. Such factories had, in addition to the workers, redundant oversight structures with directors and paradirectors, all served by several secretaries whose specializations varied from typing and answering telephones to making coffee and taking care of personal shopping for the director's family.

After the fall of communism, the new factory owners (often foreign) quickly realized that they needed only a fraction of the workers for optimal production and proceeded to fire the rest, leading to local unrest. Currently, some of the remaining factories are protected from foreign buyouts and are managed locally. A number of these companies are state-owned enterprises protected by the government from foreign investors and from competing products, such as superior steel and higher-performance tractors, by arguing that such restrictions are instituted for the **protection of markets with excess productive capacity.**

3-1b Employment Protection and Protection of Markets with Excess Labor

Under the scenario presented in Section 3-1a, "Protection of Markets with Excess Productive Capacity," the markets of Central and Eastern Europe—especially those in the countries of the former Soviet Union—are now experiencing high levels of excess labor and underemployment, all of which have led to flares of social unrest. As a result, local politicians have actively lobbied against granting import licenses for products competing with locally produced goods that are established in the market. Arguments invoking **employment protection** are used to ensure that competing multinationals do not import products manufactured elsewhere that might drive local manufacturers out of business, leading to local unemployment. The argument also is used against multinationals that might purchase local plants and fire most of the redundant workers to create acceptable levels of profitability. A related argument, invoking the **protection of markets with excess labor**, is also used to prevent foreign businesses from taking over local businesses and streamlining local operations.

protection of markets with excess productive capacity
A protectionist measure used to prevent foreign buyouts, invoking the protection of local labor.

employment protection
Protection of local employment by not granting import licenses for products competing with similar locally produced goods.

protection of markets with excess labor
The erection of barriers to imports of products competing with local offerings in an effort to protect local jobs.

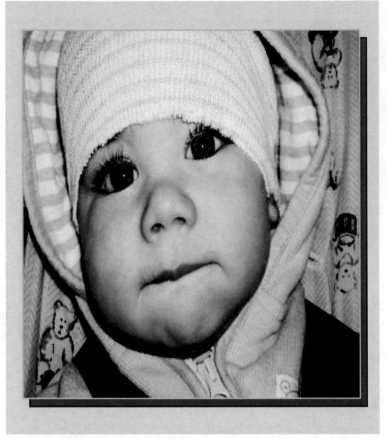

3-1c Infant Industry Arguments and Arguments Related to the Industrialization of Developing Countries

The infant industry arguments and arguments related to the industrialization of developing countries are considered valid: Developing countries need to protect their markets from competitors from countries with an established industrial base. The argument is based on the premise that establishing a new industry is a costly investment and it will take time until the industry can achieve economies of scale and become competitive. While the new industry is in the process of development, it is likely that foreign competitors with established manufacturing in markets with low-cost labor would be able to offer established brands at competitive costs and would undoubtedly undercut local manufacturers attempting to break into the market.

Western countries have used the infant industry argument dating as far back as the late 1700s, until the 1980s – until the emergence of globalization. Now that countries with emerging markets are developing new industries, they are heavily scrutinized by global trade organizations when they use similar strategies. Malaysia, India, Brazil, and Argentina are developing their respective automotive industries in partnership with established Western automobile manufacturers. However, when they attempt to erect barriers to entry to competitors using the infant industry argument, they are, nevertheless, heavily scrutinized.

3-1d Natural Resources Conservation and Protection of the Environment

The resource conservation argument is considered to be valid in international trade organization forums, especially in light of worldwide shortages of raw materials. Similarly, a balance sometimes has to be struck between free trade and legitimate arguments such as those centering on environmental protection, but governments still need to find a way of agreeing when curbs on trade can be an acceptable way to pursue a greater good.[3]

The problem with these two arguments arises when they are used arbitrarily, with a clear bias against international firms, either imposing the standards only on foreign firms or requiring them to meet higher standards than local firms.

3-1e Protection of Consumers

Protection of consumers is an often-echoed argument that ultimately favors local, over international, business. Standards that are rigidly applied against foreign businesses, quality controls that necessitate layers of costly bureaucracy, and arbitrary product origin requirements, among others, are instituted invoking this argument. Politicians in the European Union have argued that they were protecting consumers by imposing standards on imported beef: Listening to the unified voices of their constituencies and attempting to protect the local beef industry against the high-quality, cheap, corn-fed U.S. beef, the European Union banned its import, invoking the use of growth hormones in the United States.

With many countries of the European Union having previously dealt with epidemics such as mad cow and hoof-and-mouth disease, as well as with the bird flu, the U.S. beef ban is an unequivocal demonstration that over zealous consumer protection is not necessarily in the interest of the consumer.

3-1f National Defense Interests

The national defense argument is often invoked in international trade forums. Publications that attempt to destabilize the government, armament, and other similar products are legitimately under an import ban. More recently, the national defense argument has been advocated by developing countries and by countries that attempt to control and restrict access of their population to Western influence. Such nations may perceive a threat in the unrestricted imports of information-based services through electronic channels; countries such as China, Singapore, and Saudi Arabia impose restrictions on and even ban ownership of satellite dishes, whereas other nations are attempting to control citizen access on the Internet.[4] Expatriate forums in the Middle East frequently lament the restrictions on the use of the free Skype video chat, which requires individuals to use costly telephone service instead.

3-2 Tools of Government Protectionism: Tariff and Nontariff Barriers

3-2a Tariffs

Tariffs are any type of tax imposed on goods entering a particular country. Tariffs are imposed to:

- Discourage imports of particular goods, such as consumer goods, which often are not considered essential in developing countries.
- Protect local industry: For example, in 2012, the United States imposed tariffs on Chinese solar panels to protect U.S. industry and to penalize China for subsidizing solar panel exports.
- Penalize countries that are not politically aligned with the importing country, or countries that are imposing tariffs or nontariff restrictions on goods from the importing country.
- Generate revenues for the importing country.

> **tariffs**
> Taxes imposed on goods entering a country.
>
> **nontariff barriers**
> All measures, other than traditional tariffs, used to distort trade flows, used to increase prices of imports, and thus favor domestic over foreign products.

Tariffs assessed by the United States are relatively low, less than 15 percent. Some countries may set tariffs higher than 100 percent for products that compete with an infant industry. For example, in the Chinese solar panels case above, it is possible that some of the Chinese companies could face a 250 percent tariff, although the Commerce Department may require a lower amount – most of the solar panels companies will have to pay a 31 percent tariff.

3-2b Nontariff Barriers

Nontariff barriers include all measures, other than traditional tariffs, that are used to distort international trade flows; they raise prices of both imports and import-competing goods and favor domestic over foreign supply sources by causing importers to charge higher prices and to restrict import volumes.[5]

In the past 20 years, in an attempt to keep markets closed without going against the General Agreement on Tariffs and Trade (GATT) and the WTO (see Chapter 4, "Regional Economic and Political Integration"), governments have created new nontariff barriers, such as orderly market arrangements, voluntary import expansion, and voluntary export restraints, which limit market access for foreign businesses. These nontariff barriers have been erected by many countries, but most are imposed by the United States, members of the European Union, and other industrialized countries on exporting countries such as Japan, South Korea,[6] and developing countries.[7] But even local governments, such as the government of New York State, can erect such barriers, as International Marketing Illustration 3-1 describes.

Other, more traditional, nontariff barriers include quotas, currency controls, and standards—such as environmental, quality, performance, and health standards, all of which are expensive to provide and evaluate. Boycotts, embargoes, and sanctions are the most severe barriers to trade that are imposed usually to punish a company or a national government.

Nontariff barriers are constantly evolving: They are in a continuous process of refinement, aimed at avoiding scrutiny from the World Trade Organization

International Marketing Illustration 3-1

Local Trade Barriers: An Example from New York State

Direct shipping laws provide an example of nontariff barriers to trade. Such laws enacted locally—by states, for example—restrict international trade. For example, New York State law denies all firms outside the state the ability to sell directly to New York consumers. These laws restrict consumer choice, and consumers have to pay higher prices because fewer competitors are available in the market. New York consumers could order wine from a company in Alsace, France, at a lower cost than buying the same wine from a New York retailer. The ability of New York consumers to purchase wine from abroad or from other states in the United States should increase competition and lead to lower prices and more wine choices for consumers. However, this is not possible: The New York law states that New York distributors must dispense every case of wine entering the state from foreign suppliers. In effect, New York distributors have a monopoly over the market. Retailers are also affected by this law because they, too, have to purchase their wine from U.S. distributors.

A comparison of wine prices reveals that states that allow direct shipping have a lower average price than states that do not allow it. The eight states surrounding New York have restricted wine trade in different forms. For example, New Hampshire, Connecticut, and Rhode Island allow direct shipping only with a permit, which has to be obtained from the state's attorney general to allow shipping to consumers' homes.

Source: Robert Eyler, "Direct Shipping Laws, Wine, and Societal Welfare," International Journal of Wine Marketing, Vol. 15, No. 2, 2003, pp. 25–34.

or other trade organizations. Although the most frequently encountered nontariff barriers are described here, it is important to note that new variants of the barriers described are continuously emerging in the global trade arena.

Import Quotas and Orderly Market Arrangements

Quotas specify a maximum quantity (unit limit) or a value (usually specified in the national currency) of a product that may be imported during a specified period. Quotas are administered either on a global first-come, first-served basis or on a bilateral basis to restrict shipments from a specific supply source—such as the Multifiber Arrangement.[8]

The Multifiber Arrangement was initiated as a temporary measure in 1974 (but lasted 21 years!). Its articulated goals were to expand trade, to reduce barriers to trade, and to initiate a progressive liberalization of world trade in textile products, while ensuring the orderly and equitable development of this trade and avoiding disruptive effects in individual markets and on individual lines of production in both importing and exporting countries.[9] In reality, this was an **orderly market arrangement,** an intricate process of establishing quotas in the textile and apparel industries, initiated by the United States and Europe, whose textile operations were moving to Asia to take advantage of cheaper labor. The Multifiber Arrangement was nullified under the Uruguay Round of the GATT in 1995 but has since been replaced by similar nontariff barriers.

Nonautomatic Import Licenses

Nonautomatic import licenses are issued on a discretionary basis and are used to restrict imports of a given product. Licensing requirements can restrict the volume of imports, as do quotas, or they can be used to impose on the exporter or importer specific conditions that will result in fewer imports.[10] The WTO requires member countries to ensure transparency of the import-license granting process; they are asked to do so by publicizing information concerning administration of restrictions; listing information regarding the licenses granted over the most recent period; and, where practicable, providing additional import statistics of the products concerned.[11]

Automatic Import Licenses

Automatic import licenses are granted freely to importing companies. Automatic licenses are used by the importing country's government for the purpose of import surveillance: The licenses have the potential to discourage import surges, to place additional administrative and financial burdens on the importer, and to raise costs by delaying product shipments.[12]

Within most common markets, it is assumed that import licenses are automatic, if they exist at all; however, that is not always the case. For example, in 2012, Brazil decided to terminate automatic import licenses for several products, such as wheat, flour and some cheeses and wines, most imported from Argentina, another member country of MERCOSUR, the Southern Cone common market.

Voluntary Import Expansion

Under a **voluntary import expansion** (VIE), a country agrees to open its markets to imports. Voluntary import expansions increase foreign access to a domestic market, while increasing competition and reducing prices. Voluntary import expansions are not voluntary at all: A country agrees to import products as a result of pressure from another country. An example of voluntary import expansion is Japan's decision to avert U.S.-imposed trade sanctions by importing U.S. semiconductors.[13]

Voluntary Export Restraints (VER)

Voluntary export restraints (VERs), often used in the 1980s to protect local industries, are self-imposed quotas and constitute a barrier to trade. The United States, for example, used VERs to protect local steel and automobile industries. Voluntary export restraints are agreed on by both the importing and exporting countries. A country that is subject to VERs limits the quantity of products it exports to another, primarily because it attempts, by doing so, to avoid more severe, future mandatory import restrictions. Voluntary export restraints are still used today even though they have been banned by the Uruguay Round of the GATT (and by the WTO) since 1999. The United States is imposing them informally, for example, for Japanese steel imports; this protection mechanism has been used since 1969 as part of the long history of trade protection of the U.S. steel industry.[14] In a more recent example, Brazil and China have been working for some time to institute VERs for Chinese textiles to Brazil, but those negotiations failed—and Brazil is inundated with cheap Chinese textiles.

Price Controls: Increasing Prices of Imports

Price controls have a direct effect on a product mix aimed at a particular market. Increasing the price of imports to match minimum prices of domestic offer-

orderly market arrangements
Protectionist measures involving intricate processes for establishing quotas in the textile and apparel industries.

nonautomatic import license
A license issued on a discretionary basis to restrict imports of a given product or from a particular country.

automatic import license
A license granted freely to importing companies but may be used by government for the purpose of import surveillance, thus discouraging import surges, imposing administrative and financial burdens on importers, and delaying shipment.

voluntary import expansion
A government's response to protectionist threats from another country whereby it agrees to open markets to imports and to increase foreign access to a domestic market to avoid more severe protectionist action.

voluntary export restraints (VERs)
A government's self-imposed export quotas to a particular country that are established to avoid more severe protectionist action by the respective importing country.

price controls
Strategies requiring a product to sell for a particular price in the local market; price control strategies are typically used to increase the prices of imports to match the minimum prices of local competition.

ings is one such strategy that is frequently used for both products and for retailers. For example, Japan uses such controls to ensure that locally produced rice is not at a disadvantage relative to rice imports from the United States, which are of equally high quality but are sold at much lower prices. In this instance, the prices of imports are held artificially high so that local consumers would not discriminate in favor of U.S. competitors. Similarly, Walmart and other discounters and category specialists (see Chapter 12, "International Retailing") in the European Union are constantly scrutinized and often pressured by local authorities to raise prices. EU governments charge that these international retailers price products below cost to drive out smaller competitors.

Price Controls: Antidumping and Countervailing Duty Actions

Antidumping and **countervailing duty actions** were designed to counter unfair competition, such as predatory pricing. Dumping refers to selling below fair value to undermine competitors who are charging the market price or to get rid of excess inventory—with the same outcome, of undermining competition. When used as price controls, antidumping measures involve initiating investigations to determine whether imports are sold below fair value, imposing duties to offset dumping, as well as adopting other measures to counter the effects of dumping. Countervailing measures include investigations to determine whether imports are sold below fair prices as a result of foreign subsidies; such determination is usually followed by duties that are imposed to offset this practice and measures taken to offset effects of subsidies.[15]

To the detriment of international trade, such measures have become protectionist tools that are used to intimidate importers and restrict trade. The European Union has been under scrutiny in the past decade for excessive use of antidumping investigations. Such investigations probing into antidumping activity and countervailing duty investigations focus on a specific product from a particular supply source.[16]

Price Controls: Paratariff Measures

Paratariff measures are charges that increase the costs of imports in a manner similar to tariffs. Such measures include allowing an initial number of product units to enter the country duty-free and charging tariffs to subsequent shipments in excess of this quota. They also include advance import deposits, additional import charges, seasonal tariffs, and customs charges. The United States uses many of these paratariff measures to discourage shipment of certain agricultural products from developing countries.[17]

Standards

Standards as barriers to trade are frequently used as barriers to imports, primarily imposed by highly industrialized countries. Most challenging are standards that are especially strict, such as those imposed on safety grounds by the European Union against hormone-fed U.S. beef and bioengineered corn and soybeans. Standards that discriminate against foreign firms in particular, or that simply create more bureaucratic hurdles for importing firms, act as nontariff barriers to trade.

On the positive side, standards could and often do help local and international industry alike, by deterring gray markets. For example, the United States has strict environmental and manufacturing standards for automobiles. Importing an automobile that is not specifically designed according to U.S. specifications is costly: One

antidumping
Legislation designed to counter unfair price competition; lengthy antidumping investigations can also serve as an impediment to trade.

countervailing duty actions
Investigations initiated to determine whether imports are sold below fair prices as a result of foreign subsidies and the subsequent establishment of measures to offset subsidies.

paratariff measures
Additional, nontariff fees that increase the costs of imports in a manner similar to tariffs.

standards as barriers to trade
Trade barriers imposing performance, environmental, or other requirements that are primarily aimed at imports.

has to use expensive automobile conversion services and obtain the appropriate Department of Transportation authorization to use the vehicle.

Local Content Requirements and Foreign Ownership: Percentage Requirements

Governments of many emerging market economies mandate that a certain percentage of the products imported are locally produced: They mandate a **local content requirement.** This requirement can often be met by manipulating and assembling the product on the territory of the importing country—usually in a foreign trade zone. Indonesia requires that thirty-five percent of products have local content and this requirement is applied across many industries.

Volkswagen Taxis in China

China has always presented a challenge to importing firms. Multinational firms often join with Chinese partners and agents to either package or manufacture enough of the product to have it qualify based on local content requirements; firms often do tricky calculations on local services and part values to meet such local content edicts.[18] In 2006, the United States and the European Union challenged China at the WTO, taking aim at Chinese regulations intended to encourage Chinese automobile makers to use domestic, rather than imported, automobile parts. According to the United States and the EU, this, in effect, creates local content rules enacted through a complex tariff system that raises tariffs from ten to twenty-five percent if imported parts make up more than a certain proportion of the automobile.[19]

> **local content requirement**
> A protectionist measure requiring that a certain percentage of the products imported are locally produced.
>
> **boycott**
> An action calling for a ban on consumption of all goods associated with a particular company or country.

In addition to the traditional local content requirements, there are other forms of favoring local contribution and labor. For example, governments often impose regulations to protect local carriers for passenger and freight transportation. An example would be restricting foreign airlines' landing rights or ability to pick up passengers at an intermediate stop ("third freedom" rights); this requirement favors national airlines operating on international routes.[20]

Foreign ownership restrictions also are widely used. Some ownership restrictions refer to the percentage ownership in a business—for example, requiring 51 percent or more of a joint venture to be owned by a national firm. Service industries in particular are subjected to regulations that invoke foreign ownership restrictions. Creative strategies that employ an ambiguous legal environment are used to block entry of international service providers or to place them at a disadvantage relative to local competitors.

Boycott

A **boycott** is usually initiated as the result of an action group calling for a ban on consumption of all goods associated with a particular company and/or country. Often, boycotts target a company that is representative, or even synonymous, with its country of origin. For example, when the uprising in the West Bank and Gaza erupted, Coke sales in neighboring Egypt and Jordan were hit by local boycott calls.[21] McDonald's restaurants were the target of French protesters, who were against tariffs imposed by the United States on European Union countries. Exxon-owned Esso was the target of a high-profile boycott campaign by groups angered at its support of the U.S. government's rejection of the Kyoto climate change pact.[22] In another example, British Muslims have called for boycotting all the firms doing business with a U.S.-based marketing and military intelligence firm, CACI, in protest for prisoner abuse in Iraq.[23]

Nestlé has been the target of a long-standing boycott because it is perceived to contribute to the death of infants from developing countries by aggressively marketing baby formula to consumers who cannot afford to enough formula to ensure babies' healthy development. One organization, Baby Milk Action (www.babymilkaction.org), actively lobbies against Nestlé, and replaced the company's jingle "Good Food, Good Life" with "Nestlé, Good Grief."

Embargoes and Sanctions

Embargoes and **sanctions** are imposed by a country (or a number of countries) against another country. An embargo prohibits all business deals with the country that is the target of the embargo, often affecting businesses from third countries that do business with both the country imposing the embargo and the country under embargo. For example, a free-trade deal with South Korea would help the United States stem the loss of economic influence in Asia to China. For South Korea, a free-trade agreement with the United States would mean greater access to its second most important market. Nevertheless, the two countries have difficulty coming to an understanding. The United States requests greater access to the South Korean market for U.S. automobiles, rice, and pharmaceutical products. On the other hand, South Korea would like the United States to change antidumping rules enforced for its steel, cars, computer chips, and textiles. The main point of contention is that South Korea also wants products manufactured by South Korean firms in North Korea, which is currently targeted by U.S. sanctions, to be included in the agreement. The U.S. is firmly rejecting this possibility. South Korea is the United States' seventh largest trading partner. The outcome of a free-trade agreement would result in a $19 billion increase in U.S. exports to South Korea, a $10 billion increase in Korean exports to the United States. [24]

embargo
The prohibition of all business deals with the country that is the target of the embargo that is endorsed or initiated by the company's home country.

sanctions
Punitive trade restrictions applied by a country or a group of countries against another country for noncompliance.

currency and capital flow controls
All protectionist activities involving the control of capital and hard currency flows in and out of a particular country.

In 2012, the United States, the European Union, Japan and South Korea expanded the United Nations lists of goods that North Korea is not permitted to import, as a punishment for North Korea's nuclear pursuits.

Embargoes can be limited to a particular product or to particular circumstances. For example, "smart sanctions" were imposed by the United States and the United Kingdom on Iraq's oil exports, modifying the oil embargo against Iraq to allow for use of oil revenues aimed at humanitarian purposes. (The embargo has long been lifted.) Liberia also had an arms embargo imposed by the United Nations Security Council as a punishment for its support of Sierra Leone's Revolutionary United Front.

The United States has imposed, for decades, a full embargo against Cuba. The embargo covers any commercial and noncommercial relationship with Cuba, and it even prohibits visits to the country by U.S. citizens, with some exceptions. As of 2012, the embargo is still in effect, making it one of the most enduring trade embargoes in modern history. Furthermore, multinational companies from other countries doing business in the United States are prohibited, under the embargo, from engaging in any business deals with Cuba. Unfortunately for the United States, this strategy does not appear to reach its goal—punishing Cuba's leadership and its communist regime, by derailing its economy. On the contrary, Cuba is reaching out to the world by transforming itself into a hub for information technology, one where U.S. companies may be at a disadvantage relative to competition in the future. [25]

Finally, a form of nonretaliatory embargo exists: It is imposed when imports into a country that has established quotas for a particular product exceed those quotas.

Currency and Capital Flow Controls

Strategies involving **currency and capital flow controls** are used in economies under tight government control or experiencing hard-currency shortages. In the case of capital flow, countries use arguments of self-determination to ensure that regions in the country are uniformly developed or that there would not be a capital flight from the country. Such strategies affect international businesses in that they restrict market-dictated activity in the name of protectionism.

Governments use currency flow restrictions primarily to influence the stability of the national currency. Such restrictions, however, directly affect the flow of imports into the country by giving priority to desirable goods and restricting the import of less desirable goods and services. Among the currency controls used by governments are the following:

- Blocked currency
- Differential exchange rates
- Foreign exchange permits

Blocked Currency

A country using a **blocked currency** strategy does not allow importers to exchange local currency for the seller's currency. This strategy can be used as a political weapon, to create obstacles for international businesses attempting to enter the country. More often, however, the strategy is used because the country is experiencing acute balance-of-payments difficulties. Firms, fortunately, have at their disposal countertrade strategies to address this type of barrier. Under a typical scenario, the exporter sells goods in exchange for local currency and uses the proceeds to purchase local goods for sale abroad; U.S. companies in the past often bought goods from Mexico and from Eastern Europe with local currency to address this barrier.[26]

Another method that firms can use to bypass blocked exchange rates entails using unofficial (and, from the perspective of the importing country, illegal) exchange offices. Such offices exist both abroad and in the importing country; however, they offer unfavorable exchange rates and expose the company to the risk of government action against it.

Differential Exchange Rates

Two types of **differential exchange rates** can be used. The first, which is government imposed, refers to a strategy the government uses to promote imports of desirable and necessary goods, such as armament and petrol, and to discourage imports of less desirable and necessary goods, such as consumer goods and services, entertainment, and the like. Offering a less favorable exchange rate for international products and services reflects a government strategy that ultimately increases the cost of this second category of products to the final consumer and discourages its purchase.

A second type of differential exchange rate is favorable to the international firm importing products into this market. In this situation, a difference exists between the black market exchange rate and the official government exchange rate, with the black market rate being higher than the government rate. The rate difference is a reflection of economic distortion: A high black market exchange rate can signal a likely depreciation of the local currency, foreign exchange rationing by the government, or both. A large difference between the government and the free exchange rate can also be interpreted as a tax on exports and a subsidy on imports, stimulating the diversion of resources from the official to the black market sector.[27]

Foreign Exchange Permits

Countries attempting to control foreign exchange often require the use of **foreign exchange permits.** Such permits are typically provided by the central bank of the country. They also give priority to imports of goods that are in the national interest and delay access to foreign exchange for products that are not deemed essential. An exchange permit can also stipulate differential exchange rates. Most countries that experience a shortage of hard currency require foreign exchange permits. China, Ethiopia, the Czech Republic and many other countries require such permits. For imports.

blocked currency
A strategy that does not allow importers to exchange local currency for the seller's currency or a currency that the seller is willing to accept as payment (hard currency).

differential exchange rate
The rate imposed by the local government to promote imports of desirable and necessary goods; it also can be the difference between the black market exchange rate and the official government rate.

foreign exchange permit
A permit that is generally provided by a country's Central Bank in conjunction with the Department of Trade (Ministry of Foreign Trade) and that gives priority to imports of goods considered to be in the national interest.

3-3 International Trade and Trade Facilitators

Several important international and local institutions play an active role in promoting international trade and have a considerable impact on the development of international trade and marketing operations. International trade and development organizations and governmental organizations alike are working individually and jointly to increase the flow of goods, open access to products and services, and minimize costs to companies and final consumers by limiting or eliminating the layers of bureaucratic interference in the firms' international operations. Sections 3-3a through 3-3d address Ricardo's theory of comparative advantage and discuss some of the most prominent international trade and development organizations. They also address the role of national governments in promoting the international involvement of local business and in opening local markets to foreign investment—particularly foreign direct investment. It should be mentioned, however, that equally important strides have been made to date by trade agreements. The levels of economic and political integration such agreements have achieved permit free movement of labor and capital and open or nearly open access to markets by firms operating in the region; this topic will be addressed in Chapter 4, "Regional Economic and Political Integration."

3-3a The International Trade Imperative

Free trade is essential to economic development. One argument for free trade is based on economist David Ricardo's theory of **comparative advantage.** The premise for the comparative advantage argument is that countries benefit from specialization in an industry in which they have comparative advantage and from trading with one another. For example, India specializes in the software industry, achieving economies of scale in training its workforce in the necessary skills for optimal production and in the production process itself. India thus acquires the income to import other goods that meet the needs of the population. At a worldwide scale, this improves overall productivity and output of goods and increases the economic wealth of nations.

Consider the example of two countries, East and West:[28] In a year, an Eastern worker makes two bicycles or produces four bushels of wheat. A Westerner can produce only one bushel or one bike. Each country has 100 workers split evenly between producing bikes or wheat; thus, East produces 200 bushels and 100 bikes, and West produces 50 bushels and 50 bikes. East thus has absolute advantage in producing both; West has no absolute advantage, but it does have comparative advantage in producing bikes. According to the comparative advantage theory, the two countries are better off in specializing in the industry in which they have comparative advantage. If East specializes in growing wheat, moving 10 workers from making bikes to wheat, it will produce 240 bushels and 80 bikes. If West moves 25 workers from wheat production to bike manufacturing, in which it has comparative advantage, it will produce 75 bikes and 25 bushels. Subsequently, consumers in both countries can enjoy more bikes and wheat if they trade at terms at which both gain—at one and a half bushels (sold by East) per bike (sold by West).

comparative advantage
The premise that countries benefit from specialization in an industry where they have comparative advantage and from trading with one another.

Other arguments for free trade suggest that opening up the home market increases competition, thus lowering prices for local consumers. Also, the presence of efficient multinationals will encourage efficiency in local manufacturing and services as well—yet another benefit to the final consumer. Free trade also means that firms no longer have to limit themselves to the local, national market. The companies themselves can afford to increase production, achieve economies of scale, and offer lower prices to world markets.[29] In other words, free trade also means economic growth. Table 3-1 offers figures on international trade (imports and exports) in different countries and regions of the world.

Table 3-1 Trade in Goods and Services
Goods and services
($ millions)

	Exports		Imports	
	2000	2010	2000	2010
Albania	704	3,791	1,499	6,316
Argentina	31,277	81,251	33,108	67,992
Australia	83,898	261,340	87,799	246,140
Belgium	206,988	366,855	195,511	363,040
Benin	528	1,446	708	2,234
Canada	329,252	462,349	288,093	493,120
Ecuador	5,906	19,610	4,927	22,652
Germany	627,879	1,541,139	626,519	1,362,052
Moldova	641	2,292	972	4,581
UK	404,775	667,596	433,976	731,828
USA	1,072,780	1,837,576	1,449,535	2,337,607
Low income countries	32,005	105,896	45,127	156,378
Middle income countries	1,592,025	5,719,672	1,495,508	5,389,112
Lower middle income countries	369,018	1,288,993	375,652	1,374,029
Upper middle income countries	1,224,283	4,435,558	1,121,580	4,021,226
High income countries	6,357,262	13,051,331	6,409,545	12,801,007
East Asia & Pacific	612,105	2,566,113	550,904	2,271,625
Latin America & Caribbean	418,299	996,199	438,522	1,009,026
Sub-Saharan Africa	111,058	374,373	102,161	394,903
Euro area	2,298,517	4,964,584	2,262,865	4,779,448

Source: World Development Indicators, *World Development Report 2012*,
World Bank Group; http://econ.worldbank.org/wdr

3-3b International Trade and Economic Development Organizations

This chapter provides an overview of the most important trade and economic development organizations worldwide in terms of their overall impact on companies and markets. It must be noted, however, that, in addition to these organizations, other entities provide similar, but typically more targeted, input into the international trade process. They do so directly, by facilitating trade, or indirectly, by developing national infrastructures essential to the flow of goods and communication. For example, the Belgian government and the Dutch government have specific structures that operate individually and jointly, with other international development organizations, to help former colonies in East Africa and Asia, respectively. The French Ministry of Cooperation has a similar mission.

This discussion centers primarily on the WTO and the organizations that have made significant inroads with regard to the liberalization of trade in the past two decades, facilitating the marketing of goods and services in markets previously deemed inaccessible and reducing barriers to trade worldwide. It also focuses on the two Bretton Woods organizations, which have provided support for development and trade in the free world since 1944—the World Bank and the International Monetary Fund.

The World Trade Organization and the General Agreement on Tariffs and Trade

The **General Agreement on Tariffs and Trade (GATT)** was signed by 123 nations agreeing to promote trade and eliminate trade barriers. Under the agreement, the signatory countries committed to open

General Agreement on Tariffs and Trade (GATT)
The international trade agreement promoting trade and eliminating trade barriers, opening markets to international business, and creating a forum for resolving trade disputes; GATT issues are now addressed by the World Trade Organization. (See www.wto.org.)

World Trade Organization (WTO)
The largest and most influential international trade organization whose primary goal is ensure the free flow of trade; WTO's agreements (negotiated and signed by member countries, ratified in their parliaments) represent trade rules and regulations and act as contracts guaranteeing countries trade rights and binding governments to trade policies. (See www.wto.org.)

their markets to international business and to use the GATT forum to resolve trade disputes. In practice, however, trade disputes took too long to be resolved, and GATT had no enforcement power. GATT's Uruguay Round, which took place between 1986 and 1994, and was subsequently finalized at Marrakech in 1995, substantially changed international trade regulation, replacing the original GATT regulations with a newly empowered **World Trade Organization (WTO),** which currently has 150 member countries from a world total of 192, with Vietnam joining in January 11, 2007. The WTO is forever changing the way countries regulate international business on their own territory and beyond. The organization's most important trait is that membership is predicated on full implementation and adherence to all GATT agreements.

World Trade Organization candidate countries often must radically change their trade practices and, implicitly, their internal economic structures, to gain membership. For example, China attempted for 15 years to gain membership in the World Trade Organization, before being accepted in December 2001. Its impediments to access were attributed primarily to its trade restrictions (attributed to concerns about the impact of open markets on its economy) and its demands to be allowed to subsidize agricultural output at the rate of developing countries. To gain access to the WTO, China had to lower tariffs on imports such as automobiles and new technologies and to make it easier for foreign companies to establish certain types of businesses in the country.[30]

The WTO is run by member governments, and its decisions are made either by governments' trade ministers (the organization's highest authority), who meet every two years, or by official representatives, who meet regularly in Geneva, Switzerland, the organization's headquarters. Routine issues are addressed by councils, committees, working parties, and negotiating groups.[31] Ministerial meetings have met with substantial opposition in the past few years. For example, the 1999 ministerial meeting faced 50,000 protesters in Seattle; this may explain why subsequent meetings were organized in locations such as Doha, Qatar, where the government bans activities of all organizations that are critical of any other Arab government or institutions of which the respective governments are members.[32] It is significant that opposition groups see in globalization the promotion of corporate interests to the detriment of the individual, developing countries, and the environment. Today, however, the opposition to the WTO has lost some of its attraction because the organization has made important inroads in improving health and education in underserved areas, such as the African continent.

The WTO's main functions are:

- Providing assistance to developing and transition economies.
- Offering specialized help for export promotion, through the International Trade Center.
- Promoting regional trade agreements.
- Promoting cooperation in global economic policy-making.
- Reviewing members' trade policies.
- Engaging in routine notification when members introduce new trade measures or alter old ones.[33]

WTO agreements cover goods, services, and intellectual property and address issues such as:[34]

- Reducing tariff and nontariff trade barriers on specific categories of goods and services. In this regard, the WTO has made important strides in the area of manufactured goods, as well as in the area of information technology. It is still working on eliminating barriers in the area of agriculture, where GATT allowed, until recently, government subsidies and **import quotas.**
- Opening service markets to international business. The General Agreement on Trade in Services (GATS) has established rules for specific sectors, outlin-

import quota
The maximum quantity (unit limit) or value of a product that may be imported during a specified period.

ing principles that require countries to offer access to their markets. GATS initially covered banking, securities, and insurance.

• Regulating the protection and enforcement of intellectual property rights for trademarks, patents, and copyrights—under the Agreement on Trade-Related Aspects of Intellectual Property Rights (TRIPS).

• Dealing with antidumping activities.

• Addressing subsidies and trade restrictions designed to safeguard domestic industries such as technical regulations and standards, import licensing, rules of origin, and other measures that impede international trade.

• Settling disputes. Member states cannot ignore any of the dispute resolution decisions handled by the Dispute Settlement Body (DSB)—as they previously did, under GATT. Examples of disputes handled by the DSB are Venezuela's complaint against the United States over discrimination in gasoline imports (requiring higher standards for imports than for locally produced gasoline).

• Reviewing regularly individual countries' trade policies to ensure compliance with the WTO and transparency.

As mentioned in Chapter 2, one of the contentious trade issues involving the United States and mediated by the Word Trade Organization has to do with lowering trade barriers to trade of agricultural products. The United States is faulted for its farm subsidies, and the European Union for its high tariffs. The United States has called on the European Union to lower its farm tariffs by more than 50 percent. A U.S.-EU agreement on farm subsidies would not produce a breakthrough, as a global deal on trade would involve participation by India and other poor countries resisting demands that they lower barriers on farm goods. In the case of India, millions of citizens depend on subsistence farming; consequently, India is resisting lower tariffs for farm products.[35]

Group of Eight (G8)

Members of the **Group of Eight (G8)** are Canada, France, Germany, Italy, Japan, the United Kingdom, the United States, and Russia. The Group of 7 (G7), comprising the world's most industrialized countries—G8 minus Russia—was formed during the 1970s economic crisis as a forum for addressing economic and financial issues. Russia, initially an observer in the group, first participated in the organization's meetings in 1991, and it started to regularly participate in some of the meetings starting with the 1994 summit in Naples, Italy. In 2006, Russia became officially the eighth member of the group. Russia's economy, however, is the size of that of Denmark,[36] and its inclusion in the then G7 was often questioned. That is no longer the case. In fact, the 2006 summit was held in St. Petersburg, and plans are for the 2014 summit to be held in Moscow. At the more recent meetings, it was suggested that China should be invited to subsequent summits in recognition of the country's importance on the economic scene.

> **Group of Eight (G8)**
> A group of the eight most industrialized countries: Canada, France, Germany, Italy, Japan, the United Kingdom, Russia, and the United States. The group addresses issues such as biotechnology and food safety, economic development, arms control and nonproliferation, organized crime, drug trafficking, terrorism, environmental issues, digital opportunities, microeconomic issues, and trade. (See www.g7.utoronto.ca.)

The organization's yearly meetings involve heads of state, government ministers, and directors of central banks. The G8 currently addresses issues such as biotechnology and food safety, economic development, disarmament, arms control and nonproliferation, organized crime, drug trafficking, terrorism, environmental issues, digital opportunities issues, microeconomic issues, and trade.

The G8 has met with substantial criticism on a number of sectoral problems that it was unable to adequately address. Among its missteps and shortcomings are the following: a failed $24 billion aid program in 1992 to turn Russia into a market economy; the Group's inability to foresee the Mexican crisis in 1994 and the Asian meltdown in 1997; its failure to devise ways to make Japan's economy grow or Europe's to produce jobs and faster growth and to adequately respond to globalization and the challenge of emerging markets.[37] The G8 has also been criticized for its failure to challenge China on its human rights record.

Among the G8 successes are the unity developed within the group on a variety of issues. The group has addressed successfully topics ranging from debt to nuclear power control—at the very least by providing a credible forum for discussion of these issues. Of particular note is the 1989 G7 Paris meeting that created the European Bank for Reconstruction and Development to help Eastern Europe in its process of transition to a market economy.[38]

The G8 has far-reaching goals. More recently, the national science academies of the G8 countries signed a statement of commitment to global action to counter climate change. In this, they were joined by Brazil, India, and the People's Republic of China – three of the largest producers of greenhouse gases. The group explicitly endorsed the consensus of the Intergovernmental Panel on Climate Change. At the 2007 summit in Germany, members pledged $60 billion to combat HIV/Aids, malaria, and tuberculosis in Africa.

The International Monetary Fund and the World Bank

The **International Monetary Fund (IMF)** and the **World Bank** were created at the United Nations Monetary and Financial Conference, as a result of the Bretton Woods Agreement in 1944, to address the need for global economic development, stability, and rebuilding after World War II and the 1930s' Great Depression. Both the IMF and the World Bank are specialized agencies of the United Nations; membership in the World Bank requires membership in the IMF.

> **International Monetary Fund (IMF)**
> Traditionally the lender of last resort; the IMF also has assumed the position of mediator between debtors and creditors, imposing stabilization programs; debt reduction guidelines; ceilings for bank credit, budget deficit, borrowing, and international reserves; and development programs for borrowing countries. (See www.imf.org.)
>
> **World Bank**
> The World Bank Group, headquartered in Washington, D.C., is one of the largest sources of funds for development assistance aimed at the poorest countries worldwide. (See www.worldbank.org.)

The goal of the IMF was to establish an innovative monetary system and an institution charged with monitoring it. The IMF is based on the proposals put forth by Harry Dexter White in the United States and John Maynard Keynes in the United Kingdom. At its foundation lies a system that would encourage the unrestricted conversion of one currency to another by establishing a clear and unequivocal value for each currency.[39] Currently, the organization, whose mission has significantly expanded since its debut, is located in Washington, D.C. The IMF comprises more than 180 member countries who are free to join the organization—as such, they are obligated to adhere to its charter of rights and obligations—or to leave the organization (as Cuba, Indonesia, and Poland have done in the past).[40]

The IMF directly links members' voting power to the amount they contribute to the institution; as such, the United States has more than 265,000 votes (18 percent of the total).[41] The organization's civil servants are international experts and nationals of the different member countries and operate under a managing director, who is typically a European.

Traditionally, the IMF has played the role of lender of last resort. More recently, however, it has also assumed the position of mediator between debtors and creditors. Through its stabilization programs, the IMF imposes debt reduction guidelines; ceilings for bank credit, budget deficit, borrowing, and international reserves; and particular development programs that the borrowing countries have to follow. In the recent past, the IMF offered countries in Central and Eastern Europe loans for restructuring their economies. Other bailout activities focused on Brazil in 1999 and Argentina in 2000-2001. The bailout of Argentina with an $8 billion package had a unique twist: Disbursement of $3 billion of the funds hinged on a reschedule of Argentina's public debt. Brazil received a $15 billion line of credit (following a $41 billion rescue package that Brazil received in 1998), contingent on its strengthening fiscal and monetary policies and implementing a structural reform agenda.[42] These actions were necessary because these two important emerging markets were unable to attract foreign direct investment from developed countries such as the United States, Japan, and Europe, which were themselves going through a period of slow growth or recession.[43]

Among the last important bailouts before the 2008 crisis is that of Turkey, in 2001, for $20 billion, which had spectacular results, with Turkey experiencing impressive growth and development more than ten years later (see Figure 3-1).

Until the recession, experts had been asking the question whether the IMF might be obsolete because there had not been any major currency crises for many years. However, many believe that that the current global economy, with high growth and expanding trade and investment, will not last, and that,

Figure 3-1: *Turkey today is very different than Turkey a decade ago, with a building boom and an impressive transportation infrastructure on land and on water.*

over time, national governments are ill-equipped to handle cross-border crises.[44] Indeed, during the last recession, as early as 2010, the Greek government requested a loan of €45 billion from the European Union and the IMF, and, in 2012, the EU, IMF and the European Central Bank provided a second bailout of €130 billion. Ireland received a €78 billion bailout package from the IMF-EU and from the United Kingdom, Denmark and Sweden in 2010. And Portugal received €78 billion IMF-EU bailout package in 2011.

The IMF also offers training and technical assistance for monetary and financial strategists from borrowing countries through its field offices and publishes statistical information based on accurate data that member countries provide as a requirement for membership.

The World Bank is the largest international bank that sponsors economic development projects. The World Bank, headquartered in Washington, D.C., employs international specialists in economics, finance, and sectoral development. In addition, it has field offices in developing countries, overseeing projects in the area of industry, health, poultry and dairy production, among others. In the past, the World Bank's focus was in the area of industrial and infrastructure development. More recently, its priorities lie primarily in the areas of health (it provided a $500 million umbrella loan for programs to combat HIV/AIDS in sub-Saharan Africa) and information technology (the World Bank awarded $1.5 billion in contracts to information technology [IT] companies).[45] Among others, the International Finance Corporation, the World Bank's private sector arm, assigned a $320 million package to finance mobile telephone networks in sub-Saharan Africa. The investment signaled growing private sector interest in the African continent. The loan was offered to five subsidiaries of Celtel, a telecommunication group, to expand and upgrade mobile phone networks in the Democratic Republic of Congo and Sierra Leone, both recovering from civil wars, and Uganda, Madagascar, and Malawi.

In Poland, the World Bank financed the modernization of several important ports (see Figure 3-2).

Figure 3-2: *The World Bank Szczecin-Swinoujscie Seaway and Port Modernization Project had as its main charge improving the aging facilities of the port and the access infrastructure in order to promote trade with Poland.*

Both the IMF and the World Bank have met with their share of criticism. The IMF has been criticized for imposing unduly rapid or overly detailed structural adjustment programs; consequently, countries are unlikely to feel a sense of ownership of programs that stretch their capacity for implementation and, as a result, may lack the political will needed to carry them out.[46] The World Bank has been criticized for lending primarily to countries with access to private international capital; according to the Bank's own analysis, the countries that could make best use of its resources receive a comparatively small share.[47] The president of the World Bank is appointed by the United States—and the U.S. leadership has not been without controversy. In 2007, Bank president Paul Wolfowitz, in an unprecedented scandal that created turmoil among employees, was accused of breaking the Bank's code of conduct, violating staff rules, and the terms of his contract as president. He resigned and was replaced with other U.S. appointees, Robert Zoellick, until 2012, followed by Jim Yong Kim.

The accomplishments of the World Bank and the IMF and their impact on economic development and trade cannot be ignored. They have been instrumental in fostering economic and political stability in developing countries. They have protected banks from developed countries by preventing firms in volatile regions from defaulting on their debt. They have helped create viable industrial, agricultural, and infrastructure projects. Also, they have contributed substantially to the training and development of local expertise in different sectors. Furthermore, the two agencies provide reliable statistics in areas related to finance, economic development, trade, population trends, and national policies, among others.

Other Development Banks

A number of development banks with a regional focus also are instrumental in advancing economic development and in providing support for business and trade. Among the development banks are the following:[48]

- The **African Development Bank** (www.afdb.org), headquartered in Abidjan, Ivory Coast, has as a primary goal poverty reduction. It provides support and expertise in areas such as agriculture, human resources, and health services, and it emphasizes small businesses as its target recipients.
- The **Asian Development Bank** (www.adb.org), headquartered in Manila, the Philippines, focuses on the private sector. The bank sponsors projects aimed at increasing access to technology and improving the functioning of government. Together with the World Bank and the IMF, the Asian Development Bank was instrumental in Asia's recovery from the 1990s' financial crisis.
- The **European Bank for Reconstruction and Development** (www.ebrd.com) headquartered in London, United Kingdom, has as main goals reforming and strengthening markets in the transition economies of Central and Eastern Europe. Among others, it has played an important role in the development of legal and institutional frameworks, reducing barriers to foreign investment, and strengthening the countries' financial markets and their private sector.
- The **Inter-American Development Bank** (www.iadb.org), headquartered in Washington, D.C.), has as primary clients companies that do not ordinarily deal with the large development banks. Like the other banks, the IADB funds private sector projects, but it also has as priorities modernizing the governments, strengthening institutions, and overcoming the "digital divide."

United Nations Organizations

A number of United Nations (www.un.org) bodies promote the economic and financial welfare of developing countries; in particular, these organizations focus on developing the industrial, communication, and transportation infrastructure of developing countries. The impact of such development on fostering trade and foreign direct investment in these markets is substantial. Among the United Nations agencies involved in economic development are the United Nations Development Program (UNDP), headquartered in New York. The UNDP assists, coordinates, finances, and supervises various projects, ranging from institutional strengthening and support to building factories, to developing methane gas extraction facilities, to financing the building of bridges and highways or telecommunications networks. In its efforts, the UNDP, primarily a human development organization, is assisted by other specialized **United Nations organizations**—about 16 in number. Among them that are directly involved in economic development and the development of international trade are:

- The United Nations Industrial Development Organization (UNIDO), headquartered in Vienna, Austria. UNIDO offers or subcontracts expertise in industrial project design and implementation, often providing turn-key factories to countries in need.
- The United Nations Conference on Trade and Development (UNCTAD), headquartered in Geneva, Switzerland. UNCTAD assists developing countries in increasing international trade relations and promotes the integration of trade, environment, and development.
- The Regional Economic Commission for Africa; for Asia and the Pacific; for Europe, North America, and the Commonwealth of Independent States (CIS); for Latin America and the Caribbean; and for Western Asia. This regional arm of the United Nations offers support for the economic and social development of its member states, fosters regional integration, and promotes international cooperation for regional development.
- The Food and Agriculture Organization (FAO), headquartered in Rome, Italy. The FAO offers expertise in agricultural projects.

African Development Bank
A bank, headquartered in Abidjan, Ivory Coast, that has as a primary goal poverty reduction in Africa, providing support and expertise in agriculture, human resources, and health services, with an emphasis on small business. (See www.afdb.org.)

Asian Development Bank
A bank, headquartered in Manila, the Philippines, that focuses on the private sector in Asia, sponsoring projects aimed at increasing access to technology and improving the functioning of government in the region. (See www.adb.org.)

European Bank for Reconstruction and Development
A bank headquartered in London, United Kingdom, which has as main goals reforming and strengthening markets in the transition economies of Central and Eastern Europe. (See www.ebrd.com.)

Inter-American Development Bank
A bank headquartered in Washington, D.C., aiding companies in the Americas that do not ordinarily deal with the large development banks; this bank is involved in funding private sector projects, modernizing governments, strengthening institutions, and eliminating technology barriers. (See www.iadb.org.)

United Nations Organizations
The totality of United Nations bodies created to maintain international peace and security; to develop relations among nations; to achieve international cooperation in solving international economic, social, cultural, or humanitarian problems; and to encourage respect for human rights and fundamental freedoms using the venues offered by the different UN organizations. (See www.un.org.)

The United Nations agencies also provide statistical data on developing countries, with a focus on different industry sectors, health, and agriculture.

3-3c Government Organizations

Promoting international trade constitutes one of the more important tasks of the national and local governments of most countries. Most of the international marketing literature explores the different strategies used by government to protect local industry, trade, and service providers from international competition; such publications often ignore efforts of local and national government bodies in increasing exports and in promoting foreign direct investment locally. This discussion details the involvement of the United States' federal, state, and local governments in promoting international trade. Most developed countries have similar institutions to those described herein and offer similar support to local businesses attempting to market their products internationally and to international businesses entering the local market.

Regardless of the level of country economic development, most international trade issues are addressed by the national Department of Commerce, known as the **Ministry of Trade** or, more specifically, the Ministry of Foreign Trade. Frequently, the Ministry of Trade works in tandem with the State Department, known as the **Ministry of Foreign Affairs,** promoting the respective country's foreign policy.

United States Agencies: Federal and State Government

Many United States federal, state, and local government agencies promote the interests of U.S. businesses abroad, encouraging their international involvement in the form of export promotion or by providing foreign direct investment support. They also actively encourage foreign direct investment in the United States. Among the U.S. agencies supporting activities of international business are the United States Agency for International Development and the United States Department of Commerce.

United States Agency for International Development (USAID)

The **United States Agency for International Development (USAID)** is an independent agency of the federal government. Similarly to the UNDP and other development organizations, USAID engages in economic development–related operations. Unlike the development organizations previously discussed, USAID is an arm of the **United States Department of State,** supporting the economic development of and trade with developing countries aligned politically with the United States. USAID's origins are traced to the Marshall Plan of reconstruction in Europe after World War II, and it was created to advance U.S. foreign policy in developing countries by supporting economic growth and agricultural development, global health, conflict prevention, and developmental relief. In doing so, USAID gives priority to U.S. contracting firms; it has working relationships with more than 3,500 U.S. companies.[49]

Yet, in spite of USAID's success, and that of other aid organizations, not all the contributions to development are appropriately used. A case in point is the example from the Kyrgyz Republic, illustrated in International Marketing Illustration 3-2.

United States Department of Commerce

The **United States Department of Commerce** (http://www.commerce.gov/) engages in many activities that promote trade. It offers export assistance and counseling to businesses involved in international trade, provides country information and the assistance of country specialists, and helps bring buyers and sellers together through trade shows and other trade-related events. Its International Trade Administration district offices are located in the United States and in key international markets; their mission is to promote trade interests of U.S. business abroad. The Department of Commerce also regulates trade by issuing export licenses and by offering food, health, and safety inspections and certification.

Ministry of Trade
The international institutional equivalent of the Department of Commerce; it coordinates a country's international trade relations.

Ministry of Foreign Affairs
The international institutional equivalent of the Department of State; it coordinates a country's involvement in international relations.

United States Agency for International Development (USAID)
An independent agency of the federal government that supports the economic development of and trade with developing countries aligned politically with the United States. (See www.usaid.gov.)

United States Department of State
The foreign affairs arm of the United States government, in charge of promoting relations with other governments. (See www.state.gov.)

United States Department of Commerce
The U.S. governmental agency that oversees and promotes trade, offering export assistance and counseling to U.S. businesses involved in international trade, providing country information and country specialists, and bringing buyers and sellers together.

International Marketing Illustration 3-2

International Aid in Private Pockets

The newly independent Kyrgyz Republic is one of the five countries of central Asia that have emerged from the former Soviet Union and one of the few in the former Union that is making important strides toward adopting a market economy. Firms are eager to profit from consumers who are predisposed toward Western goods, unlike those of Uzbekistan, which are embracing fundamentalism and rejecting Western influence. The international aid community rapidly embraced the Kyrgyz Republic as well: Germany, Japan, the Netherlands, Switzerland, Turkey, the United States, the EBRD, the EQ, the IMF, and the World Bank have invested substantially in this country.

As aid continues to pour into the country, however, it is evident that much of it is squandered. For example, USAID sent large quantities of vegetable oil to help meet the needs of Kyrgyz consumers. However, the oil, labeled "not for sale," is sold at prices few can afford on the open market. Similarly, German bus-es were sent to replace the older Soviet models, yet few can afford the steep bus fares.

This example is not an aberration, but rather the norm in many developing countries. Agricultural automobiles are often used for personal purposes by rural mayors, aid products for flood victims often appear on local store shelves in areas of a country not affected by the floods, and government officials hire their relatives to ensure a distribution of aid products that most effectively serves their families rather than the broader target community of the aid effort.

Nevertheless, with adequate monitoring, international aid efforts ultimately raise the standard of living and the ability of countries to become attractive trade partners.

Source: Adapted from Leo Paul Dana, "Change and Circumstance in Kyrgyz Markets," Qualitative Market Research, Vol. 3, No. 2, 2000, p. 62.

An important arm of the Department of Commerce is the Export-Import Bank of the United States (the Ex-Im Bank). The Bank, created in 1934, works with city and state governments to offer export counseling and financial assistance to companies doing business in or planning to do business in international markets. Examples of the Ex-Im Bank's financial assistance are export credit insurance, guaranteed loans, pre-export financing to small and medium-sized exporters, grants for feasibility studies and project planning for projects in developing countries, and technical assistance grants, among others. The Ex-Im Bank also makes loans to foreign purchasers who purchase U.S. goods and services. [50]

State and Local Government Agencies

Examples of government agencies actively supporting international trade are the state economic development offices. Most of the 50 U.S. states have a department whose goal is to promote local firms internationally; this is typically the Department of Economic Development. States further international trade interests of local companies by setting up representative offices abroad, in key markets, such as the European Union and Japan. They often also target big emerging markets, such as those of China, Brazil, and India—countries with a large and increasingly prosperous middle class—as well as wealthier developing countries, such as oil exporting countries (for instance, Saudi Arabia, the United Arab Emirates, and Venezuela).

Among the trade services that state governments provide—often free of charge—are export counseling, full or partial sponsoring of trade promotion (primarily trade shows), and dissemination of market information.

State and local governments also actively attempt to promote international business. For example, the state of South Carolina was able to draw substantial investments from noteworthy international firms such as BMW, Michelin, and Fuji. As a result of foreign direct investment in the state, South Carolina was able to add numerous new jobs. In fact, the foreign-owned firms alone added 20,600 new jobs in the 1990s—most with higher-than-average salaries.[51] More recently, Michelin has undertaken an additional $400 million capital expansion in South Carolina: In 2012, the company employed more than 8,000 employees in the state. Similarly, BMW employed more than 5,000 employees in South Carolina in 2012. And Fuji's Medical Products Division in Greenwood, South Carolina, initiated totally integrated manufacturing of the newest generation of dry medical imaging film for the North American market.[52]

In another example, in 2006, the state of Virginia helped promote the international expansion of Electronic Development Labs, a company based in Danville, Virginia. The company approached the Virginia Economic Development Partnership to use the state's sales program to promote its heavy floor conveyors for the corrugated steel industry to the United Kingdom or to Ireland. Electronic Development Labs also received a $5,000 grant that could be used solely for marketing needs, such as translating the company's Web site into a foreign language. In addition, they received free access to international law attorneys, translating services, and freight companies. [53]

3-3d Other Institutions and Procedures Facilitating International Trade

Foreign Trade Zones

A **foreign trade zone** (FTZ), also called free trade zone or special economic zone (SEZ), is a tax-free area in a particular country that is not considered part of the respective country in terms of import regulations and restrictions. Products can be shipped to an FTZ, undergo additional manufacturing processes, and then be shipped further to the target market. Such products are not assessed any duties and cannot be subjected to tariffs or quotas unless they enter the territory of the host country of the FTZ. An FTZ is a site within a particular country that is considered to be an international area; merchandise in the FTZ, both foreign and domestic, is outside the jurisdiction of the host country's customs services. [54]

> **foreign trade zone**
> Tax-free areas in a country that are not considered part of the respective country in terms of import regulations and restrictions.

Initiated by governments, FTZs stimulate domestic and international commerce. In the United States, the Foreign Trade Zone Act of 1934 allows for the creation of FTZs for the purpose of stimulating U.S. domestic and international commerce by allowing firms to decrease tariff-related costs through their trade operations in the foreign trade zones. [55] FTZs are usually located in or near a port of entry and are usually operated as a public utility by a public entity such as the Port of Portland, the Indianapolis Airport Authority, or the Crowfield Corporate Center in Charleston, South Carolina. [56]

In the United States, FTZs are regulated by the U.S. Foreign Trade Zones Board, which is part of the U.S. Department of Commerce, and by U.S. Customs, as part of the U.S. Temporary Entry System— designed to encourage the export of goods with foreign content and the re-export of foreign goods and to reduce the costs of using foreign goods. [57]

Foreign trade zones offer advantages to both the host country and to international firms operating in these zones. In the host country, the foreign trade zone benefits:

- Domestic manufacturers, distributors, and suppliers by creating demand for their services, products, and raw materials. FTZ activities may involve manipulation, such as product inspecting, labeling, repairing, and sorting; small- and large-scale manufacturing, including manufacturing, assembling, and processing; warehousing; exhibiting; and distributing to domestic and foreign markets. [58] Such operations also create jobs in the FTZ country.

- The country's trade balance. Re-exports from the country where the FTZ is located add to the total number of exports from that country, thereby increasing its trade balance.

The international firm operating in the FTZ benefits from the following:

- Foreign goods that enter the foreign trade zone are exempt from the usual customs duties, tariffs, and other import controls, as long as the goods do not enter the country.

- For firms that ultimately export to the country where the FTZ is located, the FTZ provides flexibility by lowering or deferring tariffs for goods that are subject to tariffs. There are no time limitations for the foreign goods' presence in the FTZ. Thus, goods that are assessed tariffs on the imported components are placed in storage in the FTZ and are imported into the country only when demand for the product is high or when import quota opportunities open up.

- Rather than bringing the equipment directly into the country and paying duties immediately, equipment could be brought into the FTZ, shown to customers, and the payment of duties delayed until the goods are sold; this is especially beneficial for high-value items. [59]

- An FTZ is also a location that is used for breaking bulk. Components that are purchased from a foreign supplier to be used in a just-in-time manufacturing environment can be shipped into the FTZ in bulk to optimize quantity discounts and shipping costs. When these components are in the zone, they are repackaged into smaller quantities for shipment, which helps the company postpone the payment of duties until the items are shipped to the plant rather than when they arrive in the country. [60]

- An FTZ lowers prices for goods sold in the importing country: Unassembled goods are cheaper to transport, and duties are assessed at lower rates for unassembled, than for assembled, goods. Furthermore, duties can be avoided for goods that have been damaged in transportation.

- An FTZ also helps when an importing country imposes local content regulations on products from abroad: Local content is provided through the manipulation processes taking place in the FTZ.

- FTZs are usually bonded and must be secured and enclosed, which make them safer than most ports of entry, thus decreasing insurance costs for companies using them. In the United States, for example, unauthorized removal of goods from an FTZ is a federal offense. [61]

- Products that are manipulated in a FTZ may be labeled as manufactured in the FTZ host country. A favorable attitude toward the respective country and its products (that is, a favorable country-of-origin effect) greatly benefits the companies selling the product.

FTZs can range from no more than an assigned building close to a river port or a floor in a building adjacent to the local airport, to a gigantic operation with fully integrated multimodal access. An example of the latter is the Jebel Ali Free Zone of Dubai—one of the largest foreign trade zones in the world. The Jebel Ali Free Zone houses operations of more than 1,200 companies from 72 countries, offering state-of-the-art transport and communications facilities in its 100-square-kilometer site. More than 100 U.S. companies have manufacturing, maintenance, or transshipment operations there, including AlliedSignal, DHL, Federal Express, General Motors, Johnson & Johnson, Microsoft, and Union Carbide—and all are allowed 100 percent foreign ownership of operations, 100 percent repatriation of capital and profits, a 15-year corporate tax holiday, and a full exemption from personal income taxes. [62] In return for access to 1.5 billion consumers in the region (from countries surrounding the Persian Gulf and Red Sea), companies incur four up-front costs: a license ($954), registration as a Free Zone Establishment ($2,725), lease of space (prebuilt space and land start at $32,686 a year), and telecom hookup ($381) [63]

Other Types of Customs-Privileged Facilities

Worldwide, there are variations on the FTZ. They are similar to the FTZ in that they have some type of customs-privileged facilities that may be restricted to a region, to a plant (when such a plant is used for product assembly purposes, it is known as an **offshore assembly plant**), or to a bonded warehouse. **Special economic zones** (SEZs) in China (see later) and **maquiladoras** in Mexico are examples of customs-privileged facilities that typically exist in countries with low-cost labor. Under most arrangements, products are brought into an in-bond area, manipulated (processed, repackaged, assembled), and then re-exported to the country where the products originated. Low import tariffs are only assessed at this point and only on the value-added processing that took place in the SEZ. Some limits are typically placed on products that are imported into the SEZ country to encourage re-exporting.

offshore assembly plant
Plants located in customs-privileged bonded areas in countries with low labor costs, where products are manipulated and re-exported.

special economic zones
Customs-privileged manufacturing facilities in China where multinational companies can take advantage of low-cost labor.

maquiladoras
Customs-privileged contract manufacturing facilities in Mexico that take advantage of low-cost labor.

The Chinese Foreign Trade Zone Model: Special Economic Zones

Between 1980 and 1988, China established SEZ in Shenzhen, Zhuhai, Shantou, and Xiamen cities, as well as in Hainan Province. By 2002, the foreign trade zones (FTZ) attracted $60 billion in investments, employed two million people, and contributed a fourth to the nation's exports. [64]

Today, there are 15 FTZs in China, in Dalian (Liaoning Province); Futian, Guangzhou, Shantou, Shatoujiao, Yantian and Zhuhai (all in Guangdong Province); Fuzhou and Xiangyu (Fujian Province); Haikou

(Hainan Province); Ningbo (Zhejiang Province); Qingdao (Shandong Province); Tianjin (Tianjin Province); Zhangjiagang (Jiangsu Province); Korgas Port, in northwestern Xinjiang region, and Waigaoqiao (Shanghai municipality). These FTZs offer duty-free import and storage. To provide some understanding the magnitude of the FTZ operations, Marketing Illustration 3-3 offers some insights into the Waigaoqiao FTZ.

International Marketing Illustration 3-3

The Waigaoqiao FTZ

Shanghai's Waigaoqiao Free Trade Zone is the largest and oldest free trade zone in China – it was approved by the State Council in 1990. It covers an area of 10 km^2 northeast of Shanghai, close to the Yangtze River and the eastern coast of China. This is a perfect location considering the main functions of the FTZ include free trade, export processing, logistic warehousing and bonded commodities. It is 20 km away from Shanghai's downtown, 40 km from Shanghai's Pudong International Airport (the largest cargo airport in mainland China), and is close to Waigaoqiao Port of Shanghai. The facilities available at the FTZ provide road, sea, rail and air access. The FTZ's main road, Yanggao road, is a 50m wide and 24.5 km long highway that connects to the Shanghai beltway and other cities through suspension bridges. The FTZ is serviced by a full light rail transport system. As for air travel, it is served by Hongqiao International Airport and Shanghai's Pudong International Airport.

The main industries at the FTZ are semiconductors, automobile production and assembly, electronics assembly and manufacturing, research and development, shipping, warehousing, logistics, and distribution.

The FTZ has access to a workforce of over 16 million people, and it has attracted over 9300 companies, most of them trading companies. A total of $6.561 billion is invested into this FTZ and investors come from 127 countries and regions around the world.

Sources:

http://rightsite.asia/en/industrial-zone/shanghai-waigaoqiao-free-trade-zone

http://www.wd.gc.ca/eng/11149.asp

http://www.investing-shanghai.com/investguidance/opportunity_Waigaoqiao.asp

http://rightsite.asia/en/industrial-zone/shanghai-waigaoqiao-free-trade-zone

All accessed on July 10, 2012.

Since 2000, China has also allowed the creation of 25 export-processing zones (EPZs)—geographic areas offering special incentives to business. They are: Chengdu (Sichuan Province); Chongqing (Chongqing municipality); Dalian (Liaoning Province); Guangzhou and Shenzhen (Guangdong Province); Hangzhou and Ningbo (Zhejiang Province); Hohhot (Inner Mongolia region); Huichen (Jilin Province); Jinqiao and Songjiang (Shanghai municipality); Kunshan, Nantong, Suzhou and Wuxi (Jiangsu Province); Qinhuangdao (Hebei Province); Tianjin (Tianjin Province); Tianzhu (Beijing municipality); Weihai and Yantian (Shandong Province); Wuhan (Hubei province); Wuhu (Anhui Province); Xiamen (Fujian Province); Xian (Shaanxi Province); and Zhengzhou (Henan Province). EPZs are established only within existing economic and technological development zones.

The main difference between FTZs and EPZs is that goods delivered from Chinese companies outside the EPZs to companies inside them are treated as if they were exports, meaning that the selling company outside the EPZ is eligible for export refunds, and the buying company inside the EPZ is exempt from paying value-added tax (VAT) for the purchases. EPZs can be established only inside existing economic, industrial, and technological development zones and must obtain prior approval from the State Council (see Figures 3-3a and b).[65]

Although many of the new economic zones are exploding in the Shanghai region, Fujian Province found a niche that has attracted much government attention—and investment. Xiamen, in Fujian Province, is across the strait from Taiwan, and it is known as the Economic Zone on the West Coast of the Strait, implicitly associating it with the larger zone on the east side of the strait that includes Taiwan. In this manner, Fujian Province is playing into China's strategy of using economic integration to entice Taiwan into unification with the mainland. With this strategy in mind, the Chinese government is increasing its infrastructure investment there, increasing railway lines by more than 50 percent, cargo-handling capacity by 80 percent, and passenger capacity by 100 percent. The Chinese government expects 60 percent of the investment in the zone to come from Taiwan.[66]

Figure 3-3a: *Export processing zones in China can only be established inside existing economic, industrial, and technological development zones. This sign is for the Shanghai Qingpu Export Processing Zone.*

Figure 3-3b: *The Shangai Qingpu Export Processing Zone was established in the Shanghai Qingpu Industrial Zone, pictured here; the Industrial Zone is thirty minutes outside of the city of Shanghai.*

United States Privileged Trade Partners: Permanent Normal-Trade-Relations (PNTR) Status, the Generalized System of Preferences, and the Africa Growth and Opportunity Act

An important trade policy tool that is used by the United States is the Permanent-Normal-Trade-Relations (PNTR) Status (previously known as the Most-Favored-Nation Status).* This status grants equal tax treatment on imported products from most countries, with the exception of rogue nations. In 2007, Vietnam received the PNTR status, which means that Vietnam will be subject to the same customs and minimal tariff treatment as other PNTR countries. This also means that trade and investment in Vietnam are likely to grow rapidly.

The Generalized System of Preferences was instituted in 1976, and it allows 143 developing countries to export 4,650 specified duty-free goods to the United States.[67] Although it is still in use, it is always possible that Congress might not offer its customary extension in the future.

The African Growth and Opportunity Act (AGOA) focuses specifically on sub-Saharan Africa. AGOA was signed into law in 2001, and it offers incentives for African countries to open their economies and build free markets. Among other things, the Act allows countries in sub-Saharan Africa to use third-country fabrics and export them duty-free to the United States.

In the past, granting of the Most-Favored-Nation clause was linked to U.S. foreign policy. Receiving the MFN clause was predicated on countries' human rights records (as in the case of China in the 1990s), or as a reward for alignment with U.S. interests (as in the case of Romania before the fall of communism, when the country opposed Soviet interference in the internal affairs of Warsaw Pact member countries).

Summary

Identify different trade barriers imposed on international trade and arguments used by governments to erect and maintain these barriers. Governments impose barriers to international trade to protect national industries and nationals (consumers, employees). Arguments for protectionism include protection of markets with excess productive capacity, employment protection, protection of infant industries, protection of national resources and the environment, protection of consumers, and national defense. Governments can impose tariffs on foreign business or nontariff barriers, such as import quotas, required import licenses, voluntary imports, or voluntary export restraints. They also can impose price controls, such as simply increasing the prices of imports, filing antidumping and countervailing duty actions to delay imports, or imposing additional tariffs (paratariffs) to shipments that exceed quotas. Alternatively, they can impose currency and capital flow controls by blocking local currency exchange, charging differential exchange rates, and restricting the number of foreign exchange permits issued. Standards are also used to restrict imports, as are local content requirements. Finally, boycotts, embargoes, and sanctions restrict international trade by blocking all trade to the targeted areas.

Provide an overview of key international organizations facilitating international trade directly or by promoting economic development. Among the organizations that are most active in and have the greatest impact on promoting international trade are the World Trade Organization, which provides trade assistance and development assistance to developing countries, promotes trade agreements, and reviews member countries' trade policies to ensure that they conform to the organization's trade requirements; the Group of Eight, which is a forum of the most developed countries in the world that addresses economic and financial issues, with trade as a main focus; the International Monetary Fund and the World Bank, two specialized United Nations agencies that address the need of global economic development, imposing restructuring standards on aid recipients; other development banks; and the different United Nations organizations that promote the economic and financial welfare of developing countries, as well as their participation in international trade.

Identify government efforts involved in promoting economic development and trade. National and local governments are active in promoting international trade and development through a number of agencies and departments. Among them are the United States Agency for International Development, which supports the economic development of and trade with developing countries that are politically aligned with the United States; the Department of Commerce, which engages in activities from promoting export assistance, to organizing trade shows and events, to providing financial assistance to international business; and various state and local government agencies whose primary mission is to promote international trade involvement of local business.

Describe other trade facilitators, such as foreign trade zones, offshore assembly plants, and special economic zones, and the Normal-Trade-Relations Status. Foreign trade zones are tax-free areas in a country that are not considered part of that country from the import regulations' perspective and where products undergo additional manufacturing and are further shipped to other destination countries. They create employment in the host country, and they lower or defer import duties for the manufacturing firm. Offshore assembly plants and special economic zones are customs-privileged facilities in countries with low-cost labor where products are manipulated and then re-exported. The Permanent Normal-Trade-Relations Status offers equal trade status to most countries doing business with United States firms, with the exception of rogue nations that have been refused this normal trade relationship.

Key Terms

African Development Bank	Ministry of Foreign Affairs
antidumping	Ministry of Trade
Asian Development Bank	nonautomatic import license
automatic import license	nontariff barriers
blocked currency	offshore assembly plants
boycott	orderly market arrangements
comparative advantage	paratariff measures
countervailing duty actions	protection of markets with excess labor
currency and capital flow controls	protection of markets with excess productive capacity
differential exchange rate	protectionism
embargo	sanctions
employment protection	special economic zones
European Bank for Reconstruction and Development	standards as barriers to trade
foreign exchange permit	tariffs
foreign trade zone	United Nations organizations
General Agreement on Tariffs and Trade (GATT)	United States Agency for International Development (USAID)
Group of Eight (G8)	United States Department of Commerce
import quota	United States Department of State
infant industry argument	voluntary export restraints(VER)
Inter-American Development Bank	voluntary import expansion
International Monetary Fund (IMF)	World Bank
local content requirement	World Trade Organization (WTO)
maquiladora	

Discussion Questions

1. Discuss the different arguments used by countries invoking the protection of national industry and consumers.

2. Look up recent articles regarding China's trade restrictions. Which of these arguments does China appear to advocate?

3. What are the different financial controls imposed on international trade (i.e., price controls and currency controls)?

4. Describe the mission and accomplishments of the World Trade Organization.

5. How do international organizations overlap in their efforts to promote trade and economic development?

6. What are the U.S. equivalents of the Ministry of Foreign Trade and the Ministry of Foreign Affairs? How do they promote trade?

Chapter Quiz

True/False

1. The infant industry argument used against international firms is related to the protection of local employment in the respective country.

True

Rationale: The employment protection argument used against international firms refers to the protection of local employment. The infant industry argument is used to protect industries in their infancy.

Introduction

2. The local content requirement requires that a certain percentage of a particular product be produced in a second country.

False

Rationale: The local content requirement requires that a certain percentage of a particular product be produced locally, in the country of the company's target consumers.

Section 3-2b, "Nontariff Barriers"

3. The premise for the comparative advantage argument is that countries benefit from specialization.

True

Rationale: The premise for the comparative advantage argument is that countries benefit from specialization in an industry in which they have comparative advantage and from trading with one another. At a worldwide scale, taking advantage of countries' comparative advantage improves overall productivity and output of goods and increases the economic wealth of nations.

Section 3-3a, "The International Trade Imperative"

4. The United States Agency for International Development (USAID) has as a primary mission the promotion of trade.

False

Rationale: The U.S. Department of Commerce has as a primary mission the promotion of trade.

Section 3-3c, "Government Organizations"

Multiple Choice

1. Tariffs are meant to
    a.   discourage imports of particular goods.
    b.   generate revenue.
    c.   penalize countries imposing tariffs on goods from the importing country.
    d.   all of the above
Answer d is correct.

Rationale: Tariffs have as goals discouraging imports, penalizing countries that are not politically aligned with the country, and generating revenues.
Section 3-2a, "Tariffs"

2. Restrictions imposed by the United States on Japan to protect the U.S. automobile industry are known as

    a.   voluntary import expansion.
    b.   voluntary export restraints.
    c.   nonautomatic import licenses.
    d.   automatic import licenses.

Answer b is correct.
Rationale: Voluntary export restraints were imposed on Japan in the 1980s to ensure that Japanese automobiles did not handicap the U.S. automotive industry.
Section 3-2b, "Nontariff Barriers"

3. Which organizations were created as a result of the Bretton Woods Agreement in 1944 to address the needs of global economic development, stability, and rebuilding?

    a.   GATT and WTO
    b.   IMF and World Bank
    c.   G8 and G7
    d.   UNDP and FAO

Answer b is correct.
Rationale: The International Monetary Fund (IMF) and World Bank were created with the purpose of addressing global economic development and creating political stability.
Section 3-3b, "International Trade and Economic Development Organizations"

4. Which United Nations organization assists developing countries in creating international trade relations and promotes the integration of trade, environment, and development?

    a.   UNCTAD
    b.   UNIDO
    c.   FAO
    d.   CIS

Answer a is correct.
Rationale: The United Nations Conference on Trade and Development assists developing countries in creating international trade relations and promotes the integration of trade, environment, and development.
Section 3-3b, "International Trade and Economic Development Organizations"

5. Foreign trade zones benefit international firms in all the following ways EXCEPT

    a.   FTZs lower prices for goods sold in the importing country.
    b.   FTZs are enclosed and safer than most ports.
    c.   Just-in-time inventory can be shipped in bulk to FTZs.
    d.   Labeling, repairing, and sorting create jobs in the FTZ country.

Answer d is correct.
Rationale: The creation of jobs benefits the country, not the international firms.
Section 3-3d, "Other Institutions and Procedures Facilitating International Trade"

Endnotes for Chapter 3
1.   Victor V. Cordell and Erin Breland, "Conflicting Competition Policies in a Globalized Business Environment: Prospects for Cooperation and Convergence," *Competitiveness Review,* Vol. 10, No. 1, 2000, pp. 104–122.

2.   Ibid.

3.   "Leaders: Storm Over Globalization," *The Economist,* Vol. 353, No. 8147, November 27, 1999, pp. 15–16.

4.   Christopher H. Lovelock and George S. Yip, "Developing Global Strategies for Service Businesses," *California Management Review,* Vol. 38, No. 2, Winter 1996, pp. 64–86.

5.   Don P. Clark, "Are Poorer Developing Countries the Targets of U.S. Protectionist Actions?" *Economic Development and Cultural Change,* Vol. 47, No. 1, October 1998, pp. 193–207.

6.   Cordell and Breland, "Conflicting Competition Policies in a Globalized Business Environment," pp. 104–122.

7.   Clark, "Are Poorer Developing Countries the Targets of U.S. Protectionist Actions?" pp. 193–207.

8.   Ibid.

9.   Richard Hughes, "The Uruguay Round: New Approach for the Textiles and Clothing Sector," *International Trade Forum,* No. 4, 1995, pp. 4–11.

10.   Clark, "Are Poorer Developing Countries the Targets of U.S. Protectionist Actions?" pp. 193–207.

11.   Richard Brechter, "The WTO at a Glance," *The China Business Review,* Vol. 24, No. 3, May/June 1997, pp. 16–17.

12.   Clark, "Are Poorer Developing Countries the Targets of U.S. Protectionist Actions?" pp. 193–207.

13.   Theresa M. Greaney, "Import Now! An Analysis of Market-Share Voluntary Import Expansions (VIEs)," *Journal of International Economics,* Vol. 40, No. 1/2, February 1996, pp. 149–170.

14.   Jae W. Chung, "Effects of U.S. Trade Remedy Law Enforcement under Uncertainty: The Case of Steel," *Southern Economic Journal,* Vol. 65, No. 1, July 1998, pp. 151–159.

15.   Clark, "Are Poorer Developing Countries the Targets of U.S. Protectionist Actions?" pp. 193–207.

16.   Ibid.

17.   Ibid.

18.   Jack Robertson, "Foreign Exporters Learn to Deal with China's Local-Content Rules," *Ebn,* Issue 1258, April 16, 2001, p. 43.

19.   James Mackintosh, Raphael Minder, and Christopher Swann, "Challenge to Beijing at WTO," *Financial Times*, March 31, 2006, 5.

20.   Lovelock and Yip, "Developing Global Strategies for Service Businesses," pp. 64–86.

21.   Peter Lagerquist, Charmaine Seitz, and Harry Maurer, "Where Coke Is It—If the Trucks Get Through," *BusinessWeek,* Industrial/Technology Edition, No. 3743, July 30, 2001, p. 4EU2.

22.   James Curtis, "Body Shop Plans to Scale Down Its Political Activity," *Marketing,* July 26, 2001, p. 3.

23.   "CACI UK Hit by Iraq Torture Scandal," *Precision Marketing,* June 25, 2004, p.

24.   Choe Sang-Hun, "With New Urgency, U.S. and South Korea Seek Free-Trade Deal," *New York Times*, January 16, 2007, C8.

25.   Davis P. Goodman, "Getting Over the Slump," *World Trade,* Vol. 14, No. 7, July 2001, p. 8.

26.   Kwabena Anyane-Ntow and Santhi Harvey, "A Countertrade Primer," *Management Accounting,* Vol. 76, No. 10, April 1995, pp. 47–50.

27.   Martha de Melo, Cevdet Denizer, Alan Gelb, and Stoyan Tenev, "Circumstance and Choice: The Role of Initial Conditions and Policies in Transition Economies," *The World Bank Economic Review,* Vol. 15, No. 1, 2001, pp. 1–31.

28.   Adapted from Patrick Lane, "World Trade Survey: Why Trade Is Good for You," *The Economist,* Vol. 349, October 3, 1998, pp. S4–S6.

29.   Ibid.

30.   Elizabeth Olson, "Beijing Clears Major WTO Obstacles," *International Herald Tribune,* July 4, 2001, p. 9.

31.   www.wto.org

32.   Michael Maiello, "Hoisted by Qatar?" *Forbes,* May 14, 2001, p. 60.

33.   www.wto.org

34.   For a comprehensive overview of the WTO, see the Web site at <u>www.wto.org</u>.

35.   Steven R. Weisman, "Some Progress in Global Trade Effort," *New York Times,* January 9, 2007, C3.

36.   Barry D. Wood, "Economic Summits from Rambouillet to Cologne," *Europe,* No. 387, June 1999, pp. 18–22.

37.   Ibid.

38.   Ibid.

39.   www.imf.org

40.   Ibid.

41.   Ibid.

42.   Joseph Kahn, "I.M.F. Ready for Brazil and Argentina Rescues," *The New York Times,* August 4, 2001, A4.

43.   Ibid.

44.   *The International Economy,* "Is the IMF Obsolete?" Spring 2007, 21, 2, 9-21.

45.   Erin Butler, "New Directions for Investment in Developing Countries," *World Trade,* Vol. 16, No. 6, June 2001, pp. 24–28.

46.   Flemming Larsen, "The IMF's Dialogue with Nongovernmental Organizations," *Finance & Development,* Vol. 38, No. 1, March 2001, pp. 54–56.

47.   "Reforming the Sisters: If America's New Administration Would Like a Challenge, It Can Try Changing the IMF and World Bank," *The Economist,* Vol. 358, No. 8209, February 17, 2001, pp. 23–24.

48.   See Butler, "New Directions for Investment," pp. 24–28, for a more detailed account of each of these development banks.

49.   www.usaid.gov

50.   See www.exim.gov for information about the Ex-Im Bank.

51.   Ryan Lizza, "Silent Partner," *The New Republic,* Vol. 222, No. 2, January 10, 2000, pp. 22–25.

52.   Dennis Quick, "Globalization Has Two Sides in South Carolina," *SC World Trader,* online edition, 31 January 2007.

53.   Mac McLean, "Targeting Europe and Beyond," *Register & Bee,* December 9, 2005, 1.

54.   George F. Hanks and Lucinda Van Alst, " Foreign Trade Zones," *Management Accounting,* Vol. 80, No. 7, January 1999, pp. 20–23.

55.   Lynette Knowles Mathur and Ike Mathur, "The Effectiveness of the Foreign-Trade Zone as an Export Promotion Program: Policy Issues and Alternatives," *Journal of Macromarketing,* Vol. 17, No. 2, Fall 1997, pp. 20–31.

56.   Hanks and Van Alst, " Foreign Trade Zones," pp. 20–23.

57.   Knowles Mathur and Mathur, "The Effectiveness of the Foreign-Trade Zone as an Export Promotion Program," pp. 20–31.

58.   Ibid.

59.   Hanks and Van Alst, "Foreign Trade Zones," pp. 20–23.

60.   Ibid.

61.   Ibid.

62.   Josh Martin, "Dubai: A Model FTZ," *Management Review,* Vol. 87, No. 11, December 1998, p. 25.

63.   Ibid.

64.   Shalini S. Dagar, "How to Save the SEZs," *Business Today,* May 6, 2007, 6.

65.   *EIU ViewsWire,* "China: Trade Regulations," February 16, 2007.

66.   *The Economist,* "Asia: Digging for Victory – Fujian," Vol. 381, No. 8505, November 25, 2006, p. 73.

67.   www.ustr.gov/Trade_Development/Preference_Programs/GSP/Section_Index.html

---

Case 3-1

Transshipments: An International Trade Challenge

James Crane, a customs broker at Ship-Modal Transportation in the Port of Norfolk, was about to call a customs officer. Something about a household shipment from Germany was odd: It contained just toys, too many toys. Box after box revealed Thomas the Tank Engine, Barbie dolls, and Ninja Turtles. No beds, sofas, and other items listed in the bill of lading. They were shipped in new, large boxes, with prominent "Made in China" labels. The port agent called in a customs officer to look over the paperwork. Together, they looked over the bill of lading from a managing agent in Hamburg, Germany. The shipper was a reputable firm with offices worldwide and headquartered in the Czech Republic. The shipment was consigned to the order of a private individual living in the Norfolk, Virginia, area. The ocean carrier was Eastern Arabia, and the port of loading, Bremerhaven, Germany (the port of receipt, Hamburg, CFS). The goods were in one crate, and the description of goods stated: "Used Household Goods, HS CODE: 99909999." All seemed to be in order, except for the contents: new toys, in original boxes, rather than used household goods.

The customs officer contacted the consignee, the private individual who was supposed to pick up the shipment. He arrived at the port, filled out the paperwork, and had the shipment picked up for delivery to a warehouse. The Department of Homeland Security followed the trail of the shipment and identified a distributor who eventually delivered the goods to area toy stores. On debriefing, they found that they were dealing with a transshipment from China: the Chinese manufacturer used this distribution venue to hide the products' origin, to avoid scrutiny of the products (Thomas the Tank Engine toys) and the high tariffs and quotas imposed on Chinese products.

Transshipments—also known as laundering trade—are not unusual: when Cambodia started shipping large quantities of garlic to the European Union, analysts at Europe's Olaf antifraud office questioned it: The garlic was Chinese, shipped through Cambodia to hide its origin and avoid high EU tariffs and strict quotas. Chinese garlic production has tripled since 1995 to 13 million tons a year, but its EU export quota is only 37,480 tons. Once the quota is used up, the tariff paid climbs to 209.6 percent, up from 9.6 percent. The EU agent dispatched to Cambodia found no increase in local production; soon thereafter, Italian and U.K. customs found that a Taiwan trading company had shipped 3,000 tons of garlic from Qingdao, China, to Sihanoukville, Cambodia, and after spending two days in port, the garlic was re-exported to Naples, Italy, and Felixstowe, in the U.K. The scheme cost the EU roughly $5 million in lost tariff fees. In 2007, U.K. and Italian authorities charged the importers with fraud.

In 2007, EU officials discovered 43 operations transshipping garlic from China, with countries used as conduits including Jordan, Russia, Serbia, Turkey, the Dominican Republic, and the Philippines. The EU estimates transshipment of garlic alone has cost $80 million in lost tariff fees in the past five years. At stake are also jobs in domestic industries—from shoes to food—under threat from low-cost competition from Asia.

Chinese products are particularly scrutinized by the United States and the EU, which have imposed increasing numbers of quotas and punitive tariffs to combat Chinese dumping (i.e., pricing of goods below cost to secure market share). Another reason they are scrutinized is safety: China manufactured every one of the 24 types of toys recalled for safety reasons in the United States in 2007, including the Thomas & Friends wooden train sets—the train sets contained in the Norfolk shipment. In June 2007, 1.5 million Thomas & Friends were recalled as they were coated at a factory in China with lead paint, which can damage brain cells in children. Examples of safety violations of products made in China abound: a fake eyeball toy was recalled after it was found to be filled with kerosene; toy drums and a toy bear were recalled because of lead paint, and an infant rattle was recalled because it was a safety hazard. Overall, in 2006, a total of 467 Chinese products were recalled in the U.S. by the federal Consumer Product Safety Commission, and China is responsible for 60 percent of all product recalls. This is significant, as toys made in China make up 70 to 80 percent of the toys sold in the United States.

Transshipment is not just a Chinese phenomenon: In the EU, authorities found evidence of transshipment for 90 percent of the 91 products subject to the bloc's antidumping tariffs. In fact, customs agents in both the United States and the EU found that transshipment rings sell everything from shoes to cigarette lighters to energy-saving light bulbs. The most sensitive of all is food: Last year, the EU reported 84 instances of food transshipped from China, including duck, chicken, beef, and milk. The agents are concerned that these transshipped goods could allow unsafe or contaminated foods to leak into food chains. In other past examples, the EU discovered Brazilian sugar shipped via Serbia, after the EU had given the war-torn Balkan country a special tariff exemption to boost its economy. And, to avoid the U.S. trade embargo against Iran, U.S. companies often ship goods through Dubai.

Even though transshipment is illegal, it poses a major challenge for law enforcement: as in the case of the Norfolk shipment, the goods tend to carry documentation that looks legitimate.

Sources: The case is fictitious; other sources used are: John Miller, "Why Some China Exports Are Taking Illegal Detours," *Wall Street Journal*, May 25, 2007, Section B, p. 1; Eric S. Lipton and David Barboza, "As More Toys Are Recalled, Train Ends in China," *New York Times*, June 19, 2007, A1.

Analysis Suggestions:
1. What are the reasons behind transshipments? Address them from the perspective of U.S. law-enforcement officers and from the perspectives of Chinese manufacturers.
2. What types of barriers to trade are transshipments attempting to bypass?
3. What is the next step for the customs officers and law enforcement in the Norfolk case?

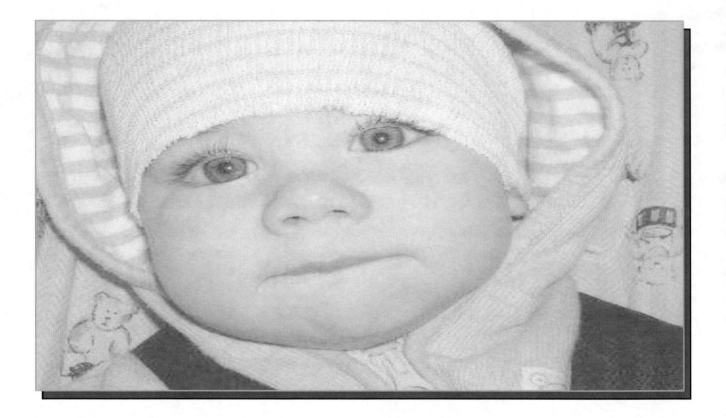

Chapter 4: Regional Economic and Political Integration

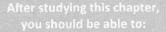

Learning Objectives

After studying this chapter, you should be able to:

- Provide an overview of the determinants of regional economic and political integration.

- Examine the different levels of economic and political integration and identify, within each world region, economic and political agreements that have met with success.

- Examine the functions of the different policy and governance bodies of the European Union.

Not long ago, shipping goods throughout Europe was a complicated process: Waiting in long lines at the border, filling out paperwork, going through customs, and paying duties were all part of the border-crossing process. Today, much of Europe has customs offices only at airports or ports, and in these locations, no companies from the European Union are subjected to customs processing and duties. Removal of restrictions in the European Union is not limited to the movement of goods; it covers movement of all capital and labor.

Countries in Europe that are not members of the European Union, such as the Ukraine and Turkey, aspire to become members and to benefit from the many advantages of integration. Countries in the rest of the world are actively building similar integrated markets, gradually removing all trade and other barriers. Companies are eagerly endorsing economic and political integration because it reduces their costs, allowing them to offer their products to customers at lower prices and to increase shareholder equity. Take, for example, IKEA, the Swedish company whose core business is functional home furnishing products at low prices.

IKEA in the European Union

IKEA has a complex product mix, consisting of its core business (functional home furnishings) and products for everyday life, such as bath and kitchen products, and even Scandinavian food products. Standardization of the product mix is one of the factors that ensure that IKEA can keep prices low. In the United States, standardization is relatively easy to accomplish because the company is, in fact, marketing to consumers in a single country. In the European Union, on the other hand, IKEA has to market to consumers in different countries—and it has done so successfully for decades. In Germany alone, the company has more than 40 stores, more than 20 in France, and 18 in Sweden, among others; in comparison, IKEA has only 30 stores in the entire United States.

European Union retailing regulations are gradually becoming uniform, and companies such as IKEA no longer have to navigate the legal complexities of each individual European country.

In terms of packaging, important content information must be translated in every single language of the countries where Ikea's products are sold. Taking one item, the Indira brand bed cover has picture signs suggesting that the product be washed in water at 40 degrees Celsius, that it should be ironed, that the dimensions are 150 by 250 centimeters, among others. It also has content information—100% cotton, 6% shrinkage—in the following languages: English, German, French, Dutch, Italian, Spanish, Portuguese, Swedish, Danish, Norwegian, Finnish, Polish, Czech, Slovene, Hungarian, Russian—as well as Chinese and Japanese (see Figure 4-1). In the entire European Union, the price of the bed cover is €10.24.

Figure 4-1: *IKEA's Indira bed cover is marketed in this package throughout the European Union.*

IKEA and its consumers are benefiting from unification: It spends less to conform to variable local legal requirements, and it can afford to charge less for its products. This level of standardization was unthinkable as recently as twenty years ago. Today, companies like IKEA are more likely to benefit from regional economic and political integration.

This chapter describes the determinants of integration, the different forms of integration, and, for each type of regional integration, it offers examples of successful agreements in all regions of the world.

4-1 Determinants of Economic and Political Integration

Numerous factors prompt countries to favor trade with other countries (neighboring countries in particular). Sharing a culture, a common language, a common history, or even common borders may lead countries to join forces in an effort to eliminate barriers to trade. The factors described in Sections 4-1a through 4-1e compel countries to lower barriers and expand trade with each other for mutual benefit.

4-1a A Common Culture

Regardless of whether a common culture was fostered by a former colonial power, people in neighboring countries often share a language, as well as other cultural elements, such as traditions, norms, and religion. As will be addressed in Chapter 5, "Cultural Influences on International Marketing," many areas in the world are characterized by cultural similarity. For example, in North Africa and the Middle East, the preponderant language is Arabic, and the environment of business, as well as everyday life, is structured in accordance with Islamic law (see Figure 4-2). Similarly, countries in Latin America share Spanish as the dominant language and Catholicism as religion and consumers in the region share rituals, traditions, and personal values.

Figure 4-2: *In Islamic countries, towers known as minarets provide a visual and auditory cue, calling the faithful to prayer. The call to prayer, five times each day — at dawn, noon, mid-afternoon, sunset, and at night — comes from the prayer hall in the mosque via a speaker located in the minaret.*

The commonality of language and other elements of culture facilitate interaction between neighboring countries and promote cooperation: In an economic relationship in which culture does not constitute a barrier to communication, individuals are more likely to understand their counterparts and their position. In addition, a common language facilitates commerce and marketing in particular. For example, Holland's Appelsientje, a Friesland Foods Dutch apple juice, is marketed to Belgian consumers nearby, who speak the same language and would understand the labels.

4-1b A History of Common Economic and Political Dominance

A history of dominance by one nation in a region often leads to shared cultural elements among the different peoples in that region, as well as to similar economic and political structures. Russia's economic, political, and cultural dominance in the former Soviet Union has resulted, for example, in the use of the Russian language from the Baltics (Estonia, Lithuania, and Latvia) and the Ukraine, to the Asian republics of the former federation, such as Uzbekistan, Turkmenistan, and Kazakhstan. The countries also shared economic and marketing structures, many of which continue to survive—for example, state-owned enterprises and large, nationwide distributors. In other examples, countries in East Africa formerly colonized by Belgium share a common second language (French), as well as extensive economic and political ties with the former colonist. And former colonies of the British Empire form the Commonwealth of Nations, a body that meets periodically to address issues of common concern and that recognizes the British monarchy as its symbolic leader.

From a marketer's point of view, such similarities facilitate a standardized approach to the market. From the countries' perspective, regional economic integration is facilitated by the similarity of economic structures established by the former colonial power and the shared language and culture.

4-1c Regional Proximity

European Union (EU)
An economic union consisting of most of the Western European countries; it is the only agreement that has achieved full economic integration and is now pursuing political integration. (See www.europa.eu)

Regional proximity is an important facilitator of economic cooperation. Although countries do not need to have a common border to engage in cooperative agreements, access that is facilitated by direct and effective transportation and communication systems greatly increases the likelihood that the economic relationship will survive over time. In the case of the **European Union (EU)** (www.europa.eu.int), the member countries are quite dissimilar culturally; however, their regional proximity and the highly developed transportation infrastructure within the region, as well as economic similarity among the different countries, have all greatly contributed to the success of regional economic and political integration.

4-1d Economic Considerations

It has been amply demonstrated that countries characterized by a similar level of economic development are more likely to be successful in establishing and maintaining regional economic integration mechanisms than countries of different levels of economic development. In the latter case, it is typical that the larger, more developed economies are likely to further their interests at the expense of countries that lag behind on economic development. In effect, countries of similar development levels are more likely to create a successful common market that assures preferential treatment for goods manufactured in the region, while also securing a substantial local consumer market. As countries prosper as a result of this proven mechanism, the regional market then opens to firms from outside its boundaries, benefiting international enterprise regardless of national origin.

As mentioned in Section 4-1c, "Regional Proximity," the EU is not characterized by a shared regional culture. The EU is successful primarily due to economic commonalities shared by member countries. Among others, they are

- A highly developed industrial base and overall productivity, translating into a high gross domestic product (GDP) per capita

- An extensive transportation and telecommunications infrastructure, which is indispensable in trading relationships
- Prosperous consumers who can afford to purchase the goods and services of local firms

It should be emphasized, however, that member countries have developed at different levels, and, often, constituents of the wealthier countries (such as Germany and the Netherlands) have deplored having to adopt policies that would benefit the lesser developed countries in the EU. Furthermore, the member countries of the EU and of other forms of regional economic integration often differ with regard to the economic and trade policies they advocate. For example, Germany and the Netherlands stress the importance of market mechanisms and interfere only minimally in the regulation of business, whereas France is more likely to intervene. France stresses social welfare at the expense of market development and is often plagued by union activity that paralyzes different sectors of the economy. (The post office and the national airline industry constitute just two examples.) Similarly, in the case of the Southern Cone Common Market (MERCOSUR), the member countries disagree with the candidate members on the common external tariffs they should impose on international business entering the region.

It should be noted that, in the EU, the economic disparity between the old members and the new members is leading to substantial controversy, as discussed in International Marketing Illustration 4-1.

The economic recession that started in 2008 created yet another, important, and most likely, lasting division, this time among the long-time members of the EU and members of the Eurozone, creating a pejorative name for the countries that have had high economic instability, huge national sovereign debts which were impossible to refinance without the assistance of the EU and/or the IMF: the PIIGS countries, Portugal, Italy, Ireland, Greece and Spain. Greece was perceived as particularly problematic after falsifying its public financial debt information – debt that was created by public sector wages and pension commitments that were difficult to sustain.

As mentioned in Chapter 3, Portugal, Ireland and Greece have received substantial rescue packages from the EU, IMF, and from other countries, most recently in 2012. In 2010, the EU finance ministers approved a rescue package of almost a trillion US Dollars to ensure financial stability.

4-1e Political Considerations

One of the more important obstacles to regional economic and political integration is the threat of losing national identity and sovereignty as part of the larger regional structure. Countries have many icons of national identity that generations have fought to maintain; such icons range from the form of government (republic, monarchy, or loose federation) to currency, language, and traditions. In the process of engaging in regional political and economic integration, member countries must choose, to a certain extent, to relinquish important aspects of their sovereignty and identity. For members of the EU, such decisions ranged from minor issues, such as the number of hours that civil servants have for a lunch break (in Spain, it is argued that it is the individual's right to have more than 1 hour—but, in 2005, they did abolish the long siesta), to completely doing away with the French franc, the German deutsche mark, and the Italian lira in favor of the common currency—the euro.

A principal consideration in accepting to relinquish part of national identity constitutes the importance of the regional group as a whole to the advancement of national priorities. A successful regional economic and political integration is one that promises a more substantial and more rapid economic development for member countries than they would otherwise experience in isolation from the country group, and one that equitably addresses and protects regional, as well as national, economic and political interests. In the case of the EU, considerations of national sovereignty and national priorities take second place to joint interests in the creation of a viable, large market that provides a credible balance to large economic and political powers, such as those of the United States, Japan, China, and Russia, among others. MERCOSUR accomplishes similar goals for its large and small South American member countries.

International Marketing Illustration 4-1
Creating a Level Playing Field in the New European Union

Meeting the new guidelines for the European Union (EU) is a challenge for the new members, the former Eastern Bloc countries, the largest body of countries to join the EU in history. These countries are facing new EU duties on imports from Asian markets and high expenses to meet EU safety, health, and other standards. For example, small farmers have to house pigs and cows in different buildings and build expensive septic tanks to conform to regulations, greatly increasing their expenses. The added hurdles and their often negative consequences force many small and medium-sized enterprises in the new member countries to fold, leading to calls for secession and renationalization.

Adding to the frustration of the joining nations are attitudes of the long-time members of the EU, who are clearly not receiving the new members with open arms: Germany, for example, intends to keep citizens of the new member countries from working there for many years. And Denmark will not offer ûn-employment benefits to the workers from the Eastern Bloc who lose their jobs. Moreover, Germany and Sweden repeatedly rebuke the new members for maintaining low tax rates that help to bring more jobs to the area, while at the same time benefiting from a generous aid package from the EU.

However, the tax controversy is likely to disappear: according to the European Commission's plans, companies will pay a common consolidated corporate tax on their business activities in the future. They would adopt a tax base for their EU-wide activities, rather than face the complexity of 27 different tax regimes.[1]

To illustrate, the corporate tax rates for the old EU members are much higher than those charged by the newcomers:

EU Member	Percentage (%) Tax Rate
Austria	25
Belgium	34
Cyprus	10
Czech Republic	26
Denmark	28
Estonia	24
Finland	26
France	34
Germany	38
Greece	32
Hungary	16
Ireland	12.5
Italy	37
Latvia	15
Luxembourg	30
Malta	35
Netherlands	31.5
Poland	19
Portugal	27.5
Slovak Republic	19
Slovenia	25
Spain	35
Sweden	28
Europe Average Corporate Tax Rate	24.1

Source: KPMG's Corporate Tax Rate Survey, 2012, www.kpmg.com.

4-2 Levels of Regional Economic and Political Integration and Examples of Integration Successes

Typically, member countries go through different stages of regional economic and political integration. Although most member countries start at the industry-specific bilateral or multilateral agreement level, theoretically at least, more complex regional agreements could jump to a more advanced stage, such as a common market, while simultaneously setting up a framework for a free trade agreement and customs union. Most commonly, however, member countries could target a more advanced framework, as their name might indicate (e.g., Common Market), but go through the different steps nevertheless. Sections 4-2a through 4-2f present the different levels of economic and political integration agreements, from the more basic to the more advanced, along with current and some past examples within each category.

4-2a Bilateral Agreements and Multilateral Forums and Agreements

Numerous examples of bilateral and multilateral agreements exist. Some are industry specific, others involve some or all products exchanged between countries. In fact, most member countries of the more complex regional economic and political forms of integration engaged, as a first step, in some type of regional cooperation. Governments could enter into agreements that are limited to a particular industry; the agreements could involve the development of an industry sector, such as participating in the development of a hydroelectric plant in an area that would serve neighboring countries, or it could entail lowering or eliminating tariffs on certain goods that are traded between the member countries, such as coal and steel. The EU had its earliest attempts at economic integration in the form of the **European Coal and Steel Community,** established in the late 1950s, and the subsequent structure, the **European Atomic Energy Community.**

What differentiates these agreements from the formal regional integration formats is that they are either limited to two countries **(bilateral agreements),** or, if they involve multiple countries **(multilateral forums and agreements),** the agreements have a less formal structure and do not aim at regional integration. Examples of bilateral agreements are infinite, and they are often the foundation for the more formal regional integration attempts. Multilateral agreements that primarily provide a forum for regional cooperation endeavors are numerous. Some are industry specific, such as the **Organization for Petroleum Exporting Countries (OPEC).** Some are military in nature, such as the **North Atlantic Treaty Organization (NATO).** Others have an economic focus—for example, the **Organization for Economic Co-operation and Development (OECD).**

A noteworthy economic organization is the **Asia-Pacific Economic Cooperation,** or APEC (www.apecsec.org.). APEC was established to mitigate the economic block and trade protection trend prevailing in the 1970s and 1980s; it was established in 1989 at a ministerial meeting in Canberra, Australia, with the mission to create an open economic alliance in the Asia-Pacific region.[2] This trade group includes all the major economies of the region (the United States and Canada are member countries), accounting for 42 percent of global trade.[3] APEC provides a forum for economic cooperation and the gradual reduction of barriers to trade and investment among member countries. Although the group does not attempt to forge an institutional integration that would be required under a free trade association or a more advanced regional economic and political integration format, APEC has nevertheless been instrumental in fostering free trade. Most of its advances so far have been made in the area of computers and the Internet: APEC members agreed on a moratorium on customs duties over the Internet, on safeguards against software piracy, and on eliminating tariffs on computers and semiconductors.[4] APEC also represents a forum for member countries to address issues critical to trade; for example, before its ascension to the World Trade Organization (WTO), China used the APEC forum to announce a number of important reductions in protectionism.[5]

Since its inception, APEC has become one of the world's most important regional groupings, with a total of 21 member countries, a population greater than 2.6 billion people, accounting for approximately 56 percent of world GDP and 49 percent of world trade. One of its current goals is to radically reduce trade transaction costs; it succeeded in reducing trade transaction costs by 2010[6] and, at its 2012 Vladivostok meeting, it redirected its focus to regional economic integration.

European Coal and Steel Community
An agreement that represents an early attempt at tariff reduction among members of the European Union.

European Atomic Energy Community
A precursor to the European Union, it addressed issues related to the use and control of atomic energy.

bilateral agreements
Regional trade cooperation between two countries aimed at reducing or eliminating trade barriers for all or for selected products.

multilateral forums and agreements
Agreements that involve multiple countries, have an informal structure, and do not necessarily have regional integration as their goal.

Organization for Petroleum Exporting Countries (OPEC)
Industry-specific (oil) multilateral agreement aimed at managing the output and price of oil. (See www.opec.com.)

North Atlantic Treaty Organization (NATO)
A military agreement among countries that were initially not part of the Soviet Bloc. (See www.nato.int.)

Organization for Economic Co-operation and Development (OECD)
An economic multilateral agreement. (See www.oecdobserver.org.)

Asia-Pacific Economic Cooperation
A trade group including all major economies of the Asia-Pacific region, it is a forum for economic cooperation and has as its goal the gradual reduction of barriers to trade and investment among member countries. (See www.apec.org.)

An example of a political agreement—which we place in this category because of its failure to achieve a substantial level of regional integration—is the **Commonwealth of Independent States** (CIS). The twelve non-Baltic successors to the EU of the Soviet Socialist Republics (the Soviet Union) formed the Commonwealth of Independent States. This organization has never had a noteworthy economic component; and, even politically, the CIS became fractured in the second half of the 1990s with the GUUAM grouping (Georgia, Ukraine, Uzbekistan, Azerbaijan, and Moldova) operating explicitly as a counter to Russian hegemony.[7] The Union of Four (Russia, Belarus, Kazakhstan, and the Kyrgyz Republic) considered creating a customs union, with Russia's tariff as the putative common external tariff, but, apart from steps toward a bilateral agreement between Belarus and Russia aimed at creating an economic union, nothing has come to fruition.[8] Finally, the Central Asian states of the former Soviet Union have drawn up numerous plans for regional cooperation—they must cooperate on nontrade matters such as the desiccation of the Aral Sea—but the establishment of a Central Asian Economic Community has had little impact to date.[9]

> **Commonwealth of Independent States**
> A political agreement among the twelve non-Baltic countries of the former Soviet Union. (See www.cis.minsk.by.)

The current official members of the CIS are Armenia, Azerbaijan, Belarus, Kazakhstan, Kyrgyzstan, Moldova, Russia, Tajikistan, and Uzbekistan, with Turkmenistan as an unofficial associate member and the Ukraine as a participating nonmember. Georgia exited the CIS in 2009, after the 2008 military conflict between Georgia on one side and Russia, South Ossetia, and Abkhazia on the other.

4-2b Free Trade Agreements

A **free trade agreement** takes place between two or more countries and involves a reduction in, or even elimination of, customs duties and other trade barriers on all goods and services traded between the member countries. Countries are free to charge their own tariffs to all entities external to the free trade market. The following are present and past examples of free trade agreements:

> **free trade agreement**
> An agreement whose goal is the reduction in, or even elimination of, customs duties and other trade barriers on all goods and services traded among member countries.

- European Free Trade Association
- Association of Southeast Asian Nations
- ASEAN Free Trade Area
- North American Free Trade Agreement
- Free Trade Area of the Americas
- Southern African Development Community

> **European Free Trade Association (EFTA)**
> A free trade agreement among Iceland, Liechtenstein, Norway, and Switzerland; previously, Sweden, Austria, and Finland were also members, but they have since joined the European Union. (See www.efta.int.)

The European Free Trade Association

The current member countries of the **European Free Trade Association (EFTA)** (www.efta.int) are Iceland, Liechtenstein, Norway, and Switzerland (see Figure 4-3). Previously, Sweden, Austria, and Finland were also members but have since joined the EU. For decades, EFTA has constituted another example of successful regional economic integration in Europe, in addition to the EU. Iceland, Liechtenstein, and Norway entered into the Agreement on the European Economic Area (EEA) in the early 1990s. Today, the contracting parties are Iceland, Liechtenstein, and Norway, the European Community, and the 27 member states. Switzerland is maintaining its independence in this relationship but has a bilateral free trade agreement with the European Union.

In 1993, EU and EFTA created the European Economic Area, representing the world's largest single market with 380 million consumers. Since then, the EU has created new regulations with the Maastricht, Amsterdam, and Nice treaties and has created new powers of authority in areas such as environmental and labor market policies.[10] EFTA countries are part of the Schengen agreement on the elimination of border controls in the EU. None of the EFTA countries have joined the European Monetary Union.[11]

At present, politicians in the EFTA countries want to be at least unofficially part of the EU but believe that public opinion at home is against further EU integration. The EU, on the other hand, does not appear to be interested in new negotiations that would offer EFTA members a greater involvement in the EU. The focus of the EU is eastern expansion, and the members are faced with the following constraints:[12]

Figure 4-3: *Member countries of the European Free Trade Association.*

- Numerous complexities related to the different stages and phases of eastward enlargement
- Possibilities of looser associated memberships
- Special rights of nonmembers
- Periods of transition to membership and special arrangements

In general, the perception of EU members is that EFTA, especially Norway and Iceland, would like to have more impact on the decision-making process within the EU, in particular on legal decisions (where nonmembers have no influence at all), and share in the benefits of the single European market, but they are not prepared to share in the costs and other obligations of membership.[13]

In spite of the national vote against joining the EU, Switzerland is engaging in bilateral negotiations, securing agreements that would help it join the EU eventually. It has negotiated issues in the area of the collection of statistics, the environment, agricultural production and customs fraud, cross-border security, youth, and education, among others.[14]

The Association of Southeast Asian Nations (and the ASEAN Free Trade Area)

The **Association of Southeast Asian Nations (ASEAN)** (www.aseansec.org) is the primary and most successful example of regional economic integration in Asia. Member countries are attempting to reduce tariffs and create an environment that promotes mutual involvement in industrial development in the region. The goal of ASEAN is ultimately to create a free trade area where tariff and nontariff barriers are eliminated and to provide a substantial market of more than 330 million consumers. Members of ASEAN are Brunei Darussalam, Cambodia, Indonesia, Laos, Malaysia, Myanmar, the Philippines, Singapore, Thailand, and Vietnam; they have signed the **ASEAN Free Trade Area (AFTA)** agreement (see Figure 4-4).

The goals of the Association are to accelerate economic growth, social progress, and cultural development and to promote regional peace and stability in the region, while adhering to the principles of the United Nations Charter. In 2003, the ASEAN leaders identified three pillars of the association as the ASEAN Security Com-

Association of Southeast Asian Nations (ASEAN)
A successful example of integration in Asia, creating an environment that promotes mutual involvement in industrial development in the region and a free trade area composed of Brunei, Cambodia, Indonesia, Laos, Malaysia, Myanmar, the Philippines, Singapore, Thailand, and Vietnam. (See www.aseansec.org.)

ASEAN Free Trade Area (AFTA)
A free trade agreement signed by members of the Association of Southeast Asian Nations (ASEAN). (See www.aseansec.org.)

Figure 4-4: *Member countries of the Association of Southeast Asian Nations.*

North American Free
Trade Agreement
(NAFTA)
An agreement among the
United States, Canada, and
Mexico, aiming to eliminate
tariff and nontariff barriers
between the countries. (See
www.nafta-sec-alena.org.)

munity, the ASEAN Economic Community, and the ASEAN Socio-Cultural Community. The ASEAN Vision 2020 is one of a partnership within a community of caring societies.[15]

ASEAN countries are pursuing free trade agreements with countries such as Japan[16] and even laying the groundwork for the formalization of currency swap agreements with Japan, South Korea, and China, whereby countries agree to give each other money to bolster foreign exchange reserves in the event of a currency crisis.[17] In addition, a China-ASEAN free trade area will be established in the near future.

The North American Free Trade Agreement

Signatory countries of the **North American Free Trade Agreement (NAFTA)** (www.nafta-sec-alena.org) are the United States, Canada, and Mexico (see Figure 4-5). The goal of the 1994 treaty was to eliminate all tariff and non-tariff barriers, such as import licenses and quotas, between the member countries and to offer free access to companies from member countries to a single market of almost 400 million consumers. As with other free trade agreements, member countries charge their own duties and other tariffs to companies from nonmember countries entering the respective markets. One of the more important decisions for NAFTA involves the rules of origin: To benefit from a duty-free status, goods must have a 60 percent North American content.

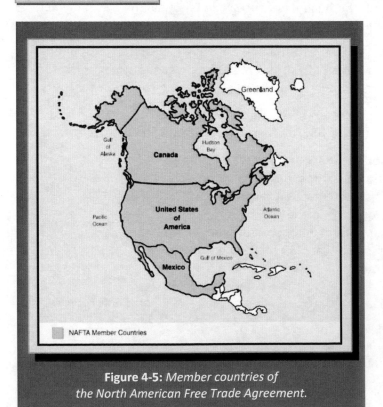

Figure 4-5: *Member countries of the North American Free Trade Agreement.*

NAFTA initially generated great fears in the United States. It was described by a former presidential candidate and NAFTA opponent as the "giant sucking sound" that would move all jobs south of the U.S. border. Indeed, U.S. workers have experienced some level of job loss that can be directly attributed to NAFTA, in the lumber and textile industries, for instance. However, it also can be argued that NAFTA created jobs in the United States. For example, in terms of trade flow, NAFTA has fared very well: U.S. merchandise exports to Mexico grew fourfold, and the United States exports to Canada more than doubled; at the same time, Mexico currently purchases just less than $100 billion in U.S. goods each year.[18] NAFTA has brought substantial foreign direct investment to Mexico,[19] creating stability in the country and lessening its dependence on the United States.

In spite of its free-market rhetoric, however, the United States has engaged in protectionist activity that hampers free trade among member countries. For example, in recent years, the U.S. Congress, pressured by domestic truck drivers, voted to keep Mexican truckers out of most of the United States, nevertheless, by 2012, trade among NAFTA countries surpassed 1 trillion US Dollars.[20]

Central American Free Trade Agreement—Dominican Republic

Central American Free Trade Agreement—Dominican Republic (CAFTA-DR) was signed in 2004 among the United States, the five countries of Central America—Costa Rica, El Salvador, Guatemala, Honduras, and Nicaragua—and the Dominican Republic (DR). It was designed to eliminate tariffs and barriers to trade and to expand regional opportunities for workers, manufacturers, consumers, farmers, and service providers of the member countries. CAFTA-DR will immediately eliminate tariffs on more than 80 percent of U.S. exports, phasing out the rest over 10 years. And CAFTA-DR countries provide reciprocal access for U.S. products.[21]

The 2011 meeting in El Salvador between members of CAFTA-DR and U.S. trade representatives concluded that the free trade agreement among the organization and the United States have had considerable success, with increasing trade flows among the countries.

The Free Trade Area of the Americas

The **Free Trade Area of the Americas (FTAA)** was an ambitious plan to create a market of about 800 million people and an annual production worth $11 trillion in the Americas.[22] The organization's initial goal was to create a free trade association by 2007, but its progress was greatly impeded by protectionist fears,[23] especially fear of U.S.-led free trade policies and Brazilian recalcitrance, as it attempts to maintain tariffs on manufactured goods, selectively liberalize services, and go slowly on intellectual property protection.[24] In addition, FTAA progress was also impeded by the rise of smaller regional free trade agreements. Member countries are the 34 democratic nations of North, Central, and South America.

However, the FTAA's future is uncertain. The heads of state and government of the different countries met in 2012 at the Sixth Summit of the Americas and addressed the topic of integration along with other topics such as poverty and security; nevertheless, no great strides were made on economic integration.

> **Free Trade Area of the Americas (FTAA)**
> A plan to create a free trade association by 2005 that would comprise all member countries of the 34 democratic nations of North, Central, and South America. (See www.ftaa-alca.org.)
>
> **Southern African Development Community (SADC)**
> A free trade organization that promotes economic cooperation among a coalition of 14 of Africa's more affluent and developed nations, designed to foster increased economic and governmental stability through the use of collective peacekeeping forces.

The Southern African Development Community

The **Southern African Development Community (SADC)** is a free trade organization that promotes economic cooperation among a coalition of fourteen of Africa's more affluent and developed nations. The organization is designed to foster increased economic and governmental stability through the use of collective peacekeeping forces and should be credited for the recent relative stability of the region.[25]

Its member countries are Angola, Botswana, the Democratic Republic of Congo (DRC), Lesotho, Malawi, Mauritius, Mozambique, Namibia, South Africa, Swaziland, United Republic of Tanzania, Zambia, and Zimbabwe (see Figure 4-6).

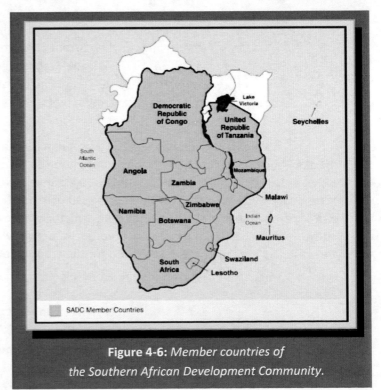

Figure 4-6: *Member countries of the Southern African Development Community.*

4-2c Customs Unions

A **customs union** is a free trade association that may have either eliminated or greatly reduced all tariffs and other trade restrictions for member countries and that has adopted common external tariffs on products imported from outside the free trade area.

customs union
A market composed of member countries imposing identical import duties and sharing import regulations.

South African Customs Union (SACU)
A customs union that includes Botswana, Swaziland, Lesotho, and Namibia. The group's main trading partner is South Africa, and member countries have partially or entirely tied their currencies to the South African rand.

common market
A market composed of member countries, characterized by the unrestricted movement of goods, labor, and capital.

Maastricht Treaty
The treaty credited with establishing the European Union, eliminating all tariffs; establishing common external tariffs; allowing for the free movement of capital and labor within its territory; and setting regulations involving common trade policies, common agricultural and industrial policies, and common monetary and fiscal policies between member countries. (See www.europa.eu.int.)

European Exchange Rate Mechanism (ERM)
A precursor of the euro, a float that included the euro, the then-theoretical currency of the European Union; the float allowed for variability in each currency.

South African Customs Union

Member countries of the **South African Customs Union (SACU)** are Botswana, Swaziland, Lesotho, and Namibia. The group's main trading partner is South Africa, and member countries have partially or entirely tied their currencies to the South African rand.

4-2d Common Markets

Member countries to a **common market** agreement eliminate all tariff and nontariff barriers to trade, adopt common external tariffs, and allow for the free movement of capital and labor within the common market. Although only the European Union has truly achieved (and surpassed) the common market stage, a number of other economic groups are forging this form of integration—among them, AnCom and MERCOSUR.

In Europe, member countries agreed at the Treaty of Rome to establish the European Economic Community (EEC), the predecessor of the European Union, eliminating all internal tariffs and duties, establishing common external tariffs, and allowing for the free movement of capital and labor within its territory. At this point, member countries also set in place regulations and bodies that would ultimately form the basis for a monetary and political union—an event that was to take place in 1992 on the occasion of the **Maastricht Treaty,** commonly known as the eagerly anticipated "Europe 1992."

An example of common monetary policies and a precursor to a monetary union is provided by the European Monetary System. In 1971, the United States decided to no longer link the dollar to the price of gold—which initially secured monetary stability after World War II—ending the system of fixed exchange rates. The EU decided to prevent fluctuations of more than 2.5 percent among the European currencies by intervening in the currency markets, thus setting up the European Monetary System (EMS) in 1979. The EMS consisted of a credit mechanism, whereby each currency transferred 20 percent of its currency and gold reserves to a common fund; a reference currency known as the ecu, consisting of a basket of all the currencies; and a float.[26]

The float was known as the **European Exchange Rate Mechanism (ERM),** also known as the "snake" because it changed its shape based on the fluctuation of the different currencies. According to the ERM, a currency could fluctuate only up to 2.5 percent of its value in either direction, as mentioned earlier. When this value was consistently surpassed, the mechanism would adjust the currency upward or downward, respectively, creating a snakelike structure. A float that performed well was an important prerequisite to the success of a monetary union; this, as we will see in Section 4-2e, "Monetary Unions," was not the case in 1992, the date established for the creation of the European Monetary Union.

Other examples of regional economic integration aiming to establish a common market are as follows:

- Latin American Integration Association
- Andean Community
- Southern Cone Common Market
- Central American Common Market
- Common Market for Eastern and Southern Africa

The Latin American Integration Association

The **Latin American Integration Association (LAIA)** was created in 1980 to replace the **Latin American Free Trade Association (LAFTA).** LAFTA was an attempt by member countries to establish a free trade association. Its demise was attributed to the disparity in the level of development of member countries and to the protectionist policies of countries with enormous foreign debt experiencing high inflation, currency devaluation, and economic crises. LAFTA is important in that it constituted a first step in an ambitious plan to create a common market that comprises all of Latin America, under the umbrella of the LAIA.

The LAIA member countries are Argentina, Bolivia, Brazil, Chile, Colombia, Ecuador, Mexico, Paraguay, Peru, Uruguay, and Venezuela. Under LAIA, member countries are encouraged to establish bilateral and multilateral agreements aimed at reducing tariff and nontariff barriers. LAIA offers differential treatment to countries of different levels of development to avoid preferential treatment of the larger countries (blamed for the failure of LAFTA). Member countries are at present members of two successful common markets—the AnCom and the MERCOSUR.

The Andean Common Market

The **Andean Common Market (AnCom),** known previously as the Andean Pact, was established in the 1970s and renamed as the Andean Community in 1996. In addition to eliminating trade restrictions (tariff and nontariff) within the Andean region, AnCom also provides for uniform external tariffs and rules for foreign investment. Its member countries are Bolivia, Colombia, Ecuador, and Peru.

AnCom's accomplishments include a sizable increase in economic and commercial links among member countries, the development of community institutions and legal provisions, the consolidation of the common market—which also entailed progress with establishing a common external tariff—and substantially increasing trade with other countries and country groups. Among the latter, AnCom participated jointly in negotiations with MERCOSUR.[27]

The Southern Cone Common Market

The **Southern Cone Common Market (MERCOSUR)** is among the most successful common markets. Initially, it started as a bilateral agreement between Brazil and Argentina aimed at eliminating trade restrictions between the two countries. MERCOSUR now comprises additional member countries: since 1991, Paraguay and Uruguay, and, since 2006, Venezuela (who pulled out of AnCom that same year). Chile, Bolivia, Ecuador, and Peru have associate status, but Bolivia is thought to be ready to apply for full-member status shortly. The countries with associate status disagree with the other members on the common tariffs (Chile insists on a much lower external tariff than the agreement provides for) to be charged to companies from nonmember countries.

Venezuela has yet to comply with all the conditions for membership, such as bringing import duties in line with the group's common external tariffs; however, its president, Hugo Chavez, is leading the charge of the group, seeking a regionwide organization that endorses his ideological, anti-imperialist vision. Meanwhile, his nationalist, anti-U.S. rhetoric and his move to centralize authority in Venezuela are raising questions about the country's compliance with the organization's requirements and vision.[28]

Initially, MERCOSUR was expected to look north, at NAFTA, for trade and cooperation accords; surprisingly, it has opted to first approach the EU in an ambitious agreement that phases out all trade barriers. However, to date, this agreement has not materialized, even though the parties have been working on it for more than a decade. MERCOSUR also has free trade agreements with AnCom. Increasingly, MERCOSUR is used as an argument against the U.S.-dominated FTAA, which would be redundant.

MERCOSUR countries are prevented from drawing up bilateral agreements with the United States. Uruguay has threatened to downgrade its MERCOSUR role to associate status so that it can make a bilat-

---

Latin American Integration Association (LAIA)
Latin America's largest trade agreement striving to establish bilateral and multilateral agreements aimed at reducing tariff and nontariff barriers.

Latin American Free Trade Association (LAFTA)
An attempt by Latin American countries to establish a free trade association; its demise is attributed to the economic disparity between member countries and to protectionist policies.

Andean Common Market (AnCom)
A trade group of the Andean countries that aspires to become a common market; it is currently in the process of agreeing on common external tariffs. (See www.comunidadandina.org.)

Southern Cone Common Market (MERCOSUR)
A free trade agreement in South America that has met with considerable success; MERCOSUR is presently in the process of becoming a viable customs union. (See www.mercosur.org.uy.)

Figure 4-7: *Member countries of the Latin American Integration Association, Andean Common Market, and Southern Cone Common Market.*

Central American Common Market (CACM)
An economic agreement among Central American countries; this agreement includes plans for forming a regional economic union similar to the European Union and to advance regional and international trade.

Common Market for Eastern and Southern Africa (COMESA)
An agreement among twenty member countries aimed at achieving economic integration; COMESA is currently eliminating all tariff and nontariff barriers to trade and is in the process of adopting common external tariffs.

eral trade deal with the United States. However, a full trade agreement is opposed by MERCOSUR, which requires members to negotiate deals collectively. Overall, MERCOSUR's status is problematic because, increasingly, Uruguay and Paraguay are looking to North America for trade relations and publicly complaining that Brazil and Argentina are denying them access to their markets. [29]

Moreover, in 2012, Brazil decided to terminate automatic import licenses for several products, such as wheat, flour and some cheeses and wines, most imported from Argentina, creating a rift between the two countries.

The Central American Common Market

The economic agreement among Belize, Costa Rica, the Dominican Republic, El Salvador, Guatemala, Honduras, Nicaragua, and Panama (with observer status), known as the **Central American Common Market (CACM),** includes plans for forming a regional economic union similar to the EU and to advance regional and international trade. The plan also encompasses political, cultural, and environmental measures. [30] However, a number of countries in the common market have had adversarial relationships, and the permanence of the pact is often questioned.

The Common Market for Eastern and Southern Africa

The **Common Market for Eastern and Southern Africa (COMESA)** plans full economic integration; it allows for the free movement of labor and capital, the free movement of people by 2014, and a currency union by 2025; it is, however, clear that the organization faces substantial political and economic obstacles given the political and economic instability in the region. [31] Specifically, the difficulties facing member countries include a poor compliance with tariff reductions and concerns over customs revenue losses; further complicating the matter is the fact that, despite diplomatic pressure, South Africa is not a member. [32] COMESA has nineteen member countries: Burundi, Comoros, Democratic Republic of Congo, Djibouti, Egypt, Eritrea, Ethiopia, Kenya, Madagascar, Malawi, Mauritius, Namibia, Rwanda, Seychelles, Sudan, Swaziland, Uganda, Zambia, and Zimbabwe.

4-2e Monetary Unions

The establishment of a **monetary union** involves the creation of a unified central bank and the use of a single currency. The following are examples of successful monetary unions:

- European Monetary Union
- West African Economic and Monetary Union
- Economic Community of West African States

It should be noted, however, that successful monetary unions do not necessarily mean successful economic integration and the elimination of all trade restrictions.

monetary union
A form of economic integration characterized by the establishment of a common central bank enacting monetary policy for the group.

European Economic and Monetary Union (EMU)
A union composed of the members of the European Union who adhere to the joint monetary policy enacted by the European Central Bank and who have adopted the euro as the single currency. (See www.europa.eu)

The European Economic and Monetary Union (Euroland)

The 1992 Maastricht Treaty had as a purpose to provide for the **European Economic and Monetary Union (EMU)** (www.europa.eu)—also known as the European Monetary Union—and to create the European Central Bank, a single currency, and fixed exchange rates. The creation of a monetary union was, however, hindered in 1992 by an exceptionally strong German mark, boosted particularly by the financing of reconstruction for East Germany (the former German Democratic Republic, part of the Soviet Bloc) and the high interest rates it offered to foreign investors. This, coupled with a recession taking place in Europe, led to a crisis that caused the other currencies—in particular, the British pound and the Spanish peseta—to lose their value overnight and to float out of the European ERM; they also left the EMS. To member countries, at the time, it appeared that the German Central Bank was likely to dominate the European body, and, for a while, the euro lost popular support, especially in Britain.

The EMU had three stages. The first (which ended in 1994), involved the free movement of all capital in the EU, the abolition of all exchange controls, the creation of structural funds to remove inequalities between countries, and convergence of economic policies. The second stage began in 1994, and it involved establishing the European Monetary Institute (EMI), made up of governors of central banks, assuring the independence of national central banks, and establishing rules to curb budget deficits. In the third stage, starting in 1999, Austria, Belgium, Finland, France, Germany, Ireland, Italy, Luxembourg, the Netherlands, Portugal and Spain adopted the euro, with Greece joining in 2001, Slovenia in 2007, Cyprus and Malta in 2008, Slovakia in 2009, and Estonia in 2011. These countries are known as the **Eurozone** or **Euroland** (see Figure 4-7).

The European Central Bank took charge of monetary policy from the EMI, defined and implemented in euros. Euro notes and coins were issued in 2002 in the twelve euro-area countries, and national

Figure 4-8: *Member countries of the European Union and the Euroland countries.*

Euroland
The nickname of the European Monetary Union. (See www.europa.eu)

West African Economic and Monetary Union (WAEMU)
One of the first attempts at economic integration in Africa. Although it is successful as a monetary union that has adopted a single currency, trade is quite modest within the WAEMU. (See www.dakarcom.com/EconReports/econ_waemu.htm.)

Economic Community of West African States (ECOWAS)
A free trade agreement that strives to achieve economic integration in West Africa; domination by Nigeria, civil unrest, and regional conflict have served as impediments in the group's success. (See www.ecowas.int.)

political union
The highest level of regional integration; it assumes a viable economic integration and involves the establishment of viable common governing bodies, legislative bodies, and enforcement powers.

Council of Mutual Economic Assistance (CMEA)
A trade agreement between the countries of the Soviet Bloc that disintegrated after the fall of communism. CMEA was an economic body similar in nature to a free trade area and approached what would be considered a political union.

currencies were withdrawn from circulation. To be admitted to the third stage, each EU country must meet the following criteria: price stability, with inflation in check; interest rates varying no more than 2 percent from average interest rates, budget deficits below 3 percent of GDP, public debt not exceeding 60 percent of GDP, and exchange rate stability.[33]

The new EU members are all due to adopt the euro, when they are able to meet the criteria. Three EU members, the United Kingdom, Denmark and Sweden, have not entered the third stage and still use their own currency today.

The West African Economic and Monetary Union

The **West African Economic and Monetary Union (WAEMU)** is one of the first attempts at economic integration in Africa. Although successful as a monetary union that has adopted a single currency—the CFA franc—trade is quite modest within the WAEMU.[34] WAEMU member countries are Benin, Burkina Faso, Ivory Coast, Guinea-Bissau, Mali, Niger, Senegal, and Togo.

The Economic Community of West African States

The purpose of the **Economic Community of West African States (ECOWAS)** is to achieve complete economic integration. At present, ECOWAS member countries are also attempting to address impediments to the integration process that are attributed to civil unrest, regional conflict, a lag in economic development compared with other market groups in the world, and the domination of the group by Nigeria.

ECOWAS's plans, however, are ambitious. Six of the fifteen members—Gambia, Ghana, Guinea, Liberia, Nigeria, and Sierra Leone—have set up a monetary union and have committed to adopting a common currency and to merge with the WAEMU. In this regard, they have pledged to meet stringent convergence criteria, such as 5 percent inflation, a maximum budget deficit-to-GDP ratio of 4 percent, and central bank financing of the budget deficit limited to 10 percent of the previous year's tax revenue, among others.[35] ECOWAS member countries are Benin, Burkina Faso, Cape Verde, Ivory Coast, Gambia, Ghana, Guinea, Guinea-Bissau, Liberia, Mali, Niger, Nigeria, Senegal, Sierra Leone, and Togo.

4-2f Political Unions

A **political union** represents the highest level of integration; it assumes a viable economic integration and involves the establishment of viable common governing bodies, legislative bodies, and enforcement powers. Although there are many examples of political unions, the European Union (www.europa.eu) is the only example to date of successful voluntary political integration. In a noteworthy past example, the countries of the Soviet Bloc were members of the **Council of Mutual Economic Assistance (CMEA),** an economic body similar to a free trade area, as well as members of the Warsaw Pact, a political/military body aimed at countering NATO. The countries formed a political union dominated by the Soviet Union, but the structures did not survive after the fall of communism. Another example of political semi-voluntary integration is the Commonwealth of Independent States, discussed in Section 4-2a, "Bilateral Agreements and Multilateral Forums and Agreements."

The EU, composed of twenty-seven member states, is an established political union. The member states are Germany, France, Italy, the Netherlands, Belgium, Luxembourg, Denmark, Ireland, United Kingdom, Greece, Spain, Portugal, Austria, Finland, Sweden, Czech Republic, Cyprus, Estonia, Latvia, Lithuania,

Hungary, Malta, Poland, Slovenia, and Slovakia, with new member states Bulgaria and Romania. Croatia, Macedonia, and Turkey are candidate countries. As a political union, the EU agreed on a common foreign policy and a common security policy that includes defense agreements, a common legal system, and a common enforcement system that works across borders for mutual purposes. As such, it has set in place a number of governmental bodies, as shown in Figure 4-9.

The **European Council,** in which heads of government meet, is the highest policy-making body of the European Union.

The **European Parliament,** located in Strasbourg, France, is a body of 754 members (as of 2012) elected every five years by direct universal suffrage. Seats are allocated among member states based on their population.

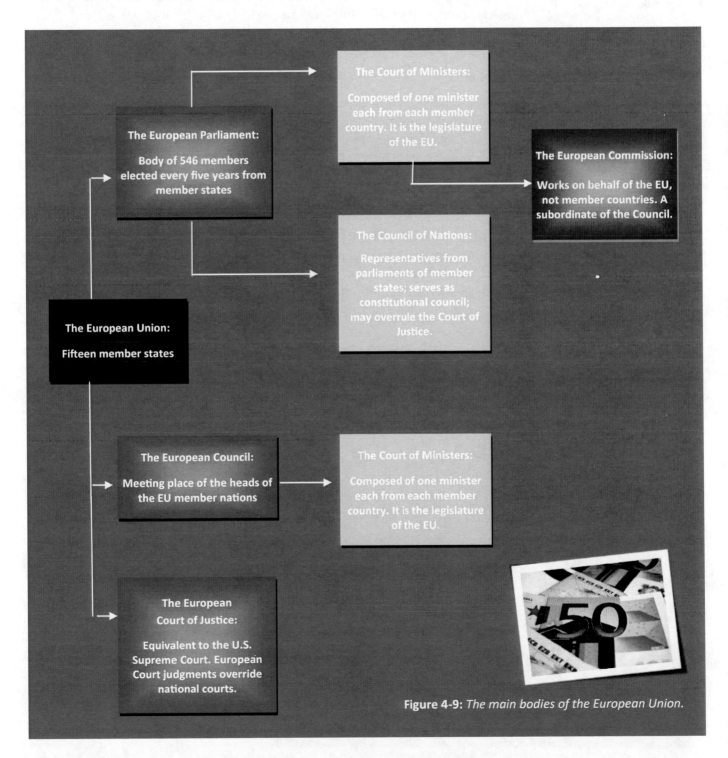

Figure 4-9: *The main bodies of the European Union.*

European Council
The highest policy-making body of the European Union. (See www.europa.eu)

European Parliament
The Parliament of the European Union, composed of members elected every 5 years by direct universal suffrage; seats in the Parliament are allocated among member states based on their population. (See www.europa.eu)

Council of Ministers
The decision-making body (the legislature) of the European Union, composed of one minister from each member country.

Council of Nations
The constitutional council of the European Union consisting of representatives from parliaments of EU member states. (See www.europa.eu)

European Commission
The body of the European Union in charge of initiating and supervising the execution of laws and policies. (See www.europa.eu)

The Parliament debates the policies and legislation in the EU. In the past, it was mainly a consultative body that passed on most of the proposed legislation with a simple majority voting. More recently, however, it has experienced extensive debates and lobbying from member countries on key international business issues. In one example, the Parliament killed a measure that would have made it easier to mount corporate takeovers; the vote is attributed to a string of hostile takeovers, such as Vodafone, the British mobile telephone company taking over its German rival, Mannesmann.[36]

The Parliament is consulted in many important matters, including those related directly to marketing in the EU. In 2007, the European Commission consulted it extensively on changes to e-commerce laws, in favor of consumers.

The **Council of Nations** consists of representatives from parliaments of member states, and it acts as a constitutional council. It has the power to overrule the Court of Justice.

The **Council of Ministers,** the decision-making body (the legislature) of the EU, is composed of one minister from each member country. The Council of Ministers passes laws based on proposals of the European Commission. Different ministers from each country, depending on the issue debated, meet at various locations to vote on directives advanced by the Commission. For example, EU energy ministers met in Stockholm to vote on EU electricity and natural gas directives to allow businesses and households to choose their electricity and natural gas suppliers.[37]

The **European Commission** is subordinate to the Council, as a civil service. The Commission consists of a president and commissioners who are appointed for a four-year term and are in charge of initiating and supervising the execution of laws and policies. This executive body of the EU is located in Brussels, Belgium. It is important to note that the European Commission acts only on behalf and in the interest of the EU, and not that of individual member states. It answers to the European Parliament.

Hemicycle of European Parliament, Strasbourg, with chamber orchestra performing.

Many of the European Commission rulings affect international business worldwide: A company that wants to do business in Europe must abide by the Commission's ruling.[38] For example, the European Commission blocked General Electric's $42 billion takeover of Honeywell International, due to the danger that General Electric could use Honeywell's strength in avionics equipment to expand its competitive strength in aircraft engines. The Commission rejected the merger of MCI WorldCom and Sprint on the grounds that the company would be able to dictate prices for Internet access in Europe, and it blocked a merger between two British travel agencies invoking the threat of collective dominance.[39] In another example, the European Commission raided nine mobile-service providers in Britain and Germany, including giants Deutsche Telekom AG, the Vodafone Group PLC, and France Telecom SA, looking for evidence of price fixing in setting roaming tariffs.[40]

The European Commission also enacted an important directive aimed at unfair commercial practices. Its Directive on Unfair Commercial Practices addresses the tangle of national bans, limits, and other restrictions that impede small and medium-sized enterprises from taking full advantage of the EU market, and provides consumers anywhere in the EU the same opportunities and protection as elsewhere in the market. The primary areas covered are misleading practices, aggressive practices, and facilitation of cross-border shopping.

Misleading practices are targeted in particular. For example, the directive would be used to outlaw the use of sports stars in food advertising directed at children. The directive bans "bait advertising" scams, whereby a product is advertised as a special offer without the retailer carrying it in stock in sufficient amounts. It also bans use of liquidation sales when in fact the retailer is not going out of business and use of pyramid schemes. Aggressive practices are also banned. For example, harassment, coercion, and undue influence in sales are banned, as is excessive solicitation. Consumers will also be able to confidently engage in cross-border shopping. Before this directive was enacted, consumers were worried that their rights would not be guaranteed to the same extent as in their home country and did not willingly purchase products over the Internet. This aspect of the directive also evens the playing field for companies in the EU. For example, companies that were unwilling to sell their products to consumers in untested areas because they were not familiar with national laws are now assured of the same protection anywhere in the European Union.[41]

In another example, the EU Commissioner for Consumer Affairs overhauled online marketing to consumers, ensuring that products are delivered in a reasonable amount of time and in good condition, and that buyers are appropriately charged for the products they order online. The overhaul also focused on enforcing consumer cancellation rights.

In yet other examples in 2012, the European Commission threatened to sue Hungary in the European Court of Justice on breaches regarding the independence of the country's central bank and its data protection authority. In reality, the Commission took on the country's authoritarian government for centralizing power and undermining democracy in Hungary, in breach of EU laws.

The current EU regulations are complex, and there are minute details that must be considered. For instance, there have even been arguments about how soon a refund must be provided based on the placement of a comma in the Distance Selling Regulations.[42]

The **European Central Bank** is charged with enacting monetary policy for the countries that share a common currency, the euro. Its goal is to maintain price stability within the European Monetary Union. The members of the European Central Bank board are appointed by the European Council by a simple majority vote. The equivalent of the Federal Reserve Bank for the United States, the European Central Bank tends to be more conservative and does not typically yield to individual countries' demands to reduce interest rates in an attempt to boost the economy during a downturn.

The **European Court of Justice** is the EU's equivalent of the U.S. Supreme Court. The Court's decisions are final, binding to member countries, and cannot be appealed in national courts. Also, European Court judgments overrule those of national courts.

In addition to these bodies, the European Union has adopted other common policies; among them are commercial policies, foreign and defense policies, and policies concerning immigration and the granting of asylum.

Other Parastatal Institutions in Europe

The EU is not the only parastatal institution in Western Europe. Other parastatal institutions have no affiliation to the EU, and yet they are significant players in the

European Central Bank
The bank of the European Union charged with enacting monetary policy for the twelve countries that share a common currency, the euro. (See www.europa.eu)

European Court of Justice
The Supreme Court-equivalent of the European Union. (See www.europa.eu)

life of this region. One such example is the Council of Europe, which is composed of forty European states that agree to accept the principle of the rule of law and guarantee of human rights and fundamental freedoms. The institution is involved in such areas as human rights; legal cooperation; cultural heritage; social, economic, and environmental planning; and local democracy. Two of its institutions are the Palais de l'Europe and the European Court and Commission for Human Rights.

Summary

Provide an overview of the determinants of regional economic and political integration. A number of factors prompt countries to favor trade with other countries. They are sharing a common culture, language, traditions, a history of common economic and political dominance, regional proximity, a similar level of economic development, and the desire to relinquish part of a nation's national identity in favor of advancing other national priorities.

Examine the different levels of economic and political integration and identify, within each world region, economic and political agreements that have met with success. The first level of integration involves establishing bilateral and multilateral agreements; these agreements involve, to some extent, opening of markets and elimination of trade barriers. At the next level, a free trade agreement involves a reduction in, or even elimination of, customs duties and other trade barriers between member countries. Examples of free trade agreements are the European Free Trade Association, the Association of Southeast Asian Nations Free Trade Agreement, the North American Free Trade Agreement, and the Southern African Development Community. The Free Trade Area of the Americas is an ambitious plan to create a market of the democratic nations of North, Central, and South America. At the next level, a customs union is a free trade area that has eliminated or greatly reduced internal tariffs and that imposes common external tariffs. An example is the South African Customs Union. A common market is an agreement to eliminate all barriers to trade, to adopt external tariffs, and to allow for the free movement of capital and labor in the region. Examples of common markets are the Latin American Integration Association, the Andean Community, the Southern Cone Common Market (MERCOSUR), the Central American Common Market, and the Common Market for Eastern and Southern Africa. The establishment of a monetary union involves the creation of a common central bank and the use of a single currency. Examples of monetary unions are the European Economic and Monetary Union, the West African Economic and Monetary Union, and the Economic Community of West African States. The only viable political unions that have survived to date are the European Union and the Commonwealth of Independent States.

Examine the functions of the different policy and governance bodies of the European Union. The different bodies of the European Union are the European Council, which is the highest policy-making body of the European Union, made up of heads of governments; the European Parliament, which debates policies and legislation of the European Union; the Council of Nations, which consists of representatives from parliaments of member states and acts as a constitutional council; the Council of Ministers, which is the decision-making body (the legislature) of the European Union that passes laws based on proposals of the European Commission; the European Commission, which is subordinate to the Council and initiates and supervises the execution of laws and policies; the European Central Bank, which is charged with enacting monetary policy for the countries that share a common currency; and the European Court of Justice, an equivalent to the U.S. Supreme Court.

Key Terms

Andean Common Market (AnCom)

ASEAN Free Trade Area (AFTA)

Asia-Pacific Economic Cooperation (APEC)

Association of Southeast Asian Nations (ASEAN)

bilateral agreement

Central American Common Market (CACM)

common market

Common Market for Eastern and Southern Africa (COMESA)

Commonwealth of Independent States (CIS)

Council of Ministers

Council of Mutual Economic Assistance (CMEA)

Council of Nations

customs union

Economic Community of West African States (ECOWAS)

Euroland

European Atomic Energy Community

European Central Bank

European Coal and Steel Community

European Commission

European Council

European Court of Justice

European Exchange Rate Mechanism (ERM)

European Free Trade Association (EFTA)

European Economic and Monetary Union (EMU)

European Parliament

European Union (EU)

free trade agreement

Free Trade Area of the Americas (FTAA)

Latin American Free Trade Association (LAFTA)

Latin American Integration Association (LAIA)

Maastricht Treaty

monetary union

multilateral forums and agreements

North American Free Trade Agreement (NAFTA)

North Atlantic Treaty Organization (NATO)

Organization for Economic Co-operation and Development (OECD)

Organization for Petroleum Exporting Countries (OPEC)

political union

South African Customs Union (SACU)

Southern African Development Community (SADC)

Southern Cone Common Market (MERCOSUR)

West African Economic and Monetary Union (WAEMU)

Discussion Questions

1.   Identify the determinants of regional economic and political integration.

2.   Describe the different stages of regional economic and political integration. What is the difference between a free trade association and a common market?

3.   There are arguments that much of the groundwork for the Free Trade Area of the Americas already has been done by other free trade agreements in the region targeted for economic integration. Which free trade agreements are operating within this area?

4.   Identify the different bodies of the European Union and describe their main function.

Chapter Quiz

True/False

1. Determinants of successful economic and political integration include a common culture, a common history, and regional proximity.

True

Rationale: Neighboring countries with a common culture and history have been successful at creating a single market.

Section 4-1, "Determinants of Economic and Political Integration"

2. Bilateral agreements and multilateral forums and agreements are different from formal regional political and economic integration.

True

Rationale: The goal of these agreements tends to be less comprehensive, focused on one industry or natural resources, for example.

Section 4-2a, "Bilateral Agreements and Multilateral Forums and Agreements"

3. The goal of NAFTA is to eliminate all tariff and nontariff barriers among the United States, Canada, and Mexico.

True

Rationale: The North American Free Trade Agreement was created to reduce and, ultimately, eliminate all tariffs and other barriers among the three countries.

Section 4-2b, "Free Trade Agreements"

4. A common market is characterized by limited movement of goods, labor, and capital.

False

Rationale: Key to the definition of a common market is the free movement of goods, labor, and capital within the respective market.

Section 4-2d, "Common Markets"

5. The European Parliament debates policies and legislation of the European Union.

True

Rationale: The European Parliament used to be a consultative body that passed on most of the proposed legislation with a simple majority voting; it now actively debates policies and legislation in the European Union.

Section 4-2f, "Political Union"

6. The European Council is the highest policy-making body of the European Union.

True

Rationale: The European Council, which is the highest policy-making body of the EU, is made up of heads of government of the member states.

Section 4-2f, "Political Union"

Multiple Choice

1.   All the following are examples of free trade agreements EXCEPT the

    a.   Association of Southeast Asian Nations.

    b.   North American Free Trade Agreement.

    c.   Southern African Development Community.

    d.   World Trade Organization.

Answer d is correct.

Rationale: The World Trade Organization is an organization that actively promotes trade by offering help for export promotion and promoting regional trade agreements and cooperation in global economic policy making.

Section 4-2b, "Free Trade Agreements"

2.   Current members of the European Free Trade Association include all the following EXCEPT

    a.   Norway.

    b.   Liechtenstein.

    c.   Sweden.

    d.   Ireland.

Answer c is correct.

Rationale: Sweden is not a member of EFTA.

Section 4-2b, "Free Trade Agreements"

3.   Which agreement is credited with eliminating all internal tariffs and creating the European Economic Community?

    a.   The Southern Cone Common Market

    b.   The Treaty of Rome

    c.   The Andean Economic Agreement

    d.   The Maastricht Treaty

Answer b is correct.

Rationale: The Treaty of Rome is credited with eliminating tariffs, establishing common external tariffs, allowing for the free movement of capital and labor within what is today the EU, and setting in place regulations and bodies that would ultimately form the basis for a monetary and political union.

Section 4-2d, "Common Markets"

Endnotes for Chapter 4

1.   "Finance and Economics: A Common EU Tax Base," *The Economist*, Vol. 383, No. 8527, May 5, 2007, p. 84.

2.   "The History of APEC," *Business Korea,* Vol. 17, No. 4, April 2000, pp. 54–55.

3.   Ibid.

4.   Laura D'andrea Tyson, "The Message from Asia: Trade Locally, Think Globally," *BusinessWeek,* Issue 3710, December 4, 2000, p. 28.

5.   Ibid.

6.   *The World Bank and The APEC Region Trade and Investment 2006*, www.apec.org/etc/medialib/apec_media_library/downloads/sec/pubs/2007.Par.0008.File.tmp/06_sec_Apec_glance.pdf.

7.   Richard Pomfret, "Reintegration of Formerly Centrally Planned Economies into the Global Trading System," *ASEAN Economic Bulletin,* Vol. 18, No. 1, April 2001, pp. 35–47.

8.   Ibid.

9.   Ibid.

10.   Robert von Lucius, "Nordic Neighbors Feel Snubbed," *Frankfurter Allgemeine Zeitung,* No. 154, July 6, 2001, p. 3.

11.   Ibid.

12.   For a discussion of the current conflict between the EU and EFTA, see Lucius, "Nordic Neighbors Feel Snubbed," p. 3.

13.   Ibid.

14.   Edward Taylor, "EU and Switzerland Resume Talks on Bilateral Accords," *Wall Street Journal Europe,* July 6–7, 2001, p. 2.

15.   www.aseansec.org/64.htm

16.   "Asia/Pacific Rim: Japan, ASEAN Set Up Free Trade Agreement Study Group," *World Trade,* Vol. 14, No. 7, July 2001, p. 18.

17.   Neil Saker, "The Foundations of Stability," *Far Eastern Economic Review,* Vol. 164, No. 20, May 24, 2001, p. 55.

18.   Alan M. Field, "A New Vision for NAFTA," *Journal of Commerce,* June 28, 2004, p. 1.

19.   Ibid.

20.   "No Time for Protectionism," *Business Week,* Issue 3742, July 23, 2001, p. 98.

21.   www.ustr.gov/Trade_Agreements/Bilateral/CAFTA/CAFTA-DR_Final_Texts/Section_Index.html, June 15, 2007; Joint Statement from 2012 NAFTA Commission Meeting, 3 April, 2012, http://canada.usembassy.gov/news-events/2012-news-and-events.

22.   Ernesto Zedillo, Former President of Mexico, "Commentary," *Forbes,* July 23, 2001, p. 49.

23.   Ibid.

24.   Gary C. Hufbauer and Yee Wong, "Grading Growth," *Harvard International Review,* Vol. 26, No. 2, Spring 2004, pp. 72–76.

25.   Ryan Fahey, "Congo Tensions: The SADC's Shortcomings," *Harvard International Review,* Vol. 21, No. 2, Spring 1999, pp. 14–16.

26.   http://europa.eu/index_en.htm

27.   www.sice.oas.org

28.   *EIU ViewsWire,* "Venezuela Politics: Hijacking Mercosur," January 22, 2007.

29.   Benedict Mander, "Uruguay Threatens to Downgrade Mercosur Role," *FT.com,* March 8, 2007, 1.

30.   www.sice.oas.org/trade/camertoc.asp

31.   *Country Monitor,* "Comesa's Free-Trade Area," Vol. 8, No. 43, November 6, 2000, p. 4.

32.   "International Economy,"*Barclays Economic Review,* pp. 29–31.

33.   http://europa.eu/abc/12lessons/lesson_7/index_en.htm, June 15, 2007

34.   Jacqueline Irving, "Point/Counterpoint: The Pros and Cons of Expanded Monetary Union in West Africa," *Finance & Development,* Vol. 38, No. 1, March 2001, pp. 24–28.

35.   Ibid.

36.   Paul Meller, "EU Parliament Rejects Bill to Ease Takeovers," *International Herald Tribune,* July 5, 2001, pp. 1, 10.

37.   "EU Energy Chief Expects Power Deal by the End of the Year," *Wall Street Journal Europe,* July 6–7, 2001, p. 3.

38.   Brian M. Carney, "Mario Monti, Central Planner: Does the European Union's Competition Commissioner Really Believe in Competition?" *Wall Street Journal Europe,* July 6–7, 2001, p. 6.

39.   Edmund L. Andrews and Paul Meller, "EU Vetoes GE's Plan to Acquire Honeywell," *International Herald Tribune,* July 4, 2001, pp. 1, 5.

40.   Philip Shishkin, William Boston, and Almar LaTour, "Nine Mobile Firms Are Raided in Probe of Roaming Tariffs: EU Antitrust Officials Look for Evidence of Collusion in Germany, U.K.," *Wall Street Journal Europe,* July 12, 2001, pp. 1, 4.

41.   ec.europa.eu/consumers/index_en.htm; and Lucy Alcock, Paul Chen, Hui Min Ch'ng, Sarah Hodson, et al., "New European Union Directive to Curb Unfair and Misleading Commercial Practices," *Journal of Brand Management,* Vol. 11, No. 2, 2003, p. 125.

42.   *New Media Age,* "UK Firms Should Get Involved in the EU Etail Consultation, February 22, 2007, 16.

43.   europa.eu./comm/enlargement/bulgaria/

44.   http://ec.europa.eu/enterprise/regulation/internal_market_package/index_en.htm, June 20, 2007

45.   http://ec.europa.eu/enterprise/eco_design/index_en.htm, June 20, 2007

46.   http://ec.europa.eu/environment/chemicals/reach/reach_intro.htm, June 20, 2007

Case 4-1

Damianov Press

Damian Damianov, a retired director of a formerly communist metallurgic factory in the capital city of Sofia, Bulgaria, bought an abandoned printing press with quality equipment in the outskirts of Sofia. His goal is to produce art books for publishers in the European Union (EU). The press, privatized in the early 1990s, after the fall of communism in Bulgaria, was recently abandoned by its previous owner because it was considered an environmental hazard by the state. The previous owner did not want to invest in new equipment needed to meet environmental requirements of the EU, which Bulgaria joined in 2007.

The fall of communism in Bulgaria created numerous opportunities for newly privatized larger companies, as well as small and medium-sized enterprises. However, many businesses were greatly challenged by the 1996 crisis, and it took years for the economic recovery to bring back entrepreneurial enthusiasm. Since the 1996 crisis, Bulgaria has achieved macroeconomic stability, it has a stable currency, and its real growth is accelerating significantly. It was considered the most attractive of the 2007 candidates for membership in the EU. It is fertile ground for aggressive expansion of multinational business, especially business from the EU. The government encourages the establishment of new small and medium-sized enterprises, in line with the EU requirements, which specify that Bulgaria should focus on resolving uncertainties in the legislative and taxation areas and reinforcing delivery mechanisms for promoting entrepreneurship. As such, Bulgaria had to implement the European Charter for Small Enterprises,[43] which would create a strong competitive position for Damianov's new enterprise.

Damianov is working with Bulgarian venture capitalists to establish a new enterprise, the Damianov Press. His goal is to produce quality art books at much lower prices than Western European presses. This would serve the publishing clients well, as the industry is characterized by strong price competition. At present, much of the art book production in the EU takes place in Spain, where costs are somewhat lower than in the rest of the EU. Damianov has just returned from the Frankfurt Book Fair, where he met with a few of the German art book publishers: Prestel, Hatje Cantz, and DuMont. The Prestel representative appeared interested in the possibility of producing lower-cost, high-quality art books. With the high costs of development, translation, and production, exhibition catalogues and art books in general are becoming quite expensive. If costs can be reduced on the production side, these books can have greater appeal to the art public in the German-speaking world and elsewhere—as art books published in Germany frequently have side-by-side English translations. Damianov Press could produce those same high-quality, contemporary art books at a fraction of the cost.

Venture capitalists are gathering at the company's primary warehouse next week for a meeting. Each representative has individually assured Damian Damianov of contributions that would assure the financial viability of the company. They understand that their charge is to finance the refurbishing of old equipment and to invest in new equipment. Damianov needs to share information on the types of equipment needed and on issues related to compliance with European Union equipment requirements.

In reviewing the EU requirements for equipment, Damianov found that, in 2007, the European Commission offered a new package of measures aimed at boosting community-wide trade that benefits primarily small and medium-sized enterprises (SMEs.) For Damianov Press, these measures make it easier to obtain high-quality, safe machinery: The EU market surveillance structures were reinforced to catch unsafe products and remove them from the market. Also, the testing, certification, and inspection bodies have greater oversight than in the past, thus assuring the safe performance of equipment. [44]

Damianov Press can also be assured that it will have access to energy-efficient equipment. The European Commission's Integrated Product Policy has accelerated, for industry, the move toward improving the efficiency of products, in terms of energy and water consumption, waste generation, and extension of lifetime. Damianov Press will be able to purchase equipment awarded the Eco-label, which guarantees its environmental efficiency. [45]

European Union regulations also require that new businesses conduct a study of environmental impact assessment, nature protection, and industrial pollution to ensure that the new company conforms to EU requirements. The study is mandated by the Bulgarian government for all new businesses. The new company also needs to conform to EU requirements in areas of antidiscrimination, equal opportunities, labor law, and occupational safety and health at the printing press. As a company that deals regularly with chemical printing components, Damianov Press must comply with the REACH Regulation. The regulation entered into force in 2007, and is under the oversight of the European Chemicals Agency. The Agency's goal is to improve health and environmental protection through better and earlier identification of the properties of chemical substances. It imposes responsibility on the business to manage risks from chemicals and provide safety information, which means that Damianov will have to pay particular attention to the processes involving the chemicals, as well as to chemical waste disposal. [46]

Analysis Suggestions

1. What are some of the challenges that Damianov Press is facing in its new business?

2. What are some of the advantages that Damianov Press derives from Bulgaria's membership in the European Union?

3. What are the costs that Damianov will incur directly due to Bulgaria's membership in the European Union?

Chapter 5: Cultural Influences on International Marketing

Learning Objectives

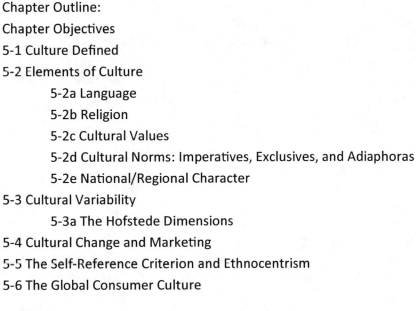

After studying this chapter, you should be able to:

- Identify the elements of culture and examine how they affect marketing practices around the world.

- Describe national and regional character based on dimensions such as time orientation, business practices, gift giving, socializing, gender roles, and materialism.

- Discuss cultural variability in terms of the Hofstede dimensions with appropriate examples and address cultural change in a marketing context.

- Address the self-reference criterion and ethnocentrism and describe how they impede mutual understanding and cooperation, with direct negative effects on marketing practices.

- Describe the global consumer culture as it manifests itself around the world.

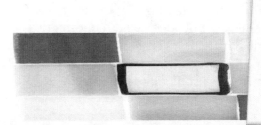

The Turkish Client

You are in the middle of negotiations with a potential Turkish client in Istanbul, over lunch, at the Conrad Hilton Hotel. You go to the self-service buffet and pile on your plate some tasty pork chops from a serving dish clearly marked "pork." You ask the waiter to bring a bottle of wine and offer some to your potential Turkish client; he declines. Your products are known for their quality in Turkey and elsewhere in the world, and your client seems receptive to your price quote. After lunch, the potential client invites you to his home for coffee; you decline and state that you need to stay at the hotel to get some work done and bid him good-bye. You come back to the United States and find that you cannot reach your Turkish client. His secretary always claims he is not in, and he does not return your calls. What went wrong?

You subsequently learn that, in Turkey, the dominant religion is Islam, and Islam bans the consumption of pork and alcohol. Could your lunch have offended your client? Probably not too much because he still seemed receptive to your offer as you were eating the "dirty animal" in front of him. Could he have been offended by your refusal to go to his house for Turkish coffee? Even though you refused, you did not tell him that you really hate the stuff and you were dreading spending even a few hours in 90-degree weather in a home that most likely was not air-conditioned. You were, after all, showing how dedicated you were to your job by staying at the hotel to work. Could the hotel staff have told him that you spent the evening next door, at another air-conditioned hotel, a former palace, having yet another bottle of wine?

This chapter examines in depth the effect of different cultural influences on consumer behavior and on a company's international operations. It examines national character and provides illustrations of behaviors in line with national character.

A full understanding of local culture in markets where one's firm is operating constitutes a minimal condition for successful global marketing operations. Although cultural understanding alone cannot guarantee a firm's success in a new international market, not fully understanding the local culture and engaging in marketing practices that may be discordant with the culture guarantees failure.

Walmart (in Germany)

The wrong strategies will quickly backfire for companies that do not fully research their target market. In Germany, Walmart banked on matching low prices with friendly service, only to find out that German shoppers just want to be left alone to shop, without the friendly chatter, which they thought was imposing, fake, and, possibly, adding to their prices.

Coca-Cola (in India)

Hindustan Coca-Cola Beverages incurred great losses in India. It was thought that the partnership with Parle, the leading local soft-drink manufacturer, was a coup. Indians were not happy about it, thinking that it would lead to the destruction of local beverage brands . . . and they were right: Coke was focusing its promotional efforts on building its international brands, phasing out Parle's Thums Up, which was the leading soft drink in India. Eventually, however, it decided to continue selling the Indian brand, which, with Coke, has 62 percent of the cola market. In other mistakes, Coke was priced too high for too long, and few consumers indulged in the product. Once they introduced returnable 200 ml bottles and reduced prices to 11 U.S. cents, sales took off. In other strategic mistakes in the Indian market, it was found that Coca-Cola's Kinley brand of bottled water had a higher level of pesticides than stipulated by European standards, and it included traces of DDT, which is banned worldwide. The company was also fined for painting its logo on rocks in the hill state of Himachal Pradesh.[1]

Microsoft

In its internationalization efforts, Microsoft has made a few costly mistakes. In the Spanish version of Windows XP, destined for Latin America, it asked users to select their gender between "not specified," "male," and "bitch"—all due to an unfortunate error in translation. When coloring in 800,000 pixels on a map of India, the company colored eight areas in a different shade of green, representing the disputed Kashmiri territory. Thus, Kashmir was shown as non-Indian, and the product was promptly banned in India. Microsoft had to immediately withdraw 200,000 versions of the program. Similar errors with maps brought Microsoft employees to face the government of China and apologize. In another example, Microsoft developed a fighting game called Kakuto Chojin, in which the fighting takes place to background chanting of the Koran. Microsoft decided, nevertheless, to issue the game in the United States, believing that it would not be noticed. But the Saudi government protested and Microsoft withdrew the game a year later.[2]

Culture is difficult to navigate in international marketing. The right product, coupled with the right local marketing decisions, can, potentially, create great customer franchise, and, implicitly, high profits. But making the right decisions is not always easy, as the previous examples illustrate. Walmart brought its low-price, consumer-friendly culture to Germany and customers responded with a shrug. Walmart's prices were low, but not that low compared with other similar long-entrenched businesses, such as Kaufland and Aldi. And a high customer focus means higher prices to German shoppers. Coca-Cola, on the other hand, proceeded in India as it did everywhere else: It bought its competitor and tried to put it on ice—to phase it out—and it priced Coke too high. Coca-Cola executives did not anticipate the adverse reaction of consumers: They were angry about the disappearance of a successful Indian brand and unhappy with the high price of soft drinks. Coca-Cola lost millions before it was able to appease the Indian public. And Microsoft lost millions as well, withdrawing products after creating ill will in their many target markets. When armed with knowledge about the local culture, companies such as Walmart, Coca-Cola, and Microsoft are in a better position to communicate effectively with the target consumer and avoid the blunders described earlier.

Culture is recognized as having a strong influence on consumption; it is expressed in the consumption of numerous products and services, in homes, offices, stores and marketplace sites, with differences noted across various subcultures and nations.[3] Cultural factors also exert a profound influence on the firm's other stakeholders, such as government representatives, national and international consumer groups and interest groups, service providers, suppliers, channel members, and shareholders, among others. Culture is the key determinant of the manner in which individuals do business or respond to a company's marketing strategy.

5-1 Culture Defined

Culture—a society's personality—is defined as a *continuously changing totality of learned and shared meanings, rituals, norms, and traditions among the members of an organization or society.*

Despite this definition, it should be noted that the notion of culture is relatively ambiguous and controversial among both practitioners and academics.[4] Some elements of culture, however, are thought to affect important aspects of marketing, and they are addressed in this chapter.

The pivotal constituents of culture are as follows:

Ecology—The manner in which society adapts to its habitat (i.e., the distribution of resources within an industrialized country versus a developing country; the desire for efficiency, space-saving devices, or green products).

Social structure—The organization of society.

culture
The continuously evolving totality of learned and shared meanings, rituals, norms, and traditions among the members of an organization or society.

ecology
The manner in which society adapts to its habitat (i.e., the distribution of resources within an industrialized country versus a developing country; the desire for efficiency, space-saving devices, or green products.

social structure
The organization of relationships in a society.

ideology
The manner in which individuals relate to their environment and to others, including their attitudes toward time, space, possessions, and referent others.

Ideology—The manner in which individuals relate to the environment and to others; this includes attitudes toward time, space, possessions, and referent others (peers).

These areas are complexly interrelated.[5]

Subcultures are components of the broad culture. Subcultures are groups of individuals with shared value systems based on ethnicity or common background. Subcultures could be based on regional differences: Southern Italian consumers have different lifestyles than Italians in the north, for example. Northern Germans have a different worldview from Germans in the southern state of Bavaria. Subcultures are also based on ethnicity or nationality: Turkish Germans maintain many of their home-country traditions and strong ties to the old country. They have larger, extended families living under one roof or nearby; they purchase products in Turkish shops, which pepper the retailing landscape in larger German cities; and they maintain their Muslim religious traditions. Subcultures can be based on religion—an important element of culture. Muslims make up a large proportion of the population of cities in Britain, and they retain their religious customs, as can be seen in the following paragraphs.

Muslim Women in the United Kingdom

London parks have many Muslim women watching their children play. The women take children to school and run errands covered from head to toe in flowing black gowns that permit only a slit for their eyes. The women say that they are targets of abuse, and Britons find that their limit of tolerance is being tested.

In fact, there are efforts underway to place legal curbs on the full-face Muslim veil. A lawyer wearing the veil was not allowed to represent an immigration client because the judge could not hear her; a teacher wearing the veil was dismissed from school; a student barred from wearing the veil to school sued and lost. And British education authorities are proposing a ban of the veil in school. The British interpret the veil as a statement that men are such brutes that if exposed to normally clothed women, they cannot be trusted to behave, and that women who do not wear a veil are indecent. People in England think the women wearing the veil are oppressed and do not speak English. However, the veil is worn by many bright, second-generation Britons, and even they are often told by Britons to go home, although they were born in Britain and their accent bears no hint of their heritage—Britain is home for these women. Among the younger women who wear the veil, many have taken it up recently as an expression of Islamic identity and as a form of rebellion against the policies of the British government overseas and at home. And many more Muslim women wear the head scarf, covering all or some of their hair, rather than the full veil. Unlike in France, Turkey, and Tunisia, where students in state schools and civil servants are banned from covering their hair, in Britain, Muslim women can wear the head scarf, and even the full veil, almost anywhere—for now.[6]

Figure 5-1: *In the Tiergarten district of Berlin, the presence of the Jewish subculture is only a memory. Jewish temples and schools were demolished starting in the late 1930s. This memorial stands at the entrance of a playground, commemorating the transport of area Jews from the Levetzowstraße Synagogue to the death camps.*

In other European examples, the Netherlands have large Indonesian and Surinamese subcultures; Austria has large Bosnian and Croatian subcultures; and Sweden has a large Ethiopian subculture. Historically, the Jewish subculture used to be the largest in many countries, in Poland, the Baltics, and Germany, but that ended in the 1930s and 1940s, when many were forced to emigrate or were deported to death camps. In some cities, there is a revival of Jewish life—Jews from the former Soviet Union account for the growth in the Jewish population—but, in many places, Jewish presence is just a memory (see Figure 5-1).

Subcultures can also be defined based on sexual preference. Gay and lesbians constitute an important market avidly courted by businesses. Among the companies that regularly target gay and lesbian consumers and sponsor exhibits at gay and lesbian events are American Airlines, America Online, Merrill Lynch, Chase Manhattan, British Airways, Virgin Atlantic, Levi Strauss, and American Express. Those companies that actively target gay and lesbian consumers have been able to reap substantial rewards: Gay and lesbian consumers have a fierce loyalty to a brand they identify as supportive.

In Section 5-2, "Elements of Culture," we describe the elements of culture that are most relevant to international marketing managers.

5-2 Elements of Culture

5-2a Language

Language has a prominent role as an element of culture: The language one learns in the community where one is born and raised shapes and structures one's worldview. Some languages, such as the Bantu languages, are broad and do not differentiate, for instance, between the "here" and the "now."[7] Other languages are precise, especially in domains such as agriculture; they may have several terms for an object or a body part, depending on the current function of the object or respective body part. For example, for the word "tail," Batwa languages have a term that refers to its use by cattle as protection against flies, another term as an illustration of joy, yet another as an indicator of attention, and so on. The key to communicating in a particular culture is understanding all the nuances and complexities of the language of the target market.

> **language**
> The vehicle used for communication in a particular culture; includes spoken and written language and nonverbal communication.
>
> **spoken/written language**
> The language used in conversation/the language used in written communications.

A number of points are relevant in this regard. At a primary level, language has two aspects: the spoken/written language and the nonverbal language.

Spoken/Written Language

Spoken/written language poses a number of concerns to marketers. First, in terms of translation, the diversity of languages creates difficulties for marketers operating internationally. Even if the same language is shared by different countries, marketers should be aware of differences in meaning: Procter & Gamble sells "nappies" in the United Kingdom, as opposed to "diapers"; the "boot" of the Ford automobile is actually its "trunk"; and housewives or househusbands who are "hoovering" in the United Kingdom may actually be "vacuuming" using an Electrolux vacuum cleaner.

Problems could arise in the process of translation: Firms have placed in jeopardy the viability of their brands by relying on primary translations and not ensuring that either the product name is appropriate in a given culture or that the communication actually conveys the intended message. Using procedures described in Chapter 6, "International Marketing Research: Practices and Challenges"—*back translation* (translation back into the original language) and *parallel translation* (translation by another translator for comparison purposes)—will diminish the likelihood that the company commits blunders when communicating with the target market. Many companies have made translation blunders, and the marketing literature is replete with examples. Using translation software increases the possibility of creating such blunders, as the Microsoft example in the introductory section illustrates.

Good translation is expensive, especially in markets where multiple languages are spoken. For example, in India, there are more than 300 minor languages and 3,000 dialects. Only 15 distinct languages are widely spoken, however; Hindi, the official language, is spoken by 30 percent of the population, and English is widely used in administrative, commercial, and political life. To effectively communicate with this promising multicultural market of approximately 1 billion, a firm's decisions on which language to use are crucial.

Marketing practitioners using the same marketing strategy in a unified market experience a similar dilemma: deciding which language to use or whether to use multiple languages. The European Union presents an interesting case: When companies target this market, product information is typically provided in, at minimum, two to three languages. An Evian bottle that has French, Dutch, and German labeling is probably sold in France, Belgium (where both French and Dutch are spoken), the Netherlands, Germany, Austria, Luxembourg, Liechtenstein, and in the German and French regions in Switzerland.

It is important to communicate in the appropriate language with the target market in areas where multiple languages are used. Marketers selling their products in the United Arab Emirates will find that a significant proportion of consumers there do not speak the national language, Arabic. These countries have a large population of guest workers from India, Pakistan, and Southeast Asia. For example, in Ajman, one of the emirates west of Dubai, only about 20 percent of the population is Emirati. In targeting these markets, firms would benefit from using English, which is widely understood, and the main language used in business, rather than Arabic.

Other aspects of the written language convey meanings as well. For example, calligraphy in China is perceived as an art, but the calligraphy itself conveys information about the writer's erudition and talent. It is said that the Chinese fine arts and the Chinese calligraphy share the same origin. Chinese characters are the only pictographic symbols among the modern languages. Writing, in fact, is perceived as an art form higher than painting in that it is more abstract. But, to appreciate the beauty of the calligraphy, "it takes deep Chinese cultural nourishment and higher intellect."[8]

Figure 5-2: *Understanding Chinese calligraphy takes deep Chinese cultural nourishment and higher intellect.*

Calligraphy is often performed in public parks, with a water brush that leaves no permanent marks. A calligrapher is usually surrounded by a crowd interested in the message and in the art. Sensitivity to and an understanding of this type of communication are essential to understanding the Chinese (see Figure 5-2).

Nonverbal Communication

Nonverbal communication includes body language, gestures, facial expressions, eye contact, and even silence. Silent communications, especially gestures, have different meanings across cultures, and marketing managers must be aware of them to avoid embarrassing or costly mistakes. Examples of nonverbal communication are provided in the next paragraphs.

Proxemics refer to the relationship between physical space and the process of communication. One of the peculiarities of American culture that most foreigners find intriguing is the "bubble," the personal space around the individual, which, if one violates, one must apologize. This "bubble" is unheard of in countries where standing in line means that the person behind another will periodically engage in a "poking exercise," pushing him or her lightly and hoping that he or she might advance somewhat. In these countries, even in polite society, apologizing for maneuvering too closely or cutting off another is not necessary.

nonverbal communication
All communication that is not written or spoken; includes body language, gestures, facial expressions, eye contact, and silence.

proxemics
The amount of physical space individuals require to feel comfortable in the process of communication.

In general, Greeks, Central and Eastern Europeans, Japanese, and South Americans feel more comfortable standing or sitting closer to strangers than do members of other nationalities.[9] Similarly, in the Middle East, even in the business world, men prefer standing close to people with whom they are conversing and take great offense if someone backs away from them.[10]

Postures, orientations, and **oculesics** refer to individuals' positioning relative to their counterpart and the use or avoidance of eye contact during communication. Individuals' approaches to greeting, for example, differ in different parts of the world. In the United States, when shaking hands, one is supposed to look his or her counterpart in the eye; this should make an impression of being forthright, as well as having a take-charge attitude. The handshake should be firm and brief. This same handshake, however, would be perceived as arrogant and aggressive by an Asian counterpart. In Asia, a soft handshake, a humble posture, and avoidance of eye contact convey an attitude of respect. In Eastern Europe, a woman may expect to have her hand kissed (this also conveys respect for her as a representative of her gender), and men typically kiss each other on the cheeks. A kiss on the cheek in Central and South American countries, France, and Mexico often is proper and perhaps even necessary (to avoid insult). But in countries such as Korea and Japan, a slight bow is a better choice; placing the hands together and bowing slightly would offer a nice welcome in India and Thailand.[11]

> **postures**
> Individuals' physical postures during conversation.
>
> **orientations**
> Individuals' positioning relative to their counterparts during conversation.
>
> **oculesics**
> The use or avoidance of eye contact during communication.

With an extensive Western presence in the countries mentioned, however, the expectation that foreigners should adhere to these patterns of behavior has diminished.

When contemplating shaking hands, it is important to be aware that touching, in many countries, especially in the Middle East, is taboo, whether through a handshake or otherwise: In Muslim and Jewish orthodox communities, it is improper for men and women to touch members of the opposite sex other than spouses or close family. Also, tipping or removing a hat may be respectable in many countries but inappropriate in Jewish and Muslim cultures, which require head coverings.[12]

Certain sitting positions may even get one in trouble; for example, a person should not cross his or her legs or show the sole of his or her shoe to another person in the Middle East and Thailand because the gesture implies that the person is "worthy of being stepped on," or, according to other interpretations, "likened to a shoe sole." And, in many countries, it is appropriate to remove shoes and socks when entering a home or a religious area. Finally, pointing with a finger is not appropriate in Asian countries, although offering direction with the full hand is acceptable.

Chronemics refer to the timing of verbal exchanges. Americans expect prompt responses and are uncomfortable with a slow response or silence. They attempt to fill in the silence and further probe into the issue at hand to ensure that their counterparts understand them. Other nationalities—the Japanese, for instance—prefer to use this "quiet time" as contemplation time in which they evaluate the message. Often, translation comes in handy in this situation, especially if the negotiating parties understand each others' languages. Consecutive translation often provides the time necessary to digest and interpret messages, thus eliminating the need for the additional contemplation time. Often, the translator familiar with the Americans' discomfort with silence will intervene and explain that the time is being used for contemplating the deal.

Haptics refer to the use of touch while conversing. Again, this nonverbal communication is rarely used by Anglo-Americans, who prefer to keep others at the periphery of their "bubble." Latinate cultures tend to make extensive use of touch in order to convey their messages. A woman could expect to have not just her shoulders, arms, and hands touched, but also her hair and face, all with good intentions.

Kinesics refer to the movement of part of the body in order to communicate. Compared with many cultures, Americans gesture very little while communicating. The French and Italians, however, use hand gestures frequently to express themselves. It is important to understand the meanings of these gestures to function efficiently in these cultures. At the same time, it is wise not to assume that the gestures used in one's home country are identical with those used in other countries. It is possible, for example, that those gestures may have no meaning in other cultures, or, worse yet, they may have meanings other than those one would like to convey. For example, the sign of "OK" commonly used in the United States signifies

> **chronemics**
> The timing of verbal exchanges.
>
> **haptics**
> The use of touch while conversing.
>
> **kinesics**
> The movement of part of the body to communicate.

"zero" in France, is a symbol for money in Japan, and is a vulgar gesture in parts of South America, as a company that had a sign printed quickly found out.[13]

Movements of the head are the most difficult to interpret. Western gestures such as shaking the head up and down to signify "yes" and from side to side to signify "no" have different equivalents in other cultures. In the Middle East, people raise their head in a haughty manner to say "no," while sometimes accompanying the gesture with a click of the tongue. "No" is conveyed with a wave of the hand in front of the face in parts of Asia, and with a shake of the finger from side to side in Ethiopia. On the other hand, the U.S. gesture to slit one's throat means "I love you" in Swaziland, folding one's arms conveys respect in Fiji and arrogance in Finland, and the list continues. . . .[14]

Paralinguistics refer to nonverbal aspects of speech that include emotional intonation, accents, and quality of voice. Again, a louder, more aggressive intonation denoting self-assurance and strength in some cultures, such as that of the United States, may be perceived as threatening or insulting by other cultures, where softness is equated with politeness and respect. In the cultures of West Africa, laughter indicates embarrassment, discomfort, or surprise, whereas in some other cultures, laughter is discouraged altogether.[15] Although many people view North Americans as fairly loud and aggressive, the Spanish speak even louder, often shouting at each other to express enthusiasm.[16]

Appearances refer to one's physical attire and overall grooming. Each culture has its own expectations and norms with regard to what is appropriate in different circumstances. For example, Western business attire for men consists of a well-tailored dark suit, complemented by a conservative shirt and tie and elegant shoes; Western business attire for women may also consist of a well-tailored suit or a conservative dress and high heels. European dress codes allow for a more casual look or a more personal style than North American dress codes. In the Middle East, depending on the country, men's business attire may consist of a *gallabeya* (a long, typically white garment) and a head cover, whereas women in business may have their hair covered and wear an equally long, conservative dress, known as the *abaya* or the *hijab*.[17]

In South Asia (India, Pakistan, Bangladesh, Nepal, and others), appropriate business attire for women may be the traditional *sari,* typically an exquisitely embroidered or designed material that is wrapped using a specific pattern. In Africa, women wear a similarly colorful outfit, but taking the form of a gown with country-specific prints—a *bou-bou* (pronounced "boo-boo"); men wear a short-sleeve shirt with a political party pin attached and a pair of slacks, with the exception of the most formal circumstances, when a coat and tie are worn.

Olfactions refer to the use of odors to convey messages. Typically, such messages have a religious meaning: Incense is frequently used to purify the air of evil presence in both temples and churches, as well as in private homes. Finally, odors are evaluated differently in different cultures. For example, U.S. culture finds body odors and garlic breath as offensive, whereas East Asian cultures avoid consumption of dairy products believed to cause intolerably bad breath.

The Nonverbal Language and High- versus Low-Context Cultures

The high-low context continuum defines the extent to which a spoken statement conveys a full message.[18] In **low-context cultures,** what is said is precisely what is meant. For example, in the United States, Canada, Germany, and Switzerland, a verbal message carries the full meaning of the sentence. In this environment, business is typically done at arm's length and change is readily accepted.

In **high-context cultures,** such as those of East Asia, the Middle East, and North Africa, the entire context of the message—the message source, his or her standing in society or in the negotiating group, level of expertise, tone of voice, and body language—is meaningful. Marketing managers must evaluate the nonverbal

paralinguistics
The nonverbal aspects of speech that include intonation, accents, and the quality of voice.

appearances
An individual's physical attire and overall grooming.

olfactions
The use of odors to convey messages.

low-context cultures
Cultures in which what is said is precisely what is meant so that the verbal message carries the full meaning of the sentence.

high-context cultures
Cultures in which the context of a message—the message source, the source's standing in society or in a group, his or her expertise, tone of voice, and body language—are all meaningful parts of the message.

communication accompanying a message and interpret the full message accordingly. In low-context cultures, business is conducted via e-mail or on paper, in contract form, whereas in high-context cultures, it is more important to establish solid personal relationships and trust in the process of conducting business. In general, relationships are highly valued in high-context cultures, and on the social side of commerce, trust is crucial: A handshake in the Middle East is as important and reliable as a paper contract.

5-2b Religion

Religion defines a society's relationship to the supernatural and, as a result, determines dominant values and attitudes. Religious beliefs are important determinants of consumer behavior: Purchase motivation; consumption preferences and

> **religion**
> A society's relationship to the supernatural.

patterns; customs and business practices; attitudes toward authority, family, peers, and foreigners; as well as attitudes toward material possessions, cultural values, and norms, among others, can all be traced to religion.

Religion, then, can be linked to cultural behaviors that can, potentially, have an impact on business. For example:

- The Protestant religion stresses hard work and frugality and is linked to the development of capitalism and economic emancipation.
- Judaism, with its disdain for ignorance and sloth, stresses education and has led to industrial development.
- Islam dictates social etiquette and consumption, and bans the use of interest rates, affecting, respectively, the relationship between men and women in society and in the workplace (as will be seen in the section "Religion and Gender Roles"); discouraging the consumption of pork products and alcohol; and requiring procedures to reconcile Islamic banking laws with Western banking practices—by, for example, charging periodic fees, rather than interest.
- The Hindu religion encourages a family orientation, and requires following strict dietary rules, discouraging the consumption of animal products—beef, in particular.
- Buddhism stresses sufferance and avoidance of worldly desires, thus, at least in principle, rejecting most aspects of business.

Assuming that Buddhism has had a negative impact on marketing and economic development is erroneous, however, because a number of the more developed economies in Asia, for instance, are predominantly Buddhist (see Figure 5-3).

It is also erroneous to assume that Islamic law affects negatively all credit-granting activity or that, because of the restrictions imposed by gender isolation, marketing to women is impossible in Islamic societies—quite the contrary: These restrictions merely require the use of creative strategies and adaptation to local practices. For example, instead of selling on credit, businesses typically offer price discounts to individuals paying the full cash value, and no discount for those paying in installments. With regard to gender, women can use creative ways to interact (though not directly) with their male counterparts. The use of e-mail and the Internet has greatly facilitated the interaction between genders at work, even in the most conservative societies.

Finally, the restrictions on consumption do not mean that the respective products are prohibited in a particular country. For example, alcohol is available at

Figure 5-3: *Woman stirring the fire at a Tibetan Buddhist temple. Tibetan Buddhists are spiritual, as well as industrious and energetic.*

diplomatic and other expatriate shops even in one of the most strict Islamic countries, Saudi Arabia; it is also readily available at regular supermarkets in expatriate enclaves. In the United Arab Emirates, alcohol can be readily purchased for home consumption in Ajman, but not in Dubai, where one has to have a license. And driving with alcohol from Ajman to Dubai could potentially get you in trouble, as you would have to drive through Sharjah, where it is illegal to carry alcohol.

Pork and pork products are readily available in Islamic countries and in Israel, targeted to the non-Muslim and non-Jewish population, respectively, and beef is available in India for consumption by non-Hindu consumers. But even in India, fast-food chains having to choose between offending Hindu consumers, by offering beef, or Muslim consumers, by offering pork, have elected to offer chicken, lamb burgers, or vegetarian burgers instead. At sacred sites, McDonald's opened vegetarian-only restaurants in 2012.

Discussions of religions and their relationship to overall consumer/market behavior and, specifically, consumption are offered in the sections "Religion and Business Days," "Religion and Gender Roles," "Religion and Gift Giving," and "Religion and Marketing Practices."

Religion and Business Days

In countries where Christianity predominates, it is customary to work full days Monday through Friday and a half-day on Saturday. In Islamic countries, businesses are closed on Friday, the holy day of Islam. And, in Israel, the Shabbos (Saturday) is the day of worship when all businesses close.

In addition to noting business days, individuals doing business abroad must also note national holidays, when businesses are usually closed, and religious events/holidays. One religious observance that can substantially affect business operations is the month of Ramadan in countries where Islam is the national or a dominant religion. During Ramadan, observers are not allowed to eat until sundown. This is typically not a productive time in the Near East and North Africa. In Israel, no business is conducted during the High Holidays (Rosh Hashanah and Yom Kippur). Russia closes down from about December 29 until sometime close to mid-January, as Russians celebrate New Year's with Champagne, fireworks, and Christmas trees, and, later, the Orthodox Christmas, on January 7. Since the long-vacation tradition started in 2005, sociologists and economists found that the extended holiday resulted in disturbing consequences: economic slowdown, seasonal spikes in fires, domestic abuse, and alcohol poisoning. Cities in Russia offer people little to do inexpensively and in bad weather. After so many days of holidays, consumers run out of money and problems are likely to start. Other countries also experience long holidays. Unofficially, Europe slows down in July and August.[19]

During the regular work week, one should not be surprised if a Muslim with whom one is talking business abruptly ends the conversation by gathering his rug, kneeling, and praying; Muslims are required to pray five times a day at specific times. In this situation, a businessman should just find a seat and wait quietly until the man is finished.[20]

Religion and Gender Roles

In the most traditional Islamic countries, women's business activities are channeled toward interaction in a women-only environment. As such, a salesman cannot engage in door-to-door selling in Saudi Arabia, for instance, in an effort to appeal to the woman of the house. In this country, women depend on men in the family for simple activities, such as driving them to and from a destination; the law does not permit women to drive cars or even to walk alone, unaccompanied by a male relative. However, a woman forbidden from driving a car in Saudi Arabia will cheerfully take the wheel when abroad, confident that the ban is not religion-based. Afghan women educated before the Taliban rule know that banning girls from school is forbidden in Islam; this encourages Afghan women to seek knowledge from cradle to grave, from every source possible. [21]

In the more traditional Islamic societies, personal services can be performed only by individuals of the same gender. For example, women can bank only at women's banks, have their hair done only by other women, and so forth. The genders typically do not interact in traditional Islamic countries except within the family. Even in the less traditional Islamic countries, women at official dinners are often seated separately from men, in a separate dining room or area.

Although business is male-dominated in Islamic countries, it should, nevertheless, be noted that women have historically held prominent government positions in countries such as Turkey and Pakistan.

Religion and Gift Giving

A more in-depth discussion of gift giving is offered in Section 5-2e, "National/Regional Character." This section will address religious holidays as important opportunities for sales. In countries where Christianity is predominant, holidays such as Christmas and Easter constitute important dates for product sales. In addition to these holidays, Saint Nicholas is celebrated on December 6 in Holland and Belgium and gifts are offered to children, usually placed in their shoes, which are nicely lined up under a window. During the time predating these holidays, promotional activity (advertising and sales promotion) is intense. In Eastern Orthodox countries, such as Greece, Bulgaria, Serbia, Romania, Russia, and the other European countries of the Commonwealth of Independent States, name days (feast days of the saints after whom one was named) are celebrated, and gift giving is a must.

Diwali is an important Hindu holiday, when the believers engage in a Puja (prayer) and typically wear new clothing. This day also is an important marketing event. The Jewish holiday of Chanukah is an eight-day-long celebration and also an occasion for gift giving.

Religion and Marketing Practices

Firms often must adapt their offering to the local culture to address consumers' religious concerns. Fast-food restaurants operating in Israel find that they can better serve their Jewish consumers by offering ample choices of vegetarian food, which does not compromise consumer kosher requirements. Keeping kosher requires the separation of milk products and meat products and of the implements used to serve or process them; vegetarian products are pareve or neutral, with regard to kosher requirements.

With regard to advertising, substantial censoring occurs in many countries. In Saudi Arabia, women should not be portrayed in advertisements; however, it is appropriate to show the covered arms and wrists of a woman demonstrating product use. For magazines of Western provenance, censorship is enforced; for example, when such magazines are brought into the country by individuals or delivered by mail, any area of a woman's uncovered body and her face in photographs are blackened with a marker. In other Islamic countries, such as Malaysia, women should not be portrayed sleeveless, whereas in the streets of Turkey, one can actually see Wonderbra billboards.

5-2c Cultural Values

Values are enduring beliefs about a specific mode of conduct or desirable end-state; they guide the selection or evaluation of behavior and are ordered by importance in relation to one another to form a system of value priorities.[22]

Values guide individuals' actions, attitudes, and judgments, which are derived from and continuously modified through personal, social, and cultural learning, ultimately affecting their product preferences and their perception of products. Cultures are set apart by their *value systems*—the relative importance or ranking of values. Western cultures (North American and Western European) place more stress on success, achievement, and competitiveness, whereas Eastern cultures are more likely to be concerned with social welfare.[23] Examples of universally held values are provided by Rokeach[24] (see Figure 5-4). According to this classification, values can be related to goals *(terminal values)* or to the processes whereby one can attain those goals *(instrumental values)*.

Members of a culture share a system of meaning, a set of beliefs about what is right or wrong. Values are learned from those with whom individuals are in contact: family, friends, teachers, clergy, politicians, and the media. The process by which individuals learn the beliefs and behaviors endorsed by one's own culture is known as **en-**

> **values**
> Enduring beliefs about a specific mode of conduct or desirable end-state that guide the selection or evaluation of behavior.
>
> **enculturation**
> The process by which individuals learn the beliefs and behaviors endorsed by their own culture.
>
> **acculturation**
> The act of learning a new culture; encompasses intercultural interaction and adaptation.
>
> **assimilation**
> The act of abandoning all home-country traditions while learning a new culture.

Instrumental Values (the means by which terminal values are achieved)	Terminal Values (goals reached buy means of instrumental values)
Ambitious	A comfortable life
Broadminded	An exciting life
Capable	A sense of accomplishment
Cheerful	A world at peace
Clean	A world of beauty
Courageous	Equality
Forgiving	Family security
Helpful	Freedom
Imaginative	Inner harmony
Independent	Mature love
Intellectual	National security
Logical	Pleasure
Loving	Salvation
Obedient	Self-respect
Polite	Social recognition
Responsible	True friendship
Self-controlled	Wisdom

Figure 5-4: *Instrumental and terminal values (Rokeach).*

culturation. Learning a new culture, which most managers must when doing business abroad, is known as **acculturation.** Acculturation encompasses intercultural interaction and adaptation, and it includes the **assimilation** of a new culture, maintenance of the new culture, and resistance to both the new and old cultures. *Consumer acculturation* refers to contact with a new culture and the resulting change for consumers in terms of their approach to consumption in the new environment, whereas *marketer acculturation* refers to contact with a new culture and the resulting change for the marketer.[25]

Acculturation does not necessarily mean abandoning all home-country traditions; that is, it does not mean complete assimilation of the new culture. For example, recent Asian Indian immigrants to the United States are less likely to be assimilated in this culture because they maintain their original religious practices, language, food consumption, housing, and friendship patterns, as well as contact with India.[23]

Although Indian Americans are not easily assimilated, they are, nevertheless, acculturated in the U.S. culture: They consume fast food; shop at supermarkets; root for their favorite baseball or basketball team; and, overall, successfully integrate in the U.S. culture, without necessarily being assimilated. On the other hand, descendants of Japanese Americans tend to quickly acculturate to the U.S. culture, and typically by the third generation, they are likely to be fully assimilated.[26]

For the marketing practitioner, acculturation means adaptation to the new culture in a manner that would render him or her more readily capable of addressing the needs of the target market in that culture.

The United States is an avid exporter of its own culture, and one can argue that the rest of the world is acculturating to American trends. Figure 5-5a and b illustrates trends exported from the United States to the rest of the world.

5-2d Cultural Norms: Imperatives, Exclusives, and Adiaphoras

Norms are derived from values and are defined as rules that dictate what is right or wrong, acceptable or unacceptable. To be successful in the markets where the firm is currently operating or where it is planning a presence, marketers need to be capable of discerning between the following:

norms
Rules that dictate what is right or wrong, acceptable or unacceptable in a society.

- What an outsider must or must not do *(cultural imperative)*
- What locals may do but an outsider cannot *(cultural exclusive)*
- What an outsider may or may not do *(cultural adiaphora)*[27]

Familiarity with the first two constitutes a minimum requirement for survival in a new country environment. Although most local employees are willing to accept that their foreign counterpart is not fully familiar with local practices, working for a firm that is planning a strong commitment to the respective market may render local representatives and clients less tolerant of ignorance of local customs.

Figure 5-5a: Exporting culture: Trends are quickly transferred from the United States. European and Asian stores carry a vast array of inline skates, basketballs, and running shoes. Running has become a trendy activity among young professionals in the larger cities in China.

Figure 5-4-5b: Western brand-name sports clothing and equipment are in high demand in China.

Imperatives

Imperatives refer to what one must or must not do in a certain culture. Respecting rank and position, especially in more formal societies, is crucial in developing a lasting relationship. In Germany, for example, individuals in a close business relationship would address each other formally, by their last names, for decades. A representative of a U.S. firm working in this environment would need to be aware of this expectation. (Although this individual may be afforded some lenience, as a foreigner, if he or she did in fact address his or her counterpart by first name.)

> **imperatives**
> The norms referring to what individuals must or must not do in a certain culture.

Also, obtaining the appropriate approval before conducting a transaction constitutes an important consideration in doing business abroad. To conduct business in many developing countries, a company needs to become acquainted with local officials at all levels of government and to seek their expertise, as part of a close working relationship. If a company does not, any operation of the firm in the country could come under scrutiny and could be subjected to complications and higher costs. Obtaining the appropriate permissions before building on company-owned grounds, conducting marketing research, or approaching potential distributors is crucial in many countries. Outcomes of noncompliance would be costly delays, the use of expensive alternative middlemen or subcontractors, or even interdiction of operations.

Other examples of imperatives are provided by the special situation women in management positions face when dealing with clients in North Africa and the Middle East. For example, women are not allowed, by law, to drive or walk in public unaccompanied by a male in Saudi Arabia. They are not allowed in the streets or in shops by themselves. A female marketing manager sent to this country would have to make arrangements to be chauffeured to client firms and to be permanently in the company of a male in public. She also would have to wear clothing to cover her wrists, ankles, hair, and face. Finally, in many firms, males are not permitted to interact with females. For example, female accountants communicate with male colleagues by e-mail and exchange hand-written material by sending a tray back and forth through a wall that divides the genders.

Another cultural imperative is the appropriate presentation of business cards in Asia. In the United States, it is common to casually hand out cards with one hand. But in Asia, the business card must be offered and received with both hands. When presenting the card, it should be done in such a way that the recipient can read the name and title. One must acknowledge the card, review it and keep it on the table in front of the recipient until the meeting concludes. One must absolutely not write on the card. Above all, never place the card in a back pants pocket. It is also important, when conducting international business, to have a card printed in multiple languages. Professionals who practice international business in different countries should have cards that are printed in multiple languages.[28]

Exclusives

exclusives
The norms that refer to activities that are appropriate only for locals and from which individuals from a foreign country are excluded.

adiaphoras
The norms that refer to customs that a foreign national may engage in but is not necessarily expected to do so.

Exclusives refer to activities that are appropriate only for locals and from which an individual from a foreign country is excluded. For example, whereas a citizen of Kenya is likely to show allegiance to the government of Mwai Kibak by wearing a pin in his party's colors bearing his picture, a foreigner wearing such a pin would not only raise eyebrows, but he or she also may be perceived as attempting to interfere in the country's internal affairs.

Adiaphoras

Adiaphoras refer to customs that a foreign representative may engage in, but conformity in this respect is not required. Eating with chopsticks in East Asia, drinking banana beer in East Africa, and greeting a woman by kissing her hand in Hungary or Romania are all examples of adiaphoras.

5-2e National/Regional Character

Each country is thought to have a distinct set of behavior and personality characteristics, characteristics that may be shared by a number of countries in a certain geographic region.[29] This section discusses some of the **national and regional characters** that are likely to influence international marketing operations.

Time Orientation

national and regional characters
A set of behavior and personality characteristics shared by individuals of a certain country or region.

monochronic time
The interpretation of time as linear, such that individuals do one thing at a time, and in sequence.

polychronic time
The interpretation of time as fluid, such that individuals can accomplish multiple tasks at once.

time orientation
The manner in which individuals view time in relation to accomplishing tasks.

An aspect of time relevant to marketers is related to the manner in which tasks are approached. **Monochronic time** (m-time) is attributed to individuals who usually do one thing at a time in sequence. These individuals tend to be prompt and to adhere strictly to agendas; countries where individuals typically operate on monochronic time are Germany, Switzerland, Austria, Scandinavian countries, the countries of Benelux, the United States, and Canada. **Polychronic time** (p-time) is attributed to individuals who tend to perform multiple tasks at once; for these individuals, time is not linear but fluid. They are less likely to adhere to schedules, and they consider business as an opportunity for socializing. Countries where individuals operate on polychronic time are Italy, France, Spain, the countries of North Africa, the Middle East, and Latin America. This aspect of **time orientation** explains some of the examples provided in this section, describing attitudes toward time in different parts of the world.

North Americans like to plan their activities or to expedite matters by setting deadlines. Arabs facing deadlines, on the other hand, may feel threatened and would back into a corner.[30] A saying translated as "God-willing tomorrow" means, loosely, "It will happen soon." At times, businessmen in the Middle East arrive late for a meeting or do not arrive at all; they believe that Allah (God) controls time, so punctuality is unimportant. One should not be surprised if a Middle Eastern businessman is not ready for an appointment. It is imperative that one does not criticize this lateness or absenteeism because the individual would most likely become offended and resentful.[31] It should be noted, however, that this behavior cannot be generalized to all business conducted, especially in many of the larger cities or in international joint ventures operating in the region, where punctuality is mandatory and expected.

This behavior is not limited to the Middle Eastern context. In many countries in sub-Saharan Africa, Southern and Eastern Europe, and Latin America, delays are common. Greeks feel that setting time limits is not only constraining, but also insulting. Latinate cultures, such as those of Latin America and Southern Europe, do not put much premium on punctuality. When one is invited to a dinner party, arriving at the specified time indicates poor manners, suggesting that the person may be very hungry. Arriving half an hour after the indicated time is considered being on time, while arriving one hour late is still no reason to apologize, especially if one is socially prominent, or, in the United Arab Emirates, if one has *wasta* (high connections or social standing). In these same countries, however, for business meetings, it is safer to arrive within 15 minutes of the agreed-on time.

Business Hours and Business Days

The hours of doing business differ from country to country. The nine-to-five schedule prevalent in the United States is unusual in many countries. In countries where the climate is too hot to permit work at midday, businesses open early, at seven, and close for two to three hours at noon, to re-open again at two or three in the afternoon. This is also the case for businesses in Latin America and in many countries in Europe, where lunchtime is spent at home having a large meal with the family, followed frequently by a nap. Nowadays, however, at least in the EU, lunchtime is restricted to just one hour. Even the staunchest supporters of siesta time in Spain had to abandon hope for a long lunch break and conform to EU regulations.

In much of Europe, it is not particularly common to find someone at the office on Friday afternoons. In many European countries, there is a move toward shortening the work week. You can have a small flood in your apartment at noon on Friday, and your management company—or landlord, if you are renting—will not be bothered until Monday morning. For a fire, however, it is very possible that things are different.

As mentioned in Section 5-2b, "Religion," working days differ, depending on the dominant religion in the different countries. Where Christianity is dominant, Sunday is a rest day; in Islamic countries, businesses are closed on Fridays; and, in Israel, businesses are closed on Saturdays. In Islamic countries, during the month of Ramadan, observers are not allowed to eat until sundown, and during the regular work week, Muslims are required to pray five times a day. The best time to be in school in Europe is the spring semester, where, in addition to a two-week-long Easter vacation, students have a nice break in February, and then celebrate several saints' days in much of March and May. Needless to mention, business is not very active during those long breaks.

Finally, vacation time—designated in Europe as the latter part of July, the entire month of August, and the last two weeks in December—tends to be slow and not very productive for most business activity, with some exceptions.

Gift Giving

Knowing what gifts are appropriate to give to one's hosts is important. Some gifts are considered inappropriate in certain cultures, whereas others may be appropriate on certain occasions and inappropriate on others. In the United States, bringing a bottle of wine to one's host is perfectly appropriate; the same gesture would not be appropriate for a similar occasion in the Middle East, where Islamic religion prohibits alcohol. This rule holds true for any other gifts that may contain alcohol, such as chocolates. Also in the Middle East, bringing food or drink to the home of one's host could represent an insult, implying that the host's food is inadequate.[32]

Other inappropriate gifts are cutlery in Latin America, signifying cutting off a relationship,[33] or handkerchiefs in Latin America and in southern and eastern Europe, signifying a final, imposed separation, usually death; handkerchiefs and small hand towels are typically given as gifts at funerals of the Eastern Orthodox faith.

gift giving
The norms regarding the gifts that are appropriate to give to others.

Although an even number of flowers (e.g., a dozen roses) constitutes the norm for **gift giving** in the United States, in Eastern Europe, odd numbers are expected because even numbers of flowers such as calla lilies are offered only at funerals or religious commemorations. Giving one's host an even number of flowers or calla lilies could even trigger superstitious fears.

In developing countries, gifts of Western provenance such as good-quality pens or t-shirts with (preferably) English writing on them for children would probably meet with appreciation. So would some products that might be unimaginable as gifts in the United States, such as cigarettes, pantyhose, and hairspray. In fact, for more than two decades before the fall of communism, Kent cigarettes constituted the gift of choice in Romania, where they had the added value as commodity money.[34]

Even the manner in which gifts are given is important. For example, in the Middle East, gifts should be presented publicly to avoid the appearance of bribery, whereas, in Asia, gifts of significance should be given privately to avoid embarrassment.[35] Nevertheless, gifts such as pens with a company logo or insignia will be graciously accepted, regardless of timing. The Chinese may refuse a gift multiple times before finally accepting it. Make it known to your client that the gift is from your company. It is advisable to express appreciation when the gift is received.[36]

Some rituals related to the giving and acceptance of gifts also should be noted. For instance, in many cultures, it is customary for the recipient to refuse the gift so vigorously that the gift giver may be tempted to withdraw it. Such a gesture, however, will meet with a noted disappointment; it is merely appropriate for the recipient to refuse the gift and then accept it reluctantly, but humbly and kindly. The ready, eager acceptance of a gift may be considered as a sign of bad manners or a confirmation of gift expectations.

In the Middle East, the mere admiration of any object in an individual's home will obligate the host to yield that object to the admirer. Although it may be appropriate to decline, such a gesture may be perceived, to a degree, as a rejection of the host's hospitality.

The example below addresses the ethics of gift giving in many parts of the world.

Gift Giving or Bribe?

Bribing is a way of life in many countries. You cannot park your car without having to bribe the policeman wandering nearby. You cannot see a doctor without paying a bribe in addition to the doctor's fee. You cannot pass your medical boards, your entrance exam into college, or obtain an exit visa without bribing the appropriate authorities. Leaving the country as a tourist may mean bribing the baggage officer to put your luggage first in line to make sure you go through customs on time; bribing the customs officer to make sure that your luggage will not be turned upside down and inside out in the process of seeking that elusive illegal gizmo, and bribing the health officer who will permit your exit from the country for a destination that may require immunizations. Does this sound outrageous? In this author's experience, it can take one case of Johnny Walker Red and a case of Kent cartons to pass the university entrance exam; the alternative is working in a factory as an unskilled worker. Does that sound attractive to the average high-school graduate? It could take a pack of Kent or Marlboro cigarettes to have access to quality red meat—meat for which you must also pay. Or it could take two packs to see a marginally competent dentist—more, if he needs to work on your teeth.

Bribing is the price one pays for survival in Russia and the former Eastern Bloc, China, India, Egypt, Indonesia, and many other countries. In these countries, individuals and firms need to bribe to lead good lives, and firms need to bribe to make reasonable profits.

Gift Giving or Bribe? (contd.)

Companies attempt to institute a code of conduct worldwide. They have the same expectations for their operations in the United States and Singapore, where there is relatively strict adherence to norms that shun corruption, as for operations in countries where they would have to offer substantial gifts to government officials, such as expensive pens, watches, or even automobiles, depending on the importance of the contract. Caterpillar states in its code of conduct that, "in dealing with public officials, other corporations, and private citizens, we firmly adhere to ethical business practices. We will not seek to influence others, either directly or indirectly, by paying bribes or kickbacks, or by any other measure that is unethical or will tarnish our reputation for honesty and integrity. Even the appearance of such conduct must be avoided."[37]

The question remains: How can a U.S. company maintain such standards and work successfully within the constraints of the U.S. Foreign Corrupt Practices Act?

Socializing

If a marketing manager is planning on a working breakfast or a working lunch or on discussing business over dinner, as is often done in the United States, it may be useful to first inquire about the extent to which such a practice is appropriate in the country where business is being conducted. Although many business partners may have been schooled in the United States and will, consequently, readily acquiesce to these types of working circumstances, other parties involved may feel uneasy if business is conducted during a meal.

In the countries of South America and in many countries in Europe, a meal is widely seen as an important occasion to personally get to know one's business counterpart; hence, the suggestion of a working lunch or dinner may indicate to the local representative a lack of interest in establishing a friendly basis for the future working relationship. For example, it is important not to plan a business meeting at first with a Mexican businessman because he usually prefers to become acquainted with his counterpart in a social atmosphere before doing business.[38]

Similarly, when first meeting a businessman in the Middle East, one should not begin right away with talk about the business at hand; instead, one should initiate "positive small talk." The first meeting in the Middle East is only to start developing a friendly relationship, not to secure business dealings.[39]

In countries such as China, knowing one's business partner socially is imperative because the relationship is seen as a long-term engagement, rather than a short-term, transaction-related one.

Gender Roles

When one engages in business internationally, it is important to understand the role that women are expected to hold in the respective society. In the countries of East Africa and in parts of West Africa (Nigeria, for example), the role of women in business, particularly in running a business and sales, is crucial and more important than the role of men. Men still hold an important decision-making role, however, when it comes to major sales or purchase decisions. In India and Pakistan, women share responsibility with men in business. It is noteworthy, however, that women play a more limited role politically, where only a few hold notable positions, despite the famous women leaders who have left important legacies in these countries.

It is important to understand the family structure and authority patterns. Addressing the wrong person in the family may jeopardize transactions. In South America, South Korea, and Japan, it may be extremely difficult to undertake business transactions with women, because they are not readily accepted in certain business settings.[40]

And, in Islamic societies, it is inappropriate for genders to mix, due to religious restrictions. A discussion of **gender roles** in Islamic societies, as well as their impact on marketing activity and consumer behavior, was provided in Section 5-2b, "Religion."

gender roles
The roles that women and men are expected to hold in a society.

Status Concern and Materialism

Related to one's background is one's concern with status, or **status concern**—maintaining it or acquiring it—and with material possessions, or **materialism.** Individuals' concern with status is related to the values placed on symbols of status and on the attainment of high status. Often, the products consumed convey messages about the consumer in the same way that language does.[41] Status—like social class, to which it is related—is easier to transcend in industrially developed countries than in developing countries. In the United States, the Protestant ethic of hard work has led to centuries of individual prosperity and, at the individual level, status advancement; in the United States, it is not perceived as shameful for prominent politicians and businesspeople to refer back to their humble beginnings.

> **status concern**
> The value placed on symbols of status and on the attainment of high status in a society.
>
> **materialism**
> Individuals' degree of concern with material possessions.

In other countries, including Great Britain, Spain, and many developing countries, one's social class is rigid, and consequently, one's status remains stable. Expatriates from these countries who have transcended their social class in the United States, for example, typically hide their lower-class origins. Those from developing countries might state, for instance, that they came from the capital city when, in fact, they did not, because of the high likelihood of low-class provenance associated with a village origin.

Due to the influence of 800 years of Moorish control, Spain still has a rigid class structure described as feudal and autocratic.[42] However, countries that historically have had a polarized class structure (for example, Mexico) are developing a middle class or merchant class in response to expanding capitalism.[43]

Within the context of highly hierarchical Asian societies, individuals are always conscious of their place in a group, institution, or society and of the appropriate behavior, dress, and speech corresponding to status. They also are extremely aware of the need to maintain their own dignity and that of others. Careful attention is given to purchasing products whose price, brand, and packaging match one's social standing. In terms of personal appearance, the color, material, and style of clothing should match an individual's status, which is defined by age, gender, occupation, and so on. In Japan, for example, a married woman's kimono is much more subdued in color than a single woman's.

One region of the world where status has undergone great changes and individuals have lost "status security" is Central and Eastern Europe. A study on status changes in Romania[44] notes that status, guaranteed during the Communist regime by one's standing in the Communist Party and one's position in the government, has undergone significant changes with the advent of democracy. In the past, nomenklatura members (top communist leaders) enjoyed the highest status and living standard, despite the Communists' goal to abolish differences between social classes. In Russia, this same privileged class, before the fall of Communism, could rent 100 square meters of living space for a ridiculous price; had the free use of a country home (dacha) in a prime vacation spot; and conspicuously consumed caviar, sturgeon, salmon, and other goods not available at regular shops—things that the average person could not aspire to. They drove foreign cars with low-numbered license plate numbers (indicative of high governmental position) at high speeds and without concern for traffic laws, dressed extravagantly, and conspicuously flaunted their Western possessions.[45]

With the transition to a market economy, former party members and intellectuals found that, to survive, they had to accept jobs below their former status, as taxi drivers, sales clerks, and street vendors. At the same time, individuals who had previously held a low status, such as gypsies and blue-collar workers who started lucrative businesses, prospered and, as a consequence, engaged in consumption behavior beyond anything imagined during the days of Communism. Take, for example, Romanian George (Gigi) Becali, a member of the European Parliament since 2009. Becali made his fortune by trading land on the outskirts of Bucharest that he did not initially own, with prime land owned by the Romanian Army. Becali was the majority owner of the Steaua Bucuresti soccer team, one of Romania's top teams, for several years, and, in 2008, he tried to open the Becali Bank by investing 30 million euros (the Romanian government did not give him permission to do so). Becali maintains a high profile by endorsing nationalist causes (he represents a nationalist party in the European Parliament), making derogatory anti-Semitic, xenophobic and homophobic statements, and getting into trouble that has landed him in prison. Nevertheless, he is one of the important faces of Romanian post-Communist elite.

Other Cultural and Behavioral Differences

Many other national and regional character differences also require companies to adapt their marketing practices. For example, as Figures 5-6 and 5-7a and b illustrate, people use different means of transportation to purchase products and get about in their daily lives. In the United States, most marketing strategies address a driving public, the shopper who can park at the supermarket and load the contents of an extra-large shopping cart into the family van. In much of the rest of the world, things are quite different. For example, Western Europeans might take the bus or their bicycles to the supermarket and use automobiles only to drive to out-of-town destinations. In Central Asia and sub-Saharan Africa, buses with crowded upper-level decks or trucks with protective grids of bars are used for local and long-distance transportation. These consumers are likely to transport goods in crowded environments where they must also keep their balance. A typical fast-food drive-through is not likely to be the most efficient means for serving these consumers.

Figure 5-6: *For visits to the local supermarkets, consumers will either walk or take the bus or local train everywhere except in the United States, where most marketing strategies address a driving public. In China, at rush hour, you can count on buses to come one after the other to pick up their passengers.*

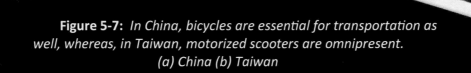

Figure 5-7: *In China, bicycles are essential for transportation as well, whereas, in Taiwan, motorized scooters are omnipresent. (a) China (b) Taiwan*

5-3 Cultural Variability

Cultural variability is the term used to identify differences between cultures using the Hofstede dimensions. All cultures can be classified based on a number of dimensions. Each dimension should be thought of as a continuum. Section 5-3a presents the Hofstede dimensions: power distance, uncertainty avoidance, masculinity, and individualism.[46]

5-3a The Hofstede Dimensions

Power Distance

Power distance refers to the manner in which interpersonal relationships are formed when differences in power are perceived. In some cultures, a vertical relationship is typical, whereas, in others, relationships are based on equality and informality. In the United States, for instance, individuals customarily address each other on a first-name basis, regardless of rank. Top managers often illustrate their solidarity with the lower ranks by engaging in work activities that they do, going to the plant floor or eating in the workers' cafeteria. Similarly, in Ireland, professional titles are not prevalent in business culture; in fact, they are perceived as arrogant. In the Czech Republic, however, titles are extremely important distinctions and are essential when conducting business.[47]

> **cultural variability**
> The classification of cultures on a number of dimensions, or continuums; Hofstede classified cultures on the dimensions of collectivism,

> **power distance**
> The manner in which interpersonal relationships are formed when differences in power are perceived.

Similarly, in Latin America, Eastern Europe, the Middle East, it is a flagrant error to address a superior informally or for a superior to mingle with underlings. In these countries, most decisions are determined by the upper-level executives and only much later disseminated to individuals in the lower positions. This is one of the reasons why, in this environment, it is particularly important to address the senior management first, before addressing other individuals in the company.[48] When doing business in a country where relationships are of a hierarchical nature, it is important to find a counterpart in the partner firm or the individual in the government responsible for regulating the activities of the firm before even approaching the business in question.

Uncertainty Avoidance

Uncertainty avoidance refers to the extent to which individuals feel threatened by uncertainty, risk, and ambiguous situations and thus adopt beliefs, behaviors, and institutions that help them to avoid the uncertainty. In countries where uncertainty avoidance is high, there is a feeling that what is different is dangerous: Consumers are resistant to change and focused on risk avoidance and reduction. In cultures low in uncertainty avoidance, there is a feeling that what is different, such as new products and services, is interesting and worth exploring. [49] In this regard, it is interesting to observe the changes taking place in the transition economies of China and Central and Eastern Europe. Traditionally, these cultures are high in uncertainty avoidance, primarily due to the Communist system's assurances of work, a home, and a minimal standard of living. During the transition period, however, attitudes toward risk manifested themselves strongly, with some (especially the older generations) holding on to the status quo and rejecting privatization and change, and with other, younger individuals taking unwarranted risks. Overall, most in this region continue to manifest symptoms of high uncertainty avoidance, electing (or supporting, in the case of China) conservative, welfare-oriented governments. Despite this trait, however, with regard to consumption, consumers here are eager to experience new products from different parts of the world and are open to new market offerings, such as food establishments and other services.

> **uncertainty avoidance**
> The extent to which individuals are threatened by uncertainty, risk, and ambiguous situations and thus adopt beliefs, behaviors, and institutions that help them to avoid the uncertainty.

In another example, Belgian consumers, who are higher in uncertainty avoidance, prefer insurance that costs more but that does not have variable fees, whereas the Dutch, who are low on uncertainty avoidance, prefer cheaper insurance with variable fees. [50]

Masculinity

Masculinity is the degree to which a national culture is characterized by assertiveness rather than nurturing. **Femininity** is the degree to which a national culture is characterized by nurturing rather than by assertiveness. Masculine societies emphasize values such as wealth, material success, ambition, and achievement, whereas, in feminine societies, benevolence, equality, caring for the weak, and preserving the environment are emphasized. [51] Another key distinction that characterizes these types of societies is that masculine societies "live to work," whereas feminine societies "work to live."

> **masculinity**
> The degree to which a national culture is characterized by assertiveness, rather than nurturing.

> **femininity**
> The degree to which a national culture is characterized by nurturing, rather than assertive, values.

In masculine societies, such as those in Australia, Canada, Great Britain, and the United States, successful marketing strategies focus on consumers' achievement motivation: Marketing communications should stress personal accomplishment and have ego appeal. In feminine societies, such as in Asian cultures, marketing strategies should steer away from a materialist, acquisitive focus and, instead, appeal to consumers' sense of good will.

Individualism versus Collectivism

Individualism refers to the degree to which people in a country prefer to act as individuals, in their self-interest, rather than as members of a group, which is a characteristic of collectivist societies. In individualist cultures, such as those of the United States, Great Britain, and Australia, the social fabric and group norms are much looser: People tend not to follow social norms but, rather, make decisions and initiate behaviors independently. [52] Such cultures stress the individuals' ability to achieve personal goals and make their way in life on their own and, in the process, seek self-fulfillment and excitement. Collectivist cultures, such as those of Latin America, Asia, and the Middle East, stress subordination to the collective (group, business, family) and require acting in the interest of the group rather than in one's self-interest. Cultures tend to evolve from collectivist to individualistic as countries become more industrialized, [53] and as individuals become less conformist.

> **individualism**
> The degree to which people in a country prefer to act as individuals, in their self-interest.

Although Asia, with 50 percent of the world's population, is culturally more heterogeneous than, for example, Europe, the emphasis on social harmony is an overriding and unifying belief across all societies. Asian societies are fundamentally collectivist. This is considered necessary in order not to disturb so-

collectivism
The degree to which individuals prefer to act in the interest of the group, rather than in their own self-interest.

cial harmony. Such thinking grounded in Confucianism, Buddhism, and Islam contrasts sharply with Western individualism. The difference is profound and has major implications for consumer behavior. Whereas Asians tend to identify themselves in terms of their social frame or relationships, Westerners define themselves in terms of personal attributes or achievements. Despite the fact that individualism has come to be considered a natural component of "modern" society, Asian cultures are now challenging this assumption. Japan, a "modern," industrialized nation by any standard, is still strongly collectivist. South Korea, Singapore, and Taiwan combine features of modern societies with a firmly entrenched **collectivism** orientation.[54] See Table 5-1 for the cultural positioning of countries on the Hofstede dimensions.

TABLE 5-1 Expected Country Dimension Scores (0 = Low; 100 = High)

	Uncertainty Avoidance	Power Distance	Masculinity	Individualism
100				
	Japan	China	United States	United States Australia
	Eastern Europe	Eastern Europe	Argentina	United Kingdom
50				
	United States	Germany, United States	China	China
1				

International Marketing Illustration 5-1 discusses one resource that students can use to learn more about the culture within a country or world region: the CultureGram.

International Marketing Illustration 5-1
Learning about National and Regional Culture

Numerous resources can be used to learn about national and regional cultures. A valuable resource is the CultureGram produced by Brigham Young University. In addition to placing the country on the world map, it also provides country background information, such as information on the land, climate, and history, as well as information on the people—population, language, religion, general attitudes, and personal appearance. Information on customs and courtesies includes greetings, gestures, visiting, and eating, whereas lifestyle information addresses issues about the family, dating and marriage, diet, recreation, the arts, holidays, and commerce. Society related discussions address the government, the economy, transportation, communication, and health. The CultureGram also has an events and trends section, which offers recipes and information on local famous people, the correct pronunciation of the country's name in the national language, and the national anthem.

To illustrate, for Bulgaria, the site offers a discussion of the preponderance of folk dance and traditions in the lives of Bulgarians. It also offers advice on interpreting gestures: For Bulgarians, "yes" is indicated by shaking the head from side to side, whereas "no" is expressed with one or two nods. The site also advises that leaving a party early is considered inappropriate and rude. In another example, we learn that Bahrain consists of thirty three islands, of which only 3 are inhabited. Bahraini citizens are highly educated in the region, but they are the minority in a country where more than two thirds do not hold Bahraini citizenship. Access CultureGrams at www.culturegrams.com.

Source: Additional sources for national culture information are the *Country Reports* of the Economist Intelligence Unit (www.eiu.com), the Department of Commerce *Country Commercial Guides* (www.ita.doc.gov), and the Sigma Two Group-Intercultural Training for International Managers (www.internationalbusinesscenter.org), among others.

5-4 Cultural Change and Marketing

Being aware of the particulars of any culture may not be enough to succeed. Culture is undergoing continuous change all over the world as a result of external influences. For example, a manager obtains textbook training in business practices in a certain country. That textbook will probably not fully prepare the manager for all the changes in the cultural environment of the respective country that he or she can expect. Cultural training should involve immersion in the culture of the country, an understanding that goes beyond the world of business. Companies that are aware of the importance of such training go to great lengths to offer it. Consider, for instance, the case of Samsung, which spends $80,000 a year per person for employees to go abroad and literally goof off (go to malls, watch people, etc.), convinced that cultural immersion is likely to better help them understand what the customers of that country want.[55]

To appeal efficiently to a new market, marketers need to identify the symbolic elements and cultural meanings that are important to a market segment and use them effectively in creating the marketing mix. For example, the meaning of a fast-food joint in the United States is quite different from its meaning in other cultures. McDonald's and Pizza Hut are perceived in some cultures as trendy, fashionable places (see Figure 5-8). Marketers can use the following checklist[56] to integrate culture when designing a marketing strategy:

1. *Research* the present and possible symbolic elements and cultural meanings in consumers' lives.
2. *Identify* cultural meanings and physical properties of the product.
3. *Design* the product and packaging accordingly.
4. *Design* the marketing campaign using symbolic elements that carry cultural meanings.

Figure 5-8: *The cultural meanings of McDonald's and Pizza Hut vary from country to country. In emerging and in other developing markets, they are not just fast-food joints; they are the hip place to take a girlfriend out on a date, the location where business is transacted, or where lifetime commitments are celebrated. The McDonald's in this photograph is in the center of Tallinn, Estonia.*

5-5 The Self-Reference Criterion and Ethnocentrism

When interpreting cultural phenomena in other countries, marketers must avoid the unconscious reference to their own value systems, to their own way of doing things; that is, they should refrain from resorting to the **self-reference criterion**, as defined by Lee.[57] Instead, they should assess each culture as objectively as possible. Lee suggests a four-step correction mechanism to address individuals' tendency to resort to the self-reference criterion, which is herein adapted to a marketing context:

1. Define the marketing problem or goal in terms of one's home-country's cultural traits, norms, and values.
2. Define the marketing problem or goal in terms of the host-country's cultural traits, norms, and values.
3. Isolate the self-reference criterion influence and evaluate it to understand how it affects the marketing problem.
4. Redefine the marketing problem and, in the process, eliminate the self-reference criterion influence. Solve the marketing problem based solely on the unique conditions of the host country.

> **self-reference criterion**
> Individuals' conscious and unconscious reference to their own national culture, to home country norms and values,

Negative outcomes of using the self-reference criterion are inflamed nationalist feelings or antiforeigner feelings targeting a particular company—even if the foreign company relies extensively on local suppliers and locally manufactures most products. The French often perceive Americans as imposing their way of life and their culture on the rest of the world without any sensitivity to the local culture. For the French, symbolizing these views are, among others, McDonald's, Coca-Cola, and Disneyland Resort Paris; Disney has often been referred to as an attempt to "McDonaldize" France. Americans are successfully selling their fast food in a country where food preparation and serving

constitute an art form; they are successfully selling mindless Hollywood action movies in a country that prizes high culture and art films; and, more recently, Americans have been arm-wrestling Europe, where natural foods are prized, into permitting the imports of hormone-treated beef. As expected, Gallic resentment and retaliation are omnipresent: A few years ago, 150 farmers in southwestern France (in Auch) occupied a McDonald's restaurant and slapped posters that said "No to the American dictatorship" and "No hormones in foie gras country." Similarly, one restaurant, Creperie Domino, charged $8 per Coca-Cola bottle, instead of a little more than $1 (its regular price).[58]

Worldwide, there is a decline in the number of people who like and use, or desire to use, American brands: NOP World, a global research firm, found that McDonald's, Coca-Cola, Microsoft, and Nike were among the brands that suffered a decline in popularity and international consumer trust. A survey of 30,000 consumers in 30 countries outside North America found that the total number of consumers who use U.S. brands fell from 30 percent to 27 percent, whereas non-American brands remained stable. Blame can be attributed to U.S. actions in Iraq, to the controversy surrounding the Kyoto agreement, and a general disaffection with U.S. culture and policies.[59]

> **ethnocentrism**
> The belief that one's culture is superior to another and that strategies used in one's home country (presumably a developed country) will work just as well internationally.

Ethnocentrism is a belief related to the self-reference criterion, that a particular culture is superior to another and that strategies used in the home country (presumably a developed country) will work just as well abroad. Many examples illustrate the fallacy of this strategy in situations in which it is unwarranted. Attempting to sell clothes dryers in rapidly developing markets where the cost of electricity continues to remain high relative to a family's monthly income has resulted in failure, as have television advertisements aired in a conservative country, depicting a woman describing in detail the use of a feminine hygiene product.

A related concept is *consumer ethnocentrism,* the belief that purchasing foreign products is wrong because it hurts the domestic economy, causes loss of jobs, and is unpatriotic.[60] Although ethnocentric attitudes are, to a degree, related to the standard of living and economic performance in a country at a particular point in time, it is important to note that consumer ethnocentrist tendencies frequently affect foreign firms. The North American Free Trade Agreement was, to a certain extent, diminished by ethnocentric feelings in the United States.

5-6 The Global Consumer Culture

Global consumer segments—consumers who associate similar meanings with certain places, people, and things—have developed worldwide and, with them, a global consumer culture. The global consumer culture is defined in terms of shared sets of consumption-related symbols, such as brands, and consumption activities that are meaningful to segment members. A global consumer culture is often attributed to the diffusion of entertainment from the United States to the rest of the world and to the dominance of English in both business and entertainment.[61] For example, MTV reaches viewers everywhere in the world, and, among teens, 8 out of their top 10 activities are media related. The direct outcome of this is a "global mall," whereby teens display the signs of this global culture by buying CDs, hamburgers, jeans, and running shoes—veritable emblems of the teen global culture.[62] In Africa, this distinctly American music video channel now beams a line-up of local pan-African stars and several U.S. stars to audiences in 48 of the 53 African nations using both satellite and terrestrial television stations. MTV Base Africa is changing the continent, and it has an impact on the 680 million people living in sub-Saharan Africa. Wireless service and deregulation in the industry have connected Africa more than ever before, affording even poor Africans access to the Internet. Even the most remote slums boast a few Internet cafés in mud homes or in converted shipping containers.[63]

The global consumer culture has been identified as involving one or more of these trends:

- The proliferation of transnational firms and their brands worldwide and the related globalized capitalism
- Globalized consumerism and the desire for material possessions (the desire for fashionable or novel goods used to gain status and social acceptance)
- Global consumption homogenization, wherein consumers worldwide eat similar foods, desire similar brand names, and are exposed to the same entertainment

In addition to the described consumption behavior, certain gift-giving occasions have been adopted in many parts of the world where both traditions and religion are different from those in the industrialized Western world. Examples of such occasions are Christmas in Muslim countries where gifts are exchanged on New Year's Day, Valentine's Day in many countries of the world (including most of Western Europe) where it was not previously celebrated, and, increasingly, Halloween. Santa Claus (even in Buddhist, Muslim, and animist cultures), much like products such as Coca-Cola, represents the symbol of a consumer paradise widely imagined to exist in the United States.[64]

In response to an increasingly global consumer culture, marketers have devised marketing programs that appeal to individuals who would like to feel one with this culture. Among such messages are "United Colors of Benetton," "ADM, Supermarket to the World," and Philips' "Let's Make Things Better," which feature individuals and synopses from different countries. Such strategies are examples of **global consumer culture positioning** and identify a particular brand as a symbol of a given global culture.[65] Such positioning is typically accompanied by the extensive use of English in environments where English is not widely spoken: As the primary language of international business, the mass media, and the Internet, English currently represents modernism and internationalism to many consumers. It is also accompanied by aesthetic styles, which increasingly belong to the global consumer culture: for example, the use of widely known spokespeople in advertising.[66] Examples of such endorsers are Halle Berry for Revlon, Billy Zane and international actress Chiara Muti from Italy, and Aishwarya Rai from India for Longines, the high-end watch maker; or, a few years ago, Harrison Ford for Kirin Beer and Jodie Foster for different Japanese soft drinks.

According to Alden et al., this strategy is different from **local consumer culture positioning**, which associates the brand with local cultural meanings, reflects the local culture, is portrayed as consumed by locals, and is depicted as locally produced for local people. For instance, Chevy trucks and Dr. Pepper have been positioned as part of the "American" way of life.

The strategy also differs from **foreign consumer culture positioning**, whereby the brand is positioned as symbolic of a foreign culture. For example, Hermès in the United States is positioned as a desirable French product. Yoplait yogurt also empha-

> **global consumer culture positioning**
> Marketing programs appealing to individuals who want to be part of a global consumer culture by purchasing a brand that is a symbol of that culture.
>
> **local consumer culture positioning**
> Positioning that associates the brand with local cultural meanings, reflecting the local culture, and portrayed as consumed by locals and depicted as locally produced for local people.

foreign consumer culture positioning
The positioning of a particular brand as symbolic of a desired foreign culture.

sizes its French origin with the slogan "C'est si bon"— "it's so good"—(whereas, in France, its slogan is "La petite fleur"—"the little flower"). And men in lederhosen sing into the Alphorn with the Matterhorn mountain as the backdrop for the Swiss Ricola cough drops, while Juan Valdez stresses the quality of pure Colombian coffee. In Japan, Coca-Cola advertising shows young Japanese driving on American desert roads, stopping for a drink at a remote truck stop, and instantly gaining locals' acceptance by consuming Coke. All these examples illustrate successful foreign consumer culture positioning strategies, focusing on desirable countries of origin for the different product categories.

Summary

Identify the elements of culture and examine how they affect marketing practices around the world. Culture, a society's personality, represents a totality of shared meanings, rituals, norms, and traditions shared by members of society. Its elements are language (verbal, written, and nonverbal), religion, values, and norms. They have a significant impact on consumer behavior and marketing practices in general, delineating gender roles, rules for gift giving, and appropriate behaviors in a business setting; they also create rules for individual interaction. International marketing managers must be familiar with local culture, practices, and expectations and behave in accordance with those rules.

Describe national and regional character based on dimensions such as time orientation, business practices, gift giving, socializing, gender roles, and materialism. Traits such as time orientation, degree of status concern, and materialism at the societal level; rules for socializing; and gender roles are important to master for one to be able to perform optimally in a country's environment. Such knowledge should be used in determining the appropriate settings for transactions, the appropriate messages that should be used in advertising, and, in general, all interactions with local society.

Discuss cultural variability in terms of the Hofstede dimensions with appropriate examples and address cultural change in a marketing context. Hofstede suggested four dimensions for classifying cultures that could benefit the marketing manager in deciding on the appropriate behavior. Those dimensions are power distance, which refers to interpersonal relationships when there are differences in power between the respective individuals; uncertainty avoidance, which refers to the extent to which individuals take risk in the respective culture; masculinity, which is the degree to which a culture is characterized by assertiveness; and individualism—the degree to which people prefer to act as individuals in their own self-interest—and collectivism—the degree to which people prefer to act as members of a group.

Address the self-reference criterion and ethnocentrism and describe how they impede mutual understanding and cooperation, with direct negative effects on marketing practices. Two impediments to cross-cultural relationships are the self-reference criterion, which is the unconscious reference to one's own values and way of doing things, and ethnocentrism, the belief that one's culture is superior to others. Marketing managers must refrain from using self-reference or from adopting ethnocentric attitudes in the process of making decisions related to local operations.

Describe the global consumer culture as it manifests itself around the world. The advent of a global consumer culture has created important opportunities for multinational firms: similar segments of consumers who share brand preferences; share a taste for similar consumer goods and services, such as fast food and entertainment; and respond similarly to a company's marketing strategies. Marketers are using three strategies to target consumers: global consumer culture positioning, which identifies brands as symbols of a particular global consumer culture; local consumer culture positioning, which targets the local consumer culture and portrays products as consumed by local consumers; and foreign consumer culture positioning, whereby the brand is positioned as symbolic of a foreign culture.

Key Terms

acculturation
adiaphoras
appearances
assimilation
chronemics
collectivism
cultural variability
culture
ecology
enculturation
ethnocentrism
exclusives
femininity
foreign consumer culture positioning
gender roles
gift giving
global consumer culture positioning
haptics
high-context cultures
ideology
imperatives
individualism
kinesics
language

local consumer culture positioning
low-context cultures
masculinity
materialism
monochronic time
national and regional character
nonverbal communication
norms
oculesics
olfactions
orientations
paralinguistics
polychronic time
postures
power distance
proxemics
religion
self-reference criterion
social structure
spoken/written language
status concern
time orientation
uncertainty avoidance
values

Discussion Questions

1. How does religion affect international marketing and international business operations in a target market?
2. What are the different cultural norms and values, and how do they differ around the world?
3. Margaret Hogan is an international marketing manager planning to accept an assignment representing her company interests in Saudi Arabia. What are some of the cultural elements that will have an impact on her performance? How can she best prepare for this assignment?
4. Many messages aimed at consumers in Central and Eastern Europe have a status message. Why? If you were assigned to work in this environment, would you, as a manager, show solidarity with the workers and symbolically work alongside them in the factory? Explain.
5. How do managers use the global consumer culture to position their goods in the local market?

Chapter Quiz

True/False
1. A sari is considered appropriate business attire for women in South Asia.
True
Rationale: The sari is appropriate business attire for Indian women.
Section 5-2a, "Language"

2. In high-context cultures, what is said is precisely what is meant.
False
Rationale: In low-context cultures, what is said is precisely what is meant. In high-context cultures, the context of the message, including the characteristics and role of the sender, is equally meaningful.
Section 5-2a, "Language"

3. Little attention to business is paid during the High Holidays month in the Islamic religion, when observers are not allowed to eat until sundown.
False
Rationale: The month of Ramadan in the Islamic religion is demanding of observers, who are not allowed to eat or drink until sundown. The High Holidays, Rosh Hashanah and Yom Kippur, are Jewish holidays.
Section. 5-2b, "Religion"

4. Acculturation is the learning of beliefs and behaviors endorsed by one's own culture.
False
Rationale: Enculturation is defined as the learning of beliefs and behaviors endorsed by one's own culture.
Section 5-2c, "Cultural Values"

5. Learning a new culture is known as assimilation.
False
Rationale: Acculturation is defined as learning a new culture. International managers need to acculturate to new cultures when they are posted abroad.
Section 5-2c, "Cultural Values"

6. In Japan, Coca-Cola advertising that includes a Japanese man driving through American desert roads is an example of foreign consumer culture positioning.
True
Rationale: The brand is positioned as symbolic of a foreign culture in foreign consumer culture positioning.
Section 5-6, "The Global Consumer Culture"

Multiple Choice
1.   Which of the following is a terminal value?
        a.   Ambition
        b.   Cleanliness
        c.   Freedom
        d.   Joy
Answer c is correct.
Rationale: Freedom is an important terminal value—a value that can be related to the goal of freedom.
Section 5-2c, "Cultural Values"

2.   The process by which individuals learn the beliefs and behaviors endorsed by their own culture is
        a.   acculturation.
        b.   enculturation.
        c.   assimilation.
        d.   none of the above.

Answer b is correct.
Rationale: Enculturation refers to learning one's own culture better and further probing into its different cultural elements.
Section 5-2c, "Cultural Values"

3.   The norms referring to what individuals must or must not do in certain cultures are
   a.   adiaphoras.
   b.   exclusives.
   c.   imperatives.
   d.   none of the above.

Answer c is correct.

Rationale: A cultural exclusive refers to what locals may do but an outsider cannot, whereas adiaphora refers to what an outsider may or may not do. Imperatives refer to what one must or must not do in a culture.

Section 5-2d, "Cultural Norms: Imperatives, Exclusives, and Adiaphoras"

Endnotes for Chapter 5

1.   *EIU ViewsWire*, "India Company: Coca-Cola's Long Road to Profit," March 12, 2003.

2.   http://news.com.com/How+eight+pixels+cost+Microsoft+millions/2100-1014_3-5316664.html

3.   Lisa Penaloza and Mary C. Gilly, "Marketer Acculturation: The Changer and the Changed," *Journal of Marketing,* Vol. 63, No. 3, July 1999, pp. 84–104.

4.   Raj Mehta and Russell W. Belk, "Artifacts, Identity and Transition: Favorite Possessions of Indians and Indian Immigrants to the United States," *Journal of Consumer Research,* Vol. 17, March 1991, pp. 398–411.

5.   Michael R. Solomon, *Consumer Behavior,* Fourth Edition, Upper Saddle River, NJ: Prentice Hall, 1999.

6.   Jane Perlez, "Muslim's Veils Test Limits of Britain's Tolerance," *The New York Times*, Online Edition, June 22, 2007.

7.   Jean-Claude Usunier, *International Marketing—A Cultural Approach,* Upper Saddle River, NJ: Prentice Hall, 1993.

8.   Lecture on Chinese Calligraphy, Prof. Tang Yi-Ming, National Chengchi University, Taiwan, May 18, 2007.

9.   For this and many other examples of blunders of translation, see David A. Ricks, *Blunders in International Business,* Oxford, U.K.: Blackwell Publishers, 1993.

10.   Sami Abbasi and Kenneth W. Holman, "Business Success in the Middle East," *Management Decision,* Vol. 31, No. 1, 1993, pp. 55–59.

11.   Mark Lee Levine, "The Impact of Cultural Mistakes on International Real Estate Negotiations, *Real Estate Issues*, Vol. 31, No. 2, Fall 2006, pp. 25–30.

12.   Ibid.

13.   David A. Ricks, *Blunders in International Business,* Oxford, U.K.: Blackwell Publishers, 1993.

14.   Ibid.

15.   Ibid.

16.   Roger Colles, "Spain—A Hot Prospect," *Resident Abroad,* November 1993, pp. 16–20.

17.   In countries where this type of dress is expected of women, those same women will be encountered only in a business environment that excludes the presence of males.

18.   E. T. Hall, *Beyond Culture,* Garden City, NY: Anchor Press, 1976.

19.   Steven Lee Myers, "Russica's Extended Winter Holidays: A Binge of Drinking and Spending," *New York Times*, January 8, 2007, A4.

20.   Abbasi and Holman, "Business Success in the Middle East," pp. 55–59.

21.   http://www.islamfortoday.com/ruqaiyyah09.htm

22.   See Milton J. Rokeach, *The Nature of Human Values,* New York: The Free Press, 1973; and Jan-Benedict E. M. Steenkamp, Frenkel ter Hofstede, and Michel Wedel, "A Cross-Cultural Investigation into the Individual and National Cultural Antecedents of Consumer Innovativeness," *Journal of Consumer Research,* Vol. 63, April 1999, pp. 55–69.

23.   Solomon, *Consumer Behavior,* 1999.

24.   Rokeach, *The Nature of Human Values,* 1973.

25.   Penaloza and Gilly, "Marketer Acculturation," pp. 84–104.

26.   Mehta and Belk, "Artifacts, Identity and Transition," pp. 398–411.

26.   See Darrell Montero, "The Japanese Americans: Changing Patterns of Assimilation over Three Generations," *American Sociological Review,* Vol. 46, December 1981, pp. 829–839; and Mehta and Belk, "Artifacts, Identity and Transition," pp. 398–411.

27.   Ricks, *Blunders in International Business,* 1993.

28.   Mark Lee Levine, "The Impact of Cultural Mistakes on International Real Estate Negotiations, *Real Estate Issues*, Vol. 31, No. 2, Fall 2006, pp. 25–30.

29.   Terry Clark, "International Marketing and National Character: A Review and Proposal for Integrative Theory," *Journal of Marketing,* No. 54, October 1990, pp. 66–79.

30.   Ricks, *Blunders in International Business,* 1993.

31.   Abbasi and Holman, "Business Success in the Middle East," pp. 55–59.

32.   Ricks, *Blunders in International Business,* 1993.

33.   Ibid.

34.   Guliz Ger, Russell W. Belk, and Dana-Nicoleta Lascu, "The Development of Consumer Desire in Marketizing and Developing Economies: The Case of Romania and Turkey," in L. McAllister (ed.), *Advances in Consumer Research,* Association for Consumer Research, Vol. 20, 1993, pp. 102–107.

35.   Ricks, *Blunders in International Business,* 1993.

36.   http://www.buyusa.gov/iowa/etiquette.html

37.   www.cat.com

38.   Perry A. Trunick, "Culture and Custom Combine with Logistics," *Transportation and Distribution,* Vol. 35, No. 1, January 1994, p. 38.

39.   Abbasi and Holman, "Business Success in the Middle East," pp. 55–59.

40.   Mark Lee Levine, "The Impact of Cultural Mistakes on International Real Estate Negotiations, *Real Estate Issues*, Vol. 31, No. 2, Fall 2006, pp. 25–30.

41.   David K. Tse, Russell W. Belk, and Nan Zhou, "Becoming a Consumer Society: A Longitudinal and Cross-Cultural Content Analysis of Print Ads from Hong Kong, the People's Republic of China, and Taiwan," *Journal of Consumer Research,* Vol. 15, March 1989, pp. 457–472.

42.   Cyndee Miller, "Going Overseas Requires Marketers to Learn More than a New Language," *Marketing News,* Vol. 28, No. 7, March 28, 1994, pp. 8–10.

43.   Trunick, "Culture and Custom Combine with Logistics," p. 38.

44.   Dana-Nicoleta Lascu, Lalita A. Manrai, and Ajay K. Manrai, "Interpersonal Influences on Shopping Behavior: A Cross-Cultural Analysis of Polish and Romanian Consumers," in J. Bloemer, J. Lemmink, and H. Kasper (eds.), *European Marketing Academy Proceedings,* Vol. 3, 1994, pp. 1369–1371.

45.   Ibid.

46.   Geert Hofstede, *Culture's Consequences: International Differences in Work-Related Values,* London: Sage, 1984.

47.   http://www.buyusa.gov/iowa/etiquette.html

48.   Abbasi and Holman, "Business Success in the Middle East," pp. 55–59.

49.   Steenkamp, Hofstede, and Wedel, "A Cross-Cultural Investigation," pp. 55–69.

50.   Ibid.

51.   See Hofstede, *Culture's Consequences,* 1984; and Steenkamp, Hofstede, and Wedel, "A Cross-Cultural Investigation," pp. 55–69.

52.   Steenkamp, Hofstede, and Wedel, "A Cross-Cultural Investigation," pp. 55–69.

53.   Harry C. Triandis, "The Self and Social Behavior in Differing Cultural Contexts," *Psychological Review,* Vol. 96, July 1989, pp. 506–520; and John A. McCarty and Patricia M. Hattwick, "Cultural Value Orientations: A Comparison of Magazine Advertisements from the United States and Mexico," *Advances in Consumer Research,* Vol. 19, 1992, pp. 34–38.

54.   Hellmut Schutte, "Asian Culture and the Global Consumer," *Financial Times,* November 1998, Mastering Marketing, Part Two: Understanding Consumers, pp. 2–3.

55.   "Korea's Biggest Firm Teaches Junior Execs Strange Foreign Ways," *Wall Street Journal,* December 31, 1991, 1.

56.   Adapted from Grant McCracken, "Culture and Consumer Behavior: An Anthropological Perspective," *Journal of the Market Research Society,* Vol. 32, No. 1, January 1990, pp. 3–11.

57.   James A. Lee, "Cultural Analysis in Overseas Operations," *Harvard Business Review,* March–April 1966, pp. 106–114.

58.   Craig R. Whitney, "Food Fight: French Impose Own Tariffs," *The International Herald Tribune,* July 31–August 1, 1999, p. 9.

59.   "How the American Dream Became a Global Nightmare," *Marketing Week,* June 3, 2004, p. 32.

60.   Terence A. Shimp and Subhash Sharma, "Consumer Ethnocentrism: Construction and Validation of the CETSCALE," *Journal of Marketing Research,* Vol. 24, No. 3, August 1987, pp. 280–289.

61.   See Dana L. Alden, Jan-Benedict E. M. Steenkamp, and Rajeev Batra, "Brand Positioning through Advertising in Asia, North America and Europe: The Role of Global Consumer Culture," *Journal of Marketing,* Vol. 63, No. 1, January 1999, pp. 75–87; and Guliz Ger and Russell W. Belk, "I'd Like to Buy the World a Coke: Consumptionscapes of the 'Less Affluent World,'" *Journal of Consumer Policy,* Vol. 19, No. 3, September 1996, pp. 371–404.

62.   Chip Walker, "Can TV Save the Planet?" *American Demographics,* Vol. 18, May 1996, pp. 42–49; and Alden, Steenkamp, and Batra, "Brand Positioning through Advertising," pp. 75–87; and Edna Gundersen, "MTV, at 20, Rocks on Its Own," *USA Today*, August 1, 2001, http://www.usatoday.com/life/television/2001-08-01-mtv-at-20.htm.

63.   Quentin Hardy, "Hope & Profit in Africa," *Forbes*, Vol. 179, No. 13, June 18, 2007, p. 92.

64.   See Ger and Belk, "I'd Like to Buy the World a Coke," pp. 371–404.

65.   Alden, Steenkamp, and Batra, "Brand Positioning through Advertising," pp. 75–87.

66.   Ibid.

Case 5-1

Walmart: An Anatomy of Failure in the German Market

When the retail giant Walmart entered the German market, it made every conceivable mistake, looking past the country's restrictive polices on store hours and new development, difficult economic conditions, unfavorable demographics, and intense price competition and entered the country with great confidence stemming from its past success in the United States. First, it bought 21 profitable, large-format Wertkauf stores in 1997, followed by 74 Interspar stores that were smaller and unprofitable, and it had a difficult time coordinating business with the two chains.

Walmart's greatest challenge was that it did not understand the German market, the consumer culture, and the employee culture.

The Retailing Market and Competition

When Walmart entered Germany in 1997, success was nearly impossible: Retail sales growth was stagnant, and profit margins in German retailing, especially in the food businesses, were lower compared with other European countries; Walmart's net margins were less than 1 percent. Walmart encountered fierce competition: Frugal Germans already had a number of well-established alternatives. Among competitors were: Aldi and Lidl, the privately owned discounters; Globus; Real (Metro), the country's largest listed retailer; Kaufland, Lidl's sister operation, which competed directly with Walmart's hypermarkets; and Toon (Rewe Group).

All of these competitors had efficient if drab out-of-town sites and offered economies of scale. Furthermore, these competitors had greater geographic penetration in Germany, which enabled them to adopt "zone pricing" tactics to match Walmart prices in areas where it was a key competitor. In the ensuing battle over prices, all the retailers suffered. At the end of the day, price pressure was so intense that Walmart's formula of clear price leadership did not work.

Regulations

The German regulatory environment was demanding. Until 1996, opening hours were restricted to 6 P.M. on weekdays and 2 P.M. on one Saturday each month. These restrictions have been lifted since then to allow an additional 10 hours per week, including Saturday opening until 4 P.M. Other regulations prohibited loss leader pricing—that is, pricing a product under cost to draw traffic into the store. More importantly, German law dealt a blow to Walmart's signature pricing strategy, everyday low pricing (EDLP). Under German law, an item must be sold at the same reduced level for 2 months to be classified as EDLP.

The Customer

Walmart believed that the German market was similar to that of its home state in the United States, Arkansas, and the German consumer would, similarly, desire low prices but excellent customer service. Walmart's strategy for Germany was to improve in-store appearance and ambience and emulate its U.S. and Canadian success by achieving price leadership through cost leadership. It would also deliver high quality customer service and act as a "market spoiler" on the service attribute. Walmart offered free shopping bags in a market where consumers were used to paying for bags, bag packing service, maximum allowed opening hours, credit card acceptance, baby trolleys and hospitality, especially greeters at the store entrance. The retailer was attempting to break customer perceptions in Germany away from their narrow focus on price as main the attribute for store choice—all the while advertising low pricing.

Walmart fully misunderstood Germans, who like to bargain hunt on their own, without cheerful assistants to hover around. Moreover, customers also failed to see what all the fuss was about because Walmart's low-price message played in a very low-price marketplace. To illustrate, most German discounters make Walmart look downright luxurious. Germany's so-called "hard discounters" tear open shipping cartons, set them on the floor and let consumers pick out the products. Discounting means no frills-open boxes and just bare fluorescent bulbs. And consumers in Germany like a bargain and are used to hunting for one.

They also have not taken kindly to the smiley face logo or traditional greeters, as homey charm does not work well in a country that leans more toward staunch traditionalism. In general, Germans are not quick adopters, as they tend to have set habits. It is difficult to get them to switch retailers if they do not consider themselves to be underserved. The typical German consumer is also loyal to national manufacturers' brands, buys on price, and pays cash. A retailer accepting credit cards is not particularly attractive to Germans, who do not have the benefit of the loyalty programs that credit cards offer in the United States.

It should be mentioned, however, that some of Walmart's efforts elicited positive response from German consumers. The retailer adapted to local tastes, adding fresh carp at Easter, and consumers responded well. Walmart also launched singles shopping events on Friday nights. Walmart workers greeted customers with a glass of sparkling wine and freshly shucked oysters, took their photo, and tacked it on a singles bulletin board, along with their age, interests, and the qualities sought in a prospective partner. Walmart stated that about 30 couples found each other at a singles shopping night, and its employees were fighting to work Friday evening shifts.

Employees

From the beginning, German employees were somewhat antagonistic toward Walmart's practices. First, when Wertkauf's Karlsruhe headquarters closed in favor of Interspar's, some talented people resigned. And Walmart bought the Interspar chain after committing to retain 200 hand-picked employees, many of whom were poorly trained, prompting consumers to complain about inferior service. In general, the employees resisted the company's customer-service culture and stood stone-faced as exuberant U.S. managers did the company cheer.

Even more problematic was that Walmart managed its international operations from its home office in the United States, rather than delegating decision-making and buying functions to the local Walmart team. In fact, Walmart's person in charge in Germany spoke no German and insisted that his managers work in English. The next in charge, an Englishman, ran the show from England.

Employees were in uproar when they learned that Walmart's ethics code included a ban on relationships at work and a hotline for employees to report on colleagues' violations of the rules. The clause infuriated workers' councils in Germany and prompted a lawsuit. A German labor court ruled that parts of the U.S. retailer's ethics code contravened German law.

Walmart also encountered other cultural problems, clashing with Ver.di, Germany's service workers' union on other issues and refusing to participate in national wage negotiations.

The End of Walmart's German Venture

Walmart conceded to failure after nearly a decade of courting Germany, leaving the German market in 2006. It was an expensive lesson for the retail giant, who sold its stores to Metro—the end result for Walmart was a $1 billion pretax loss. German retailer Metro Group AG said its acquisition of Walmart Stores Inc.'s stores helped almost double the company's net profit in 2006. Metro had 66.7 billion euros ($81.64 billion) in annual sales in 2011, and it is one of the world's largest retailers; it operates about 2,400 stores in 30 countries in a mix of department stores, wholesale stores that sell to other businesses, consumer electronics stores, and supercenters under its Real and Extra brands. It closed 15 of Walmart's stores and converted 22 into Real stores, which are Walmart-style supercenters.

Walmart may be right to forget about Europe. It has a growing joint venture in China, though there is a threat that its 30,000 employees may be unionized, while, in India, it has a procurement operation and big plans, although foreign investors cannot own supermarkets. And the company is doing better than ever in its North American markets: United States, Canada, and Mexico.

Sources: Cecilie Rohwedder, "Metro's Walmart Deal Helps Boost Profit," *Wall Street Journal*, online edition, March 22, 2007; Mike Troy, "Walmart Bids Auf Wiedersehen, Ends Nine-Year Grind in Germany, *Retailing Today*, Vol. 45, No. 14, August 7, 2006,pp. 1–2; *The Economist,* "Business: Heading for the Exit; Retailing, Vol. 380, No. 8489, August 5, 2006, p. 54; Gerrit Wiesemann and Jonathan Birchall, "Why Walmart Decided to Pack Its Bags in Germany," *FT.com*, July 29, 2006, p. 1; Betina Wassener, "German Blow to Walmart Ethics Code," *Financial Times*, June 17, 2005, 23; Laura Heller, "Cracking the German Code Not So Easy This Time Around," *DNS Retailing Today*, Vol. 23, December 13, 2004, pp. 55–56; Ann Zimmerman and Almut Schoenfeld, "Walmarts in Germany Redefine the Term 'Checkout Aisle,'" *Wall Street Journal*, November 9, 2004, B1; John Fernie and Stephen J. Arnold, "Walmart in Europe: Prospects for Germany, the UK, and France," *International Journal of Retail & Distribution Management*, Vol. 30, No. 2/3, 2002, pp. 92–102.

Analysis Suggestions

1. Do an analysis of the German food retail consumer. How do consumers in Germany differ (or do they?) from consumers in the United States?
2. What assumptions did Walmart make regarding German consumers that were incorrect? Why did the company make erroneous assumptions?
3. How did Walmart's employee culture clash with Germany's employee culture?

Case 5-2
Disneyland Post Paris, Taking on China: Reflections on the Past, Plans for the Future

Disneyland Resort Paris started out as an epic failure, as Euro Disney, in its first incarnation on the European continent. After its launch in April 1992, many name changes were made with the purpose of distancing the company from the bad publicity. The company learned many important lessons, and then pursued an Eastward expansion.

The Paris Experience

The idea of expanding the Disney magic to Europe proved to be a project that involved more attention to marketing than even this advertising giant could handle. Many Europeans did not want the American dreamland to distract their children, economy, and countries from their own homegrown successful entertainment. David Koenig, author of *Mouse Tales: A Behind-the-Ears Look at Disneyland,* commented, "To the Parisian intellectuals, Disneyland was a symbol of everything contemptible about America: artificial, unstimulating, crass, crude, for the masses. Yet here was a 5,000 acre Disneyland springing up half an hour from the Louvre."

Disney believed that locating the theme park in close proximity to Paris, France, would both ensure growth for Disney and offer an opportunity for it to incorporate different European cultures. It envisioned a Discoveryland that incorporated the histories of European countries through its fairy tales: Italy for Pinocchio, England for Alice in Wonderland, and France for Sleeping Beauty's chateau.

In its first incarnation as Euro Disney, the company failed in many aspects of its marketing strategy:

Euro Disney failed to target the many different tastes and preferences of visitors from dissimilar countries, such as Norway, Denmark, and Germany, on one hand, and Spain, Italy, and France, on the other.

Disney's admission costs were 30 percent higher than a DisneyWorld ticket in the United States, and the company refused to offer discounts for winter admissions.

Euro Disney ignored travel lifestyles of Europeans, accustomed to taking a few long vacations, rather than several short trips, which fit with the Disney model. The company also neglected to consider national holidays and traditional breaks when Europeans are more likely to travel.

Its restaurants did not appeal to visitors. A Rhode Island firm designed classic American-style restaurants, which most Europeans consider exotic and unusual – and the Europeans did not respond well to this format.

Euro Disney assumed that all Europeans wanted gourmet meals, which is not the case. Although French consumers tend to live a more lavish lifestyle and spend more for gourmet meals, many other consumers in Europe do not. Meal scheduling was also problematic: The French, for example, are accustomed to having all businesses close down at 12:30 for meal time, but the park's restaurants were not made to accommodate such large influxes for meals, leading to long lines and frustrated visitors. Finally, Euro Disney initially had an alcohol-free policy, which did not fit with local traditions, where wine is an important part of the culture.

Disney's failed marketing strategy for Euro Disney led to below-average attendance levels and product sales and the park was on the edge of bankruptcy in 1994, with a loss per year of more than a billion dollars. Changing strategies—as well as its name, to Disneyland Resort Paris—eventually led to increased revenues . With a full-scale change in the company's marketing direction, Disneyland Resort Paris has been successful in attracting visitors from many countries. Access was a priority for Disney. The company worked on access to the park via the fast train—the TGV; it also worked deals with the EuroStar and Le Shuttle train companies. Disney negotiated deals with trains and airlines to reduce prices, a move that ultimately benefited all. New Disney offices were established in London, Frankfurt, Milan, Brussels, Amsterdam, and Madrid and were given the task of tailoring package deals to the vacation lifestyles of the different European segments. Disney also offered discounts for the winter months and half-price discounts for individuals going to the park after 5:00 P.M.

The resort hotels also lowered their room rates and offered less expensive menu choices in their restaurants. The restaurants created more suitable food options, catering to different regional European tastes, but continued to offer large American-size portions. Crepes and waffles are on the menu of almost every street stand in the park.

Mickey Mouse and Donald Duck have French accents, and many rides were renamed to appeal to French visitors: in Adventureland, one can find Le Ventre de la Terre (Galleries under the tree), l'Ile au Tresor (Treasure Island), La Cabane des Robinson (Robinsons' Cabin); in Fantasyland, Sleeping Beauty's Castle, rather than Cinderella's Castle at Disney World, United States, and in Discoveryland, L'Arcade des Visionnaires, Le Visionarium (a time-travel adventure with Jules Verne), among others.

Disney capitalized on its European success by offering yet another grand theme park adjacent to Disneyland—the Walt Disney Studios. Disney promoted Walt Disney Studios in a manner that did not cannibalize attendance at Disneyland Resort Paris.[81] Among its attractions are a Rock'N'Roller Coaster Starring Aerosmith, capitalizing on the U.S. band's success in Europe; Animagique; and Cinemagique. The park is dedicated to the art of cinema, animation, and television, and it focuses on the efforts of many Europeans who made it possible to bring fantasy to reality.

The Shanghai Disney Resort

In 2011, Walt Disney Company broke ground on a $4.4 billion theme park in Shanghai, in an effort to attract many of China's 1.3 billion consumers. Like the Paris Disney venture, its first theme park in China, opened in Hong Kong in 2005, ran into trouble, once again because the company did not understand the local culture. Disney expected consumers to linger no more than 20 minutes at its restaurants, as is the case for the other Disney resorts, but, in Hong Kong, the average amount of time is 40 minutes; this resulted in many consumer complaints. In addition, the government and some consumers, much like in France, disliked that Disney was exporting American culture.

The Shanghai theme park, expected to open in 2015, will have a 225-acre Magic Kingdom-type $3.7 billion park with various themed areas and a castle.

The Disney experience will include two hotels, a lake, and a shopping area, eventually stretching for over 1,730 acres – and it will be much larger that the Hong Kong Disneyland. Disney is playing its cards close to its chest, to avoid copycats; once it announced its rides for Hong Kong, several parks were built nearby having very similar attractions. Whereas the Hong Kong Disneyland is very similar to the U.S. versions, the one in Shanghai is expected to bow primarily to the Chinese culture. For example, it will not have a Main Street theme at the entrance characteristic of all Disney resorts; and the castle will be huge...

<CAS>*Sources:* David Barboza, "Disney Plans Lavish Park in Shanghai," *The New York Times*, April 7, 2011 (www.nytimes.com); "Disney Parks and Resorts Plan New Attractions, Expansion in 2007, Both Land and Sea," *Financial Wire*, January 5, 2007, 1; "Euro Disney SCA: Revenue Increases by 13% on Back of Solid Attendance," *Wall Street Journal*, July 27, 2006, B8; "Business: Trouble in the Royaume Magique: Euro Disney," *The Economist*, Vol. 372, No. 8387, August 7, 2004, p. 57; Juliana Koranteng, "Taking It to the Tube: Parc Asterix to Unleash National TV Campaign," *Amusement Business,* February 11, 2002, p. 6; Juliana Koranteng, "Euro Disney Revenues Rise," *Amusement Business,* August 6, 2001, p. 38; Juliana Koranteng, "Future May Be Bright for Euro Disney," *Amusement Business,* May 21, 2001, p. 19; "Euro Disneyland SCA," International Directory of Company Histories, Vol. 20, December 1997, pp. 209–212; Harriet Marsh, "Variations on a Theme Park," *Marketing,* London, May 2, 1996, p. 14; "The Kingdom inside a Republic," *The Economist,* April 13, 1996, Vol. 339, No. 7961, p. 66; David Koenig, *Mouse Tales: A Behind-the-Ears Look at Disneyland,* Irvine: Bonaventure Press, 1994; Gail Ghetia, "As American as French Fries: Euro Disneyland, When It Opens, Will Feature Typically American Restaurants," *Restaurant Hospitality,* August 1990, p. 20; Barbara J. Mays, "French Park Still Negotiating for Airline Partnership," *Travel Weekly,* April 20, 1992; Barbara Rudolph, "Monsieur Mickey: Euro Disneyland Is on Schedule, but with a Distinct French Accent," *Time,* March 25, 1991, pp. 48–49.

Analysis Suggestions

1.   How do the values and lifestyles of European and Chinese consumers differ from those of consumers in the United States? Discuss the Disney failure to address European and Chinese (Hong Kong) consumers' preferences based on values and lifestyles.

2.   How did Disneyland Resort Paris manage a turnaround? What did it do to convince consumers to come back? What lessons were there to learn in Hong Kong? How the Shanghai venture different?

3.   Is there a world amusement-park consumer segment that is similar across different cultures? Discuss.

P A R T   3

International Marketing
Strategy Decisions

Chapter 6: International Marketing Research: Practices and Challenges

Learning Objectives

After studying this chapter, you should be able to:

• Define international marketing research and provide a description of its immense scope; offer examples of each type of research conducted in international marketing.

• Describe the steps involved in the international marketing research process while addressing the international constraints involved for each step.

• Introduce the concept of decision support systems for international marketing and describe the sales forecasting process.

International marketing managers operating in unfamiliar environments need to have a thorough understanding of their target market if their marketing efforts are to be successful. Numerous marketing plans fail due to an incomplete understanding of the market. Companies selling consumer products are especially prone to experiencing difficulties in foreign markets. Many such examples exist: European and U.S. multinationals have entered many low- and medium-income markets with large and expensive bottles of cleaning products and tubes of toothpaste, only to find that consumers will not purchase them, in spite of the fact that they prefer Western brands. As soon as those products were packaged in cheap, small sachets, consumers started purchasing large volumes. As we have seen in earlier chapters, sales of Coke packaged in 200 ml recyclable bottles took off instantly in India. Unlike in the United States, where 24-packs of any drink fly off the shelves, internationally, products sell better when they come in smaller packages. In fact, smaller-sized products do better in general, as the following example illustrates.

Living in an Apartment in Berlin

It is not unusual for a European family of four to live in a one-bedroom apartment. That apartment can very well be on the fourth floor (according to U.S. floor counting—on the third floor, counting the "European" way) in a five-story building with no elevator. Try to sell this family a package of 12 giant Bounty-brand rolls of paper towels, and they will ignore your product and go on to the next aisle. Sell them just one giant Bounty roll of paper towels and they will think twice. Do they really need paper for cleaning and drying when they can use and reuse their kitchen towel? Environmentally conscious Western Europeans will think twice before they create more waste because waste is expensive and difficult to unload. Figure 6-1 shows a typical garbage disposal site shared by a number of homes: It is kept under lock and key to prevent nonresidents' access, and because containers can fill up quickly, one is often forced to hold on to waste until the garbage trucks come around the following week.

Figure 6-1: *Guarded garbage: Garbage disposal areas for apartments and homes in Europe are only available with key access. The garbage must be separated into paper, plastic, organic waste, bottles, metal, and, well . . . garbage.*

Let us assume that our Western European shoppers are at least open to the idea of using Bounty paper towels for a limited number of jobs. Where will they store this giant Bounty? Kitchens are tiny, so hanging a roll above the sink will impede access to the sink, and the few inches of countertop has to be free to allow for food preparation (see Figure 6-2).

Figure 6-2: *A typical kitchen sink in an apartment: it can barely contain a European plate—a large American plate would only fit lying on the side. Woks are popular, but this author has always wondered if they are cleaned in the bathtub to accommodate their size.*

Western European apartments are not unique. In Japan, many apartments are small, with just 500 square feet and paper-thin walls. Storage space is limited and products are best sold in small quantities. In Japan, as in Europe, products for the consumer market should be smaller in size. Procter & Gamble did not take into consideration women's needs for a thinner diaper due to high frequency of changes and limited storage space, and their market share was quickly eroded by a local competitor that provided thinner diapers that were in line with market demands.[1]

Companies must conduct research in their local markets to understand consumers, their needs and wants, and consumption patterns. This chapter defines marketing research and examines its broad scope across all components of the marketing mix (product, place, price, and promotion). The chapter addresses the international marketing research process and the complexities of the process in an international setting.

6-1 The Need for International Marketing Research

Marketing managers need to constantly monitor the different forces affecting their international operations. Marketing information, which should constitute a basis for all executive action, must be taken into consideration to improve the chances of success in a complex global environment. Such information, although amply available in highly developed, industrialized nations, needs to be carefully evaluated and viewed in light of the purpose for which it was collected. In developing countries, relevant data may not be available at all, and if available, it is often questionable in terms of both quality and integrity. For example, production and sales data reported may be tainted by pressures of governments on factories to exceed unrealistic plans or production quotas.

International marketing research is especially complex. International managers are likely to encounter not only the obstacles they have learned to master when conducting research in their own countries, but also obstacles laden with the specifics of the international market where they are conducting the research, specifics that may differ substantially from those of their national market. Consider, for instance, a male marketing researcher working for a hair care firm interested in launching its lines in the beauty salons of the Middle East. In the United States, it is perfectly appropriate for this individual to assess interest in the company's product line by collecting data in beauty salons. In most countries in the Middle East, however, women's beauty parlors cater exclusively to women (men's barber shops cater exclusively to men), and the presence of males in this environment would constitute a breach of Islamic law, which forbids males from seeing a woman's hair if they are not closely related.

Another aspect of the difficulty of engaging in research internationally is readily observable in Eastern Europe, where consumers remain suspicious of attempts by foreigners and locals to investigate local markets and related consumer behavior. Consumers prefer not to participate in opinion polls and regard such attempts as an intrusion or as suspect. And, since instituting a market economy over 20 years ago, prospective respondents feel that they understand business and they will promptly demand payment for any time and effort demanded by the investigation.

These and many other environmental factors encountered in international marketing research complicate the task of marketing researchers, who should have not only an expertise in the most advanced techniques of scientific inquiry, but also a profound understanding of the markets under investigation.

6-2 -Defining International Marketing Research

We define **international marketing research** as follows:

International marketing research is the systematic design, collection, recording, analysis, interpretation, and reporting of information pertinent to a particular marketing decision facing a company operating internationally.

This definition of international marketing research contains a caveat also present in the general definition of marketing research: an acquired understanding of the market environment. In an international setting, the environment is particularly com-

> **international marketing research**
> The systematic design, collection, recording, analysis, interpretation, and reporting of information pertinent to a particular marketing decision facing a company operating internationally.

plex, and it displays obvious and important subtle differences in culture, religion, customs and business practices, and general market characteristics from the environment of the company's home country.

6-3 The Scope of International Marketing Research

International marketing research has a broader scope than domestic research: Managers need additional information to compensate for lack of familiarity with the foreign environment. Sections 6-3a through 6-3f describe some general research categories (see Figure 6-3).[2]

Figure 6-3: *The Scope of international Marketing Research.*

Research of industry, marker characteristics, and market trends

Buyer behavior research

Product research

Distribution research

Promotion research

Pricing research

6-3a Research of Industry, Market Characteristics, and Market Trends

Studies of industry, market characteristics, and market trends—often in the form of acquisition, diversification, and market-share analyses—are conducted regularly by marketing research suppliers and shared with subscribers. This topic will be further addressed in the "Secondary Data" section. Export research is yet another type of research in this category; it is prompted by the shortening of the product life cycle and the intensity of international competition, as well as by the rapid technological change that increases the need to segment markets more frequently.[3] The research techniques range from formal methods, such as focus groups and concept testing,[4] to more informal approaches.

6-3b Buyer Behavior Research

> **buyer behavior research**
> Research examining brand preferences and brand attitudes.

Examining brand preferences and brand attitudes falls into the category of **buyer behavior research.** To the uninformed, China is an emerging market that cannot afford many luxuries. However, buyer behavior research found that the Chinese luxury market is growing, and this market is demanding. Researchers at General Motors (GM) know that well.

Cadillac in China

General Motors conducted extensive buyer behavior research in China to find that luxury consumers responded well to special treatment. Its Chinese dealerships greet visitors with cigars and Napa Valley wines on black-marble bars, VIP rooms with leather sofas, and movie shots of the brand. GM has done well with Buick and Chevrolet, and now it is ready for a sales offensive that will ensure that Cadillac will succeed in this market. Cadillac is expensive because the Chinese government adds a 25 percent import tax. Models sold in China are 4 inches longer than the U.S. model, which is in deference to Chinese customers who tend to have chauffeurs.

Buyer behavior research found that luxury automobile brands are the fastest growing segment in the Chinese market and that consumers desire luxury-brand automobiles and related accessories (see Figure 6-4).

Figure 6-4: *Large cities in China boast several showrooms for luxury automobiles.*

Consumers in China tend to go for established luxury brands, such as Rolls Royce, BMW, Audi, and Cadillac. In fact, in most Asian countries, uncertainty is strongly avoided, resulting in high brand consciousness, brand loyalty, greater insistence on quality, and consumers' active reliance on reference groups and opinion leaders. People tend to shop in groups, and they are slower to accept new products. Whereas consumers worldwide are concerned about monetary, functional, physical, psychological, and social risks, Asians tend to be more sensitive to social risk than Westerners.[5]

Brand awareness research and **purchase behavior studies** are often conducted by companies to assess their position in the market. Hilton Hotels, in an attempt to change the way customers perceive them, engaged in a worldwide study of brand awareness of the Hilton brands, including its limited-service offerings.

Other useful studies that belong to this category are **consumer segmentation studies,** which are conducted to identify market segments. Such studies are also used to identify profiles of heavy product consumers and occasions for consumption. Cosmetics companies, for example, have conducted research looking at

brand awareness research
Research investigating how consumers' knowledge and recognition of a brand name affect their purchasing behavior.

purchase behavior studies
Research aimed at evaluating consumers' reaction to and interaction with a company's products.

consumer segmentation studies
Research conducted to identify market segment profiles.

emerging market cosmetics consumers in Eastern Europe and China. The segments behave differently when it comes to cosmetics, as the following examples illustrate, and cosmetics companies need to devise marketing strategies accordingly.

Hilton Hotels

Hilton Hotels Corp. aims to create a truly global company and expand the Hilton brand in Asia, Europe, and the Middle East. In China and India, it is partnering with companies to convert underutilized office buildings and retail space into limited-service, home-away-from-home type hotels, such as the Hilton Garden Inn, Hampton Inn, and Double Tree hotel. In Europe, it is also focusing on the limited-service sector, where comparable, lower-service hotels are nonexistent.

Hilton studied consumer hotel perceptions worldwide and brand awareness of its own Hilton brand. In Europe, it found that, except for resorts, consumers perceive them as expensive and snooty, with hired doormen to keep out riff-raff. Accordingly, many Europeans are unaccustomed to staying in hotels in the first place. Based on the studies, Hilton believes that limited-service hotels could do the most to create brand loyalty among travelers. The company is working to change consumer awareness of the broader Hilton brand, and to position their limited-service offerings as an extension of the home, without an imposing exterior and without the grand entrance. [6]

Eastern European and Chinese Cosmetics Consumer Segments

Russians want to impress at any price. Russian women focus primarily on outward appearance and strive to make a bold personal statement. They spend heavily on cosmetics: Many twenty-something professionals spend $300 a month on cosmetics, and even students manage to spend $150 in spite of little or no income. In fact, Russia spends 1.3 percent of GDP on cosmetics and toiletries, double what Western Europeans spend. Russian women have high awareness of and receptivity to Western brands. Russian women desire opulence and are drawn to audacious retail environments. In line with these research findings, brands such as Olay are marketed as prestige brands, rather than products for the mass market—a strategy used in Western Europe and the United States.

In comparison, Polish women are more concerned with products that make a difference from the inside out. They desire Western cosmetics, which are heavily advertised, but they are also price conscious and have high ethnocentric purchase tendencies. Consequently, much of their cosmetics expenditure goes to high-quality domestic brands. They expect retailers to be knowledgeable about the cosmetics they sell.

Chinese cosmetics segments, on the other hand, are receptive to different strategies. They prefer less color and simple graphics and typography. White is the preferred color for all skin products because it projects luminescence and clarity of skin. Black is acceptable as well, as an indicator of quality and brand status. Consumers enjoy going through skin care regimens and rituals, unlike Western women, who have less patience for rituals. They also respond better to prestige messages than Western consumers. [7]

concept development and testing studies Concept tests usually performed in developed countries evaluating the product/service offering and the related marketing mix in light of the different international target markets.

6-3c Product Research

Concept development and testing studies are usually performed in developed countries by the firms' research and development departments. When going international, multinational firms usually already have a successful product to bring to the marketplace. Nevertheless, it is still important that they evaluate the product/service they offer and the related marketing mix in light of the different regional and local target markets. And, although the initial concept development and testing studies are performed in high-income countries, increasingly, they are being performed in important emerging target markets, such as China.

brand name generation and testing
The testing of brand names and logos; necessary when companies market their products internationally.

Brand name generation and testing is used not only in the consumer goods industry, where its importance is obvious, but also in companies that have traditionally marketed their products regionally, such as agricultural goods companies. These companies need to test brand names when they market their products internationally. The annals of marketing are replete with examples illustrating the importance of testing a brand name in different countries. International Marketing Illustration 6-1 addresses challenges that marketing managers have faced in the process of deciding on brand names.

International Marketing Illustration 6-1

Naming the Brand

Marketers, historically, rushed to international markets with proven brands, and immediately proceeded to market them. However, brand names have hurt companies' efforts in many markets: name-related blunders are amply documented in the history of international marketing. As a result, companies have changed strategies accordingly, researching the appropriateness of the brand name for their target markets—and changing it, if necessary. Examples of U.S. brands in China with extensively researched local names are: *Coca-Cola*, which means "tastes good and makes you happy," *Keebler*, which means "rare treasure," *Ford*, which means "happy and unique or special," and *Marlboro*, which means "a road with 10,000 treasures." Choosing an appropriate brand name is more than simply a translation exercise; the translation should consider the local culture, norms, tradition, and history to ensure an optimal appeal.

In the case of global products, it is important to research their meanings in different languages. Kodak, Exxon, Xerox, and Ajax are examples of product names selected only after extensive testing. Frequently, companies may have to come up with different names for products to ensure their acceptance in each region or country. As a result of brand-name–testing research, Maxwell House introduced its product under the name Maxwell Kaffee in Germany, Legal in France, and Monky in Spain.

It is, however, important to note that brand names that were selected because of their effectiveness in the languages of key target countries are not necessarily particularly resonant in other countries. For example, the name "Accenture" was created by combining the words accomplishment, enthusiasm and future. In an English or French business setting, these connotations have value; however, in other languages, the meaning is lost.

Sources: Lily C. Dong, "Brand Name Translation Model: A Case Analysis of U.S. Brands in China," *Journal of Brand Management,* Vol. 9, No. 2, 2001, pp. 99–115; Charlotte Clarke, "Language Classes," *Marketing Week,* Vol. 20, No. 17, July 24, 1997, pp. 35–39; and David Ricks, *Big Business Blunders,* Homewood, IL: Dow Jones, 1983.

Product testing identifies the extent to which the product conforms to local tastes. For example, PepsiCo Foods International decided to undertake extensive product testing in China before introducing its Cheetos snack food brand. The outcome of the test was not favorable: Respondents indicated that they did not like the cheesy taste of the snack. As a result, PepsiCo's local joint venture, Guangzhou Frito-Lay, decided to get rid of the cheese and replace it with cream and steak flavors. Sales increased dramatically.[8]

Other types of studies that would be appropriate are competitive product studies, which are helpful in determining the overall product strategy for the product, the price that the market will bear for the respective product category, the promotion that is appropriate in light of the competition, and so on.

As for **product packaging design studies,** firms need to take into consideration consumers' reaction to the package, the extent to which the package adequately communicates information to the consumer, and the distribution implications of the packaging decisions. For instance, in many emerging markets, packaging distinguishes between local products and international products. In the Czech Republic, Poland, and Romania, many local dairy products are available in recyclable glass jars, have no brand name (just the product name, such as yogurt, kefir, etc.), and may contain only the dairy's address information. International products, on the other hand, come in colorful, sophisticated, disposable packaging. To the local consumers, however, simple packaging represents freshness and a lack of additives. After researching this phenomenon, Tesco Extra, the U.K. hypermarket, is selling its Tesco brand packaged in the same no-frills packaging.

The choice of package color is another important dimension that necessitates research. One color could have different meanings in different countries: Green signifies abundance in North Africa and the Middle East, disease in the Amazon region, and healthful contents in North America and Western Europe. In Western Europe, bio (organic-type) foods are most often presented in green packaging.

In another example, Primus, a Belgian beer manufactured under license in Rwanda, is sold in one-liter bottles, rather than in the 33 cl bottles that most other Western beers use in this market. In researching the Rwandan market, Primus found that the Rwandan consumer typically drinks beer at night, sharing with family and friends. Research also showed that beer is usually purchased and transported on foot for distances of one or two kilometers. Consequently, the bottles are typically sold in crates of 12, fitted such that they could be easily transported on one's head, allowing the individual to also carry other goods.

Test marketing is another important research procedure belonging to the product research category. Procter & Gamble test marketed Swiffer, a disposable mop, in Cedar Rapids, Iowa, and Sens, France, among other international markets. The company hoped to craft an international new-product success with the goal of evaluating whether a consistent brand image could be achieved in a number of major markets.[9] This research was the first step in the company's strategy to introduce the product worldwide in 18 months, rather than in the traditional four to five years.[10]

6-3d Distribution Research

The distribution function is particularly important in international marketing, where special attention should be given to import/export regulations and practices, and where companies are well advised to engage in comprehensive analyses. For example, **import/export analyses** aid companies in identifying the logistics companies most capable of handling the paperwork and getting products through customs in a timely and cost-effective manner. Federal and state governments in the United States are often instrumental in helping with this type of research.

Researching individual exporter and importer expertise and the firm's local influence are crucial to the success of the firm in a particular market. In one example, a private shipper from the U.S. attempted to export older, high-quality Louis XV armchairs from Romania to the United States. In the process, the firm obtained the appropriate documentation from the State Patrimonium Commission, attesting

product testing
Studies that estimate product preference and performance in a given market.

product packaging design studies
Studies that evaluate consumers' reaction to a package, the extent to which the package adequately communicates information to the consumer, and the distribution implications of the package.

test marketing
Testing new-product performance in a limited area of a national or regional target market to estimate product performance in the respective country or region.

import/export analyses
Analysis research that aids companies in identifying the necessary logistics that serve their needs in a timely and cost-effective manner.

to the fact that these armchairs were not antiques or important local historical artifacts. However, the large local export company (a vestige of the former communist firm ROMTRANS) encountered obstacles involving the local customs office that prevented it from exporting the armchairs. Only after contacting a different and much smaller firm, owned by a well-connected former government official, was it possible to export the armchairs. This same influential firm arranged for the chairs to be shipped via the Romanian airline directly to New York at a fraction of the cost of the shipment quote from the initial top shipping firm, by ship. Had the U.S. shipper researched the local import/export service providers, it would have found that influence is crucial in facilitating shipments.

Trade with Turkmenistan serves as an example of the importance of researching specific requirements imposed on importers by the local government. The government of Turkmenistan tightly monitors all foreign trade through the State Commodity and Raw Materials Exchange. All import and export contracts must be registered with the exchange at a 0.3 percent commission. According to foreign companies, connections with someone holding a seat on the exchange facilitate registration.[11]

Consider another example. Kazakhstan is a small but growing market for U.S. consumer goods. Distributing products in this large and sparsely populated country is a challenge. Geography and the inexperience of local wholesale distributors require exporters of consumer products to pay close attention to developing and maintaining a distributor network in this region—a task that is not easy to implement. Most of the population is located in two areas: the southeast, around Almaty, and the north and northeast, the republic's industrial and mining centers. Some existing infrastructure already supports distribution. An extensive railway network carries products within Kazakhstan, to other Commonwealth of Independent States countries, and to Europe. On the other hand, poor roads and bad telecommunications, when combined with geography, make it virtually impossible to rely on just one regionally based distributor. Smaller foreign companies may wish to start with a small, regionally located distributor and gradually build a countrywide network from there. Larger firms may consider a larger up-front investment to establish their own infrastructure in Kazakhstan.[12]

Another important type of study is that of **channel performance and coverage studies,** which may reveal either that channels need to be further developed at significant expense to the company, or that, in certain markets, particular channels dominate much of the activity in a particular area. In Japan, channel performance research reveals that the dominant firms that can offer the most efficient and broad distribution for the firms that can afford their high fees are the large trading companies, such as Mitsui and Mitsubishi. This research also finds that distribution in Japan is multilayered, with many distributors involved at each level. Much channel performance and coverage research has been conducted to date by U.S. multinationals in Asia to devise ways in which to adjust U.S. distribution practices to better fit with local market practices.

Finally, **plant/warehouse location studies** are important, as are evaluations of the transport infrastructure (roads, shipping, and warehousing infrastructure). In countries with an underdeveloped infrastructure or a mountainous terrain, warehousing is available only in the main cities or just in the capital city. Consequently, distribution to a more remote location is complicated, and firms may elect to avoid it altogether. Research in this regard is important. For example, in the case of Ecuador, transportation between the capital city, Quito, and its second largest city, Cuenca, is facilitated by the well-developed highway system between the two cities, both of which are at a high altitude in a plateau region. Moving products from one location to another should not present problems because the transportation infrastructure is adequate and warehousing facilities exist in both cities. If, however, a firm is to transport goods to Guayaquill from the capital city, it is likely to encounter difficulties because the transportation infrastructure between these two locations is complicated by the terrain. Guayaquill is easily accessible by sea—the route taken by most imported goods and services aimed at the islands' tourist market. Goods from Quito are more likely to be transported by air than by truck.

channel performance and coverage studies
Studies investigating whether existing channels are appropriate for communication, if channels exist at all, or whether they are appropriate for international marketing communications.

plant/warehouse location studies
Studies that evaluate the appropriateness of plant or warehouse location to ensure that it is in accordance with the limitations of the national environment and with the needs of a company.

6-3e Promotion Research

Promotion research is crucial for companies doing business internationally. By doing such research, the firm evaluates the extent to which it effectively communicates with the market, it ensures that certain promotional strategies are appropriate for that particular market, and, finally, it evaluates the extent to which the local media are appropriate for developing the intended message.

First, in terms of **studies of premiums, coupons, and deals,** it is important to identify the practices in each country where the specific promotion will run. When an agency has developed an idea to run in a

number of countries, it first needs to check on the legality of premiums and coupons across those markets. As individual European Union (EU) countries are relaxing their limits on consumer promotions to align their retail policies with those of the EU, IKEA decided to introduce a new loyalty program. It conducted a full year of testing of an innovative family-loyalty promotion, testing the family club card in the United Kingdom. It offered cardholders a 25 percent discount on selected "family" products in the store—for example, bicycle helmets, luggage, silverware, and bathroom accessories. The goal for the card was to also create a useful vehicle for direct marketing. After the year-long test of the card, the company decided to launch the promotion across Europe. [13]

Some examples of family card promotions are 9 euros for a lamp table that normally costs 25 euros, a 24-piece silverware set for 1.49 euros, and 11 euros for two children's tennis rackets. IKEA even has a magazine publication called *IKEA Family Live,* which is supposed to cost 1.75 euros but is actually available for free, promoting the family card and living with IKEA products. The magazine carries advertising from Hilton Hotels for family deals and other travel-related advertising.

It is important to determine whether consumers are likely to respond to promotions as expected. According to sales promotions experts, the most difficult aspect about promoting in Eastern Europe is that consumers are just not accustomed to entering competitions and sending off coupons. [19] In the EU, on the other hand, consumers are keen on in-store promotions, going shopping in droves to take part in competitions for free product giveaways and the like. In Latin America, research conducted by ACNielsen in Argentina, Brazil, Chile, Colombia, and Mexico found that the diverse consumers had diverse reactions to consumer promotions, but that, in general, promotions clouded price perception accuracy for consumers, acting as a driving force for the increase in the bargain-hunting segments. [14]

studies of premiums, coupons, and deals
Studies that help identify the practices in each target country where a promotion is planned by investigating the practice and legality of premiums, coupons, and special deals.

advertising effectiveness research
Studies conducted to examine the effectiveness and appropriateness of advertisements aimed at individual markets.

Advertising effectiveness research is often conducted to examine the effectiveness and appropriateness of advertisements aimed at individual markets. Frequently, ads that are initially developed for home-country markets and tested there are later used abroad. Such ads are frequently dubbed and do not fit with the culture of the local environments where they are broadcast. Tailoring the ads to the local market will always pay off, but it is more expensive.

Advertising must appeal to the target customer to be considered effective. In one example, Switzerland's tourism authority launched an advertising campaign aimed at soccer widows (women temporarily abandoned by their husband spectators). The ads showed beefy, waxed men in various states of undress performing uniquely Swiss tasks, forking hay at the farm, sawing logs, milking cows. In the ad, Switzerland invites women to visit because Swiss men would pay more attention to them. What the ad created was, in fact, a homegrown version of the Village People, and it ended up attracting more gay men as a result. The ad was effective in promoting tourism to Switzerland, but not in the way the tourism authority had intended. [15]

Media research also is important. In particular, it is important to determine the appropriate media outlets for advertising the company's products. In many countries, television advertising is broadcast only in between programs, rather than at 10-minute intervals as in the United States, and consumers often use the advertising time to take a break from television. In many developing countries, the primary local television channel is government owned and often will not broadcast advertising for consumer products—they might advertise programming and city events, but they might not offer commercial advertising opportunities.

Researchers do not always have access to information regarding programming audiences. They can find out who are the formal cable subscribers or satellite dish users, but they may not necessarily identify all the viewers. In Germany, for example, many purchase a digital box to append to the television set (for about $30) and are able to receive numerous subscription programs. Thus, even though satellite dishes dominate the apartment landscape (see Figure 6-5), research cannot possibly identify the millions of users of digital boxes and fully understand their viewing behavior.

Finally, studies pertaining to personal selling activities, such as **sales force compensation, quota, and territory studies,** are crucial in helping to determine the appropriate strategies for different markets. Even the highly industrialized countries with a tradition of a well-trained sales force have deficits with regard to sales force compensation. For example, sales research in the electronic component supply industry shows great dissatisfaction with sales operations among salespeople in Europe, as seen in the following discussion.

Figure 6-5: *Many apartment dwellers in Germany have satellite dishes.*

media research	sales force compensation, quota, and territory studies
Studies that evaluate media availability and appropriateness of the medium for a company's message.	Different studies pertaining to personal selling activities; they are crucial in helping to determine the appropriate strategies for certain international markets.

Sales Commissions for European Electronic Component Suppliers

Many electronic component suppliers are encountering disappointing results from their sales operations in Europe. First, there has been a mass exodus of production to China. Second, many are still using the same geographic orientation and sales commission structures they had in place in the late 1990s, which have added to their costs and eroded the motivation of their salespeople. European component suppliers need to develop a worldwide structure and a more logical and consistent approach to determining and awarding sales commissions—otherwise, Europe will be squandering its last chance to remain a major player in high-tech industry.

For example, design centers, where purchasing decisions often start, tend to be far from manufacturing centers, where parts orders are scheduled and shipments are received. Thus, it is difficult to determine which sales team should receive a commission and how much it should earn. To deal with this problem, the companies split the commission among different regions based on complex and arbitrary methods. As a result, sales staff motivation suffers. [16]

6-3f Pricing Research

Internationally, pricing research is much more problematic than when it is performed locally, in a developed country. Studies projecting demand, such as **international market potential studies, sales potential studies, sales forecasts, cost analyses, profit analyses studies, price elasticity studies,** and **competitive pricing analyses,** which are typical of most pricing research studies conducted by U.S. firms in the United States. In addition, however, the firm also must look at issues regarding countertrade and currency issues, inflation rates, and a national tradition of bargaining for every transaction, all of which have implications for pricing decisions. These points will be further addressed in Section 6-4e, "Designing the Data Collection Instrument," as well as in Chapter 16, "International Pricing Strategy."

At the retail level, pricing decisions could make or break a product. In countries where salespeople typically keep the change, it is important to price the product a few pennies/centimes below the amount that can be paid using larger currency denominations. For example, for a product costing $10.00, pricing it at $9.50 will give the salesperson a $.50 "tip" because customers would not demand change—an important consideration, especially in markets where salespeople have considerable latitude as to which product they make available to the consumer.

In industrial marketing, research in cost analysis might reveal that high product certification costs could significantly contribute to the price of a product and ultimately adversely affect its marketability. This is the case in Russia, where the lack of transparency connected with certifying products confronts both foreign and domestic companies. Although such companies are awaiting political solutions to these problems, marketers should be aware and plan ahead for certification. Often, the process may be cumbersome. Generally, there is some choice among the certification centers inside and outside Russia that are accredited to certify a given type of product or equipment. In some cases, however, the product itself may fall into several categories, and two certificates may be required.[17]

6-4 The International Marketing Research Process

Effective international research involves the steps shown in Sections 6-4a through 6-4g. Researchers attempting to obtain accurate and reliable information regarding a problem experienced in the firm's international operations are likely to encounter a number of difficulties, such as translation and cross-cultural comparison complications, which do not, as a rule, affect firms engaging only in domestic research. These difficulties will be addressed for each step in the subsections titled "International Constraints."

6-4a Defining the Research Problem and Research Objectives

The first step in the international marketing research process requires the international marketing manager and marketing researcher defining the research problem and jointly agreeing on the research objectives. The complexity of the environment of international operations does not afford marketing researchers the opportunity to have a clear idea of the specifics that the research study should examine. Instead, they may need to engage in **exploratory research** of the problem to define the relevant dimensions of the problem investigated. Exploratory investigations may help to further define the problem, suggest hypotheses, or even actually identify additional problems that need to be investigated. **Descriptive research,** on the other hand, portrays a situation—for instance, how frequently shoppers in Cairo shop for food items; whether they prefer to shop for meat products in state stores, which are cheaper but offer inferior-quality products, or in private stores, which are more expensive but offer a higher quality and assortment of meat products. Finally, **causal research** examines cause-and-effect rela-

international market potential studies
Studies conducted to evaluate the potential that a particular country offers for a company.

sales potential studies
Studies forecasting optimal sales performance.

sales forecasts
Projected sales for a particular territory.

cost analyses
Methods used for projecting the cost of research.

profit analyses studies
Studies that estimate product profit in specific international markets.

price elasticity studies
Studies examining the extent to which a particular market is price sensitive.

competitive pricing analyses
Pricing studies that determine the price the market will bear for the respective product category.

exploratory research
Research conducted early in the research process that helps further define a problem or identify additional problems that need to be investigated.

descriptive research
All research methods observing or describing phenomena.

causal research
Research that examines cause-and-effect relationships.

tionships, such as the extent to which Sony's offer of financial incentives to electronics salespeople in Ahmedabad, India, is likely to increase sales of the Sony brand.

Managers must note that a fine line should be maintained between identifying the problem too broadly—"What are French consumers' entertainment needs?"—or too narrowly—"Will enough French consumers pay an additional 4 euros to gain access to a specific American movie channel to make an investment in such a business worthwhile?" Better questions are: "What should be the price of this service in order to draw sufficient subscribers?" "What is the interest of French audiences in the movies carried by this channel?" "To what extent would anti-American sentiment affect subscriptions?"

At this point, the researcher, in conjunction with the marketing manager, sets specific research objectives identifying:

1. What is the interest of French audiences in the types of movies offered by the American movie channel?

2. How many subscribers will the company have if the subscription costs four euros? Three euros? Two euros?

3. Will the channel gain customers in spite of the anti-American feelings in France?

6-4b Developing the Research Plan

The research plan is a blueprint for the study, indicating all the decisions to be made with regard to information sources; research methods; data collection instruments; sampling procedures; data collection methods data analysis; and, based on these decisions, the projected costs of the research.

6-4c Deciding on Information Sources

After the international manager and researcher define the problem and set the objectives, the researcher must determine the extent to which available information may shed further light on the problem at hand. The researcher starts by identifying useful information pertaining to the issue that has been collected either by the company itself (internal) or by some other firm or agency (external)—**secondary data.** The secondary data may, if needed, help the researcher more clearly define the problem and set better objectives. It also helps the researcher pinpoint the type of information that needs to be gathered for the goals articulated in section 6-4a, "Defining the Research Problem and Research Objectives"; the data collected to address the problem at hand is known as **primary data.**

> **secondary data**
> Data collected to address a problem other than the problem at hand.
>
> **primary data**
> Data collected for the purpose of addressing the problem at hand.

International Constraints (for Both Secondary and Primary Data)

Conceptual Equivalence. Concepts have different meanings in different cultural environments. For example, the meaning of "household" in the United States is different from the meaning of "household" in many developing countries. In the United States, a household typically consists of a nuclear family, although this meaning is changing to include increasing numbers of single parents with children or of households with roommates. In the urban centers of Western Europe, a household typically consists of roommates, or unmarried long-time companions and their children, whereas the new immigrants tend to have a more traditional family consisting of married parents and their children, or even an extended family under one roof. In developing countries, the household may include the extended family with distant relatives, as well as servants who have chosen to live with the respective families for the rest of their lives.

Another issue that deserves mention is that many marketing applications in the United States are designed for the typical American who drives a car; shops once a week at a supermarket; and, when the need arises, drives to the mall to purchase department-store goods. In most other countries of the world, however, the population is largely "pedestrian." Consumers shop daily for food, as they are unlikely to have refrigerators, or, if they do, the refrigerators are small, fitting under the countertop. And they may have to make special and costly plans to take a long trip—using public transportation, rather than a personal car—to a larger city to shop for department-store type items. How, then, should researchers study these markets differently than they study the U.S. market? Clearly, practices such as mall-intercept interviewing will have a bias towards those motivated to go the distance to shop there, rather than simply reflect consumers in the general area.

Also imagine, for instance, conducting a research study at the Khan El Khalili bazaar in Cairo or at the "Russian markets" in the Ukraine or Poland where Russians sell household goods. In both scenarios, even a study based solely on observation is logistically complicated, given the crowded, aggressive environment where consumers can barely keep their balance and get around, let alone respond to interviews.

Retailers and service providers differ greatly from one country to another. A drug store in much of the rest of the world outside the United States is known as a pharmacy or apothecary. A mall in the United States typically is one huge structure anchored by large department stores; in other countries, a mall could be a centrally located shopping avenue that may or may not be covered or a pedestrian shopping zone. However, that is changing rapidly, as more and more countries adopt the U.S. covered mall concept. Figures 6-6 and 6-7 show covered malls in Asia and Europe. They are not much different from those in the United States

Figure 6-6 (top): *Taiwanese mall: Different country, same scene; as in the United States, in Taiwan, young consumers are avid shoppers and spend weekends at the mall with friends.*

Figure 6-7: *German malls are similar structures to malls in the United States and Taiwan; however, do not expect to find premium brands at these malls—premium brands prefer a location in a prime downtown shopping district or inside a luxury department store.*

Functional Equivalence. Products themselves may be used for different purposes in different country environments. Whereas, in many countries, jewelry is used to advertise status and style and to reflect concern with appearance, in countries such as India and Pakistan, jewelry is used as a way to accumulate wealth. In other examples, refrigerators might be used in the United States to chill soft drinks, whereas, in much of the rest of the world, soft drinks are consumed at room temperature or with just one ice cube. In the United States, ice is consumed in large quantities, so the refrigerators have ice makers. But in much of the rest of the world, ice is consumed in small amounts, and ice trays are common. Companies manufacturing plastic wrap also make plastic bags with small compartments that are filled with water and frozen. Then, the ice is squeezed out, as needed.

> **conceptual equivalence**
> The extent to which meanings remain the same in different cultural environments.
>
> **functional equivalence**
> The difference in the purposes for which products may be used in different country environments.

In another example, coffee, in southeastern Europe and the Middle East, is the quintessential drink for socializing. It is ground finely, boiled with water in a special container called the ibrik, and then poured into cups carefully, reserving the foam, which is added at the end. Close friends socializing over a cup of coffee might, when finished, turn the cup over to read each other's fortune in the grounds. In France, making coffee is perceived as an art, reflecting the ability and talent of the host. In Italy, people linger with friends in outdoor restaurants with a cup of coffee, and many cigarettes later, they may still continue to socialize. In Austria and Germany, coffee is also a tradition called the kaffeehaus tradition. Smoky, elegant coffee houses pride themselves on the coffee and cakes they serve. The instant coffee popular in Britain would not work in these markets. In Asia, tea replaces coffee, and the tea ceremony is central to many cultures there. With all these traditions, it is an impressive feat that Starbucks has done so well worldwide.

Problems also are encountered when companies assume that, if individuals have a certain purchasing power, the market is ripe for timesaving devices that appeal to Western consumers. Standard of living is not necessarily an indicator of such needs, particularly in countries where a wide gap exists between the haves and the have-nots. In many middle-class and upper-class families worldwide, household work is done by hired workers, and there is little likelihood that much thought would be given to facilitating their work. Moreover, servants themselves perceive timesaving devices as a threat to their job security.

In fact, the immense popularity of Western luxury goods among high-income earners and teenagers in Asia is not necessarily proof that they have joined the rest of the world's Western consumers. They may try some goods, but for different reasons. Brand name goods such as Louis Vuitton bags may be bought more for "face" reasons and the importance of the regard of others than from an individual preference for the product. Remy Martin cognac and Lafitte red wine may not be consumed because consumers really prefer it over local liquor or beer but because of peer pressure. Strong market position can therefore be built on foundations different from those in the West and require different marketing activities—in other words, an approach especially geared toward globalization but more efficient in terms of creating value for the consumers, and, as a result, earning higher returns.[18]

In yet another example, consumers shop differently worldwide. Marketing Illustration 6-2 compares shoppers in China and the United States—clearly, shopping has different meanings in each of the two cultures.

International Marketing Illustration 6-2
A Comparison between Shoppers in China and the United States

ACNielsen's annual reports on Chinese shoppers' habits suggest that foreign retailers have focused on the wrong things, assuming that consumers want a one-stop-shopping experience when, in fact, they do not. Mass retailers such as Carrefour SA and Wal-Mart Stores, Inc., have built hundreds of look-alike sprawling stores offering food, appliances, and housewares but have met with declining sales per store and little consumer loyalty. What went wrong? These retailers built these stores around the Western one-stop, infrequent shopping concept. But consumers in China prefer to go daily to open-air markets selling fresh produce, meat, and dry goods (see Figure 6-8). In fact, these markets account for more than 80 percent of food expenditures.

Yet, when Chinese consumers do go to supermarkets, they spend more than 1 hour there, expect the experience to be relaxing and entertaining, and spend relatively little money, compared with consumers in Europe and the United States. Indeed, U.S. consumers expect some entertainment—hence the success of creative supermarket retailers such as Stew Leonard's, who have mooing cows and singing farmer puppets, and the fun product sampling experiences provided by many retailers. However, in the process of enjoying their shopping experience, U.S. consumers spend substantially more compared with their Chinese counterparts.

In other differences, U.S. supermarket consumers shop in bulk at supermarkets or warehouse clubs once a week, loading the family automobile with large packages of food, freezing the meat and some of the vegetables for later consumption, or purchasing these products frozen. In contrast, Chinese consumers place little value on convenience. Overall, Chinese households spend 72 percent on fresh food, 9 percent on frozen food, 9 percent on convenience food and canned food, and the 10 percent on basic necessity food items such as packaged rice, edible oil, sauces, and chicken stock. The fresh food products most often purchased by consumers in China are oranges, apples, and bananas, Chinese cabbage, lettuce, bean curd, pork, pork soup bone, pork spare ribs, and mandarin fish, golden thread, and big head fish.

What do consumers in the U.S. and China have most in common? They pursue good value over lower prices when it comes to retailer choice and they report the highest coupon use of all consumers in the world.

Sources: Shopping & Saving Strategies around the World: A Nielsen Report, A.C. Nielsen, October 2011 (http://hk.nielsen.com); "World Watch," Wall Street Journal, March 21, 2003, A12.

Figure 6-8: *Market stall in Lhasa, Tibet. Consumers here purchase daily products such as grains, yak butter, and meat.*

Secondary Data

Researchers first must determine whether information is available, and if so, how much. Doing so may aid in gaining insights into the problem at hand. Secondary data are defined as *data collected for a problem other than the problem at hand.*

Secondary data are typically examined first, and they offer the advantage of low cost and ready availability in many of the more-developed countries.

Secondary data can be categorized as *internal,* collected by the company to address a different problem, or collected by the company to address the same problem but in a different country, or *external,* collected by an entity not affiliated with the company.

Internal Secondary Data

Assuming that Reynolds aluminum foil is available in Saudi Arabia but not in Sudan and assuming that the firm has no prior experience in Sudan, **internal secondary data** are useful only if the company has collected similar information from relevant respondents in a country with a similar environment (Saudi Arabia). For example, after considerable research, Reynolds' advertising in Saudi Arabia portrays the hands (with the wrists covered) of a woman preparing a sandwich for storage. An authoritative male voice describes the use of the foil and endorses its use. Because, from a religious perspective, the two countries are similar (although Sudan is less conservative), transferring this advertisement to Sudan will probably work. In this case, an analogy approach is appropriate.

If the environments of the countries are different, however, internal secondary data collected in one country are not useful in the second country. For example, Philip Morris International advertises its Lark and Parliament brands in Japan using glamorous American images—scenes of the New York skyline at night and the Golden Gate Bridge. These advertisements were created as a result of extensive research in Japan, which revealed that Japanese consumers are admirers of many things American. In advertising to the Chinese, Philip Morris found that it cannot communicate using such advertisements: The Chinese are reluctant to fully buy into U.S. values. The primary type of media communication that Philip Morris offers to this market is, typically, an elaborate advertisement, glorifying Chinese culture, on the occasion of the Chinese New Year. Transferring research findings on effective advertising appeals from the Japanese market to China is clearly not appropriate.

External Secondary Data

Marketing researchers in developed countries have ample access to different sources of **external secondary data.** They include government sources, provided by different government ministries departments or bureaus—such as the Census Bureau, international agencies, such as the World Bank, the various United Nations agencies, professional associations, various publications, and Internet sources.

> **internal secondary data**
> Data collected by a company to address a problem not related to the current research question.
>
> **external secondary data**
> Data collected for purposes other than the problem at hand.

Secondary Data Sources

Researchers must check established sources of information on countries, regions, markets, competitors, and consumers. As a first step, researchers can conduct online searches using search products such as Dialog, Lexis-Nexis, and others, as well as Google, Yahoo, and other similar search engines or portals. Additional useful country resources are the CultureGrams produced by Brigham Young University, previously mentioned in International Marketing Illustration 5-1 in Chapter 5, "Cultural Influences on International Marketing." They provide succinct country background information, information on the people, language, customs, lifestyles, government, economy, and other important facts useful for a summary country analysis (see www.culturegrams.com).

As a second step, researchers can access various publications and national and international marketing associations; examples are offered in Table 6-1.

Table 6-1: Sources for Secondary Data: Publications and Professional Associations

Professional Organizations	Publications
Academy of International Business	*Advertising Age*
Academy of Marketing (U.K.)	*Adweek*
Academy of Marketing Science	*Brand Marketing*
Advertising Research Foundation	*Brandweek*
American Academy of Advertising	*Catalog Age*
American Marketing Association	*Chain Store Age*
American Psychological Association	*Discount Store News*
Asia Pacific Marketing Federation	*Marketing*
Association Française du Marketing	*Marketing and Research Today*
Association for Consumer Research	*Marketing Management*
Australia-New Zealand Marketing Academy	*Marketing News*
Center for Service Marketing	*Marketing Research*
Chartered Institute of Marketing	*Mediaweek*
Direct Marketing Association	*Sales & Marketing Management*
European Direct Marketing Association	*Target Marketing*
European Marketing Academy	
Hong Kong Institute of Marketing	
Institute for the Study of Business Markets	
Institut fuer Qualitative Markt und Wirkungsanalysen, Germany	
Interactive Marketing Institute	
Japan Marketing Association	
Market Research Society, U.K.	
Marketing Research Association	
Marketing Science Institute	
Medical Marketing Association	
Sales & Marketing Executives Association	

Research suppliers such as ACNielsen and others offer subscribers extensive information on different markets. Overall, secondary data collected by different research suppliers is quite useful. In the past, U.S. research suppliers dominated the market; nowadays, there are more and more international players. The leading firms in all areas of market research are ranked in Table 6-2.

Researchers searching secondary data internationally are likely to encounter a number of constraints, which are addressed in the next section.

Table 6-2: The Top 10 Market Research Organizations

Rank	Rank	Organization (Country)	Revenue (US$m)	Growth
1	1	Nielsen (U.S.)	4,958	6.5
2	2	Kantar (U.K./U.K.)	3,183.6	3.9
3	3	IMS Health (U.S.)	2,211.6	0.3
4	4	GfK (Germany)	1,716.2	7.3
5	5	Ipsos (France)	1,512.8	8.3
6	6	Synovate (U.K.)	884.8	5.9
7	7	SymphonyIRI Group (U.S.)	727	4.6
8	8	Westat (U.S.)	455.3	-9.4
9	10	Intage (Japan)	416.2	4.7
10	9	Arbitron (U.S.)	395.4	2.6

Source: Adapted from Brian Tarran, "Honomichl sees 'healthy turnaround' for global top 25, *Research*, 16 August, 2011 (http://www.research-live.com, accessed June 1, 2012).

International Constraints

In many international markets, information sources may be limited and inaccurate. Although information accuracy is usually closely linked to the level of country development, the data collected may have shortcomings attributed to factors other than development, such as translation, correspondence, and so forth. The following are some of the shortcomings of secondary data in international markets:

Availability—In many markets, little data are available. The detailed data readily available in developed countries may not exist in numerous regions in developing countries, where, for example, population censuses are frequently collected based on estimates made by village elders. If, for instance, demographic information—reliable and readily available in developed countries—is deemed important to the project but is not available for the local market to be researched, the researcher may have to collect this type of data. Also, data on income and sales from tax returns can be inaccurate in countries where this information is not declared.[19] Finally, state-run research organizations are often reluctant to disclose the details of the data collection method and process used; no information may be available on response rates, questionnaire development, and the nature of the sample.[20]

Reliability and **validity**—Governments in developing countries often exaggerate poverty figures to solicit international aid. On the other hand, in many dictatorial environments where the government desires to project prosperity, figures attesting to the success of the economic policies may be inflated. Such was the case for many of the communist governments of Africa, Asia, and Eastern Europe, where figures demonstrating that workers were surpassing the five-year plans abounded, although, in fact, these same economies were experiencing severe shortages (typically attributed by government officials to consumer hoarding).

reliability
The extent to which data is likely to be free from random error and yield consistent results.

validity
The extent to which data collected is free from bias.

Errors also may be unintentional, attributed to lack of education, or mere carelessness. Regardless, unless the researcher is convinced of the credentials of the research firm performing the study, it is best that the secondary data be regarded with skepticism.

Overall, the accuracy of government-published secondary data is questionable. Published statistics contain high margins of error, beyond the tolerance range of reliability.[21] In addition, published data may be fragmented or aggregated in inconsistent formats by different research organizations; researchers may pull the data for estimation, but, in most instances, they are likely to view the data with skepticism.[22]

Some reliable sources of data are the World Bank, the United Nations Development Program, and the Organization of Economic Co-operation and Development. But even countries whose research reporting has been questionable for decades are revamping their data collection and reporting systems. For example, the Chinese government started to improve its marketing research infrastructure in the 1980s, introducing criteria for high-quality statistical service: accuracy, timeliness, relevance, diversity, and richness.[23] Overall, the State Statistics Bureau has expanded its role from data collection and compilation to a role similar to that of a business consultant.[24]

Regardless of the source, secondary data must be carefully scrutinized and interpreted. Researchers may construct a checklist to determine the extent to which the data are usable. This list may contain items such as:

- Who collected the data and for what purpose? Was this actual research, or was it used to support a decision already taken (i.e., is it pseudo-research)?

- When was the data collected? What were the environmental country-conditions then?

- What stakes did the firm managers have in the study?

- What stakes did the researchers have in the study?

- Who else may have a stake in the findings of the study (government entities, businesses)?

- What methods were used?

- How consistently were the methods applied?

Do the findings appear to be consistent with the findings of previous studies or with studies conducted in similar countries?

Primary Data

Primary research is used internationally far less than it should be. Cost-benefit analyses suggest that spending on research in remote markets of questionable value is unwise; consequently, the temptation is to use secondary data to serve all research functions.[25]

Often, even the largest firms use a wide variety of quick, ad hoc research techniques and look at databases and online information to get their projects off the ground.

Yet many U.S. firms are interested in conducting research in the international markets where they operate. In an interview of 313 executives at major U.S. corporations who were responsible for conducting research and hiring outside research firms, 61 percent indicated that they would devote a larger percentage of their research budgets to international research over the following 3 years.[26]

Most international marketing research projects involve the collection of primary data, *information collected for a specific purpose, to address the problem at hand.* It requires substantial expertise in both instrument design and administration and, as a consequence, it is expensive and time consuming.

International Constraints

Lack of Marketing Infrastructure. The costs of collecting primary data in foreign markets are likely to be much higher, given the lack of a marketing infrastructure. Many markets do not have research firms or field-interviewing services; consequently, the sponsoring firm would have to invest in developing sampling frames and training interviewers.[27]

6-4d Determining Research Approaches

When collecting primary data, researchers may use qualitative and quantitative **research approaches.** Qualitative research methods typically have some of the following characteristics:

- Fewer respondents belonging to a nonrandom sample
- Open-ended answer format
- Nonsystematic observation
- Researcher involvement as participant

Qualitative Research

Qualitative research has been particularly useful either as a first step in studying international marketing phenomena—when conducting exploratory research—or as one of the methods of exploring the problem at hand in a multiple-method approach. Focus group research and observation fit in this category. In certain countries, such as France and Italy, there is a preference for qualitative data as a complement to quantitative data, whereas in others, such as Germany, the United States, and Scandinavian countries, quantitative data are deemed as most valuable.

Focus Group Interviews and Depth Interviews

Focus group interviews typically involve 6 to 12 participants recruited to meet some previously decided characteristics—for instance, ethnic background, certain age group, social class, tribal allegiance, and use of certain products—and a moderator who guides the discussion based on a certain discussion agenda. Often, representatives from the sponsor observe the group's deliberations through a one-way mirror or on closed-circuit television. A video camera or video chat systems may also be used to record the group's deliberations on a certain topic of interest to the sponsor. The participants are typically given a small financial reward for participating in the study or products such as free beer and food, product samples, and the like.

Depth interviews are one-on-one attempts to discover consumer motivations, feelings, and attitudes toward an issue of concern to the sponsor using a loose and unstructured question guide. They are typically used if the issue under study is a complex behavioral or decision-making consideration or an emotionally laden issue.

research approaches
The method used to collect data.

qualitative research
Research that uses nonsystematic processes, such as nonrandom sampling and open-ended data, as well as involves the researcher as participant.

focus group interviews
A qualitative research approach investigating a research question using a moderator to guide discussion within a group of subjects recruited to meet certain characteristics.

depth interviews
A qualitative research method involving extensive interviews aimed at discovering consumer motivations, feelings, and attitudes toward an issue of concern to the sponsor using unstructured interrogation.

International Constraints

Focus groups, consumer panels, and depth interviews are frequently problematic to apply in international settings. In Eastern cultures, responses are likely to be affected by "acquiescence bias" or "good-subject role," whereby consumers agree to please the interviewer. When conducting international research using focus groups, researchers should be aware of the significance of culture in the dialogue because many societies do not condone open exchange and disagreement between individuals.[28] Also, topics such as domestic and consumption habits are considered too private and embarrassing to discuss with strangers. In these environments, researchers would benefit more from using observational approaches.[29]

observational research
A research approach used frequently in international markets, whereby subjects are observed interacting with a product and the related components of the marketing mix.

Observation

One type of **observational research** that is particularly useful in international research is naturalistic inquiry. Naturalistic inquiry requires the use of natural rather than contrived settings because behaviors take substantial meaning from their context.[30] The researcher is the data collection instrument and part of the behavior, verbal and nonverbal. The analysis performed by the researcher is inductive, rather than deductive; that is, unlike in conventional research methods, the researcher does not rely on previous theory in the process of developing hypotheses, but, rather, theories are developed from data. Ethnography—the study of cultures—is largely based on naturalistic inquiry. Both academic researchers and practitioners have used observation to better understand international consumers and consumer motivations. It is often used by researchers who attempt to increase the validity of their studies by acquiring an intimate knowledge of a culture's daily life through personal observation[31] (see Figure 6-9).

Figure 6-9: *Observing consumers shopping collectively or on their own in the shopping districts reveals dynamics of the shopping experience (interpersonal influences, atmospheric influences, etc.) more readily than conducting an interview with the respective shoppers.*

Other observational methods—such as the study of garbage (garbology); physiological measurement methods, which measure a respondent's nonvoluntary responses to stimuli; eye tracking, which is used in packaging research and in advertising; and response latency, which measures the time interval between the question and the response to that question—are used only to a limited extent in international research, usually in developed countries. They are costly because they require sending expensive experts to the research site abroad and obtaining data only on limited, usually nonrepresentative samples.

Information technology provides new sources for observation-based information, such as point-of-sale (POS) store scanner data, which can offer outlets high-quality, instant, as well as longitudinal, information on the movement of goods. Such resources are amply available in the United States, Canada, and the countries of the European Union. Increasingly, they are available in Asia and in the emerging markets of Latin America. This information is used for tracking, as well as for managerial decision making. This topic will be addressed in Section 6-5a, "Sales Forecasting." Other sources for observation-based information include people meters, used to identify television audience watching behavior. In the United States, ACNielsen also links this type of data with self-reported purchase behavior of consumers.

International Constraints

Observation can have a number of shortcomings. Individuals in different cultures may react differently if they note that their behavior is being observed. Also, the observer may need to be familiar with all the different languages spoken at the study site.[32]

Quantitative Research

Quantitative research methods are more structured, involving either descriptive research approaches, such as survey research, or causal research approaches, such as experiments.

Content Analysis

Content analysis, an example of descriptive research, is a quantitative analysis that entails counting the number of times preselected words, themes, symbols, or pictures appear in a given medium such as printed material or any medium with verbal or visual content. Content analysis is particularly useful in international marketing research, helping international marketing practitioners understand the complex multicultural environments in which they compete. At the same time, content analysis makes them aware of the subtle qualitative differences—such as taste, tradition, and symbolism—that are especially useful in market segmentation.[33]

One area where content analysis is used extensively is advertising research, in an attempt to discover themes that are more popular in certain countries, for particular product categories. One study examined differences in the portrayal of women in magazines of different countries.[34] Using U.S. and international male and female judges, the study found that, in general, North American and Western European magazines portrayed women displaying more positive emotions, compared with Latin American, East European, and African magazines. In addition, the women from Latin America appeared to be older, sexier, and more aggressive than their Western counterparts. Table 6-3 (next page) is a partial content analysis questionnaire used to gather this data.

> **quantitative research**
> A structured type of research that involves either descriptive research approaches, such as survey research, or causal research approaches, such as experiments.
>
> **content analysis**
> Method that assesses the content of advertisements in a medium with verbal and visual content.
>
> **survey research**
> Descriptive research that involves the administration of personal, telephone, or mail questionnaires.

Survey Research

Survey research, another example of descriptive research, typically involves the administration of personal, telephone, mail, or Internet questionnaires. The use of the questionnaires assumes that respondents are both capable and willing to respond to the questions. A cheap survey method involves the use of mail questionnaires; however, this method is fraught with obstacles in many developing countries. And, in most developing countries, there is a high level of illiteracy, which renders impossible the use of mail surveys. Nevertheless, this method is most popular in international marketing research, especially because it can be effectively used in cross-national comparisons.

International Constraints

Respondent Factors. In certain countries, researchers may not have access to certain household members. For example, a male researcher collecting data in Djeddah, Saudi Arabia, will not have access to female respondents; in fact, he may even get into trouble if he attempts to approach a woman in any environment. Companies are advised to hire local female interviewers for any study that may involve women and male interviewers for studies that involve male respondents. Procter & Gamble, for example, a Western company with a substantial presence in the Saudi market, conducted a study examining the consumer behavior of Saudi women. The marketing department invited the husbands and brothers of Saudi women to participate in a focus group study. In spite of its obvious limitations, the study produced useful results that helped Proctor & Gamble develop appropriate strategies for this market.[35]

Table 6-3: Partial Content Analysis Questionnaire

Women are frequently used in advertising. Advertisers portray them differently, depending on the mood/feeling they would like to convey. Please look at each ad and indicate to what extent you believe that THE WOMAN IN THE AD appears to have the following characteristics by circling the corresponding number, as follows:

1 = if the ad/woman DOES NOT AT ALL HAVE the respective characteristic
2 = if the ad/woman DOES NOT HAVE the respective characteristic
3 = if the ad/woman SEEMS TO HAVE the respective characteristic
4 = if the ad/woman HAS the respective characteristic
5 = if the ad/woman DEFINITELY HAS the respective characteristic

The woman in the ad appears to be . . .

Soft	5	4	3	2	1
Cool	5	4	3	2	1
Seductive	5	4	3	2	1
Scornful	5	4	3	2	1
Kitten-like	5	4	3	2	1
Optimistic	5	4	3	2	1
Maternal	5	4	3	2	1
Loving	5	4	3	2	1
Practical	5	4	3	2	1
Proud	5	4	3	2	1
Comic	5	4	3	2	1
Calm	5	4	3	2	1
Superior	5	4	3	2	1
Elegant	5	4	3	2	1
Caucasian	5	4	3	2	1
Afro-American	5	4	3	2	1
Hispanic	5	4	3	2	1
East Asian	5	4	3	2	1
Asian Indian	5	4	3	2	1

The woman is looking at . . .

People	5	4	3	2	1
An object	5	4	3	2	1
Nothing	5	4	3	2	1
The reader	5	4	3	2	1
Herself	5	4	3	2	1

The woman's age is approximately _____ years.

In Eastern Europe, there continues to be considerable suspicion of any attempts to gain personal information. In fact, the word used for "research" is a variant of the Slavic ankieta, meaning inquiry (of the same type as that conducted by the former, feared secret police). Intercepting middle age or older consumers in the marketplace typically meets with minimal response and with possible attempts to discredit the interviewer. A better method is "the apartment intercept," whereby the interviewer randomly chooses apartment buildings—typical mass structures found in most communist and formerly communist countries—located in representative neighborhoods and then attempts to interview every nth individual. The individuals approached may either live in the building, visit someone who lives there, or do business (shopping, renting videocassettes, etc.) in one of the apartments. An advantage of this method is the private environment protected from weather elements that may impede interaction.[36] Yet, even this method does not yield a high response rate because respondents may still suspect the interviewer's intentions. Moreover, Eastern European respondents believe that, in capitalism, people do not give something for nothing, and they almost always ask to be paid for their time.

In conclusion, it is crucial that researchers have a good understanding of the culture and local practices to be able to obtain adequate response rates.

Infrastructure Factors. Research using the telephone as the contact method has changed greatly in the past decade alone. It used to be that, in many countries, the use of telephones limited the data collection to a handful of individuals who had access to a landline. However, today, with cheap access to prepaid cell phones, pretty much anyone can be reached. Because most subscribers do not have to pay for phone calls they receive, telephone interviewing is much easier than in the past. Random digit dialing is probably the best method to use to ensure a representative sample of the population. Using the telephone book as the sampling frame is problematic because it restricts the sample to landline subscribers, and many today choose not to have a landline.

Using mail surveys is problematic in many international markets where mail is unreliable and slow. Even in India, which has one of the best home delivery mail systems in the entire developing world, mailing surveys to consumers' homes or offices has never been a part of the business culture of Indian society; similarly, in Saudi Arabia, which has one of the most efficient mail systems in the world using the most modern technologies, studies cannot be conducted through this venue because the system restricts the use of mail surveys.[37]

In the lowest-income countries, another obstacle to the mail survey approach is the low literacy rate, which eliminates many potential respondents. Here, a personal interview is the preferred data collection approach.

Internet research has become a viable approach to data collection worldwide; however, response rates can be a problem. Moreover, the sampling frames needed for data collection (Internet subscribers, mailing lists, telephone books, or other relevant databases) may not be available. In business-to-business research, sampling frames such as industry-association directories are often used – if they are at all available.

> **experimental research**
> Research that examines cause-and-effect relationships; it has the highest validity and reliability of all types of research.

Experimental Research

Experimental research has the highest validity and reliability of all types of research. This research looks at cause-and-effect relationships, eliminating or controlling other extraneous factors that may be responsible for the results, and eliminating competing explanations for the observed findings. It requires the use of matched groups of subjects who are subjected to different treatments to ascertain whether the observed response differences are statistically significant.

Given the many constraints that this type of research imposes on the researcher, experimental research findings are difficult to transfer to other countries where the control factors behave differently. Given the fact that results are not easily generalizable to similar environments, and that this type of research can be costly, experimental research is rarely used in international research.

6-4e Designing the Data Collection Instrument

International marketing phenomena are particularly difficult to measure and require an intimate knowledge of the culture. Themes that are functionally and conceptually equivalent across nations, such as the universal concept of "affection," manifest themselves differently in different environments; for instance, hugging, a common manifestation in the West, is inappropriate in Eastern cultures and taboo in others.[38] Given these differences, phenomena specific to each culture are best measured by **emic instruments,** which are constructed for each nationality to measure the particular factor. The instrument employed must then conform to the specific characteristics of each culture.

In other examples, the type of store referred to as a "supermarket" in the United States is typically a large store belonging to a national or regional chain. It carries a wide assortment of competing brands in each product category, including its own brand, a couple of dealer brands, and numerous national brands. Supermarkets in Europe, such as *Migros* in Switzerland, *Edeka* in Germany, and *Albert Heijn* in the Netherlands, carry a larger variety of products, but not as wide an assortment of competing brands as their U.S. equivalents. Alternatively, supermarkets in sub-Saharan Africa, such as *Alirwanda* and *La Galette*, in Kigali, Rwanda, are more similar to Western specialty shops, carrying primarily fresh meat and dairy products, and expensive brand name products such as confectionery items, alcoholic drinks, jams, and Belgian and French magazines and newspapers. Studying the supermarket shopping experience should be done using market-specific measures. Comparing consumer choice behavior across the different environments is not possible because the choice variables are different for each market. Consequently, an emic measure is needed for each market.

International managers are frequently faced with problems related to the need for survey instruments that can be used across different cultures, especially for comparative evaluation of market characteristics such as response to an advertising campaign and other types of multicountry research. For this type of study, **etic instruments,** which are culture neutral and extremely difficult to develop, can be used to measure the same phenomenon in different cultures. Going back to the supermarket example, studying consumer behavior at the cash register can easily be measured with an etic measure. Some dimensions that such a study can capture are the payment method, the degree of yielding to store-aisle impulse purchases, as well as the emotion during the purchase transaction, among others. Then, these measures can be compared across the different countries.

emic instruments
A data collection instrument constructed for each nationality to measure a particular factor; it is the best measure for culture-specific phenomena.

etic instruments
A culture-free data collection instrument that can be used to measure the same phenomenon in different cultures.

data collection instrument
The instrument used to collect data, such as a printed questionnaire, a paper-and-pencil measure, or an electronic measurement device.

open-ended questions
Questions with free-format responses that the respondent can address as he or she sees appropriate.

When deciding on the **data collection instrument,** the researcher needs to come up with an appropriate format and to offer precise instructions. Frequently, respondents may not answer entire sections of the questionnaire, unless advised that full completion is essential for the integrity of the study. A typical *semantic differential* scale, anchored by words with opposite meanings (good . . . bad, important . . . not important) could be confusing to respondents as well. Clear instructions, preferably with examples, help respondents in filling out the questionnaire appropriately. A variant of the semantic differential scale follows (note the detailed explanation of the numbers to be circled). The typical Likert scale anchored by "strongly disagree" and "strongly agree" is unfamiliar to respondents in many cultures. Explaining the procedure in detail, as well as the meaning of circling a particular response, is essential. See the questionnaire in Table 6-4 for a variant of the Likert scale.

An easier approach (from the point of view of the respondent, and certainly not from the perspective of the individual coding and analyzing the data) is to use **open-ended questions** that elicit the appropriate answer from the respondent. This format allows the interviewer to probe in depth into the issue at hand and the respondent to fully address the points.

Table 6-4: Sample Partial Consumer Research Questionnaire
(Version Translated into Romanian, Bulgarian, and Hungarian)

Please indicate the extent to which you agree or disagree with the statements below by circling 5 if you strongly agree, 4 if you agree, 3 if you neither agree nor disagree, 2 if you disagree, or 1 if you strongly disagree with a statement. Please answer every question; the questionnaire cannot be used unless you do so.

	Strongly Agree				Strongly Disagree
1. I don't care to find out about what types of brand names of appliances and gadgets my friends have.	5	4	3	2	1
2. I often read advertisements just out of curiosity.	5	4	3	2	1
3. I rarely read advertisements that just seem to contain a lot of information.	5	4	3	2	1
4. When I hear about a new store or restaurant, I take advantage of the first opportunity to find out more about it.	5	4	3	2	1
5. Companies are usually out to make money even if it means violating ethics and taking advantage of consumers.	5	4	3	2	1
6. Most durable products could be made to last much longer but are made to wear out quickly to necessitate repurchase.	5	4	3	2	1
7. If people really knew what businesses do to deceive and take advantage of consumers, they would be up-in-arms.	5	4	3	2	1
8. Most Western products I buy are overpriced.	5	4	3	2	1
9. Most local products I buy are overpriced.	5	4	3	2	1
10. Businesses could charge lower prices and still be profitable.	5	4	3	2	1

Sources: Dana N. Lascu, Harold W. Babb, and Julie Bodine, "Western and Own-Country Product and Service Evaluations: Perspectives from Eastern Europe," *Journal of East-West Business*, Vol. 4, No. 4, 1999, pp. 49-67.

International Constraints

Instrument Translation. Instruments developed in one country require translation into the language of the country where they will be administered. Many concepts, however, are likely to lose some of their meaning when translated into another language. Idioms are particularly problematic, and their literal translation has led to numerous marketing blunders.

In cross-cultural research, all steps should be performed by individuals fluent in both the original language of the questionnaire and in the language of the country where it will be administered. First, a questionnaire is translated from the language in which it was originally written into the language in which it will be administered. There are two possible alternatives to further ensure that the instrument has been translated as intended. One is **back translation**, whereby the translated questionnaire is again translated into its initial language by a different individual. Another possibility is **parallel translation**, whereby the questionnaire is translated from its original language by two different individuals and the two versions are compared. The successive translation (by different translators) of the instrument between the original language and the language of administration with the purpose of obtaining an instrument that is closest in meaning to the original questionnaire is known as **decentering**.

The consumer research questionnaire in Table 6-4 contains a number of scales developed in marketing in the United States, among which are attitudes toward business ethics, pricing practices, comparison shopping, dogmatism, fashion concern, dress conformity, and information searches. The translated scales performed well and were considered highly reliable when used in the different country environments.

Instrument Reliability. Even if the same scale is used in different cultures and has been subjected to decentering techniques, it is likely to have different reliabilities (i.e., the extent to which the scale is likely to be free from random error and yield consistent results) when administered in different countries because respondents in one country might be more likely, for example, to give answers that would please the interviewer. This provides yet another argument against simple comparison of research results in international marketing.[39]

Other Instrument Issues. In certain environments, such as the United States, respondents are unwilling to answer questions about income, whereas in others, such as France, respondents more readily volunteer such information. In other cultures, age is a taboo subject. It is important to take these differences into consideration when designing questionnaires. Creating categories of income rather than asking the precise figure tends to have a better success for data collected in the United States. Regardless, it is best if all demographic data are placed at the end of the questionnaire to ensure response.

6-4f Deciding on the Sampling Plan

The sampling plan calls for the manager and researcher to jointly decide on the following issues:

- **Sampling unit**—Determining who will be included in the survey

- **Sample size**—Determining how many individuals will be surveyed (the larger the sample, the higher the study reliability)

- **Sampling procedure**—Determining how the sampling units will be selected (the most representative sample is a random probability sample)

Determining the sampling plan is likely to be affected by some of the same problems discussed previously. First, the sampling unit itself may have a different

---

back translation
The translation of translated text back into its original language, by a different individual, to ensure that the instrument has been translated as intended.

parallel translation
The process of translating the original instrument by different translators and comparing the translations.

decentering
The successive translation (by different translators) of an instrument between the original language and the language of administration with the purpose of obtaining an instrument that is closest in meaning to the original.

sampling unit
The entity included in the study; it may be individuals or representatives belonging to particular groups.

sample size
The number of study participants necessary to obtain a high study reliability.

sampling procedure
A decision involving the selection of sampling units.

definition, depending on the country where the data are collected. In developed countries, for example, research examining family consumption patterns typically surveys a nuclear family, whereas in many developing countries, an extended family, including relatives living with the nuclear family, is scrutinized. Similarly, as already mentioned, the concept of household varies across different countries.

The sampling procedure also presents a problem, as previously discussed, especially the **sampling frame** (the list from which sample units are selected). Mailing lists are inadequate, and telephones are available to only a small percentage of the population in many countries of the world.

6-4g Collecting, Analyzing, and Interpreting the Information

In the final stage of the marketing research process, the researcher or research team is ready to collect the primary data. This expensive undertaking can be eventful. Researchers are frequently faced with respondents who have never had any experience participating in surveys. *Nonresponse* (inability or, more frequently, refusal to participate in the study) can be a particularly serious problem, as previously seen. Even lateral processes that do not involve data collection per se, such as *briefing the field force* (training the interviewers) and *evaluating the fieldwork quality,* can be particularly difficult if the marketing researcher is not a national because communication may be encumbered by language and cultural differences. Ideally, local researchers should be in charge of implementing the data collection process because they are aware of the particulars of the environment that may have an impact on the data collection.

Finally, it is important that marketing managers not base all their decisions on the data collected because even proper planning of the data collection effort does not exclude the possibility of shortcomings in the study. For example, after one market research firm indicated that there was a substantial market for a specific product, a Swiss pharmaceutical firm built an $8 million manufacturing firm in Southeast Asia. The researchers, however, overlooked an important aspect of that market: the black market controlled by government officials. The added competition of the black market led to lower earnings for the company.[40]

> **sampling frame**
> The list from which sample units are selected.
>
> **decision support system**
> A coordinated collection of data, systems, tools, and techniques, complemented by supporting software and hardware designed for the gathering and interpretation of business and environmental data.

6-5 -Decision Support Systems for Global Marketing

A **decision support system** is defined as "a coordinated collection of data, systems, tools, and techniques, complemented by supporting software and hardware designed for the gathering and interpretation of business and environmental data."[41] In a global environment, the environmental data takes into account home-country and host-country developments, as well as developments in other global markets that may affect operations.

Ideally, a global marketing decision support system should be:[42]

- *Computerized*—Having a computerized support system is now possible in the case of many global markets, including those of developing countries, due to the increase in the capability of personal computers to perform more complex tasks.

- *Interactive*—Managers can use online instructions to generate reports on the spot, without assistance from a programmer, who now may need to be present in the country of operations only periodically for system updating and training. This, of course, reduces the number of expatriates necessary at the operations site and the overall costs to the company.

- *Flexible*—Managers can access and integrate data from a variety of sources and manipulate the data in a variety of ways (producing averages and totals, sorting the data, etc.). The system should allow managers to access information about firm operations in similar markets where the firm may be present and competitors' operations in the respective market where such information is available.

- *Discovery-oriented*—Such systems should produce diagnostics that reveal trends and identify problems.

In a global environment, there are different, country-specific information systems. Integrating the different approaches may lead to operational difficulties; managers must continually take into consideration such differences as they interact with the system.

A number of areas lend themselves well to marketing decision support systems (MDSS). In Section 6-5a, "Sales Forecasting," we discuss different possible applications for such systems.

6-5a Sales Forecasting

Different approaches to sales forecasting are discussed in this section. The more complex these techniques are, the more their efficiency can be improved in an MDSS environment. Nevertheless, input obtained from using the simpler methods (sales force composite estimates, jury of executive opinion, and the Delphi method) can be used to cross-validate the estimates given by the more sophisticated forecasting techniques (time series and econometric models).

Sales Force Composite Estimates

Forecasts from **sales force composite estimates** are based on the personal observations and "hunches" of the local sales force. These people are in the closest contact with the international consumer, and they are likely to find out about consumer desires and overall changing market trends. The sales force is likely to be constituted of locals who have a good understanding of the market. They, in turn, report to the manager, who may or may not be an expatriate sent abroad by the home office. Ideally, the individual occupying this position is schooled under both home- and host-country systems; if not, it is recommended that this individual should undergo at least some training in host- or home-country approaches, respectively, to doing business. This training is important because this individual is typically responsible for interpreting the predictions of the sales force.

Jury of Expert Opinion

Forecasts from the **jury of expert opinion** are based on the opinions of different experts about future demand. The experts' opinions are then combined, and an aggregate demand estimation is offered. Because experts could come from both home and host country, as well as countries where other companies, or the company in question, may face similar problems, obtaining a consensus perspective or aggregate forecast may be more difficult to achieve. At the same time, the awareness of the different possible outcomes or individual perspectives may prove invaluable in gaining insight on demand, particularly for a market new to the company.

The Delphi Method

sales force composite estimates
Research studies wherein sales forecasts are based on the personal observations and forecasts of the local sales force.

jury of expert opinion
An approach to sales forecasting based on the opinion of different experts.

Delphi method
A method of forecasting sales by asking a number of experts to estimate market performance, aggregating the results, and sharing this information with the said experts; the process is repeated several times until a consensus is reached. selection of sampling units.

The **Delphi method** entails asking a number of experts to estimate market performance, aggregating the results, and sharing this information with the experts. This process is repeated several times until a consensus is reached. Clearly, such an approach would be most cumbersome when dealing with a global company. First, in addition to impositions on executives' time, the company also must incur expenses related to the logistics of bringing together experts from different countries. Second, should the company attempt to use the Delphi method by mailing forecasting surveys, there is always the risk that international mail may impose, in addition to the high likelihood of noncompliance by executives, who may perceive such an exercise as an imposition on their time. Typically, these types of studies are performed at yearly or quarterly meetings of international managers.

The Delphi method has been used in within-country studies to identify the needs for professional training for life insurance sales representatives and to examine the competencies needed by those sales representatives in the United States and in Taiwan. Sales representatives of the same company receive the same training in both the United States and Taiwan, but the Taiwanese did not exhibit the same high performance levels as their U.S. counterparts. A study using the Delphi technique revealed that the company needed to offer additional training to the Taiwanese salespeople especially in problem solving, communication, and information technology utilization.[43]

Time Series and Econometric Models

Time series models use data of past performance to predict future market demand. Typically, these models give more weight to recent developments. These methods assume that the future will be similar to the past. **Econometric models,** on the other hand, take into account different deterministic factors that affect market demand—factors that may or may not depend on past performance trends.[44]

An example of an application of econometric models to global marketing is provided by the application of an autoregressive moving average (ARMAX) to predict consumer demand for beer in the Netherlands.[52] The variables used as predictors of the demand for beer were temperature, price, consumer expenditures, and company advertising expenditures. The study concluded that advertising expenditures are not good predictors for beer demand; the authors suspected that the reason is a saturated market where all competitors advertise extensively and where additional advertising efforts may go unnoticed.

Time series and econometric models are dependent on the availability of historical data, data that are mainly available in developed countries but not in developing countries. For these markets, then, it is appropriate to estimate demand *by analogy,* noting responses of markets with similar relevant characteristics, levels of economic development, cultural characteristics, and so forth.

Analogy Methods

The **analogy method** is an estimation method that relies on developments and findings in markets with similar levels of economic development, markets where the product is in the same development stage, or markets with similar cultural characteristics, or it may be based on sales of a related product in the key market of study. For example,

- To estimate anticipated adoption rate of cell phones in Latvia, it may be appropriate to identify the proportion of new adopters in a more advanced country in the Baltic region—Estonia, which is more developed—where cell phone service is widely available, but which shares a similar history and similar geopolitics with Latvia. This is an example of *country performance analogy.*

- To estimate the adoption rate of Internet service in Sri Lanka, it may be appropriate to evaluate the adoption rate of computers in this country. This is an example of *product performance analogy.*

Typically, in the country performance analogy, adjustments are made based on development level, cultural differences, trade barriers, competition, and so on. In the product performance analogy, adjustments are made for consumer traits such as purchase power, consumer innovation rate, and competitive environment.

Point-of-Sale Based Projections

Point-of-sale based projections are made with the help of store scanners, which are increasingly used by research suppliers, particularly in the United States (ACNielsen and Information Resources, among others), to assess market share and other relevant market dimensions. Weekly or biweekly store audits reveal the movement of goods within the store and from warehouses. Internationally, although scanning technology is widely available, it is mainly used for inventory purposes, rather than for research purposes. For example, British retailer Marks & Spencer uses bar code and wireless local area network (LAN) technology to improve operations in its stores. The company installed a Symbol Technologies Spectrum24 wireless LAN, mobile computers, and bar code laser scanners to increase accuracy and efficiency and to improve customer service at its more than 300 European-based stores. The scanners send data over the LAN, allowing Marks & Spencer to reconfigure POS stations or add and subtract stations based on need.[45] Overall, scan rates are lower in Europe when

time series models
Models that use the data of past performance to predict future market demand.

econometric models
Models that use the data of past performance to predict future market demand.

analogy method
A method for estimation that relies on developments and findings in similar markets or where the product is in the same life cycle stage.

point-of-sale–based projections
Market share and other relevant market dimensions assessed by the use of store scanners in weekly and biweekly store audits.

compared with the United States, but higher than rates elsewhere around the world (with the exception of Canada); Europe, Great Britain, and France have 100 percent scanning for most food products.[46] Surprisingly, in the United Kingdom, unlike the United States, consumer data collection is dominated by face-to-face interviewing, which still accounts for more than 50 percent of U.K. research, whereas retail data collection is still dominated by the conventional retail audit. The use of scanners at POS and the difference in the level of development in the major store groups make it impossible to construct a nationally representative sample of scanner stores.[47]

Summary

Define international marketing research and provide a description of its immense scope; offer examples of each type of research conducted in international marketing. International marketing research involves gathering information for international marketing decisions. It is wide in scope, covering industry research, market traits and trends, buyer behavior, and the marketing mix. Examples of product research are product testing, product package studies, and competitive product analysis. Distribution research covers areas such as import/export analysis, international channel performance and coverage, as well as plant/warehouse location studies. Promotion research has the widest scope, with studies of premiums, coupons, and deals; advertising effectiveness; media research (which is especially important in highly industrialized countries); and sales force analyses. Pricing research involves studies projecting demand, as well as international market potential studies, sales potential studies, cost analyses, and profit analyses.

Describe the steps involved in the international marketing research process while addressing, for each step, the international constraints involved. The first step of the international research process involves defining the research problem and setting the research objectives; this is usually done in conjunction with a local team and international experts and consultants. The development of the research plan involves deciding on the information sources—primary and secondary (evaluating the validity and reliability of secondary data)—and determining the appropriate research approach. The research approach may involve collecting qualitative data, using focus groups or observation methods, or quantitative data, using descriptive (surveys, content analyses) or causal research methods (experimental research). They, in turn, determine the contact methods. The next step requires the researcher to design the data collection instrument and translate it into the local language(s). Next, the sampling plan must be determined: selecting the sampling procedure and sample size, frame, and unit. Finally, the researcher must collect, analyze, and interpret the information.

Introduce the concept of decision support systems for international marketing and describe the sales forecasting process. Decision support systems represent a coordinated approach to collecting and interpreting business and environmental data. International sales forecasting techniques can be improved in this environment. Methods used in international sales forecasting are international sales force composite estimates, jury of expert opinion, the Delphi method, time series and econometric models, the analogy method, and point-of-sale–based projections, all of which can be used in an international setting with various degrees of success.

Key Terms

advertising effectiveness research

analogy method

back translation

brand awareness research

brand name generation and testing

buyer behavior research

causal research

channel performance and coverage studies

competitive pricing analyses

concept development and testing studies

conceptual equivalence

consumer segmentation studies

content analysis

cost analyses

data collection instrument

decentering

decision support system

Delphi method

depth interview

descriptive research

econometric model

emic instrument

etic instrument

experimental research

exploratory research

external secondary data

focus group interview

functional equivalence

import/export analyses

internal secondary data

international market potential studies

international marketing research

jury of expert opinion

media research

observational research

open-ended questions

parallel translation

plant/warehouse location studies

point-of-sale–based projections

price elasticity studies

primary data

product packaging design studies

product testing

profit analyses studies

purchase behavior studies

qualitative research

quantitative research

reliability

research approach

sales forecast

sales potential studies

sales force compensation, quota, and territory studies

sales force composite estimates

sample size

sampling frame

sampling procedure

sampling unit

secondary data

studies of premiums, coupons, and deals

survey research

test marketing

time series model

validity

Discussion Questions

1.   Describe the broad scope of marketing research with a focus on promotion-related research.

2.   You have been hired to evaluate the purchase behavior of adolescents in Latvia. What types of research studies could you conduct?

3.   What are some of the limitations of secondary data available to international marketing researchers?

4.   Describe the challenges that researchers experience when designing and administering questionnaires in countries that are culturally dissimilar from their own.

5.   Discuss the quantitative data collection methods that researchers can use in an international study and the problems they pose to the validity and reliability of the findings.

6.   Describe the international sales forecasting methods that marketing managers can use to better monitor and more efficiently react to information in the local environment.

Chapter Quiz

True/False

1. Brand awareness research and purchase behavior studies are often conducted by companies to identify the profiles of heavy consumers of the product.

Answer: False

Rationale: Consumer segmentation studies are used to select profiles of heavy product consumers. Brand awareness research and purchase behavior studies are conducted by companies to assess their position in the market.

Section 6-3b, "Buyer Behavior Research"

2. Advertising effectiveness research uses studies that evaluate media availability and the appropriateness of the medium.

Answer: False

Rationale: Advertising effectiveness research is conducted to examine the effectiveness and appropriateness of advertisements aimed at individual markets.

Section 6-3e, "Promotion Research"

3. Research that examines cause-and-effect relationships is also known as causal research.

Answer: True

Rationale: Causal research examines cause-and-effect relationships using experimentation as a method of investigation.

Section 6-4a, "Defining the Research Problem and Research Objectives"

Multiple Choice

1. Which product research method mainly deals with testing new-product performance in a limited area of a national or regional target?

    a.   Test marketing
    b.   Product testing
    c.   Competitive product studies
    d.   Brand name generation and testing

Answer: a is correct.

Rationale: Test marketing is a product research procedure that attempts to evaluate new product performance in a particular region characterized by demographics that are representative of the international target audience.

Section 6-3c, "Product Research"

2. Which product research method attempts to identify the extent to which the product conforms to local tastes?

    a.   Test marketing
    b.   Product testing
    c.   Competitive product studies
    d.   Brand name generation and testing

Answer: b is correct.

Rationale: Product testing identifies the extent to which the product conforms to the tastes of the local target market.

Section 6-3c, "Product Research"

3. Kraft's research on identifying the top distribution firm in Hong Kong is a good example of which distribution research method?

    a.   Plant/warehouse location studies
    b.   Channel performance and coverage
    c.   Import/export analyses
    d.   None of the above

Answer: b is correct.

Rationale: Kraft, after researching channel performance and coverage, identified the top distributor in Hong Kong and enlisted the company to carry its products.

Section 6-3d, "Distribution Research"

4. Which of the following is a stage of the research plan?

    a.   Deciding on the research methods
    b.   Deciding on the information sources
    c.   Deciding on the sampling procedure
    d.   All of the above

Answer: d is correct.

Rationale: When designing a research plan, the researcher, together with top local management, decides on the research methods, the information sources, and sampling procedures appropriate for the research.

Section 6-4b, "Developing the Research Plan"

5. Data collected by a company on previous occasions to address a problem not directly related to the current research question is also known as

    a.   first-tier data.

    b.   primary data.

    c.   internal secondary data.

    d.   external secondary data.

Answer: c is correct.

Rationale: Internal secondary data are collected from sources within the company. The data were collected previously to address similar issues in another market or in the present market.

Section 6-4c, "Deciding on Information Sources"

6. Qualitative research methods include

    a.   survey research.

    b.   focus group research.

    c.   experiments.

    d.   all of the above

Answer: b is correct.

Rationale: Focus group research typically involves 6 to 12 participants and a moderator who guides the discussion based on a certain discussion agenda. The outcome of focus group research is a qualitative analysis. Survey research and experiments, on the other hand, involve data and measurement; they are thus quantitative research methods.

Section 6-4d, "Determining Research Approaches"

7. A sampling plan relies on specific decisions for a

    a.   sampling unit.

    b.   sample size.

    c.   sampling procedure.

    d.   all of the above

Answer d: is correct.

Rationale: The sampling plan specifies the sampling unit, the sample size, and the sampling procedure.

Section 6-4f, "Deciding on the Sampling Plan"

Endnotes

1.   Alecia Swasy, *Soap Opera: The Inside Story of Procter & Gamble,* New York: Times Books, 1993.

2.   This section is organized based on a framework provided in a table in Thomas C. Kinnear and Ann R. Root, eds., *1988 Survey of Marketing Research: Organization, Functions, Budgeting, and Compensation,* Chicago: American Marketing Association, 1989, p. 43.

3.   See Rolf F. H. Seringhaur, "Comparative Marketing Behaviour of Canadian and Austrian High Tech Firms," *Management International Review,* Vol. 33, No. 3, Third Quarter 1993, p. 247; and James D. Hlavacek and B. C. Ames, "Segmenting Industrial and High-Tech Markets," *Journal of Business Strategy,* Vol. 7, October 1986, pp. 39–51.

4.   William L. Shanklin and John K. Ryans, Jr., "Organizing for High-Tech Marketing," *Harvard Business Review,* Vol. 62, 1984, pp. 164–171; and Seringhaur, "Comparative Marketing Behaviour," p. 247.

5.   Hellmut Schutte, "Asian Culture and the Global Consumer," *Financial Times,* November 1998, pp. 2–3.

6.   Joe Gose, "Hilton Builds Brand Awareness Worldwide," *National Real Estate Investor Worldwide*, Vol. 48, No. 10, October 2006, p. 115.

7. Liz Grubow, "Branding Eastern European Shoppers," *Global Cosmetics Industry*, Vol. 173, No. 2, February 2005, pp. 30–32.

8. Helen Johnstone, "'Little Emperors' Call the Shots," *Asian Business,* Vol. 32, No. 9, September 1996, pp. 67–68

9. James I. Steinberg and Alan L. Klein, "Global Branding: Look Before You Leap," *Brandweek,* Vol. 39, No. 43, November 16, 1998, pp. 30–32.

10. "P&G Goes Local," *Country Monitor,* Vol. 47, No. 3, October 27, 1999, p. 9.

11. Irina Begjanova and Lisa Palluconi, "Trade with Turkmenistan," *BISNIS Bulletin,* September 1996, p. 5.

12. Kevin Lyons, "Distribution in Kazakstan," *BISNIS Bulletin,* November 1996, pp. 1, 5. This article was adapted from the *Country Commercial Guide* for Kazakstan, produced by the U.S. Commercial Service in Almaty.

13. Richard Cuthbertson, "Ikea's Card Is a Global Drive for Local People," *Promotions & Incentives*, March 2007, p. 13.

14. Guillermo D'andrea, Martin Schleicher, and Fernando Lunardini, "The Role of Promotions and Other Factors Affecting Overall Store Price Image in Latin America," *International Journal of Retail & Distribution Management*, Vol. 34, No. 9, 2006, p. 688.

15. Tyler Brule, "Good Summer Holiday Idea? Find a 'Badi" in Switzerland," *Financial Times*, August 5, 2006, 18.

16. Derek Lidow, "Global Industry, Global Approach," *Electronic Business*, Vol. 30, No. 4, April 2004, p. 72.

17. Judith Robinson, "Product Certification in Russia," *BISNIS Bulletin,* August 1996, p. 6.

18. Schutte, "Asian Culture and the Global Consumer," pp. 2–3.

19. William R. Dillon, Thomas J. Madden, and Neil H. Firtle, *Marketing Research in a Marketing Environment, Second Edition,* Burr Ridge, IL: Irwin, 1993.

20. T. K. Sherriff Luk, "The Use of Secondary Information Published by the PRC Government," *Journal of the Market Research Society,* Vol. 41, No. 3, July 1999, pp. 355–365.

21. Naresh Malhotra and J. Agarwal, "Methodological Issues in Crosscultural Marketing Research: A State of the Art Review," *International Marketing Review,* Vol. 13, No. 5, 1996, pp. 7–43.

22. Luk, "The Use of Secondary Information," pp. 355–365.

23. Ibid.

24. Ibid.

25. Michael R. Czinkota and Ilkka A. Ronkainen, "Market Research for Your Export Operations: Part II—Conducting Primary Market Research," *International Trade Forum,* Vol. 1, 1995, pp. 16–26.

26. Allison Lucas, "Market Researchers Study Abroad," *Sales and Marketing Management,* Vol. 148, No. 2, February 1996, p. 13.

27. Ibid.

28. Czinkota and Ronkainen, "Market Research for Your Export Operations," pp. 16–26.

29. Choudry, Y.A. 1986. "Pitfalls in International Marketing Research; Are you speaking French Like a Spanish Cow?" *Akron business and Economics Review* (Winter): 18-28.

30. See Yvonna S. Lincoln and Egon G. Guba, *Naturalistic Inquiry,* London: Sage Publications, 1985; Laura A. Hudson and Julie L. Ozanne, "Alternative Ways of Seeking Knowledge in Consumer Research," *Journal of Consumer Research,* March 14, 1988, pp. 508–521.

31. Jerome Kirk and Marc L. Miller, *Reliability and Validity in Qualitative Research,* London: Sage Publications, 1986.

32. Czinkota and Ronkainen, "Market Research for Your Export Operations," pp. 16–26.

33. David R. Wheeler, "Content Analysis: An Analytical Technique for International Marketing Research," *International Marketing Review,* Vol. 5, No. 4, Winter 1988, pp. 34–40.

34. Dana-Nicoleta Lascu, "Women in Advertising: A Cross-Cultural Study of Emotion," working paper.

35.   Zafar U. Ahmed, Dana-Nicoleta Lascu, and D. Neil Ashworth, "International Management and Marketing Research in Developing Countries," in *Proceedings of the Sixth Annual Meeting of the American Society of Business and Behavioral Sciences,* Vol. 10, February 1999, pp. 9–14.

36.   Dana-Nicoleta Lascu, Lalita Manrai, and Ajay K. Manrai, "Marketing in Romania: The Challenges of the Transition from a Centrally-Planned Economy to a Consumer-Oriented Economy," *European Journal of Marketing,* Vol. 27, No. 11–12, 1993, pp. 102–120.

37.   Ahmed, Lascu, and Ashworth, "International Management and Marketing Research in Developing Countries," pp. 9–14.

38.   The material in this section is adapted from Choudhry, "Pitfalls in International Marketing Research," pp. 18–28.

39.   Ravi Parameswaran and Attila Yaprak "A Cross-National Comparison of Consumer Research Measures," *Journal of International Business Studies,* Spring 1987, pp. 35–49.

40.   Ricks, *Big Business Blunders,* 1983.

41.   William R. Dillon, Thomas J. Madden, and Neil Firtle, *Marketing Research in a Marketing Environment,* Burr Ridge, IL: Irwin, 1993.

42.   Ibid.

43.   Chiang Ku Fan and Chen-Liang Cheng, "A study to identify the training needs of life insurance sales representatives in Taiwan using the Delphi approach," *International Journal of Training & Development,* Vol. 10, No. 3, September 2006, p. 212.

44.   William R. Dillon, Thomas J. Madden, and Neil Firtle, *Marketing Research in a Marketing Environment,* Burr Ridge, IL: Irwin, 1993.

45.   "British Retailer Goes Wireless," *Automatic I.D. News,* Vol. 14, No. 11, October 1998, p. 14.

46.   Gerry Eskin, "POS Scanner Data: The State of the Art, in Europe and the World," *Marketing and Research Today,* Vol. 22, No. 2, May 1994, pp. 107–108.

47.   Tim Bowles, "Data Collection in the United Kingdom," *Journal of the Market Research Society,* Vol. 31, No. 4, October 1989, pp. 467–477.

Case 6-1:

Hilton Sorrento Palace

Two hours south of Rome to Naples by the Eurostar, the Italian high-speed train, and an additional hour west along the Bay of Naples via the Circumvesuviana regional railway is the town of Sorrento. The Hilton Sorrento Palace reigns high on the hills of Sorrento, overlooking Mount Vesuvius, the now-dormant volcano (since 1944) that buried the towns of Pompeii and Herculaneum in the year 79 CE.

Sorrento is a small resort town, known well throughout Europe, an ideal vacation destination for its picturesque location and mild weather. A favorite of British travelers, the town of Sorrento has 10,000 beds according to Mr. Ziad Tantawi, director of business development at the Hilton Sorrento Palace. The Hilton Sorrento Palace is the largest of all hotels in the small resort town, with 383 rooms. Owned by the Sorrento Palace Gruppo since its year of construction (1981), the hotel became part of the Hilton chain in May 2001, and is now under Hilton management. One of the few hotels open in the winter in Sorrento, the Sorrento Palace boasts an average occupancy rate of 60 percent, with an average occupancy of 30 percent from November to March and more than 85 percent from May to October.

The Hilton Sorrento Palace faces competition from three categories of competitors. Family-run lodging, such as a bed and breakfast, is very popular. The bed and breakfasts are competitively priced at or below the room rates of leading hotels in the area. Most bed and breakfast accommodations are open year round.

Sorrento is also a popular destination for cruise lines during the summer months. For cruise ship passengers, Sorrento offers easy access to the ruins of Pompeii, Mount Vesuvius, and the Isle of Capri. Overall, prices for cruise ships are higher than that of hotels, but they include meals and entertainment, as well as airfare to Italy.

Other local hotels compete directly with the Sorrento Hilton. The historic Europa Palace Grand Hotel, for example, offers close views of the Bay of Naples and the cliffs of Sorrento.

The Hotel Offerings

The four-star Hilton Sorrento Palace is situated on a hill overlooking the town and the Bay of Naples, a short walk from downtown's busy tourist markets. Surrounded by residences and lemon and orange groves, the hotel is modern and elegant. Its restaurant, L'Argumento, is situated amidst blooming cannas and orange and lemon trees. Le Ginestre has frescoes and elegant columns and an indoor pool with a lush painted background. Its other four restaurants abound in blooming bougainvillea and oleander and have a splendid view of the Bay of Naples and Mount Vesuvius.

The indoor lounge has excellent performers scheduled every evening and boasts a view of the city and the bay. The executive lounge is situated on the top floor of the hotel and has a splendid view of the gulf and town. It also boasts a swimming pool at the highest altitude in the region. The lounge serves complimentary food and drinks to executive guests and to gold- and diamond-level Hilton Honors members.

The hotel has a total of six outdoor swimming pools of different depths, flowing into each other, a tennis court, and a relatively well-equipped fitness center. Among the services offered at the hotel pool is the Hilton Kids Club: Every day, from 10 to 12 in the morning and from 2 to 4 in the afternoon, the children staying at the hotel can enjoy entertainment by the pool (uno spazio giochi per bambini).

Marketing Strategies

The hotel's targeting strategies focus primarily on meetings: Its meeting space is one of the largest in Europe. The Centro Congressi (congress center) has a full range of rooms for conferences and conventions of any type or size, from the 1,700-seat auditorium to smaller rooms, a 2,300-square-meter exhibition space, a banquet facility that can accommodate 1,000 people, and parking facility that can accommodate 300 automobiles. In addition, the Centro also offers conference interpreting systems (six conference interpreting booths) and audio-visual presentation equipment, including a megascreen, making it an ideal venue for international events. About 65 percent of all hotel guests are conference participants. Hilton's sales offices in Italy (Milan) and overseas (in Germany, the United Kingdgom, France, Sweden, and the United Arab Emirates) are responsible for conference sales.

Tour operators constitute a second target group, accounting for 25 percent of the hotel's business. Their demand is highest in the months of July and August, when demand exceeds supply—Sorrento's location on the Bay and up a steep hill does not allow for space that could accommodate additional hotels. Only 10 percent of the hotel's business comes from individual bookings, the Internet, and telephone reservations.

The Hilton Sorrento Palace's main target market is Italy. In addition, the hotel also actively targets groups from the United Kingdom, Germany, Belgium, France, and Japan—in that order, according to Mr. Tantawi. Visitors from the United States previously constituted a large proportion of guests at the hotel, particularly in the summer, in organized tours. However, the number of American guests decreased considerably in recent years, starting with the terrorist attacks of September 11, 2001. Today, the numbers are even lower, as tourists from the United States have to cope with the radically increased value of the euro relative to the U.S. dollar and often restrict their visits to the main tourist attractions in Rome, Milan, Venice, and Florence.

However, as European economies tend to follow a similar economic cycle, it is preferable for the hotel to diversify and to attract more visitors from the United States. Recently, the hotel made extensive marketing attempts aimed at Japanese tour groups, with great success. The hotel's management would like to repeat those successes with U.S. visitors. They would like to find out how to best direct the hotel's marketing strategies to U.S. travelers visiting Italy and to persuade them to spend a weekend in a peaceful, semi-tropical paradise at the Hilton Sorrento Palace. The hotel is close to Rome, very close to Naples, and just a short flight from Milan—the primary airport for U.S. visitors. The hotel management would also like to increase conference attendance at the hotel in the off-season (November to March). Hilton managers are wondering how to attract professional groups from the United States using the organizations' counterparts in Italy. They had some initial discussions with an area business school about hosting an international management conference at the hotel. They would like to identify similar opportunities that would entail working with other local, regional, and national university groups, pharmaceutical companies, and medical organizations that would be able to bring U.S. guests to the Hilton Sorrento Palace.

Analysis Suggestions:

1. Conduct a study for the hotel (provide the entire research design) to identify U.S. travelers who have already committed to visit popular destinations in Italy (not including Sorrento).

2. Your research has a second step: to persuade U.S. travelers who have already committed to visit popular destinations in Italy to spend a weekend at the Hilton Sorrento Palace.

3. Conduct a third study to identify area businesses and organizations that are planning to host conferences at the Hilton Sorrento Palace during the off season.

4. For each of the previous studies, provide a complete research design and provide sample questionnaires that will be used in the research conducted with each segment.

Chapter 7: International Strategic Planning

Learning Objectives

After studying this chapter, you should be able to:

• Develop a general understanding of international marketing strategy at the different levels of the international organization and provide some insights into the international marketing planning process of selected companies.

• Identify the rationale for adopting a target marketing strategy in international markets.

• Identify the requirements necessary for effective international market segmentation.

• Introduce the concept of country attractiveness analysis and offer a blueprint for conducting the analysis.

• Identify the bases for consumer segmentation and offer company application examples.

• Describe the three targeting strategies used by companies worldwide.

• Describe the six positioning strategies that international companies can use to position their brands in the minds of target consumers.

VOLKSWAGEN

Ford, Motorola, Procter & Gamble: Reorganizing to Better Serve Customers

Ford, responding to rapid changes in the global economy, implemented a major reorganization, ending competing regional fiefdoms by consolidating engineering, design, and development within new global divisions developed to serve customers more efficiently. Motorola, faced with aggressive Asian competitors and falling profits, adopted a similar plan, replacing decentralized and competing businesses with three distinct global groups focusing on retail customers such as cell phone users, telecommunications companies, and government and industrial clients. Procter & Gamble initiated the broadest overhaul in its industry, transforming four business units based on geographic regions into seven global entities based on product lines such as baby care and food and beverage.[1]

In another example, SANYO engaged in a global reorganization of TV business. SANYO Electric formed a strategic alliance in its global TV business with Quanta Computer of Taiwan, hoping to use their joint strengths to implement a standard product platform and joint purchasing of materials and components—and thus ensure lower prices for customers. The new company is responsible for purchasing for all of SANYO's TV business for all world regions. In this reorganization, SANYO's TV business headquarters were transferred to North America, where it changed its name to SANYO TV International Corporation. The corporation created two business groups, a flat panel TV business for North America and Europe and a Cathode Ray Tube (CRT) TV business for emerging markets. SANYO's TV business in emerging markets set up in Hong Kong as SANYO TV International Asia, with SANYO BPL in India, P.T. SANYO Electronics Indonesia, and in China, Dongguan Huaqiang SANYO Electronics Co., Ltd., and Shenzhen Huaqiang SANYO Technology Design Co.[2]

International companies such as Motorola, Procter & Gamble, and SANYO need to consider the fit between their external environment and company characteristics and goals that optimally serve their target consumers. In the previous examples, the firms adapted to their environment based on consumer needs and preferences. In the case of SANYO, flat panel televisions are managed by an organization headquartered in the United States, for a target market located in North America and Europe.

This chapter offers an overview of international marketing strategy and provides insight into the international marketing planning process. The chapter covers tools for macro- and microsegmentation and strategies for targeting international consumers; it also identifies the different product positioning strategies that companies use in world markets.

7-1 Developing an International Marketing Strategy

An international marketing strategy involves developing and maintaining a strategic fit between the international company's objectives, competencies, and resources and the challenges presented by its international market or markets. The international strategic plan forges a link between the company's resources and its international goals and objectives in a complex, continually changing international environment. Given the changing nature of the environment, the international company's strategic plan cannot afford a typical long-term focus (a 5- or 10-year plan); rather, the planning process must be systematic and continual, and it must reevaluate objectives in light of new opportunities and potential threats.

Another dimension of international marketing strategy is linked to the company's commitment to its international markets. Some companies use international marketing only to test the waters or to unload overproduction. This approach to international marketing, although it might open long-term opportunities to the company, does not indicate a substantial commitment to internationalization and is not a premise for success in the long term. A long-term international commitment that entails substantial investment in terms of resources and personnel is likely to bring the company the greatest rewards. Such a strategy makes the company a stronger competitor in the world market, as well as at home. Appendix A, "The International Marketing Plan," offers guidance for the development of an international marketing plan.

International strategic planning takes place at different levels (see Figure 7-1):

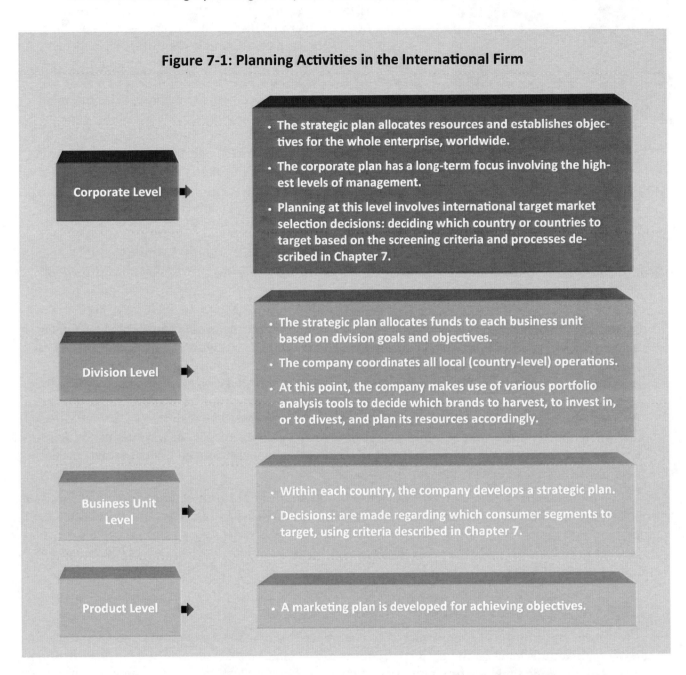

Figure 7-1: Planning Activities in the International Firm

Corporate Level

- The strategic plan allocates resources and establishes objectives for the whole enterprise, worldwide.
- The corporate plan has a long-term focus involving the highest levels of management.
- Planning at this level involves international target market selection decisions: deciding which country or countries to target based on the screening criteria and processes described in Chapter 7.

Division Level

- The strategic plan allocates funds to each business unit based on division goals and objectives.
- The company coordinates all local (country-level) operations.
- At this point, the company makes use of various portfolio analysis tools to decide which brands to harvest, to invest in, or to divest, and plan its resources accordingly.

Business Unit Level

- Within each country, the company develops a strategic plan.
- Decisions: are made regarding which consumer segments to target, using criteria described in Chapter 7.

Product Level

- A marketing plan is developed for achieving objectives.

- At the *corporate level,* the strategic plan allocates resources and establishes objectives for the whole enterprise worldwide. The corporate plan has a long-term focus and involves the highest levels of management. For example, PepsiCo Beverages headquarters (including its international headquarters) are located in Purchase, New York. The company's corporate plan is developed there. Planning at this level involves international target market selection decisions, deciding which country or countries to target based on the screening criteria and processes described in this chapter.

- At the *division level,* the strategic plan allocates funds to each business unit based on division goals and objectives. In the PepsiCo example, its divisions are organized regionally—for example, in Eastern Europe, its regional division is located in Vienna, Austria. From there, the company coordinates

all regional operations. At this point, PepsiCo may use various portfolio analysis tools to decide which brands to harvest, to invest in, or to divest, and plan its resources accordingly. PepsiCo's product portfolio for North America is the most comprehensive, with brands such as Pepsi-Cola (diet or regular), Pepsi Twist (regular and diet), Wild Cherry Pepsi, Pepsi Blue, Pepsi One, Pepsi Vanilla, Mountain Dew (regular and diet), Mountain Dew Code Red (regular and diet), Mountain Dew LiveWire, Mountain Dew Blueshock, Mountain Dew AMP energy drink, Mug, Sierra Mist (regular and diet), Slice, Lipton (in partnership), Dole juice, FruitWorks juice drinks, Aquafina (water), Frappuccino coffee and Starbucks DoubleShot (in partnership), SoBe juice drinks, and SoBe energy drinks. For the international market, it offers Pepsi-Cola, Pepsi Light (same as diet), Pepsi Limón, Pepsi Max, Mirinda, 7UP, Kas, Teem, Manzanita Sol, Paso de los Toros, Fruko, Evervess, Yedigun, Shani, Fiesta, Radical Fruit, and, under license, D&G and Mandarin. [3]

- At the *business unit level,* within each country, decisions are made regarding which consumer segments to target, using criteria described in this chapter. At this level, PepsiCo develops a strategic plan.

- At the *product level* (line, brand), a marketing plan is developed for achieving objectives. In the United Kingdom, Pepsi's marketing plan involves a heavy emphasis on advertising. Pepsi is the king of big budget, star-studded television commercials. Their intention is for viewers to talk about the ads as much as about the programming on which the ads appear. Pepsi stars have been the "who's who" of the pop world, starting with Michael Jackson in the 1980s, continuing with Madonna and Ray Charles in the 1990s, then with the Spice Girls, Robbie Williams, Britney Spears, Pink, Enrique Iglesias, Boyzone, Mariah Carey, and, more recently, Nicki Minaj. It also signed up with U.K.'s ITV's series *Pop Idol* when it first started in 2002, and with its series *I'm a Celebrity* in 2004. As a consequence, Pepsi was the United Kingdom's 33rd biggest brand. U.K.'s ITV channel has been a key partner, making possible Pepsi's close relationship with British consumers. [4]

In other company examples, at division level, Kraft has its Kraft North America Commercial division, its largest division with many offerings (beverages, dairy, grocery, snacks and cereals, foodservice, among others), and its Kraft International Commercial division, which is organized on the geographic region it serves, not on the products it sells—Asia Pacific, Eastern Europe, Middle East and Africa, European Union, and Latin America. [5]

7-1a Developing an International Marketing Plan

At this stage of the planning process, the international company develops marketing strategies for the target market, deciding on the product mix for the local target market, as well as on the other components of the marketing mix (distribution, promotion, and pricing); plans the international marketing programs; and manages (organizes, implements, and controls) the marketing effort.

The decision on which elements of the marketing mix to use in a particular target market is closely linked to the product's life cycle and to the market entry strategy selected. A product in the early stages of its life cycle, such as the Palm Pilot, will most likely be sold to consumers in highly industrialized countries for a high price, accompanied by heavy promotion. Such a product will most likely be manufactured in a developed country and exported to the rest of the world. Alternatively, a product in the later stages of its life cycle, such as a videocassette recorder, will be sold to consumers worldwide, regardless of country development level. The company selling the product will heavily compete on price and, thus, most likely manufacture the product in a developing country, where labor is inexpensive, to sell all over the world. Most likely, the company will have at least one subsidiary located in the country of product manufacture.

Kraft Foods

Insights into the marketing strategies that companies use to target international markets reveal that marketing mix decisions are complex and based on extensive research. Kraft Foods (www.kraftfoods.com), a company based in the United States, has made interesting product mix decisions. It sells coffee products and confectionery products that cover the spectrum of target consumers—and the brands often overlap in terms of their target market! In addition, Kraft Foods has different mix strategies for each market. And it sells to the U.S. consumer only a fraction of its international coffee and confectionery offerings, some of which are positioned as premium European imports.

Among the many brands of coffee Kraft Foods offers [6] are:

Maxwell House—"America's favorite coffee," this brand is also doing well in China, Taiwan, and South Korea, France, Germany, Poland, Russia, the United Kingdom, and Ireland.

Jacobs Coffee—This product sells mainly in Central and Eastern Europe. Its target countries are Austria, the Czech Republic, Germany, Hungary, Latvia, Lithuania, Poland, Slovakia, Switzerland and Turkey. Jacobs coffee is popularly known as a quality German brand. Kraft purchased Jacobs Suchard in the early 1990s, gaining the famed European confectionary items (Suchard, Milka, and Toblerone chocolates) along with Jacobs coffee for its portfolio.

Gevalia Coffee—This brand is aimed at the Scandinavian market and imported into the United States as a gourmet product sold exclusively by mail order.

Kaffee HAG—Especially known for its decaffeinated coffee, it is available in Austria, Germany, and Italy.

Carte Noire—A super-premium brand, leading the premium category in France, and gaining market share in Belgium, Ireland, and the United Kingdom.

In the company's international product portfolio, there are also country-specific offerings, such as *Maxim* in Japan, which is also available in South Korea; *Kenco* in Ireland and the United Kingdom; *Blendy* in Japan; *Saimaza* in Spain; and *Tassimo* and *Jacques Vabre* in France.

Kraft uses a similar strategy with its numerous confectionery brands. Its *Toblerone* chocolates are available all over the world; its *Suchard* and *Milka* chocolate brands are available in most of Europe, and *Milka* is now available in the United States as a premium brand, even though, in Europe, it is among the cheapest chocolates, selling for just under 3 euros for a 10.6 ounce bar at the supermarket Edeka in Germany. Its *Côte d'Or* brand is available in Belgium, Netherlands, France, and Italy, with the rest of its brands focusing primarily on a target country or region. In this category are *Marabou* and *Daim*, available in the Nordic countries; *Freia* in Norway; *Sonho De Valsa* and *Laka* in Brazil—among many other offerings.

How did Kraft decide on the previously described markets and the combinations of offerings for each market or world region? Through a careful evaluation of the local consumers and their preference and an equally thorough evaluation of its own capabilities, and overall internationalization goals. Like Kraft, companies entering new countries, buying local products, and bringing their own international brands to these markets, have to make important decisions regarding their local and regional portfolios. And, in the process, they must monitor not only the constantly changing marketing environment, but also changes in competitive intensity, competitor product/service quality strategies, supply chains, and consumer expectations. This will then help them to carefully target international market segments and appropriately position their products relative to those of the international and local competition.

target marketing
The process of focusing on those segments that the company can serve most effectively and design products, services, and marketing programs with these segments in mind.

segmentation
The process of identifying consumers and international markets that are similar with regard to key traits, such as product-related needs and wants, and that would respond well to a product and related marketing mix.

7-2 The Rationale for Target Marketing

With the exception of narrow markets, one single company, however large its resources and capacity, could not possibly serve all customers. Consumers worldwide are too numerous, and their needs and wants are too diverse. Companies must focus on those segments that they can serve most effectively and design products and services with these segments in mind; that is, they must engage in international **target marketing.**

International target marketing is used by companies to:

• Identify countries and segments of international consumers that are similar with regard to key traits, who would respond well to a product and related marketing mix (international market segmentation).

• Select the countries and segments that the company can serve most efficiently and develop products tailored to each (international market targeting).

• Offer the products to the market, communicating, through the marketing mix, product traits and benefits that differentiate it in the consumer's mind (market positioning).

7-3 International Market Segmentation

International market segmentation involves identifying countries and consumers that are similar with regard to key traits, such as product-related needs and wants, and that would respond well to a product and related marketing mix. International **segmentation,** thus, must be performed at the country level (macrosegmentation) and at the consumer level (microsegmentation).

At the country level, segmentation analysis identifies countries that are similar in aspects relevant to the company. If a company produces luxury goods, for example, economic variables can help determine whether a sufficient number of consumers can afford to purchase the company products. At the consumer level, segmentation analysis identifies consumers who are looking for the same benefits in the product. Although all consumers seek an efficient mode of transportation when they purchase an automobile, they also fulfill other desires. Consumers in rural Scotland may seek a small, versatile vehicle that can maneuver through tight single-lane roads, whereas executives in Dubai or Abu Dhabi of the United Arab Emirates may want a luxury automobile that exudes high status and elegance to navigate on impeccable roads.

7-3a Requirements for International Segmentation

Regardless of whether the segmentation analysis is performed at the country level or at the individual consumer level, several requirements must be met for market segmentation to be effective. The requirements, which apply equally to country and consumer segmentation, are shown in Figure 7-2.

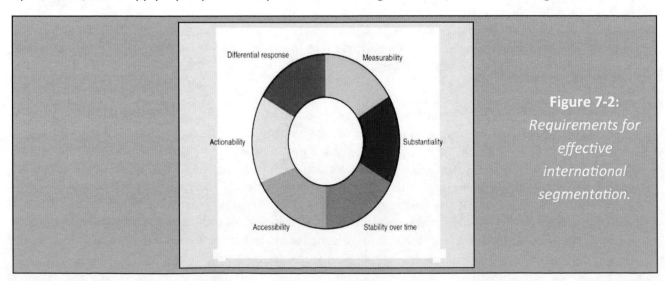

Figure 7-2: *Requirements for effective international segmentation.*

Measurability

measurability
The ability to estimate the size of a market segment.

substantiality
The extent to which the market is large enough to warrant investment.

Individual market segments should be easy to identify and measure, thus ensuring **measurability.** International market segments pose numerous challenges in this regard. First, in many developing countries, reliable population statistics, including market size and economic development data, are difficult to come by. Even if the International Monetary Fund and other development organizations' data are reliable and valid, international companies still run into difficulties when evaluating culture-related dimensions, such as product preferences, especially food products, and benefits sought. Collecting data on such variables also presents many challenges.

For example, working backward, from product performance to segmentation, the Wonderbra has sold well in Islamic countries. What benefit could women seek when purchasing the Wonderbra in an environment where many women are fully covered in thick clothing in public? Research would find that women dress primarily to impress other women in many Islamic countries, in a friendly competitive way. To be able to reach such conclusions, the research study would have to explore motivations beyond basic product benefits. Furthermore, the subjects must be willing to share such information.

Substantiality

The segment should be large enough to warrant investment. Assuming that the segment can be measured, this step—determining **substantiality**—is relatively easy. Even if research determines that the local market segment is not large enough, it can be grouped together with an identical segment in another country and targeted jointly. Another dimension that must be evaluated is the segment's growth potential. Such data must be evaluated with surrogate statistics, such as economic development measures (i.e., as an increase in GDP per capita or income per capita), employment data, the level of foreign direct investment in the country, exports from the country, and trends in consumer spending. An important consideration here is also the intensity of competition directed at the same segment. All of these examples constitute important variables that must be evaluated to determine the market's viability in the future. A substantial and growing market is listeners of world beat music; see International Marketing Illustration 7-1.

International Marketing Illustration 7-1

Naming the Brand

World beat—or world music—is a popular genre of music that has been around since the late 1980s. It is a mix of techno and Latin beats, hip-hop, and African or Arab beats, with a synthesized ethnic melodic touch. This music is marketed effectively to the world beat consumer segment worldwide. Some classify world beat as a catch-all that does not include the music genres popular in the United States—such as top 40, rock, country, classical, jazz, and so forth. World beat (groups accessible at www.cdnow.com) ranges from more traditional Europop groups to African hip-hop or reggae, Afropop, Bhangra, and Latin American jazz groups—such as Cuba's Buena Vista Social Club. Even heavy metal groups have dabbled in world beat, starting as early as the 1970s, with Led Zeppelin's album Kashmir, to current bands such as Tool and Nile.

National Public Radio is popularizing this format in the United States. However, worldwide, this genre has much broader appeal.

The market for world beat is the world beat consumer. This genre of music appeals across cultures and across age groups; in Europe, Asia, and Africa, listeners range from teenagers to forty-somethings. The opportunities that this segment presents to entertainment companies are immense. In North America, this type of music is especially popular in Canada. In one example, the International Jazz Festival in Montreal, attended by hundreds of thousands yearly, is, in fact a world beat event, featuring contemporary world music artists such as Keith Jarrett, Anouar Brahem, Tord Gustavsen, Nik Bärtsch's Ronin, and Stefano Bollani.[7]

stability over time
The extent to which preferences are stable, rather than changing, in a market segment.

target market
Consumers and international markets that are similar in aspects relevant to the company.

accessibility
The ability to communicate with the international target market.

actionability
The extent to which the target market segment is responsive to the marketing strategies used.

differential response
The extent to which international market segments respond differently to marketing strategies.

Stability over Time

In the past, stability of a segment over time was a primary consideration mainly for developed countries. Today, however, **stability over time** is an important consideration in a world environment where products are in different life-cycle stages and where preferences are continually changing with the advent of the Internet and online ordering across borders from countries of all development levels. In a rapidly changing environment, it is important to constantly reevaluate this segment.

Accessibility

The ability to communicate with the **target market,** determining the market's **accessibility,** is essential as well. Internationally, the differences in language in individual countries may pose obstacles, greatly increasing the cost of advertising and other promotions. Marketing in large emerging markets, such as India and China, could present challenges for different reasons: Communicating with Indian consumers outside of the large metropolitan areas necessitates expensive translation into the many local languages. Similarly, communicating with Chinese consumers in the countryside may be difficult because the large rural population has a more limited access to technology. The ability to serve the market is also essential. Companies should be able to freely access the market; the market must be open to international companies and reachable (i.e., topography and local governments and local media should permit access to the target market).

Actionability

Actionability refers to the idea that the market should respond to the marketing strategies used, assuming that the company is targeting the market with the appropriate marketing mix. Consider, for example, the Colgate-Palmolive strategy for Latin America and the Balkans. In both markets, the company noted that its dishwashing liquid was not selling well. Research revealed, for this large market segment, a different approach to washing dishes—using soap slivers in a tub. As soon as the company developed a tub with dishwashing paste and promoted the product to the market, sales took off. The segment responded as intended to the strategy. The segment was actionable.

Differential Response

The segments should be easy to distinguish from each other and should respond differently from other market segments to marketing strategies; they should have a noticeable **differential response.** If consumers all over the world are similar or have identical preferences—and this is hardly the case—there is no need for international target marketing.

7-3b Macrosegmentation: Country Attractiveness Analysis

Companies have different criteria that they consider essential for committing to a particular market. PepsiCo International did not consider profit as the main criterion when it approached the former Soviet Union to establish a countertrade agreement; rather, market size and the ultimate potential of the market were the company's primary concerns. As a first step in the segmentation process, companies engage in macrosegmentation, grouping countries based on such criteria as economic performance, evaluating the potential of a particular market; political, legal, and financial environment; marketing support infrastructure; the company brand's standing or potential standing relative to existing competition; and the degree of market fit with company resources, policies, and goals. These criteria, in turn, are used in the screening process to select and target the countries that present the highest potential to the company.

Firms could use the following criteria to group countries and, based on these criteria, select those countries that offer the most opportunity for the company and those countries that should be targeted:

- Market potential
- The political, legal, and financial environment of the country

- The marketing support infrastructure in the country

- Brand/company franchise relative to competing products/companies

- Degree of market fit with company policies, goals, and resources

Market Potential

Countries can be grouped based on market potential. The potential of a market can be evaluated based on the rate of economic development, as expressed through validated, reliable market indicators, such as:

- Gross domestic product (GDP) per capita

- Industrial and agricultural sectors statistics

- Market size and potential

- Consumer buying power

- International investment figures, such as foreign direct investment data and other trade statistics

Such indicators identify countries and markets where the company should invest important resources and engage in long-term commitment. Attractive big emerging markets, such as Brazil or China, have initially presented many challenges to international companies. Brazil in the 1970s and 1980s was plagued by runaway inflation and instability, whereas China was an unpredictable market closed to international scrutiny and influence.

With time, both countries have opened their markets to international investment, which has led to rapid economic development and prosperity. In the case of Brazil, statistics demonstrate enormous growth. With a population of more than 190 million, of which almost half are younger than 20 years old, and with a GDP growing from US$800 billion in 1997 to more than US$2.3 trillion in 2011, Brazil is performing well. As a result, Brazil is a viable player in the world trade arena.[8]

Similar potential is now presented by the countries of the former Soviet Union. These countries, despite being plagued by inflation and instability, all have a literate, educated workforce and an excess of highly qualified labor on one hand and a consuming public that is eager to experience new products on the other. Among attractive markets of the former Soviet Union are the Baltic republics (Estonia, Latvia, and Lithuania), Russia, and Belarus, all of which are being actively targeted by multinationals; Estonia adopted the euro in 2011 and, since then, business is booming with cross-border shoppers. See Figure 7-3

Figure 7-3: *Cross-border shoppers are abundant in Estonia. Full ships, carrying Finnish consumers returning home with large quantities of alcoholic drinks, taking advantage of lower prices in Estonia. As of 2011, Finnish consumers shopping in Estonia no longer have to deal with the hassles and the costs of converting currency - they can pay in euros.*

Of interest in the future are many of the former republics of the former Soviet Union, such as Armenia, Azerbaijan, Georgia, Kazakhstan, the Kyrgyz Republic, Turkmenistan, and Uzbekistan. A number of these countries have made important inroads on the path to economic development and prosperity: Kazakhstan, the Kyrgyz Republic, Uzbekistan, and oil-rich Turkmenistan are rapidly developing their banking systems and have adopted pro-market structural reforms. Many companies that initially only exported to these countries are now committing greater resources or even engaging in aggressive foreign direct investment.

The Political, Legal, and Financial Environment of the Country

Countries also can be grouped based on their political, legal, and financial environment. Some of the following criteria should be considered when evaluating a potential country for entry:

- Ethnic conflict in the region
- History of war engagement
- Antiforeigner rhetoric
- Recent nationalization activity
- Legal ambiguity—especially in business
- Trade barriers erected by government to protect local business
- Exchange rate controls

Companies are not likely to succeed in markets where there is high political risk. Sri Lanka, a small country located southeast of the Indian subcontinent, is no longer even a viable export market. Tensions between the Sinhalese majority and the Tamil minority have escalated out of control, with Tamil separatists targeting Sri Lanka's airport. Over two decades, the conflict has practically demolished the country economically, driving the once-booming tourism industry out of Sri Lanka.

Even oil-rich countries could present a risk for companies considering entering these markets. Sudan, for example, discovered substantial oil reserves; however, its initially modest exports have only further fueled an ethnic civil war that has been raging for more than two decades. Today, increased oil production coupled with high oil prices, a revived light industry, and expanded export processing zones have helped sustain GDP growth at about 10 percent.[9] However, in spite of a strong GDP growth, Sudan represents a risk for long-term investment due to continuing clashes between rebel factions and government-armed militia.

Ambiguities in the legal system create an environment that renders companies vulnerable to competitive theft, lack of trademark protection, bribery pressures, and employee theft. In such an environment, where everything is perceived as allowed unless expressly forbidden, even exporting can pose difficulties. For example, it can force firms to incur bribery costs that cannot be justified to the headquarters or to the home-country government for mere access to the market. Finally, exchange-rate controls can restrict the types of products that can be exported to the target market and impede the repatriation of profits.

One related issue is whether the country is a member of the World Trade Organization (WTO) or of a regional block, such as the European Union or the Southern Cone Common Market (MERCOSUR). Countries that adhere to regulations of the WTO and that have the supra-national controls of regional integration are more likely to have a stable environment that promotes trade and investment.

The Marketing Support Infrastructure in the Country

The marketing support infrastructure of the target country is an important determinant of country attractiveness. Important to international firms are the availability and reliability of distribution and logistics providers to ensure that the product is delivered in a timely fashion at locations convenient to consumers.

Countries also can be grouped based on the availability of competent partners for firms contemplating international partnerships. A firm entering a new market should have access to capable local firms.

In many developing countries, only few such firms may be available, and all other competitors will attempt to approach them. For instance, for large multinationals attempting to enter the Turkish market, Sabanci Holdings is in great demand and already boasts joint-venture and distribution partners in companies as varied as Carrefour supermarkets, Danone dairy products, Dresdner Bank, DuPont, IBM, Mitsubishi, Philip Morris, and Toyota.

The information technology available to members of the local distribution chain is an important consideration in that it maximizes supply chain efficiencies and minimizes warehousing and logistics costs to the company. The level of local telecommunications development is also essential in ensuring adequate data flow and access to suppliers, clients, and company headquarters. Countries also should be evaluated on the availability of adequate local advertising support, such as local advertising talent and open access to media for advertising and other communication purposes. Finally, the availability of other service providers, such as marketing research firms, financial firms, and management consulting firms, is also essential for company performance in the market.

Brand/Company Franchise Relative to Competing Products/Companies

Markets where a brand or company name is already established with local consumers—either by reputation, through advertising, or experience (for consumers who have bought the product abroad or have heard of the company)—offer greater potential to the company.

This situation is especially true if the company has only few viable direct competitors. Markets can thus be segmented based on the reputation of the product and company in the market and on the competitive density in the market for the company's products. Here, a related dimension is also useful: that of *lead country* (a country where products are first adopted) versus *lag country* (a country where products are last adopted). The lead/lag concept also is closely linked to the level of economic development and is particularly relevant to firms at the forefront of technology. These firms usually first introduce their products in lead countries.

Degree of Market Fit with Company Policies, Goals, and Resources

For companies that have the resources and the goal to saturate the world market, such as McDonald's and Coca-Cola, no market is too small. Other companies that have the resources but whose products cater only to the luxury market will most likely ignore countries with a limited number of elite consumers and focus on industrialized countries or countries with substantial revenues from national resources, such as oil and diamonds. Yet other companies have limited resources and can afford to target consumers in only one or a few countries. For these companies, it is essential to select those markets that are perceived as the most appropriate for their goals and that provide the lowest level of risk.

7-3c Microsegmentation: Focusing on the Target Consumer

The purpose of microsegmentation is to identify clusters of consumers that respond in a similar fashion to a company's marketing strategies. Identifying individual market segments enables the company to produce products that meet the precise needs of target consumers with a marketing mix that is appropriately tailored for those segments. The international company typically conducts extensive marketing research to identify such segments.

Bases for Segmentation

In the process of analyzing consumer demand and identifying clusters of consumers that respond similarly to marketing strategies, firms must identify those bases for segmentation that are most relevant for its products or service offerings. The features that identify the bases for segmentation that companies may use in the process of analyzing their international markets are described next.

Demographic and Psychographic Segmentation

Demographics are statistics that describe the population, such as age, gender, race, income, education, occupation, social class, life-cycle stage, and household size. Demographics are easy to measure and to compare across countries; for this reason, they are widely used by international companies.

Consumers worldwide exhibit many differences with regard to **demographic segmentation** variables. The following examples demonstrate how these differences have important implications for marketing:

- *Age*—Countries that have a rapidly aging population (the Scandinavian countries, for example) present different challenges and opportunities to international firms than countries with half of their population younger than 20 (such as Brazil and most countries in sub-Saharan Africa) (see International Marketing Illustration 7-2).

- *Urbanization and social class*—Industrialized countries, such as the United States, Japan, and the countries of Western Europe, are primarily urban and have a large middle class with substantial buying power. China's rural consumers are poor and have limited buying power. Its urban consumers fall into four segments: "working poor" and "salaried class"—together accounting for 80 percent of the urban population; "the little rich," 15 percent of the urban population; and young urban professionals, or "yuppies," representing nearly 5 percent of the urban households.[12] Although multinationals such as Coca-Cola and Kodak actively target middle class consumers in the industrialized countries with their global brands, in China, they target their global brands primarily to yuppies; for the remaining 95 percent of the population, multinationals have developed or acquired local brands in addition to their premium global brands.[13]

- *Education*—Most developed countries, countries that were formerly communist, and countries that are under a communist rule (China, for example, where the literacy rate is close to 90 percent) have a high literacy rate and heavily emphasize education. In contrast, countries in sub-Saharan Africa have a lower literacy rate; here, education is a privilege. Companies that target these consumers have to adapt the marketing mix, describing product use pictorially in their communications. Countries where education is stressed present opportunities for educational institutions intending to expand globally, to firms selling training technology and software, and so on.

Demographics are closely linked to psychographics, which include lifestyles, values, attitudes, interests, and opinions. It is difficult to describe psychographics without demographics. Cultural variables such as religion, norms, and language influence consumer product preferences as well. As such, these variables can be used as bases for segmentation. For example, Hofstede's dimensions—described in Chapter 5, "Cultural Influences on International Marketing"—can be used to segment countries based on individualism/collectivism, masculinity/femininity, uncertainty/avoidance, and power/distance. A study conducted with consumers in Europe[14] found that consumers in the Scandinavian countries have a small power/distance (are more egalitarian), have a low uncertainty/avoidance (take more risks), rate high on individualism, and have a low level of masculinity (low ambition and competitiveness). These consumers share certain traits that marketers can stress: They seek variety and prefer environmentally friendly products.

---

demographic segmentation
The process of identifying market segments based on age, gender, race, income, education, occupation, social class, life cycle stage, and household size.

psychographic segmentation
The use of values, attitudes, interests, and other cultural variables to segment consumers.

global youth segment
A psychodemographic global group of teenagers considered to be astute consumers with precise desires for brand name clothing products and entertainment.

Many management consulting firms have come up with systems for segmenting consumers, clustering them on different behavioral and psychological dimensions, or **psychographic segmentation.** In the United States, a popular classification system is *Acorn*, which classifies individuals based on ZIP code. Another classification of lifestyles is provided by SRI Consulting Business Intelligence, which offers the *VALS 2* (www.sric-bi.com) psychographic consumer segmentation system. Upon completing a questionnaire containing lifestyle and demographic questions, individual respondents are categorized based on resources and on the extent to which they are action oriented. VALS also has a survey that is especially designed for the Japanese market.

Global market segments present important opportunities for standardized marketing. Among the global psychodemographic (a combination of psychographic and demographic segments) segments that have emerged are the following:

- **Global youth segment**—Psychographically, teenagers are described as astute consumers with precise desires for brand name clothing products and entertainment. They are described in International Marketing Illustration 7-2.

International Marketing Illustration 7-2
The Global Youth Consumer Segment

Worldwide, the global youth consumer segment presents an important opportunity for U.S. corporations to leverage their investment. The global youth segment has a purchasing power of more than $100 billion; in the United States, only 21 percent of the population is aged 14 or younger, but in many other countries, especially in Asia, the youth market far outnumbers that of the United States—for example, in India, 35 percent of the population is younger than 14. There are emerging similarities in youth culture across the globe. For example, technology is a major focus of the youth market. And brands and styles preferred by young people around the world are surprisingly alike: The more exposure they have to common information—through the Internet, for instance—the more homogeneous young people appear to become.[10]

Global youth purchase products such as Levi's and Diesel jeans, Nike shoes, and Ralph Lauren clothing. They see newly released movies, listen to popular musicians, go to discos, and are interested in music in general. Marketers find this segment particularly attractive: Coca-Cola has successfully targeted global teenagers and preteens (see Figure 7-4) with messages that use local and international celebrity endorsers; Nike is continually producing new designs for them.

Coca-Cola is presently targeting the youth segment worldwide with a major global interactive marketing initiative called iCoke, aimed at reconnecting with young people through digital music and mobile and branded entertainment. It launched its iCoke Web sites worldwide, starting with China, Canada, and the United Kingdom, followed by the rest of the world. It offered on-pack promotions aimed at driving customers to the iCoke Web sites. It also partnered with mobile music company Shazam Entertainment for a joint ringtones and downloads promotion across 275 million Coke and Diet Coke cans.[11]

Figure 7-4: *These representatives of the global youth segment listen to rap, adore Niki Minaj, and are increasingly fashion conscious.*

- **Global elite**—The global elite have the highest income of all consumers. From a psychographic perspective, they travel the globe, often have homes in more than one country, and spend money on luxury brands, such as Rolex, Prada, and Mercedes (the E-Class models and beyond). The marketing mix typically used to target this group focuses on status: exclusive distribution, high price, and status-oriented advertising messages.

global elite
A psychodemographic group worldwide characterized by high income and desire for status brands and exclusive distribution.

- **Global gay and lesbian segment**—This psychographic segment has received much focus from marketing in recent years. The gay and lesbian segment has been identified as a loyal segment, purchasing brands that are positioned as gay-friendly. It has also been identified as a segment with a high percentage of disposable income—and with a willingness to spend it for travel, entertainment, and luxury items (see Figure 7-5).

Figure 7-5:

Christopher Street Day Parade, Berlin: Gay-friendly brands in this parade included Ford Motor Company, which had its own automobile featured in the parade, Red Bull, Smirnoff Vodka, and Nivea, as well as local goods and services. Nivea, in its promotional giveaways (shampoo, hair gel, lotion), was positioning itself as "a man's thing."

Benefit Segmentation

Benefit segmentation also is a useful tool for identifying uniform consumer segments. Marketers who understand the motivation behind consumer purchases are able to send the appropriate message to the relevant market segments. Internationally, important differences exist between the benefits sought from purchasing a particular product. Consumers in the United States purchase soft drinks such as Coke and Pepsi to quench their thirst on a regular basis. In Eastern Europe, Asia, and Africa, these brands are purchased primarily as special-occasion drinks.

In other examples, the majority of consumers in developing countries are not as much interested in brand names as they are in product performance and value. Marketing strategies catering to these preferences have succeeded in China. Philips Electronics introduced a popular combination video/CD player, which Chinese consumers perceived as good value for the money.[15] And, although consumers in the United States seek speedy service, quality food, and convenience in fast-food chains, consumers in emerging markets are particularly attracted to the clean environment, pleasant ambience, polite staff, and air conditioning.[16]

Usage and User Status Segmentation

Usage rate indicates the extent to which individuals are:

- Nonusers
- Occasional users
- Medium users
- Heavy users

Consumers worldwide can be segmented based on these **usage segmentation** dimensions. Segments of consumers identified as heavy users of a product category would constitute prime target markets for new brands in the category. For example, French women are heavy users of perfume, have a refined understanding of scent, and use different brands (often of the same company) at different times of day and for different occasions. Similarly, German, Dutch, and Belgian consumers are heavy users of beer. In each country, hundreds of breweries carry specialty beers, and each country is also an exporter of global beer brands.

User status refers to the status as:

- Users of competitors' products (nonuser)
- Ex-users
- Potential users
- First-time users
- Regular users

In terms of **user status segmentation,** the ideal consumer is the regular, heavy user! Companies introducing a product for the first time to a market of nonusers face enormous and costly challenges, in that they have to educate consumers about the product and convince them to buy, but these companies also can reap huge rewards, especially if they are first in the market. The paper towel offering in Europe was practically nonexistent before the introduction of the Procter & Gamble Bounty brand; consumers typically used cloth towels in the kitchen. Bounty introduced its quality, heavy-duty paper towels in the late 1990s, accompanied by heavy promotion—particularly direct mail samples. In the Netherlands, those samples consisted of just one towel, nicely folded, and mailed in a plastic bag. The brand quickly took off, and now many households have an accessory previously nonexistent in European households: a paper towel holder. It is, however, much smaller than its U.S. counterpart—about half the height, with the roll also half the width.

Geographic Segmentation

Geographic segmentation can be performed at the macrosegmentation level—country analysis, membership in international trade forums, regional blocks, and so on—as well as within the country. Consumers differ within countries with regard to demographics and psychographics, such as ethnicity, religion, and language spoken. Even in small countries such as Switzerland, the marketing mix needs to be adapted for German Swiss, French Swiss, and Italian Swiss consumers. They constitute segments that differ not only linguistically, but also with regard to other aspects of culture, and consequently are likely to respond differently to marketing strategies. Belgium also is a case in point: A Dutch-speaking Flemish culture thrives in the north; in the French-speaking south, people view themselves as Wallonians rather than Europeans or Belgians; and a small German-speaking community exists in the southeast.[18]

> **geographic segmentation**
> Market segmentation based on geographic location, such as country or region.

7-4 Targeting International Consumers

7-4a Target Market Decisions: Country Screening and Selection

Companies engage in processes that involve extensive evaluation of countries' attractiveness for the purpose of market entry. In this evaluative process, a company must ensure that it does not overlook countries with potential and that it does not target markets in countries that do not provide sufficient potential or that present a high risk. To ensure that markets that present the most promise to the company—based on the company's goals and resources—are selected, countries are submitted to a screening process. Most often, screening of potential markets follows a variant of these three stages:

- Assigning an importance score to country screening criteria
- Evaluating country performance on each of the screening criteria
- Calculating the country attractiveness score

Assigning an Importance Score to Country Screening Criteria

An international company would typically aggregate a selection of criteria—discussed in Section 7-3b, "Macrosegmentation: Country Attractiveness Analysis"—that the company deemed important. Among these criteria are market potential, determined using economic indicators; the degree of political and financial stability; the extent to which the legal system is transparent and predictable; the state of the marketing infrastructure in the country; the degree to which consumers have a preference for company brands; the extent of competitive intensity in the market; and the market fit with company goals, policies, and resources. The criteria deemed important are selected from brand managers in different international markets, salespeople, industry country specialists working for management consulting firms, and international suppliers and distributors. Each criterion is then assigned an importance weight that denotes the extent to which the company considers a particular trait important in its decision to enter the market.

Evaluating Country Performance on Each of the Screening Criteria

In the second stage of country screening and selection, potential target countries are rated on each of the criteria enumerated. The rating process may involve the same evaluators as in the first stage.

Calculating the Country Attractiveness Score

In the third stage of country screening and selection, the importance score is multiplied by the performance score for each of the screening variables. The total score for each country is then calculated by adding the resulting scores. This is the country attractiveness score that can be used to compare potential target countries.

7-4b -Target Market Decisions: The Target Market Strategy

Companies that have ample resources can, and often do, address the needs of all segments of consumers. Procter & Gamble, Henkel, and Kraft attempt to target all consumers with the products they sell, filling the supermarket and discount store shelves with what seemingly are competing brands and saturating the media with their communication, meeting all related needs of the global consumer at a nice profit. Other companies with sufficient resources choose to focus on one well-established brand, improving it continuously, offering alternatives under the same umbrella brand name. Boeing uses such a strategy and, to date, it has only one true direct competitor—Airbus Industries. Not all international companies have the resources of the companies mentioned here. Frequently, small and medium-sized businesses are quite successful internationally as they are in the home-country market, by best addressing the needs of one segment, or a niche. One common trait of all these international companies is that they research closely their consumers and target and position their products accordingly.

Companies can use the three main strategies in Table 7-1 to target their international markets.

Table 7-1: International Targeting Strategies

Strategy	Purpose
Differentiated targeting strategy	Differentiated targeting strategies identify, or even create, market segments that want different benefits from a product and target them with different brands, using different marketing strategies.
Concentrated targeting strategy	Companies select only one market segment and target it with a single brand. Companies that cannot afford to compete in a mature market with an oligopoly may choose to pursue a small segment—a niche.
Undifferentiated targeting strategies	The product is aimed at all markets using a single strategy, regardless of the number of markets and countries targeted.

Differentiated Targeting Strategy

Companies that use a **differentiated targeting** strategy identify, or even create, market segments that want different benefits from a product and target them with different brands, using different marketing strategies. Some companies have the necessary resources to offer at least one product to every conceivable market segment. Procter & Gamble, for example, offers a variety of laundry detergents and fabric care products in North America: Bounce, Cheer, Downy, Dreft, Era, Febreze, Gain, Ivory, and Tide. To Western European consumers, the company offers Ace, Antikal Ariel, Bounce, Bonux, Dash, Daz, Dreft, Fairy, Febreze, Gama, Lenor, and Vizir.[18] Each of these laundry detergents appeals to a different market: consumers who want a detergent that has an excellent cleaning ability, consumers who need whitening, consumers who need fabric softening agents in the washing process, consumers who need a product for sensitive fabrics or for babies' sensitive skin, and consumers who may be allergic.

differentiated targeting
A targeting strategy identifying market segments with different preferences for a particular product category and targeting each segment with different brands and different marketing strategies.

concentrated targeting
The process of selecting only one market segment and targeting it with a single brand.

Concentrated Targeting Strategy

Not all companies can afford to offer something for everyone, and not all companies want to meet the needs of all consumers. In fact, many companies select only one market, and segment and target it with one single brand, using a **concentrated targeting** strategy. Mont Blanc, a company manufacturing pens and fountain pens, offers a relatively limited product selection that it markets using the same theme worldwide—"the art of writing." This product is targeted at the professional class.

Undifferentiated Targeting Strategies and Standardization

undifferentiated targeting
A targeting strategy aiming the product at the market using a single strategy, regardless of the number of segments.

The existence of similar consumer needs worldwide presents opportunities for international firms. They can reap the benefits of standardization by achieving economies of scale in the manufacturing process and in distribution and promotion. Pure standardization can be described as an **undifferentiated targeting** strategy, in which the product is aimed at the market using a single strategy regardless of the number of countries targeted and regardless of the locations where it is marketed.

Yet even products that are created as pure global brands, such as Coke, are not marketed using a standardized, undifferentiated strategy. Coke is sold primarily in recyclable glass and plastic bottles requiring a high deposit in Africa and Europe, whereas, in the United States, it is sold in disposable cans and plastic bottles. Its taste differs depending on the market. Diet Coke is sold as Coca-Cola Light elsewhere in the world. Heineken, the Dutch beer that bills itself as the world's most international brewery, uses a global positioning strategy of premium pricing and high quality, whereas, in Holland, the beer is positioned as a product for the masses. It costs slightly more than a one-liter bottle of Coke. And in North America and Europe, Volkswagen's Passat has been offered under different brand names in the international market. Among these names are Santana, Dasher, Quantum, Magotan, and Corsar. Santana has the highest name recognition of all the automobile brands in China and most taxicabs in Shanghai, for example, are Santana automobiles (see Figure 7-6).

Figure 7-6

Shanghai Volkswagen, a partnership between Shanghai Automotive and Volkswagen, sells the Santana automobile, the automobile that has the highest brand awareness among Chinese consumers.

7-5 Positioning the Brand

Positioning entails placing the brand in the consumer's mind in relation to other competing products, based on product traits and benefits that are relevant to the consumer. Such a process entails identifying the international and local competitors, determining how the competitors are perceived and evaluated by local consumers, determining the competitors' positions in the consumers' mind, analyzing the customers, selecting the position, and monitoring it.[19]

Brands are positioned using a theme—a unique selling proposition. This theme could be unique to each market, for companies that customize their offering to local markets, or uniform, throughout the world. A third approach also is common: a uniform positioning strategy that still allows local offices free-

attribute/benefit positioning
Positioning that communicates product attributes and benefits, differentiating each brand from the other company brands and from those of competitors.

price/quality positioning
A strategy whereby products and services are positioned as offering the best value for the money.

use positioning
The process of marketing a precise product application that differentiates it in the consumers' minds from other products that have a more general use.

applications positioning
The marketing of a precise product application that is differentiated in the consumers' minds from other products that have a more general use.

dom for adaptation, if necessary. Coca-Cola, for example, formulates its worldwide positioning at its Atlanta headquarters but enables its affiliates in different markets to alter the strategy as needed.

The six international positioning strategies are illustrated in Sections 7-5a through 7-5f.[20]

7-5a Attribute/Benefit Positioning

Procter & Gamble focuses on product attributes and benefits to position its products. An **attribute/benefit positioning** strategy uses product or service attributes and benefits to position it in the consumers' mind relative to competitors' products and services. The following are examples of product positioning by the company:[21]

- Cheer, in powder or liquid, with or without bleach, is positioned as protecting against fading, color transfer, and fabric wear.

- Dreft is positioned as a detergent that removes tough baby stains and protects garment colors.

- Gain, as a liquid and powder detergent, is positioned as having exceptional cleaning and whitening.

- Procter &Gamble's premium product worldwide, Tide, in powder or liquid, with or without bleach, is positioned as a laundry detergent with exceptional cleaning, whitening, and stain removal.

Such precise positioning, which is reflected in the company's communication with its respective segments, clearly differentiates each brand from the other company brands and from those of competitors such as Unilever and Colgate-Palmolive.

7-5b Price/Quality Positioning

Products and services can be positioned as offering the best value for the money. The **price/quality positioning** strategy is especially useful for companies marketing in developing countries. Manufacturers such as Toyota, Daewoo, and Philips and retailers such as Wal-Mart and Sears emphasize the value aspect of their offerings.

Alternatively, products and services can be positioned at the other end of the price/quality continuum as the best product that money can buy. In addition to stressing high price and high quality, such positioning also entails an exclusive distribution or access, an expert sales force and service, and advertising in publications aimed at the global elite. Mercedes-Benz claims that, in a perfect world, everyone would drive a Mercedes. Kempinski Hotels and Resorts, an upscale German chain, "reflects the finest traditions of European hospitality, luxurious accommodation, superb cuisine and unrivalled facilities—complemented by impeccable service."[22]

7-5c Use or Applications Positioning

Uses or applications are often used to position products in the **use positioning** or **applications positioning** strategies, respectively. Procter & Gamble's Era is positioned as a high-technology detergent that pretreats and washes fabrics to suspend dirt. This precise application differentiates it in the consumers' minds from other laundry detergents that have a more general use.

Sometimes the uses or applications differ from one market to another: A bicycle manufacturer would most likely position its offerings in Asia and Europe as efficient transportation machines, whereas, in the United States, it would position them as high-performance recreation instruments.

7-5d Product User Positioning

The **product user positioning** strategy focuses on the product user, rather than on the product. The marketing mix for the Mont Blanc pen is targeted at the business executive anywhere in the world. The pen is usually pictured along with a quality business letterhead, with a passport, and with an attaché case. In this case, the product is understood to be among the highest quality pens around, so it receives only associative emphasis.

7-5e Product Class Positioning

Disney sells magic, not just entertainment. Harley sells excitement, not just motorcycles. And Parliament sells a glamorous, romantic America all over the world, not just cigarettes. Products using a **product class positioning** strategy differentiate themselves as leaders in a product category, as they define it.

7-5f Competitor Positioning

When a firm compares its brand with those of competitors, it uses a **competitor positioning** strategy. Some comparisons are direct, if the local legal environment allows it. Others are somewhat subtle. When Airbus asks readers of *The Financial Times* whether they would be more comfortable with two or four engines when they are up in the air, it makes implicit reference to Boeing.

All positioning, ultimately, is relative to competition, only not always explicitly so. Even symbols hint at competition: Merrill Lynch is bullish on the market (it is embodied by the bull); all other competitors are probably wimps. Quick, a local competitor of McDonald's in France, advertises cheaper prices: Its restaurants are quick and they are cheaper than McDonald's—and they are right across the street.

> **product user positioning**
> A positioning strategy that focuses on the product user, rather than on the product.
>
> **product class positioning**
> A strategy used to differentiate a company as a leader in a product category, as defined by the respective company.
>
> **competitor positioning**
> The process of comparing the firm's brand with those of competitors, directly or

Summary

Develop a general understanding of international marketing strategy at the different levels of the international organization and provide some insights into the international marketing planning process of selected companies. Planning takes place at different levels. At the corporate level, the strategic plan allocates resources and establishes objectives for the whole enterprise worldwide. At the division level, the strategic plan allocates funds to each business unit based on division goals and objectives, whereas, at the business unit level, within each country, decisions are made on selecting target consumer segments. At the product level (line, brand), a marketing plan is developed for achieving objectives. An important decision is which product mix to use in the different countries where the company is present.

Identify the rationale for adopting a target marketing strategy in international markets. International target marketing is used to identify countries and segments of international consumers that are similar with regard to key traits, who would respond to a particular marketing mix (i.e., segmenting the market); to select the countries and segments that the company can serve most efficiently and develop products tailored to each (i.e., targeting the market); and to offer the products to the market, communicating, through the marketing mix (i.e., positioning), product traits and benefits that differentiate it in the consumers' minds.

Identify the requirements necessary for effective international market segmentation. For segmentation to be effective, segments must be easy to measure, stable over time, accessible, actionable, and respond differentially from other segments to a company's marketing strategy.

Introduce the concept of country attractiveness analysis and offer a blueprint for conducting the analysis. Country attractiveness can be assessed by measuring market potential using indicators such as GDP per capita, industrial and agricultural sectors statistics, market size, and consumer buying power. It also can be assessed by evaluating international investment figures, such as foreign direct investment data and other trade statistics; the political, legal, and financial environment in the country; the existing marketing support infrastructure; the existing brand and/or company franchise for the product and/or company, and for competitors' products and/or companies; and the degree of market fit with company policies, objectives, and resources.

Identify the bases for consumer segmentation and offer company application examples. Consumers are segmented on demographics, psychographics, geography, usage and user status, and benefits sought from purchasing the product or service. International firms segment based on the criteria that are most appropriate for their product or service. The job of the international marketing manager is facilitated by the emergence of homogeneous demographic segments worldwide, such as global teenagers and the global elite.

Describe the three targeting strategies used by companies worldwide. These strategies are differentiated marketing, whereby companies address the needs of different segments by offering them different brands and using different marketing mix strategies; concentrated marketing, whereby companies address a single consumer segment that is large and stable enough to warrant the investment; and undifferentiated marketing, whereby a company can reap the benefits of standardization by using the same strategy to market to all consumers worldwide.

Describe the six positioning strategies that international companies can use to position their brands in the minds of target consumers. International companies can position products by focusing on product attributes or benefits; by positioning the brand as a high-price/high-quality product or as the best value for the money; by positioning the brand based on use or applications; by positioning the brand based on product users; or by positioning it as the best product in its class.

Key Terms

accessibility

actionability

applications positioning

attribute/benefit positioning

benefit segmentation

competitor positioning

concentrated targeting

demographic segmentation

differential response

differentiated targeting

geographic segmentation

global elite

global youth segment

measurability

price/quality positioning

product class positioning

product user positioning

psychographic segmentation

segmentation

stability over time

substantiality

target market

target marketing

undifferentiated targeting

usage segmentation

use positioning

Discussion Questions

1. International planning involves planning activities at different levels of an organization. Describe the planning processes that take place at each level of an international company.

2. International marketing managers use a number of criteria to ensure that segments are useful. Describe the effective types of segmentation and offer examples for each.

3. Macrosegmentation refers to country-level segmentation, and microsegmentation refers to consumer-level segmentation. What bases and strategies do marketing managers use for segmenting their international markets using macro- and microsegmentation?

4. Describe the principal targeting strategies. Go to the Mercedes-Benz USA (www.mercedes.com) home page. What targeting strategy does the company use? Explain.

5. Go to the VALS 2 web page and read the description of each population segment; also, go to the PRIZM web page. What segments would you ascribe to Mercedes users based on VALS 2?

6. What are the six positioning strategies? What strategies does Mercedes-Benz USA use for its U.S. market? Does Mercedes use different strategies for its international market? (Go to the other English-language Mercedes sites to answer this question.)

Chapter Quiz

True/False

1. International positioning involves identifying countries and consumers that are similar with regard to key traits and would respond well to a product and related marketing mix.

Answer: False

Rationale: International segmentation involves identifying countries and consumers that are similar with regard to key traits and would respond well to a product and related marketing mix. Positioning entails placing the brand in the consumer's mind in relation to other competing products, based on product traits and benefits that are relevant to the consumer.

Sections 7-3, "International Market Segmentation," and 7-4, "Targeting International Consumers"

2. Measurability refers to the requirement that the segment should be large enough to warrant investment.

Answer: False

Rationale: Substantiality refers to the requirement that the segment should be large enough to warrant investment. Measurability refers to the ability to measure the size of the segment.

Section 7-3a, "Requirements for International Segmentation"

3. Actionability refers to the ability to communicate with the international target market.

Answer: False

Rationale: Accessibility refers to the ability to communicate with the market and to serve the respective market.

Section 7-3a, "Requirements for International Segmentation"

4. Macrosegmentation involves grouping countries together based on their political, legal, and financial environments.

Answer: True

Rationale: Macrosegmentation involves grouping countries based on such criteria as economic performance, evaluating the potential of a particular market; on their political, legal, and financial environment; on their marketing support infrastructure; on the company brand's standing or potential standing relative to existing competition; and on the degree of market fit with company resources, policies, and goals, among others.

Section 7-3b, "Macro-Segmentation: Country Attractiveness Analysis"

5. Identifying markets based on age and gender is an example of demographic segmentation.

Answer: True

Rationale: Demographics are defined as statistics that describe the population; gender and age statistics are examples of demographic variables.

Section 7-3c, "Microsegmentation: Focusing on the Target Consumer"

Multiple Choice

1. Target marketing involves

    a.   market segmentation.

    b.   market targeting.

    c.   market positioning.

    d.   all of the above

Answer: d is correct.

Rationale: International target marketing identifies countries and consumer segments similar with regard to key traits that would respond well to a product and related marketing mix (international market segmentation); selects the countries and segments that the company can serve most efficiently and develops products tailored to each (international market targeting); and offers the products to the market, communicating, through the marketing mix, differentiating product traits and benefits (market positioning).

Section 7-2, "The Rationale for Target Marketing"

2. Which segmentation requirement refers to the ability to communicate with the international target market?

    a.   Actionability

    b.   Substantiality

    c.   Accessibility

    d.   Measurability

Answer: c is correct.

Rationale: Accessibility refers to the ability to communicate with the market and to serve the respective market.

Section 7-3a, "Requirements for International Segmentation"

3. Proctor & Gamble offers a variety of laundry detergent brands to European consumers, which appeal to different market segments. This is a good example of

    a.   undifferentiated targeting.

    b.   concentrated targeting.

    c.   differentiated targeting.

      d.   none of the above

Answer: c is correct.

Rationale: Differentiated targeting refers to identifying, or even creating, market segments that want different benefits from a product and targeting them with different brands, using different marketing strategies.

Section 7-4b, "Target Market Decisions: The Target Market Strategy"

4. Which type of positioning focuses on offering the best value for the money?

      a.   Applications

      b.   Price/quality

      c.   Product class

      d.   Attribute/benefit

Answer: b is correct.

Rationale: Companies using price/quality positioning present the products and services as offering the best value for the money. This strategy is especially useful when marketing to consumers in developing countries.

Section 7-5b, "Price/Quality Positioning"

Endnotes

1.   Jeffrey E. Garten, "Cutting Fat Won't Be Enough to Survive This Crisis," *Business Week,* No. 3603, November 9, 1998, p. 26.

2.   Chris Lui, "SANYO in Global Reorganization of TV Business, Alliance with Quanta," *JCNN News Summaries,* August 15, 2006, p. 1.

3.   www.pepsico.com

4.   "Brandfame: Pepsi," *Marketing*, September 2005, p. 38.

5.   www.kraft.com

6.   Ibid.

7.   www.montrealjazzfest.com/Fijm2007/splash.aspx

8.   www.cia.gov/library/publications/the-world-factbook/print/br.html

9.   www.cia.gov/library/publications/the-world-factbook/print/su.html

10.   Tim Stock and Marie Lena Tupot, "Common Denominators: What Unites Global Youth?" *Young Consumers*, Vol. 7, No. 2, 2006, pp. 36-43.

11.   "Coca-Cola Prepares iCoke for Global Youth Marketing Drive," *New Media Age*, May 19, 2005, p. 1.

12.   Geng Cui and Qiming Liu, "Executive Insights: Emerging Market Segments in a Transitional Economy: A Study of Urban Consumers in China," *Journal of International Marketing,* Vol. 9, No. 1, Spring 2001, pp. 84–106.

13.   Ibid.

14.   Sudhir H. Kale, "Grouping Euroconsumers: A Culture-Based Clustering Approach," *Journal of International Marketing,* Vol. 3, No. 3, 1995, pp. 35–38.

15.   Cui and Liu, "Executive Insights," pp. 84–106.

16.   Ibid.

17.   Art Weinstein, "A Primer for Global Marketers," *Marketing News*, Vol. 28, No. 13, June 20, 1994, p. 4.

18.   www.pg.com

19.   Adapted from David A. Aaker and Gary J. Shansby, "Positioning Your Product," *Business Horizons*, Vol. 25, No. 3, May/June 1982, pp. 56–62.

20.   See Aaker and Shansby, "Positioning Your Product," pp. 56–62.

21.   www.pg.com

22.   www.kempinski.com

Case 7-1

Prosperity Painting Equipment

James Vreeland is an international marketing manager with Prosperity Painting Equipment in Kunming, in the Yunnan Province in southwestern China. He was previously a manager for Baker Equipment, an equipment manufacturer on the East Coast of the United States, a former Peace Corps volunteer in Nepal, and an MBA graduate—with a marketing concentration—of the College of William and Mary in Virginia. He recently married a Chinese woman from Kunming and decided to settle there.

Prosperity Painting Equipment is a supplier of painting equipment for three small automobile manufacturing firms—three out of many in China's booming automobile industry—and is a medium-sized firm with reasonable potential for growth in a rapidly expanding market. Prosperity Painting Equipment's competitors are medium-sized and large state-owned enterprises, as well as smaller private firms. The firm's director, Zhang Chen, hired Vreeland for his excellent English and his polished presence, and to date, his primary task was to learn about China's automobile industry. Zhang Chen had important decisions to make regarding the future growth of the company and Vreeland was going to play an important part in his plan.

The Chinese Automobile Market

Vreeland found that, in 2007, Chinese automobile manufacturers had a combined share of 29.1 percent of China's market, the world's second largest. Chinese automakers were ahead of the Japanese, who had 28.3 percent of the market share. Still, the Chinese market is dominated by big-name foreign brands, holding 70.9 percent of the market share, with most automobiles produced in China by joint ventures. China accounted for 17 percent of BMW's sales in 2011, and its Chinese revenue increased 37 percent in 2011, from 2010. China was BMWs fastest-growing market in 2012, and, for the first time, exceeded BMW's U.S. sales.

In all categories other than the luxury market, however, Chinese-made automobiles are ahead of competition. This is attributed to price, especially in the large-vehicle segment, where, for the price of one foreign heavy truck, one can purchase three Chinese ones. Automobile buyers are pickier, but a cheap automobile appeals to many Chinese consumers.

The best-selling brand in China is the Chery (see Figure 7-7), produced by Chery Automobile, which was founded in 1997 and is government-owned. Its most popular model, the Chery QQ, appeared six months earlier than GM's Chevy Spark, the car it copied successfully, because a Chinese firm somehow got hold of the blueprints. The Chery sold more cars than Shanghai GM, which makes Buicks, Chevrolets, and Cadillacs. But it lagged behind Shanghai General Motors, a joint venture between Shanghai Automotive Industry Corp and GM, and Shanghai Volkswagen, a partnership between Shanghai Automotive and Volkswagen. It sold 50,000 automobiles overseas in 2006, with its primary markets in the Middle East and Eastern Europe. It is currently eyeing the U.S. and Western European markets, hiring expertise that will help it launch the Chery in these markets.

Another important player in the Chinese automobile industry is SAIC GM Wuling Automobile Co., a Chinese joint venture with General Motors (with the Chinese partner owning 50.1 percent), situated about 1,200 miles west of Shanghai. It makes commercial minivans and the Chevrolet Spark minicar. Wuling's automobiles are tiny, with the best-selling Sunshine van at a third the size of GM's Chevrolet Tahoe SUV. The starting price of a Wuling Sunshine van with a 1-liter engine is $3,700, about the same price of a low-end Chevy Spark. Wuling's sales were 460,000 vehicles in 2006. Production capacity goals are as much as 600,000 to 700,000 vehicles. Wuling's target customers earn $200 to $600 a month, do not own a car, and travel on bicycles, scooters, or motorized three-wheel vehicles. Wuling's automobiles—the Sunshine, and the more upscale Hongtu—are not

Figure 7-7: *The Chery automobile is the best-selling car in China; it is produced by Chery Automobile, which is government-owned.*

designed for mature markets, such as the United States: The engine and wheels are small, and air bags are optional. At the Wuling factory, workers do the jobs that are performed by robots at Western GM plants, taking advantage of low wages. Wuling is a model closely studied by GM operations in other locations, such as India.

In other examples, the Changan Automobile Group Co. is an important newcomer to the automobile industry, with BenBen, a microvan that has been on the market since 2007. BenBen quickly became the number two seller in China's booming microvan segment, averaging about 7,000 cars a month. Its target market is Chinese farmers and small business owners in smaller provincial towns. Shanghai Automotive, in turn, acquired design rights for U.K.'s Rover and is planning to offer an automobile with a higher sticker price, positioned upmarket.

For Chinese consumers, automobile brands with the highest brand recognition are Santana, Red Flag, Mercedes, Beijing Jeep, Shanghai VW, BMW, Honda, Volkswagen, Toyota, and Buick, according to the Gallup Research Co. LTD. Today, these brands will include many more local makes, including the Chery.

Chinese Automobile Exports

Vreeland also reviewed the state of Chinese automobile exports and quickly concluded that this is a growth market. Chinese automobile manufacturers exported 340,000 vehicles in 2006, bound primarily for developing countries in the Middle East, Russia, and Southeast Asia. About 25 percent of the passenger cars China exports are made by Japan's Honda Motor Company, which owns a plant in Guangzhou that manufactures cars specifically intended for overseas markets. Honda exports its Jazz compact cars to Europe from this plant.

Predictions of Europe and the United States being flooded with cheap and popular Chinese cars may be premature, as Chinese manufacturers must first build cars that meet European and U.S. safety and environmental standards, and, equally important, consumers' standards for quality. Jiangling Motors' Landwind, a copy of Opel's Frontera, spectacularly failed European crash tests. International joint ventures in China, with the exception of Honda, have little interest in selling automobiles outside of China, because they would face political and economic disadvantages. Instead, they are focusing on tapping the growing Chinese market. But, even if only few of China's automobiles are available in the West (Chrysler has signed a letter of intent with Chery to build a small car in China for Chrysler to sell in North America), they are likely to heighten competition for U.S. automobile manufacturers worldwide. In the face of growing political pressure in the U.S. and Europe to address China's large trade surplus, this may spell trouble for Chinese exports in general in the future.

The Task

Zhang Chen set up a meeting with James Vreeland. They started their conversation casually exploring Vreeland's take on the Chinese automobile industry. Zhang Chen informed him that the supplier of painting equipment for the SAIC GM Wuling Automobile Co., the GM joint venture, has just been contracted to supply General Motors' operations worldwide. Zhang Chen would like Prosperity Painting Equipment to enter into a similar relationship, supplying the worldwide operations of a large automobile manufacturer with painting equipment.

James Vreeland's task is to create a presentation for the company's investing partners that will segment the automobile market in China based on dimensions such as degree of focus on the Chinese market, joint-venture partnership, export orientation, and brand recognition. Then, Vreeland is to present a targeting strategy that is appropriate for his firm. The strategy proposed must convince investors to provide the necessary funding for Prosperity Painting Equipment's growth.

Sources: Xiaoguang Fang, Vice Chairman/Senior Strategic Consultant, Gallup Research Co. LTD, lecture on consumer trends in China, May 23, 2007, University of Richmond Faculty Seminar, Beijing, China; Bruce Einhorn, "The Surge in China's Auto Sales May Soon Slow," *Bloomberg Businessweek*, April 5, 2012 www.businessweek.com/articles/2012-04-05/chinas-auto-sales-surge-may-soon-slow/.

"The Chinese Carmakers," *Financial Times,* Asia Edition, April 25, 2007, 16; Gordon Fairclough and Joseph B. White, "China Car Makers Pull Ahead at Home," *Wall Street Journal*, April 23, 2007, A9; Joseph B. White, "For GM in China, Tiny Is Mighty; Wuling Venture Plans Expansion as Sales of Small Cars Surge," *Wall Street Journal*, April 20, 2007, A9; "Business: The Sincerest Form of Flattery—Counterfeit Cars in China," *The Economist*, Vol. 383, No. 8523, April 7, 2007, p. 76; Gordon Fairclough, "China Auto Exports May Roil Rivals," *Wall Street Journal,* February 16, 2006, A2.

Analysis Suggestions:

1. Provide a competitive analysis for Prosperity Painting Equipment.

2. What are the bases for segmentation appropriate for Prosperity Painting Equipment's industry? Refer to the automobile industry in your analysis.

3. Identify the different automobile-manufacturing segments based on the degree of focus on the Chinese market, joint-venture partnership, and export orientation.

4. Present a targeting strategy that is appropriate for Prosperity Painting Equipment.

Chapter 8: Expansion Strategies and Entry Mode Selection

Learning Objectives

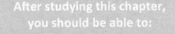

After studying this chapter, you should be able to:

- Offer an understanding of company expansion strategies, entry mode selection, and the risks involved at each level.

- Describe different types of strategic alliances involving international companies.

Dial your airline or your Internet service provider, and you will likely have someone in Bangalore, India, make your reservations or help you pay your subscription. You may be dealing with Delta or United Airlines, AOL, and many other service providers, but you will no longer hear a Southern accent at the other end—nor someone addressing you as "honey"; instead, you may hear a precise Indian accent with softened v's that sound like w's. And, if you make a joke, your customer representative may quickly steer you on to business, without letting on that he or she does not quite understand you. Ask your service rep where he or she is located, and the response may be India—or even China. Then look around you in your community, and you will find individuals recently laid off by service companies, such as credit card businesses, software companies, and customer service providers. The chances are high that their jobs were outsourced.

Companies join forces to broaden their market access and appeal and to take advantage of economies of scale. National airlines become instant worldwide carriers by establishing strategic alliances. For example, Delta Airlines started partnerships with Air France, AeroMexico, Air Jamaica, China Southern, Czech Airlines, Korean Air, Singapore Airlines, and South African Airlines, to name a few. These partnerships involve, in addition to code sharing and mutual partner booking in areas not serviced by the airline, other types of advantages that ultimately benefit consumers, such as a frequent-flyer miles exchange. In addition to helping airlines cut costs and increase their customer base, the alliances may even help individual carriers weather temporary financial challenges. Other airlines actually share routes, with a flight bearing numbers of two airlines. Such sharing enables firms to have multiple flight options to a destination; it also lowers airport access fees. Examples of airlines sharing routes are United Airlines with German company Lufthansa, Air France/KLM with Northwest, and Air France/KLM with Alitalia.

8-1 Going International: Evaluating Opportunities

Managers of small and medium-sized enterprises and multinational firm managers alike must evaluate the costs of delivering their products and services to their target markets. They need to take into consideration a number of important factors in their decisions related to the manufacturing and distribution of their goods. In Chapter 1, "Scope, Concepts, and Drivers of International Marketing," we examined the different drivers of international expansion in the environment, such as competition, regional economic and political integration, economic growth, technology and converging consumer needs, and the firm-related international expansion drivers, such as product life-cycle considerations, new product development costs, experience transfers, and labor costs. Many firms cross borders in search of lower factor costs, such as low-cost labor, capital, and land. As Table 8-1 illustrates (next page), hourly compensation costs for production workers in manufacturing in the United States are quite high, averaging around $23.00. However, in Singapore and Korea, average hourly costs are $7.44 and $11.52, respectively; considering the high productivity of these countries' highly educated workforce, Singapore and Korea may be attractive labor markets for skilled manufacturing work. Moving manufacturing to Mexico would further lower labor costs to less than $3.00 per hour.

It should be noted, however, that wages are only part of the cost of production. Other costs are equally important—capital equipment, components, and land, for example. Firms must look at the full spectrum of costs and opportunities when deciding which markets to enter. An international manufacturing presence could ultimately mean greater access to the respective international markets facilitated by local governments that favor firms engaging in foreign direct investment. Companies need to examine the fit between the costs of international involvement (and the opportunity costs that they would incur if they ignore the international market), company resources, and market potential. They should also evaluate exactly how much risk they are willing to take in the process of going international and how much control they desire to maintain over the marketing mix.

Table 8-1

Hourly Compensation Costs in U.S. Dollars for Production Workers in Manufacturing

Country	Compensation (in US$)	
	1997	2010
Norway	26.38	57.53
Switzerland	30.00	53.20
Belgium	29.12	50.70
Denmark	24.09	45.48
Germany	29.15	43.76
Finland	22.35	42.30
Netherlands	23.40	40.92
Australia	19.10	40.60
France	24.88	40.55
Ireland	17.03	36.30
Canada	18.84	35.67
United States	23.05	34.74
Italy	19.67	33.41
Japan	22.28	31.99
United Kingdom	18.50	29.44
Spain	13.92	26.60
Greece	11.56	22.19
Israel	12.32	20.12
Singapore	12.15	19.10
Argentina	7.43	12.66
Slovakia	2.86	10.72
Brazil	7.07	10.08
Hungary	3.05	8.40
Taiwan	7.04	8.36
Mexico	3.47	6.23
Philippines	1.28	1.90

Source: http://stats.bls.gov, December 21, 2011.

8-2 Control versus Risk in International Expansion

In broad terms, companies need to decide whether to use middlemen in the process of taking their products internationally or to market directly to the international market. Using middlemen requires a company to relinquish control: The distributors or agents sell the product. Middlemen allow the company to become involved in international business, while minimizing the typical risks involved in international marketing. On the other hand, direct international involvement exposes the company to substantial risk, but it also affords the company significant control of the marketing mix. Figure 8-1 illustrates the control and risk trade-off facing international firms in the process of selecting the international entry mode.

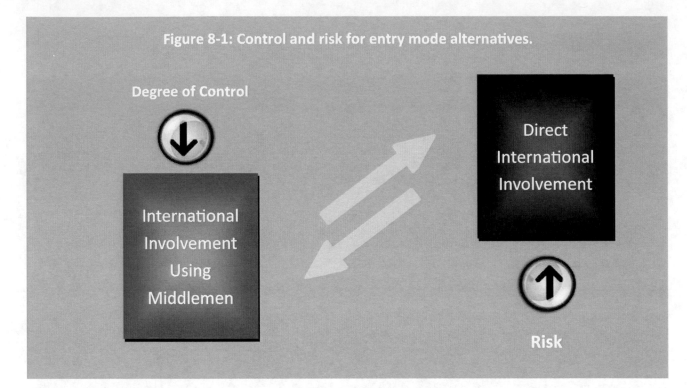

Figure 8-1: Control and risk for entry mode alternatives.

International expansion using middlemen may represent a first step in going international. Firms often test their international markets using distributors and, in a quest for higher profits and greater market share, eventually opt for direct international involvement. Section 8-3 addresses the different international entry mode selection and expansion strategies for international markets.

8-3 Deciding on the International Entry Mode

The **entry mode** classifications offered in Sections 8-3a to 8-3i follow a general model of low to high control and risk, respectively. That is, company control over operations and overall risk increases from the export mode to the wholly owned subsidiary entry mode. In general, companies tend to use the export mode in their first attempt to expand internationally and in environments that present substantial risk, and they tend to approach markets that offer promise and lower risk by engaging in some form of foreign direct investment. There are, however, many exceptions: Companies that have been present for decades in international target markets, such as Airbus Industries and Caterpillar, continue to export to those markets, rather than manufacture abroad. For example, Airbus has a strong market in Asia, where it is fulfilling orders for 30 A320 and 20 A330 aircraft; it also has an order from Singapore-based Tiger Airways for 30 A320 aircraft.[1] However, in spite of doing business for millions of dollars in Asia, Airbus has no intention of locating its manufacturing there.

Similarly, many new small businesses find that they can manufacture products cheaply abroad and distribute them in those markets without making a penny in their home country; this is increasingly becoming a possibility for companies selling their products using the Internet.

8-3a Indirect Exporting

Indirect exporting means that the company sells its products to intermediaries in the company's home country who, in turn, sell the product overseas. A company engaging in indirect exporting can use middlemen such as export management companies, trading companies, or agents/brokers (described in Chapter 11, "Managing International Distribution Operations and Logistics") to distribute its products overseas. Alternatively, the company can use **cooperative exporting,** also referred to as **"piggybacking"** or **"mother henning."** With cooperative exporting,

entry mode
The approach to international expansion a company chooses based on desired control and on the risk it can afford.

indirect exporting
An export entry mode whereby a company sells its products in the company's home country to intermediaries who, in turn, sell the product overseas.

cooperative exporting
Using the distribution system of exporters with established systems of selling abroad who agree to handle the export function of a noncompeting (but not necessarily unrelated) company on a contractual basis; also called mother henning and piggybacking.

companies use the distribution system of exporters with established systems of selling abroad who agree to handle the export function of a noncompeting (but not necessarily unrelated) company on a contractual basis. Such companies are paid on commission or are charged a discount price for the product. They are larger companies with extensive experience in and knowledge of the target international market. The companies facilitating indirect exporting may have different names in different countries. The primary indirect exporters in the United Kingdom are known as export houses. They cover a variety of different organizations. For example, export houses might buy goods for export, acting on their own behalf, or act on behalf of an overseas principal wishing to purchase U.K. goods. As such, the export house is similar to wholesalers selling goods internationally.[2]

Using indirect exporting does not require market expertise or a long-term commitment to the international market. The company essentially sells its product to a distributor with little investment and without having to learn about the international market. The company's risk also is minimal; at most, it can lose a product shipment. Among disadvantages are lack of control over the marketing of its products, which could eventually lead to lost sales and a loss of goodwill that might ultimately affect the perception of the company and its brands in other markets where it has a greater commitment.

Some companies use indirect exporting as a first step toward a greater degree of involvement. After a sufficient consumer franchise is secured and the market is tested with the initial shipment, a company might commit resources for additional investment in the market. It should be mentioned, however, that indirect exporting in the long term does not necessarily mean that the company is not committed to the market; it simply means either that the company does not have the resources for greater involvement or that other markets are performing better and need more company resources.

One of Europe's leading car makers, Volkswagen, operates through independent importers and distributors in Belgium, the Netherlands, Switzerland, and Austria, whereas in France, Germany, Italy, and Spain, which together account for the largest percentage of European sales, it controls its wholesale operations directly.[3]

piggybacking
Using the distribution system of exporters with established systems of selling abroad who agree to handle the export function of a noncompeting (but not necessarily unrelated) company on a contractual basis; also called mother henning and cooperative exporting.

mother henning
Using the distribution system of exporters with established systems of selling abroad who agree to handle the export function of a noncompeting (but not necessarily unrelated) company on a contractual basis; also called piggybacking and cooperative exporting.

direct exporting
An export entry mode whereby a firm handles its own exports, usually with the help of an in-house exporting department.

8-3b Direct Exporting

Companies engaging in **direct exporting** have their own in-house exporting expertise, usually in the form of an exporting department. Such companies have more control over the marketing mix in the target market: They can make sure that wholesalers and retailers observe the company's marketing policies, charging the suggested sale price, offering the appropriate promotions, and handling customer requests promptly and satisfactorily. More control, however, is expensive. Companies carry the cost of their export department staff and the costs involved in selecting and monitoring the different middlemen involved in the distribution process—freight forwarders, shipping lines, insurers, merchant middlemen, and retailers—as well as other marketing service providers, such as consultants, marketing researchers, and advertising companies.

One venue that opens new opportunities for direct exporting is the Internet. With a well-developed web site, companies now can reach directly to customers overseas and process sales online. And many companies do: Catalog retailers and dot-com companies, such as Lands' End, long ago made their first international incursions by exporting their products to consumers abroad and have successfully expanded their international operations. They were quickly joined by businesses ranging from small and medium-sized enterprises in emerging markets to designers.

The Mexx eShop

Mexx is a chain selling clothing and accessories for men, women, and children under the Mexx brand. The store started in the Netherlands as two clothing brands, Moustache, for men, and Emanuelle, for women; the names of the two companies were merged as ME plus XX, the English sign for two kisses. Liz Claiborne owned Mexx Europe for a decade, from 2001[4] until 2011. The Mexx brand, which cleverly advertised and promoted using the catwalk concept, sells in the United States exclusively at Mexx stores. Elsewhere, Mexx-branded apparel retails in 7,500 stores, in more than 40 countries, with sales of more than $1.5 billion.

The brand is also sold online through the Mexx eShops, which, however, are only available in France, Germany, and the Netherlands, where it advertises free delivery for each order, and sales and more sales. The brand's allure is the same high style (think Diesel) and moderate prices (think H&M). The lines targeting the younger, high-fashion market feature gold on kitsch items, such as poodles, but, overall, the clothes and accessories are not particularly edgy or innovative.[5] In Germany, in 2012, you could purchase either a Lemon Soda yellow or Carmen Red handbag called canvas shopper with enormous attached flowers for €29.95, which includes a value added tax of 19.6 percent.[6]

In the case of the Mexx eShop, it would be interesting to find out why the eShop is not available in other European Union (EU) countries. Selling in the different countries in the EU should not be difficult, as transactions take place in one currency, and through banks that have branches throughout the area. The challenges for companies using the Internet to export their products involve securing the appropriate credit in environments where credit cards and personal checks are uncommon and, finally, having sufficient sales to warrant staff expenditures needed to process and handle sales.

The primary export destinations for U.S. products are listed in Table 8-2. Note that our neighbors to the north and south—Canada and Mexico, respectively—are the primary purchasers of U.S. exports.

Table 8-2: Top Purchasers of U.S. Exports
(Ranked by 2011 U.S. Total Export Value for Goods, in millions of U.S. dollars)

	May 2011	May 2012
1 Canada	249,105	280,890
2 Mexico	163,473	198,378
3 China	91,881	103,939
4 Japan	60,486	65,706
5 UK	48,414	55,881
6 Germany	48,161	49,156
7 Korea	38,846	43,415
8 Brazil	35,425	42,944
9 Netherlands	34,939	42,351
10 Hong Kong	26,570	36,449
11 Singapore	29,017	31,223
12 Belgium	25,456	29,899
13 France	26,969	27,803
14 Australia	21,798	27,542
15 Taiwan	26,043	25,889
16 Switzerland	20,687	24,425
17 India	19,250	21,501
18 Italy	14,219	16,007
19 Chile	10,905	15,986
20 UAE	11,673	15,900

Source:
http://www.ita.doc.gov/td/industry/otea/
(accessed June 3, 2012)

8-3c Licensing

A popular international entry mode, **licensing** presents more risks to the company but also offers more control than exporting. Licensing also offers substantial flexibility to the company, allowing for rapid international expansion and high brand awareness worldwide. Licensing often does not require knowledge of the local market, and it may not even require any capital investment, allowing for a low-cost market penetration.

Licensing involves a **licensor** and a **licensee.** The licensor offers know-how, shares technology, and often shares a brand name with the licensee. The licensee, in turn, pays royalties. The licensor may license the product without the name, or it may license the product allowing the use of the brand name.

A licensor is selective when choosing a licensee, ensuring that products manufactured under license are of the highest quality. When quality cannot be guaranteed, either because the licensee does not allow the licensor sufficient control and scrutiny or because the licensee cannot guarantee quality, it is preferable for the products produced under license not to carry the licensor's brand name.

In the early 1970s, Italy's Fiat granted a license to AvtoVAZ, Russia's largest automobile manufacturer, to manufacture Lada, Russia's most popular automobile and an important export to neighboring and other developing countries. Under a similar arrangement, France's Renault granted a license to build Dacia brand automobiles in Romania in the 1960s. Today, the automobile, which continues to sell under the Dacia name, is as popular as ever, and in 1999, Renault acquired a 51 percent stake in the company.

Licensors can decide to adapt the names of their products when they have a greater confidence in the capability of the licensee's workforce. One example is Poland's Polski Fiat. Fiat was confident of the reliability of Polish manufacturing and did not require the use of a different name for the product. Today, the company no longer licenses the Fiat name to Polish manufacturers; it has set up a subsidiary with multiple operations, Fiat SpA, which manufactures many of the Fiats sold in Eastern Europe under the Fiat brand name (primarily lower-priced models, such as Fiat Punto and Seicento).

Licensing is a lower-risk entry mode that allows a company to sell a product all over the world and offers the brand a global distribution. Beverly Hills Polo Club, for example, conducts business in more than 100 countries around the globe,[7] producing apparel licensed under its own name, all licensed apparel for Harvard University, as well as "Kulanui" (Hawaiian handbags), Beverly Hills Athletic Club, and Kinloch Anderson—a line that sells kilts, tartans and Highland dress. In fact, companies may choose to engage in trademark licensing, whereby brand names appear on merchandise without any design input from the parent company. For example, Eskimo Pie ice cream—a Nestlé brand – is sold around the world, but the product is not manufactured according to its original recipe. The only constant for this brand, in international sales, is its name.

Licensing permits the company access to markets that may be closed or that may have high entry barriers. However, without full control in these markets, manufacturers need additional protection. For instance, they may elect to license the product processing know-how, while deciding against allowing the use of the company's brand name. In the examples in the "Licensing without the Name" section, Lada and Dacia were sold in the countries of manufacture, the Soviet Union at that time, and Romania, at low prices, while automobile imports were charged tariffs at rates ranging from 50 to 100 percent.

Companies that engage in licensing agreements also limit their exposure to economic, financial, and political instability. In the event of a national disaster or a government takeover, the licensor licensing without the name incurs only the loss of royalties. The licensor that permits the use of the name may suffer a loss of reputation in the short term if the products are manufactured without li-

licensing
An international entry mode that involves a licensor, who shares the brand name, technology, and know-how with a licensee in return for royalties.

licensor
The owner of a product license who agrees to share knowhow, technology, and brand name with the licensee in return for royalties.

licensee
The purchaser of the license who pays royalties to the licensor for the rights to use the licensor's technology, know-how, and brand name.

censor supervision and if they do not uphold the licensor's standard. In the latter case, the licensor has some control, at least in international markets. For example, it can bring to the attention of international trade bodies the sale of products that are illegally using its brand name, assuming the company has international trademark protection; in most markets, it also can sue the former licensee.

A downside of licensing is that it can produce a viable competitor in the licensee, who is well equipped to competently compete with the licensor. Training locals in company operations, particularly technology, can lead to the development of skills for future competitors.

8-3d Franchising

Franchising is a principal entry mode for the service industry, and it is the service industry's equivalent to licensing. The **franchisor** gives the **franchisee** the right to use its brand name and all related trademarks and its business know-how, such as secret recipes and customer interfacing techniques; the franchisor also may provide the franchisee with advertising and sales promotion support—all in return for royalties.

The popularity of U.S.-based franchises worldwide is undisputed: McDonald's Golden Arches decorate the picturesque Scottish countryside, elegant buildings in the downtown of centuries-old European cities, at train stations (see Figure 8-2), and strip malls in Holland (where one franchise commissioned a giant Michael Jackson sculpture). They also border the suks (bazaars) in the Middle East and position themselves in strategic corners on crowded Shanghai streets (see Figure 8-3). Among other fast-food franchises present all over the world are Pizza Hut, KFC, and Burger King. Many of these franchises are adapted to the local market, serving spicy vegetarian dishes (and no beef) in India and Sri Lanka and beer and wine in

Figure 8-2: *There are few noteworthy train stations in Europe without a McDonald's.*

Europe. Although some of the products might differ (as do the sizes of portions—gigantic in the United States, minuscule in the rest of the world), the franchises look quite similar. They also offer the same courteous service, air conditioning, and clean toilets, and they run similar promotions.

Surprisingly, some franchises are successful even if the premise of the service's primary offering (hamburgers) runs counter to the local culture (religious ban on eating beef). When a company sets up franchises, it is especially important to evaluate the market's acceptance of the offering and to envision how the company can fit in the life of the local consumers, as the following Starbucks example illustrates (next page).

Figure 8-3: *A busy KFC in downtown Shanghai, with a Pizza Hut on the second floor.*

Starbucks

In a bold move, Starbucks decided to compete with Austria's coffee houses. Although Austria is a good market for coffee consumption, with an annual consumption of 56.8 gallons per person, Starbucks encountered some challenges: It was unwilling to relax its global no-smoking policy, which is daring in a country with a high proportion of smokers. Also, the company's concept runs counter to an environment that perceives American coffee and the pace of life associated with American cafés as being different from the Austrian café business perfected over the course of 200 years[8]—the kaffeehaus tradition. Nevertheless, the company has done well, positioned as a place to relax. Its signs inside read "Aroma protection through smoke-free spaces," and the company thanks customers for their understanding. [9]

Starbucks is also prominently present in China. In fact, until July 2007, there was a Starbucks in Beijing's Forbidden City, in a centuries-old building that used to be the home of Chinese emperors and is now a museum. It was popular with tourists, and helped pay for the upkeep of the 178-acre complex. Starbucks' presence at this location had been controversial since the very beginning, in 2000, when the company opened in China. Chinese nationalists perceived the company's presence in the Forbidden City as an act of disrespect by a U.S. company of China's values and traditions and have demanded that the Starbucks shop be closed down.[10] Starbucks, at first, refused to relent, but made some changes, toning down its prominent presence at the site by removing the large logo outside, and sharing space with other small Chinese retailers. However, ultimately, the company gave up and moved out, intent on maintaining the Chinese consumers' good will. And, if one wants a Starbuck's latte, a shop is always nearby, anywhere in China.

Franchises, in their close association in the consumer's mind with the franchises' country of origin—for consumers, the franchise may, in fact, be representative of its country of origin, which may be high on the target list for individuals who do not agree with the politics of the franchise home country, as exemplified in International Marketing Illustration 8-1 (next page).

The advantages and disadvantages of a franchise system are similar to those of licensing. The franchisor experiences less risk and a higher level of control over operations and offerings to the target market. Franchising also is a method that allows for rapid market penetration, which is important especially when new markets open their doors to foreign firms. On the downside, franchising can create future competitors who know the ins and outs of the franchise's operations. In fact, one hears many stories of former employees from fast-food restaurants who offer a precise replica of the original franchise, while offering better prices. Ideas of franchises can also be copied (see Figure 8-4). As soon as Esso (Exxon) stations in Europe started offering a Tiger Mart (a convenience store affiliated with the Esso franchise), local competitors immediately set up their own version that was even better adapted to local demands—selling, for example, potted flowers at discounted prices in affiliation with local growers. Aral, a pan-European gas station franchise, has its own shopping mart. In addition to products serving each market with convenience items, the mart also accepts recycling goods, offering cash back for plastic and glass bottles.

Figure 8-4: *Franchises often find that their concept is easily copied. This Burger King has to compete with a similar burger joint a few feet away.*

International Marketing Illustration 8-1

Successful U.S. Franchises in a Hostile World

Franchises have often been the scapegoats for action groups protesting U.S. politics, trade, and health policies, and globalization in general. In their use of English, with the corollary loss of stature of other languages, franchises are perceived as an imperialist enemy, driving out local traditional operations and imposing U.S. culture and traditions on developed and developing countries alike. KFC operations in India were closed by the government on grounds of compromised hygiene. A McDonald's franchise was vandalized in France and access to McDonald's was blocked in France and Belgium; a McDonald's was bombed in Xian, China, and another in Istanbul was a target of a pipe bomb. Other franchises were bombed in Beirut, Moscow, Riyadh, and in an eastern Indonesian town.

In yet another example, in Islamabad, Pakistan, angry crowds protesting against derogatory cartoons published in European newspapers, attacked and damaged two McDonald's restaurants and a Pizza Hut, before pelting the Holiday Inn hotel and some government buildings with stones.

Still, U.S. franchises continue to do well abroad, even in hotbeds of anti-U.S. sentiment. Franchises stress the local origin of the products they sell, the local labor they employ, and their stature as local citizens. They even make fun of their U.S. origins to appeal to the local consumers; for example, in France, McDonald's ads feature cowboys who boast that the McDonald's franchises refuse to import American beef to guarantee maximum hygienic conditions. In fact,

in France, McDonald's ceased using Ronald McDonald as the company mascot, replacing him with Asterix, a popular French comic book hero.

To position themselves as local brands, U.S. franchises also support nationalist and local ethnic causes of broad appeal. For instance, in Serbia, McDonald's hands out free burgers at rallies and has added a Serbian nationalist cap to the golden arches, using the slogan "McDonald's is yours." And in Saudi Arabia, for every Big Mac purchased during a Ramadan promotion, McDonald's offers a 30 cent contribution to the Red Crescent Society and to a hospital in Gaza treating Palestinians.

The survival of U.S. franchises in a world that, for now, is somewhat hostile toward the United States is also due to the franchises' efforts to adapt to the local markets. They sell wine and beer in Europe, pastries in France, miso soup in Japan, and other local favorites. McDonald's fries come with mayonnaise in Belgium and the Netherlands, but there, the mayonnaise is more of a yellow cream with a slight mustard-taste.

And, in spite of often-ignited anti-U.S. feelings, consumers worldwide maintain a certain preference for all things American: for an American education, medicine, airplanes, and the Internet—and for American franchises.

Source: Adapted from B. Muralidhar Reddy, "Protests Turn Violent in Pakistan" The Hindu, February 15, 2006, 1; Philip F. Zeidman, "The Global Brand: Asset or Liability?" Franchising World, Vol. 35, No. 4, 2003, p. 52.

It should be mentioned that licensing and franchising can be used instead of exporting, but also in addition to this approach to ensure rapid international expansion.

8-3e Joint Ventures

Joint ventures involve a foreign company joining with a local company, sharing capital, equity, and labor, among others, to set up a new corporate entity. Joint ventures are a preferred international entry mode for emerging markets. In developing countries, joint ventures typically take place between an international firm and a state-owned enterprise; in this case, the company's partner is the local government. As such, the company is assured instant local access and preferential treatment.

> **joint venture**
> A corporate entity created with the participation of two companies that share equity, capital, and labor.

Many developing countries welcome this type of investment as a way to encourage the develop-ment of local expertise, of the local market, and of the country's balance of trade—assuming the resultant production will be exported abroad. In most developing countries, the international firm typically provides expertise, know-how, most of the capital, the brand name reputation, and a trademark that is internation-ally protected, among others. The local partner provides the labor, the physical infrastructure (such as the factory and access to the factory), local market expertise and relationships, as well as connections to gov-ernment decision-making bodies.

It is typical for the local government of the developing country to limit the joint-venture ownership of international firms to less than 50 percent. It is also typical for the local government to encourage the reinvestment of profits into the firm, rather than the repatriation of profits by the international firm. As such, the government, in effect, leads the international firm to engage in transfer pricing, a method where-by the parent company of the international joint-venture partner charges the joint venture for equipment and expertise, for instance, above cost.

Joint ventures could constitute a successful approach to a greater involvement in the market, which is likely to result in higher control, better performance, and higher profits for the company. Success-ful joint ventures abound. In one example, British Petroleum PLC established a joint venture in Russia, un-der the name Petrol Complex, with ST, a powerful local partner with close ties to the Moscow city govern-ment. The company owns 30 BP gas stations, each of which sells an average of 3.5 million gallons of gaso-line a year, four times the average of a gas station in Europe.[11] BP offers Russian drivers good service (a rare commodity in this market), as well as minimarkets with espresso bars and a wide selection of wines; this is in stark contrast to the Russian gasoline stations where customers pay for gasoline by stuffing cash through a tinted window and where they communicate with the salesperson through a microphone.[12]

The joint-venture entry mode is not limited to developing countries. Numerous joint ventures are operating throughout Europe, and they are increasingly coming under the scrutiny of the European Com-mission, which assesses their impact on competition. Typically, the Commission appoints a task force to investigate the impact of the joint venture on competition and then issues a statement of objections within six to eight weeks, giving the companies involved a chance to respond and request a hearing before the Commission makes its final decision with regard to the joint venture. Whenever no such statement is is-sued, the deal is assumed to be on its way for approval.[13] One joint venture that the European Commission has examined involves the diamond giant De Beers Centenary AG (the world's largest diamond-mining company) and the French luxury goods company LVMH Moët Hennessy Louis Vuitton SA (which owns Chris-tian Dior, Moët & Chandon, Louis Vuitton, and Donna Karan). The company would produce De Beers-branded jewelry and open a network of exclusive shops all over the world.[14]

In another example, Polo Ralph Lauren Corp., the fashion giant, entered a joint venture with Gene-va-based watch and jewelry concern Compagnie Financiere Richemont AG to design and market luxury watches and fine jewelry. The venture is named Polo Ralph Lauren Watch and Jewelry Co. Polo and Richemont and each partner owns 50 percent of the new company. Starting in 2008, the joint venture de-velops and distributes the products through Ralph Lauren boutiques and through independent jewelry and upscale watch retailers around the world. This is Polo's first venture into the fine jewelry and luxury watch business, and it is Richemont's first joint venture with a fashion designer.[15]

Companies can, to a certain extent, control the chances for success of the joint venture by carefully selecting the joint-venture partner. A poor choice can be costly to the company. Factors that will increase the success of the international joint venture are the firm's previous experience with international invest-ment and the proximity between the culture of the international firm and that of the host country; a great-er distance erodes the applicability of the parent's competencies.[16]

But, even with careful planning, multinational firms have little recourse when local governments take actions favoring the local partner companies. For example, a national government may step in to con-trol energy sources, offering an advantage to local competitors, who are then in a position to take over. A joint venture recently started by BP in Russia offers an example of this.

BP in Russia

In 2003, BP announced, with great pomp, a landmark investment of $6.15 billion in Russia, in the form of a joint venture, the TNK-BP. The joint venture is the second largest private oil company in Russia, after Lukoil, and the only Russian energy company with partial foreign control.

However, four years later, the Russian government stepped up its control over its natural resources. State-controlled energy companies Gasprom and Rosneft quickly responded by showing interest in purchasing additional shares in TNK-BP, moving rapidly in a direction that would leave BP at a disadvantage. TNK-BP has been a very successful investment for BP, accounting for almost a third of the company's production, 27 percent of its reserves, returning $19 billion in dividends. Nevertheless, the obstacles posed by the government are such that BP has actively attempted to sell its shares in the company — without much success, as the Russian joint venture partners are blocking the sale.[17]

Like licensing and franchising, joint-venture partners can turn into viable competitors that know the firm's operations and competitive strategies. In this case, the local partner will undoubtedly become a formidable competitor in the region, where the firm will be protected by the government. Internationally, however, the international firm has some capability to combat the new competitors through controls and agreements with the supply chain and distributors that will prevent access to equipment or to markets, for example.

8-3f Consortia

Consortia involve three or more companies. An example of a successful consortium that involves some companies with a substantial percentage of government ownership is Airbus Industries. Airbus is an international consortium involving France (Aerospatiale with a 37.9 percent ownership), the United Kingdom (British Aerospace, with a 20 percent ownership), Germany (DaimlerChrysler DASA subsidiary, with a 37.9 percent ownership), and Spain (Construcciones Aeronauticas, with a 4.2 percent ownership).[18]

Most national governments and trade organizations are concerned with the monopoly effect that a consortium would create. In the case of Airbus, it was successfully argued that a single European country would not have the resources necessary to provide a challenge to Boeing, the U.S. manufacturer. In general, companies are allowed to set up consortia in the area of research and development, where they can share the cost of developing products that are at the forefront of technology.

Interestingly, consortia can have international subsidiaries. For example, Airbus has subsidiaries in the United States, Japan, and China. In the United States, the newest Airbus engineering facility—and largest as well—is in Wichita, Kansas. It is the first design and engineering venture of the company in North America, and its 140 engineers worked on the largest Airbus aircraft, the A380, the company's twenty-first century flagship airplane. At its 10th anniversary in June, 2012, the Airbus Engineering Center operations employed more than 350 engineers working on the design and stress work for wings and fuselages on new as well as existing models of Airbus aircraft.[19] Most of the other non-European subsidiaries deal primarily with customer service training and support services.

consortia
A company created with the participation of three or more companies; allowed in underserved markets or in domains where the government and the marketplace can control its monopolistic activity.

wholly owned subsidiary
The entry mode that affords the highest level of control and presents the highest level of risk to a company; it involves establishing a new company that is a citizen of the country where the subsidiary is established.

8-3g Wholly Owned Subsidiaries

Companies can avoid some of the disadvantages posed by partnering with other firms by setting up wholly owned subsidiaries in the target markets. The assumptions behind a **wholly owned subsidiary** are that:

- The company can afford the costs involved in setting up a wholly owned subsidiary.

- The company is willing to commit to the market in the long term.

- The local government allows foreign companies to set up wholly owned subsidiaries on its territory.

> **greenfielding**
> Developing a brand new subsidiary.

The company can develop its own subsidiary, referred to as **greenfielding,** which represents a costly proposition, or it can purchase an existing company through acquisitions or mergers. Many opportunities for acquisitions have recently emerged in developing and developed markets alike: Governments have been desocializing services and industries and rapidly privatizing industries that were formerly government owned or operated. Opportunities have emerged in the area of telecommunications, health care, energy, and even the national mail service.

The most important advantage that a wholly owned subsidiary can provide is relative control of all company operations in the target market. In particular, a subsidiary offers the company control over how to handle revenue and profits. Wholly owned subsidiaries also carry the greatest level of risk. A nationalization attempt on the part of the local government could leave the company with just a tax write-off.

Additional difficulties could arise when a company decides to acquire or merge with another. In the case of DaimlerChrysler, Daimler quickly found out that Chrysler was not performing up to par and quickly proceeded to restructure, weeding out former Chrysler employees. Daimler ultimately sold Chrysler in 2007.

In general, the company acquiring another or building its wholly owned subsidiary is not be able to share risks with a local partner, nor will it benefit from a partner's connections; it must build its own. Yet, even selling the subsidiary can eventually haunt the company years later. Harrods Buenos Aires was originally set up as a subsidiary of Harrods London but became an independent company in 1913 and changed hands several times. Today, Harrods Buenos Aires operates in Argentina and has no relationship whatsoever with Harrods London—which cannot address this issue successfully in the local courts in Argentina.

8-3h Branch Offices

The primary difference between subsidiaries and branch offices is that subsidiaries are separate entities, whereas branch offices are entities that are part of the international company. Companies that set up branch offices abroad often must engage in substantial investments. For example, Stihl, a German manufacturer of chain saws, has a branch office in Bucharest, Romania, that handles all company operations in the country. In addition to overseeing product sales, Stihl also ensures that servicing contracts are appropriately honored and that the representatives have adequate training. In low-income countries in sub-Saharan Africa, where Mercedes-Benz is a standard of luxury, but where only a few locals and a handful of expatriates can afford to purchase the brand, Mercedes must still incur substantial investment costs. At the minimum, it must invest in a sales office that has substantial staffing requirements and in a showroom that displays a few models. The company also is likely to engage in the distribution of parts to service stations and in the training of mechanics in handling Mercedes parts.

Branch offices of service providers typically engage in a full spectrum of activity in the domain of their specialization: The Chase branch offices in different European capitals handle the banking needs and credit to corporate and individual clients, in effect serving these markets the same way they serve the home markets.

Branch offices, like subsidiaries, also offer companies a high level of control over operations and profits in international markets. In terms of risk, however, the company invests much less in the market that can be lost in a government takeover attempt, compared with a subsidiary.

Companies also can have a presence in international markets in other formats that could be informal or more formalized. For example, the company could have a sales office (low risk, especially if the company does not carry any inventory in the country; some control). Alternatively, the company could be part of a strategic alliance, which varies in the level of control it provides the international company, as well as in the level of risk to the company, depending on the type of alliance and resource commitments. Strategic alliances are described in section 8-3i.

8-3i Strategic Alliances

All joint ventures and licensing and franchising agreements are occasionally loosely referred to as **strategic alliances** between companies attempting to reach joint corporate and market-related goals. This textbook, however, adheres to the mainstream thought that strategic alliances are formats that tend to be more short term in nature and that do not entail the same level of commitment as the previously described categories. Such alliances crop up frequently and have various forms and degrees of "alliance." They vary from a contract manufacturing agreement that requires the contracting firm to provide raw material and training to the contracting factory in return for production that could last for two years, to an exchange of loyalty points (hotel, frequent flyer) between companies. The following are some examples of alliances:

- Manufacturing alliances
- Marketing alliances
- Distribution alliances
- Outsourcing

Manufacturing Alliances

The category of **manufacturing alliances** covers many types of alliances, from **contract manufacturing** to technological, engineering, and research and development alliances. A typical example of a manufacturing alliance is that between the U.S. company Motorola, Inc., and Singapore's Flextronics International, Ltd., whereby the Singapore-based electronics manufacturer would make billions of dollars' worth of Motorola products. At present, Flextronics has manufacturing contracts for infrastructure and cell phones, among others.[20] In another example, Porsche has engaged in different types of technical alliances with Harley-Davidson, the U.S. motorcycle icon, primarily helping it develop low-noise, low-emissions motorcycles; most recently, Porsche helped Harley-Davidson develop its water-cooled Revolution engine.[21]

In another example—one that necessitates heavy investment on the part of both partners and commitment for the longer term—China's Chery Automobile Co. will produce Daimler's A1 hatchback, a small Mercedes automobile, for sale in the United States.[22]

Marketing Alliances

Some **marketing alliances** focus on all aspects of marketing. Historically, marketing alliances have taken on a variety of formats. Many marketing alliances focus on sales; for example, U.S.-based Northwest Airlines is in charge of all sales in the United States for the KLM Royal Dutch Airlines. One of many examples of marketing alliances is one between AOL Deutschland (Germany) and eBay, and, together with Google, it has a marketing alliance with several travel web sites:

www.TicketPoint.de, www.spartours.de, www.ReisepreisVergleich.de, and www.lastminute-express.com.

Distribution Alliances

Distribution alliances are common as well. Mitsui and Mitsubishi have set up distribution alliances with Coca-Cola in Japan, bottling and distributing all Coke products in this market. Numerous distribution alliances exist under various formats and in countries of all levels of development. Emerging markets are well served by such alliances. In an example, Carrier Aircon distributes Toshiba's high-end air conditioners in India. The Toshiba air conditioners are positioned as a super premium product catering to a wealthy niche market. Carrier set up a separate exclusive distribution network for them.[23]

strategic alliance
Any type of relationship between one or more companies attempting to reach joint corporate and market-related goals; term used to refer to most nonequity alliances.

manufacturing alliance
A nonequity relationship between two firms, in which one firm handles the other's manufacturing or some aspect of the manufacturing process.

contract manufacturing
A relationship between two companies wherein one company contracts with another to manufacture products according to the contracting company's specifications and for a specified period of time.

marketing alliance
A nonequity relationship between two firms, in which one firm handles the other's marketing or some aspect of the marketing process.

distribution alliance
A nonequity relationship between two firms, in which one firm handles the other's distribution or some aspect of the distribution process.

Outsourcing: A Rapidly Growing International Expansion Mode

Outsourcing is defined as the strategic use of outside resources to perform activities that are usually handled by internal staff and resources.[24] Outsourcing has established itself as an effective cost-cutting technique for companies around the world, because, in most cases, it involves transferring service-sector jobs to overseas locations where labor is competent and cheap—hence, outsourcing is also known as **offshoring.** Millions of jobs have gone from high-income countries to low- and medium-income countries, such as India and China.[25]

outsourcing
The strategic use of outside resources to perform activities that are usually handled by internal staff and resources.

offshoring
The strategic use of outside resources to perform activities that are usually handled by internal staff and resources.

Outsourcing has been around for a long time, but, until the late 1990s, much of the outsourcing was in the technology industry. Today, it is present in many domains and prominent in providing activities usually handled by internal staff, such as customer service and billing. Outsourcing offers opportunities for strategic alliances for the service industry—and even for manufacturing businesses using outside resources to perform activities normally handled by internal staff. The growth of the global outsourcing market has been phenomenal, and all indications suggest that this trend will continue, with the outsourcing market pegged at US$100 billion and growing. Forrester Research predicted that 3.3 million U.S. service-sector jobs will move offshore by 2015, at a rate of about 300,000 jobs per year.[26]

Asia has emerged as the outsourcing hub and back-office of the Western world, and India, China, the Philippines, and Singapore are competing for the business. India has initially received the lion's share of outsourcing opportunities, starting with information technology: A software developer in India costs US$6 per hour, compared with one in the United States, who costs US$60 per hour.[27] Subsequently, many other businesses turned to India for outsourcing, taking advantage of the low-cost, educated, and English-speaking labor force of about 150 million. As seen in the introductory section, Delta Airlines and AOL outsource many customer service functions to India. Tata Consultancy Services, the largest outsourcing firm in India, became the first information technology company in India to make more than $10 billion in revenues (in March 2012).[28]

China had initially focused on providing back-office support for financial services, telecom, software, and retailers in neighboring Asian countries because its operators can easily talk to people in Taiwan, Japan, and Korea in their native languages—China has plenty of Japanese and Korean speakers. However, China is rapidly making inroads as an outsourcing base for English-speaking nations, a business initially dominated by India.[29] Nevertheless, workers in the United States and in other English-speaking countries should be less concerned about a challenge from China, which comes largely in manufacturing, and more concerned about the challenge from India, which comes in the area of services. Moreover, information-service jobs are the easiest to outsource because of the efficiency with which they can be performed electronically. Another industry that has outsourced many jobs is the mortgage industry: It was recently reported that "the total annual value of such outsourcing contracts around the world is about $10.9 billion."[30]

In other examples, United Airlines is outsourcing its maintenance on Boeing 777 aircraft to China. And electronic medical records and computerized physician-order entries are increasingly managed offshore: X-rays from the United States, for example, are sent to India, where qualified medical personnel evaluate them for a fraction of the cost.

Although outsourcing offers many benefits, it requires careful planning and implementation. Nearly half of all outsourcing deals end in failure, with 60 percent of the problems due to errors in communication: New employees are capable and understand the technology, but not the goals of the company.[31]

The success of outsourcing strategic alliances is contingent on the use of the right strategy, as seen in the following:[32]

- Outsourcing must be done carefully, and with clear objectives and expectations of outsourcing activities.

- Outsourcing partners must be selected based on their expertise in the outsourcing activity and based on their cultural fit with the firm.

- The outsourcing firm must provide its partner in the strategic alliance with adequate training and skills that will help the partner adapt to other cultures.

- The outsourcing plan should provide clear expectations, requirements, and expected benefits during all phases of the outsourcing activity.

Outsourcing has been challenged in the United States. Government representatives, urged on by their constituencies who are directly affected by the job losses attributed to outsourcing, are attempting to ban outsourcing, especially business process outsourcing. Some experts in the United States, the United Kingdom, and other European countries worry that this trend will spell the end of their economic domination. Moreover, consumers are not keen on outsourcing, as they feel that their personal information is not well protected when handled by employees in countries where U.S. consumer protection laws may not be enforced.[33] In fact, outsourcing is not necessarily an ideal method for cost cutting: JetBlue, for instance, found that U.S. call-center operators cost about the same as Indian call-center operators, especially after communications and start-up costs are factored in.

Other experts argue that radical changes have occurred in the past, with Western nations benefiting most. They suggest that, for every dollar going offshore, the U.S. economy gets back more than $1.12 in income, whereas the countries doing the work gain 33 cents.[34]

It is important, however, that policies on trade, education, and social welfare, for instance, be modified to accommodate the radical societal changes linked to outsourcing. With time, different geographic locations and economies will develop different comparative advantages. According to this argument, outsourcing will not cause massive unemployment in the United States; rather, it will require job creation in other industries.[35]

Summary

Offer an understanding of company expansion strategies, entry mode selection, and the risks involved at each level. A company can use different entry modes to enter a new market. They range from the lowest-risk mode and the mode that provides the least control to the highest-risk/highest-control mode. Exporting is at the lowest level of control and risk. Indirect exporting requires minimal internationalization and involves selling the product to distributors, such as export management companies, trading companies, or export agents in the company's home country, who then distribute the product internationally. Direct exporting requires in-house exporting expertise, usually in the form of an exporting department. Such companies have more control over the marketing mix in the target market than indirect exporters. Licensing and franchising are popular entry modes that allow flexibility and allow for rapid international expansion and high brand awareness. Joint ventures, consortia, and wholly owned subsidiaries are examples of foreign direct investment; wholly owned subsidiaries offer the greatest commitment to a particular market but also present the highest risk to investors.

Describe different types of strategic alliances involving international companies. A company can use various forms of strategic alliances (manufacturing, marketing, distribution, and outsourcing alliances) to enter a new market. Such alliances are industry-specific, and they have various degrees of stability over time.

Key Terms

consortia

contract manufacturing

cooperative exporting

direct exporting

distribution alliance

entry mode

franchisee

franchising

franchisor

greenfielding

indirect exporting

joint venture

licensee

licensing

licensor

manufacturing alliance

marketing alliance

mother henning

offshoring

outsourcing

piggybacking

strategic alliance

wholly owned subsidiary

Discussion Questions

1. What is the difference between international franchising and international licensing? Explain.

2. Briefly describe each type of international entry mode, from exporting to wholly owned subsidiary, and address the risks and controls characterizing each entry mode.

3. There are many types of international alliances. Go to the home page of U.S. Airways (www.usairways.com/awa/content/dividendmiles/default.aspx) and identify the company's alliances.

Chapter Quiz

True/False

1. Companies need to examine the fit between the costs of international involvement, company resources, and market potential.

Answer: True

Rationale: Companies need to examine the fit between the costs of international involvement (and the opportunity costs that they would incur if they ignore the international market), company resources, and market potential.

Section 8-1, "Going International: Evaluating Opportunities"

2. Licensing is an international entry mode that presents less risk to the company but offers more control than exporting.

Answer: False

Rationale: Licensing is higher risk than exporting, but it also offers more control.

Section 8-3c, "Licensing"

3. One of the benefits of franchising is that it keeps out new competitors.

Answer: False

Rationale: Franchising has the potential of creating competitors among local employees who can learn the business and transfer the know-how to a local competitor.

Section 8-3d, "Franchising"

4. Competing companies are allowed to work in consortia in industry sectors where the government can control their monopolistic activity.

Answer: True

Rationale: Competing companies are allowed to form consortia and work in domains where the government can scrutinize their activities.

Section 8-3f, "Consortia"

5. Outsourcing involves the strategic use of outside resources to perform activities that are usually handled by internal staff and resources.

Answer: True

Rationale: Outsourcing is defined as the strategic use of outside resources to perform activities that are usually handled by internal staff and resources.

Section 8-3i, "Strategic Alliances"

Multiple Choice

1. Which of the following is correct about using international middlemen?

     a.   They increase company control over marketing strategy.

     b.   They subject the company to less risk than direct international involvement.

     c.   They maximize control for the company in the target market.

     d.   All of the above

Answer: b is correct.

Rationale: Using international middlemen subjects the company to less risk than direct international involvement.

Section 8-2, "Control versus Risk in International Expansion"

2. Direct international involvement has as a result which of the following?

     a.   The company is exposed to less risk than if it used middlemen.

     b.   The company has greater control over marketing strategies.

     c.   The company faces greater risk in the market.

     d.   b and c only

Answer: d is correct.

Rationale: The company has greater control but also faces greater risk if it opts for direct international involvement.

Section 8-2, "Control Versus Risk in International Expansion"

3. Companies may choose direct exporting because it allows them to

    a.   monitor retailers.

    b.   control suggested sale prices.

    c.   observe the handling of customer complaints.

    d.   all of the above

Answer: d is correct.

Rationale: Advantages of direct exporting are the ability to monitor retailers, control prices, and address customer concerns.

Section 8-3b, "Direct Exporting"

4. Franchising constitutes a primary entry mode for the _____ industry.

    a.   automobile

    b.   technology

    c.   service

    d.   machine-tools

Answer: c is correct.

Rationale: The preferred entry mode for services is franchising—the process whereby the franchisor gives the franchisee the right to use its brand name, related trademarks, and its business know-how, such as secret recipes and customer interfacing techniques, in return for royalties.

Section 8-3d, "Franchising"

5. Which of the following is a reason for the failure of joint ventures?

    a.   Natural disasters

    b.   Poor performance by a partner

    c.   Partners becoming competitors

    d.   All of the above

Answer: d is correct.

Rationale: Many joint ventures fail; the primary reason for failure is usually attributed to one partner—although reasons outside the partners' control, such as the economy or natural disasters, can lead to the demise of the joint venture.

Section 8-3e, "Joint Ventures"

6. Porsche helping Harley-Davidson to produce its water-cooled Revolution engine is an example of which type of strategic alliance?

    a.   Distribution

    b.   Marketing

    c.   Manufacturing

    d.   None of the above

Answer: c is correct.

Rationale: The Porsche–Harley-Davidson alliance, in this situation, involves only manufacturing processes, not distribution or marketing.

Section 8-3i, "Strategic Alliances"

Chapter 8 Endnotes

1. David Pearson, "Airbus Courts Buyers for New Aircraft," *Wall Street Journal*, June 22, 2007, A7.

2. Jacqui Bishop, "Entry Strategies," *Supply Management*, Vol. 11, No. 3, February 2, 2006, p. 37.

3. Frank Bradley and Michael Gannon, "Does the Firm's Technology and Marketing Profile Affect For eign Market Entry?" *Journal of International Marketing,* Vol. 8, No. 4, 2000, pp. 12–36.

4. Emily Scardino, "Mexx Feeds Market Madness for Value-Based Euro Glam," *DNS Retailing Today*, Vol. 43, No. 11, June 7, 2004, pp. 9–10.

5. Ross Haxton, "Retail Choice: Mexx, Oxford Street, London," *Marketing*, March 1, 2006, p. 12.

6. http://www.mexx.de/women/taschen/c-1733 (accessed July 9, 2012).

7. www.bhpc.com

8. "Starbucks Targeting Austria's Coffeehouses," *International Herald Tribune,* Frankfurt Edition, July   5, 2001, 12.

9. "Starbucks Company Invades Austria," *Austria Information,* Vol. 55, November/December 2002, http://www.austria.org/nov02.

10. www.associatedpress.com, March 13, 2007.

11. Sabrina Tavernise, "In Russia, BP Profits at the Pump," *International Herald Tribune,* Frankfurt Edition, July 5, 2001, 12.

12. Ibid.

13. Brandon Mitchener and Deborah Ball, "EU Clears De Beers-LVMH Venture," *Wall Street Journal Europe,* July 6–7, 2001, 3.

14. Ibid.

15. Terry Agins, "Polo, Richemont Team Up In Watch and Jewelry Venture," *Wall Street Journal* online edition, March 5, 2007.

16. Harry G. Barkema, Oded Shenkar, Freek Vermeulen, and John H. J. Bell, "Working Abroad, Working with Others: How Firms Learn to Operate International Joint Ventures," *Academy of Management Journal,* Vol. 40, No. 2, April 1997, pp. 426–442.

17. Catherine Belton and Guy Chazan, "Oligarchs threaten BP's Russia sale plans," *Financial Times,* June 4, 2012, p. 1; Andrew Kramer and Heather Timmons, "After Setbacks, BP May Be Forced to Give Up Some Control of Joint Venture in Russia," *New York Times*, January 16, 2007, C3.

18. www.airbus.com (accessed June 20, 2012).

19. Ibid.

20. "Motorola Scales Back Flextronics Outsourcing Deal," *International Herald Tribune,* Frankfurt Edi tion, July 4, 2001, 11.

21. Tim Burt, "Porsche Fires Revolution at Harley," *Financial Times,* July 14–15, 2001, p. 8.

22. Gordon Farclough and Stephen Power, "Chery Will Make Hatchback for Daimler," *Wall Street Journal*, March 15, 2007, p. A9.

23. "Friendly Rivals," *Country Monitor,* Vol. 11, No. 16, 2003, p. 5.

24. Dean Elmuti, "The Perceived Impact of Outsourcing on Organizational Performance," *Mid-   American Journal of Business,* Vol. 18, No. 20, 2003, pp. 33–36.

25. Tom Holman, "A Passage to India," *Bookseller*, Vol. 5246, 2006, pp. 6-7.

26.   Alan S. Blinder, "Offshoring: The Next Industrial Revolution?" *Foreign Affairs*, Vol. 85, No. 2, March – April 2006, p. 113.

27. Pankaj Mishra, "US Proposes Ban on Outsourcing," *Asia ComputerWeekly,* February 16, 2004, p. 1.

28. Business Standard, "TCS beats $10-bn revenue mark in FY12 Posts 23% growth in net profit," April 24, 2012 (http://www.business-standard.com/india/news/tcs-beats-10-bn-revenue-mark-in-fy12/472437; accessed May 14, 2012).

29. Bruce Einhorn and Manjeet Kirpalani, "Move Over India, China Is Rising Fast as a Services Outsourcing Hub," *BusinessWeek,* August 11, 2003, p. 42.

30. "Home and Away," *The Economist,* July 10, 2006, Vol. 381, No. 8499, p. 82.

31. "Outsourcing Success Is All about the Relationship," *eWeek*, October 18, 2006, p. 1.

32. Dean Elmuti, "The Perceived Impact of Outsourcing on Organizational Performance," *Mid-American Journal of Business,* Vol. 18, No. 20, 2003, pp. 33–36.

33. "Home and Away," p. 82.

34. Pankaj Mishra, "US Proposes Ban on Outsourcing," *Asia ComputerWeekly,* February 16, 2004, p. 1.

35. Alan S. Blinder, "Offshoring: The Next Industrial Revolution?" *Foreign Affairs* Vol. 85, No. 2, March-April 2006, p. 113.

Case 8-1

Danone in a Bind

Background

For Danone, China is one of the most attractive markets. With two joint ventures and its own subsidiary operations, it was China's largest bottled water maker, with 39 percent of the market, and the largest seller of soft drinks, with an 18 percent share. Danone created the Wahaha joint venture with Hangzhou Wahaha, its local partner, in 1996. Danone owned 51 percent of the joint venture, which brought in $1.4 billion in sales in 2006 alone. The relationship between the joint venture partners was smooth at first. However, in 2007, Groupe Danone SA of France filed suit against the joint venture partner, accusing it of creating a parallel manufacturing and distribution structure for the Wahaha brand, against the terms of the joint venture agreement.

The Hangzhou Wahaha Group Co., Ltd.

Anyone traveling to China has drunk at least one bottle of Wahaha water or some of the company's other drinks. ("Wahaha" in Chinese, mimics the sound of a baby laughing.) The Hangzhou Wahaha Group Co., Ltd., is China's leading *domestic* beverage producer. Its predecessor, the Hangzhou Shangcheng District School-Run Enterprise Sales Department, funded its start-up operations in 1987 with a government loan and Zong Qinghou, the company's founder, and two retired schoolteachers initially sold milk products and popsicles at the local school store. With the support of the Hangzhou government, the company bought a large, old state-owned enterprise and changed its name to the Hangzhou Wahaha Group Co.

After joining with Danone, in 1996, Hangzhou Wahaha's production increased dramatically. Today, the company has 70 subsidiaries and 40 manufacturing bases in China, with a workforce of 10,000. The state owns a majority share of Danone's joint-venture partner, Hangzhou Wahaha, and the company has foreign investment, as well as Chinese investment. Zong, its founder and chair, has played such an active role in the company, that, in the Chinese marketplace, Hangzhou Wahaha is regarded as a private enterprise. Its products are sold in France, Germany, Hong Kong, Japan, Malaysia, the Netherlands, Spain, Taiwan, Thailand, and the United States. Its product mix includes milk and yogurt drinks, purified and mineral water, carbonated soft drinks, fruit and vegetable juice, sports drinks, tea, as well as rice porridge, canned food, and health products, such as children's vitamins. The company expanded into children's clothing in

2002, and is planning to diversify into personal care products, including shampoo and toothpaste. One of its brands, Future Cola, is positioned as a challenger to Coke and Pepsi.

The company emphasizes its Chinese origins, encouraging consumers to support their country by selecting the Wahaha brand.

The Conflict

In May 2007, Groupe Danone SA of France filed suit against the joint venture partner, Zong Qinghou, and his daughter. It filed for arbitration with a body in Sweden specializing in commercial disputes involving China. Danone accused Zong of producing and selling Wahaha products outside of the joint venture structure established in 1996. Danone found evidence of the existing parallel business in 2005. Danone, which owned 51 percent of the 39 joint ventures with Wahaha, accused Wahaha of setting up independent companies to sell products identical to those sold by the joint ventures. In the lawsuit, Danone demanded a 51 percent stake in the Wahaha companies that are not part of the joint venture—the Wahaha group rejected the demand.

In response, Zong Qinghou, Hangzhou Wahaha's founder and chairman, used nationalistic imagery, accusing Danone of trying to control subsidiaries that were not part of the partnership. He claimed that the terms of the joint venture were not fair.

Danone also decided to use Western courts to challenge its joint venture partner, filing a lawsuit in the United States against one of Wahaha's subsidiaries and two of Zong's relatives owning an offshore company. It claimed that a Wahaha company registered in the British Virgin Islands has been illegally selling the joint venture's drinks. In response to this action, the joint venture partner accused Danone of utilizing global pressure to force Wahaha to concede.

Chinese customs, in response, seized 118,000 liters of Evian mineral water—a Danone brand—which officials claimed had unacceptable levels of bacteria. Danone claimed that this seizure was directly related to its actions against Hangzhou Wahaha.

The founder and chairman of the joint venture, Zong Qinghou, resigned in June 2007. Since then, Zong and Hangzhou Wahaha have actively battered Danone in public, posting venomous letters on the Internet and vowing to punish Danone for its evil deeds and destroy the company. Wahaha employees even showed up at Danone's Shanghai headquarters protesting against the company.

By 2009, Danone gave up the fight and Wahaha agreed to pay cash to acquire Danone's 51 percent, ending the joint venture. The two companies also agreed to drop all legal proceedings. In an unrelated story, in December 2011, Danone also closed a yogurt factory in China. The future of the company in China might not look as promising as once thought.

Sources:

David Barboza, "Danone Exits China Venture After Years of Legal Dispute," *The New York Times*, September 30, 2009 (www.nytimes.com); James T. Areddy, "Danone Seeks Ways to Fix China Venture; Vow Not to Walk Away Follows Resignation of Partner Amid Tussle," *Wall Street Journal*, June 13, 2007, A8; David Barboza, "Wahaha Executives Threaten to Quit Danone," *International Herald Tribune,* Online Edition, June 13, 2007; Geoff Dyer, "Danone Files US Lawsuit Against Wahaha," *Financial Times*, June 6, 2007, 28; Adam Jones, "Chinese Seize Cases of Danone Water," *Financial Times*, May 31, 2007, 27; Paula M. Miller, "The Chinese Beverage Company's Expansion Is No Laughing Matter," *China Business Daily Online*, September – October 2004.

Analyses Suggestions:

1. Describe the joint venture between Danone and Hangzhou Wahaha. What were some of the important ownership characteristics? Who contributed what to this relationship?

2. What were the advantages to Danone, and to Hangzhou Wahaha in setting up the joint venture?

3. What were the disadvantages to Danone and to Hangzhou Wahaha in this joint venture relationship?

PART

4

Managing the
International Marketing Mix

Chapter 9: Products and Services: Branding Decisions

Learning Objectives

After studying this chapter, you should be able to:

- Describe drivers for international standardization and offer an overview of the international standardization–local adaptation continuum and respective company strategies.

- Examine country-of-origin effects on brand evaluations in relation to product stereotypes and consumer ethnocentrism.

- Examine challenges faced by service providers in international markets.

- Address issues related to brand name protection and the reasons behind widespread international counterfeiting.

- Address the marketing of industrial products and services and related product and service standards.

The world has been gradually moving toward one large, global marketplace. As Chapter 4, "Regional Economic and Political Integration," illustrated, a fragmented Europe is merging into one large, unified market, as is South America. The Asian market also is gradually removing barriers and allowing more access to Western multinationals. Mature products in many industries are addressing the needs of consumers worldwide with the same brands and only minimal, market-specific modifications. Panasonic (Japan) markets the Viera flat panel television set using similar marketing strategies worldwide, with its daring commercials toned down somewhat for the U.S. market. Braun and Krups (Germany) sell kitchen appliances using the same marketing mix across continents with only minor mandatory adaptations (voltage, cycles, television systems).

Similarly, franchises such as KFC, Pizza Hut, McDonald's, and Burger King are only minimally altering their offerings to meet local demands, offering wine and beer in some European countries, vegetarian burgers in India, and so on. U.S. consumers are more demanding and they get more—free refills, free ketchup and mayonnaise, lower prices and much bigger portions. A "small" is a "giant" elsewhere in the world, and a "supersize" is simply unimaginable elsewhere. Ask for a large Coke at McDonald's in Amsterdam and you get a drink in something the size of a vial. Moreover, you still need to negotiate for one of those hard-to-come-by ice cubes to cool it off.

Mineral water distributors, such as Gerolsteiner (Germany), Evian, and Volvic (France), and food manufacturers, such as the Kraft International confectionery products, are modifying only their labels to conform to local labeling requirements when selling their products across different continents. Toblerone bars look the same in Seattle, Cairo, Quito, Paris, Addis Ababa, Budapest, and Beijing, and they taste exactly the same.

Yet, for certain product categories that appeal to local preferences, international firms have to adapt their offerings to effectively compete with local manufacturers and service providers and to more directly cater to the individual needs of local markets. Advertising agencies and numerous financial and legal service providers, for example, typically partner with local firms to create successful campaigns and strategies aimed at individual markets.

This chapter examines the driving forces behind a company's decision to standardize, or to partially or fully adapt, its offerings to individual international markets. It also addresses barriers faced by brands from private-label offerings and by service providers from local government. The chapter addresses brand name protection issues and reasons behind the proliferation of counterfeiting activity worldwide.

9-1 Standardization versus Adaptation

The topic of standardization versus **adaptation,** to a certain extent, parallels the concepts introduced in Chapter 1, "Scope, Concepts, and Drivers of International Marketing," addressing geocentric, regiocentric, and polycentric orientations. Global standardization reflects a geocentric company orientation, regional standardization reflects a regiocentric orientation, and local adaptation reflects a polycentric orientation, respectively (see Figure 9-1). It must be noted, however, that multinational companies may adopt a combination strategy, depending on the particulars of individual markets. For instance, PepsiCo is a global company with, most likely, a geocentric orientation; however, it has only recently moved from a localized strategy to a regional strategy in terms of its distribution and purchasing.

> **adaptation**
> The strategy of altering a product to better meet the needs of a local market.

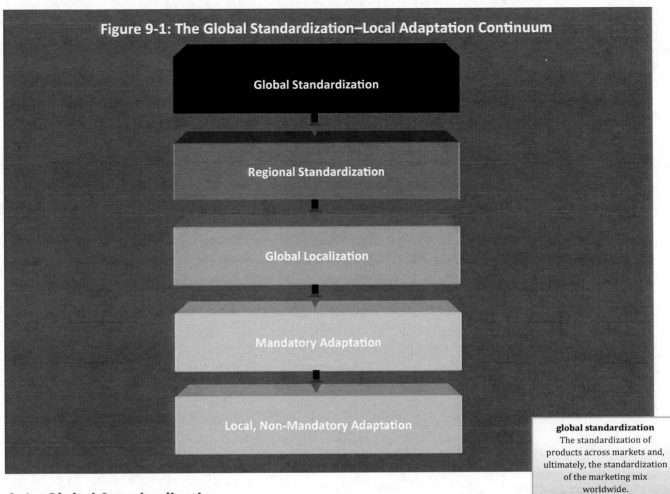

Figure 9-1: The Global Standardization–Local Adaptation Continuum

Global Standardization

Regional Standardization

Global Localization

Mandatory Adaptation

Local, Non-Mandatory Adaptation

> **global standardization**
> The standardization of products across markets and, ultimately, the standardization of the marketing mix worldwide.

9-1a Global Standardization

Global standardization, frequently used interchangeably with the term "glocalization," refers first to standardization of products across markets and, ultimately, to the standardization of the marketing mix worldwide. This latter definition is used in this textbook.

The main reason why firms favor global standardization is obvious: It is cheaper to have the same product and the same integrated marketing communication strategy worldwide. And standardization is possible because consumers increasingly have the same product preferences.

The primary reason for uniform preferences is the media, the instant penetration of Internet and television in homes everywhere in the world. In the most remote areas in developing countries, technology makes it possible to have Internet cafés and television. In many countries worldwide, in addition to premium international channels, such as MTV and CNN, access to neighboring countries' television programs is commonplace. Serbian television is preferred by many viewers in western Romania, as the following example illustrates.

Serbian Television: Who Would've Thought?

In the city of Timisoara, in western Romania, one has access to all the national Romanian programming and regional Transylvanian programming. One also has access to Hungarian and Serbian television programs and to Italy's Rai Uno, as well as MTV and CNN for those who have subscriptions.

Serbian television has had a long tradition in this part of Romania. Before the fall of communism, Serbian television programs carried much more Western programming than Romanian TV, and the nightly news was more informative and honest. As a result, there are generations of Romanians who made an effort to understand Serbian to understand the programming. Today, those same viewers continue to have a preference for Serbian television programs and to watch them regularly.

Exposure to overlapping media increases exposure to brand advertising: Companies are able to build brand awareness beyond the borders intended for the diffusion of the respective media. In the previous example, Kraft advertising on Serbian television will reach Romanian viewers, who are also exposed to Kraft advertising on Romanian television channels. In addition, the Internet provides individuals with opportunities to compare notes on brands and product styles with others of similar age and interest. See the following examples from Greenland and Denmark.

Greenland and Danish Youth

A young man in isolated Greenland found that his Internet chat-buddies in the U.S. live the same way: sleep, watch television, listen to music, party, and go to school—riding a motorcycle or scooter, whereas the individual in Greenland rides a snow-scooter to school. The youth market categorizes itself similarly, whether in the United States or in Denmark. For example, a young man in Denmark describes his peers' styles: the typical girl who listens to pop music and imitates Britney Spears' style of dress, wearing tight trousers that are a bit wide at the bottom and shirts that are so tight that the breasts almost jump in your face; the girl who listens to techno music wearing wide, baggy trousers with traffic-safe colors, who likes to party at a Copenhagen night-club well-known for its techno music and drug scene; the typical boy who prefers pop music and who is probably trendy and wears a tight t-shirt and nice clothes but also might wear a frumpy sweater; and the skater-look, which is a bit like hip-hop style, with more earth-colors and the characteristic skater shoes. This individual is fully committed to the Copenhagen hip-hop scene, and spends most of his money on clothes, music, and electronic equipment.[1]

Another reason for similar consumer preferences is international travel. In spite of increasing gasoline prices, it is still cheap to travel, especially at nonpeak times. And, as more consumers cross borders, they are exposed to more brands and brand advertisements.

As a result of the exposure, the interests and product/service-related needs of consumers are becoming more and more homogeneous worldwide. Consequently, products and, indeed, brand preferences are gaining a common definition across continents, leading to the emergence of **global consumers.**

global consumers
The homogeneous consumer group worldwide sharing similar interests and product/brand preferences.

Inline skates, skateboards, and scooters are in great favor with preteens in New York, Copenhagen, Warsaw, and Delhi. Blonde, svelte Barbie dolls and Barbie-doll look-alikes are on the wish lists of little girls in developed countries and developing countries. Nike sneakers, Coke, Levi's jeans, and Timberland shoes are in with the preteen to college segment. Business people watch CNN, and practically everyone, young and old, especially outside of the United States, watches MTV and owns an iPod.

The strategy used to address these increasingly homogeneous consumer needs is global branding. A global brand has the same name, logo, image, and positioning everywhere in the world. Main streets in most world capitals and malls worldwide advertise and sell brands such as Ralph Lauren, Escada, and Donna Karan, while logos of Pepsi, Coca-Cola, and Camel and Kent cigarettes adorn umbrellas in many central squares and beach resorts (see Figure 9-2). These are global brands, enjoying worldwide reputation and recognition, demanded by consumers in Shanghai, Antananarivo, and Paris alike. These brands have a high awareness among consumers worldwide and are perceived to be of high quality.

Figure 9-2: *Pepsi umbrellas at a Polish resort on the Baltic Sea warm up the landscape.*

Standardization is particularly important for product research and development. Economies of scale can be achieved if there is a concentration in research and development, and coordination also gives a firm flexibility in responding to competitors' R&D efforts.[2] Such coordination is expensive. Moreover, governments may restrain the flow of information and people, which are required to coordinate research and development activities.[3]

With regard to the other components of the marketing mix, advertising savings can be achieved by having a uniform advertising strategy in each country. PepsiCo, for example, saves millions as a result of using the same film for television advertising in different international markets, and Levi Strauss typically uses one series of TV commercials around the globe.[4] These companies are lowering their media expenditure costs while benefiting from advertising consistency and from the brand image consistency they have created.

Similarly, the standardization of supply chains has resulted in cost reductions in transportation and distribution, with significant cost reductions and overall shorter transportation times. In addition, research and development, purchasing, packaging, and customer service, among others, have also benefited from standardization.[5] The standardization of point-of-sale (POS) systems is creating efficiency within the supply chain. McDonald's has standardized its point-of-sale system worldwide, using the NewPOS, produced by Savista Corp. The new system was introduced in the more than 30,000 restaurants, replacing the decentralized system McDonald's used in the past, which made it difficult for the chain to mandate technology standards. Almost 65 percent of all McDonald's restaurants worldwide are operated by franchisees, and as recently as 2001, McDonald's operations featured "800 combinations" of POS hardware and software and back-office applications. Today, McDonald's views POS not just as a commodity, but as yet another strategic asset that helps in the process of standardizing McDonald's processes of supply-chain management and customer interface.[6]

Issues related to the standardization of distribution and promotion will be further examined in Chapter 11, "Managing International Distribution Operations and Logistics," and Chapter 13, "The International Promotional Mix and Advertising Strategies."

9-1b Regional Standardization

A variation of global standardization, a **regional standardization** strategy refers to the use of a uniform marketing strategy within a particular region. This strategy is becoming more appealing to companies as regional market integration is gaining strength worldwide, with the European Union, MERCOSUR, and NAFTA in particular gaining ground as veritable unified markets. Pan-European brands are becoming common, even for U.S. multinationals, such as Procter & Gamble (whose Ariel detergent was its first Pan-European product; today, the brand is available in most markets, with the exception of North America).

> **regional standardization**
> The use of a uniform marketing strategy within a particular region.

In addition to regional branding strategies, companies also benefit from economies of scale by concentrating certain marketing activities regionally. We have seen earlier in this chapter the Levi Strauss attempts to standardize its communication as much as possible—even having one TV commercial worldwide, whenever possible. However, with a large corporation and with consumers perceiving it as a premium brand in some parts of the world and as an everyday, basic brand in its home country of the United States, Levi Strauss is forced to engage in some level of adaptation, as the following example illustrates.

Levi Strauss

Levi Strauss is reconciling its efforts to standardize its offering through regional standardization, organizing its operations into three regional divisions: Levi Strauss, the Americas, based in San Francisco; Levi Strauss Europe, Middle East, and Africa, based in Brussels, Belgium; and the Asia Pacific Division, based in Singapore.[7]

For the United States, Levi Strauss' strategy has always been one of offering a quality brand at lower prices, whereas, internationally, the company has been charging premium prices. However, with consumers worldwide learning of the lower jeans prices in the U.S., and demanding cheaper brand-name jeans, Levi Strauss has had to adapt and offer a "value range of clothing" at about $50 a pair, at least $30 cheaper than its ordinary offerings. The company distributes this new line in France, Germany, and the U.K. through discount hypermarkets Tesco and Asda.[8]

In other examples, PepsiCo centralized purchasing across all of its European businesses, thus achieving volume savings from sugar, cooking oil, flour, and packaging materials, for a total savings of $100 million per year.[9] In terms of distribution, Nike has traditionally utilized local warehousing to supply retailers; the company has replaced more than 20 national warehouses in Europe with one single distribution center located in Belgium, thus using a strategy similar to that used in the United States, where Nike has successfully centralized its American operations in Memphis, Tennessee.[10]Another example of a company using regional standardization is Mercedes-Benz.

Mercedes-Benz

Mercedes-Benz (www.mercedes.com) engages in regional standardization of its offerings. Its operations in the United States are centralized under the Mercedes-USA umbrella organization. One of the reasons behind the regional standardization is that Mercedes' premium positioning in the United States market was undercut by gray marketing channels in the 1970s, when many lower-priced Mercedes automobiles were shipped from Europe and sold to customers in the United States at prices lower than those of U.S. dealers.

As a result of the regional standardization, the European[11] offerings are different from those in the United States. For passenger cars, the Mercedes A-Class, a lower-priced series (see Figure 9-3),[12] is available everywhere except in the United States. Among the A-Class are the A-150 to A-200, which also comes in a turbo model. Mercedes also offers the B-Class, with the B-150 to B-200, which comes in a turbo model as well. Both the A- and B-Classes are not available in the United States.

In the case of its compacts, the C-Class, for much of the rest of the world, Mercedes offers the Classic, the Elégance, and the Avantgarde models in the C-180, C-200, C-220, C-350 versions. For the U.S. market, the C-Class is limited to C-230, C-280, and C-350 models, and the cheapest C-Class automobile starts at $30,000. Clearly, for the United States, Mercedes insists on being only a luxury automobile, at least for the time being.

Figure 9-3: *The A-Class Mercedes is about as large as a Ford Focus; it even looks like one.*

A product often must be adapted to the demands of the local market because consumers might have specific preferences. Alternatively, adaptation might be dictated by the political and legal environment, by the technological environment, or by other particulars of the market (trade relationships, climate, etc.). The degree of economic development in a market also is a factor that determines the degree of product adaptation needed. The lower the level of economic and market development, the more the product needs to be changed to serve the needs and demands of the market.[13]

Host governments affect the globalization of products by imposing local content requirements, standards (technical, emission, etc.), and ownership restrictions and requirements on technology transfer; in the case of services, consumer participation in production may be affected by government barriers to global strategy.[14] Banking in the Middle East is gender-based: Women's banks are separate from banks used by men, and cross-access is restricted. Government restrictions affect not only international banking: China, Singapore, and Saudi Arabia ban the private ownership of satellite dishes, and China is restricting citizen access to the web (see the following example).[15]

Googling in China

If you are attempting to do any Internet searches in China, be warned: You will have access only to selected web sites. As soon as you attempt to use the Google engine, you are restricted to Google China—as in www.google.cn. Should you search any topics that are sensitive, and thus are under the scrutiny of the Chinese government, you will find that your results will be limited. Type "Dalai Lama" and you will only find information on the Chinese government approved Panchen Lama, rather than on His Holiness. Type Tiananmen Square and you will get basic information about the square, with no information about the protests of 1989. When the same search is entered at www.google.com in the United States, the landmark student protests in 1989 are prominently featured.

9-1c Global Localization

In the Levi Strauss example, one size of jeans does not fit all. First, culture can limit the types of jeans for a particular market. For example, in Islamic countries females are discouraged from wearing tight fitting attire, whereas Japanese consumers prefer tighter fitting jeans than the American counterparts. Secondly, average height can dictate product specifications. Jeans for the East Asian market, where the average height of individuals is less than in the West, require shorter inside leg measurements than for Western countries.[16]

In general, few products and services can succeed through a purely global strategy, where the product undergoes no changes, and where the promotional mix, distribution, and pricing remain the same. A degree of adaptation to local conditions is frequently imperative for company success. According to marketing experts, the idea of marketing a standardized product with a uniform marketing plan around the world remains purely theoretical. Although a product concept may be universal, it must still be adapted to differences in local culture, legislation, and even production capabilities.[17] The term **global localization,** or **glocalization,** is frequently used to describe the practice of global branding and localized marketing adaptation.

Product managers must decide on which aspects of a product they want to standardize across markets and which aspects of the product to localize. In this decision, they resort to two approaches: One involves offering parts (modules) that can be assembled worldwide in different configurations, depending on the needs of the market—**modular adaptation;** the other, standardizing the core product/service, but allowing for easy modification from market to market—**core product strategy.** In an instance of the latter, the core product is identical from one country to another, but certain aspects of the offering differ from market to market. To illustrate this concept, marketers with brands heralded as global icons often act using a local strategy: McDonald's Golden Arches are omnipresent throughout the world. Its offerings, however, are adapted to the local culture. At its restaurants in New Delhi, where most Indian consumers consider cows sacred and do not eat beef, McDonald's offers the Maharaja Mac (two all-mutton patties, special sauce, lettuce, cheese, pickles, onions on a sesame-seed bun). Similarly, Volvo, unlike Mercedes (as mentioned in Section 9-1b, "Regional Standardization"), has a similar core product in every market. However, it offers air conditioning as a standard feature only for the U.S. market.

Similarly, other fast-food restaurant services have adapted their offerings from market to market (see Figure 9-4). The Yum! Brands companies (Pizza Hut and KFC, in particular), Burger King, and McDonald's offer beer and wine in Europe, and most multinational fast-food companies offer miso soup in Japan. Along with this type of adaptation are other examples: McDonald's in the Netherlands offers its large Coca-Cola Light (Diet Coke)[18] in containers slightly smaller than the medium drink containers it serves in the United States. Pizza Hut in Germany sells cans of Pepsi from take-home windows—outside a café-restaurant on Leopoldstrasse, a street

global localization or glocalization
The practice of global branding and localized marketing adaptation to differences in local culture, legislation, and even production capabilities.

modular adaptation
The localization across markets of the product by offering parts (modules) that can be assembled worldwide in different configurations, depending on the needs of the market. Mandatory

core product strategy
The strategy of using the same standard core product/service worldwide, but varying certain aspects of the offering (product ingredients, advertising) from market to market.

Figure 9-4: *This Starbucks, near the Great Wall, is an elegant coffee house. Here, and in its former location in the Forbidden City, in Beijing, there was barely any mention of the brand name that one could readily spot.*

lined with cafés, in Munich, for instance. KFC found that, for its Japanese consumers, it needed to change its product's shape and size because the Japanese prefer morsel-sized food.

In another example, Disney, as a global company, decided to allow its regional organizations to create their own programming. The company first decided to localize production for its shows in India. Disney's first television show in India, *Vicky Aur Vetall,* was based on an Indian myth about a prince and a genie-like figure. After this successful venture, it decided to offer the Indian market a show called *Dhoom Machaoo Dhoom* (Hindi for "let's have a blast"), aimed at teenagers. The show is about two teenage girls and is popular with Indian audiences of all ages. *Dhoom* is a breakthrough because it is one of the few programs produced for teenagers—specifically, for girls—in this market. This is similar to family serials: It is real and close to the lives of teenagers. After its success in India, Disney decided to expand its localization efforts in Britain and Japan as well.

Disney's competitors are quickly following suit. Time Warner is offering an Indian version of *Sesame Street* called *Galli Galli Sim Sim,* using some material from the popular U.S. show, but set on Indian streetscapes and anchored by local Muppets. Big Bird is replaced with a big lion called Boombah.[19]

9-1d Mandatory Adaptation

To render products usable, manufacturers of appliances adapt their products to local requirements. Such **mandatory adaptations** involve electricity—220 volts and 50 cycles for Europe, whereas, in the United States, the standard is 110 and 60 cycles. Other such adaptations involve telephone jacks, and television/VCR systems (NTSC in the United States, PAL and SECAM I and SECAM II in the rest of the world).

In other examples, automobiles must be adapted to driving on the left side of the road in the United Kingdom, Ireland, and Australia. The United States requires a conversion to local specifications (emissions and other standards) for any imported automobiles that were not manufactured according to U.S. standards. Subsequent to conversion, the U.S. Department of Transportation must approve the conversion for the vehicle to be registered locally, which makes this, overall, a costly undertaking.

Other types of mandatory adaptation abound. For example, a number of Middle Eastern countries continue to restrict the import of products that have components manufactured in Israel. Food products, in particular, must be scrutinized: Alcohol content is prohibited from distribution without special and limited authorization in many countries in North Africa and the Middle East, and food products containing pork have limited appeal and face inspections and other restrictions in this same region. Magazines are either marked with a black marker where a woman's body or face is evident or not allowed through at all in Saudi Arabia, and the list continues.

mandatory adaptation
The adaptation of products to local requirements so that the products can legally and physically function in the specific country environment.

9-1e Local, Nonmandatory Adaptation

Many global companies adapt their offerings to better meet the needs of the local market, thus performing a local, **nonmandatory adaptation.** Examples of multinational companies offering products aimed at local markets abound. In most instances, the products result from a buyout. Unilever and Procter & Gamble bought numerous brands in Central and Eastern Europe; for instance, Unilever bought Romania's Dero, a detergent that is now part of the company's product mix in that country. It is also one of the few Romanian communist brands that has survived post-communism, inspiring artists to use the name in titling works dealing with Romanian society. In other examples, Unilever also has a Bulgarian dressing, Kaliakra, in its mix, as well as a Serbian margarine, Sunce.

Multinational companies also have developed new brands for individual local markets: Häagen-Dazs Japan offers its customers Royal Milk Tea ice cream, a full-bodied, creamy green ice tea; Weight Watchers offers consumers in France Mousse Legeres in two different four-pack combinations—Cherry/Green Tea, Pear/Jasmine, Apricot/Orange Flower, and Peach/Ginger; in the United Kingdom, Nestlé offers a drinkable fruit yogurt named Squizzos, which sports Disney characters on its packaging.[20]

9-2 Private-Label (Retailer) Brands

Private-label (retailer) brands pose an increasing challenge to manufacturers' global or local brands. European food retailers, such as Sainsbury in the United Kingdom and Albert Heijn in the Netherlands, as well as North American retailers, offer quality products with the "Sainsbury" and "ah" brands, respectively, packaged impeccably and positioned on the shelves side-by-side with popular multinational/national brands.

Among the best known **private labels** is the Tesco brand, which is a reliable brand that has the same appeal in the Czech Republic and Hungary as it does at home, in the United Kingdom. Among other European private labels that have broad appeal are Marks & Spencer, from the U.K. and Dallmayr, a specialty store offering gourmet food from Munich, Germany, whose specialty goods are now available in many supermarkets in Germany and neighboring countries.

It used to be that private-label brands appealed to consumers primarily during downturns in the economy, when they were more likely to make their brand selection based on price; however, that is no longer the case. Consumers worldwide have become more price conscious, demanding higher quality at lower prices. The private-label brand offering serves well this mind-set, as does the proliferation of discounters such as Wal-Mart, Aldi, Metro, Costco, and Toys "R" Us, which are increasing price competition by offering their own dealer brands.

9-3 -Global Branding and Country-of-Origin Information

Country of origin is defined as the country with which a particular product or service is associated. The country could be the **country of manufacture,** in the case of products, or the country where the company headquarters are located, for both products and services. The key to determining a product's perceived country of origin depends on which of the two (country of manufacture or home country of the company) elicits the stronger association. For example, many of the appliances Philips sells are manufactured in Asia; however, the Philips' headquarters are in the Netherlands. The country of origin for Philips appliances, then, is not the particular country in Asia where they are manufactured, but the Netherlands. A new, unknown brand, however, will be associated more strongly with the country of manufacture.

In the absence of other product information, the country of origin of a product or service affects consumers' evaluations of that product or service. Country-of-origin information constitutes a product trait that is external to the product itself,

> **nonmandatory adaptation**
> The strategy of adapting a product to better meet the needs of the local market, without being required to do so.
>
> **private labels**
> Brands sold under the brand name of a retailer or some other distributor.
>
> **country of origin**
> The country with which a particular product or service is associated.
>
> **country of manufacture**
> The country in which a particular product is manufactured.

acting as a surrogate for product quality, performance, reliability, prestige, and other product characteristics that cannot be directly evaluated.[21] In general, products manufactured in highly industrialized countries are perceived as being of higher quality and having greater prestige than those manufactured in developing countries. Consumers from highly developed countries tend, in general, to evaluate home-country products more favorably than products from other countries. The opposite is true for consumers in developing countries and newly marketizing economies[22] who evaluate home-country products as inferior to products from developed countries.

When consumers have additional product information, however, such as brand name, or if they purchase the product at a store known for its quality—and especially premium-quality—products, country-of-origin information is no longer a primary source consumers use for product quality evaluation. And, increasingly, with products manufactured using components made in various countries and assembled in yet other countries, determining the "true" country of origin of a product is difficult. For example, BMWs for the U.S. market are manufactured in South Carolina, rather than in Bavaria; Michelin tires are also manufactured in South Carolina; the Mercedes M-Class is manufactured in Alabama; and many software products used by U.S. businesses are developed in India.

In many developing countries, local brands have difficulty competing with multinational firms, and when they are successful, they are often quickly bought by multinational competitors. Marketing Illustration 9-1, however, suggests that Chinese brands are slowly gaining brand recognition and adoption—and the respect—of the Chinese consumers.

International Marketing Illustration 9-1
Multinational versus Chinese Brands

One of the most noteworthy developments in the Chinese marketplace is the coming battle and shrinking disparity between multinational and local brands: Can Chinese brands compete at home against Western, Japanese, and Korean brands preferred by China's 1.3 billion consumers? Chinese brands have differentiated themselves primarily on price and distribution, rather than quality or brand attributes, which are known to create consumer loyalty and high profit margins. On the other hand, multinational brands are ubiquitous and heavily advertised: On the way to Shanghai from Pudong International Airport, one of the first billboards is for the Hooters chain of restaurants. Michael Jordan smiles from a Hanes ad in taxis, and iPods are everywhere. According to Gavin Heron, managing director of TBWA/Shanghai, China is a story of international brands, not local ones, and as soon as a local brand has traction, it is quickly bought out by a multinational. J. Alfonso A. De Dios, associate director of Procter & Gamble's Greater China Media Department, suggests that China should innovate and move from "made in China" to "created in China."

Xiaoguang Fang, vice chairman/senior strategic consultant, Gallup Research Co. LTD, suggests that, since 1994, Chinese brands have come a long way. In 1994, the brand recognition rate was highest for non-Chinese brands: Hitachi, Coca-Cola, Panasonic, Tsingtao, Toshiba, Toyota, and Marlboro, among others. Today, the top 10 brands in terms of brand-recognition rate in China are Wahaha (bottled water), Bank of China, Coca-Cola, Tsingtao beer, China Telecom, Chang Hong, Haier, Santana (VW automobile joint venture in China), China Mobile, and Head & Shoulders. In fact, Wahaha has a 94 percent brand recognition rate.

The top automobile brands in China in terms of brand recognition are: Santana, Red Flag, Mercedes, Beijing Jeep, Shanghai VW, BMW, Honda, Volkswagen, Toyota, and Buick. However the best-selling automobile is the Chery, produced by Chery Automobile, which was founded in 1997 and is government-owned.

For cosmetics, the top brands in terms of recognition are Western multinational brands: Colgate, Head & Shoulders, Procter & Gamble, Avon, and Johnson & Johnson.

When asked who makes the best products, Chinese responded, in the following order: Japan, United States, Germany, France (especially for luxury goods), Britain, Korea (for its successful brands, such as Samsung and LG), Taiwan (for its information technology expertise), and China. China has gone far in terms of brand development and building, but it has a long way ahead.

Sources: Xiaoguang Fang, Vice Chairman/Senior Strategic Consultant, Gallup Research Co. LTD, lecture on consumer trends in China, May 23, 2007, University of Richmond Faculty Seminar, Beijing, China; Scott Donaton, "Chinese Challenge: Local Brand More Copycats than Creators," *Advertising Age*, Vol. 76, No. 49, December 5, 2005, p. 21.

9-3a Product-Country and Service-Country Stereotypes

product-country stereotypes
Product-specific stereotypes that associate the country of origin as a certification of quality.

Kenyan or Colombian coffee, Chinese silk (see Figure 9-5), German beer and electronics, French perfume, Italian fashion, Swiss chocolate, and Russian caviar are examples of strong **product-country stereotypes** of quality held by consumers in the United States. Among such stereotypes shared elsewhere in the world are Iranian pistachios and rugs, Polish vegetables, Israeli oranges, and Czech and Italian crystal, to name a few. Such stereotypes are product specific and do not apply usually to other products from that particular country.

Advertisements often emphasize these stereotypes. In the United States, Colombian coffee is touted as a certification of quality. Petrossian in New York stresses its reputation as the authentic retailer of Russian beluga and sevruga caviar. Toblerone chocolate stresses its European origins, despite the fact that it is a U.S. brand owned by Kraft. Häagen-Dazs chocolate-dipped ice cream is really a product produced locally, in the United States; its name suggests an association with Europe, again affirming the quality association with European chocolate. But sometimes a product's Italian reputation may be the only thing Italian about it (see International Marketing Illustration 9-2).

Figure 9-5: *Chinese silk factory: Chinese silk is perceived by consumers worldwide as a high-quality silk.*

International Marketing Illustration 9-2

Italian Olive Oil from Spain and Greece: A New Perspective on Country of Origin

Superb Italian olive oils have achieved a remarkable reputation worldwide: Italian olive oil is a strong product-country stereotype of quality that helps it command a high price and sell well. Berio olive oil is exported from the fabled Italian countryside—a countryside with tanker trucks that bring the oil from Spain, Tunisia, and Greece for processing and export. No, the Berio olive oil does not come from Lucca in the celebrated olive-growing region of Tuscany, where the Berio olive oil factory is located. In fact, Italy does not grow enough olives to even satisfy the Italian market, let alone export the product to the rest of the world. Less than 20 percent of the Berio brand olive oil is made with Italian olives. Berio's rival, Bertolli, also has its roots in Lucca and uses foreign oil.

Berio's management justifies that it is not important where the olives are picked and pressed, but, rather, where the oil is refined and blended; the oil acquires its Italian cachet through processing by skilled Italian experts. This is a rather novel country-of-origin argument and one that the marketplace has not yet altogether dismissed because Belgian chocolate made with cocoa from the Ivory Coast is, in fact, Belgian, and not African chocolate.

This deceptive marketing strategy may be challenged in the future, however. Italian olive oil producers are up in arms because Italian exporters are more likely to purchase cheaper oil from abroad than from the promoted Tuscan olive groves.

And consumers in the United States are being deceived by advertising that claims the oil is "born in the Tuscan Mountains."

Source: Clifford J. Levy, "The Olive Oil Seems Fine. Whether It's Italian Is the Issue," *The New York Times*, May 7, 2004, A4.

Services too have their own stereotypes. Eastern European cosmeticians, for example, are popular in the West. Names such as Ilona of Hungary, Frederic Fekkai, and Erno Laszlo cosmetics are prominent on Madison and Fifth Avenues in New York. Tourists going to Eastern Europe often use the services of local beauticians or even go for extended stays to spas specializing in mud baths and life-renewal therapies.

Unfortunate negative stereotypes also exist. French waiters have received unfair evaluations in the United States, where they are perceived as arrogant. U.S. consumers also perceive them as not liking American consumers in particular. But that is absolutely not the case, as American consumers tip about 20 percent (at least until they live in the country long enough to learn about the local norms), whereas French and European consumers tip less than 10 percent. Consumers from the United States are, in fact, preferred worldwide as they tend to tip substantially more than locals or to tip where the tradition is not to tip at all, as the service charge is included in the bill. In general, customer service tends to be less enthusiastic in most other countries. Employees do their job and expect a set salary in return—there is rarely a premium for service that is above and beyond expectations.

9-3b Country of Origin and Ethnocentrism

We have learned about **ethnocentrism** as a company philosophy, an approach to international marketing as an extension of domestic marketing with minimal adaptation to the needs of the international consumers and the peculiarities of the local market. This second definition of ethnocentrism, used in relation to country of origin, is related to consumers' beliefs that purchasing foreign products is morally wrong.[23] Ethnocentric consumers believe that purchasing imported products hurts the economy, causes loss of jobs, and is unpatriotic, and consumers purchasing foreign products are worthy of contempt.[24] This concept then translates into a preference for products from one's own country (i.e., "buy American") and a rejection of products with a foreign country of origin. This attitude can exist at the individual consumer level or at the aggregate societal level.

Companies often try to circumvent any ethnocentric tendencies of local consumers by marketing their products as local, trying to persuade locals that the brand is their own, or, at least that a part of the product is locally produced. The ad in Figure 9-6 illustrates a Swiss McDonald's ad stressing that the bread used in its buns is local.

ethnocentrism
The belief that one's culture is superior to another and that strategies used in one's home country (presumably a developed country) will work just as well internationally.

Governments also frequently engage in practices in which they favor locally produced products and local service providers for government-sponsored work. In Section 9-4, similar restrictions and related philosophies are explored in the area of services.

Figure 9-6: *In Italian-speaking Switzerland, McDonald's is advertising hamburger buns as being of Swiss origin.*

9-4 -The Service Side: Tariff and Nontariff Barriers to Entry

service barriers
Barriers encountered by services in different markets, such as requirements for local certification, local providers, and other requirements that favor local over international service providers.

This section examines challenges that service providers face in their international involvement. These challenges, or **service barriers,** in one form or another, represent a manifestation of ethnocentrism at the firm level, government level, or consumer level. Among such challenges are:[25]

- The requirement to use national services. This requirement is a form of protectionism: Company or government policies provide implicit or explicit preference for a domestic supplier, which makes it difficult for international service providers to survive.

- The prohibition against the employment of foreign nationals or other barriers—for example, demanding a local certification such as certified public accountant (CPA), which requires a degree in accounting from a U.S. institution as well as passing the CPA exam.

- Direct competition from government providers, such as a local government monopoly over natural gas and electricity.

- Restrictions on movement—for example, limiting access for tourists in a particular region or the number of flights allowed into the country.

- Tariffs imposed on international service providers.

Frequently, the challenges posed to international service providers can be attributed to the close cultural link between a society and services.[26] Section 9-5 addresses the relationship between products, services, and culture.

9-5 Products, Services, and Culture

Service encounters are primarily social encounters, and rules and expectations related to services vary from culture to culture.[27] Studies in marketing reveal that it is important for international service providers to understand the factors that affect customer considerations in service evaluations and to emphasize the various dimensions of service quality accordingly.[28] To illustrate, Japanese consumers do not expect special treatment in a medical environment. Medicine is perceived as a public good, and it would be selfish of anyone to expect special attention. Similarly, the Japanese also hold doctors in high esteem, and customers expect and accept rudeness from doctors.[29] They also expect to be treated with a greater degree of formality by all service providers compared with consumers in the United States, whereas consumers in the United States prefer a greater degree of service personalization.[30]

Culture also influences the perception and evaluation of a brand in a particular country. Kent cigarettes continue to hold a high market share and are prominent in Romania due to the status they held as commodity money and a prestige product before the fall of communism.[31] Pepsi and Coca-Cola continue to market their diet brands as Pepsi Light and Coca-Cola Light in much of the rest of the world, where the word "diet" refers to a medically restricted diet. In Rwanda, Fanta Citron is a preferred mixer for most hard liquor. Housewives in the United Kingdom are "hoovering" when they are vacuuming (regardless of the brand of vacuum cleaner they are using), and they buy Jell-O in a semi-gelled, rather than powder, format.

Culture also determines the degree of brand loyalty. Consumers from more collectivist cultures, such as Latin American and Asian consumers, tend to prefer established brands and purchase them in the maturity stage. European consumers tend to be brand name conscious and are especially loyal to top brands. In urban areas, high-priced designers such as Prada, Escada, Dolce & Gabbana, and Diesel jeans are common among middle- and upper-middle-class consumers who might otherwise live in small rental apartments.

Chapter 10, "International Product and Service Strategies," addresses strategies of manufacturers and service providers aimed at meeting the challenges imposed by culture.

9-6 Protecting Brand Names

Brand names are valuable assets to a company. Companies pay millions to protect their brand names from dilution by registering them anywhere they are present and defending them in court, primarily because counterfeit merchandise harms the brand's reputation as well as company profits. The Uruguay round of the General Agreement on Tariffs and Trade (GATT) addressed standardizing global trademark legislation that is now incorporated under the World Trade Organization (WTO) umbrella. The question that remains is whether individual governments can and will enact this legislation. To illustrate, Yiwu, a city five hours from Shanghai, is one of the largest wholesale centers of China, where 200,000 distributors purchase up to 2,000 tons of goods daily. It also is China's counterfeit capital, where counterfeit products bearing established brand names—such as Procter & Gamble's Safeguard soap and Rejoice shampoo, Gillette razor blades, and other brands belonging to companies such as Philip Morris, Anheuser-Busch, Prada, Robert Bosch, Kimberly-Clark, and Nike, are sold at a fraction of their genuine counterparts' cost.[32] Counterfeiters in China range from manufacturers of shampoo and soap in back rooms to large state-owned enterprises and joint-venture partners making their profits selling knockoffs of soft drinks and beer, to factories producing car batteries, motorcycles, and even mobile CD factories with optical disc machines. These products are distributed all over the world, including the United States.[33]

9-6a Identifying Types of Counterfeiting

Examples of counterfeiting are design counterfeiting and brand name counterfeiting.

Design Counterfeiting

Copying designs or scents, known as **design counterfeiting,** is quite common and risk free. The Ralph Lauren Polo-style shirt is replicated by many companies, with a design that approximates the logo of the polo rider. The design of women's Peugeot watches is close to that of the Rolex Oyster Perpetual. Unknown perfume manufacturers suggest that their brand is similar in scent to a particular brand of perfume, which they name in their product packaging and advertising.

> **design counterfeiting**
> Copying designs or scents of another company.

At some point, though, color and design cease to be distinctive if broadly adopted; then, it is longer be appropriate to refer to them as design counterfeits. The traditional Hermès orange leather handbag with its distinctive color and pronounced leather grain has maintained its clear identity until about 2012, when many designers, luxury or not, started to use the color with a similar grain in their own handbag designs. The purse in Figure 9-7 is by a competing luxury designer. Here, it is elegantly displayed on sale, with another object of status consumption, Veuve Cliquot champagne. There are, however, many other handbags in the marketplace which are not particularly faithful copies of the very expensive Hermès Birkin bag that is distributed only in limited quantities to the company's boutiques. These design counterfeits have similar saddle stitching and an identical color, with the distinctive locks in a clochette and the top flaps closing with the two buckles.

Figure 9-7: *The bag portrayed in this display is a distinctive orange color, much like that of Hermès handbags. However, it is not a design counterfeit – the orange color of Hermès is now omnipresent in window displays.*

Brand Name Counterfeiting

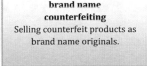

> **brand name counterfeiting**
> Selling counterfeit products as brand name originals.

At the next level is **brand name counterfeiting.** In Cairo, for about a dollar one can purchase simple, cotton shirts with the Christian Dior name on the label. Purses with names such as Prada, Fendi, and Louis Vuitton are sold practically on the steps of the actual retailers, in many capital cities, as are fake Rolex watches. Bazaars in Istanbul and Cairo are known for their "quality" fakes. Hong Kong markets where counterfeit products are sold are popular with tourists. Counterfeit products even make it to flea markets in the United States. In different countries, Pizza Hut and Domino's Pizza restaurants are quite different from the originals, and are not legitimate franchises. In the city of Shanghai, even stores carry names that invite scrutiny (see Figure 9-8).

Multinational businesses need to address several factors that contribute to the counterfeiters' success:

- Consumer factors
- Technology factors
- Distribution factors
- Local government factors

Figure 9-8: *This shoe store in central Shanghai Is called Nibe, and its symbol is a version of the Nike swoosh.*

Consumer Factors

On the consumer side, there is a high willingness to purchase counterfeit goods. Studies have shown, for example, that a large proportion of consumers are likely to select a counterfeit apparel item over a genuine product when there is a price advantage, primarily because function risks are low for apparel, whereas prestige gains are high.[34] In this sense, products that are visible and consumed publicly are more likely to be in demand than products that are less visible and not consumed publicly.

To consumers in both emerging markets and high-income countries, the difference between a brand and its counterfeit is often not obvious. However, consumers in high-income countries can rely on the guarantees from the legitimate retailers with exclusive brand distributorships, whereas consumers in many emerging markets have to rely on guarantees from retailers who themselves do not have guarantees that they are selling the real thing.

Technology Factors

The spread of advanced production technology (affordable, quality, color-copying machines), as well as production lines supplied by pirates or know-how stolen from joint-venture multinationals required to transfer technology to local partners, has made it possible for counterfeiters to make perfect replicas of the original products. Frequently, neither the manufacturer nor the consumers can tell fakes from the real product.[35] Especially problematic is the fact that advanced technologies allow for the marketing of fake car parts, as described in International Marketing Illustration 9-3 (next page).

Distribution Factors

Supply chains are not adequately controlled. Traders use Internet chat rooms and unauthorized dealership networks to sell the products and mix counterfeit products with legitimate products sold on the secondary gray market.[36]

Local Government Factors

Governments in many developing countries are reluctant to crack down on counterfeiting, especially when state-owned enterprises are involved in the operations. In the case of China, for instance, local governments hesitate to crack down on product pirates because they create thousands of jobs and keep the local economy going. And, even when local authorities take action against counterfeiters (most of whom evade taxes), persuading them to close down the state-owned factories engaging in illegal production is impossible.[37]

International Marketing Illustration 9-3

Taking Counterfeiting to New Heights

Global counterfeiting is at an all-time high. It is estimated to account for seven percent of world trade, or US$500 billion a year. Counterfeiters from China, Taiwan, India, and South Korea have managed to create knockoffs not just for clothing, apparel items, and videos, but also for car parts, which now account for $12 billion a year in sales. Bootleggers are selling the most frequently used parts, such as fluids, brake pads, fan belts, oil and fuel filters, spark plugs, batteries, and windshields, all packaged with fake logos. These products are selling rapidly in North America, but the largest market for these products is the Middle East; fake Ford break pads go for $30, whereas the legitimate product costs $47.

The problem facing large automobile manufacturers, however, is not just the loss of sales. If someone purchases a fake part, which causes injury to the passengers, these leading automakers have to prove that the parts are not theirs.

Counterfeiters are using acceptable technology to manufacture these goods. And they are investing primarily in computer scanners to duplicate trademark labels that they can then attach to these knockoffs.

Sources: Murray Hiebert, "Chinese Counterfeiters Turn Out Fake Car Parts," *Wall Street Journal*, March 3, 2004, A14; Joann Muller, "Stolen Cars," *Forbes*, Vol. 173, No. 3, February 16, 2004, p. 58.

Counterfeit products are openly available in many developing countries. Here, consumers, as well as customs representatives inspecting the counterfeit product shipments, are not familiar with many international brand names. Further, customs officials in many developing countries often are not sufficiently trained in identifying illegal trade in mass-market products. And, as mentioned, counterfeit products are also widely available in developed countries. The prevailing reason is that in the industrialized countries, customs officers inspect the contents of only a small fraction of the goods that go through customs.

9-6b Combating Counterfeiting

Multinational companies have used a number of strategies to combat counterfeiting. Lobbying the U.S. government, as well as the governments involved, is a first step. This process involves filing appeals to the World Trade Organization and lobbying other governmental organizations in the United States and abroad regulating trade. The outcome is uncertain, however. For example, even though member countries of the World Trade Organization are expected to abide by the organization's antipiracy provisions, they are not entirely successful in combating the sales of counterfeit products.

Alternatives involve a concerted action on the part of companies to combat counterfeiting by changing a product's appearance to differentiate authentic products from fakes. Budweiser embedded in its beer bottles special images that appear only when the product is chilled, rendering them difficult to copy. Microsoft included holograms on its software boxes and inside user manuals, but pirates quickly learned the trick.[38]

The most successful attacks have been launched with the cooperation of local governments. In China, a raid was launched by seven battery makers, including Gillette, Energizer, and Panasonic, with the help of 200 government agents, on 21 factories in a southwestern city. As a result of the raid, 150 pieces of manufacturing equipment and three million counterfeit batteries (with Russia as their destination) were confiscated.[39]

9-7 International Perspectives of Industrial Products and Services

Marketing industrial products and services across borders has certain similarities to the marketing of consumer goods. However, there are also important differences. For example, in the marketing of consumer products, culture plays a key role, and firms must be aware of norms, values, and traditions in the target country. However, cultural differences are not readily relevant in the production process, in the types of products that businesses purchase, such as major equipment, buildings, land, accessory equipment, fabricated and component parts, process material, maintenance and repair parts, operating supplies, raw materials, goods for resale, and business services. Culture is relevant when it comes to the selection of suppliers. Typically, the decision to purchase industrial products rests with management—and often with top management at the company's headquarters in the home country for the most expensive products—and the purchase process often takes several months.

In many countries, the national government in the country of operation has substantial input in the supplier decision, favoring national suppliers over foreign businesses. National government input can be even more restrictive when it comes to the purchase of business services. For professional services, which include legal services, auditing and consulting services, and medical services, the national government can directly restrict the company to local service suppliers, or it can require that the respective service providers have local licenses and other credentials, which could essentially mean hiring local businesses. For operating services, which include Internet services, telephone service, shipping, and insurance, which are typically contracted out for a fixed period of time, the national government can require the business to hire local providers. If not, the business can handle those services using the most cost-effective approach, which could still mean resorting to local services or even outsourcing them to a third country where labor costs are lower. Many companies launch a request for bids for these types of services on an annual basis, and the national government could require that, all things being equal, the national company must be selected.

Industrial consumers are manufacturers, wholesalers, retailers, government agencies, and non-profit organizations. Unlike consumer markets, business-to-business markets are characterized by fewer buyers and a larger purchase volume. In addition, the business-to-business market has important geographic concentrations. The world banking centers and advertising centers are concentrated in New York, London, and Tokyo. And the world insurance centers are Geneva, London, and Munich. And demand for industrial products is derived from demand for consumer products and thus is much more volatile: Small changes in demand for consumer products can lead to substantial changes in demand for industrial products. Plus, fluctuations in the world marketplace readily affect industries worldwide. For example, the surplus of steel in China and the former Soviet Union has dealt a blow to the steel industry in industrialized countries, to the point that most have contemplated protectionist measures.

In designing industrial products and services for international markets, firms must consider the formal buying process, starting with the identification of needs, establishment of specifications, identification of product solutions and vendors, evaluation and selection of vendors, and negotiation of purchase terms. The decision to purchase a particular product is contingent on the entire package offering—the product, the service contract and availability of replacement parts, and the product price. For example, in the process of identifying product solutions and vendors, the firm needs to evaluate whether the product comes with installation, training, and other after-sales service. Even the local availability of aftermarket replacement parts may constitute an important factor in the purchase decision. Replacement parts are often expensive, but, if they are readily available locally at a significantly lower cost than having to ship them to Thailand from New Jersey, the respective brand becomes much more attractive.

9-7a Product Standards

The discussion in Section 9-1, "Standardization versus Adaptation," is less relevant in industrial marketing because common industrial consumer needs have led to a high degree of standardization of industrial products and services. In addition, the world industrial community is attempting to create standards for each industry. And, with quality taking an important place in the competition for global markets, businesses are adhering to the international quality standards set by the International Organization for Standardization (ISO), which was established in 1946 as a nongovernmental federation of national standards bodies.

The organization issues the **ISO 9000 certification,** which addresses quality management, whereby quality refers to all product or service features that are required by the customer. In ISO terms, quality management implies that the organization ensures that the products or services it sells satisfy customer requirements and comply with any regulations applicable to those products or services. In broad terms,

> **ISO 9000 certification**
> Certification that specifies that the organization must meet customer and regulatory requirements and follow its policies and procedures while advancing quality through continuous improvement.

ISO 9000 specifies that the organization must meet customer and regulatory requirements and follow its policies and procedures while advancing quality through continuous improvement. It addresses issues such as the phases of product development from the initial design phase to the delivery phase. It also requires performance measurement throughout the process through performing internal audits, monitoring customer satisfaction, and taking corrective action.[40]

In 1992, the United Nations Conference on Environment and Development (UNCED) requested that the ISO introduce the ISO 14001 four years later. This would be the first of the ISO 14000 family of environmental management system standards designed to help businesses reduce their impact on the environment and to facilitate sustainable development and foster international trade by providing an international system of standards. **ISO 14000 certification** guidelines discourage multinational firms from engaging in hazardous environmental practices, such as locating plants that generate hazardous emissions in poor countries with weak environmental regulations, and ensure that corporate policies promoting environmentally sound, efficiency-embracing, innovative technologies and processes will contribute to establishing twenty-first century production and distribution systems that are far less environmentally degrading and wasteful. To receive this certification, multinational companies have to develop environmental management systems (EMS) similar to the ISO 9000 standards for total quality management and a policy that stresses a commitment to continual improvement and prevention of pollution, assurances that the company will comply with relevant laws and regulations, and a framework for setting and regularly reviewing environmental objectives and targets. The respective policy must be documented, communicated to all employees, and made available to the public. [41]

ISO 14000 certification
Certification that a company follows guidelines that discourage firms from engaging in hazardous environmental practices, and ensures that corporate policies promoting environmentally sound, efficiency-embracing, innovative technologies and processes will contribute to establishing twenty-first century production and distribution systems that are far less environmentally degrading.

Both ISO 9000 and ISO 14000 address the production process, rather than the product. However, it is implied that the process affects the product. In the context of both, certification refers to the issuing of a certificate by an independent external body that has audited the organization's management system and verified that it conforms to the requirements of the standards. The auditing body then registers the certification in the client's register. ISO 9000 and ISO 14000 are implemented by about 776,608 organizations in 161 countries. The top 10 countries with ISO 9001–2000 certificates are listed in Table 9-1.[42]

Table 9-1: Top 10 Countries with ISO 9001Certificates

Rank	Country	Number of Certifications
1	China	297,037
2	Italy	138,892
3	Russian Federation	62,265
4	Spain	59,854
5	Japan	59,287
6	Germany	50,583
7	United Kingdom	44,849
8	India	33,250
9	United States of America	25,101
10	Korea	24,778

Source: ISO Survey Certifications 2010, December 1, 2011, www.iso.ch.

Table 9-2 lists the distribution of ISO 9001 certifications worldwide. Note that Europe has the largest share of ISO 9001 certifications, followed by the Far East. One reason for Europe's lead is the fact that the European Union's directives on quality management and environmental management pressure companies into becoming ISO certified.

Table 9-2: ISO 9001 Certifications Worldwide

Region	Total	Percent Share	Number of Countries
Africa and West Asia	63,357	5.7	58
Central and South America	40,655	3.7	27
North America	36,632	3.3	3
Europe	530,722	47.8	48
Far East	428,755	38.6	23
Australia and New Zealand	9.784	0.9	2.46

Source: ISO Survey Certifications 2010, December 1, 2011, www.iso.ch.

Summary

Describe drivers for international standardization and offer an overview of the international standardization–local adaptation continuum and respective company strategies. The emergence of uniform market segments, such as global consumers (global teenagers, the global elite), increased international travel, and a general consumer preference for products of higher quality at a lower price, led to opportunities for global standardization strategies. Such strategies offer numerous benefits, primarily the capability for a firm to market its goods at lower costs and higher profits. A purely global strategy, however, will invariably result in ignoring specific segment preferences and in targeting strategies that have a higher likelihood of failure. Some adaptation can be attempted using a global localization strategy, where the main module of the strategy is maintained, while making minor modifications from market to market. Sometimes, however, adaptation may be required (mandatory), or the adaptation is necessary to better meet the needs of the local market.

Examine country-of-origin effects on brand evaluations in relation to product stereotypes and consumer ethnocentrism. Country-of-origin information is used in making product evaluation inferences in situations in which little other information (brand name, for instance) is available to evaluate the product. Country information also can be used to exclude products from the consideration set. For example, ethnocentric consumers, who believe that purchasing foreign products is morally wrong, will refuse to purchase products unless they are made in their home country.

Examine challenges faced by service providers in international markets. Service providers face numerous barriers to entry in international markets. In addition to tariffs, international service providers may be prohibited from hiring international employees, or they may be required to have certain certifications that are difficult to obtain and can be obtained only locally. They might also face direct competition from government providers, such as a local government monopoly, or they could face restrictions on movement.

Address issues related to brand name protection and the reasons behind widespread international counterfeiting. Counterfeiting, ranging from direct copying to design counterfeiting, is flourishing due to improved technology, inadequate channel control, lax enforcement locally and worldwide (despite World Trade Organization involvement), and consumer demand.

Address the marketing of industrial products and services and related product and service standards. Industrial products and services are marketed differently than consumer products and services are: They are not as culture dependent and are more standardized. In an effort to create quality standards for products worldwide, the ISO 9000 certification addresses quality management standards, and the ISO 14000 certification addresses environmental management standards.

Key Terms

adaptation

brand name counterfeiting

core product strategy

country of manufacture

country of origin

design counterfeiting

ethnocentrism

global consumers

global localization

global standardization

glocalization

ISO 9000 certification

ISO 14000 certification

mandatory adaptation

modular adaptation

nonmandatory adaptation

private labels

product-country stereotypes

regional standardization

service barriers

Discussion Questions

1. Describe the global standardization–local adaptation debate. What are the drivers for globalization and for adaptation? Explain.

2. Give examples of mandatory and nonmandatory adaptations.

3. How do private-label (retailer) brands compete with international and local brands? Give examples.

4. Discuss the different barriers to entry that international service providers face worldwide.

5. What are the reasons behind counterfeiting, and what efforts are taking place to combat it? Are they successful?

Chapter Quiz

True/False

1. Overlapping media among countries makes it easier to create awareness of a product.

Answer: True

Rationale: Consumers are exposed to the message frequently brand in different environments, thus increasing product awareness.

Section 9-1a, "Global Standardization"

2. Global branding creates different images for the product in the different regions where the product is sold.

Answer: False

Rationale: A global brand has the same name, logo, image, and positioning everywhere in the world.

Section 9-1a, "Global Standardization"

3. A product's country of origin is always the country where the product was manufactured.

Answer: False

Rationale: Country of origin is defined as the country with which a particular product or service is associated. That country may be different from the country where the product is manufactured; the company may have moved production in the country of manufacture to take advantage of lower labor costs.

Section 9-3a, "Product-Country and Service-Country Stereotypes"

4. Multinational companies often try to combat counterfeiting by differentiating their products with signature traits.

Answer: True

Rationale: Along with lobbying governments, firms can combat counterfeiting by changing a product's appearance and features to differentiate authentic products from fakes.

Section 9-6b," Combating Counterfeiting"

5. Wal-Mart and Tesco products sold under the respective company's umbrella name are known as private-label brands.

Answer: True

Rationale: Products sold under a retailer's brand name are also known as private-label brands.

Section 9-2, "Private-Label (Retailer) Brands"

6. Culture is essential in the marketing of industrial products.

Answer: False

Rationale: In the marketing of consumer products, culture plays a key role, and firms must be aware of norms, values, and traditions in the target country. However, culture does not play as important a role in the production process or in the types of products that businesses purchase.

Section 9-7, "International Perspectives of Industrial Products and Services"

Multiple Choice

1. Girls around the world participating in similar pastimes such as inline skating or playing with Barbie dolls are an illustration of

  a.   differentiated consumer preferences.

  b.   global consumers.

  c.   international production.

  d.   none of the above

Answer: b is correct.

Rationale: Global consumers want the same products worldwide—and share the same pastimes and interests.

Section 9-1a, "Global Standardization"

2. Ford's success in promoting "world cars" like the Ford Focus is a successful example of

    a.   international positioning.

    b.   international travel.

    c.   satisfying consumer preferences.

    d.   all of the above

Answer: c is correct.

Rationale: Consumers worldwide are willing to sacrifice product-related features, function, and design to obtain higher quality at a lower price; with the Ford Focus, the company was able to address uniform consumer preferences worldwide.

Section 9-1a, "Global Standardization"

3. Promoting its products globally and altering parts of their promotion based on specific areas is common of a company focused on

    a.   nonmandatory adaptation.

    b.   global standards.

    c.   glocalization or global localization.

    d.   none of the above

Answer: c is correct.

Rationale: The practice of global branding and localized marketing adaptation is known as global localization, or glocalization.

Section 9-1c, "Global Localization"

4. The following is an example of mandatory adaptation for the United States market:

    a.   U.S. automobile emission standards

    b.   110 volts

    c.   NTSC television

    d.   all of the above

Answer: d is correct.

Rationale: All of the above are requirements for the U.S. market. The U.S. Department of Transportation enforces emission standards for imports. Most appliances in the U.S. work only on 110 volts, and televisions are all on NTSC.

Section 9-1d, "Mandatory Adaptation"

5. Philips is headquartered in the Netherlands, but many of its appliances are manufactured in Asia. The country of origin of Philips

    a.   is the Netherlands.

    b.   is the country in Asia where the product is manufactured.

    c.   depends on the perception of the consumer.

d.   none of the above

Answer: a is correct.

Rationale: The country of origin of Philips products is, in the minds of most consumers, the Netherlands.

Section 9-3, "Global Branding and Country-of-Origin Information"

6. Which of the following are examples of products that businesses purchase?

a.   Major equipment, buildings, land

b.   Accessory equipment and fabricated and component parts

c.   Process material and maintenance and repair parts

d.   All of the above

Answer: d is correct.

Among the products that businesses purchase are major equipment, buildings, land, accessory equipment, fabricated and component parts, process material, maintenance and repair parts, operating supplies, raw materials, goods for resale, and business services.

Section 9-7, "International Perspectives of Industrial Products and Services"

Chapter 9 Endnotes

1.   Dannie Kjeldgaard and Søren Askegaard, "The Glocalization of Youth Culture: The Global Youth Segment as Structures of Common Difference," *Journal of Consumer Research*, Vol. 33, No. 3, 2006, pp. 231–247; Dannie Kjeldgaard and Søren Askegaard, "Consuming Modernities: The Global Youth Segment as a Site of Consumption, Barbara E. Kahn and Mary Frances Luce (eds.), *Advances in Consumer Research*, 2004, p. 31.

2.   Shaoming Zou and Aysegul Ozsomer, "Global Product R&D and the Firm's Strategic Position," *Journal of International Marketing*, Vol. 7, No. 1, 1999, pp. 57–76.

3.   Ibid.

4.   Demetris Vronitis and Peri Vronitis, "Levi Strauss: An International Marketing Investigation," *Journal of Fashion Marketing and Management*, Vol. 8, No. 4, 2004, p. 389.

5.   Susan Segal-Horn, "The Limits of Global Strategy," *Strategy & Leadership,* Vol. 24, No. 6, November–December 1996, pp. 12–17.

6.   Alan J. Liddle, "McD's Global Standardization Strategy Enhanced by Vendor Sale," *Nation's Restaurant,* Vol. 40, No. 19, May 8, 2006, p. 22.

7.   Demetris Vronitis and Peri Vronitis, "Levi Strauss: An International Marketing Investigation," *Journal of Fashion Marketing and Management*, Vol. 8, No. 4, 2004, p. 389.

8.   Ibid.

9.   Segal-Horn, "The Limits of Global Strategy," pp. 12–17.

10.   Ibid.

11.   www.mercedes-benz.de/content/germany/mpc/mpc_germany_website/de/home_mpc/passenger_cars/home/products/new_cars/a_class_3door.html

12.   www.mbusa.com

13.   John S. Hill and Richard R. Still, "Adapting Products to LDC Tastes," *Harvard Business Review,* March–April 1984, pp. 92–101.

14.   Christopher Lovelock and George S. Yip, "Developing Global Strategies for Service Businesses," *California Management Review,* Vol. 38, No. 2, 1996, pp. 64–87.

15.   Ibid.

16.   Vronitis and Vronitis, "Levi Strauss," p. 389.

17.   Cyndee Miller, "Chasing the Global Dream," *Marketing News,* Vol. 30, No. 25, December 2, 1996, pp. 1–2.

18.   This is yet another example of adaptation, this time by Coca-Cola, for consumers in Europe, to whom the term "diet" signifies medically imposed eating restrictions.

19.   Vikas Bajaj, "In India, the Golden Age of Television Is Now," *New York Times*, February 11, 2007, Sunday Business section, 1, 4.

20.   Donna Gorski Berry, "Global Dairy Food Trends," *Dairy Foods,* Vol. 99, No. 10, October 1998, pp. 32–37.

21.   For a review of the country-of-origin effects literature, see Lalita A. Manrai, Dana-Nicoleta Lascu, and Ajay K. Manrai, "Interactive Effects of Country of Origin and Product Category on Product Evaluations," *International Business Review,* Vol. 7, 1998, pp. 591–615.

22.   Ibid.

23.   Saeed Samiee, Terry Shimp, Subhash Sharma, "Brand Origin Recognition Accuracy: Its Antecendents and Consumers' Cognitive Limitations, *Journal of International Business Studies* Vol. 36, No. 5, 2005, pp. 379–397.

24.   Ibid.

25.   For an in-depth description of these and additional restrictions, see Lee D. Dahringer, "Marketing Services Internationally: Barriers and Management Strategies," *Journal of Services Marketing,* Vol. 5, No. 3, Summer 1991, pp. 5–17.

26.   P. B. Kenen, *The International Economy,* Englewood Cliffs, NJ: Prentice Hall, 1989; and Ikechi Ekeledo and K. Sivakumar, "Foreign Market Entry Mode Choice of Service Firms: A Contingency Perspective," *Journal of the Academy of Marketing Science,* Vol. 26, No. 4, 1998, pp. 274–292.

27.   John A. Czepiel, "Service Encounters and Service Relationships: Implications and Research," *Journal of Business Research,* Vol. 20, 1990, pp. 13–21; and Kathryn Frazier Winsted, "Evaluating Service Encounters: A Cross-Cultural and Cross-Industry Exploration," *Journal of Marketing Theory and Practice,* Vol. 7, No. 2, Spring 1999, pp. 106–123.

28.   Naresh K. Malhotra, Francis M. Ulgado, J. Agrawal, and I. B. Baalbaki, "International Services Marketing: A Comparative Evaluation of the Dimensions of Service Quality Between Developed and Developing Countries," *International Marketing Review,* Vol. 11, No. 2, 1994, p. 515.

29.   Frazier Winsted, "Evaluating Service Encounters," pp. 106–123.

30.   Ibid.

31.   Guliz Ger, Russell W. Belk, and Dana-Nicoleta Lascu, "The Development in Consumer Desire in Marketizing and Developing Economies: The Cases of Romania and Turkey," in L. McAllister (ed.), *Advances in Consumer Research,* Association for Consumer Research, Vol. 20, 1993, pp. 102–107.

32.   Dexter Roberts, Frederik Balfour, Paul Magnuson, Pete Engardio, and Jennifer Lee, "China's Pirates: It's Not Just Little Guys—State-Owned Factories Add to the Plague of Fakes," *BusinessWeek,* No. 3684, June 5, 2000, pp. 26, 44.

33.   Ibid.

34.   Peter H. Bloch, Ronald F. Bush, and Leland Campbell, "Consumer 'Accomplices' in Product Counterfeiting," *Journal of Consumer Marketing*, Vol. 10, No. 4, 1993, pp. 27–36.

35.   Roberts, Balfour, Magnuson, Engardio, and Lee, "China's Pirates," pp. 26, 44.

36.   Ibid.

37.   Ibid.

38.   Ibid.

39.   Ibid.

40.   www.iso.cf

41.   Dennis Rondinelli and Gyula Vastag, "International Environmental Standards and Corporate Policies: An Integrative Framework," *California Management Review*, Vol. 39, No. 1, 1996, pp. 106–122.

42. www.iso.ch

Case 9-1:

smart fortwo: One Car for Narrow European Alleys . . . and for High U.S. Gasoline Prices

Mercedes-Benz would be a consistently profitable business, had it not been trying to fix its small car business. The Smart, its iconic, but troubled brand, has been in the red ever since its launch in 1998. In 2005, the Smart cost the company more than $2 billion in charges for job losses and cutbacks. In the process of restructuring to reduce Smart's fixed costs, the company had to cut 600 jobs in Germany and 100 in France.

However, things are looking up for the smart fortwo. Initially designed as a cute cobble-stone negotiator in crowded European alleys, the little car is planning to help U.S. consumers better negotiate their often shrinking gasoline purchasing power in the land of SUVs . This is a story of market adaptation. Sort of.

The Story of Smart

In the world of joint ventures, the smart fortwo has a distinguished history. The smart fortwo was propelled to stardom in the mini-automobile category in the early 1990s, as a joint venture between Mercedes-Benz and Swatch. Daimler is the luxury automobile manufacturer that has created the Mercedes automobile, the worldwide standard for luxury on the road. Swatch is a creative and quirky company that makes Swatches, watches with colorful designs. The smart fortwo joint venture was created with the purpose of enhancing the Mercedes portfolio with an "ultra-urban" automobile that negotiates well narrow European alleys, fits neatly on the sidewalk if the parking spaces are all taken, and otherwise makes the driver look good (see Figure 9-9).

Figure 9-9: *The smart fortwo is present everywhere in Berlin. On a city walk, there was a smart fortwo every eight cars or so, in your average-middle-class neighborhood – this yellow smart fortwo demanded a double-take.*

Though small, the smart fortwo protects its passengers well. It has a tridion safety shell, a hard shell that protects occupants in case of impact. It is also equipped with electronic stability control, which prevents it from flipping over, and antilock brakes. It has a high driving position to ensure the greatest visibility on the road. The design team focused on creating an energy efficient automobile using recyclable materials. Compared with the luxury Mercedes line, the smart fortwo is affordable: A two-seat, 9-foot-long smart fortwo costs about $11,000 for the bare model, reaching about $15,000 for convertibles. Its gas consumption is 40 miles per gallon, and it reaches 90 miles per hour on the highway. It seats two and is so small that two cars can fit in a traditional parking spot.

The smart fortwo's problem, however, is that its market performance has been poor. Although Smart's global sales have grown steadily since its launch thanks to the introduction of new models, it has consistently missed its targets. The company launched the forfour model to compete in the saturated, highly competitive compact-car segment, but it was quickly discovered that the new model hurt the brand, ultimately resulting in its withdrawal from the market. In a parallel development, the company also intended to build the formore, designed for the U.S. SUV market. However, after steep losses, coupled with additional problems—Mercedes had to recall 1.3 million vehicles, including its luxury E-Class – the company reconsidered its strategy.

The Turnaround

At first, Mercedes-Benz had considered eliminating Smart, but quickly determined that it had too much brand franchise and bailing out the brand was the best option from a shareholder point of view.

Its recovery plans included having Mercedes take over purchasing, sales, and service operations, and creating a better fit with the needs of European consumers. Smart has been testing several prototype models using alternative fuels, including an electric-powered Smart, a compressed natural gas version, and a hybrid model. Smart's proposition of being the "ultimate urban solution" will be even more relevant now that more cities in Europe are looking to introduce congestion charging.

The U.S. Launch

The new fortwo model, launched in Europe in 2007, was introduced in the U.S. in 2008. The company first decided to use Roger Penske's United Automotive Group Inc., to distribute the product to the United States, serving as the interface between dealers and Daimler, ordering cars for the U.S. market and distributing them to about 60 dealers affiliated and nonaffiliated with the chain.

In the United States, smart fortwo was targeted at younger buyers, urban residents, baby boomers, and retirees. In order to target younger buyers, Penske followed the example of Toyota Motor Corp. and BMW AG, both of which successfully launched new small cars, the Scion and the Mini, respectively. Penske used a largely Internet-based advertising model that targeted niche buyers, which included younger buyers and other trendsetting groups. The company staged a 50-city road tour so people could drive the car and attracted 10,000 test drivers.

After a rip-roaring start, sales went down precipitously, to the point that Penske threw in the towel as the automobile's distributor in 2011. A redesign for the 2013 model provides some reassurance, with a stronger front bumper. However, the cost of gas has been stable and U.S. consumers don't seem to be in a hurry to buy the Smart when there are other, cheaper and somewhat larger options on the market. Thus, the main question remains: How will Smart drivers feel confident of their safety as they share the road with America's large SUVs?

Sources: Doron Levin, "U.S. sales of Smart cars hit a wall," CNN Money, February 19, 2011, http://money.cnn.com/2011/02/18/autos/smart-car-penske-mercedes.fortune/index.htm; John D. Stoll, "Smart Car a Shrewd Move?" *Wall Street Journal*, June 27, 2007, A8; Gina Chon and Stephen Power, "Can an Itsy-Bitsy Auto Survive in the Land of the SUV? *Wall Street Journal*, January 9, 2007, B1; "Smart Car: Engineering a Recovery," *Marketing Week*, May 11, 2006, p. 28; Paul Eisenstein, "Smart Struggles to Survive," *Professional Engineering*, April 13, 2005, Vol. 18, No. 7, p. 28; www.smartusa.com/company.html.

Analysis Suggestions:

1. What strategies does Smart use in the European market? Is the automobile adapted to consumers' driving needs in Europe?

2. Why is the Smart not changing to adapt to the U.S. market, dominated by large trucks and sports utility vehicles? Will the lack of adaptation hurt sales in the United States?

Chapter 10: International Product and Service Strategies

Learning Objectives

After studying this chapter, you should be able to:

- Evaluate the stages of the international product life cycle and identify the locus of operations and target markets at each stage.

- Identify the different dimensions of the international product mix with company illustrations.

- Examine the new product development process and the activities involved at each stage in international markets.

- Examine degrees of product newness and address international diffusion processes

Energy Drinks

Red Bull, an Austrian energy drink, has systematically taken over energy drink marketing around the world. The drink was adopted by consumers in the rest of Europe in the early 1990s and took the U.S. market by storm in 1997. It was, a decade later, in nearly every retail shop in the United States. By the year 2000, Red Bull single-handedly created and then propelled the energy drink category to $75 million in sales.[1]

In 2001, Hansen Natural, a Southern California beverage company, introduced a successful challenger to Red Bull: Monster. Five years later, the company had sales close to $500 million and claimed second place behind Red Bull in the $5.7 billion energy drink category. Copycats continue to battle for shelf space where they are joined by newcomers from Coca-Cola, such as Full Throttle and RockStar, which are privately held but distributed by Coke's top bottler, and PepsiCo. While Red Bull sponsors NASCAR and professional soccer, Monster prefers to claim visibility at the fringes, selecting endorsers who are up-and-coming athletes in obscure sports, sponsoring freestyle motocross stud Mike Metzger, who was originally paid just $600 a month to endorse the brand.

The energy-drink category has grown rapidly, at 10 percent in 2010, and at 15 percent in 2011. But it is well possible that those numbers might go down due to a potential backlash against energy drinks. For example, regulators in Norway and France have kept Red Bull off the shelves for some time before allowing it to enter the market. In Canada, the product comes with a long warning label. In the United States, the Food and Drug Administration has recently held a public hearing addressing health claims of "brain boosting" attributed to energy drinks. The future of this product category is by no means certain.[2]

The international marketing environment creates complex challenges for products and services. For example, during the product life cycle, firms must coordinate their marketing activities with international trade and investment decisions to remain price competitive in the face of increased competition from manufacturers in developing and developed countries alike. New product development decisions involve consumers in target markets that differ from home-country consumers in their attitudes, interests, and opinions. The challenges of new product/service launches are amplified by the complexities of the marketplace and the competition from both local and multinational firms. And managing the product mix and the product portfolio in line with company strategy and the demands of different consumers offers many dilemmas to brand managers. This chapter attempts to shed light on some of these challenges.

10-1 The International Product Life Cycle

Products pass through distinct stages, during which profits may rise and fall. As a consequence, products require different marketing strategies in each stage. The **international product life cycle (IPLC)** involves a complex relationship between the product life cycle stage and international trade and investment. At a basic level, the premise of the IPLC is as follows: Firms from developed, industrialized countries produce products for domestic consumption in the early stage of the product life cycle primarily because product specifications and the manufacturing process are not yet stable. As the product advances to the **maturity stage,** product specifications and the manufacturing process stabilize. At this point, price competition becomes intense, and international markets emerge, prompting firms to move production abroad to benefit from lower manufacturing costs.[3]

Figure 10-1 describes the international trade and investment activity of an international corporation and of local competition during each stage of the international product life cycle (from the perspective of the international corporation). During the introduction and growth stages, production takes place in the home country or in another industrialized country, and the company exports the products to developing countries. At maturity, manufacturing moves overseas, and the product is imported to the home country and other industrialized countries. Local competitors then emerge; they compete with the international corporation in its home country or in other industrialized countries. During the decline stage, international sales keep the company afloat.

international product life cycle (IPLC)
A product life cycle theory, which states that firms from developed countries engage in domestic production in the early stage of the product life cycle, marketing the product to industrialized countries; as the product reaches maturity, product specifications and the manufacturing process stabilize, price competition becomes intense, and markets in developing countries become essential to the firm's success.

maturity stage
A stage of the international product life cycle characterized by a slowdown in sales growth as the product is adopted by most target consumers and by a leveling or decline in profits primarily due to intense price competition.

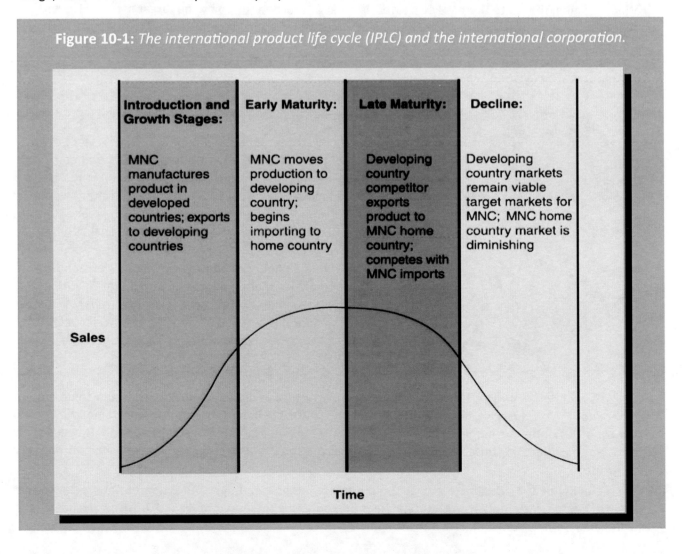

Figure 10-1: *The international product life cycle (IPLC) and the international corporation.*

10-1a The Product Introduction Stage

During the **introduction stage,** products are developed in industrialized countries and supported by firms' substantial research and development budgets and by highly skilled product research teams. To quickly recover the high costs of product development and launching, a firm markets products in industrialized countries to consumers who can afford the high prices charged to recover the high costs, while it still has control of the market (it is the only manufacturer or one of the few manufacturers of the product). According to the initial IPLC theory (see Section 10-1, "The International Product Life Cycle"), these products were first marketed in the products' country of origin. Assuming a reasonable adoption rate in highly industrialized countries, the product also becomes available in developing countries, where it is exported by the firm. Examples of offerings in the introduction stage are provided by GrandCentral, which consolidates all individuals' phone numbers and personalizes the cell phone device consumers already have; EQO, which circumvents the carriers' steep rates for international calls, and Spinvox and SimulScribe, which turn voicemail into text (although, with iPhone 4S and similar competing offerings, it can be argued that turning voicemail into text might already be in the growth stage). New mobile start-ups are attempting to find ways to release consumers from the established carriers' grip by using the web to get around carrier control and by training users to switch carriers for better add-ons.[4]

introduction stage
The first stage of the international product life cycle when products are developed and marketed in industrialized countries.

growth stage
The stage of the international product life cycle characterized by increasing competition and rapid product adoption by the target market.

10-1b The Growth Stage

The **growth stage** is characterized by increasing competition, with new product variants offered to the market, as well as rapid product adoption by the target market. Toward the end of this stage, the focus is on developing economies of scale in the manufacturing process. Price competition increases at this point and a standard is reached. An example of a product in the growth stage is the Apple iPhone 4S, which is experiencing rapid adoption in high-income countries.

The iPhone

By all accounts, the iPhone is a reliable, cool calling tool that is easy to use, fun to play with, and comes in a stylish, sexy shell. Unlike the leading cell phones, the iPhone allows one to watch films from iTunes, video podcasts, and YouTube hits. It uses a touch screen, but you can ask Siri to perform many tasks, such as find stores, look up traffic, or write e-mails. It offers 8 hours of talk time, 24 hours of music, or 250 hours of stand-by time, and allows sharing photos by e-mail (taken with its 2-megapixel camera) with just a couple taps of the screen. And it has a global positioning chip which allows you to let everyone know where you are at all times.[5]

As mentioned earlier, the iPhone is in the growth stage in high-income countries and some emerging markets. The product was not available as recently as 2012 in Belarus, Georgia, the Ukraine, the Central Asian countries of the former Soviet Union, and in most Sub-Saharan African countries soon. However, it is likely that consumers in these countries will have access to it or to a competitive alternative in the very near future.

Clearly, new products are not adopted instantly across the board. Adoption of new technology is uneven at best in each market, with urban areas first adopting the brand, followed, possibly decades later, by rural areas. Television in India is a case in point.

Television in India

In India, television is in the growth stage, whereas in most Western countries, television is in a long-established maturity stage. In India, before the early 1990s, a single government broadcaster provided a handful of channels. Today, there is a crowded field of domestic and international broadcasters, including Sony Entertainment, News Corporation, and Walt Disney. Television ownership is growing fast, and it is ready for further expansion. There are 105 million homes with televisions— about the same as in the United States. However, 98 percent of U.S. households have a television set, whereas only half of Indian households do. Advertising spending has increased to $1.6 billion, at a rate of about 21 percent a year since 1991, and these double-digit growth rates are expected for years to come, according to ZenithOptimedia, which tracks advertising worldwide. Many media companies, such as News Corporation, Disney, Time Warner, and Viacom, as well as advertisers, are losing viewers in their core Western markets and turning their sights to more profitable markets, such as the booming Indian market. India is a country of contrasts. Digital technology is only available in the largest four cities. However, 40 percent of households have black and white television sets, whereas 56 percent of households do not even have electricity.[6]

In high-income countries, such as Japan (see Figure 10-2), the United States, and the countries of Western Europe, consumer electronics typically pass quickly through the growth stage and reach maturity. There will always be a new offering that will attract the attention and the wallets of consumers

Figure 10-2: In Japan, consumer electronics quickly pass through the growth stage and reach maturity, as consumers are keen on the new models with new capabilities.

At the end of the growth stage, the product is standardized – a particular standard is reached, such as a flat screen for television sets. During the growth stage, production continues to take place in industrialized countries and manufacturers in industrialized countries continue to export their products in developing countries.

It should be noted that fast growth does not necessarily mean vast recovery of company investments in the market. For example, India is the fastest growth market for cell phones, but phone companies are not bringing in great profits. Rather, cell phone companies are investing in this market on the premise that, in the future, consumers will afford to pay for the phone services. For now, even those who make only $3 dollars a day can afford cell phones. How? They pay only for the calls they dial, hang up, and wait to be called back. A cellular service provider, in many instances, has to practically offer the service for free. Western callers pay more than $500 a year for their cellular service; Indian callers pay only $110. Nevertheless, phone companies compete for the Indian consumer: Among competitors are the Vodafone Group of Britain, the world's largest cellphone operator, Japan's NTT DoCoMo, and Teléfonos de Mexico. Multinational giants, including General Motors, Unilever, Coca-Cola, and many others have learned to make money with cheaper offerings, as India makes up for cheap prices with volume and breakneck growth.[7]

10-1c The Maturity Stage

Usually the longest stage in the product life cycle, the maturity stage is characterized by a slow-down in sales growth as the product is adopted by most target consumers and by a leveling or decline in profits primarily due to intense price competition. At this point, manufacturing moves to developing countries to save on labor costs. For example, the U.S. electronics company Motorola selected Krakow, Poland, as its first European software center and the location of a chip plant,[3] while Siemens AG, Macronix, and Intel Corp. are engaging in semiconductor manufacturing in Thailand, in a consortium with a local company.[4] Products manufactured abroad are then imported in the home country and other industrialized countries. These products successfully compete on price in the respective developed countries. Examples of products in maturity are television sets, stereo equipment, and video cameras. In the United States, mobile phones belong in this category as well.

The Mobile Phone Oligopoly

A sign of maturity is an established oligopoly—and that is precisely what characterizes the mobile-phone system in the United States, much like television networks in the 1980s. The market is dominated by Verizon, Sprint, AT&T, and T-Mobile, which control nearly 90 percent of the market. The mobile-phone service carriers have used their oligopoly power to control the networks. When a client signs up for the service, he or she can only use the services the carrier provides. As consumers in the United States are trying alternative services, such as ringtones from other companies (in one example, the "Crazy Frog" ringtone earned more than $70 million) The phone carriers fight back by restricting the features available on the cell phones (e.g., by controlling the billing for add-ons. And new companies selling ringtones and games must work with the phone carriers to be able to gain a foothold in the market. In effect, the oligopoly presents multiple barriers to entry to up-starts that might, potentially, compete with their own offering. [8]

In other high-income countries, however, consumers have some alternatives to the established mobile-phone service carriers. In fact, developments in the industry are creating new competitive turbulence in the market, with new technologies that are keeping the mobile-phone industry in what has been a prolonged growth stage. Governments are encouraging new entrants in the business as well. In one example, the German government keeps auctioning additional UMTS-spectrum radio frequencies for mobile phones, allowing operators to meet rising demand for data-intensive services. This is likely to lure new operators into the German mobile-phone market. This auction creates a burden for the established provider, market leader Deutsche Telekom, which now faces more competition, while at same time losing market share in its fixed-line business.[9]

As companies establish strategic alliances with firms from developing countries or engage in contract manufacturing, or, alternatively, develop a wholly owned subsidiary, they train local talent and are likely to create local competitors. These competitors from developing countries then sell products in industrialized countries, competing directly with the multinational firm in its home market and in other developed countries. Examples of successful companies from developing countries exporting their products in developed countries abound. "Made in India" is a sign of high-quality software; in this market, top software companies include subsidiaries of U.S. companies, such as Motorola India Electronics Ltd. and IBM

Global Services India, as well as local companies such as Satyam Computer Services Ltd., Tata Consultancy Services, and Wipro Infotech.[10]

10-1d The Decline Stage

Products in the **decline stage** are rapidly losing ground to new technologies or product alternatives. Sales and, consequently, profits are declining at this stage, and a firm might consider whether its presence in the market is warranted. However, having an international presence during the decline stage, particularly in developing countries, could be an advantage. One of the main benefits of going international and engaging in international marketing is the ability of a firm to extend the product life cycle. A product may be in the decline stage in the lead country, where it was developed, as well as in other industrial economies, and, at the same time, in a stable maturity stage in most developing countries.

Conceptually, the international product life cycle makes sense. Products are produced in developed countries where they are first adopted; then they are later made available in developing countries. However, consumers in today's industrializing nations do not wait for unrolling of small electronics gadgets on the basis of the life cycle addressed here. These consumers want their portable cell phones and other devices right now. For example, wireless telephones have made tremendous advances in transition economies because the traditional wired systems often have reception problems—more so than wireless phones. Nations in Europe, Latin America, and Asia are often ahead of the United States on many fronts (e.g., public transport, cellular technology, etc.).

10-2 Managing the International Product and Service Mix

The product portfolio of a firm is usually diversified into products that are in different stages of the product life cycle, such that profits from successful mature products can be used to invest in new products and products that have a lower market share. Most multinational corporations tend to have both local and global brands that they nurture through their life cycle. The international **product mix** is the complete assortment of the products that a company offers to its target international consumers, and it has a number of important dimensions. One important dimension of the product mix is the **product line,** a number of related brands in the same product category. Companies use different line strategies to achieve market share and profitability goals. For example, companies engage in line extensions to target consumers who otherwise cannot afford a particular product. In the fashion realm, for example, numerous top designers target the masses with bridge offerings (secondary, more affordable lines): Escada with Laurel, Anne Klein with Anne Klein II, Donna Karan with DKNY, Armani with Emporio Armani, and so forth.

To illustrate the remaining product dimensions, we will use the example of Unilever (www.unilever.com), one of the largest consumer product companies in the world. Unilever is actually composed of two companies, Unilever NV and Unilever PLC, operating as one company linked by a series of agreements and common shareholders, and headquartered in London, United Kingdom, and Rotterdam, the Netherlands, respectively.[11] Although Unilever is organized primarily into two divisions, the foods division and the personal care division, the company has a number of product lines that are addressed as separate strategic business units.

Another important dimension of the product mix is **product consistency.** This term refers to the extent to which the different product lines are related, use the same distribution channels, and have the same final consumers. The Unilever brands are consistent within each of the company divisions. The Corporate Venture Activities (see Table 10-1) is the only venture that might break this pattern of consistency.

The other dimensions of the product mix, as illustrated by the Unilever example in Table 10-1, are product length, width, and depth.

decline stage
The stage of the international product life cycle in which products are rapidly losing ground to new technologies or product alternatives, causing a decrease in sales and profits.

product mix
The complete assortment of products that a company offers to its target international consumers.

product line
All the brands the company offers in the same product category.

product consistency
The extent to which a company's different product lines are related, use the same distribution channels, and have the same final consumers.

Table 10-1: *Unilever Products*

Category	Product	Category	Product
Culinary products	Ragú Spaghetti Sauces	Diet	Slim Fast
	Calvé Whisky Cocktail Sauce	Household care	Domestos
	Hellmann's Mayonnaise		Cif
	Knorr Soups	Detergents	Omo
	Bertolli Pastas		Ala
	Amora Vinaigrettes		Surf
	Wishbone Salad Dressing		Radiant
	Colman's Mustard		Snuggle
	Pepperami		Comfort
	Pot Noodle		Persil
Frozen foods	Findus 4 Salti in Padella	Deodorants	Rexona/Sure
Ice cream	Magmum		Axe
	Cote D'Or		Dove
	Cornetto		Degree
	Klondike Bars		Impulse
	Solero	Shampoos	SunSilk
	Bryers		ThermaSilk
	Ben & Jerry's		Organics
	Viennetta	Personal care	Lux
	Wall's		Lynx
Margarine	I Can't Believe It's Not Butter		Dove
	Rama Margarine		Vaseline Intensive Care
	Becel Spreads		Pond's
	Flora Spreads		Lifebuoy
	Blue Band	Oral care	Signal
	Country Crock		Close-Up
	Doriana Light Spread	Corporate Venture Activities	Unilever Technology Ventures
	Stork		
Cream alternative	Elmlea		Unilever Ventures
Spread	Marmite		Langholm Capital
Cheese	Boursin		
Fruit drinks	Adez		
Tea	Lipton		
	Bovril (UK)		
	PG Tips (UK)		
	Scottish Blend (UK)		

10-2a Length

The **product length** is the total number of brands in the product mix—all the brands sold by the company. Counting the Unilever brands in Table 10-1, the total product length is 65.

10-2b Width

The **product width** is the total number of product lines the company offers. Counting the different product lines in Table 10-1 (culinary products, frozen foods, ice cream, margarine, cream alternative, spread, cheese, fruit drinks, tea, diet, household care, detergents, deodorants, shampoos, personal care, oral care, and corporate venture activities), the total product width is 17.

product length
The total number of brands in the product mix.

product width
The total number of product lines that a company offers to its target international consumers.

product depth
The number of different offerings for a particular brand.

10-2c Depth

The **product depth** refers to the number of different offerings for a product category. For example, in the detergent category, Unilever offers Omo, Ala, Surf, Radiant, Snuggle, Comfort, and Persil (Figure 10-3). Unilever's product depth for the detergent line is thus 7. Product depth for the detergent line is calculated by adding all the brands in the detergent category. In another example, Unilever has only one brand in its diet category: Slim Fast. The product depth for the diet line is 1.

Figure 10-3:
In Europe, Unilever brands dominate the shelves in the laundry detergent category— in the United States, the dominant company is Procter & Gamble. Persil is a major presence, from supermarket to supermarket, while Procter &Gamble's Ariel is often in a secondary position.

Companies alter their product mix by purchasing existing international or local brands. For example, Unilever purchased the Ben & Jerry's Ice Cream brand. Companies also develop new brands and products that they can add to their portfolio. Section 10-3 discusses new product development.

10-3 New Product Development

To maintain their competitive advantage and to ensure survival and growth locally, regionally, or globally, companies must develop and introduce new products and services that meet the needs of their markets. International new product development is a costly process that involves the firm at all levels. If successful, product/service development is the key to a company's success and future.

In general, new product development involves substantial risks and costs. The complex environment of the international marketplace adds considerably to both the risks and costs. Consider, for example, the case of Freeplay Energy, a company that started in Cape Town, South Africa.

Freeplay Energy

Freeplay Energy started in Cape Town, South Africa (its headquarters are now in London, United Kingdom), developing wind-up, self-powered radios for the African market. The product initially failed in Africa, where consumers preferred to purchase batteries, rather than incur a one-time expenditure of about $50 for such a radio. The company, however, remained in business primarily due to its success in the United States and Europe.[12] After refocusing on developed markets, Freeplay developed its products with a sophisticated, Western consumer in mind. With the initial product, the radio had to be wound 20 seconds to produce 30 minutes of radio time; a lighter, smaller version produced one hour of playing time. Subsequent to its success in Europe, the product started selling in developing countries as well. The product is marketed using different strategies worldwide: In Japan and the United States, the product is marketed as part of earthquake and tornado survival kits; in Germany, interest in the product is fueled by environmental concern; whereas in the United Kingdom, consumers take pride in owning such an invention.

Interestingly, the same company made a second attempt to fulfill the needs of the African market: Freeplay developed a self-powered generator intended to enable consumers in developing countries to charge their satellite telephones. The entrepreneurs developing this product believed that most of the growth in cell phones is in the developing world. However, most African countries cannot afford the infrastructure needed, leaving satellite communication fueled by either expensive disposable batteries or self-powered technology as the only options. This and many other Freeplay products are today used to increase self-sufficiency for consumers in developed countries

Currently, the Freeplay markets itself as a leading brand of clean, dependable energy products that harness human, solar, and rechargeable energy and convert it into electricity, replacing battery-operated systems. Their product range consists of radios, torches, lanterns, mobile phone chargers, and standalone foot-powered generators. Its affordable Companion Radio, for example, has a compact AM-FM radio, which doubles as a flashlight and a mobile phone charger, and it is self-charging, using solar power.[13] Freeplay is a global company today, manufacturing its products in emerging markets —some of its wind-up electronic products are made on production lines in Guangdong, China. Freeplay has signed a deal for 1.1 million wind-up mobile-phone chargers for sub-Saharan Africa and the Caribbean, worth $13 million a year. Freeplay is also developing rechargers for U.S. Agency for International Development's One-Laptop-per-Child program. [14]

These examples of Freeplay's innovations illustrate some of the complexities involved in developing new products internationally. The following are examples of risks and difficulties companies face when developing new products:

- International and local competitors could appropriate the product/service idea and deliver the final product or service to the market more swiftly, economically, and with stronger company backing (brand reputation, financial support) than the initial product/service developer.

- International target consumers might not respond as anticipated to the offering (as in the case of Freeplay's wind-up radio) because it does not meet their needs, because they cannot afford it, or because they prefer to adopt a product later in the product life cycle stage.

- Local governments or the home-country government might impose restrictions on product testing procedures (in the case of pharmaceuticals, for example).

- The technological infrastructure of the market is substandard and cannot support the new product.

The steps that companies typically follow in the product development process are essentially the same as those involved in domestic product development. Figure 10-4 illustrates the international product development process. At each step, the process can be either terminated or restarted for each individual product idea; consequently, a product must go through each stage to reach the international product launching stage.

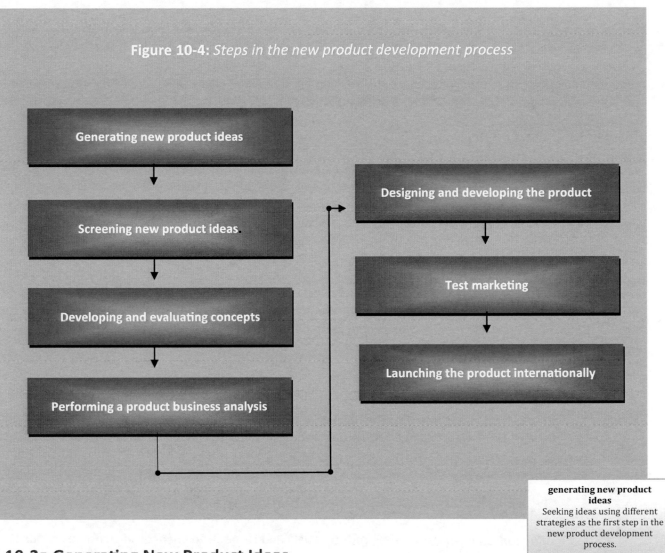

Figure 10-4: *Steps in the new product development process*

generating new product ideas
Seeking ideas using different strategies as the first step in the new product development process.

10-3a Generating New Product Ideas

The first step in the new product development process is **generating new product ideas.** Depending on the products provided and company philosophy, ideas are sought using different strategies. Most product and service firms are driven by the marketing concept, and their product development decisions are based on identifying the needs, wants, and desires of consumers. For technology-driven firms, the focus is more likely to be on the product itself, and thus the research and development division is likely to be responsible for developing product ideas. Even in this second instance, however, products are developed with the needs of the consumer in mind. Freeplay Energy, with its wind-up radio, is an example of a product -focused company. An inventor created the radio independent of the market, and a marketer identified a market for the product—consumers in Africa who do not have electricity, use batteries for their radios, and could benefit from using wind-up radios.

Companies use multiple sources for ideas. Among the most common are consumers, competitive analyses, and some additional sources such as channel members, company employees, and so on.

Consumers

The most obvious sources for ideas are consumers in the home-country market of the firm. Other sources of product ideas are consumers in the company's international markets. Although, traditionally, products of U.S. multinational firms were driven entirely by consumers in the United States, these companies are now increasingly drawing on consumers around the world for new product or service ideas. A growing number of companies are developing products for one market and successfully marketing them in markets that are substantially different. Häagen-Dazs developed a caramel-flavored ice cream called Dulce de Leche for Argentina. The company brought this flavor to the United States, where it is second only to vanilla in sales, and to Europe, where it is moving from seasonal-flavor to year-round-flavor status.[15] In other examples, Nike found that a soccer cleat designed and worn by Ronaldo, a player on the Brazilian soccer team, was popular with consumers in the United States. Similarly, Levi Strauss, the quintessential all-American jeans manufacturer, offered a dark version of denim jeans, that was popular for a few years with consumers in Japan, to U.S. consumers, who responded favorably to it.[16]

Competitive Analyses

Competition represents an obvious source for product and service ideas. Products that are in the test market phase or that are just being launched are always vulnerable to having their ideas copied. For example, Kao, a Japanese detergent manufacturer, developed a super-absorbent diaper, causing Procter & Gamble's Pampers to lose its lead in the Japanese market. However, Procter & Gamble promptly developed its own super-absorbent version of Pampers, selling it aggressively worldwide.[17]

Additional Sources

Other sources of ideas are channel members, who are closer to consumers than the manufacturer; company employees, such as sales personnel, engineers, or even top management; inventors; consultants; nonprofit research laboratories; universities; and research firms, among others. Research conducted by the firm in the form of brainstorming sessions and qualitative research also can be used in the process of generating product ideas.[18]

10-3b Screening New Product Ideas

In the process of **screening new product ideas,** it is best to consider both the extent to which the product fits with the target consumers, as well as with the overall mission of the organization. At this stage, a checklist is usually developed to screen for product ideas that do not meet these criteria. In a study of European, North American, East Asia, and Australian consumer packaged-goods firms,[19] researchers identified screening factors that appear to draw the line between new product adoption or rejection in a detailed screening:

- The support and endorsement of senior management
- Superior consumer fit—does the product satisfy and respond to changes in customer needs and values?
- Lucrative market potential
- Clearly defined promotional plan and clearly identified brand strategy
- Alignment with product-led strategy and technological advantage
- Demonstrating strengths in both market attack strategy and product-led strategy
- Likely trade adoption (retailers, supermarket chains)
- Resistance to brand switching

10-3c Developing and Evaluating Concepts

screening new product ideas
Eliminating product ideas that do not fit with the target consumers and the overall mission of the organization.

developing and evaluating concepts
Determining how consumers will perceive and use a new product; a step in the new product development process.

The next stage, **developing and evaluating concepts**, is very important for firms developing products for international markets. Key activities at this stage are to determine how the product will be viewed by consumers and how it will be used. Typically, the process involves developing a detailed description of the product and asking prospective consumers to evaluate it and to indicate their willingness to purchase the hypothetical product. Most often, this is done using a focus group of representative target consumers.

Even in cases in which firms are exporting products initially developed for the home-country market, it is essential that they engage in market research in the international target market. The shortening of the product life cycle and the intensity of international competition increase pressure on exporters to evaluate and reevaluate their international target market in light of rapid technological change and to conduct concept-testing research that ranges from formal methods, such as focus groups, to ad hoc information gathering.[20]

One method that is frequently used at this stage is conjoint analysis. In this method, respondents receive descriptions of different hypothetical products with varying levels of the same attributes, which they are then asked to rank. Analysts can determine the ideal combination of attributes, ascertain the importance of each attribute, and, assuming the data were collected from a sufficiently large sample of the target population, estimate market share.

10-3d Performing a Product Business Analysis

Performing a product business analysis should include calculating projected project costs, return on investment, and cash flow and determining the fixed and variable costs for the long term.[21] However enthusiastic the target consumers queried, if these figures do not fit the company budget, the project will be high risk. For many product categories, product price is a critical characteristic; at this stage, it is important to identify the price level at which revenue or profit best fit the manufacturer's goals.[22]

10-3e Designing and Developing the Product

At the next stage, **designing and developing the product,** product prototypes are developed. It is important that product prototypes precisely match the concept description developed in the concept development and evaluation stage. If the company strays from the initial description, testing the revised product description is crucial.[23]

The product now acquires a name—a brand identity—and the marketing mix is developed. The cross-functional team developing the product—research and development, engineering, operations, marketing, finance—must come together for this process.[24] This team must be focused on the project in such a way that a large percentage of team members' time is devoted to the project, rather than to other projects. It also is important that the team acts as a unit, focusing on project, rather than departmental, interests.[25]

For multinational companies, coordination takes place across subsidiaries, or in conjunction with international partners. Companies such as Boeing and Motorola coordinate research and development activities globally by establishing worldwide information systems to coordinate product and design development. For example, in developing the Boeing 777, the company used real-time computer-aided technology to design components jointly with Japanese partners.[26] Companies also tend to encourage communication among research and development facilities in different countries. Procter & Gamble, for example, requires extensive communication and information sharing among units to develop new offerings, such as single-dose laundry tablets, which they introduced in 2012.[27] Products must fit client needs and specifications, so coordinating with clients is essential. In one example, the Airbus A380 was designed to hold more people and handle more cargo, creating efficiencies for the airlines. The issue that had to subsequently be resolved is where to land and to park the enormous aircraft, and how to handle passenger processing (see International Marketing Illustration 10-1).

It should be mentioned that product development activities increasingly take place in emerging markets. India is one country where there is intense work performed in the area of new product development, as the example on the top of the next page illustrates.

performing a product business analysis Calculating projected costs such as return on investment and cash flow and determining the fixed and variable costs for the long term.

designing and developing the product Developing product prototypes and giving the product a name, a brand identity, and a marketing mix; a step in the new product development process.

New Product Development—in India[28]

Yokagawa's J-Team (standing for H.B. Jayanthi), is a group of 60 Indian engineers working for Yokagawa, the Japanese industrial control systems manufacturer, in Bangalore. The Team was trained to speak Japanese so they can communicate effectively with colleagues in Japan while collaborating on product development. Of Yokogawa's development engineers, 350 are based in India—and the number is increasing —while 1,000 are based in Japan. This is an example of offshored product development taking place in India. Revenues from this type of activities are about $500 million annually and growing at 25 percent a year. And India is not alone in this regard. The Czech Republic, China and Russia are closely following in its footsteps.

Among other companies offshoring new product development to India are Johnson Controls, the U.S. vehicle parts maker and a big producer of seats and vehicle interiors, which employs 50 engineers in product development focused on the Indian market; Quest, another U.S. company with 650 engineers working on product development outsourcing contracts on behalf of customers such as U.K.-based aerospace company Rolls-Royce and General Electric; and Philips, the Dutch electronics manufacturer, which has just less than 1,000 employees developing new products, from projects such as low-power lighting systems for houses that work off rechargeable batteries to developing transportable health screening equipment, connected by satellite to hospitals.

International Marketing Illustration 10-1
Airbus 380: The Superjumbo Double-Decker

The Airbus 380 is touted as the world's largest airplane, the world's only twin-deck airliner, with a dedicated three-deck, 150-ton, long-range freighter. This giant is more fuel efficient than the average person's car. Its modern technology and economies of scale provide 15 percent lower seat-mile costs than today's most efficient aircraft. Thus, it is capable of offering passengers luxury travel at much more affordable prices—a cruise ship for the skies, the company claims.

The plane, which seats 555 passengers comfortably in a three-class interior layout, a superjumbo double-decker aircraft, advertises itself as 50 percent larger than the Boeing 747, with plenty of extra space that would allow passengers to lounge about in cozy conference rooms and attend chic in-flight gatherings. In reality, however, airlines could choose to pack 880 passengers in the A380, which, in all likelihood, they might if they are going to opt for running a highly profitable operation. At present, the lowest seat count is on board of Korean Airlines aircraft at 407 seats, and the highest is on Air France with 538 seats – with a comfortable layout, in this author's opinion.

When such an aircraft is in use, it requires an entirely new infrastructure to support it. For example, airports had to increase their baggage handling capacity and increase the number of customs and immigration personnel to handle customs at one time. Taxiways and gates needed to be modified to accommodate an airplane that has 12 doors and four aisles. In 2012, there were 28 airports in the world with the capacity to handle the aircraft.

After entering service in 2007, the A380 has quickly claimed ground lost as a result of early production problems that delayed production by 2 years. The company slashed profit forecasts as it had to pay out compensation for delays to its customers. Moreover, because jets trade in dollars, the dollar weakness relative to the euro also eroded the company's profits.

Nevertheless, it is expected that the jet giant will account for a large proportion of the Airbus revenue, even if it is a small fraction of the aircraft sold by the company. At a price of more than $300 million— early customers received large discounts—this jet is supposed to rake in the profits. However, Airbus continues to face challenges: UPS cancelled its order for 10 A380 freighters after Airbus said it was unable to deliver the planes until 2014, at the earliest. And FedEx Corp. and International Lease Finance Corp. cancelled their orders in 2006. Airbus is now concentrating on the A380 passenger version, where it has 253 orders (it has 72 aircraft in service).

Not least of the company's challenges is Boeing's 787 Dreamliner, the only large commercial aircraft on the market. The Dreamliner is made primarily of carbon fiber, rather than aluminum, and it is touted as the most environmentally-friendly airplane ever built, more fuel efficient, and producing 20 percent less carbon dioxide than competitors. The Dreamliner is not a direct competitor for the A380, which is much larger; nevertheless, it is an important challenger to Airbus, as both the A380 and the Dreamliner are positioned as large commercial aircraft.

Sources: International Airport Review, "Continued Handling of the A380," 6 June, 2012 (http://www.internationalairportreview.com/tag/a380/); Rebecca Christie, "Airbus's Leahy Expects Few '07 A380 Orders, Surge in '08-'09," *Dow Jones Newswires*, March 26, 2007, 5:46 p.m.; Steve McGrath, "Airbus Puts A380 Freighter on Ice to Focus on Passenger Version," *Wall Street Journal*, March 2, 2007, p. 1; Joe Sharkey, "Where Do You Park a 747 on Steroids?" *The New York Times*, May 4, 2004, C7; www.airbus.com; Ham Granlund, "Are Airports Ready for A380?" *Aviation Week & Space Technology*, Vol. 160, No. 16, April 19, 2004, p. 6.

10-3f Test Marketing

Test marketing a product can provide a good indication of how the product will be received when it is in the market, but this stage can also be expensive, time consuming, and open to competitive sabotage. The following are test marketing options firms can choose to evaluate the reaction of the market to their product. At the lower involvement level is **simulated test marketing,** which is not as costly and does not give competition much information about the product. Controlled test marketing is limited to a few stores, is thus also less costly, and gives only limited exposure of the product to competition. Actual test marketing necessitates important strategic decisions and commitments that involve channel members, intensive promotion, and high promotional expenses; test marketing could create conditions that make the product vulnerable to competitive reactions.

Simulated Test Marketing

Because eight out of ten products fail, simulated test markets are often used to reduce the risks a company would incur in terms of marketing, sales, and capital expenses; cannibalization of the parent brand through line extension; and competitive reaction to the new product.[29] Among the simulated test marketing research systems employed today are LITMUS, which is used especially for new packaged goods, consumer durables, and services; ASSESSOR, which is used for packaged goods; BASES, which is used primarily for food and health and beauty products; and ESP, which is used primarily for packaged goods.[30]

To illustrate, the LITMUS simulated test marketing study recruits about 600 representative consumers who participate in a research study in a central facility in a number of markets.[31] After responding to questions about their product-related attitudes and purchase behavior, they view advertising of the new brand and of competitive brands that are embedded in a television program. The respondents then comment on the television program and advertising and then proceed to a simulated store stocking test brands and competitive brands where they can buy the products at a substantial discount. The proportion of individuals purchasing the test brand is then used to estimate product **trialability.**

Controlled Test Marketing

Usually conducted by a research firm in industrialized countries, **controlled test marketing** involves offering a new product to a group of stores and evaluating the market reaction to it (consumer reaction as well as competitive reaction). In the process, different aspects of the marketing mix are varied—price, in-store promotion, placement in the store, and so on. A more informal controlled test marketing involves simply asking a number of stores to carry the product for a fee. Depending on the outcome, the manufacturing firm may decide to produce the product on a larger scale.

Actual Test Marketing

A number of important decisions are involved in full-blown test marketing. Companies at this stage must decide on the cities that are most appropriate for testing the product, based on the availability of retailers and other necessary distribution and logistics service providers, and on availability of the infrastructure needed to conduct the test market, such as the necessary media, research firms, direct mail providers, and so forth. Multinational companies do not limit test marketing or product launching to their home countries. For example, MasterCard continually tests new products in the Netherlands and Germany by using direct mail. This strategy also appeals to service providers from developing countries. For example, Mexican exporters often use direct mail to test a market in the United States or Canada. However, this approach is problematic because the national mail service can be unreliable, ZIP codes are missing from database lists, and so on.[32] Test marketing exclusively using direct mail works well when it is aimed at a narrow, well-defined target market. Although this approach is possible in Europe, Canada, and the United States, where segmentation is a precise science, based on refined methods of demographic and psychographic assessment, in developing countries, such well-defined databases are not always available.[33]

test marketing
Testing new-product performance in a limited area of a national or regional target market to estimate product performance in the respective country or region.

simulated test marketing
Test marketing simulating purchase environments where samples of target consumers are observed in their product-related decision-making process.

trialability
The ability of the consumer to experience a product with minimal effort.

controlled test marketing
Test marketing that involves offering a new product to a group of stores and evaluating the market's reaction to it.

Although test marketing can provide valuable information for the manufacturer, anticipating product performance in the short run, its usefulness is often questioned given the high expense it necessitates. In a rapidly changing competitive environment, being first in the market constitutes an important competitive advantage, the first-mover advantage. As such, the company is the first to attract consumers and to commit channel members for its new product. A company is also vulnerable to competitive reaction during the test marketing stage. On one hand, competition could appropriate the product idea and be the first to offer the product to the market; on the other, competition could sabotage the new brand, cutting prices for all competitive offerings.

Test marketing, nevertheless, can be a reliable predictor of national market share, costs, and profitability, and it can be a tool to assess and compare alternative product strategies. Yet, surprisingly, this tool is frequently overlooked in international marketing.[34] According to international marketing experts, some of the errors to avoid in international test marketing are incorrect forecasts, unrealistic market conditions, incorrect media translations, and choice of the wrong test market.[35]

10-3g Launching the Product Internationally

launching the product internationally
Introducing a new product to the international market as the last step in the new product development process.

Strategies for **launching the product internationally** have an impact on later product performance. Products launched using a successful strategy have a higher rate of success and score high ratings on profitability, technical success, and positive impact on the company.[36] "Goodness of launch" is characterized by the following, in order of impact: high service quality, on-time shipment and adequate product availability, quality sales force and enough sales effort and support, quality of promotion, and sufficient promotional effort.[37]

Product Launch Decisions: Consumers and Countries

In international marketing, an important decision at the launching stage is in which countries to launch the product. Whereas, in the recent past, most launching was aimed at consumers in the manufacturers' home countries, increasingly, multinationals launch products in countries that have the best consumer-product fit. Coca-Cola, for instance, launched Coke Blak, a coffee-flavored cola hybrid, simultaneously in the United States and France in 2006, banking on receptive consumers in both countries toward a cola product with a coffee flavor. Both countries have a strong coffee tradition, and a preference for coffee-flavored desserts and drinks. Unfortunately, the brand did not perform well and it was pulled from the market a few years later.

Timing of Launch

Another important decision is the timing of the new product launch. Companies often attempt to gain the first-mover advantage by being the first to launch the new product. Alternatively, they could engage in later entry. The advantage of this approach is that the competitors would have to incur the costs of informing the market about the new product and its features. Also, the company could market the product as a "me-too" product, reducing advertising costs significantly.

Marketing Mix Decisions

Other important decisions at the product-launching stage involve setting the price that the target consumer is willing to pay for the product. Prices might be higher if the product is launched in industrialized countries with a wealthy consumer base—typically on par with competing products. For consumers in emerging markets, the product is usually launched at a lower price to initiate trial.

Figure 10-5: *In the United States, Ajax' offering is limited to just a few products, compared to most European markets, where the company offers a multitude of cleaning products in different scents, as those available in this Estonian supermarket.*

Firms typically choose to vary their product mix from one market to another. For example, in the United States, Colgate-Palmolive's Ajax offering is limited to a few cleaning products, compared to the company's Ajax offering in Europe (see Figure 10-5).

Promotion, in the form of sales promotion, personal selling, and advertising, is crucial during the launching process. The introduction of Coca Cola Zero in 2007 in Europe was accompanied by heavy advertising in metro stations, on busy street corners, anywhere one could imagine it. The message the ad sported in large, almost graffiti-like print against a gothic background was "As it should be: real taste and zero sugar."

Channel members constitute an important element of the marketing mix during the launching stage. Decisions such as shelf positioning, often contingent on the payment of slotting fees to retailers, as well as questions on inventory, trade allowances, and financing, are addressed at this stage. As will be seen in Chapter 11, "Managing International Distribution Operations and Logistics," there are significant variations in the channels of distribution worldwide for individual product categories, with fragmented channels in markets such as Japan, concentrated channels in command economies, and so on. This factor adds to the complexity and expense of the product-launching effort.

10-4 Degree of Product/Service Newness

Innovation is thought of as the creation of a better product or process and may range from the substitution of a cheaper material in an existing product to a better way of marketing, distributing, or supporting a product or service.[38] **Degree of product/ service newness** refers to the extent to which a product or service is new to the market. Organizations that have a good record of innovation pursue innovation systematically, actively searching for change and supporting creative individuals who are internally driven.[39]

Innovation takes on many forms, and marketing literature uses various classifications for different categories of innovation. At a basic level, new products and services can be classified in one of five categories:[40]

- **New product to existing market, new product to existing company**—These categories account for 33.7 percent of products.

- **New line**—This category represents a new product or product line to a company, but for a company already operating in that market. It accounts for 16.8 percent of products.

- **New item in an existing product line** for the company—This category accounts for 11.9 percent of products; these products are likely to have the highest success rate (83 percent) and the greatest impact on company sales and profit.

- **Modification** of an existing company product—This category accounts for 18.8 percent of products.

- **Innovation,** new product to the world—This category accounts for about 18.8 percent of products.

Another popular classification organizes innovation into the radical, dynamically continuous, and continuous categories. **Radical innovations** (also known as *discontinuous innovations*) create new industries or new standards of management, manufacturing, and servicing, and they represent fundamental changes for consumers, entailing departures from established consumption.[41] Examples of radical innovations are the Internet and endoscopy/endoscopic surgery. **Dynamically continuous innovations** do not alter consumer behavior significantly, but they represent a change in the consumption pattern; cell phones are an example of such innovation. **Continuous innovations** have no disruption on consumption patterns and involve only product alterations, such as new flavors, or a new product that is an improvement over the old offering. They usually are congruous, in the sense that they can be used alongside the existing systems; for example, a new Microsoft Windows version will work with computers that are

innovation
A product new to the world.

degree of product/ service newness
The extent to which a product is new to the market in general or to a group of consumers.

new product to existing market
A product never before offered to the market.

new product to existing company
A new product that the company offers to the market; the product competes with similar competitor offerings.

new line
A new product category offered by the company.

new item in an existing product line
A new brand that the company offers to the market in an existing product line.

radical innovations
The creation of new industries or new standards of management, manufacturing, and servicing that represent fundamental changes for consumers, entailing departures from established consumption.

modification
The alteration of an existing company product.

dynamically continuous innovations
Innovation that does not alter significantly consumer behavior but still entails a change in the consumption pattern.

continuous innovations
Product innovation where there is no disruption in consumption patterns; such innovations involve product alterations such as new flavors or new products that are improvements over the old offerings.

only a few years old or older computers with enhanced capacity. Geox shoes, described in International Marketing Illustration 10-2, are an example of a continuous innovation.

International Marketing Illustration 10-2
An Innovation That Could Relaunch the Italian Economy

Mario Moretti Polegato, a former winemaker in northern Italy, was attending a wine convention in Nevada and went hiking to explore the area. He was hot and uncomfortable, so he poked some holes in his sneakers to cool off. This led him to go into the shoe business with a new product idea. He decided to bring to the world an innovation: a patented membrane on the soles of his Geox brand shoes. The Geox membrane has dozens of tiny openings that allow sweat to evaporate while blocking water entry, thus making them more breathable than other shoes—a difficult-to-prove claim. This membrane is referred to as the "Geox breathes" ("Geox respira") patented system. Moretti Polegato claims that this material is superior to leather, which aspirates water and keeps feet wet. The membrane he patented blocks water entry.

The company has been growing by leaps and bounds, faster than any other Italian shoe company, projecting sales of 15 million pairs a year in the short term. At the basis of its growth is the company's international expansion; in fact, the Geox brand is already present in 68 countries. Moretti Polegato's goal is to open several stores in the United States (the company's flagship store opened in New York City in May 2004), one of the largest world markets for shoes. It is also planning to open more than 100 stores in China and in many other countries.

Moretti Polegato claims that his is an innovation that could relaunch the Italian economy, which is quite a claim, considering that most of the Geox shoes are manufactured in Romania and Slovakia. Yet, using an image-based marketing strategy in a market where image is essential, he may just be successful. The Geox stores are located in Via Montenapoleone in Milan and on Madison Avenue in New York, next to luxury retailers Prada, Gucci, and Armani. Geox shoes are available at higher end shops; for example, in the United States, they are sold at Nordstrom and Dillard's.

Sources: Eric Sylvers, "Not Footloose but Fancy-Free, An Italian Comes Calling," *The New York Times*, March 18, 2004, W1, W7; www.geox.biz; www.geox.com.

Most of the innovation taking place today is continuous. However, a radical innovation, the Internet, has revolutionized all aspects of the marketing mix, with important implications for international marketing. As a distribution tool, it renders products accessible instantly worldwide, regardless of the firm's experience and size. It is an equal-opportunity distribution tool for companies from industrialized and developing countries alike, allowing for creative and innovative market penetration.

In one example demonstrating how the Internet can be used successfully in promoting developing country exports, the International Trade Center organized the world's first online coffee auction, selling Brazilian specialty coffee to bidders around the world via the Internet; the auction drew buyers around the world and generated high prices for Brazilian growers.[42]

In another example, Pavex Parquet, an SME in Transylvania, Romania, used the Internet to research custom-made hardwood borders, a product used in elaborate, high-end parquet flooring and to sell the product.

Pavex Parquet

Pavex Parquet (www.pavexparquet.com) is a Romanian company that specializes in the manufacture of hardwood borders for parquet flooring. Their borders are used to enhance the esthetics of parquet and other hardwood flooring. What is especially noteworthy about this company is that it relied on the Internet to evaluate the market for hardwood borders and to sell its products to consumers and businesses around the world.

The company first conducted research on the Internet, to identify designs, and improved on them to create a portfolio of well-designed, well-structured borders. The hardwood borders include well-known patterns, such as the Greek key (see Figure 10-6); lesser-used patterns, such as weaver lines and Victorian patterns; and truly unique patterns, such as the chain, the grill, and infinity. The company also used the Internet to research the market. It studied its competitors, the wood they used, and the specifications of their parquet flooring. Finally, the company conducted research to identify appropriate outlets for its Pavex Parquet brand.

Figure 10-6: *Pavex Parquet's Greek key pattern in the company's showroom.*

Photo Courtesy of Pavex Parquet SRL.

In its promotional mix, Pavex Parquet relied heavily on the Internet as well. It used FLICKR.com and WEB-SHOTS.com to show how the borders can improve the esthetics of the room once they are inserted into parquet flooring. In 2006, Pavex Parquet introduced its offering using a new, sleek website, at www.pavexparquet.com. On the website, the company educates prospective consumers about hardwood borders and how they can integrate the elegant borders into their home-improvement or new-home-building efforts. The company promotes the hardwood borders primarily through the main three search engines, Google, Yahoo, and MSN.

Pavex engaged in additional communication with prospective customers by publishing articles about parquet in different flooring, home-improvement, and remodeling forums.

The company has distributors in the United States, United Kingdom, and Germany, and it also distributes directly to final consumers and businesses worldwide.

10-5 Product Diffusion

Product diffusion refers to the manner in which a product is adopted by consumers worldwide—the speed of adoption by various groups. The consumer adoption process is addressed in Section 10-5c, "Consumer Adopters." A number of factors influence the speed of product adoption in different countries; they are discussed in Sections 10-5a through 10-5c.

10-5a Product Factors

In general, a number of attributes of an innovation are likely to accelerate the rate of adoption of a product or service.[43] First, the new product or service must offer a *relative advantage* compared with the other offerings available on the market and must be *compatible with the needs of consumers*. In addition, the product/service use must be *observable* (or communicable to others) and have a high trialability (for example, consumers can try the product on a limited basis, by renting it, for instance). Both product and country determinants of adoption rates are illustrated on Figure 10-7.

10-5b Country (Market) Factors

New products tend to be adopted at different rates in different international markets. Countries where the product or service is first introduced and adopted are referred to as **lead countries,** and countries where the product or service is adopted at a later stage are known as **lag countries.** This process is similar to the traditional two-step **diffusion process,** whereby products are first offered to wealthy consumers and, subsequently, to the mass market. By analogy, consumers in high-income, industrialized countries (lead countries) adopt the product first, whereas consumers in low-income countries (lag countries) adopt the product later.

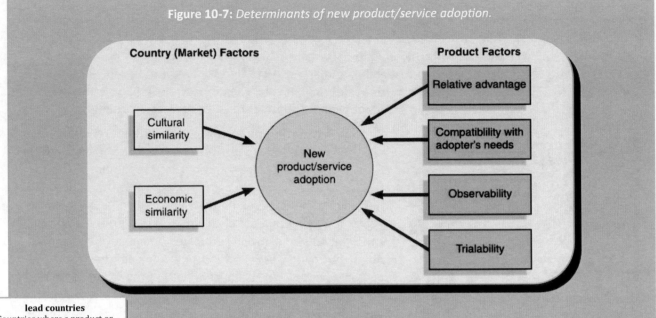

Figure 10-7: *Determinants of new product/service adoption.*

lead countries
Countries where a product or service is first introduced and adopted.

lag countries
Countries where a product or service is adopted after already being introduced in lead countries.

diffusion process
The process by which a product is adopted by consumers worldwide.

Generally, the diffusion rate tends to be faster in lag countries, as consumers learn from the experiences of adopters in lead countries. Moreover, the later in the product life cycle the product or service is introduced in a lag country, the faster the adoption rate.

In the past, geographic proximity was also an important factor in rapid diffusion. However, today that is no longer the case. Television and the Internet have contributed to the instant adoption of styles and innovations worldwide for products that do not need a specialized technology infrastructure (see Figure 10-8). A more important factor affecting product adoption is the country's cultural similarity to the country where the product was invented (the innovation center). Also, a country's wealth is a good indicator of the possibility of rapid adoption of the new product.[44]

Figure 10-8: *Music rapidly diffuses from the United States to Germany. What is particularly interesting is the age of consumers – adopters are often older consumers, as the ones portrayed here listening to a new group on tour, playing New-Orleans-style blues.*

10-5c Consumer Adopters

Target consumers—national, regional, or worldwide—can be segmented based on the manner in which they adopt new products throughout the respective products' life cycle. The segments are:

- **Innovators**—These few (2.5 percent of the total market) risk takers can afford to pay the higher purchase price charged by companies during the introduction stage of the product (to recoup investment costs). See Figure 10-9. In developing countries, these consumers are the well-to-do business owners and leading government ministers and their families.

Figure 10-9: *Top designers use creative fashion displays to attract fashion innovators who are able and willing to purchase the latest and most innovative designs.*

innovators
Risk takers who can afford to pay the higher purchase price charged by companies during the introduction stage of a product; they account for 2.5 percent of the total market.

early adopters
Consumers who purchase a product early in its product life cycle and who tend to be opinion leaders in their communities who take risks, but with greater discernment than innovators; they account for 13.5 percent of the total market.

early majority
Consumers who enjoy the status of being among the first in their peer group to purchase a popular product; they account for 34 percent of the total market.

late majority
Individuals of limited means who are likely to adopt products only if the products are widely popular and the risk associated with buying them is minimal; they account for 34 percent of the total market.

laggards
Consumers who are the last to adopt new products and do so only in late maturity because they are risk averse and conservative in their spending; they account for 16 percent of the total market.

- **Early adopters**—The next consumers to purchase the product tend to be opinion leaders in their communities who take risks, but with greater discernment than innovators. They constitute about 13.5 percent of the total population.

- **Early majority**—These consumers, who account for 34 percent of the total market, are more risk averse than individuals in the first categories but enjoy the status of being among the first in their peer group to buy what will be a popular product.

- **Late majority**—These consumers, who account for 34 percent of the total market, are individuals of limited means who are likely to adopt products only if the products are widely popular and the risk associated with buying them is minimal. The products themselves are much more affordable at this stage.

- **Laggards**—These consumers, who account for 16 percent of the total market, are the last to adopt new products and do so only in late maturity. In general, laggards are risk averse and conservative in their spending.

The categories of adopters vary greatly in markets of different development levels. For example, all categories of consumers have significantly higher means in highly industrialized countries, compared with consumers in developing countries. Nevertheless, the segments are similar in terms of their risk propensity, their status in society, and their wealth relative to the rest of the consumers in the country where they live.

Chapter Summary

Evaluate the stages of the international product life cycle and identify the locus of operations and target markets at each stage. Most products are introduced in developed countries, where consumers can afford the high costs charged by manufacturers to recoup product development costs. During growth, the international company faces increasing competition worldwide from products also produced in the developed country. At maturity, standardized products compete primarily on price; manufacturing moves overseas to take advantage of cheaper labor. The company has a sales focus on emerging markets. In a product's middle and late maturity stages, competitors from developing countries enter the company's world markets and compete for consumers. In the product's decline stage, the company seeks new markets in countries of lower development levels.

Identify the different dimensions of the international product mix with company illustrations. Companies use different product mix strategies for different markets. The product mix refers to the totality of brands the company offers to its target markets. A company such as Unilever offers products in many categories—for example, coffee, ice cream, detergent, and others—but does not offer many varieties of each. Unilever, thus, has low depth but high product width, and its product offering is not consistent because it includes products for different uses. Other companies may offer high depth in certain markets and have a very limited offering in yet other markets.

Examine the new product development process and the activities involved at each stage in international markets. The new product development process starts with idea generation, in and outside the company. The next step involves idea screening using predetermined criteria, followed by concept development and evaluation. Product business analysis determines the extent to which the product is likely to be viable. In the next stage, product design and development, product prototypes are developed and evaluated by target consumers. Test marketing involves great expense on the part of the company, but it also leaves the company vulnerable to competitive idea theft. Often, companies use international markets as testing grounds for new products. The final stage, launching, requires significant commitment to the product and to the target market.

Examine degrees of product newness and address international diffusion processes. There are different types of new products: products that are new to an existing market or new to an existing company; new lines (i.e., new products or product lines to a company but for a company already operating in that market); new items in an existing product line for the company; modifications to an existing company product; and innovations (i.e., products that are new to the world). New products are first diffused in lead countries, typically industrialized countries where consumers can afford the products; here, the diffusion rate is slow. The countries where the product is adopted last are known as lag countries; in these countries, the diffusion rate is faster because consumers learn from the adoption experiences of consumers in lead countries.

Key Terms

continuous innovation

controlled test marketing

decline stage

degree of product/service newness

designing and developing the product

developing and evaluating concepts

diffusion process

dynamically continuous innovation

early adopters

early majority

generating new product ideas

growth stage

innovation

innovators

international product life cycle (IPLC)

introduction stage

lag countries

laggards

late majority

launching the product internationally

lead countries

maturity stage

modification

new item in an existing product line

new line

new product to existing company

new product to existing market

performing a product business analysis

product consistency

product depth

product length

product line

product mix

product width

radical innovation

screening new product ideas

simulated test marketing

test marketing

trialability

Discussion Questions

1. Describe the international product life cycle and the activities involved in developed and developing countries.

2. What are the activities involved at each stage of the new product development process? Where are most new products developed?

3. Many products are advertised in the United States as "new and improved." What does this description mean in terms of new product classifications?

4. Describe the differences between lead and lag countries in terms of adoption status and adoption rate.

Chapter Quiz

True/False

1. A product line is defined as the complete assortment of products that a company offers to its target international consumers.

Answer: False

Rationale: The product line is defined as all the related brands a company offers in the same product category.

Section 10-2, "Managing the International Product and Service Mix"

2. Product length is defined as the total number of product lines that a company offers.

Answer: False

Rationale: Product length is defined as the total number of brands in the product mix—all the brands sold by the company worldwide.

Section 10-2a, "Length"

3. Test marketing has a number of disadvantages: It is expensive, time consuming, and subjects the company to competitive sabotage.

Answer: True

Rationale: Although test marketing provides a good indication of how the product will be received when it is in the market, it can be expensive and time consuming; plus, it exposes the company to competitive sabotage.

Section 10-3f, "Test Marketing"

4. Product trialability interferes with the diffusion process.

Answer: False

Rationale: Trialability is an important attribute of an innovation: It tends to accelerate the rate of adoption of a product or service.

Section 10-5a, "Product Factors"

Multiple Choice

1.   The iPhone is relatively expensive. Companies are presently selling them to consumers in industrial-ized countries. In which stage of the international product life cycle is the iPhone?

    a.   Product introduction

    b.   Growth stage

    c.   Maturity stage

    d.   Decline stage

Answer: b is correct.

Rationale: Innovations and inventions are targeted at first to consumers in developed countries; during the introduction stage, these products were targeted primarily to innovators. Today, as this technology be-comes more popular, they are targeted to the early adopters; thus, the iPhone is in the early growth stage.

Section 10-1a, "The Product Introduction Stage"

2.   DVD players are most likely in which stage of the international product life cycle?

    a.   Growth stage

    b.   Maturity stage

    c.   Decline stage

    d.   Product introduction

Answer: b is correct.

DVD players are widely adopted and thus are in the maturity stage of the product life cycle.

Section 10-1b, "The Growth Stage"

3.   Anne Klein II is an example of a

    a.   line extension.

    b.   product mix.

    c.   product length.

    d.   none of the above

Answer: a is correct.

Rationale: A company is likely to increase the number of lines (related brands in the same product catego-ry) it offers to capture more loyal consumers. Anne Klein offers the Anne Klein II line extension to consum-ers who could otherwise not afford its expensive main product line.

Section 10-2, "Managing the International Product and Service Mix"

4.   The many different flavors of Unilever's Ben & Jerry's ice cream illustrate Ben & Jerry's

    a.   product length.

    b.   product width.

    c.   product depth.

    d.   all of the above

Answer: c is correct.

Rationale: Product depth refers to the number of different offerings in a particular product category.

Section 10-2c, "Depth"

5.   New product ideas can be found through

  a.   competitive analyses.

  b.   international employees.

  c.   international customers.

  d.   all of the above

Answer: d is correct.

Rationale: Sources of new product ideas are, among others, competitors and company employees and consumers.

Section 10-3a, "Generating New Product Ideas"

6.   When a company screens new product ideas, what are the most important factors to consider?

  a.   Unique benefits to users

  b.   Product requirements versus resources

  c.   Narrowly specified target markets

  d.   a and b

Answer: d is correct.

Rationale: It is important for the company to match its resources with the new product requirements and to identify the benefits the products will have for new users.

Section 10-3b, "Screening New Product Ideas"

Chapter 10 Endnotes

1.   Kenneth Hein, "Bull's Market," *Brandweek*, Vol. 42, No. 22, May 28, 2001, pp. 21, 23.

2.   Alex Planes, "A Leap of Faith: Monster Beverage," *Daily Finance*, February 29, 2012 (http://www.dailyfinance.com/2012/02/29/a-leap-of-faith-monster-beverage/); Matthew Boyle and Dana Vazquez Castillo, "Fueled by Its Energy Drink, Hansen Natural's Stock Has Been on a Rocket Ride," *Fortune*, Vol. 154, No. 13, December 25, 2006, pp. 116—122.

3.   See Raymond Vernon, "International Investment and International Trade in the Product Cycle," *Quarterly Journal of Economics*, Vol. 80, No. 2, 1966, pp. 190–207; Raymond Vernon, "The Product Cycle Hypothesis in a New International Environment," *Oxford Bulletin of Economics and Statistics*, Vol. 41, 1979, pp. 255–267.

4.   Jeremy Caplan,"The iPhone Kick-Starts the Competition," *Time*, Vol. 169, No. 27, July 2, 2007, p. 36.

5.   Ibid.

6.   Vikas Bajaj, "In India, the Golden Age of Television Is Now," *New York Times*, February 11, 2007, Sunday Business section, 1, 4.

7.   Andand Giridharadas, "Big Names Competing for India's 2-Cents-a-Minute Caller," *The New York Times*, January 10, 2007, C9.

8.   Jeremy Caplan, "The iPhone Kick-Starts the Competition," *Time*, Vol. 169, No. 27, July 2, 2007,   p. 36.

9.   Gerrit Wiesmann, "Berlin Plans Frequency Auction," *Financial Times*, February 7, 2007, p. 19.

10.   Michael Cusumano, "'Made in India' a New Sign of Software Quality," *Computerworld,* Vol. 34,   No. 9, February 28, 2000, p. 36.

11.   Unilever is described in detail at www.Unilever.com, a source for some of the material in this section.

12.   These examples are detailed in Harriet Marsh, "Adapting to Africa," *Marketing,* March 30, 2000,   p. 39.

13.   http://www.freeplayenergy.com (accessed May 12, 2012).

14.   "Freeplay Energy," *Investors Chronicle*, October 6, 2006, p. 1.

15.   David Leonhardt, "It Was a Hit in Buenos Aires—So Why Not Boise?" *BusinessWeek,* Vol. 3594, September 7, 1998, pp. 56–57.

16.   Ibid.

17.   C. Samuel Craig and Susan P. Douglas, "Configural Advantage in Global Markets," *Journal of International Marketing,* Vol. 8, No. 1, 2000, pp. 6–26.

18.   Gordon A. Wyner, "Product Testing: Benefits and Risks," *Marketing Research,* Vol. 9, No. 1, Spring 1997, pp. 46–48.

18.   Lisa Susanne Willsey, "Taking These 7 Steps Will Help You Launch a New Product," *Marketing News,* Vol. 33, No. 7, March 29, 1999, p. 17.

19.   John Saunders, Veronica Wong, Chris Stagg, Mariadel Mar Souza Fontan, "How Screening Criteria Change During Brand Development," *Journal of Product and Brand Management*, Vol. 14, No. 4/5, 2005, pp. 239–250.

20.   F. H. Rolf Seringhaus, "Comparative Marketing Behaviour of Canadian and Austrian High Tech Firms," *Management International Review,* Vol. 33, No. 3, 1993, pp. 247–270.

21.   Willsey, "Taking These 7 Steps," p. 17.

22.   Wyner, "Product Testing," pp. 46–48.

23.   Robert S. Doscher, "How to Create New Products," *Target Marketing,* Vol. 17, No. 1, 1994, pp. 40–41.

24.   Willsey, "Taking These 7 Steps," p. 17.

25.   Robert G. Cooper, "How to Launch a New Product Successfully," *CMA,* Vol. 69, No. 8, 1995, pp. 20–23.

26.   Shaoming Zou and Aysegul Ozsomer, "Global Product R&D and the Firm's Strategic Position," *Journal of International Marketing,* Vol. 7, No. 1, 1999, pp. 57–76.

27.   Melanie Healy, North America and Global Hyper-Super-Mass Channel Group President, University of Richmond lecture, February 15, 2012.

28.   Peter March, "Feast of a Movable Workforce: India's Revolution Part II," *Financial Times*, May 17, 2006, 12.

29.   Kevin J. Clancy and Robert S. Shulman, "It's Better to Fly a New Product Simulator than Crash the Real Thing," *Planning Review,* Vol. 20, No. 4, July/August 1992, pp. 10–16.

30.   Ibid.

31.   The LITMUS test is the creation of Kevin J. Clancy, who describes the procedure used in Clancy and Shulman, "It's Better to Fly a New Product Simulator," pp. 10–16.

32.   Stacey Ramirez, "Hand Outs," *Business Mexico,* Vol. 6, No. 5, May 1996, pp. 12–16.

33.   Ibid.

34.   Tamer S. Cavusgil and Ugur Yavas, "Test Marketing: An Exposition," *Marketing Intelligence and Planning,* Vol. 5, No. 3, 1987, pp. 16–20.

35.   Ibid.

36.   Robert G. Cooper, "Debunking the Myths of New Product Development," *Research Technology Management,* Vol. 37, No. 4, July/August 1994, pp. 40–50.

37. Ibid.

38. Nicholas Valery, "Survey: Innovation in Industry: Industry Gets Religion," *The Economist,* Vol. 350, No. 8107, February 20, 1999, pp. S5–S6.

39. Ibid.

40. Cooper, "Debunking the Myths," pp. 40–50.

41. Michael-Jorg Oesterle, "Time-Span Until Internationalization: Foreign Market Entry as a Built-in-Mechanism of Innovations," *Management International Review,* Vol. 37, No. 2, 1997, pp. 125–149.

42. "World's First Internet Coffee Auction a Success," *International Trade Forum,* No. 1, 2000, pp. 37–38.

43. Everett M. Rogers, *Diffusion of Innovations, 3rd Edition,* New York: Free Press, 1983.

44. Sanna Sundqvist, Lauri Frank, and Kaisu Puumalainen, "The Effects of Country Characteristics, Cultural Similarity and Adoption Timing on the Diffusion of Wireless Communications, *Journal of Business Research*, Vol. 58, No. 1, 2005, pp. 107–110.

Case 10-1

FrieslandCampina

Royal FrieslandCampina is a multinational dairy cooperative with 14,391 member dairy farms in the Netherlands, Belgium, and Germany with sales over 9.6 billion euros, and with 19,000 employees in 25 countries. A European company that remains close to its Dutch roots, FrieslandCampina's image evokes picturesque Dutch cow pastures and healthy lifestyles. The company's history can be traced to southern Holland, in the Eindhoven area. A dairy cooperative with the name "De Kempen" was created in 1947 and used the brand name "Campina." In 1964 the cooperative merged with another cooperative in the Weert region in Holland and formed Campina (named after a regional moor—its meaning is "from the land").

After several consecutive mergers, most recently, in 2008 with another Dutch dairy behemoth, Friesland Foods, FrieslandCampina became one of the largest dairy cooperatives in the world, active from London to Moscow and from the United States to Japan. The company's products are milk, desserts, yogurt, dairy drinks, butter, cheese, condensed milk, powdered milk, and caseinate, and it has a large brand portfolio. It is also a company that takes corporate social responsibility seriously, and, as a result, it is well positioned in the industry, especially when it comes to relationships with consumers and public authorities.

FrieslandCampina must buy all the milk the farmers produce, while the farmers must finance the cooperative, and, in return, they obtain a yield of the products sold. FrieslandCampina itself is a nonprofit organization. Member farmers receive all the company profits. They have voting rights in the company that are proportional to the amount of milk they deliver, and they are represented by the Members' Council, which is the highest managerial body of the cooperative.

Industry Trends

The European Union remains the world's top dairy producer, manufacturer, and trader of dairy products. Because the EU is a mature dairy market, the emphasis is on value growth and processing milk into products with high added value. Among the trends in the industry is consolidation. Another important trend is the focus on convenience (a packaging issue) and on value-added nutrition for functional foods (a product ingredient issue). Changes include creating new packaging and unique containers for innovative products. For example, Germany-based Schwalbchen Molkerei offers Go! Banana, the first milk-energy drink made from fresh milk and real, pureed bananas, packaged in 330 ml Tetra Prisma cartons with fluted sides. Spain's Pascual Dairy offers milk-based energy drink Bio Frutas in two flavors: tropical and Mediterranean. German milk processor Immergut produces Drinkfit Choco Plus, a vitamin-fortified, chocolate-flavored milk, in the same carton as Go! Banana. The United Kingdom company Miller offers dual-compartment, side-by-side containers of refrigerated yogurt, while a drinkable fruit yogurt from Nestlé SA is offered in the United Kingdom under the name Squizzos, sporting Disney characters on a triangular-shaped package that is easy to tear, squeeze, and drink.

FrieslandCampina is also a creative innovator when it comes to convenience, giving a new twist to dairy desserts. The company's new strudel is two product layers swirled into a single portion pack. It gives consumers a dessert that looks striking and offers a surprising combination of flavors, according to the company. FrieslandCampina was the first company to apply the swirl effect in desserts, and thereby setting a trend. The two layers remain stable and do not run into each other.

Functional ingredients (health foods or ingredients that enhance the nutritional value of products) represent yet another important trend in the dairy industry. In this category are a number of heath foods and other milk-based nutritional supplements sold to consumers. Examples are input products for pharmaceutical products, food ingredients, and ingredients used to enhance nutrition.

Finally, another industry trend is internationalization. FrieslandCampina is a veritable international company, present in Belgium, Denmark, Germany, Spain, Greece, the Netherlands, Poland, the European Union, Russia, Thailand, Vietnam, India, China, Japan, Argentina, and the United States, among others.

Meeting Competitive Challenges at FrieslandCampina: Adopting a Market Orientation

Historically, milk production was supply driven, and excess milk was used to produce cheese and powdered milk. This strategy led to excess cheese/commodities on the market and the need for subsidies. FrieslandCampina initiated a change in this practice. Since the late 1980s, the company has been demand driven: Farmers are assigned production quotas that they are not allowed to exceed.

According to R. J. Steetskamp, formerly a director of strategic business development at Campina (presently, involved in the FrieslandCampina's international operations), the company examines consumer behavior to determine where to fit products in consumers' lives. As such, the company offers four categories of products:

1. Indulgence products. This category constitutes an important growth area for the company. FrieslandCampina produces numerous milk-based desserts, with the exception of ice cream—primarily due to the product's seasonality and the logistics strategies involved in the transportation and storage of ice cream, which differ from those for the rest of the company's offerings.

2. Daily essentials. This category includes FrieslandCampina products that shoppers purchase routinely, such as milk, buttermilk, yogurt, coffee cream, butter, cheese, and others. FrieslandCampina, using a strategy employed by all its competitors, also sells daily essentials under dealer (store) brands, rather than under its own brand name. For example, in Holland, it sells milk, plain yogurt, butter, Gouda cheese, and vla (chocolate or vanilla custard) under the Albert Heijn brand name. Albert Heijn is a dominant, quality supermarket chain in Holland that is owned by Royal Ahold—a large conglomerate that also owns supermarket chains in the United States (BI-LO, Giant, and Stop & Shop). The company also sells daily essentials under dealer brands in Germany.

3. Functional products. According to Mr. Steetskamp, this product category needs to be further explored and defined by the company. In this category are health foods and other milk-based nutritional supplements sold to consumers. DMV International, a FrieslandCampina division present all over the world, produces pharmaceutical products, food ingredients, and ingredients used to enhance the nutrition of consumers and their pets, such as proteins and powders with different functions. All these products are milk-based, and many of them are well known. For example, Lactoval is a popular calcium supplement.

4. Ingredients (food and pharmaceutical ingredients). This product category is targeted at other food product manufacturers, rather than at the individual consumers. The primary purpose of the food and pharmaceutical ingredients is to enhance the quality, taste, texture, and nutritive content of the products manufactured by FrieslandCampina's clients. The company's Creamy Creation unit specializes in blending dairy and alcohol to make various cream liqueurs, leading to both healthy and indulgent drinks. In this category are meal replacement drinks and high protein drinks. With this category, FrieslandCampina becomes a supplier to other manufacturers, rather than a product manufacturer distributing to supermarkets.

International Expansion at FrieslandCampina

One of the most important undertakings at FrieslandCampina in the past two decades was to expand beyond the Netherlands. In its first expansion effort, the company bought Belgium's Comelco, another dairy cooperative. In Belgium, the company boasts the Joyvalle dairy products and milk brand and the Passendale, Père Joseph, and Wynendale cheese brands, all marketed under the FrieslandCampina umbrella brand.

FrieslandCampina expanded into Germany, purchasing a number of cooperatives: Sudmilch (southern Germany), Tuffi (western Germany), and Emzett (Berlin). In Germany, its primary brand is Landliebe; here, the company sells Landliebe milk, cream, yogurts (seasonal, fruit, and plain, in different types of containers); different types of puddings, including rice pudding, ice cream, cheese, and qwark (a uniquely flavored creamy cheese) plain or with fruit; yogurt drinks (with fruit flavors such as banana, cherry, lemon, peach, and orange); and different milk drinks with flavors such as vanilla and chocolate. The company also offers products such as coffee machines, cups, and spoons, for purchase online at its site, www.landliebe-online.de.

As a result of these acquisitions and mergers, FrieslandCampina is the market leader in the Netherlans, Germany, and Belgium. The company is further expanding in the European Union and in other international markets. Currently, it produces, among others, liquid milk and drinks in Belgium, Germany, the Netherlands, Russia, Thailand, and Vietnam; yogurt and desserts in Germany, the Netherlands, and Russia; cheese and butter in Belgium, Germany, and the Netherlands; ingredients for the international food and pharmaceutical industries in Belgium, Germany, the Netherlands, and the United States; cream liqueurs in the Netherlands; and baby-animal feed in the Netherlands. It has sales organizations for consumer products in Belgium, Germany, the Netherlands, Russia, the United Kingdom, Spain, Greece, Thailand, and Vietnam. Its sales organizations for industrial products are in the Netherlands, Denmark, Poland, the United Kingdom, Spain, United States, Argentina, India, China, and Japan.

Sources: www.FrieslandCampina.com (accessed on May 12, 2012); www.prnewswire.co.uk/cgi/news/release?id=197343, May 2006; "An Overview of the World's Largest Functional Foods Companies," *Just Food*, July 2006, pp. 6–22; Arno Mathis, "Corporate Social Responsibility and Policy Making: What Role Does Communication Play?" *Business Strategy and the Environment*, Vol. 16, No. 5, July 2007, p. 366; Sarah McRitchie, "Europe Shrinks to Expand," *Dairy Foods,* Vol. 100, No. 1, January 1999, pp. 75–79; Donna Berry, "Global Market Basket," *Dairy Foods*, September 2005, Vol. 106, No. 9, September 2005, pp. 32–36.

Analysis Suggestions:

1.   Perform a broad product mix analysis for FrieslandCampina. Calculate product width by examining *only* the product categories that the company carries.

2.   Comment on the product consistency across the different product lines. Is product consistency important for a dairy company? What do all the lines have in common—in addition to FrieslandCampina ownership?

3.   Look at the main Dutch brands on the Campina website. Click on some of them and look at their history. Click also on Napolact, a Transylvanian dairy in Romania. How is it different from the rest of the FrieslandCampina portfolio, and how is it similar?

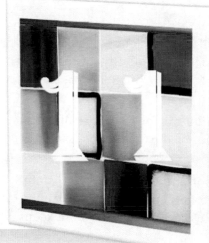

Chapter 11: Managing International Distribution Operations and Logistics

Learning Objectives

After studying this chapter, you should be able to:

- Describe the functions of home-country and host-country intermediaries involved in international distribution.

- Identify the different facilitators of international distribution and logistics and describe their involvement in the international distribution process.

- Address the challenges encountered by distribution in countries of different development levels.

International distribution channels link manufacturers and final international consumers. Internationally, distribution channels vary greatly from one region to another and from one market to another. For most markets, consumer product channels of distribution tend to be longer than industrial product channels. Beyond this general trait, however, channel characteristics differ worldwide. The following are examples of such differences:

• In Japan, there are many more levels of distributors for consumer products than in most other countries, whereas, for most industrial goods, the large trading companies deal directly with retailers.

• In economies where the state plays an important role in business, state-owned enterprises may act as massive distributors that frequently carry unrelated products. In these countries, China and Russia included, the state keeps a close oversight of distribution activities.

• In emerging markets and low-income countries, network marketing is rapidly becoming a popular channel of distribution.

This chapter addresses all the aspects of managing international distribution, offering an overview of the different intermediaries involved in the international distribution process, the facilitators involved in international distribution and logistics, and the challenges facing the distribution process.

11-1 Issues Related to International Distribution

Some international markets have an underdeveloped distribution system for many industrial sectors and, to a lesser extent, for consumer goods. Distribution to these markets may be opportunistic and not adequately organized, or distribution channels may not exist at all. Alternatively, the complex structure of certain international channels may serve as a barrier to multinational company entry in an international market new to the company. The company first must determine whether it can use established channels or build its own.

11-1a Using Established Channels

Entering a new market can be problematic for companies. In most cases, competitors already have a hold on existing channels and are thus likely to *block* them for new entrants. In addition to competitors, there are other obstacles to using **established channels.** For example, the amount charged by distributors could be so high that the company may be unwilling to use them. This was the case for Kraft Foods in its attempt to enter the Hong Kong market with its products.

> **established channels**
> Distribution channels that already exist in a particular market.

The initial channel selection decision is important. Once in a channel relationship, a company may be bound to that relationship and may not legally be allowed to change distributors.

Kraft: Successfully Navigating Blocked Channels

Kraft used to team up only with the biggest logistics company in each region. However, in Hong Kong, in the mid-1990s, the leading distributors charged an exorbitant amount to distribute Kraft products. At first, the company refused to pay the price, and the distribution structure at the time blocked their access into the market. Years later, Kraft yielded, deciding to use the same overpriced distributors to sell its Kraft brand in Hong Kong and then China—for a few years longer, according to Bill Campbell, former Philip Morris chief executive officer (Kraft was a Philip Morris company at the time).

Kraft entered mainland China in the mid-1990s by setting up two joint ventures: Kraft Tianmei Foods in the northern city of Tianjin, which makes Tang, a fruit-flavored instant drink mix, and Sugus fruit-flavored chews; and Kraft Guangtong Food in the southern province of Guangdong, producing Maxwell House coffee. When entering these markets, Kraft, as usual, teamed up with the largest logistics companies, but changed its strategy after sometimes experiencing delays in its orders. In 2005, under its pledge to the World Trade Organization, China opened its logistics sector to foreign competition. However, Kraft's current distribution operations continue to be handled by Chinese or joint ventures.[1]

11-1b Building Own Channels

Although **building channels** is expensive, this strategy is especially necessary in situations in which no channels exist at all or no channels conform to the needs of the company. The example of Coca-Cola in Eastern Europe after the fall of communism is a case in point. Although Pepsi had been present in the region since the late 1960s, Coke did not enter many of the countries until the 1990s. When Coca-Cola decided to enter this market, it found old state-enterprise-owned channels selling beverages and operating with low efficiency. Consequently, it decided to create its own channels of distribution that fit well with the market structure by working with independent truck drivers who had some experience working with soft-drink retailers.

11-2 Intermediaries Involved in International Distribution

Depending on company involvement in a particular market, a company can use home-country intermediaries or host-country intermediaries. A company that uses intermediaries in its own home country is likely not to be as involved in managing the marketing mix in the country where the target market is located. **Home-country intermediaries** typically provide all marketing services for firms that do not wish to enter the foreign market or do not have the capability to do so. Companies relying on home-country intermediaries relinquish their control of the marketing mix to their distributors in the target-market foreign country.

A company using intermediaries in the host country is likely to have a presence there, in the form of a sales office, at the lowest level of direct international involvement, or in the form of a wholly owned subsidiary, at the highest level of direct international involvement. The company, by using host-country intermediaries, also seeks to have a greater degree of control of the marketing mix in the target-market foreign country.

11-2a Home-Country Intermediaries

Export Management Companies

Export management companies are highly specialized in certain industries, such as endoscopic surgery instruments or networking products, and typically represent smaller companies in a region of the country. Some of their activities include researching the international market, representing a company at trade shows and exhibitions, screening and selecting international distributors, shipping the company's product, and handling all the necessary export documentation, such as customs forms and export licensing. An example of such a firm is Amex, Inc., a company based in Minneapolis, Minnesota, that offers export trading services for Midwestern technology companies.

> **building channels**
> Creating new distribution channels, especially necessary in situations where there are no channels at all, or there are no channels that conform to the needs of the company.
>
> **home-country intermediaries**
> Intermediaries in the home country.
>
> **export management companies**
> Companies specializing in the export function for client companies in a particular industry.

Amex, Inc.

An established export management company, Amex, Inc., offers export trading services to high-tech network, computer, and medical diagnostic device manufacturers from the Midwest. It, essentially, works as the outsourced international department of these exporting firms and manages all the export functions for them. The company markets the clients' products using a professional sales force and established distribution networks, handling all export licensing and regulatory approvals, and taking title and assuming foreign credit risk—thus eliminating the costs of managing complex international credit and collections.

Its clients are manufacturers of data communication products, networking products, medical and medical electronic products, and telecommunications products in the Midwestern United States.[2]

Firms such as Amex, Inc. typically work as a company's export department. In the United States, the Office of Trading Company Affairs in the U.S. Department of Commerce can help companies identify the appropriate export management company for the companies' target country.

Trading Companies

The Japanese Model

Japanese **trading companies** (also known as **sogo-shoshas**) existed for more than four centuries, when the House of Mitsui was created, soon followed by Mitsubishi and Sumitomo. As Japan was short on natural resources, it was heavily dependent on foreign markets for necessities and had no foreign exchange to pay for them. As a result, they specialized in the movement of goods. Currently, Japanese general trading companies account for about 10 percent of world export trade, and their operations range across finance, distribution, technology, mining, oil and gas exploration, and information. Over time, they have changed from pure traders to more financially sophisticated investment holding companies. Their basic functions are to serve as an intermediary for all marketing and import and export transactions and to perform financial intermediary activities and information gathering. Today, they also perform logistical and warehousing services and are involved in trading and distribution, management consulting, manufacturing, risk-hedging to deal with exchange rate and price fluctuations, domestic and overseas importing and exporting of technology, and joint ventures to develop foreign industrial markets. They act as intermediaries for half of Japan's exports and two thirds of its imports.[3]

The biggest and the best of the traders are members of **keiretsus,** which are families of firms with interlocking stakes in one another. Here, the trading companies' role is to act as the eyes and ears of the whole group, spotting business trends, market gaps, and investment opportunities. The top sogo-shoshas, or general trading companies, are Itochu Corp., Sumitomo, Marubeni, Mitsui, and Mitsubishi.[4]

Japanese export trading companies are presently facing competition from companies in every domain of their activity. They are also increasingly facing competition from manufacturers, who are setting up their own distribution networks. As a result, they are handling a smaller proportion of Japan's exports. On the other hand, their other domains of activity help them maintain a prominent profile across industries.

The U.S. Model

In the United States, export trading companies are, primarily, consortia of smaller suppliers, service-oriented firms, multinational corporations, and quasi-public organizations or public entities.[5] In 1982, the U.S. Congress passed the **Export Trading Company (ETC) Act** to encourage the formation of export trading companies to promote U.S. exports and to facilitate the formation of export intermediaries.

trading companies
Large companies that specialize in providing intermediary services, risk reduction through extensive information channels, and significant financial assistance to manufacturing firms.

sogo-shosha
A large Japanese trading company that specializes in providing intermediary services, risk reduction through extensive information channels, and significant financial assistance to manufacturing firms.

keiretsu
A Japanese trading firm that consists of families of firms with interlocking stakes in one another.

Export Trading Company (ETC) Act
Legislation, passed in 1982, that encourages the formation of export trading companies by competing firms to promote U.S. exports without violating antitrust regulation.

The U.S. Export Trading Company Act

The Act expected small and medium-sized firms to join an export trading company with a bank to provide major financing. The Act relieved some of the restrictions placed on U.S. companies by the antitrust laws. It also created the Export-Import Bank (Eximbank), an independent U.S. government agency whose purpose is to guarantee loans to export trading companies. Each year approximately 100 such guarantees are provided by the Eximbank. The loan guarantees range anywhere between $10,000 and $25 million. The Eximbank usually provides a repayment guarantee of 90 percent of the loan value. In most cases, the terms of the loan are 12 months.

In response to the ETC Act, in 1982, Sears formed its Sears World Trade Organization, intending to export and import trade with low-income countries, and General Electric also established a trading company. Both failed and agreed that it was due to the lack of expertise and qualified managers in trading. Moreover, the Act limited U.S. trading companies to exports, which limited in turn their viability, and the administrative burdens of obtaining certification created too many hurdles for the firms to follow. Among the U.S. trading companies that registered some success are Cyrus Eaton World Trade, which is involved in many ventures, including financing, marketing of countertrade products and services, working out contracts, and handling products such as agricultural items, beverages, petroleum, natural gas, metal ores, chemicals, fertilizer, pulp, paper, rubber, building materials, textiles and apparel; the Coca-Cola Trading Company; the Rockwell International Trading Company, which assists Rockwell divisions in negotiating and implementing offset and countertrade programs; and the Caterpillar World Trading Company, which finances exports of CAT equipment through counterpurchase of minerals, agricultural commodities, and raw materials.[5]

The Office of Trading Company Affairs in the U.S. Department of Commerce can help companies identify the appropriate export trading or export management company for the company's target country as is shown in see International Marketing Illustration 11-1.

International Marketing Illustration 11-1
Aiding Export Joint Ventures: The Office of Trading Company Affairs

For companies interested in partnering with competitors to export internationally, the Office of Trading Company Affairs can provide help. Under Title III of the Export Trading Company Act, any U.S. resident, business association, group of firms, or state or local government entity may apply to this office for a Certificate of Review. The certificate provides antitrust preclearance for the export activities of the certificate holder, essentially minimizing the application of U.S. antitrust laws to export activities and the related risk of expensive antitrust litigation. The Certificate of Review provides exporters with immunity from both government antitrust suits and with procedural advantages in private antitrust suits. The Export Trade Certificate of Review application is a free and quick process: The Department of Commerce determines whether the Certificate meets the certification standards contained in the Export Trading Company Act, obtains the concurrence of the Department of Justice, and then issues the final Certificate within 90 days.

Some of the activities that could receive the Export Trade Certificates of Review are joint establishment of export prices; exclusive agreements with domestic suppliers and foreign representatives; joint export marketing/selling arrangements among domestic competitors; allocation of export markets, territories, or customers; refusals to deal; exchanges of business information; and the joint licensing of technology.

Among the competitive advantages offered by export joint ventures are economies of scale and spreading of risk among the participating firms, which benefits most small and medium-sized enterprises that may be new to exporting or may have limited exporting experience.

Examples of partnerships may take place in the areas of:

- Market research
- Market development, reducing the individual costs of attending trade shows or trade missions, and sharing the cost of generic advertising
- Overseas joint bidding
- Transportation and shipping, thus negotiating volume discount and guaranteeing carriers sufficient cargo
- Establishment of uniform minimum export prices to avoid price rivalry with each other
- Service and promotional activities

In one example, an Export Trade Certificate of Review was awarded to Florida Citrus Exports of Vero Beach, Florida. Florida Citrus Exports operates as an export service umbrella for its nine members, including grower-owned cooperatives and packing houses, sharing transportation and market development costs, engaging in joint promotion, preparing joint bids, assisting each other in maintaining quality standards, and spreading the risk of international involvement. In another example, the Export Trade Certificate of Review allows the American Film Export Association of Los Angeles, California, to engage in international licensing agreements and create financing documents that are the standard for the independent film and TV industry. It permits the organization to produce a membership sales survey to measure the licensing of motion picture and television products in 33 territories. It also facilitates the sharing of credit data on more than 500 film and television buyers from 56 countries.

In an example of facilitation, the American Film Export Association ran a Regional Market in Bangkok, Thailand, which opened opportunities for U.S. film companies to enter Vietnam, where cinema representatives were eager for the companies' business and were especially interested in learning how best to fight piracy. In another example, the American Film Export Association performed a study that found that countries such as Australia, France, Germany, Italy, Japan, Taiwan, Spain, and the United Kingdom can each provide revenues of $50,000 to $200,000 in theater, video, television, cable, and satellite markets.

Sources: www.filmfestivals.com/afm/afnewb4.htm; www.mothermuse.com/markets.htm; www.ita.doc.gov/td/sif/office_of_export_trading_company.htm (accessed on May 16, 2012).

Home-Country Brokers and Agents

Home-country **brokers and agents** bring international buyers and sellers together in the company's home country and do not carry title to the product. They can handle different export functions and specialize in certain product categories.

Alternatively, they may represent a certain manufacturer on a commission basis for a particular deal; they are known as **manufacturer's export agents.** Or they may be buyers located in the firm's home country, representing different firms located abroad; in this case, they are known as **buying offices.**

Cooperative Export Arrangements

Cooperative export arrangements, also referred to as piggybacking or mother henning, involve exporters agreeing to handle export functions for unrelated companies on a contractual basis. Generally, cooperative exporters are large multinationals with substantial in-house know-how and resources, as well as extensive knowledge of international markets. The piggybacked products are noncompetitive with the cooperative exporter's own products but may be, nevertheless, similar; an example is an auto manufacturer in the United States who agrees to market tires or seat covers for a much smaller company that is new to international marketing.[7]

Two types of firms are generally involved in cooperative export arrangements: **complementary export agents** and **complementary export merchants.** Complementary export agents export complementary products. This category includes individual firms exporting other firms' products that are complementary to their offerings (along with their own products). If these firms carry the other firms' products for a fee/commission, they act as complementary export agents. If, instead of operating on a fee/commission, the firms actually take title to the complementary products distributed and are compensated in the form of a discount in a buy-sell arrangement,[8] they act as complementary export merchants.

Webb-Pomerene Associations of Exporters

Webb-Pomerene Associations, established under the Webb-Pomerene Act, also are involved in cooperative exporting. Webb-Pomerene Associations are

---

brokers and agents
Intermediaries who bring international buyers and sellers together; they do not carry title to the product.

manufacturer's export agents
Agents in the firm's home country handling the exporting function of a certain manufacturer on a commission, per deal, basis.

buying offices
Buyers representing different firms located abroad.

cooperative export arrangements
Agreements that involve the use of a distribution system of exporters with established systems of selling abroad, who agree to handle the export function of a noncompeting (but not necessarily unrelated) company on a contractual basis; also called mother henning or piggybacking.

complementary export agents
Firms that export other firms' products that are complementary to their offerings, along with their own products, for a fee/commission.

export merchants
Intermediaries who take title to and possession of the products they carry; they are responsible for shipping and marketing the products to the target market.

composed of competing companies that join resources and efforts to export internationally. The companies are granted immunity from antitrust prosecution under the Webb-Pomerene Act so that they can export products manufactured in the United States to compete effectively internationally, especially in world markets in which cartels are active. Examples of Webb-Pomerene Associations under Webb-Pomerene Act filings with the Federal Trade Commission in 2010 are the American Cotton Exporters Association, American Natural Soda Ash Corporation, American-European Soda Ash Shipping Association, Inc., Phosphate Chemicals Export Association, Inc., Overseas Distribution Solutions, LLC, and Specialty Crop Trade Council.[9]

Tax Incentive-Based Structures for Internationalism

For decades, the Foreign Sales Corporation (FSC) has been an important instrument for internationalization, but that is likely to come to an end. The FSC was initially set up as a sales corporation overseas. Establishing an FSC allowed for a portion of a U.S. tax-paying firm's foreign-source income to be exempt from U.S. income tax. To qualify for tax exemption, the FSC had to have a foreign presence, meeting certain management requirements and certain economic process requirements with regard to both the extent and nature of the sales activities undertaken abroad; and incurring abroad a minimum level of direct costs in sales activities, in areas such as marketing, advertising, and order processing.[10] After the World Trade Organization found the FSC to essentially constitute an illegal export subsidy, which saved U.S. companies about US$5 billion per year, the Extra Territorial Income (ETI) Act was instituted to replace the FSC. The ETI Act, however, did not modify the export subsidy scheme, and, consequently, the European Union (EU) challenged it before the World Trade Organization (WTO). Four years later, in March 2004, the EU imposed countermeasures consisting of customs duties of 5 percent on a list of U.S. products, followed by automatic, monthly increases by 1 percent up to a ceiling of 17 percent to be reached on March 1, 2005, if compliance had not happened. But, in May 2004, the U.S. Senate adopted the JOBS Act, a bill that repeals the FSC/ETI.

Yet, in spite of the repeal, the subsidies that U.S. business received under the FSC and its successor, the ETI, continue to be scrutinized by the WTO. The European Commission charged Boeing, the world's leading aerospace and defense group, for receiving subsidies from the United States totaling $23.7 million, in breach of WTO rules—in the biggest trade conflict ever handled by the WTO. The Commission claimed that this allowed Boeing to engage in aggressive pricing of its aircraft. In particular, the Commission claimed that Boeing received tax breaks, under the U.S. Foreign Sales Corporation and successor legislation, for an amount totaling $2.2 billion.[11]

Export Merchants

Export merchants are intermediaries who take title to and possession of the products they carry. They are responsible for shipping and marketing the products to the target market. In this sense, they have full control over the products' international marketing mix. Generally, they can carry competing brands. One type of export merchant is the *export jobber,* who carries primarily commodity goods but does not take physical possession of the products. Another type of export merchant is the **Norazi agent,** who deals in illegal and gray market products. This agent might deal in legitimate exporting, but, among the exported goods, the agent will also deal in arms, untaxed liquor, or items of contraband. The Norazi agent will also engage in exporting legitimate merchandise to countries where governments prohibit exports. See also Section 11-4b, "Parallel Imports," later in this chapter.

11-2b Foreign-Country Intermediaries

Foreign-country intermediaries can be placed in two broad categories: merchant middlemen, who take title to and possession of the products they carry, and agents and brokers, who bring buyers and sellers together but do not carry title to and take possession of the products they deal with.

Webb-Pomerene Associations
Associations of competing companies that are granted immunity from antitrust prosecution and that join resources and efforts to export internationally.

export merchants
Intermediaries who take title to and possession of the products they carry; they are responsible for shipping and marketing the products to the target market.

Norazi agent
An export agent dealing in illegal and gray market products.

foreign-country intermediaries
Intermediaries who help distribute products in a target foreign market.

Merchant Middlemen

Merchant middlemen are intermediaries who carry the manufacturer's product line in a particular country. They usually both carry title to and have physical possession of the products they distribute in the foreign target market. Companies often have close relationships with their international intermediaries; such relationships allow them to have control over their products' international marketing mix. Selecting one's intermediaries carefully is important because, in many markets, the relationship with a distributor might be difficult or impossible to dissolve. A particular type of merchant middleman in a foreign country is an **import jobber,** who usually purchases commodity goods from the manufacturer to sell to the trade (wholesaler, retailer, business-to-business client) in the target market. In addition, wholesalers, retailers, and industrial consumers may import products directly for resale. As such, they act as merchant middlemen.

Agents and Brokers

A company can select from many different types of agents and brokers in its foreign target market. An agent can represent the manufacturer exclusively in this market, acting thus as a **manufacturer's representative.** This individual usually works practically as the company's sales representative and is paid on a commission basis. The **managing agent,** often called the **comprador,** has an exclusive arrangement with the company, representing its operations in a particular country. This individual does not take title to the goods and is usually paid as a percentage of sales of the company he or she manages.

11-2c Alternative International Distribution Structures

One type of alternative distribution structure is **network marketing,** a mode of distributing goods using acquaintance networks. Network marketing companies are gaining access to emerging markets all over the world, and many continue to find potential in developed countries. Because network marketing serves primarily a retailing function—all distributorships engage in selling to the final consumer—this topic is addressed in Chapter 12, "International Retailing."

11-3 International Logistics

The international distribution function is supported by a number of service providers. Among them are distribution centers, transportation firms, home-country freight forwarders and customs brokers, government agencies, nongovernmental organizations, logistics alliances, and other firms. They are described in Sections 11-3a through 11-3c.

Logistics costs account for a large percentage of a company's gross revenues (between 10 and 30 percent) and for a large percentage of GDP (almost 10 percent in the United States), making logistics the single highest operating cost.[12] The largest percentage of multinationals' logistics costs is spent on transportation; thus, money saved in this area is likely to lead to lower prices for the end consumers.

The primary functions of international logistics are transportation, warehousing, inventory control, and order processing.

11-3a International Transportation

Transportation is important in international marketing. The choice of transportation determines whether products arrive at the international destination on time and in good condition. The cost of transportation is also essential because transportation costs can increase the product price in the target country. Important for transportation is the transportation infrastructure of the country where the company is doing business. Transportation networks are excellent in industrialized countries, with the countries easily accessible by rail, air, and water. Highly industrialized countries with water access have numerous sea and inland waterway ports that can handle cargo shipments efficiently. Emerging markets are also quickly developing their port facilities to handle the brisk traffic of cargo and passengers. See International Marketing Illustration 11-2.

International Marketing Illustration 11-2
Ports Facilitating Trade

The Port of Sète in southern France is one of many ports in France that offer international access to the French market and that allow French businesses to engage in international commerce. The port handles container vessels, conventional vessels, ferries, heavy lift ships, ocean-going barges and tugs, floating pontoons, livestock carriers, navy vessels, and military cargoes. It handles over three million metric tons of goods and hundreds of thousands of passengers. This port offers easy access to the rest of France via rail and truck. It also serves various developed local industries, among them seafood processing, wine and spirits, chemicals, building, clothing manufacturing, and aquaculture. The port is served by numerous shipping agents, freight forwarders, terminal operators, shipyard operators, naval services, and other logistics facilitators.

The Port of Sète also handles cruise vessels along the Mediterranean coast and from Bayonne to Dunkirk on the Atlantic, Channel, and North Sea range, to and from Morocco, and from Monaco to Sète, the latter a less-traveled destination that has much to offer.

Emerging markets are also developing their cargo and passenger facilities. There are still some complex geopolitical issues that affect transportation. For example, Kaliningrad Oblast is a Russian Federation enclave located between Lithuania and Poland where many Western companies manufacture products for tax-free shipping to Russia. Cadillac manufactures luxury sedans there since 2011 and BMW has made its 3 and 5 Series models there since 2007. The Russian government plans to turn the area into the Russian Hong Kong.

The Port of Kaliningrad on the Baltic Sea is huge and of strategic importance when it comes to trade with the Russian Federation. LukOil, Russia's main petrol company, even has its own terminal in the port, loading tankers going to different international destinations. However, there is one factor that could potentially be problematic if there is any regional discord: shipments to and from mainland Russia have to pass through Lithuania and Belarus (see Figure 11-1).

In other examples, the Port of Tallinn, in Estonia, has several harbors, some handling containers and solid bulk goods, such as coal, and liquid bulk goods, and some handling loads of passengers on day trips or cruise trips to St. Petersburg, Russia, Helsinki, Finland, and Stockholm, Sweden. The Port of Saint-Petersburg, in the Russian Federation, is the largest port in North-West of Russia and one of the oldest — it is the famous Port of Leningrad of the communist era, shipping dry goods to the rest of the European continent, and welcoming tours from the West for a rare glimpse of majestic art beyond its rigid iron curtain.

The Port of Istanbul, Turkey, has been a bridge and a barrier for cultures, religions, and imperial powers for over 2,500 years. It is the region's largest port with annual cargo surpassing six million metric tons and it can handle 1,200 vessels a year. The port has excellent railway and truck access facilities. See Figure 11-2.

Sources: www.sete.port.fr/; www.agenatramp.fr/index.htm; www.portoftallinn.com; www.worldportsource.com/ports/TUR_Port_of_Istanbul_3090.php; www.en.seaport.spb.ru (accessed on May 18, 2012).

Figure 11-1: *This cargo, photographed 10 miles from Vilnius, Lithuania, is traveling from Kaliningrad to mainland Russia. Good relations between Lithuania and the Russian Federation are important to be able to maintain cheap rail access as a transportation venue for products made in the enclave of Kaliningrad.*

Figure 11-2: *Port of Istanbul, a busy destination for cargo and passengers.*

Transportation firms are key players in international distribution, especially firms that can handle intermodal transportation, using two or more different transportation modes (truck, rail, ship [inland and sea/ocean shipping]). Intermodal transportation has been greatly facilitated by containerization. For example, goods can be placed into containers at the factory, taken by truck to a train-loading facility, transported to a port, and loaded aboard a ship. After crossing the ocean, the containers are loaded on a truck and transported to their final destination. All these maneuvers can be accomplished using the initial containers—thus providing a greater protection for the products, which do not have to be shifted individually from one vessel to another—at lower cost because loading the individual products from/into vehicles is more expensive than using containers. Table 11-1 offers information on the value of U.S. international merchandise trade by mode of transportation. Note that access for most of the imports and exports into the United States, in terms of dollar amounts, is by water.

Table 11-1:

Value of U.S. International Merchandise Trade by Mode of Transportation
(in millions of US Dollars)

	1990	2010
Total merchandise trade	889,004	3,189,596
Exports	392,976	1,277,504
Imports	496,028	1,912,092
Air, total trade	201,383	836,953
Exports	110,471	392,634
Imports	90,912	444,319
Water, total trade	434,233	1,434,259
Exports	150,827	455,460
Imports	283,406	978,799
Road, total trade	N	556,884
Exports	N	284,698
Imports	N	272,186
Rail, total trade	N	131,228
Exports	N	45,748
Imports	N	85,480
Pipeline, total trade	N	62,933
Exports	N	5,189
Imports	N	57,744
Other, total trade	N	167,337
Exports	N	93,774
Imports	N	73,564

N = Data are nonexistent

Sources: U.S. Department of Transportation, Bureau of Transportation Statistics, *Pocket Guide to Transportation*, International Merchandise Trade, 2012, http://nats.sct.gob.mx/nats/sys/tables.jsp?id=19&i=3.

The different transportation modes offer advantages and disadvantages in terms of flexibility, cost, and speed. Table 11-2 summarizes the flexibility, cost, and speed characteristics of each mode of transportation.

Table 11-2: Flexibility, Cost, and Speed Characteristics of Each Mode of Transportation				
Mode	Flexibility (in Terms of Area coverage)	Cost	Speed	Product Examples
Truck	High	Higher	Higher	Consumer goods, perishables, automobiles
Rail	Medium	Medium	Lower	Coal, gasoline, forestry products, grains, automobiles
Air	High	High	Highest	Jewelry, electronics, expensive low-volume products
Water	Low	Low	Low	Grains, gasoline, forestry products, cement and fertilizers
Pipeline	Low	Lower	Low	Oil and gasoline, chemicals, semi-liquid coal, refined products

Tankers, barges, and other freighters in the sea and inland waterways account for a substantial proportion of international traffic. Waterways are used for transporting over long distances high-weight, high-volume products that have a low per pound value, such as grains, gasoline, forestry products, cement, and fertilizers. Refer to International Marketing Illustration 11-2 earlier in this section, which offers a discussion of the Port of Sète.

Railways remain the primary mode for intracontinental freight transportation. Cargo that has a high-weight, high-volume, and low per pound value are transported by rail, with some exceptions. Examples of rail cargo are coal, gasoline, forestry products, and grains. Higher value products, such as equipment and automobiles, may also be transported by train. Railways are a low-cost, low-speed mode of transportation, and mobility is restricted to designated areas for freight handling.

Truck transportation handles smaller shipments over shorter distances. Much of the local transportation—within cities, for example—is handled by trucks, which offer high flexibility at competitive rates. Often, trucks transport products carried by ship and rail to the final product destination. Trucks may have refrigeration and processing capabilities, which allow them to carry a variety of products, such as consumer

Figure 11-3: In Europe, trucks are found in rest areas on the highways, or parked outside of the city centers on the weekends, as they are not allowed on the highways.

goods, perishables, and automobiles. Trucks offer high flexibility and competitive rates in Europe; however, a company should not expect delivery over the weekend even to key clients: In many countries, trucks are not allowed to drive on highways on Sundays (see Figure 11-3).

Air freight is used for products that are low-volume and low-weight but high-value, such as jewelry and electronics. They are also used in situations in which handling documents or materials expeditiously is essential.

Pipelines provide a low-cost mode of transporting liquid or semi-liquid products from the source to the target market in a continuous manner, where there are no interruptions (unless interruptions are voluntary), and where intermediate storage is not necessary. Examples of pipelines are Basin, Bonito, and Capline for offshore and onshore crude oil; Harbor System and Wolverine Line for refined products; and the large, remote, and technically difficult pipeline, the Trans-Alaska Pipeline,[13] a feat of engineering running from northern to southern Alaska across rough terrains and performing well in extreme weather conditions, transporting more than 1.4 million barrels of crude oil daily. Pipelines are typically owned by the producer or by joint ventures, and they are expensive to maintain.[14]

Pipelines encounter many challenges. Brazil needs more energy sources to meet its energy needs, and the Amazon jungle has huge oil and gas reserves. Petrobras, Brazil's state-controlled oil company, invested more than $7 billion in Amazon exploration, finding important resources there in 1986. But only now, after overcoming geographic, logistic, environmental, and political challenges, is it able to build the pipelines. The first pipeline carries gas more than 400 miles, from the Amazon jungle to the city of Manaus, a large port city at the junction of Brazil's largest two rivers. Petrobras worked extensively to make this possible; but even now, it faces challenges. Its reputation tarnished after oil pipeline leaks and the collapse of an offshore drilling platform elsewhere in the country, the company still managed to woo its fellow citizens. It offered promises of economic benefits and it consulted scientists and environmentalists on how to minimize damage to the jungle, which alone covers a territory as large as Britain, France, Germany, and Italy put together. A second pipeline, going in a southern direction for more than 300 miles, to Porto Velho, faces challenges not only from environmentalists, but also from indigenous people, as it crosses Indian lands. It is also competing for government money with two large dams. The difficulties faced by Petrobras do not bode well for Venezuela's ambition to build a 5,000 mile north-south pipeline from Caracas, Venezuela, to Buenos Aires, Argentina, a plan also conceived with the intention to bring South America together.[15]

11-3b Logistics Facilitators

Moving goods from the place of origin, normally a manufacturer, to the place of sale, normally the retailer, requires some type of facilitation. The two most common logistics facilitators are distribution centers and freight forwarders, but governmental and nongovernmental organizations handle similar functions as well.

Distribution centers are designed to speed up warehousing and delivery by channeling operations to one center (hub) that is particularly well equipped to handle the distribution of products to their destination. This function is becoming a popular choice of multinational firms that have to efficiently warehouse and distribute their goods in target markets situated thousands of miles from their home country. Certain locations have become important players as hubs to a number of multinational firms. For example, Singapore is a leading regional and international logistics hub and host to virtually every major logistics player; logistics account for about seven percent of Singapore's gross domestic product.[16]

Freight forwarders and customs brokers arrange for transportation, customs clearance, and document filing for products exported abroad. Often, they specialize in geographic locations or other areas of expertise, such as commodities, for example, flowers, seafood, and other types of perishable products. Many freight forwarders are adapting to fit the needs of their corporate consumers, pursuing different value-added techniques, such as developing distinctive competencies in terms of geography, type of business, or specific commodities. For example, Kuehne & Nagle (www.kuehne-nagel.com) is well respected for its ability to expertly handle museum art and valuable exhibition material. The company has also developed expertise with respect to arranging trade fairs and art exhibits, as well as aid and relief for developing countries. Another freight forwarder, DHL (www.dhl.com), has particular expertise in shipping for several industry sectors, including health care, fashion, electronics, and live animals, including 15 5-foot-long jellyfish.[17]

The Internet poses the greatest threat to freight forwarders and customs brokers because it provides a venue for importers to use dot-com companies to arrange for transportation, customs clearance, document filing, and other activities. Moreover, the Department of Commerce, the U.S. Customs Service, and the WTO have rulings, forms, and other useful documentation posted on the web.[18]

Today, customers ask more of freight forwarders – they are required to keep their inventory for them at sea or in the air, and customers want to be able to track their packages every minute of the day. Moreover, forwarders are often the ones who are taken to task if the shipment is late, which happens often in the United States, ever since the terrorist attacks of September 11, 2001. European companies, in particular, have a difficult time understanding the situation. America is at war and security is a top priority, with customers being a second priority. Customers now have to pay demurrage charges for delays caused by inspections that can be performed by Customs, FBI, the Drug Enforcement Agency, and they potentially can face delays of up to 15 days, and demurrage charges can be as much as $10,000 per container.[19]

In many countries, governments are directly involved in the international distribution process. Often, private distributors are not permitted by law to engage in any type of direct international transaction. This is the case for many developing countries and countries where national currencies are under strict control. Government involvement in distribution and logistics processes is not limited to developing countries. In many developed countries, the governments are involved in the following processes:

- As promoters of national security interests and national regulations
- As promoters of international involvement of firms, particularly of small and medium-sized businesses
- As financing and insurance providers for higher-risk international ventures

In the United States, international distribution and logistics involvement are shared by a number of different government agencies—most of which are affiliated with the U.S. Department of Commerce (http://home.doc.gov):

- The International Trade Administration in the U.S. Department of Commerce offers export assistance to international firms and to small to medium-sized businesses. It offers trade education, mentoring programs for exporters (assistance from an experienced exporter), access to a market research database, country analysis information, and economic data, as well as business counseling in the form of expert assistance from trade specialists. It also helps firms with export documentation (applications, licenses, declarations, etc.).

- The Bureau of Export Administration in the U.S. Department of Commerce advances U.S. national security, foreign policy, and economic interests by regulating exports of products and technologies that could affect those interests. This agency regulates exports of products such as high-platform computers and weapons, and imposes sanctions against certain countries (such as Burma, Cuba, North Korea, and Iran); it enforces compliance with those regulations and cooperates with other nations in monitoring the trade of sensitive goods.

- The U.S. Commercial Service promotes and protects small and medium-sized U.S. business interests in key export markets. It operates Export Assistance Centers, which offer companies a range of export facilitation services.

- The Export-Import Bank of the United States (Exim Bank) is an independent government agency that aids the financing of international sales of U.S. products and services. It guarantees loans and makes loans to international buyers of U.S. goods; it also insures many business ventures that international or local banks will not insure due to their high risk. The Exim Bank does not compete with commercial lenders and insurance firms.

- The United States Trade and Development Agency creates jobs for Americans by helping U.S. companies pursue overseas business opportunities. Although not directly involved in distribution and logistics, this agency funds feasibility studies, training, business workshops, and technical assistance aimed at infrastructure and industrial projects in developing countries, covering the cost of logistics and distribution.

Equivalent structures exist in most other countries, typically housed under the Ministry of Foreign Trade (the equivalent of the Department of Commerce in the United States).

In addition to country-specific agencies, international bodies could facilitate distribution and logistics. One example is the International Chamber of Commerce (ICC), a business organization that represents enterprises from all sectors in every part of the world engaging in international business. The ICC makes voluntary rules that govern the conduct of business across borders, and it provides important services, such as the ICC International Court of Arbitration, the world's leading arbitral institution.

Among other service providers are banks and insurance agencies financing and insuring international distribution transactions, marketing research firms providing information on the target markets and trade, and various types of consultants that specialize in facilitating international distribution and logistics activities.

logistics alliances
Distribution alliances between two firms involving product transportation and warehousing.

In the process of setting up a firm's distribution activity in the target market, the firm needs to set up successful logistics relationships. Many **logistics alliances** in Europe have been successful and are characterized by an atmosphere of openness between the customer and the provider, mutual trust, and a clear line of communication. Successful logistics alliances typically are formed using the following steps:[20]

1. Establish objectives and selection criteria. Because choosing a logistics provider is a long-term decision, it is important to choose a partner that is likely to be a good match.

2. Identify qualified providers, with the help of consultants.

3. Express needs and wants. Here, issues such as integrating computer systems with that of the partner and other information-sharing needs should be expressed.

4. Evaluate bidders and select the partner, preferably after a site visit and interview.

5. Develop an integration plan. Because logistics involves many players, it is important to engage in system-wide integration.

6. Create a win-win relationship, based on continuous communication.

7. Measure and analyze performance.

8. Redefine goals and objectives.

11-3c Warehousing and Inventory Control

In international marketing, warehousing is of great importance. One of the critical decisions involves determining the number of warehouses and distribution centers needed to optimally implement the logistics function. In some countries, private warehouses, owned or leased by the company and operated by firms storing their own products, may be easy to come by and might provide more control and safety for the shipping firm than public warehouses. In other countries, public warehouses, used by firms that cannot afford to have their own facilities or that do not have a need for storage on a regular basis, represent a viable option: They are safe, have the necessary capacity, and are dependable in terms of other capabilities, such as refrigeration.

In most industrialized countries, distribution centers are an option for the international firm. They receive goods from different producers, take orders from buyers, and distribute them promptly.

Warehouses located in free trade zones or those warehouses that are themselves customs privileged facilities are typically also facilities where product assembly and packaging may be conducted.

Worldwide, companies are attempting to address customer demand while reducing inventory costs. Multinational firms adopt a just-in-time inventory system where this is possible, reducing inventory by ordering products often and in lower quantity, creating product flow rather than stock. Also, where possible, all intermediaries use the Universal Product Code (UPC), which links suppliers' and customers' inventory systems through electronic data interchange, facilitating the flow of products. Both of these approaches aimed at reducing storage costs are widely adopted in developed countries. In developing countries, multinationals tend to adopt them, spending large sums to link suppliers to their own systems.

11-4 Challenges to International Distribution and Logistics

Firms selling across borders encounter numerous challenges. The two most cited challenges are distribution in developing countries and parallel imports.

11-4a Challenges to Distribution in Developing Countries

One challenge faced by multinationals distributing their products in developing countries is the transportation infrastructure. Dirt roads are often impassable when wet, and, in tropical climates, cool temperatures must be maintained to ensure the quality of perishable goods such as pharmaceuticals. Containerization also poses problems: Most of the ports in West Africa have shallow drafts and cannot handle larger vessels. Furthermore, unloading the products from the container may take weeks, or the container may be held indefinitely for customs inspection.[21]

11-4b Parallel Imports

Parallel imports are products purchased in a low-price market and diverted to other markets by means of a distribution system not authorized by the manufacturer; this is also known as a *gray market*. A low-price market is one where the products can be purchased for a lower price either because the company is in a competitive situation in which it must lower the price or because local taxes do not significantly increase the price of the products. Most often, however, gray market goods come from authorized dealers who are getting rid of excess inventory by selling the products to discounters. [22]

> **parallel imports**
> A distribution system not authorized by the manufacturer whereby the products purchased I n a low-price market are diverted to other markets; also called gray market.

The Netherlands, for example, is a low-price market for Similac, an infant formula manufactured by Abbott Laboratories. There, a 900-gram can of Similac sells for 6.99 euros, or $8.58 at the Etos, Kruidvat, and DA Drogist drug stores in 2012. A can of Similac weighing 658 grams sells in the United States for $22.99 at Target in the United States. The reasons Abbott Laboratories engages in the differential pricing of Similac may be numerous. First, it might be attempting to further penetrate the market: Although the product is well known in the United States, it is not popular in Europe. Second, it is priced just less than the other, local, competing products: The company might be using a penetration-pricing strategy. Third, the Dutch government might have required the company to sell at a lower price (unlikely, but possible). Consequently, the Netherlands constitutes a low-price market for Similac. If an entrepreneur decided to bring Similac from the Netherlands to sell it in the United States, he or she would be engaging in parallel imports. He or she would be selling the product on a gray market that is not authorized by the manufacturer – but would be doing something entirely legal. When such products are available for sale in the unintended market, parallel imports then compete with the manufacturer's products intended specifically for this market, cutting into profits.

Examples of gray markets abound, and "gray" businesses take advantage of price differences between different markets, buying products from low-tax areas and selling them in high-tax areas, for instance. Purchasing cigarettes from the state of Virginia, where cigarette taxes are low, and selling them in the European Union, where cigarette taxes are high, would create a pretty nice profit. It would also create unauthorized cross-border trade, which would be heavily scrutinized by EU authorities, who benefit from these taxes. Products with a long history of parallel imports are automobiles (Mercedes-Benz in the 1970s, before the company decided to engage in regional standardization), pharmaceuticals, and cigarettes.

Multinational corporations can choose from a number of alternative actions in the process of combating parallel imports (see Figure 11-4 on next page):

- *Charge similar prices worldwide*—If price differences are not substantial enough, there will not be a gray market. Although this strategy does not quite conform to the marketing concept—selling consumers products at prices they can afford and are willing to pay—it is, nevertheless, successful in preventing the success of a gray market for that particular brand.

- *Create products for low markets that are not as attractive or are not a perfect fit with an up-market*—Mercedes-Benz, after creating Mercedes USA, its subsidiary in the United States, attempted to create different automobiles for the European and the U.S. market. To the European consumers, Mercedes offers the A-Class, which is not available in the United States, and lower-level models that are too small to meet U.S. consumers' demands for comfort. The same level C-Class and E-Class are sold for comparable prices in the European and the U.S. markets.

- *Complicate the repair and servicing process for the gray market goods*—Individuals purchasing gray market Mercedes-Benz automobiles in the United States will find that, often, replacement parts for their automobiles must be ordered from Stuttgart, Germany, making the cost of maintenance prohibitive.

- *Inform consumers about the perils of buying gray market products*—Possible perils of gray market products might be that the product is new but technically outdated or that the product will not benefit from manufacturer warranties.

- *Litigate*—Unlike in the case of counterfeit products, litigating is often not possible in many of the integrated markets, such as the European Union, where the free movement of goods is guaranteed by law. Nevertheless, it is recommended that manufacturers keep up with the changing regulations to be able to take on unauthorized distribution when that is possible.[23] Frequently, loopholes in the national laws may allow parallel distribution, but states and localities may pass stringent gray market legislation; examples are Colorado, Michigan, and Georgia in the United States, which do not allow the importation of gray market cigarettes.

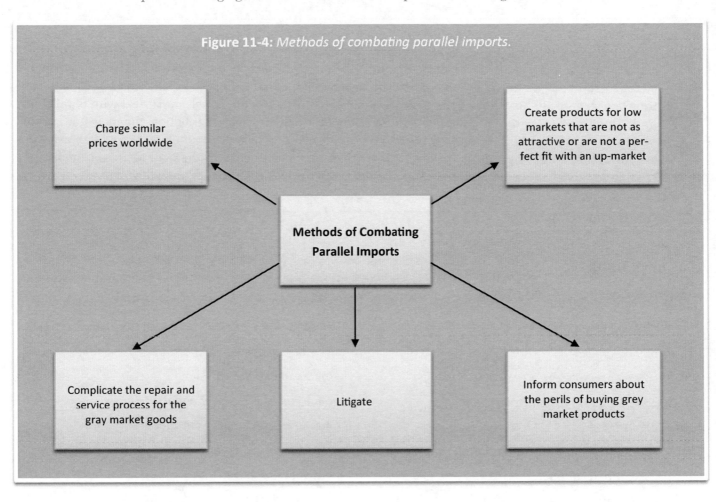

Figure 11-4: *Methods of combating parallel imports.*

Summary

Describe the functions of home-country and host-country intermediaries involved in international distribution. Examples of home-country intermediaries involved in international distribution are export management companies, which specialize in a particular industry; Japanese trading companies, whose operations range from distribution to manufacturing, mining, and technology, and U.S. trading companies, which are export consortia of small businesses; brokers and agents who do not carry titles and export merchants who carry titles to products; cooperative export arrangements, whereby exporters handle other firms' unrelated products on a contractual basis; Webb-Pomerene Associations, which allow competitors to join forces in exporting; and Foreign Sales Corporations, which allow for a portion of a firm's foreign income to be tax exempt. Foreign-country intermediaries involved in logistics are merchant middlemen, who carry title to and have possession of products, and agents and brokers, who do not.

Identify the different facilitators of international distribution and logistics and describe their involvement in the international distribution process. Among facilitators are distribution centers, which use a hub for efficient channeling of operations; transportation companies; freight forwarders and customs brokers, both in the home and the host country, who arrange for transportation, customs clearance, and export documentation; governmental and nongovernmental organizations, such as the International Trade Administration, the Bureau of Export Administration, the Export-Import Bank, and the International Chamber of Commerce, which promote and facilitate international involvement of companies.

Address the challenges encountered by distribution in countries of different development levels. Multinationals operating in developing countries often must face challenges related to the transportation infrastructure, containerization (e.g., ports with shallow drafts that cannot handle large vessels), and customs inspections. In both developed and developing countries, multinationals must deal with parallel imports (gray markets), from a low-price market to another market using distribution channels not authorized by the manufacturer. Increasingly, companies are combating such distribution by charging similar prices worldwide, creating products for low markets that are not attractive to the high market, complicating repair and service processes, informing consumers about buying such products, and litigating.

Key Terms

brokers and agents

building channels

buying offices

complementary export agents

complementary export merchants

comprador

cooperative export arrangements

established channels

export management companies

export merchants

Export Trading Company (ETC) Act

foreign-country intermediaries

home-country intermediaries

import jobber

keiretsu

logistics alliances

managing agent

manufacturer's export agents

manufacturer's representative

merchant middlemen

network marketing

Norazi agent

parallel imports

sogo-shosha

trading companies

Webb-Pomerene Associations

Discussion Questions

1.   Companies either can build new channels or use existing channels in new markets they plan to serve. What are the determinants of this choice? Explain.

2.   Who are the different distributors available in your home country? Who can distribute your products abroad?

3.   Who are the different distributors in your target market (host country)? Who can manage a company's distribution in the host country?

4.   How does the U.S. government help companies in the process of distributing their goods internationally?

5.   What types of distribution and logistics challenges do firms face in the process of going international?

Chapter Quiz

True/False

1. Using established channels can be costly for multinational firms, but paying the high price may also erect barriers to entry for competitors.

Answer: True

Rationale: Penetrating markets in China or Japan may mean doing business with the established channel members that dominate the market; the disadvantage of such channel relationships is cost, but the relationship also constitutes a barrier to entry for potential competitors. Coca-Cola and Kraft have benefited from their relationship with the most powerful channel members in these markets.

Section 11-1a, "Using Established Channels"

2. Home-country intermediaries are instrumental in providing all international marketing services for firms that otherwise would not be able to enter a foreign market.

Answer: True

Rationale: Companies relying on home-country intermediaries relinquish their control of the marketing mix to their distributors in the target foreign country. Home-country intermediaries provide all the necessary international marketing services for these firms.

Section 11-2, "Intermediaries Involved in International Distribution"

3. Buying offices are located in the target market country and carry title to the product.

Answer: False

Rationale: Buying offices consist of buyers located in the firm's home country, representing different firms located abroad.

Section 11-2a, "Home-Country Intermediaries"

4. Neither merchant middlemen nor agents and brokers carry title to products.

Answer: True

Rationale: Agents and brokers do not carry title to products. Merchant middlemen usually both carry title to and have physical possession of the products they distribute in the foreign target market.

Section 11-2b, "Foreign-Country Intermediaries"

5. Truck transportation handles larger shipments over longer distances.

Answer: False.

Rationale: Truck transportation handles smaller shipments over shorter distances. Most of the local transportation is handled by trucks, which offer high flexibility at competitive rates.

Section 11-3a, "International Transportation"

Multiple Choice

1. What services do Japanese trading companies offer their suppliers?

    a. Risk reduction

    b. Specialization in intermediary services

    c. Financial assistance

    d. All of the above

Answer: d is correct.

Rationale: Japanese trading companies offer their suppliers three primary services: specialization in providing intermediary services, risk reduction through extensive information channels, and significant financial assistance.

Section 11-2a, "Home-Country Intermediaries"

2. What aspect of international distribution and logistics is facilitated by containerization?

    a. Distribution research

    b. Freight forwarding

    c. Intermodal transportation

    d. Government agencies

Answer: c is correct.

Rationale: Intermodal transportation has been facilitated by the use of containers: Goods can be placed into containers, taken by truck to a train-loading facility, transported to a port, and loaded aboard a ship—all using the initial container, providing protection for the products at lower cost.

Section 11-3a, "International Transportation"

3. DHL uses hubs that hold products it delivers regularly so it always has them on hand. This is an example of what international distribution and logistics facilitator?

    a. Freight forwarders

    b. Distribution centers

    c. Transportation firms

    d. Government agencies

Answer: b is correct.

Rationale: Distribution centers are designed to speed up warehousing and delivery, by channeling operations to one center (hub) that is equipped to handle the distribution of products to their destination.

Section 11-3b, "Logistics Facilitators"

4. Which government agency offers export assistance to international firms and, in particular, to small to medium-sized businesses?

    a. U.S. Department of State

    b. Bureau of Export Administration

    c. U.S. Trade and Development Agency

d.   International Trade Administration

Answer: d is correct.

Rationale: The International Trade Administration in the U.S. Department of Commerce offers export assistance to international firms and, in particular, to small to medium-sized businesses.

Section 11-3b, "Logistics Facilitators"

5.   Which of the following constitutes a possible strategy to combat parallel imports?

a.   Charging similar prices worldwide

b.   Complicating the repair process for parallel imports

c.   Informing customers of problems when buying gray market products

d.   All of the above

Answer: d is correct.

Rationale: Possible perils of gray market products might be that the product is new but technically outdated or that the product will not benefit from manufacturer warranties; informing customers of such problems could deter them from purchasing. Similarly, charging the same prices in all markets and complicating the repair process for parallel imports could deter future buyers.

Section 11-4b, " Parallel Imports"

Chapter 11 Endnotes

1.   Cui Rong, "Privileged Position," *Far Eastern Economic Review*, Vol. 167, No. 31, August 5, 2004, pp. 46-48.

2.   www.amexinc.com (accessed May 15, 2012).

3.   Paul Herbig and Alan T. Shao, "American Sogo Shosha: American Trading Companies in the Twenty-First Century," *Marketing Intelligence & Planning*, Vol. 15, No. 6, 1997, pp. 281–290.

4.   "Japanese Trading Companies: The Giants That Refused to Die," *The Economist,* Vol. 319, No. 7709, June 1, 1991, pp. 72–73.

5.   Lyn S. Amine, Tamer S. Cavusgil, and Robert I. Weinstein, "Japanese Sogo Shosha and the U.S. Export Trading Companies," *Journal of the Academy of Marketing Science,* Vol. 14, No. 3, Fall 1986, pp. 21–32.

6.   Material in this section adapted from Herbig and Shao, "American Sogo Shosha," pp. 281-290.

7.   Ernest R. Larkins and Fenwisk Huss, "Establishing Trade Relations in Russia," *The CPA Journal,* Vol. 65, No. 8, August 1995, pp. 26–31.

8.   Ibid.

9.   www.ftc.gov/os/statutes/webbpomerene/index.shtm (accessed May 18, 2012).

10.   Rob Lee, "Boeing in the Middle," *Airfinance Journal,* Vol. 236, February 2001, pp. 34–36.

11.   Kevin Done, "WTO to Hear of 'Lavish' Boeing Aid," *Financial Times*, March 22, 2007, 34.

12.   Joseph Bonney, "Logistics Costs Rise," *The Journal of Commerce Online*, June 6, 2007, 1.

13.   Randy R. Irvin, "Pipeline Owners Must Reassess Utility of Undivided-Interest Ownership," *Oil & Gas Journal,* Vol. 99, No. 30, July 23, 2001, pp. 60–65.

14.   Ibid.

15.   Larry Rohter, "Vast Pipelines in Amazon Face Challenges Over Protecting Rights and Rivers," *New York Times*, January 21, 2007, 14.

16.   David Biederman, "Intelligent Island Links the Globe," *Traffic World*, Vol. 264, No. 10, December 4, 2000, pp. 28–31.

17.   www.danzas.com

18.   Lara L. Sowinksi, "It's Sink or Swim for Freight Forwarders and Customs Brokers," *World Trade*, Vol. 14, No. 2, February 2001, pp. 54–56.

19.   Peter T. Leach, "With Philippe Naudin, SDV USA," *Journal of Commerce*, May 7, 2007, p. 1.

20.   Adapted from Prabir K. Bagchi and Helge Virum, "Logistical Alliances: Trends and Prospects in Integrated Europe," *Journal of Business Logistics,* Vol. 19, No. 1, 1998, pp. 191–213.

21.   See Anthony Coia, "The Global Supply Chain Pill," *Traffic World,* Vol. 259,   No. 13, September 27, 1999, p. 17.

22.   Alexandra Alger, " 'Gray' Watches," *Forbes,* Vol. 160, No. 3, August 11, 1997, p. 151.

23.   Matthew B. Myers and David A. Griffith, "Strategies for Combating Gray Market Activity," *Business Horizons,* Vol. 42, No. 6, November/December 1999, pp. 2–8.

Case 11-1

Kraft's Distribution Challenges in China

Tom Shu, Kraft Foods' warehouse and distribution manager in China, is on top of things when it comes to local logistics companies. He lines up, along with hundreds of other workers, to work as a day laborer for local logistics companies and to find out how the companies are running the business. He feels that it is important to find out as much as possible about potential logistics providers because he needs to rely on them to handle the movement of Kraft products between production plants, distribution centers, and wholesalers.

Logistics companies are essential for large multinationals and small and medium-sized enterprises alike: They ensure that products arrive on time and in good shape. They also make sure that the manufacturer and the wholesaler do not have to store the product for prolonged periods because this creates additional costs and the potential for merchandise loss. In China, in particular, this is important, as the country's fast economic growth has contributed to serious transport bottlenecks. Although the government attempts to make sure the infrastructure is adequate, building highway networks to adequately serve the needs of the population, it still happens that shipments are stuck in traffic (see Figure 11-5) or even disappear, as highway robbery of shipments is not unusual.

Figure 11-5: *China has been investing massively to improve the road infrastructure. In Beijing, eight-to-ten-lane highways often have traffic jams. In this sprawling city it is not unusual for a drive across town to take as long as three hours.*

Kraft partnered with Chinese firms to enter China in the mid-1990s: One of its companies, Kraft Tianmei Foods, in Tianjin, makes Tang instant drink mix and Sugus chews, and the other, Kraft Guangtong Food, in Guangdong, produces Maxwell House coffee. In 2000, as part of the Nabisco acquisition, Kraft gained two more plants in Beijing and Suzhou that produce Oreo, Chips Ahoy! and Ritz brands cookies and crackers. Kraft has not yet brought its full product line to China, but its presence in this market is expanding rapidly.

Kraft has trimmed down its number of regional distribution centers in China from 13 to 5 to reduce costs. Each center has networks radiating into several neighboring provinces that are managed by third-party logistics, providing warehousing service and delivering goods to Kraft's designated wholesalers around China. One strategy that has helped the company is to hire mid-size logistics companies, rather than to go with the top companies. Going with the largest companies used to be Kraft's mantra in the past. In its relationship with the logistics firms, Kraft wants to be their number one client, to ensure that the company's needs are met first. In China, if a company is the third or fourth largest client, its orders are often delayed when there is a shortage of vehicles.

Kraft, however, has rigorous standards for storage and delivery. All the products are sealed in dry-food containers for transport. Once Kraft's sales manager approves an order, the logistics firm has only one to three days to deliver, which is not a problem in the United States, but it is in China where roads are often narrow and where local officials often demand additional fees from truck drivers (see Figure 11-6). The reason for the short delivery time is that Kraft insists on keeping its inventory down at its five warehouses. The highest cost incurred by distribution centers is attributed to inventory, not to management fees.

Figure 11-6: *Local officials in China often request additional fees from truck drivers, delaying them and making it hard for them to reach their destination on time. At toll stops, trucks tend to take much longer than other vehicles.*

Another logistics challenge that Kraft faces in China is the pilfering of goods transported by rail. Often dozens of boxes are missing at destination. With rail, the company does not have many choices other than to keep its fingers crossed—or to hide the more expensive goods at the bottom of the container.

Yet another challenge is that China is clamping down on overloaded trucks, which will take a big bite out of Kraft's bottom line. Trucks drive around China with huge loads, a practice adopted by logistics companies to keep costs down, but which poses a threat to road safety. Now, these companies are forced to distribute the same loads over two or three trucks, increasing their costs.

Sources: Cui Rong, "Privileged Position," *Far Eastern Economic Review*, Vol. 167, No. 31, August 5, 2004, pp. 46–48; "Getting a Foothold in China: Kraft Foods Works on Improving Its Recipe for Distributing Goods," *The Wall Street Journal*, August 3, 2004, A9.

Analysis Suggestions:

1. What types of products in Kraft's product mix can the company transport by truck? What are the advantages and disadvantages of truck transportation for Kraft's China operations?

2. What types of products in Kraft's product mix can the company transport by rail? What are the advantages and disadvantages of rail transportation for Kraft's China operations?

Case 11-2

Shipping Doo Kingue

Doo Kingue is a baby mountain gorilla, a member of one of the two most endangered species of apes in the world. There are only approximately 655 mountain gorillas alive today, all in the wild in the mountainous forests of northwest Rwanda, southwestern Uganda, and eastern Democratic Republic of Congo. Mountain gorillas in this region are constantly threatened by poaching, continuous encroachment on the national parks for agricultural use, extensive harvesting of wood for fuel, and a landscape covered with land mines as a result of fighting between the different tribes in the region. Doo Kingue, whose tribe perished as a result of water contamination, was able to survive—barely—and is currently experiencing a difficult-to-treat pulmonary infection.

The director of Karisoke Research Center in Volcano National Park in Hawaii—founded by the late American anthropologist Dian Fossey in 1968 and run by the Dian Fossey Gorilla Funds, a U.S. nongovernmental organization—recently approached the National Zoo in Washington, D.C., and asked for help. The Center obtained permission from the regional government of Ruhengeri and the national government of Rwanda to send the gorilla to the National Zoo, provided the zoo takes responsibility for shipping and hospitalization. John James, one of the directors of conservation and science at the zoo, is excited about having a mountain gorilla for its primate exhibit, and Doo Kingue seems like the ideal candidate.

John's plan is to work with one of the transportation companies doing business in sub-Saharan Africa, to bring the gorilla quickly and painlessly to Washington, D.C., and to start aggressive treatment on the pulmonary infection. Clearly, in this decision, time is of the essence. His staff is familiar with some of the companies that provide quick, reliable service for transporting animals, ensuring that they are transported safely to zoos whose mission is focused on animal welfare and on maintaining the earth's biodiversity (see Figure 11-7).

One of the companies he is considering is Animal Port Houston (www.pettransport.com), a company with expertise in the relocation of pets and animals, offering services that include housing, transporting, and preparing relevant health certificates and permits. Animal Port Houston is a member of the American Zoo Association (AZA), the International Animal Transportation Association

Figure 11-7: *These endangered Grevy Zebras in the Berlin Zoo originate in Kenya and Ethiopia, where there are only 2,000 animals left, due to habitat loss, water shortages, and hunting. The European Conservation Breeding Program ensures that the offspring of these zebras populate European zoos from Lisbon to Moscow.*

(AATA), the International Pet and Animal Transport Association (IPATA), the American Animal Sciences Association (AALAS), the United States Animal Health Association (USAHA), and the U.S. Air Forwarders Association.

Another company that seems a viable candidate for the transportation job is FedEx (www.fedex.com). FedEx has, for example, donated the use of its express transportation network and relocated six endangered polar bears from San Juan, Puerto Rico, to their permanent zoo homes. The company flew the bears from San Juan to the FedEx Hub in Memphis, Tennessee, onboard a DC-10 aircraft. Later in the day, the bears were transloaded to three other aircraft in Memphis to fly to their final destinations near Seattle, Washington; Detroit, Michigan; and Charlotte, North Carolina. FedEx Express used its customs clearance expertise to expedite the animals through U.S. Customs. John found out that FedEx has considerable experience in transporting animals, including elephants, rhinos, lions and gorillas. The company even transported animals to the National Zoo. FedEx provided air transportation, ground support, and logistic expertise to deliver two giant pandas from Chengdu, China, to the National Zoo in Washington, D.C. FedEx also transported six rare white tigers from Memphis, Tennessee, to Bangkok, Thailand, to ensure that work could continue on an endangered species breeding program.

Sources: Valerie May, "Animals on the Move," *Smithonian* Zoogoer, 39(1) 2010, p. 1; http://www.zoo-berlin.de/index.php?id=210&tx_ttnews[backPid]=12&no_cache=1&tx_ttnews[tt_news]=953 (accessed July 12, 2012); www.scienceinafrica.co.za; Paul R. Murphy and James M. Daley, "Profiling International Freight Forwarders: An Update," *International Journal of Physical Distribution Logistics Management,* Vol. 31, No. 3, 2001, pp. 152–168; www.fedex.com.

Analysis Suggestions:

1. Weigh the advantages and disadvantages of using Animal Port Houston and FedEx to transport Doo Kingue to Washington, D.C.

2. Arrange for intermodal transportation for Doo Kingue from Ruhengeri, Rwanda, to Kigali, the capital city of Rwanda, and to the United States. Note that none of these companies, nor any U.S. airlines, fly to Rwanda. Attempt a few routes by looking at airlines' Web sites, at the Animal Port Houston site, and the FedEx site to find out what markets they serve. Find out how animals can be transported downtown to the National Zoo from Dulles Airport outside of Washington, D.C.

Chapter 12: International Retailing

Learning Objectives

After studying this chapter, you should be able to:

- Provide an overview and description of the general merchandise retailing category and offer examples and illustrations.

- Provide an overview and description of the food retailing category and offer examples and illustrations.

- Provide an overview and description of the nonstore retailing category and offer examples and illustrations.

- Address issues related to legislation, taxation, and retailing practices around the world.

Worldwide, retailing is experiencing a revolution. Markets are changing, retailing technology is changing, consumers are changing, and retailers face challenges in every aspect of their operations. On the other hand, opportunities abound for retailers with astute, responsive market approaches. International retailing conglomerates are using creative strategies in their mature home markets to retain profitable consumers, and expanding rapidly into emerging markets, fighting equally aggressive international and local competition, navigating government restrictions and regulations, and courting the ever increasing and appealing local middle class. Take, for example, the world's leading retailer, Walmart.

Walmart in China

Walmart had $312 billion in retail sales in the fiscal year ending in 2006, accounting for more than 10 percent of the total sales of the world's top 100 retailers. In spite of its exit from Germany and South Korea, the chain keeps growing, surpassing by far its competitors. It assumed the top position in 1990 and has held on to it ever since.[1]

The retailing titan has been active in China since early 1996. It presently operates 370 stores in 140 cities in China, including supercenters, Sam's Clubs, and Neighborhood Markets. With its Global Procurement Center located in Shenzhen, Walmart is also a major exporter from China. Its direct and indirect purchases from China have steadily increased, with $18 billion worth of exports annually. To date, it has relationships with about 20,000 suppliers in China.[2]

In the city of Kunming, in southwestern China, there are four Walmart Superstores serving a population of about six million. Their location is convenient, but not obvious. The location shown in Figure 12-1 is barely visible from a spaghetti junction at the edge of town. However, consumers know well its location, and local guides proudly announce the chain's presence in the city, as an indicator of the city's cosmopolitan nature.

Figure 12-1: *A Walmart store in Kunming, in the province of Yunnan, southwestern China, which is not as obvious and as dominant in the landscape as the stores are in the United States.*

Large retailers from emerging markets are also expanding, entering markets in neighboring countries, and eyeing consumers on other continents. Small and medium-sized retailers from emerging markets, or even from low-income countries, are breaking through national boundaries, selling their products to buyers in high-income countries. Consumers are selling products on auction websites and competing with established retailers.

This chapter offers insights into the internationalization efforts of retailers, describing different categories of retailers and their international involvement and expansion, and issues related to legislation and taxation that affect retailing operations. The chapter also illustrates retailing practices around the world.

12-1 International Retailing Defined

International retailing is defined as *all the activities involved in selling products and services to final international consumers for their personal consumption.*

International retailing differs from local retailing as defined in marketing management in that it addresses operations of international retailers beyond home-country borders, as well as operations of local retailers in different countries worldwide—in general and in response to the presence or entry of international retailers aiming for their target market. As such, an examination of international retail operations must include an evaluation of global and local retailing formats, retail practices, and an overview of local retailing environments. The next section provides an overview of developments in the process of the international expansion of retailing.

12-2 International Expansion of Retailers

Retailers are rapidly expanding internationally to gain competitive advantage and to increase sales, profits, and overall firm performance. As they expand beyond their home-country borders, retailers also can take advantage of cost savings and learn from experiences in a way that could further enhance home-country operations. The 10 largest retailers, 5 U.S. companies (Walmart, Home Depot, Kroger, Costco, and Walgreen), and 5 European companies (Carrefour, Metro, Tesco, Schwartz, and Aldi), dominate the market (see Table 12-1 on the next page). In general, diversified retailers, operating across the food, apparel, and hard goods sectors enjoyed the highest growth.[3]

French and German retailers have been, by far, the most globally active in the past decade. In 2012, they generated more than 40 percent of sales abroad and they have substantially reduced their dependence on the home markets, where sales have stagnated since the beginning of the recession. Of the top 250 global retailers, French companies are the most international, expanding beyond France, in an average of over 30 countries. And, of this same group, fashion retailers are the most global of all product groups, and North American retailers are the largest, with an average size in excess of $19 billion, and more than half of the area's top 250 retailers operate only within their own country's borders. Finally, in many of the slowing economies, retailers targeting upscale consumers have done well.[4]

In the process of internationalization, many retailers continue the trend of consolidation in the food and general merchandise sectors. Past examples of consolidation are offered by Walmart's acquisition of one of the largest U.K. grocery chains, the Asda Group; and the merger between two medium-sized French Walmart look-alikes, Promodes and Carrefour [5] to form the second largest retailer worldwide, the French retailer Carrefour. Carrefour is present in Argentina, Brazil, Chile, Colombia, Mexico, and the Dominican Republic in Latin America; in China, Japan, Indonesia, Malaysia, Singapore, South Korea, Taiwan, and Thailand in the Asia; Egypt, Oman, Qatar, Tunisia, Turkey, and the United Arab Emirates in North Africa and the Middle East; and France, Belgium, Italy, Switzerland, Spain, Portugal, the Czech Republic, Slovakia, Poland, Romania, and Greece in Europe. Carrefour is currently the largest foreign chain in China with 61 hypermarkets; after 10 years of operation, it employs more than 23,000 people in China and is generally considered the most aggressive of the foreign operators in terms of store development.[6]

To understand the changes in the vibrant world of international retailing, one needs to gain some insight into the many categories of retailers (local and multinational) and their modus operandi in different

Table 12-1: *The Top 10 Global Retailers*

Rank	Country of Origin	Retailers	Format	Sales (US$ millions)
1	U.S.	Wal-Mart Stores, Inc.	Discount, Hypermarket, Supermarket, Superstore Warehouse	418,952
2	France	Carrefour	Cash & Carry, Convenience, Discount, Hypermarket, Specialty, Supermarket	119,642
3	U.K.	Tesco	Convenience, Department Hypermarket, Supermarket, Superstore	92,971
4	Germany	Metro	Cash & Carry, Department, DIY, Hypermarket, Specialty, Superstore	88,931
5	U.S.	Kroger	Convenience, Discount, Specialty, Supermarket, Warehouse	82,189
6	Germany	Schwartz	Discount, Hypermarket, Supercenter/Superstore	79,119
7	U.S.	Costco	Warehouse	76,255
8	U.S.	Home Depot	DIY, Specialty	67,997
9	U.S.	Walgreen Co.	Drug Store/Pharmacy	67,420
10	Germany	Aldi Einkauf GmbH & Co.	Discount Store	67,112

Source: "2012 Global Powers of Retailing," January 2012, www.stores.org.

parts of the world. It also is important to understand how international retailing differs from retailing as defined in marketing management texts. Both of these topics are addressed in Sections 12-2 and 12-3.

12-3 Retail Formats: Variations in Different Markets

There are three main retail formats: general merchandise retailing, food retailing, and nonstore retailing. Sections 12-3a through 12-3c describe the retailers in each category and address the different international variations for each retail format, with a focus on local markets.

12-3a General Merchandise Retailing

Specialty Stores

Specialty stores offer a narrow product line and wide assortment. In this category are clothing stores (usually further specialized into women's, men's, or children's clothing stores), bookstores, toy stores, office supply stores, and consumer electronics stores.

In many markets, specialty stores—chains in particular—are expanding at the expense of all forms of nonfood retailing. For example, specialty store chains are taking market share away from traditional department stores worldwide. U.K. specialty retailers have made great strides in international expansion: Marks & Spencer is rapidly expanding in France, and retailers such as Virgin Megastores have already made substantial inroads into the U.S. market. They are also present in Ireland, France, Greece, and Germany (see Figure 12-2), in Europe, as well as in Japan, Australia, and throughout North Africa and the Middle East in the Kingdom of Bahrain, Egypt, Qatar, Kuwait, Lebanon, and the United Arab Emirates (Abu Dhabi and Dubai).

specialty stores
Retailers that offer a narrow product line and wide assortment.

Figure 12-2: *The Virgin Meg-astore left Germany in 1994, complaining that the laws governing store opening hours were too restrictive, but they returned to Germany and opened a new store in Berlin's ultra-modern central train station in 2006.*

For apparel retailing, many European companies are rapidly entering new markets: Mango, the Spanish retailer specializing in youth fashion, has 400 shops in 44 countries, including Israel, Eastern Europe, and South America.[7] Rival Spanish chain Zara, with its distinctive brushed-steel staircases, and Swedish chain H&M are competing for these same consumers and are proving to be successful in mature markets worldwide. Esprit, a German apparel company, sells its international youthful lifestyle clothing brand worldwide: It offers 12 product lines of women's wear, men's wear, kid's wear, youth wear, as well as shoes and accessories through more than 770 directly managed retail stores (see Figure 12-3) and more than 12,000 wholesale point-of-sales worldwide. The company is present in more than 40 countries.[8]

In most developing countries, specialty stores represent the main retail format. Although Western and local specialty chain stores are quite popular and have done well for decades, developing country markets are dominated by independent (usually family-owned) specialty stores, such as apparel stores, cosmetics stores, and local arts and crafts stores aimed at the tourist market (see Figure 12-4), as well as other traditional retail systems as exemplified by specialized markets.

Figure 12-3: *Esprit stores are popular worldwide: Esprit has more than 770 stores in more than 40 countries.*

Figure 12-4: *Tibetan shopping street where vendors sell local arts and crafts.*

<table>
<tr><td>

specialized markets
Markets that contain specialty stores specializing in a particular product category.

</td></tr>
</table>

Specialized Markets

Specialized markets contain specialty stores focusing on a particular product category. Examples of such markets exist worldwide, in both developed and developing countries. Examples of specialized markets are the Cairo Gold Market in the Khan El Khalili bazaar, the Jade Market in Hong Kong, and the Gold Market and the Spice Market in the Covered Bazaar in Istanbul, Turkey (see Figure 12-5). Specialized markets may even cover entire cities. For example, the town of Otavalo, Ecuador, houses large and small retailers of leather goods.

Figure 12-5: *The Covered Bazaar in Istanbul, Turkey, is the prime destination for Turkish food and spices.*

In addition to these markets, local specialty stores affiliated with a project sponsored by governmental or nongovernmental organizations also are prevalent in many developing countries. Examples may be a poultry shop partially owned by local investors selling poultry raised in a project funded by the World Bank and the United Nations Development Program aimed at helping a developing country become self-sufficient with regard to meat production, or a folk art outlet selling handmade embroidery produced by young girls in a convent. In other examples, the Chinese government heavily promotes what are known as Government Friendship Stores (see Figure 12-6). The stores are owned by the government and Chinese tour guides are advised to take their busloads of foreign tourists to these destination retailers to unload their foreign currency. The stores specialize in the local crafts: in Shanghai, they sell silk and jade, and in Beijing, they sell cloisonné, for example. The stores advertise that prices are reasonable and there should be no bargaining —but one has yet to find a government store in China where bargaining is not going to result in a better deal.

Figure 12-6: *This Government Friendship Store is situated in the proximity of Beijing, adjacent to a cloisonné "factory"— a little shop where a handful of workers decorate a handful of cloisonné vases. The retailing operation adjacent to the "factory," however, is massive, selling thousands of dollars' worth of jade pieces, in addition to large, medium, small, and miniature cloisonné vases.*

Department Stores

Department stores offer a broad variety of goods and wide assortments. Among the products they carry are clothing for men, women, and children; household appliances and electronics. Kitchenware; china; home furnishings; and toys and games. Outside the United States, department stores typically also have large supermarket sections, and some may even carry fresh produce: the more elegant the department store, the more upscale the supermarket section.

The Supermarket in the Department Store

One would not normally link a department store with a supermarket. Bloomingdale's, in its Manhattan store, has a handful of gourmet products, and plenty of chocolate, especially at holiday time. And your local Macy's might carry some Cellar-brand products such as nuts, cookies, dog chews. But your European department store comes with a full-scale supermarket. No, it is not your average Kroger-in-the-basement variety; rather, it is as comprehensive and fancy as the store itself.

Take, for instance, the German Kaufhaus des Westens (KaDeWe) or the French Galeries Lafayette, or Printemps. All three have huge spaces dedicated to lively displays of fresh exotic fish, posing as predators or as filets, smoked, fried, toasted, elaborately decorated and in ample quantities. Next to the fish displays, vegetables and fruit color the retail space and lure visitors toward a labyrinth of ethnic foods that includes a display of American goodies, including Oreo cookies, Swiss Miss hot chocolate, marshmallows, and French's mustard. The cold cuts are from every imaginable European source, in multiple displays that suggest endless ways to roast, smoke, preserve, and slice that ham. The cheese and the wine sections are immense, with every country of origin represented.

In the United States and Canada, department stores have suffered substantial losses since the 1990s, mostly attributed to the rise in discount stores, off-price retailers, and category killers. In an attempt to conquer new markets, however, a number of chains have been looking overseas for expansion: Sears Roebuck and JCPenney, in particular, have been looking at the Latin American market, with JCPenney opening a number of stores in Mexico and Chile.[9]

In Europe, department stores typically tend to address the needs of home markets, with efforts to expand mainly in the European Union. In the United Kingdom, the self-proclaimed "most famous shop in the world," Harrods department store in London (Knightsbridge), was established in 1849 and, by the end of the nineteenth century, was flourishing, selling airplanes and elephants, jewelry and pineapples, golf clubs and snuff boxes. Today, it attracts an exclusive clientele to its 300 departments, covering a million square feet of selling space, and to its 21 restaurants.[10]

In the Netherlands, three department stores dominate: Vendex (Vroom & Dreesman), HEMA, and Bijenkorf. (The latter two belong to the KBB Group.) A similar concentration is encountered in Germany, where KarstadtQuelle owns numerous department stores, such as Karstadt, Hertie, KaDeWe (see Figure 12-7), Wertheim, Alsterhaus, and others. French department stores

Figure 12-7: *German retailer Kaufhaus des Westens— KaDeWe, or the Department Store of the West—was founded in 1905 by Adolf Jandorf. It was destroyed in the 1940s and rebuilt in 1950. It is the largest store in Western Europe.*

are surviving despite the dominance of specialty shops and the increasing popularity of category killers and discount shops. Among the leading department stores in France are Bon Marché, and Galeries Lafayette, and Printemps (see Figure 12-8). Galeries Lafayette made an unsuccessful attempt to enter the U.S. market by locating in the heart of Manhattan. It also opened a store in the former East Berlin—an architectural landmark, by famous architect Jean Nouvel, which is moderately empty most of the time, in this author's experience. In Spain, the leading department store is El Corte Inglés, which dominates the Madrid retail scene.[11]

Figure 12-8: *Printemps is much like your typical U.S. department store, but more edgy and much more expensive. In the summer of 2010, a pair of Dockers sold at Costco in the United States for about $25; at Printemps that exact same pair was on sale for 64 euros, or about $78. On the roof of its Paris store, there is a surprisingly affordable restaurant selling decent crêpes.*

In Central and Eastern Europe department stores abound. The former communist regimes found that large department stores offered economies of scale in terms of distribution and sales management. Consequently, department stores dominate the retailing environment of most large cities. With names such as Centrum or the Central Store in Central and Eastern Europe and GUM in Russia, or bearing the name of the capital city or of socialist and nationalist symbols ("Victory," "Liberty," "Unity," etc.), these stores continue to thrive in a slightly different format. In addition to their merchandise, they also have a substantial presence of leased departments. The leased departments are noteworthy in that they carry merchandise that directly competes with the store's offerings and with that of other leased departments. For example, the Bucur Obor department store in Bucharest has at least three leased departments selling chandeliers. Alternatively, store space may be rented to retailers that are not traditionally associated with department stores, such as automobile retailers.

In Asia, department stores have different histories. Japanese department stores started out as kimono shops that originally sold textiles. At present, Japan's department store groups (Mitsukoshi, Daimaru, ADO, the Seibu stores and affiliates, and Takashimaya) are designed to be cradle-to-grave providers of goods and services. Japanese department stores have also expanded in China and Hong Kong, where they control 50 percent of the market. In Taiwan, most department stores either come from Japan, or have sought affiliation with foreign—especially Japanese—department stores. Examples of department stores here are Mitsukoshi, Takashima, Pacific Sogo (see Figure 12-9), Sesame, and Evergreen.[12]

Although department stores remain a dominant retail outlet in Asia, they are currently displaying symptoms of decline, such as oversupply, over-duplication of merchandise, fierce competition, and declining profits. Shanghai alone witnessed the demise of five department stores. Existing department stores in this city have done well when changing their format—for example, specializing in European-style clothing and furnishings, or emulating the hypermarket environment by offering lower prices and maintaining a customer-friendly environment.[13]

Figure 12-9: *The Sogo department store in Taipei, Taiwan, is located on one of the busiest streets of a busy city, receiving high consumer traffic.*

General Merchandise Discount Stores

General merchandise discount stores sell high volumes of merchandise, offer limited service, and charge lower prices. Discount stores are divided into two categories: **all-purpose discount stores,** which offer a wide variety of merchandise and limited depth, and **category specialists (category killers),** which carry a narrow variety of merchandise and offer a wide assortment.

The all-purpose category is dominated by stores such as Walmart, Sears, and Target in the United States. Internationally, this retailer category tends to draw a substantial portion of profits from its supermarket section; consequently, it will be addressed in Section 12-3b, "Food Retailers." In the all-purpose category, Walmart has more than 4,500 stores internationally (many of the international stores are hypermarkets). The company is present in Canada, Mexico, Puerto Rico, Costa Rica, Nicaragua, El Salvador, Guatemala, Honduras, Argentina, Brazil, China, Japan and the United Kingdom. It serves more than 50 million international customers weekly in these markets, and it has a total of 2.1 million employees.[14]

Category specialists, also known as category killers or stores with category dominance, are large specialty stores that carry a narrow variety of merchandise and a wide assortment. Among examples of category specialists that are successful internationally are office supply stores, such as Staples, OfficeMax, and Office Depot; home improvement centers, such as Home Depot; bookstores, such as Borders, which are especially well received in East Asia; children's stores, such as Toys "R" Us, which leads sales in this product category from Scandinavia to South Africa; and furniture stores, such as IKEA, which dominates the modern, basic furniture market. Of the first category, office supply stores, Staples is present internationally in 26 countries in North and South America, Europe, and Asia; it has over 2,000 stores.[15] OfficeMax has division headquarters in the United States, Canada, Mexico, Europe, Australia, and New Zealand, and, in partnership with Lyreco, a business-to-business distributor of office supplies, it serves businesses in 36 countries. Office Depot sells its products through more than 400 stores outside the U.S., operating through wholly owned retail stores, joint ventures, licensing and franchise agreements under the Office Depot; it also sells office products and services through direct mail, internet sites, and through its sales force.[16]

Many of the established international specialty retailers and numerous newcomers are attracting consumers with innovative approaches to merchandising. In the furniture business, IKEA has redefined furniture retailing for more than three decades with its impressive merchandising core competencies, its sourcing economies of scale, and the savings it passes on to consumers.

Off-Price Retailers

Off-price retailers sell brand name and designer merchandise below regular retail; the products they sell may include overruns, irregular products, as well as products from previous seasons. Among examples of off-price retailers are factory outlet stores. Close-out retailers, with broad, inconsistent assortments; and single-price retailers. Although this type of retailing is popular in the United States and Canada, in the rest of the world, there are only limited possibilities, other than store sales, for purchasing brand names at a discount. For example, Hugo Boss has an outlet store in southern Germany, close to its factory, near Stuttgart, and Zurich has a famous designer outlet mall; Italy also has a few outlet stores for its famous designers. None of these examples come close in depth and variety to the North American off-price retailer presence, but that is about to change, as more and more international consumers demand similar deals as the ones offered in the United States.

Often, American companies must build their own outlet stores in environments where this type of retail format is unknown. In the Tokyo suburb of Sagami-Ono, for instance, American Malls International opened an outlet mall for companies such as Guess! and Laura Ashley to sell discontinued merchandise at a discount.[17]

general merchandise discount stores
Retailers that sell high volumes of merchandise, offer limited service, and charge lower prices.

all-purpose discount stores
General merchandise discount stores that offer a wide variety of merchandise and limited depth.

category specialists (also known as category killers)
Large general merchandise discount stores that carry a narrow variety of merchandise and a wide assortment; also called category killers.

off-price retailers
Retailers who sell brand name products and designer merchandise below regular retail prices.

Catalog Showrooms

Catalog showrooms usually offer high-turnover, brand name goods at discount prices. A typical format for a catalog showroom is one in which customers order from a catalog in the showroom where the product is only displayed and then pick up the merchandise at a designated location. Internationally, the goods sold in this retail format are not typically brand name goods, but, rather, they are goods that have not sold in season through a company's catalog. For example, Neckermann and Quelle, well-known German catalog retailers, have catalog showrooms in many of Germany's largest cities where they sell their catalog store brands. In addition, IKEA uses this strategy to sell to consumers worldwide. Customers receive a catalog, which is also available in the showroom; based on the offerings displayed in the catalog and in the showroom, customers order in the store the product they would like to purchase and pick it up from a designated location in its unassembled state.

12-3b Food Retailers

Conventional Supermarkets

Food retailers include **conventional supermarkets,** which are self-service retailers with annual sales greater than $2 million and less than 20,000 square feet of store space. Such supermarkets abound worldwide, with local retailers and regional international retailers most prominent in this retail category.

Superstores

The **superstores** category includes **combination stores** (food and drug) and **hypermarkets** (which combine supermarket, discount, and warehouse retailing principles). In the United States, combination stores have been quite successful; all-purpose general discount stores, such as Walmart and Kmart, are often transformed into superstores to facilitate one-stop shopping for consumers. In their new, enhanced formats, these stores are known as the Walmart Superstore and Big K, respectively, and they carry an extensive food selection but have a limited refrigeration space and fresh produce offerings, similar to that offered by a supermarket. Leading worldwide in the superstore category are, in addition to Walmart, France's Carrefour; Germany's Metro, with its Interspar superstores, and the Schwartz group; and U.K.'s Tesco.[18]

Warehouse Clubs or Wholesale Clubs

Warehouse clubs, also called **wholesale clubs,** require members to pay an annual fee and operate in low-overhead, warehouse-type facilities. They offer limited lines of brand name and dealer-brand groceries, apparel, appliances, and other goods at a substantial discount. They sell to final consumers who are affiliated with different institutions, as well as to businesses (in this capacity, they are wholesalers, rather than retailers). This retailing concept is presently pioneered worldwide by Sam's Club (part of Walmart) and Costco.

Sam's Clubs are in China, Brazil, Puerto Rico, and Mexico.[19] Costco has 605 warehouse clubs in the United States and Puerto Rico, Canada, South Korea, Taiwan, Japan, Canada, Australia, the United Kingdom,[20] and Mexico, where it has a joint venture with the retail conglomerate Controladora Comercial Mexicana.[21] San Diego-based PriceSmart Inc. has been forming joint ventures and licensing agreements with foreign partners to set up wholesale clubs in Latin America and Asia-Pacific countries.[22] Currently, it is the largest warehouse club in Central and South America and the Caribbean, with a presence in Colombia, Costa Rica, El Salvador, Guatemala, Honduras, Nicaragua, Panama, Aruba, Barbados, Dominican Republic, Jamaica, Trinidad and Tobago, and the U.S. Virgin Islands.[23]

catalog showrooms
Showrooms displaying the products of catalog retailers, offering high turnover, brand name goods at discount prices.

conventional supermarkets
Self-service food retailers with annual sales of more than $2 million and with an area less than 20,000 square feet.

superstores
Large retailers such as combination stores or hypermarkets that sell food, drugs, and other products.

combination stores
Medium-sized retail stores that combine food and drug retailing.

hypermarkets
Large retail stores that combine supermarket, discount, and warehouse retailing principles.

wholesale clubs (or warehouse clubs)
Stores that require members to pay an annual fee operating in low-overhead, warehousetype facilities, offering limited lines of brand name and dealer-brand groceries, apparel, appliances, and other goods at a substantial discount.

convenience stores
Small retailers located in residential areas, open long hours, and carrying limited lines of high-turnover necessities.

Convenience Stores

Convenience stores are small retailers located in residential areas, convenient to consumers. They are open long hours, carry limited lines of higher-turnover necessities, and offer the possibility of a one-stop shopping experience. Formats of convenience stores vary worldwide—from small independent retailers to chains such as 7-Eleven; from large stores offering a one-stop shopping opportunity for convenience goods and fast food to kiosks selling food items and alcoholic beverages obtained through both legal and illegal channels; from convenience stores-cum-pharmacies in a city's town square to seventh-floor apartments with a large opening in the front door selling milk, cheese, bread, and different types of chocolate. Convenience stores abound in both developing and developed countries, with many chains developing in conjunction with gas stations.

12-3c Nonstore Retailing

Internet Retailing

Also known as **interactive home shopping** or **electronic retailing**, selling through the Internet has quickly become an important retail format. In the **Internet retailing** category, dot-com companies and traditional retailers are attempting additional market penetration by making it convenient for loyal customers to purchase their products, as well as attempting market diversification by expanding their market to consumers who otherwise would not normally shop in their particular retail establishment.

With the Internet and the increase in the number of Internet users worldwide, providing retailing services through a website that is accessible globally becomes much easier. Local retailers can easily become international retailers without making investments in store leases, aesthetics, atmospherics, and so forth.

Internet retailing provides opportunities for retail firms to define their market beyond their target regions. At the same time, it presents dilemmas with regard to customer service and control of the retail transactions (due to international and regional differences in mail reliability and in customer orientation and skill of local service representatives). Many companies with e-commerce capabilities turn away international orders, primarily because they do not have a way to ship the merchandise overseas or lack the processes necessary for international shipments.[24]

In developed countries, Internet purchasing is consumption market driven and not experience driven: Consumers shop for needs and wants but do not view Internet surfing as a pleasure trip, as would consumers going to a mall or a store.[25] Consequently, shopping via the Internet for consumers in countries where attractive shopping alternatives are available, such as malls and stores with great merchandise assortment and variety, is quite different from shopping in many developing countries, where alternatives are limited, and where both retailers and the products they sell are inferior. If it were not for the Internet and for catalog retailing, consumers in this second category would be able to purchase higher quality goods only if they went abroad.

Consumers in developed countries might also have to contend with unethical retailers. Whereas brick-and-mortar retailers can be sued in a local court of law for nonperformance, Internet retailers are more elusive; the issue of the appropriate jurisdiction further complicates the situation. Using the more established Internet retailers—the well-known brick-and-mortar retailers or the established catalog stores, such as Neckermann from Germany and IKEA from Sweden, which are now also selling through their own web pages—may be a safer alternative.

The Internet also provides a venue for émigrés shopping for their relatives in their home countries as described in International Marketing Illustration 12-1.

convenience stores
Small retailers located in residential areas, open long hours, and carrying limited lines of high-turnover necessities.

interactive home shopping
A venue for selling through the Internet using Web sites to increase market penetration and market diversification; also called electronic retailing and Internet retailing.

electronic retailing
Selling through the Internet using Web sites to increase market penetration and market diversification; also called interactive home shopping and Internet retailing.

Internet retailing
Selling through the Internet using Web sites to increase market penetration and market diversification; also called interactive home shopping and electronic retailing.

International Marketing Illustration 12-1
Retail Opportunities for Émigrés:
Repatriating Food and Clothing to Home-Country Relatives

In the past, helping out relatives with money or with food packages was expensive. Traditionally, émigrés living in developed countries sent money periodically to their relatives in their home country—a developing country. Typically sent through money wire transfers or by check, the sums were often decimated by fees by the time they reached a recipient in a developing country or in an emerging market. For example, sending a check from the United States would require the recipient in Ecuador, India, or Slovakia to go to a local bank to cash it. The money would be released as long as a month later, after the check was cashed, and the recipient, who did not normally have an account at the international bank, would be charged hefty fees. It would not be unusual for the recipient of $100 check to cash out $70 or less, even if the remittance services promised free money transfer and excellent exchange rates.

In the pre-Internet past, émigrés also helped their families with food packages: Most diaspora newspapers advertised the shipping of consumer products to the home country at competitive prices (they still do today, but the Internet has taken a large bite of their business). Merz Pharma, a German pharmaceuticals firm, has been catering to East European émigrés for decades. All one had to do was pick up the phone and order the goods for delivery, paying for them with a credit card. Because shipping was involved, costs were a bit steep and prices were not quite a bargain.

Today, a greater accessibility of goods in the home country, coupled with Internet-facilitated transactions, allows émigrés to order goods for the family at competitive prices and with free shipping for orders higher than a particular amount. This variant is so attractive that it is not unusual for émigrés from Latin America and Eastern Europe to purchase food and other necessities for family members in the home country, in some cases as often as three times a month.

To illustrate, shoppers in Oregon can place grocery orders for their relatives in Argentina through Discovirtual.com, an online site of Argentine retailer Disco SA, owned by Dutch chain Royal Ahold. Peruvian supermarket chain E. Wong launched an online store that taps Peruvians abroad shopping for their families, doubling its online transactions in one year. Similarly, Brazil's Pao de Acucar found that it can sell an average of 5,000 grocery items a day through its website. And Mexico's Grupo Gigante is also actively pursuing this market.

Even though many Latinos living in developed countries do not have Internet access, it is likely that this will become big business in the future. Latino immigrants and their descendants living in the United States repatriate close to $20 billion yearly. Immigrants from Haiti and Nicaragua remit more than 20 percent of the respective home-countries' GDP yearly, that is, $810 and $610 million, respectively. Immigrants from El Salvador and the Dominican Republic remit close to $2 billion yearly. And, in Somalia, remittance companies, known as hawala, transfer $750 million to $1 billion a year from Somalis abroad to families and businesses in their home country.

E-tailers have good prospects for tapping into the remittance market.

Sources: DiscoVirtual.com.ar (accessed May 21, 2012); Nicole Raymond, Di Pinheiro, and Alejandro Bianchi, "Emigres Send Food Online to Old Country—Retailers Seek to Tap into Billions Repatriated by Latino Immigrants to the U.S.," *Wall Street Journal*, November 6, 2002, B3; and this textbook author's remittance experiences.

---

vending machines
Interactive modes of retailing convenience goods.

Vending Machines

With the advent of the Smart Card, vending machine retailing has become more popular than ever (and, increasingly, more **vending machines** worldwide accept credit cards). Technology is now facilitating a more interactive consumer relationship, where videos illustrate product use and provide more information. The extent to which vending machines are used as a retail venue varies from country to country. Vending machines are used most in Japan, where they sell just about anything one can think of, including beer, hot food, cold food, ice cream (see Figure 12-10), cameras, and so on. Coke alone has over 1 million vending machines in Japan (see Figure 12-11). [26] In fact, in central locations in Japan's major cities, there are so many vending machines that they interfere with pedestrian traffic.

Figure 12-10: *Japanese vending machines offer ice cream, cold drinks, hot food, and beer, as well as many nonfood items.*

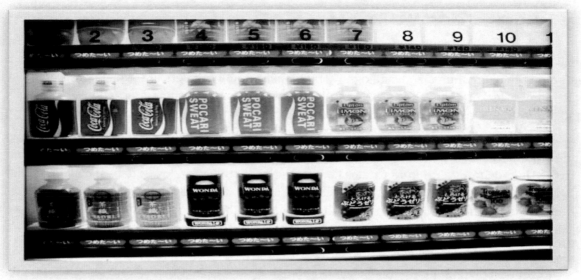

Figure 12-11: *Cold drink vending machines in Japan, selling Coca-Cola, and Tropicana, as well as local favorite Pocari Sweat.*

Vending machines are encountered in different configurations around the world. In the Netherlands, for instance, one can enter an outfit known as an Automatiek and select sausages, meatballs, salads, and beverages from the different machines, all replenished frequently by a full-time employee. In Munich, Germany, a vending machine for fresh flowers is located in the center of town. In much of the rest of the world, with the exception of the United States and Canada, cigarettes are readily available in the streets at all times of the day. In Europe, condoms are sold in vending machines outside pharmacies.

Television Home Shopping

> **television home shopping**
> Retailing through cable channels selling to consumers in their homes, through infomercials, and through direct response advertising shown on broadcast and cable television.

The **television home shopping** category includes cable channels selling to consumers in their homes, infomercials, and direct response advertising shown on broadcast and cable television. Television shopping networks, much like QVC and the Home Shopping Network in the United States, operate in many developed countries. The Home Shopping Network has three international channels, Home Shopping Europe in Germany; SHOP Channel, Japan; and TVSN Ltd. China. And QVC is also present in international markets, in the United Kingdom, Germany, and Japan. Local television home shopping channels are sprouting everywhere, from the United Kingdom, which has many shopping channels—Telewest now owns all the SitUp TV shopping channels[27]—to China, where the largest TV shopping network is Acorn International, in a country where television home shopping is a $2 billion market.[28]

Peter Justesen

All career diplomats know about Denmark's Peter Justesen, a catalog for five decades, and now the Internet website. Some have bought, on occasion, alcoholic drinks and chocolate, "shipment outside Europe at customer's risk." Others have bought households full of furniture—at diplomatic prices, of course. Some products are a bargain: cheap perfume, much cheaper than at Parfumerie Douglas, even cheaper chocolate and chocolate spread. But don't turn in your Sam's Club or Metro membership card yet: by the time you add shipping costs, these products become expensive. On the other hand, if you are buying a Rolex Daytona steel/gold for 9,168 euros, and add shipping (to Bali), you still have a bargain. Peter Justesen is a direct marketer, serving diplomats, embassies and consulates, the United Nations, and other international organizations. Its customers are expatriates who enjoy duty-free products worldwide, in more than 160 countries.[29]

Catalog Retailing and Direct Mail Retailing

Retailers of all categories are expanding internationally through catalog sales and **direct mail retailing.** Marketers are using consistent marketing communications worldwide, coordinating their advertising with direct mail brochures and catalogs. [30] Traditional **catalog retailers** are expanding internationally as well. Germany's Neckermann, and Otto Versand are actively expanding their international operations. Otto Versand, for example, offers specialty goods to consumers in Europe, the United States, and Japan.

U.S. retailers have established themselves in the United Kingdom in the 1990s with catalogs such as Lands' End, Peruvian Connection, and Talbots. Ten years later, British catalogs are finally coming full force to the United States: Furniture catalog Europe by Net, clothing catalog Boden, and shoe retailer Shipton & Heneage are just some of the catalogs crossing the Atlantic. U.K. catalog companies are going primarily to Germany, due to the proximity of the market and the ease of transactions, and to the United States, due to the size of the market and its preference for British brands. [31]

Catalog sales provide challenges to businesses not familiar with local practices. For example, catalog and Internet retailers found that consumers in Japan expect to first receive the product and only then pay for it. The key to success of catalog retailing is adaptation to local market needs and practices. U.S. personal planner cataloger DayTimers mails its catalogs in North America, the United Kingdom, Australia, New Zealand, Central Asia, and Germany; for its German calendars, which are translated into German, the company made Monday, rather than Sunday, the first day of the week and increased the size of the planners to accommodate Germany's larger paper sizes. Although Germans are accustomed to buying from catalogs, they are not used to the privileges considered standard in the U.S. catalog industry, such as 24-hour service, liberal return policies, or even lifetime guarantees from apparel catalogers. Such guarantees were unheard of in Germany, and a group of German retailers took Lands' End to court, accusing it of "unfair" competition (and lost). [32]

The potential for catalog sales remains high internationally and is greatly enhanced by the facilitations provided by the Internet. To offer some examples, [33]

- 30% of the world's population is online, and the global time spent online per month is equivalent to 3,995,444 years;

- In Southeast Asia, Singaporeans spend an average of 25 hours online per week, and Filipinos and Malaysians are close behind, at 21.5 and 19.8 hours, respectively, while Indonesians spend 14 hours per week;

- In 2011, at least one retailing website was among the top web brands for: Germany (Amazon, eBay); Japan (Amazon); Australia (eBay); UK (Amazon, eBay).

In some developing countries, however, many obstacles affect catalog retailing. First and foremost, the infrastructure must be sufficiently developed to warrant investment. For catalog companies, it means that telephone service and mail service must be reliable. In many countries—even in emerging markets—consumers must often purchase cell phone service because standard telephone service is inadequate or is not available. In addition, the mailing system is lax and mail is often intercepted and opened, such that only a portion of a package's content may arrive at its destination. Finally, in many developing countries, average income is a fraction of the average income in developed countries. Thus, products sold via catalog, such as clothing, appliances, housewares, and so on, are prohibitively expensive.

direct mail retailing
Retailing using catalogs and other direct mail, instead of brick-and-mortar stores.

catalog retailers
Retailers selling products through mail catalogs.

direct selling
Selling that involves a salesperson, typically an independent distributor, contacting a consumer at a convenient location—at his or her home or workplace, demonstrating product use and benefits, taking orders, and delivering the merchandise.

Direct Selling and Network Marketing

In the **direct selling** retail format, a salesperson, typically an independent distributor, contacts a consumer at a convenient location such as his or her home or workplace, demonstrates product use and benefits, takes orders, and delivers the merchandise. Direct selling is in the growth stage in most of the developing world; here, a number of impediments restrict firms' capability to successfully carry out their selling activity. Among these impediments are low per capita income, unreliable postal services, high levels of bureaucracy, lack of credit cards, few telephones, and a lack of mailing lists or access to mailing lists.

> **network marketing**
> Using acquaintance networks through an alternative distribution structure for the purpose of distribution; also called multilevel marketing.
>
> **multilevel marketing**
> Using acquaintance networks through an alternative distribution structure for the purpose of distribution; also called network marketing.

Direct selling firms are most active in growth markets, such as the emerging economies of China and Southeast Asia, Central and Eastern Europe, and Latin America. American direct selling firms, such as Avon Products, Nu Skin, and Mary Kay Cosmetics, are active in these markets, as well as worldwide. Avon, for example, earns more than half of its revenues from markets abroad, especially from developing countries.

Network marketing, or **multilevel marketing,** is a variation on direct selling and an approach to selling at the same time. It involves signing up sales representatives to go into business for themselves with minimal start-up capital. Their task is to sell more "distributorships"—that is, to identify more sales representatives from their own personal network, to buy the product, and to persuade others to buy the product. Network marketing is experiencing rapid growth, especially in emerging markets. In South Africa, for example, the poor transportation infrastructure that presents a challenge to many multinationals does not present a problem to network marketing. This and the fit with elements of traditional African culture make network marketing one of the most significant avenues for growth within the post-apartheid economy.[34] Among the most successful network marketing firms that have international operations are Amway, Herbalife International, and Equinox International.

12-4 Issues in International Retailing

12-4a Legislation and Regulation

Country regulations differ from one market to another, and legislation can have a profound impact on a firm's operations. Protectionist rules in India, for example, keep out the world's biggest retail names — Walmart, Tesco, and Carrefour are vying for this market, but they continue to be barred legally from setting up and running their own stores in India.[35] In China, direct sales were completely banned in 1998 due to pyramid schemes that caused social unrest, only to be allowed again in 2005. However, retailers now have to contend with new restrictions. For example direct-sales commissions must be capped at 30 percent, and companies cannot have sales promoters who are health-care professionals, civil servants, foreigners, or students. In addition, salespeople can derive income only from product sales and not from recruiting other sellers and receiving a commission on their sales — in other words, network marketing as a form of distribution is out.[36] To further complicate matters for retailers, in many markets (including China), retail legislation and rules differ from province to province, as well as at the national level.[37] For example, regulations allow foreign retail joint ventures to operate in more cities throughout China and to engage in wholesaling for the first time; however, most rural areas are off-limits to international retailers.[38]

Other types of regulations restrict expansion of superstores and hypermarkets (United Kingdom, France, and Belgium); limit the hours of operation to protect smaller stores (the Netherlands, Spain); require that stores locate in downtown areas (Germany); control disposal of packaging used for transportation (Germany); limit the use of promotional pricing (France, Germany);[39] and limit the period for sales. French companies, for example, rarely offer an extra product free because the amount companies are allowed to give away is minimal. In Germany, offering three products for the price of two or other bundling offers is illegal, and cash discounts to the consumer are limited.

Legislation has also created stores that limit access of local consumers. In addition to shops created for the use of different categories of consumers, such as diplomatic shops or shops for the military, different countries have shops that are open to all consumers except nationals. This is the case in countries where locals are not allowed access to hard currency, which must be channeled through the Central Bank, and where all hard currency retail transactions are conducted only with expatriates. The only advantage these stores offer is that they might carry select merchandise that is not readily available in the market. However, overall, the quality of the merchandise is not necessarily higher than that of goods in the open market.

12-4b Taxation and Cross-Border Shopping

In countries where consumers are not charged duties for products they purchase from a neighboring country (if the neighboring country belongs to the same free trade area, for example), **cross-border shopping** affects most retailers in the higher-tax countries. The United Kingdom, the Irish Republic, and Denmark charge much higher taxes than the rest of the European Union members. To avoid the large value-added tax on most products for personal consumption, consumers in these countries cross borders into countries where this tax is substantially lower. In this sense, consumers' purchase decisions are driven by tax differences rather than by underlying differences in producer prices, and cross-border shopping causes an inefficient allocation of resources, leading to significant reductions in sales by domestic retailers and manufacturers, reduced profits, and job losses.[40]

cross-border shopping
Purchasing products from a neighboring country where the consumers may be charged lower duties.

In other situations, retailers in neighboring countries suffer from the low taxes imposed by a tax haven nearby. Examples of consumer tax havens are Port Said in Egypt, and Bermuda or the Bahamas in North America, among others. In setting up retail operations overseas, a company must assess and seek the most favorable environment from the taxation perspective.

Alternatively, consumers may cross borders in search of quality, variety, and novelty, as in the case of Mexican consumers purchasing products at the Imperial Valley Mall in El Centro, California, located 10 miles north of the Mexican border. The mall targets about one million potential consumers living in Mexicali, Mexico.[41]

12-4c Variation in Retail Practices: A Consumer Perspective

Retail practices vary from one market to another. Consumers in the United States prefer to shop less frequently and purchase products in bulk, whereas consumers in Japan prefer to purchase products in smaller quantities, packaged individually. In Asia, store demonstrations are popular, and in Japan and Korea, Saturday is a major shopping day, when shopping and attending the respective demonstration are a family affair. Consumers in Asia and the United Kingdom prefer products of the highest quality and are willing to pay the price. In Argentina and Saudi Arabia, consumers prefer to purchase food products at mom-and-pop stores, rather than at the supermarket, whereas in Mexico consumers continue to go to farmers' markets for fresh produce. Even bugs on fruit are important to consumers in the Philippines; they indicate that the fruit is ripe. Finally, in the United Kingdom, store name is a better indicator of quality for food products than brand name. Hence, private labels are thriving for popular stores.[42]

12-4d Variation in Retail Practice: Salespeople and Management

Sales service differs greatly from one market to another. Whereas in the United States it is customary to have friendly salespeople waiting on customers, treating them with respect, in many other countries this is not always the case. In Eastern and southeastern Europe, for example, salespeople tend to be curt, bordering on unfriendly. A Pizza Hut employee trained in customer service according to U.S. specifications sounds terribly out of place in Poland. In fact, the language used with customers appears to be unnatural. In the early 1990's, the telephone line of a Delta Airlines office in Bucharest sounded constantly busy. On arriving at the respective office, it was evident that two telephones were intentionally placed off the hook, while the agents were drinking coffee, chatting loudly with friends, ignoring their clients' presence. Customers were casually waited upon by one single agent.

In other examples, in China, the sales staff tend to be overly conscientious. If a customer forgets to pick up the change after a sale is complete, the salesperson will most likely follow him or her into the street to return the change. In other countries, the situation is quite the contrary. Salespeople keep the change and sell only those products that are priced under an even amount so that they can claim they do not have the change if a customer dares challenge them. In countries where there may be shortages of certain products, salespeople are bribed with money and other goods such as coffee, cigarettes, and perfume.

Finally, certain stores charge an admission price to ensure that individuals permitted to enter can actually afford the products sold there (an example is an antique store selling what locally would be considered masterpieces or national treasures). In these stores, it is also appropriate for customers to dress well so that they do not look "suspect." Similarly, not dressing well in environments considered upscale locally (despite the fact that, in most of the world, the respective retail environment would be perceived as average at best) could easily result in denial of service.

12-5 Trends and Issues in International Retailing[43]

Among the trends to watch for in international retailing are those related to technology and consumers. With regard to technology, retailers worldwide are integrating their different customer and supplier databases to create an efficient shopping environment for consumers. In developed countries, new technology, such as Fujitsu's Transaction Solutions' Pervasive Retailing Framework (PRF), is able to coordinate independent retailing applications—such as point-of-sale hardware, wireless shopping cards, and loyalty software—into an efficient customer experience. As customers use their PDA to access their loyalty account on the grocer's website, they download their shopping list and the shopping cart guides them through the store, interacting with kiosks at the deli and pharmacy, offering personalized coupons, and helping them proceed to checkout.

Technology is also increasing the transparency of the marketplace. This has an impact on prices, but it also applies to every attribute of the brand mix. The use of child labor, environmentally unfriendly suppliers, and other questionable activities can easily be discovered. Technology also creates highly informed consumers and eliminates the need for retail staff that try to sell consumers products. Finally, technology also means that more consumers will become retailers through auction sites or other e-commerce venues, taking share away from conventional retailers.

In developing countries, there will be faster retail growth as the populations remain relatively young. In addition, there will be two billion middle-class consumers at the end of this decade, most of them in developing countries, with more disposable income to spend on clothing and home goods, rather than just on food products. For this reason, more and more specialty stores are successfully pursuing international expansion.

In developed countries, consumer demographics present a problem to retailers, as their aging consumers' spending on services (travel, health care) will increase faster than spending on goods. Moreover, in these countries, customers are taking charge, defining for retailers their preferences for quality, convenience, and low price, making it difficult for retailers to make a solid profit.

Summary

Provide an overview and description of the general merchandise retailing category and offer examples and illustrations. In the general merchandise retailing category are a number of retailers. Specialty stores, offering narrow assortments and deep product lines, are rapidly increasing their presence internationally. From The Gap to Mango to Marks & Spencer, retailers find success well beyond their national borders. Specialized markets are omnipresent worldwide. Department stores are experiencing a decline, with some exceptions. Innovative stores that position themselves creatively have more success. In Asia, the more successful department stores are those that position themselves as European retailers. General merchandise discount stores are rapidly expanding, with great success. Walmart, in particular, has made great strides in conquering international markets. Category specialists, specializing in one product category, are also very successful in their international pursuits. Off-price stores, a staple of U.S. retailing offering brand name products at lower prices, are in great demand in other countries. Recently, such retailers have made substantial inroads into markets in Asia and Europe. Catalog showrooms, selling high-turnover, brand name goods at discount prices, are also successful internationally, with many competing players. The IKEA "model" has been the most successful to date.

Provide an overview and description of the food retailing category and offer examples and illustrations. Food retailers include conventional supermarkets, which are dominated by national and regional chains. Superstores can be combination stores (food and drug) or hypermarkets, which are successful abroad but are slow to become mainstream retailers in the United States. Warehouse clubs are becoming popular worldwide, and many U.S. retailers in this category are doing well. Convenience stores abound in both developing and developed countries, with many chains developing in conjunction with gas stations.

Provide an overview and description of the nonstore retailing category and offer examples and illustrations. Nonstore retailing is one of the areas with the highest growth and unlimited opportunities. Internet retailing has vastly expanded opportunities for small and medium-sized retailers all over the world. Vending machines are increasing in sophistication and have different formats and capabilities in each market where they are available; the products they can carry also differ. Television home shopping is attracting more audiences and also offers opportunities to brick-and-mortar retailers to expand. Catalog retailers are still strong, expanding rapidly beyond their home-country borders. Direct selling and network marketing are gaining ground rapidly, especially in developing countries.

Address issues related to legislation, taxation, and retailing practices around the world. Retailers have many restrictions imposed on them, and those restrictions vary from one market to another. The restrictions cover hours of operation, sales activity, and pricing techniques; or the restrictions may limit access to local consumers. Retailing practices vary from one market to another. Salespeople may be more courteous and solicitous in some countries, and consumers may be more demanding in certain markets, shop more or less frequently, and may or may not rely on a product's brand name as an indication of quality.

Key Terms

all-purpose discount stores	general merchandise discount stores
catalog retailers	hypermarkets
catalog showrooms	interactive home shopping
category killers	Internet retailing
category specialists	multilevel marketing
combination stores	network marketing
convenience stores	off-price retailers
conventional supermarkets	specialized markets
cross-border shopping	specialty stores
department stores	superstores
direct mail retailing	television home shopping
direct selling	vending machines
electronic retailing	warehouse clubs
food retailers	wholesale clubs

Discussion Questions

1.   What is the difference between a specialty store and a category specialist?

2.   Describe the state of the department store around the globe. What strategies appear to be more successful for department stores?

3.   Hypermarkets are a dominant retailing format in Europe but not in the United States. What are hypermarkets? Give examples of successful hypermarkets worldwide.

4.   Direct selling and network marketing have found great success in emerging markets. What is the difference between the two categories of retailers, and how do they gain access to consumers?

5.   What are some of the challenges that retailers face in international markets?

Chapter Quiz

True/False

1. General merchandise discount store retailers sell high volumes of merchandise and offer limited services; they also charge lower prices.

Answer: True

Rationale: General merchandise discount retailers sell high volumes of merchandise, offer limited service, and charge lower prices.

Section 12-3a, "General Merchandise Retailing"

2. Factory outlet shops are an example of off-price retailers.

Answer: True

Rationale: Among examples of off-price retailers are factory outlet stores and close-out retailers, with broad, inconsistent assortments, as well as single-price retailers.

Section 12-3a, "General Merchandise Retailing"

3. Internet purchasing is experience driven in developed countries.

Answer: False

Rationale: In developed countries, Internet purchasing is consumption market driven and not experience driven. Consumers shop to satisfy their needs and wants but do not view Internet surfing as a pleasure trip, as would consumers going to a mall or a store.

Section 12-3c, "Nonstore Retailing"

Multiple Choice

1.   The three main retail formats are

    a.   general merchandise, food, and nonstore.

    b.   automotive, food, and nonstore.

    c.   general merchandise, automotive, and luxury.

    d.   none of the above

Answer: a is correct.

Rationale: The primary retail formats are general merchandise retailing, food retailing, and nonstore retailing.

Section 12-3, "Retail Formats: Variations in Different Markets"

2.   Retailers that offer a narrow product line and a wide assortment—for example, office supply stores—are examples of

    a.   specialized markets.

    b.   specialty stores.

    c.   department stores.

    d.   all-purpose discount stores.

Answer: b is correct.

Rationale: Retailers that offer a narrow product line and a wide assortment like office supply stores are known as specialty stores; large specialty stores are also known as category specialists or category killers.

Section 12-3a, "General Merchandise Retailing"

3.   Harrods of London exemplifies which of the following retail formats?

    a.   specialized markets

    b.   all-purpose discount stores

    c.   specialty stores

    d.   department stores

Answer: d is correct.

Rationale: Harrods is a department store, carrying a broad variety of goods and wide assortments.

Section 12-3a, "General Merchandise Retailing"

4.   Walmart and Target are all examples of

    a.   category specialists.

    b.   specialized markets.

    c.   all-purpose discount stores.

    d.   specialty stores.

Answer: c is correct.

Rationale: Walmart and Target are examples of stores in the all-purpose discount store category; they offer a wide variety of merchandise and limited depth.

Section 12-3a, "General Merchandise Retailing"

5.   Food retailers include which of the following?

    a.   superstores

    b.   convenience stores

    c.   warehouse clubs

    d.   all of the above

Answer: d is correct.

Rationale: Superstores, convenience stores, and warehouse clubs carry food products, among other goods.

Section 12-3b, "Food Retailers"

6.   Vending machines constitute a primary mode of retailing in

    a.   the United States.

    b.   the Netherlands.

    c.   Japan.

    d.   Canada.

Answer: c is correct.

Rationale: Vending machines are ubiquitous in Japan, where they sell just about anything one can think of, including beer, sausage, rice, life insurance, eggs, cameras, and pantyhose.

Section 12-3c, "Nonstore Retailing"

Chapter 12 Endnotes

1.   *Stores*, "2007 Global Powers of Retailing," Deloitte-Touche Tohmatsu, January 1, 2007.

2.   www.wal-martchina.com/english/walmart/index.htm (accessed May 18, 2012); *China Business Review*, "Profiles of Select Beijing Retailers," Vol. 32, No. 6, November/December 2005, pp. 14–17.

3.   *2012 Global Powers of Retailing*, Deloitte-Touche Tohmatsu, January 1, 2012.

4.   Ibid.

5.   For a discussion of these mergers, see Allyson L. Stewart Allen, "Ensure Success by Studying Europe's Lessons," *Marketing News,* Vol. 34, No. 4, February 14, 2000, p. 11; and "Global Retailing," *Chain Store Age,* pp. 69–82.

6.   *China Business Review*, "Profiles of Select Beijing Retailers," Vol. 32, No. 6, November/December 2005, pp. 14–17.

7.   "Mango Hires BBJ to Boost Brand in UK Stores Launch," *Marketing,* February 17, 2000, p.4.

8.   www.esprit.com

9.   See John S. Hill and Giles D'Souza, "Tapping the Emerging Americas Market," *The Journal of Business Strategy,* Vol. 19, No. 4, July/August 1998, pp. 8–11.

10.   www.harrods.com

11.   Dana-Nicoleta Lascu, Jose Fernandez-Olano, and Thomas D. Giese, "Holiday Shopping: A Cross-Cultural Examination of Spanish and American Consumers," in R. King (ed.), *Proceedings of the Fourth Triennial AMS/ACRA National Retailing Conference,* 1994, pp. 147–149.

12.   Brenda Sternquist, *International Retailing,* New York: Fairchild Publications, 1998.

13.   Andrew Ness, "Retail Space to Let," *The China Business Review,* Vol. 26, No. 3, May/June 1999, pp. 44–49; and "China: Shanghai Retail Sector in Transition," *International Market Insight Reports,* July 26, 1999, pp. 1–4.

14.   www.walmartstores.com, June 2011 Data Sheet (accessed May 18, 2012).

15.   www.staples.com (accessed May 18, 2012).

16.   http://about.officemax.com/html/officemax_company_faqs.shtml;

http://investor.officedepot.com/phoenix.zhtml?c=94746&p=irol-faq (accessed May 18, 2012).

17.   Peter Landers, "Stores and Stripes," *Far Eastern Economic Review,* Vol. 161, No. 52, December 24, 1998, pp. 48–50.

18.   *Stores*, "2012 Global Powers of Retailing," Deloitte-Touche Tohmatsu, January 1, 2012.

19.   http://samsclubanswercenter.custhelp.com/app/answers/detail/a_id/278/~/sam%27s-club-international (accessed May 18, 2012).

20.   http://phx.corporate-ir.net/phoenix.zhtml?c=83830&p=irol-homeprofile (accessed May 18, 2012); "Loyalty Helps Drive Club Sales Gains," *Discount Store News,* Vol. 38, No. 15, August 9, 1999, p. 65; "Costco Expands into Korea," *Discount Store News,* Vol. 37, No. 14, July 27, 1998, p. 54; Doug Desjardins, "Costco ramps up for international growth," *DSN Retailing Today,* Vol. 44, No. 4, February 28, 2005, pp. 4-6.

21.   "A Partnership," *Discount Store News,* pp. 85, 179.

22.   "Rio-to-Manila-to-Jakarta," *Communications News,* Vol. 35, No. 4, April 1998, p. 64.

23.   www.pricesmart.com/Investor (accessed May 18, 2012).

24.   Lynda Radosevich, "Going Global Overnight," *InfoWorld,* Vol. 21, No. 16, April 19, 1999, pp. 1–3.

25.   "Sticking to the Web," *Chain Store Age,* Vol. 74, No. 7, July 1998, pp. 153–155.

26.   Dean Foust, "Doug Daft Isn't Sugarcoating Things; He's Already Shaking Up Coke. But Can He Bring Back the Fizz?" *BusinessWeek,* Industrial/Technology Edition, No. 3667, February 7, 2000, p. 36.

27.   Emiko Terazono, "BBC and Channel 4 in Talks Over UKTV Stake Media," *Financial Times*, June 1, 2005, 20.

28.   *China Venture News,* "Saif Partners Picks China TV Home-Shopping Network as the Next Big IPO," August 15, 2005, www.chinaventurenews.com.

29.   www.pj.dk

30.   Sarah Lorge, "A Priceless Brand," *Sales and Marketing Management,* Vol. 150, No. 11, October 1998, pp. 102–111.

31.   Heather Retzlaff, "British Invasion," *Multichannel Merchant*, August 2006, Vol. 23, No. 8, August 2006, p. 7.

32.   Shannon Oberdorf, "U.S. Mailers Blitz Germany," *Catalog Age,* Vol. 15, No. 2, February 1998, p. 2.

33.   Nielsen, "Surging Internet Usage in Southeast Asia Reshaping the Media Landscape," November 10, 2011, http://blog.nielsen.com/nielsenwire/global/surging-internet-usage-in-southeast-asia-reshaping-the-media-landscape; www.mindjumpers.com/blog/2012/05/time-spend-online (accessed on June 3, 2012); Nielsen, "Digital Consumer Report Q3/Q4,"2011, http://nielsen.com/us/en/insights/reports-downloads/2012/us-digital-consumer-report.html.

34.   Adrian Sargeant and P. Msweli, "Network Marketing in South Africa: An Exploratory Study of Consumer Perception," *Journal of International Consumer Marketing,* Vol. 11, No. 3, 1999, pp. 51–66.

35. Jason Burke, "India postpones plan to allow in Walmart and Tesco," *The Guardian*, 5 December, 2011, 12; Joe Leahy, "Indian Regulations Hampers Retail Growth Protectionist Rules Keep Big Foreign Names Away, But Domestic Operators Are Targeting the Market," *Financial Times*, October 26, 2006, 25.

36.   Mei Fong, "Avon's Calling, But China Opens Door Only a Crack," *Wall Street Journal*, February 26, 2007, B1.

37.   "China: The Grandest Opening Ever," *Chain Store Age,* Supplement: "Global Retailing," December 1997, pp. 32–35.

38.   "China: Shanghai Retail Sector in Transition," *International Market Insight Reports,* July 26, 1999, pp. 1–4.

39.   See Sternquist, *International Retailing,* 1998; and David Reed, "Country Practice," *Marketing Week,* Vol. 20, No. 4, July 3, 1997, pp. 45–49.

40.   Ian Crawford and Sarah Tanner, "Bringing It All Back Home: Alcohol Taxation and Cross-Border Shopping, *Fiscal Studies,* Vol. 16, No. 2, May 1995, pp. 94–115.

41.   Connie Robbins Gentry, "Border Malls," *Chain Store Age,* Vol. 80, No. 4, April 2004, p. 81.

42.   Terry Hennessy, "International Flavors," *Progressive Grocer,* Vol. 78, No. 8, August 1999, pp. 67–73.

43.   Adapted from *Stores*, "2007 Global Powers of Retailing," Deloitte-Touche Tohmatsu: January 1, 2007.

Case 12-1

Stefanel Canada

Jean Luc Rocher, formerly with a leading department store in Montreal, is contemplating opening a clothing specialty store with European flair that would appeal to the city's large middle class. In his many years with various specialty retailers and department stores, he noted the strong appeal of European stores to the local market.

Stylish department stores abound. Holt Renfrew, for instance, founded as a hat shop in Quebec City, is known for its many exclusive designers, branded lines, and its Holt Renfrew Private Brand collections. L'Aubainerie offers excellent product selections at competitive prices. Other popular department stores are La Baie and Hoda. In addition, numerous specialty clothing stores draw Canadian consumers and Montreal visitors alike: Gap, Benetton, Abercrombie & Fitch, and Canadian clothing shops are among many retailers present in the city.

Jean Luc knows that Montreal is a mature market for clothing stores but believes that there is sufficient demand for a clothing store that carries with it personality, as well as a history of success in Europe. Ever since his last visit to Europe, where he shopped at Stefanel, a clothing specialty store on Rue de Rennes, in Paris, and on Theatinerstrasse in Munich, Jean Luc has contemplated the idea of bringing the popular chain to Canada.

Stefanel started more than 40 years ago in Ponte di Piave, close to Venice, Italy, where Carlo Stefanel produced knitwear in his factory, the "Maglificio Piave." At first, the company sold its products through Italian wholesalers. In the 1970s, the company diversified to offer sportswear, denimwear, and prêt-a-porter collections, selling the merchandise in modern, stylish retail outlets. The company continues to produce knitwear, which is its core business, in a plant in Salgareda, Italy. In 2000, Stefanel further expanded into Germany in a take-over of Hallhuber GMBH, a clothing retail chain in Munich, and it has a 50 percent stake in Nuance, the leader in airport retailing.

The company's brand is well known in much of Europe: Its stores in many Western European countries are located centrally, in the main downtown shopping centers. They are stylish and have daring ads. Joakim Jonason, the talent behind the provocative Diesel jeans advertisements, is now in charge of the Stefanel advertising account at MADE, a Leo Burnett company. An ad aimed at movie audiences in Europe opens at dawn at the Boom Boom Circus, where the daughter of the dwarf ringmaster has just spent the night with the bearded lady's husband, resulting in chaos, until the husband wakes up from his dream. The tagline used is "Stefanel. Now you wake up." Stefanel uses "Now" in all its ads, on shopping bags, and on its website.

Stefanel also has several stores in East Asia—in Hong Kong, South Korea, Taiwan, and Thailand—and in the Middle East—in Kuwait and the United Arab Emirates. In 2007, it opened its first store in China, in Shenzhen. Stefanel had actually opened a store in China in 1992, but it did not make any headway then due to the immaturity of the Chinese market. It is working in cooperation with Hong Kong High Fashion Group to subsequently expand to Beijing, Shanghai, Macao, and Hong Kong. It is currently solidifying an expansion in the former Eastern Bloc, into Croatia, the Czech Republic, Slovakia, Slovenia, Romania, and Russia. In the Americas, Stefanel is present only in Los Angeles and Chicago in the United States; in Hamilton, Bermuda; and in Santiago de Chile. A retail franchise in Canada may be attractive to the company and appeal to Canadian consumers as smart, casual clothing with European flair.

Jean Luc Rocher is presently consulting with investors to evaluate the likelihood of success of a Stefanel retail outlet in Montreal. He learned that Stefanel has important and costly requirements for new franchises. For example, the stores must be located on the main commercial streets of cities with a population of at least 50,000; they should have a surface area between 120 and 250 square meters and numerous wide store windows. The franchise is permitted to use only Stefanel's furnishings that distinguish the store from those of other companies. Stefanel would provide the franchisee with architects free of charge; with training seminars for the store's personnel; and with shop-window designs, posters, and images. Stefanel will lease software for sales and inventory analysis and the appropriate hardware to ensure coordination and profitability. Although the company protects franchises in the sense that it limits same-store competition, Stefanel has just partnered with Pino Venture to pursue Internet shoppers.

Jean Luc's questions include: What would be the appropriate expansion strategy into the Canadian market? Would his Montreal store be the first leg in the company's international expansion into Canada? Would Stefanel sell other franchises to competitors? To what extent will Internet sales cannibalize Jean Luc's brick-and-mortar operation? How should he most effectively sell the Stefanel franchise to his investor friends?

Sources: http://www.holtrenfrew.com; http://www.hbc.com/bay; http://www.stefanel.it/; *China Retail News,* "Stefanel Opens First Store in China," May 9, 2007; Laure Wentz, "The World," *Advertising Age,* Vol. 73, No. 37, September 16, 2002, p. 14.

Analysis Suggestions

1.   Identify the retail category of Stefanel.

2.   What are some of its competitors worldwide? How is Stefanel different from its competitors?

3.   What is the company's international expansion strategy? How does Jean Luc Rocher's proposal fit into the company's expansion plans?

Chapter 13: The International Promotional Mix and Advertising Strategies

Chapter Outline:
Chapter Objectives
13-1 The International Promotional Mix
13-2 The International Communication Process
13-3 Advertising
      13-3a The Media Infrastructure
      13-3b The Advertising Infrastructure
      13-3c The Advertising Strategy

Summary
Key Terms
Discussion Questions
Chapter Quiz
Notes

Case 13-1 Selling the Donnelly Brand in Romania

Learning Objectives

After studying this chapter, you should be able to:

- Describe the international promotional mix and the international communication process.

- Explore the international advertising formats and practices around the world.

- Describe the international advertising and media infrastructure and infrastructure-related challenges in different markets.

- Describe advertising strategies and budgeting decisions and offer examples of international applications.

Promotion and, as an element of promotion, advertising are omnipresent in all countries of the world. Promotion has become part of the world landscape, framing highways, lighting crowded downtowns, projecting glamour on walls of slums, and shading street cafés. It reaches consumers in high-income and low-income countries alike, on their doorsteps, in mail or e-mail, and via blasting stereos or drumbeats. Promotion is daily life in the markets of Dar es Salaam, in the blazing Shanghai skyline at night, and on the famous avenues of wanton consumption in Buenos Aires and Manhattan. Promotion is condemned for creating unaffordable consumption desires and celebrated for its creativity and for setting new trends in general, and in the relationship between consumers and business, in particular. Unilever can claim both, based on the following example, illustrating the Dove and the Axe campaigns.

Unilever's Advertising Strategy: Dove vs. Axe

"Evolution," Dove's famous viral video, and other new media ads were the big winners at the Cannes Lions International Advertising Festival in 2007. Dove's spot, from Ogilvy, Toronto, was a 60-plus-second spot that barely qualified for the category. It first went viral on the Web and garnered more attention than a Super Bowl ad. Dove had the foresight to run the ad just once on TV, so it qualified for the Lions award. The Lions award also reflects a change in the realm of promotion. Most of the awards went to new media (Internet) ads.[1]

The "Evolution" video shows a woman undergoing a complete makeover, from human to billboard model. It presents a succession of stylists poking and lining the face and teasing the hair and a computer elongating the neck and enhancing the eyes for a billboard-ready look. The ad is part of Dove's "Campaign for Real Beauty." The campaign fights the definition of beauty that uses narrow, stifling stereotypes and tries to build an acceptance that real beauty comes in many shapes, sizes, and ages. The tool the campaign uses is advertising that inspires women and society to think differently about what is defined as beautiful.[2]

In the campaign, Dove—a Unilever company specializing in skin, body cleansing, and hair care products—uses the "Evolution" video, as well as other advertisements on television, in magazines, and Internet advertising, to portray women older than 50 as beautiful, whether they are nude or dressed up or down. The company websites in most of Europe, Australia, and New Zealand, as well as in Japan, South Korea, Chile, Canada, and the United States, portray women of all sizes, ethnicities, and ages, with wrinkles, moles, pimples and all. In the Romanian website, the Dove campaign asks women to submit a photo that indicates how beautiful they are for a contest where, if selected, they win a cruise on the Mediterranean. The site lists the winners' names as well.[3]

Interestingly, in 2012, Unilever received the Creative Effectiveness Grand Prix at the Cannes Lions International Advertising Festival for its Axe "Excite" campaign, portraying voluptuous, sexy angels falling upon a small town from the heavens, walking until they stop in front of a man wearing Axe deodorant, and one by one, they rip off their halos and smash them. The tagline states, "Even Angels Will Fall." Unilever, through its advertising agency, BBH London, is treading aggressively into a territory where women are presented in all of the 75 countries where Unilever sells Axe as irresistible victims to men's charms. Previously it drew the attention of the Campaign for a Commercial Free Childhood (CCFC), a respected Boston-based activist group, for promoting Axe with the phrase "Bom Chicka Wah Wah," a musical expression associated with pornographic movies, and interpreted as a slang term for a sexual encounter: When a thin, attractive woman smelled Axe on a man nearby, she would blurt out "Bom Chicka Wah Wah." In its online campaign, the company webpages showed a map that depicted areas where women fell prey to Axe, and viewers were asked to find an area on a local map where they could click and watch women lose their minds... and their clothes.[4]

Much like the Dove advertisements, the Axe ads went viral and received much publicity – positive and negative. When comparing Unilever's two contradictory campaigns, Dove's Real Beauty and Axe's Excite, many are accusing the company of hypocrisy. Is this good marketing?

The previous Dove/Axe examples illustrate Unilever's creative and controversial approach to promotion, from advertising to sales promotion to public relations. This chapter discusses the international promotional mix and the international communication process. Of the mix items, the chapter focuses on advertising and illustrates advertising formats, practices, and infrastructure-related issues around the world.

13-1 The International Promotional Mix

The components of the **international promotional mix** are international advertising, international sales force management, international sales promotion, and public relations and publicity (see Figure 13-1). Companies use the promotional mix to communicate with international consumers about their products and services. In the process of expanding internationally, companies are faced with numerous challenges to their plans for communicating with the world's consumers. Many of the challenges are attributed to differences in culture. As described in Chapter 5, "Cultural Influences on International Marketing," understanding the norms, motivations, attitudes, interests, and opinions of the target market is crucial to company success in marketing to and communicating with different cultures around the globe. Companies also must be prepared to handle the challenges presented by the local media, local advertising infrastructure, and the different layers of government regulating all aspects of communication with the target market.

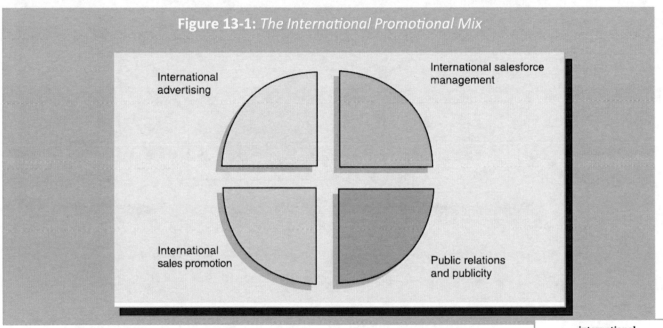

Figure 13-1: *The International Promotional Mix*

Section 13-2 describes the international communication process, and Section 13-3 presents the topic of international advertising. Chapter 14, "International Publicity, Public Relations, and Sales Promotion Strategies," and Chapter15, "International Personal Selling and Personnel Management," will address the remaining elements of the international promotional mix: sales force management and the expatriate sales force, international sales promotion, international public relations, and international publicity, completing the topic of the international promotional mix.

13-2 The International Communication Process

The **international communication process** involves using the entire promotional mix to communicate with the final consumer (see Figure 13-2). Regardless of the elements of the promotional mix involved, the communication essentially has the same format. The international sponsor **(sender),** usually represented by an advertising agency, encodes a message into words and images. The message is then translat-

international promotional mix
The different modes of communication with international consumers about products and services, using international advertising, international sales force management, international sales promotion, public relations, and publicity.

international communication process
The communication process that takes place between the product sponsor and the international target market.

sender
The sponsor of an advertisement, usually represented by an advertising agency, who encodes the message into words and images and communicates it to the target market.

ed into the language of the target market and transmitted through a **channel of communication,** or **medium,** to the international consumer in the target market **(receiver).** The medium may be a **nonpersonal medium:**

- A **print medium,** such as a newspaper, magazine, billboard, pamphlet, or a point-of-purchase display

- A **broadcast medium,** such as television and radio

- An **interactive medium,** such as a web page or a computer terminal on the retailer's premises

channel of communication
The medium used to communicate a message about a product to the consumer.

medium/media
The channel(s) of communication that a company uses to send to the target consumer a message about its product or services.

receiver
The target market that receives the advertising message from a sender.

nonpersonal medium
A channel of communication such as a print medium, a broadcast medium, or an interactive medium that does not involve contact between the seller and the consumer.

print medium
A nonpersonal channel of communication such as a newspaper, magazine, billboard, pamphlet, or point-of-purchase display.

broadcast medium
A nonpersonal channel of communication such as television or radio.

interactive medium
A nonpersonal channel of communication such as a Web page or a computer terminal on the retailer's premises.

personal medium
A communication channel that involves contact between the seller and the consumer.

telemarketing
A personal channel of communication that involves a salesperson calling on consumers.

noise
All the potential interference in the communication process.

feedback
Information regarding the effectiveness of a company's message.

encoding
The process whereby the advertiser puts the company's message about the product into words and images that are aimed at the target consumer.

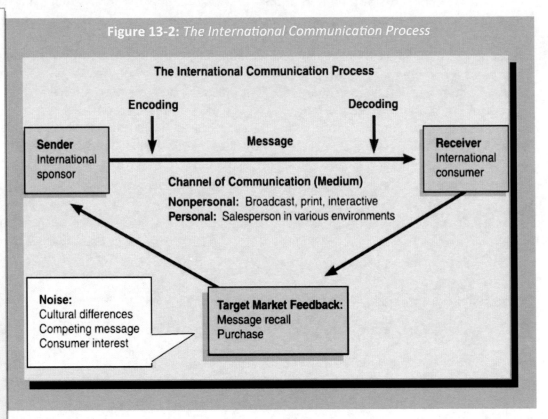

Figure 13-2: *The International Communication Process*

Alternatively, the channel may be a **personal medium:**

- A salesperson calling on a supplier or a door-to-door salesperson calling on consumers

- A telemarketer calling on consumers **(telemarketing)**

- A trade show, where one can address questions to an individual who is knowledgeable about the product

The international consumer (receiver) receives the message and decodes it into meaning. Ideally, the meaning of the decoded message should be identical to the meaning of the encoded message. However, **noise**—all the potential interference in the communication process, particularly noise attributed to cultural differences—may impede communication. During the message transmission and delivery processes, noise may interfere with proper message reception. The sponsor (sender) collects and relies on information regarding the effectiveness of the message **(feedback)** to evaluate the success of the promotional campaign. Such information may be provided by sales data or by advertising research evaluating message recall rates.

Each step of the international communication process presents challenges to the message sponsor beyond those encountered when marketing to home-country consumers. First, when **encoding** the message, the source determines whether the attitudes, interests, and motivations of consumers in the international target market are different from those in the home-country target market. Manufacturers of Peugeot bicycles in France selling their product in Belgium and the United States need to be aware that consumer motivations behind the purchase differ. In Belgium, the main purpose of using the Peugeot bicycle is transportation. Major cities have bicycle paths on the sidewalks, and pedestrians and automobiles are not allowed to block them. Bicycle paths also have their own signals at intersections. In the countryside, paths, in parallel with the main roads or highways, are reserved for bicycles. A Belgian consumer who purchases a Peugeot bicycle wants a product that is reliable and can perform optimally, regardless of weather. Communication about the product, then, should stress durability, reliability, and quality. In the United States, a Peugeot bicycle is used primarily for recreation. Communication about the product is more likely to be successful if it focuses on a weekend recreational activity and on performance.

Similarly, Pizza Hut in the United States and the United Kingdom is a staple family restaurant for busy families who do not have time to cook. Pizza Hut advertising focuses on deals for the entire family. In Poland, Pizza Hut is the in-place for dinner accompanied by techno music before consumers descend to the downstairs disco in the city of Wroclaw. It is also the place for a business lunch in Warsaw's prestigious Marriott building, located strategically between stores selling haute couture. Consequently, communication about Pizza Hut in Poland should not limit itself to a family focus.

When encoding the message, one must ensure that the message is appropriately translated. In the process of translating the message, one should note that language is closely related to advertising strategy. For example, English requires less space in print and less airtime for broadcast advertising. This is one of the reasons it is widely used in advertising (see Figure 13-3). Translated into German, Dutch, or French, the headline, body copy, and tag line require more space for a print advertisement and more airtime for a broadcast ad.

Figure 13-3: *Lucky Strike's cigarettes' English message for German-speaking consumers: "iSmoke" – plays on the statement "I Smoke" and on the name of the trendy iPhone.*

From product name to the entire marketing communication, all must be monitored to ensure that the meanings intended are the meanings conveyed. There is an explosion of naming consultancies, set up as offshoots of advertising agencies, which develop product names that are intended to work worldwide. Because consumers travel everywhere, it is important that brand names are consistent in any country where they are sold.[5] From names such as Vauxhall's Nova automobile, meaning "no go" in Spanish, to airlines claiming that one will fly "naked" (as opposed to "on leather") in first class, companies have made many mistakes when communicating with international consumers.

Sending the message through the appropriate channel is often a challenge. The media infrastructure might be such that the most appropriate medium cannot be successfully used. In countries where mail is less reliable, such as India and Mali, it is advisable not to send direct mail containing samples. In other countries where the mailing system is reliable, such as Saudi Arabia, mail might not constitute a traditional medium for sending samples, and a direct mail package might be perceived as suspicious. In Rwanda and Burundi, the only broadcast medium available is the radio; however, international brands are rarely advertised on this medium. To reach the mass market in these two countries, the only appropriate communication medium is the billboard. Furthermore, it is preferable that the advertisement has few words and relies on pictorials to convey the message because many target consumers are illiterate.

All this competition, including other noise, such as audience inattention, from other channels of communication and from programming could negatively affect the **decoding** process, such that the target consumer does not fully comprehend the communication. To lessen the impact of these communication impediments, companies do the following:

> **decoding**
> The process whereby the target consumer receives the message from the advertiser and translates it into meaningful information.

- Hire research firms to evaluate the message in multiple international environments.
- Evaluate the effectiveness of the communication in attracting target market attention, using recall tests and other memory-based procedures.
- Evaluate the effectiveness of the communication in getting consumers to purchase the product.
- The company then uses this feedback in modifying or designing future communication strategies.

13-3 Advertising

International advertising is becoming increasingly complex. More local and international companies are competing for consumers who are increasingly sophisticated and demanding. International advertising is defined as *a nonpersonal communication by an identified sponsor across international borders, using broadcast, print, and/or interactive media.*

13-3a The Media Infrastructure

The **media infrastructure** provides different challenges in countries of different levels of economic development. And, even though the media structure is essentially the same in most industrialized countries, challenges still arise in terms of business practices: A medium might not be considered appropriate for advertising. For example, newspapers might not constitute the right medium for advertising a particular product in one country, whereas, in other countries, advertising a particular type of product or service might be restricted or prohibited in other media—for instance, television.

Media infrastructure challenges are discussed below. However, one additional caution is in order: It is not just the infrastructure that poses challenges in a target market, but also the status of promotion and the extent to which management considers promotion to be an important strategic tool. Take, for instance, the following case.

The Lower Status of Advertising in Germany

Germany's advertising market is the third largest in the world, behind the United States and Japan. However, German companies hold advertising in low regard. There, business strengths are linked to technical talent rather than to marketing talent. And, when the economy does not perform well, the first to go is advertising expenditures. As a result, ad agencies had to change their management styles. For example, executives at Leo Burnett in Frankfurt started becoming more involved in the agency's daily business, participating in all client meetings and even attending focus groups, to express their commitment to their clients. Also, the advertising companies have become more selective about the accounts they take on instead of going after every potential business.[6]

Media Challenges

Some of the challenges firms encounter on the media front are availability, reliability, restrictions, and costs.

Media Availability

An important issue facing the international marketing manager is **media availability,** the extent to which the media needed for a particular communication exist locally, and if they do exist, how they can be used as intended for the company communication. Certain types of media simply might not be available in a company's target markets. In many countries in sub-Saharan Africa, for example, there are no local television stations and access to television programming is possible only via satellite. Alternatively, there may be one or two government-owned or government-controlled stations that do not permit advertising or that limit advertising to certain

media infrastructure
The media vehicles and their structure in an international target market.

media availability
The extent to which media are available to communicate with target consumers.

times. Although some television owners might have access to international satellite and cable television, especially in the emerging markets in Asia and Latin America, many more cannot afford a satellite dish or a subscription to cable television. Access to these consumers, then, is limited. And, even though more and more consumers have access to Internet advertising worldwide, such access primarily favors consumers from more developed countries, or wealthy consumers and government employees from developing countries. See the following example of media in the Democratic Republic of Congo and Angola.

Media in Angola and the Democratic Republic of Congo[7]

Angola, a country in central southern Africa, is characterized by a rapidly growing media sector in a rapidly growing economy. The government is still grappling with the notion of a free media. There are 20 television sets and 68 radio sets per 1,000 people. There are 6 television stations, with a government-supervised station broadcasting in Portuguese being the most widely watched; a second is private and broadcasts in Portuguese; a third is TV Globo, which broadcasts in Portuguese in Brazil and Angola and is popular for its soaps; and the fourth is DStv, broadcasting in English from South Africa. In terms of newspapers, Angola has 4 dailies, 8 weeklies, and more than 14 Pan-African magazines. Cinema is not a viable advertising medium as there are too few cinemas available, but outdoor advertising offers a full range of opportunities. There are 172,000 Internet users, out of 15.9 million Angolans, and one Internet service provider.

In comparison, the Democratic Republic of Congo in eastern central Africa is a vast country with a surprisingly large and comprehensive media industry and with huge potential. There are 20 television sets and 358 radio sets per 1,000 people. There are 75 television stations, 3 national or almost national (1 government-owned and 2 private), and 72 regional, mostly private, television stations. There are about 170 radio stations, 13 of which are government-owned. There are 250 newspapers of all types, as well as French and Pan-African magazines. Cinema is not a viable advertising medium, but outdoor advertising offers a full range of opportunities. There are 140,600 Internet users, out of 57.5 million Congolese, and one Internet service provider.

Those consumers who can, indeed, afford satellite and other pay TV services have access to numerous programs, including programming from the United States, such as the MTV Base Africa channel. MTV Base Africa is a 24-hour, English-language music television channel, reflecting the tastes and interests of African youths through African and international music videos, mainly driven by the pounding beat of rap and hip-hop. As in its other international markets, MTV is using local management teams to create and market programming that connects with the local audiences. It is currently broadcasting to 48 countries in sub-Saharan Africa, reaching approximately 1.3 million households via the multichannel operators DStv, Trend TV, CTNL, and FSTV.[8]

Media Reliability

Media reliability, the extent to which the existing media reliably reach the target consumer in the intended format and within the intended time frame, is also an important consideration. In some cases, media may be unreliable. Magazine or newspaper issues might not be printed on time, or publishers might accept more advertisements than they can print. The quality of the medium itself may be questionable. Local newspapers might not be of a high enough quality to print advertising for a global brand. Television stations might go off the air indefinitely at inopportune times, such as when a company's advertisement is scheduled to air. This often happens to small television stations that compete with government stations for viewers' attention.

> **media reliability**
> The probability of the media to air advertising messages on time, at an acceptable quality, and with the agreed on frequency.

Media Restrictions

Media restrictions refer to the different limitations that existing media pose on the sponsor. For example, the media could limit the types and number of advertisements aired or published. As mentioned in Chapter 5, "Cultural Influences on International Marketing," advertising in a number of Islamic countries might not permit

> **media restrictions**
> Legal or self-imposed restrictions on the types and the number of advertisements aired or published.

the portrayal of women, whereas in other countries (China, for instance) the media do not readily encourage the advertising of feminine hygiene products. Airtime might be limited; for example, the European Union allows only 12 minutes per hour for advertising on each television station.

Advertising also might be clustered and separated from editorial content in newspapers or magazines or from television programming. Many television stations in Europe, as well as in South America (Brazil, for instance), broadcast television advertising only between programs, in clusters. Consumers typically choose to engage in other activities in the home during that time. In these countries, a better venue for firms that need to send their message using visuals in broadcast media is movie advertising. In Europe, cinema advertisements are typically shown before films to a captive audience. Usually, viewers see about 25 minutes of product and service advertising and just five minutes of movie trailers. Films also have an intermission, when viewers are urged to purchase products that the movie theater offers (soft drinks, popcorn and the like). In many developing countries where the literacy rate is low, advertising is primarily limited to billboards that do not display words other than the company logo and brand name.

Media scheduling also constitutes a restriction. Lag times between the submission of the advertisement and printing could reach as much as one year for some publications, primarily due to space restrictions allotted to advertising. Also, a contract that requires a publication or a television station to print or air an advertisement on a particular date is not backed by guarantees in many countries.

Media Costs

Media costs differ greatly between countries, and even within a particular country. Factors that account for this difference range from income per capita of a target market and competition for media by advertisers, to firm status (a local firm is charged less than an international firm in Eastern European countries, China, Cuba, and Vietnam).

Costs are high in countries where the advertising campaign must be translated into multiple languages. India is an interesting case in point. A campaign aimed at a more educated consumer can be communicated effectively in either Hindi or English. To reach the masses in southern India and penetrate this target market, however, translating the advertisements into Malealam, Tamil, and Telegu would be important.

Media Formats, Features, and Trends around the World

Advertising Posters on Kiosks and Fences

Advertising posters appear on kiosks and fences in the United States to a more limited extent than in much of the rest of the world. In the United States, some kiosks display neighborhood announcements, and construction fences in larger cities display advertisements for plays, concerts, and art exhibits (see Figure 13-4). In much of the rest of the world, especially in developing countries, kiosks display advertisements for the international products they sell. Kiosks are valuable and relatively inexpensive communication venues for multinationals. They are typically required to have posters displayed in exchange for having the rights to carry particular brands.

Fences and other display structures are omnipresent in international capitals and small towns alike (see Figure 13-5). In France, the *affichiste* movement of modern art, whose works are displayed in major museums worldwide, used layers of posters that had been displayed for decades and then torn off walls and placed on canvas.

Figure 13-4: Kiosks have many formats. Some are used just for the display of advertising, as the one in this figure, while others are used for the purpose of retailing – the latter might also carry advertisements.

Figure 13-5: *Advertisements are ever-present on fences in large urban areas.*

Advertising on the Sides of Private Homes

Typically located in high traffic areas, homes from Bangladesh to Bulgaria display advertising for international brands. This advertising constitutes a substantial source of revenue for the homeowners and owners of larger commercial buildings (see Figure 13-6).

Figure 13-6: *Advertising on the side of these private homes benefits the apartment owners in Taipei, Taiwan.*

Advertising on Outdoor Umbrellas

In the United States, outdoor umbrellas, if they contain any information at all, typically display the name of the restaurant where they are located. In other locations worldwide, umbrellas display international brand names, such as Marlboro, Coca-Cola, Pepsi, and others (see Figure 13-7).

Figure 13-7: *Outdoor umbrellas in Lhasa, Tibet, compete with colorful local ads and public information.*

The Omnipresent Billboard

Although **billboards** are quite common in the United States, in other parts of the world they dominate the landscape. Examples of billboard advertisements include elegant advertisements for Coca-Cola in Russia and for the same brand at the railway station in Barcelona, Spain; ads for new housing developments that promise the good life in Shanghai, where they are allowed (in Beijing, the mayor is attempting to ban them); or for a new movie in Beijing, just outside the movie theater where it is playing. An especially interesting development is the fact that, increasingly, local ads are of comparable quality and compete effectively with ads of multinational firms. This new development is attributed to the proliferation of computer technology and lower technology costs.

Smaller billboards are used in captive environments such as bus and metro stations. Figure 13-8 portrays a billboard used in a Czech bus station.

Figure 13-8: *Billboards are common in train and bus stations.*

The Dominance of Global Media

Late-night talk show host Jay Leno's jokes are a staple around the world, as are Conan O'Brien's. CNN and Bloomberg broadcast all over the world, including in sub-Saharan Africa. CNN is a popular television station in Ethiopia for those who can afford a television set; in fact, Addis Ababa, its capital city, often has a more accurate forecast of the next day's weather in Hong Kong from the CNN satellite than for drought-prone regions in Ethiopia itself.[9] European television stations have competitors such as CNN Europe, Sky, and NBC. Asian stations compete with global companies such as CNN, MTV, NBC, Turner Broadcasting, Walt Disney/Capital Cities ABC, and the Cartoon Channel. ESPN Asia broadcasts American basketball in the Philippines and baseball in Taiwan, and millions of Chinese viewers watch badminton and U.S. National Basketball Association games.[10] Rupert Murdoch alone owns Star Plus, Star Plus Japan, Star Chinese Channel, and Star Movies in Asia, and has, among other media interests, resonant media companies such as Fox Broadcasting, 20th Century Fox, 20th Century Television, as well as investments in BskyB, Vox Channel, El Canal Fox, Australia's Channel 7, and 130 newspapers worldwide. All these stations can sell international brands to consumers all over the world.

Magazines such as *Glamour, Cosmopolitan,* and *Mademoiselle* are published in languages ranging from Mandarin and Italian to Polish and Japanese. These magazines are vehicles for global, regional, and local advertising campaigns of multinational companies.

Infomercials and Television Shopping Networks

Infomercials and **television shopping networks** once were a North American phenomenon. Currently, infomercials and television shopping channels exist in much of the industrialized world and in many emerging markets. Not only have QVC and the Home Shopping Network expanded in Europe, Latin America, and Asia, but also local competition is growing rapidly. Home Order Television in Germany has created a strategic alliance with Quelle, the catalog store discussed in Chapter 12,

---

billboards
Advertisements in public areas appearing on large posters or electronic panels.

infomercials
Long television advertisements (one-half to one full hour in length) that are positioned as programming.

television shopping networks
Cable channels that sell products to a television audience.

"International Retailing," selling its products to television shoppers, and Acorn in China is the leading local shopping channel in this rapidly growing sales medium.

English in Local Advertising

Section 13-2, "The International Communication Process," stressed some of the benefits of using English for advertising. Other reasons for using English, particularly in advertising by local firms to local consumers, are to stress a cosmopolitan attitude and to endow a product or service with status. Words such as "very quick" are used in advertising for a tire inflation service *(vulcanizacion)* in Ecuador and "super wonderful" to describe the travel bags sold by a company in Poland. This is true also for product and service brand names—for example, the Romanian-American University and American Gold for a brand of gold-plated jewelry—when the products or services really have little to do with the United States, Canada, or Mexico. Figures 13-9 through 13-11 show some examples of advertisements using English in non-English–speaking countries, aimed at local consumers. Also, they show some examples of English names for products and retail establishments appealing to local consumers in non-English–speaking countries.

Figure 13-9: Use of English in Estonia, appealing to Estonian consumers, promoting Big Milk ice cream.

Figure 13-10: A bus advertisement for Chinese consumers: La Maison (with a wants-to-be-French-but-it's-not spelling) and advertised in English: New! opening . . . for a restaurant-cum-cabaret establishment.

Figure 13-11: *Swedish brand Zewa sells toilet paper and advises customers, in English, that it is a "big pack" and suggests that they should "open here."*

Product Placement

Product placement involves placing brands in movies with the purpose of promoting the products to viewers. Studies have found that product placement can produce a greater level of advertising recall than television advertising.[11] Year after year, films exported by the United States have swept the globe and, as a result of the world dominance of Hollywood films, product placement is likely to be a venue providing high exposure for international brands.

However, there are restrictions against product placement. The most restrictive has been the European Union (EU), where, until recently, product placement has been illegal in many EU countries. And, in spite of changes in EU law in 2007, Hollywood's product-placement continues to be problematic.

> **product placement**
> The strategy of placing brands in movies with the purpose of promoting the products to viewers.

Product Placement in the European Union

In 2007, the European Union's (EU) national governments approved sweeping changes to the bloc's television-broadcasting rules, extending the amount of advertising allowed and allowing product placement in TV shows. The rules now allow product placement, although only under certain conditions. For example, the products featured must not be too prominent and must come with repeated disclaimers to viewers. In addition, they are banned from children's programs, news programs, and documentaries. These restrictions apply to all EU programming, including shows created outside the EU, which means it would be difficult or even illegal for broadcasters to show many U.S. programs, which are often laden with product placements.

EU film and TV companies have lobbied hard against product placement, and, in general, for tough limits on Hollywood imports. Of additional concern to European television broadcasters is that the EU has instituted no Internet regulations, and now the broadcasters are facing increased competition from services such as YouTube and mobile-multimedia companies, which places them at a competitive disadvantage.[12]

Advertising Regulations

Advertisers encounter numerous restrictions in their efforts to deliver communication to consumers worldwide. Most regulations are imposed by national (host-country) governments. Alternatively, local firms have established traditions and self-imposed regulations that must be observed by newcomers to the local advertising scene. Among advertising restrictions are the following:

- **Comparative advertising**—In the past, continental Europe condemned comparative advertising as denigration and unfair competition. However, Directive 2006/114/EC of the European Parliament and of the European Council of 12 December, 2006, acknowledges that comparative advertising, when it compares material, relevant, verifiable, and representative features and is not misleading, may be a legitimate means of informing consumers of their advantage. Considerations of comparative advertising should determine if the advertising is detrimental to competitors, distorts competition, or have an adverse effect on consumer choice. Comparative advertising should take EU trademark law into consideration. As such, firms are not allowed to use competitors' trademarks and other copyrighted materials.[13]

  Worldwide, comparative advertising is typically not used, even if laws allow it, and consumers have difficulty understanding comparative ads. For example, a company that engages in comparative advertising in the Arab world may be taking a risk, because the Arabic consumer is not accustomed to it. This lack of exposure to comparative ads, and not a lack of sophistication, may lead to confusion between the advertised brands.[14]

- **Advertising to children**—This is a contentious issue in high-income countries, but a non-issue in developing countries and emerging markets. In the EU, the European Union Directive Concerning Television Broadcasting does not permit advertising that directly exhorts minors to buy a product or a service, that directly encourages minors to persuade their parents to purchase the goods advertised, that exploits the trust minors place in adults, or that shows minors in dangerous situations. Local law restricts advertising to children further: French law limits the use of children as endorsers in advertising and prohibits the use of children's heroes as endorsers.[15]

- **Advertising vice products**—The European Union Directive Concerning Television Broadcasting prohibits television advertising for tobacco products and prescription drugs.[16]

- **Other regulations**—The French have regulations requiring advertisers (and all broadcasters) to keep the language pure and not to use English terms or anglicized French terms (Franglais). Singapore does not permit advertising that is sexual in nature. The use of sex in advertising is also banned in most Islamic countries. Other challenges are posed by the need to copyright the advertising message in different languages in countries where multiple languages are spoken.

One of the most restrictive marketing regulations in Europe ended in December 2006—a ban on television advertising by supermarkets, hypermarkets, department stores, and other merchants. In January 2007, retailers responded like shoppers, rushing to advertise on television. The purpose of the ban was to safeguard advertising revenue for French local newspapers and to protect small retailers from advertising blitzes by large chains. In 2004, the European Commission forced France to drop the restriction on retailers. France continues to uphold a restriction regarding the television advertising of films. This restriction is intended to protect French movie producers from big-budget Hollywood marketing.

Before this regulation expired, retailers spent 38 percent of their budget on print ads, 34 percent on radio ads, and 23 percent on outdoor advertising. Television advertising by retailers will have a negative impact on the other media. The print media, however, may retain a competitive edge: To protect them from a free-fall of advertising revenue, advertisers are allowed to include detailed information on product prices and sales in newspapers ads but are prohibited from mentioning prices or sales in their television advertisements.[17]

13-3b The Advertising Infrastructure

Advertising Agencies

The approach to advertising varies from one company to another, and the strategies used by different companies are numerous. Advertising decisions may be determined based on the product strategy. In one example, Henkel, a leading German manufacturer of household and cleaning products, uses a Pan-European approach to advertising. The company attempts to achieve efficiency in advertising production and advertising impact by identifying how a particular product addresses target market needs (for consumers in Europe or a larger area); by assigning that specific need or benefit to one product with one brand name; by assigning that brand to one brand manager and to one advertising agency to develop and market; and by not permitting the use of that individual brand's benefit, name, or creative campaign for any other brand in the company.[18] This strategy results in the use of multiple advertising agencies, depending on the brand involved. Alternatively, the choice of the advertising agency in international markets may be based on a long-standing relationship with a particular agency in the home market. An advertising agency could follow a leading global brand anywhere in the world. This has been the case of McCann Erickson, the advertising agency that has been handling the Coca-Cola account in 60 countries since 1942[19]until recently—it has been replaced in a number of markets with its competitor, Leo Burnett.

A company can approach its international advertising strategy using one or more of the following options: developing local ads for the international markets in-house; developing ads using local advertising agencies, home-country agencies, or international advertising agencies with local offices; or using a combination strategy. The home-country agency and the in-house options by themselves are not likely to allow for local participation if they are located away from the target market.

The most common types of relationships between international corporations and the agencies providing advertising support are as follows:

- Hiring local advertising agencies
- Hiring international advertising agencies
- Hiring local advertising agencies to implement international agency messages

Hiring Local Advertising Agencies

A company that uses a localized strategy, targeting each individual market, is more likely to hire a local advertising agency. Hiring a local advertising agency is appropriate, especially when knowledge of the market is important. The Swedish furniture company IKEA, for example, engaged in a branding campaign aimed at the San Diego market. The company left it up to the San Diego IKEA franchise to hire a firm to build the IKEA brand in the San Diego market. It hired AM Advertising, a Los Angeles firm boasting top local talent.[20]

In a relatively uniform market, such as the Latin American market, advertisers often use Spanish and Portuguese to communicate with consumers. When a company advertises to the 25 countries of Latin America and the Caribbean, however, it is preferable to translate into each country's regional dialect to avoid presenting the company as an outsider.[21] A local agency could better design the campaign for each individual market. In addition to its knowledge of the local market, a local agency also offers the advantage of being capable of facilitating interaction with local media and government.

On the negative side, the quality of advertising is not at the level offered by a large international advertising agency. With the proliferation of technology, local companies, even in developing countries, are increasingly able to provide higher quality graphics, comparable to those produced by larger international advertisers. Nevertheless, if a company decides to hire local advertising agencies, it will not be able to coordinate a global, standardized advertising campaign.

Hiring International Advertising Agencies

In general, if a company uses a standardized (global) strategy for its products or services, it is more likely to use an international agency with local offices that can manage advertising in the respective markets. Most of the leading advertising agencies have branches in important international markets. In Eastern Europe, companies such as Leo Burnett, Young and Rubicam, and Ogilvy & Mather are represented in practically every capital city. Other companies select primarily markets of interest to their clients. For example, J. Walter Thompson is present as J. Walter Thompson/ARK Communications in Prague, the Czech Republic; as Partners J. Walter Thompson Budapest in Hungary; and as Scala JWT Advertising in Bucharest, Romania.

The list of top advertising agency groups worldwide is led by Dentsu, the Japanese ad firm. Dentsu is followed by seven Madison Avenue, New York firms: McCann, Young & Rubicam, DDB, Ogilvy & Mather, BBDO, TBWA, and others.[22] (see Table 13-1).

Table 13-1: The Top 10 Agency Networks (Ranked by 2010 Worldwide Network Revenue)

Rank	Company	Headquarters	Worldwide Revenue (US$ millions)
1.	Dentsu	Tokyo	3,028
2.	McCann Worldgroup (Interpublic)	New York	2,671
3.	Young & Rubicam Brands (WPP)	New York	2,651
4.	DDB Worldwide Communications Group (Omnicom)	New York	2,223
5.	Ogilvy & Mather (WPP)	New York	1,754
6.	BBDO Worldwide	New York	1,671
7.	TBWA Worldwide (Omnicom)	New York	1,518
8.	EURO RSCG WORLDWIDE (Havas)	New York	1,206
9.	DRAFTFCB (Interpublic)	New York	1,175
10.	JWT (WPP)	New York	1,119

Source: *Advertising Age*, "Top 10 Consolidated Agency Networks," April 26, 2011, http://adage.com.

International advertising agencies benefit from access to the parent company's experience and talent, as well as technology and research capabilities. They also can take advantage of local representatives' expertise and relationships with the media and government. Increasingly, international advertising agencies are present with more than one type of agency in important markets. For example, Rapp Collins Worldwide opened an office of its interactive arm, Rapp Digital, in Brazil. Because Latin America is advanced from the point of view of technology, the market has high potential for interactive services.[23] Grey Global Group is present in Europe with Grey Direct, its direct marketing arm; Grey Desire, a London-based customer relationship management consultancy for Europe;[24] Grey Interactive, GCI (one of the largest public relations firms in the world); and Grey Worldwide, the company's advertising arm.

Hiring Local Advertising Agencies to Implement International Agency Messages

Hiring an international advertising agency with local offices does not preclude the use of local advertising agencies. For example, although Coca-Cola uses leading global agencies to design its message for advertising worldwide, it also encourages each country office to appoint local agencies to implement the brand message. In fact, Interpublic generates ideas at a global level, which are then translated by local marketers as part of Coke's "think global, act local" strategy.[25] International Marketing Illustration 13-2 offers insights into the agency choice of one of the corporate sponsors of advertisements, McDonald's.

International Marketing Illustration 13-1
The Giant Sponsor and the Small Advertising Boutique:
An Unlikely Pairing for a Global Advertising Campaign

McDonald's surprised the agency world by selecting a small advertising agency to lead its worldwide campaign. It hired the fifteenth largest agency in Germany, Omnicom's Heye & Partner, a company with a reputation for lacking creativity. But Heye, led by chief executive Jurgen Knauss, was able to gain the trust of McDonald's. McDonald's was also ready to take greater risks in its international advertising because its brand outside the United States is relatively young. Today, Heye & Partner is so closely associated with the chain that it is often referred to as the McDonald's agency. Heye also has as clients other top multinationals, such as Johnson & Johnson and Esso (Exxon), but McDonald's, one of the largest ad spenders in the world, is its top client. To best serve this client, Heye employees eat at McDonald's on a regular basis and even work behind the counter.

Going against the German tradition, which shuns humor in advertising, the Heye ads show a man stuck in traffic and a kid in another automobile making faces at him. The man, in revenge, holds up McDonald's fries and eats them demonstratively. This ad is used for most world markets, with the exception of the United States. Heye also won the McDonald's competition between several agencies for a tag line—"I'm lovin' it"—and it is used for all the company's ads in English. In another ad, aliens are shown ready to eat humans standing in line at McDonald's, with one urging the other to wait until the humans have eaten the burgers because they taste better afterward. The ads are funny and emotional—and it is difficult to imagine

that a German company came up with them. The ad campaign communicates a youthful spirit and the idea that something is changing at McDonald's—something that its franchisees are not especially keen on. In October 2006, Heye won yet another award, the GWA Effie award for the "McDonald's Once One is One" campaign.

To date, McDonald's sales have increased, posting the biggest sales gain in five years.

Sources: www.mcdonalds.de/produkte/biggestmacs.html (accessed July 8, 2012); www.mcwww.gwa.de/Press.1441.0.html, June 2007; Erin White and Shirley Leung, "How Tiny German Shop Landed McDonald's," *Wall Street Journal*, August 6, 2003, B1; Kate MacArthur, "McD's Sees Growth, But Are Ads a Factor?" *Advertising Age*, Vol. 74, No. 47, November 24, 2003, p. 3.

13-3c The Advertising Strategy

Standardization versus Adaptation in Creating Message Strategies

standardization of the advertising strategy
The process of globalizing a company's promotional strategy so that it is uniform in all its target markets.

adaptation of the advertising strategy
The act of changing a company's promotional mix to each country or market or creating local campaigns.

One of the most important decisions of firms designing their international promotional mix is whether to standardize (globalize) their promotional strategy **(standardization of the advertising strategy),** to adapt their promotional mix to each country or market **(adaptation of the advertising strategy),** or to create local campaigns. Practitioners are divided on this issue. Sponsors, as well as advertising agencies, agree that using a standardized strategy worldwide presents substantial advantages. This is most obvious from a cost perspective: Costs are reduced considerably if companies do not need to duplicate the creative effort and the resultant communication campaign in each market. In addition, as product life cycles shrink, companies are pressured to accelerate worldwide rollout of new products. Developing communication strategies for each market would delay launch.[18] Moreover, world consumers are developing common product preferences and increasingly share similar frames of references with regard to products and consumption because they are exposed to the same sources of influence (broadcast and print media, in particular, as well as blockbuster films and tourists, among others).

High-profile advertisers, including Mercedes-Benz, Hewlett-Packard, Walt Disney, and Coca-Cola, have started, or announced plans to start, worldwide ad campaigns. Some of these marketers have previously eschewed global campaigns or have gone back and forth between local and regional approaches. Now, however, there is clearly a shift in the strategy of multinational firms. Standardization versus adaptation decisions come down to a battle between marketing and sales—marketing emphasizes a global approach, whereas sales insists on being local.[26]

Typically, marketers end up in between, with a consistent overall image, but tailoring the ads for perceived local differences. McDonald's, in the earlier example, has been using this strategy since 2003, with its theme "I'm lovin' it."[27] The campaign, however, adapts to appeal to local markets, assuring consumers that McDonald's products are local.

Other companies whose brand identities had become fragmented through regional or country-specific advertising have also moved toward global campaigns. Coca-Cola, for example, has moved to unify its advertising under the theme, "The Coke side of life." The auto industry, which has for many years rejected this approach, is changing as well at the insistence of local sales branches: Mercedes hired the advertising agency BBDO to develop a single global ad campaign for its new C-Class. Hewlett-Packard rolled out the first global advertising campaign for its personal computer division in 2006, and Disney started a global campaign for its theme parks. This approach makes sense, as it costs less for one ad agency to create a single global ad campaign than it does for multiple agencies to create separate campaigns. Moreover, new technology makes it easier to adapt a global campaign for individual markets, and procurement officials know this, putting further pressure on agencies to cut costs. Most big marketing campaigns now include a substantial online presence, and the enormous popularity of social networking and video-sharing web services means ads and videos quickly zip across borders.[28]

In the case of Mercedes-Benz, it introduced the new C-Class using a comprehensive integrated marketing campaign, with the slogan "C-for Yourself," developed by the advertising agency BBDO France. The campaign attempted to convince customers based on the world of qualities of the new C-Class sedan, its design, comfort, agility, and safety. Interestingly, Mercedes decided that all communication measures for the C-Class should be geared toward direct contact with customers and potential buyers. Specifically, magazines and newspapers with high circulation featured ads inviting customers to test-drive the sedan.[29]

In Germany, a 30-/40-second television commercial was launched on all prominent public and commercial stations, featuring the Formula 1 world champion race car driver Fernando Alonso. At the end of the ad, Alonso, who drives for the Vodafone McLaren Mercedes Formula 1 team, symbolically hands over the keys to a new C-Class to the audience at home, inviting them to test-drive the vehicle. Mercedes coupled this campaign with the more local "Exclusive Driving Experience" campaign, which allowed 80 consumers from all over Europe to experience the C-Class. In Barcelona, participants drove an off-road course—and King Juan Carlos of Spain and founding partner of Mercedes-Benz attended the event. Vacationers at Robinson Club Resorts and Westin Hotels & Resorts facilities in Germany, Austria, Scotland, Italy, Spain, Portugal, and Greece were also offered the opportunity to test-drive the new C-Class.

In addition to its traditional advertising strategies, Mercedes combined direct communication at driving events with interactive films on the Internet. The online presentation at www.mercedes-benz.com/c-class allowed viewers to select the vehicle of their choice and see it displayed against realistic backdrops. The site also offered several interactive films featuring individuals describing details of the new C-Class as they took the vehicle for a drive.[30]

Differences between countries, however, might render standardization a challenge, or even impossible. The following are barriers to advertising standardization:

- The communication infrastructure is one barrier: A particular medium might be inappropriate or not available for advertising.

- International advertising agencies might not serve a particular market.

- Consumer literacy level constitutes another major barrier. Consumers might not be able to read the body copy of the advertisement, so the information conveyed to the consumer should be visual.

- Legal restrictions and industry self-regulation might also impede standardization: Comparative advertising is not permitted in many countries, whereas, in others—Korea, for example—Confucianism forbids the public criticism of others.[31]

- Values and purchase motivations differ across countries and cultures, as illustrated in Chapter 5, "Cultural Influences on International Marketing." Targeting consumers with a campaign that stresses the good life, exemplified by driving a luxury car and having a blonde on one's side, might be inappropriate in countries where consumers are living a subsistence existence and just as improper in highly developed, cultured environments. Consumers from collectivist cultures will also question the values suggested by such ads. The decision of whether to standardize is most often contingent on the degree of cultural similarity between the sponsor and the target market. Standardization of communication is recommended when similarity exists between senders and receivers in the communication process.

- Attitudes toward the product or service country of origin create another barrier, especially in environments where there is some level of hostility toward the United States and its economic and cultural dominance, it might be best to change an advertising campaign that stresses the product's country of origin.

- The elements of the promotional mix—particularly advertising[32]—are especially difficult to standardize because communication is language and culture specific.

Budgeting Decisions for International Advertising Campaigns

Companies use the following approaches to advertise spending decisions.

Objective-and-Task Method

Companies using the **objective-and-task method** first identify advertising goals in terms of communication goals such as target audience reach, awareness, comprehension, or even purchase. As a next step, research is conducted to determine the cost of achieving the respective goals. Finally, the necessary sum is allocated for the purpose.

This method is the most popular one used by multinational corporations in the process of deciding on their advertising budgets because it takes into consideration the firms' strategies. A comprehensive international study suggests that this method is more frequently used by firms from Canada and Singapore and less frequently by Swedish and Argentinean firms.[33]

> **objective-and-task method**
> An advertising budgeting method in which the company first identifies advertising goals, conducts research to determine the cost of achieving the respective goals, and allocates the necessary sum for the purpose.

Percent-of-Sales Method

The **percent-of-sales method** determines the total budget allocated to advertising based on past or projected sales. This method is difficult to adopt for firms entering new markets, which are more likely to benefit from budgeting methods such as competitive parity or objective-and-task. The problem with this method is that it causes advertising expenditures to decline as sales decline; at this point, the company should increase advertising spending.

For firms that have been in a particular international market for some time, this method is used by almost half of the respondents in the study on transnational advertising practices. This study found that the percent-of-sales method is most popular in Brazil and Hong Kong and less popular in Germany.[34]

Historical Method

Firms using the **historical method** base their advertising budget on past expenditures, usually giving more weight to more recent expenditures. The percent-of-sales method uses the historical method as a first step, if the percentages allocated to advertising are based on past, rather than projected, sales. This method is not recommended for firms that operate in unstable economic, political, or competitive environments.

Competitive-Parity Method

The **competitive-parity method** uses competitors' level of advertising spending as benchmarks for a firm's own advertising expenditure. This approach is not recommended for a firm entering a new market and whose brands are not known locally. Moreover, this method suggests that a firm's goals and strategies are identical with those of competitors, which, most likely, is not the case.

Executive-Judgment Method

In the **executive-judgment method,** executive opinion is used in determining the advertising budget. A third of the responding firms queried in the study on transnational advertising practices reported relying on executive judgment.

All-You-Can-Afford Method

Most small and medium-sized enterprises entering a new market do not have the large budgets of multinational corporations. The **all-you-can-afford method** best suits the financial limitations of these firms. Unfortunately, this approach completely ignores strategic issues.

U.S. advertising spending used to account for more than half of world totals. That is, however, no longer the case. According to the *Advertising Age*, the largest top 100 media spenders boast $98.27 billion in global media spending. The top spender, by far, is Procter & Gamble Co. with $8.19 billion, followed by Unilever, at $4.27 billion; General Motors Corp., at $4.17 billion; and Toyota Motor Company, at $2.8 billion. The top 100 spent $47.46 billion in the United States—or 48.2 percent of the total—followed by Europe, at $30.17 billion or 30.7 percent. Noteworthy is also China, where media spending has been growing at more than 35 percent per year, or 15.8 percent of total spending ($15.57 billion) (See Table 13-2 on the next page).[35]

percent-of-sales method
An advertising budgeting method that determines the total budget allocated to advertising on the basis of past or projected sales.

historical method
An approach to budgeting that is based on past expenditures, usually giving more weight to more recent expenditures.

competitive-parity method
The strategy of using competitors' level of advertising spending as a benchmark for the company's own advertising expenditures.

executive-judgment method
A budgeting process that allocates the company's advertising budget based on the opinions of executives.

all-you-can-afford method
The process of allocating the maximum amount possible to advertising; this method is used by small and mediumsized corporations.

Table 13-2: *Top 10 Global Marketers*

Rank	Company	Headquarters	Media Spending (U.S.$ millions)
1	Procter & Gamble Co.	Cincinnati	9,731
2	Unilever	London/Rotterdam	5,717
3	L'Oreal	Clichy, France	4,040
4	General Motors Corp.	Detroit	3,674
5	Toyota Motor Corp.	Toyota City, Japan	3,203
6	Coca-Cola Co.	Atlanta, Georgia	2,673
7	Johnson & Johnson	New Brunswick, New Jersey	2,601
8	Ford Motor Co.	Dearborn, Michigan	2,448
9	Reckitt Benckiser Slough	Berkshire, U.K.	2,369
10	Nestlé	Vevey, Switzerland	2,314

Source: Advertising Age, "Top 100 Global Marketers," November 30, 2010, pp. 1–53.

Summary

Describe the international promotional mix and the international communication process. The components of the international promotional mix are international advertising, international sales force management, international sales promotion, and public relations and publicity. The international communication process involves the sender encoding a message and sending it via a medium to the receiver, who then decodes the message; the goal is to have the message sent be identical to the message received. In an international communications context, the process is complicated by interferences (noise) injected by cultural and language differences between the advertiser, sponsor, and the target audiences.

Explore the international advertising formats and practices around the world. International advertising—defined as a nonpersonal communication by an identified sponsor across international borders, using broadcast, print, and/or interactive media—faces many international challenges. The primary challenge is attributed to the lack of uniformity in media infrastructure, formats, and practices accepted in different markets. Among such challenges are media availability and reliability issues, such as media's inability to work with company deadlines and television going off the air frequently. The media could limit the types and the number of advertisements aired or published, or they might not permit the portrayal of women or advertising of certain products. They also might isolate advertising from programming or from editorial content. Media costs, formats, features, and trends may differ around the world.

Describe the international advertising and media infrastructure and infrastructure-related challenges in different markets. Advertising worldwide is dominated by U.S. advertising agencies; however, that fact is quickly changing. Firms from the United Kingdom and Japan are competing with large full-service agencies from the United States, and boutique advertising agencies worldwide are winning important accounts and awards for quality advertising. Multinationals today have increasing advertising agency choices. Depending on the availability of local talent and capability, companies advertising in international markets have a choice between advertising using a local agency, using an international agency, or using a local agency to advertise international agency messages.

Describe advertising strategies and budgeting decisions and offer examples of international applications. An important decision facing international firms is whether to use a standardized message worldwide or to adapt the message to local markets. Standardization would lead to great economies of scale and cost savings; in reality, standardization may not be possible because of variations in the advertising and media infrastructures due to differences in consumer literacy, motivations, or consumer interests, and due to differences in advertising legislation. Advertising budgeting may involve one of the following methods: objective-and-task, whereby marketing managers set objectives and then calculate the cost for reaching the objectives; percent-of-sales, whereby the advertising budget is set as a percent of sales; historical, whereby spending is based on past expenditures; competitive-parity, whereby spending is based on competitors' spending; executive-judgment, whereby the firm's executives make the decisions; and the all-you-can-afford method.

Key Terms

adaptation of the advertising strategy

all-you-can-afford method

billboards

broadcast medium

channel of communication

competitive-parity method

decoding

encoding

executive-judgment method

feedback

historical method

infomercials

interactive medium

international communication process

international promotional mix

media availability

media infrastructure

media reliability

media restrictions

medium/media

noise

nonpersonal medium

objective-and-task method

percent-of-sales method

personal medium

print medium

product placement

receiver

sender

standardization of the advertising strategy

telemarketing

television shopping networks

Discussion Questions

1.   Describe the challenges involved in the international communication process and suggest how each challenge could be addressed by a firm's international marketing manager in conjunction with an advertising agency.

2.   What are some important traits of the international media infrastructure that are likely to affect local advertising strategies?

3.   Describe how media formats, features, and trends differ around the world.

4.   What are the advertising agency choices that international companies have for communicating with local markets? Describe each choice, its advantages, and disadvantages.

5.   Ideally, multinationals should standardize their message worldwide to benefit from economies of scale and other cost savings. What prevents companies from using a standardized message worldwide?

6.   How do multinational firms determine their budget for advertising?

Chapter Quiz

True/False

1. In the international communication process, the sender can evaluate the effectiveness of the message with appropriate feedback from the target market.

Answer: True

Rationale: The sender can determine whether the communication program launched to the international target market is effective by evaluating the market response to the communication.

Section 13-2, "The International Communication Process"

2. Homeowners worldwide often agree to display advertising on the walls of their homes.

Answer: True

Rationale: Advertising on the sides of homes is very popular in many countries; individuals are usually remunerated for allowing the advertisements to be displayed on the wall.

Section 13-3a, "The Media Infrastructure"

3. *Glamour, Cosmopolitan,* and *Mademoiselle* are all examples of global media.

Answer: True

Rationale: Magazines such as *Glamour, Cosmopolitan,* and *Mademoiselle* are published in languages ranging from Mandarin and Italian to Polish and Japanese. These magazines are vehicles for global, regional, and local advertising campaigns of multinational companies.

Section 13-3a, "The Media Infrastructure"

4. The European Union Directive Concerning Television Broadcasting limits all advertising of tobacco and prescription drug products in all media.

Answer: False

Rationale: The European Union Directive Concerning Television Broadcasting prohibits only tobacco and prescription drug advertisements on television.

Section 13-3a, "The Media Infrastructure"

5. Adaptation of the promotional strategy refers to changing a company's promotional mix so that it is uniform in most of its target markets.

Answer: False

Rationale: Adaptation of the promotional strategy entails changing the promotional mix for optimal appeal to each individual country or market.

Section 13-3c, "The Advertising Strategy"

Multiple Choice

1.   Which of the following is a nonpersonal medium of the International Communication Process?

    a.   personal selling

    b.   trade shows

    c.   television

    d.   telemarketing

Answer: c is correct.

Rationale: Television is the only nonpersonal medium of the four. Personal selling and trade shows involve the presence of sales people, whereas telemarketing involves the presence of a telemarketer who would be handling the sales call.

Section 13-2, "The International Communication Process"

2.   Which of the following refers to interference in the communication process attributed to cultural differences, competing messages, and degree of consumer interest?

    a.   encoding

    b.   decoding

    c.   noise

    d.   none of the above

Answer: c is correct.

Rationale: Noise refers to all the potential interference in the communication process, particularly noise attributed to cultural differences, which may interfere with proper message reception.

Section 13-2, "The International Communication Process"

3.   Local newspapers that are unable to produce high enough quality in a print ad for a global brand are an example of what media challenge?

    a.   media availability

    b.   media costs

    c.   media reliability

    d.   media restrictions

Answer: c is correct.

Rationale: Media reliability refers to the extent to which the existing media reliably reach the target consumer in the intended format and within the intended time frame.

Section 13-3a, "The Media Infrastructure"

4.   Which of the following is not an example of media restriction?

   a.   prohibiting advertising to children

   b.   prohibiting the advertising of vice products

   c.   keeping the local language pure

   d.   all of the above

Answer: d is correct.

Rationale: Media restrictions refer to the different limitations that can be imposed on media: Media could limit the types and the number of advertisements aired or published, limit air time, or prohibit advertising to children or advertising vice products, among others.

Section 13-3a, "The Media Infrastructure"

5.   The budgeting decision that is mostly used by small and medium-sized corporations' campaigns is the

   a.   percent-of-sales method.

   b.   executive-judgment method.

   c.   competitive-parity method

   d.   all-you-can-afford method.

Answer: d is correct.

Rationale: Most small and medium-sized firms are limited in terms of their advertising expenditures and cannot afford to copy competitors' strategies or spend enough for the desired impact; consequently, they use the all-you-can-afford method.

Section 13-3c, "The Advertising Strategy"

Chapter 13 Endnotes

1.   Laurel Wentz, "'Evolution' Win Marks Down New Cannes Era," Vol. 78, No. 26, June 25, 2007, pp. 1–2.

2.   www.unileverusa.com/brands/hygiene/dovecampaignforrealbeauty (accessed May 28, 2012);

3.   www.dove.de; www.dove.ro

4.   Rupal Parekh, "Creative Effectiveness Cannes Lion Goes to Unilever's Axe," *Advertising Age*, June 19, 2012, http://adage.com/author/rupal-parekh/4468; Daniel O'Donnell, "Unilever's Dove and Axe: Examples of Hypocrisy or Good Marketing?" *Case Study Competition*, 2008 (Arthur W. Page Society): 39–51.

5.   Sam Solley, "Developing a Name to Work Worldwide," *Marketing,* December 21, 2000, p. 27.

6.   Erin White, "For Germany's Ad Agencies, Recovery Is Distant Prospect, *Wall Street Journal,* August 14, 2002, B5; Erin White and Shirley Leung, "How Tiny German Shop Landed McDonald's," *Wall Street Journal,* August 6, 2003, B1; Robert J. Coen, *Universal McCann's Insider Report,* December 8, 2003, www.universalmccann.com.

7.   Adapted from www.omdmedia.co.za

8.   Anver Versi, "MTV Rolls Out Africa Channel," *African Business*, Vol. 305, January 2005, pp. 58-59.

9.   Anita Franklin, "Whose News? Control of the Media in Africa," *Review of African Political Economy*, Vol. 25, No. 78, December 1998, pp. 545–550.

10.   Helen Johnstone, "Asian TV Companies Take Lead in Local Content," *Asian Business*, Vol. 32, No. 10, October 1996, pp. 26–33.

11.   See Pola B. Gupta and Kenneth R. Lord, "Product Placement in Movies: The Effect of Prominence and Mode on Audience Recall," *Journal of Current Issues and Research in Advertising*, Vol. 14, No. 1, Spring 1998, pp. 47–59; and Steven J. Gould, Pola B. Gupta, and Sonja Grabner-Kräuter, "Product Placements in Movies: A Cross-Cultural Analysis of Austrian, French, and American Consumers' Attitudes Toward This Emerging International Promotional Medium," *Journal of Advertising*, Vol. 29, No. 4, Winter 2000, pp. 41–68.

12.   Anne Jolis, "EU Backs Rise in Advertising on Broadcast TV," *Wall Street Journal*, May 25, 2007, B3.

13.   http://eur-lex.europa.eu

14.   Morris Kalliny and Lance Gentry, "Cultural Values Reflected in Arab and American Television Advertising," *Journal of Current Issues and Research in Advertising*, Vol. 29, No. 11, Spring 2007, pp. 15–21.

15.   See Ross D. Petty, "Advertising Law in the United States and European Union," *Journal of Public Policy & Marketing*, Vol. 16, No. 1, Spring 1997, pp. 2–13.

16.   Ibid.

17.   Eric Pfanner, "Reins Off, French Retailers Rush to Buy TV Time," *New York Times*, January 9, 2007, C6.

18.   William Wells, John Burnett, and Sandra Moriarty, *Advertising Principles and Practice*, Fifth Edition, Upper Saddle River, NY: Prentice Hall, 2000; and *Advertising Age*, "10 Biggest Stories of 2003," Vol. 74, No. 51, December 22, 2003, p. 4.

19.   Hillary Chura, "Coke Brands IPG as Global Ad Strategist," *Advertising Age*, Vol. 71, No. 50, December 4, 2000, p. 50.

20.   David Lipin, "San Diego Ikea Hires a Local Ad Agency," *Adweek*, Vol. 50, No. 51, December 18, 2000, p. 4.

21.   Peter Rosenwald, "Surveying the Latin American Landscape," *Catalog Age*, Vol. 18, No. 2, February 2001, p. 67.

22.   *Advertising Age*, "Top 10 Consolidated Agency Networks," April 26, 2007, http://adage.com.

23.   Cara Beardi, "Grey's Global Desire," *Advertising Age*, Vol. 71, No. 48, November 20, 2000, pp. 22, 24.

24.   Ibid.

25.   Cordella Brabbs, "Can Coke and IPG Truly 'Think Local'?" *Marketing*, December 7, 2000, p. 7.

26.   Eric Pfanner, "On Advertising: Passport to Success?" *International Herald Tribune*, August 6, 2006, online edition.

27.   www.mcd.com

28.   Eric Pfanner, "On Advertising: Passport to Success?" *International Herald Tribune*, August 6, 2006, online edition.

29.   "C-for Yourself": Mercedes-Benz launches integrated marketing campaign for the new C-Class, Stuttgart, March 19, 2007, Official Press Release, www.mercedes-benz.com/c-class.

30.   Ibid.

31.   Michel Laroche, V. H. Kirpalani, and Rene Darmon, "Determinants of the Control of International Advertising by Headquarters of Multinational Corporations," *Revue Canadienne de l'Administration*, Vol. 16, No. 4, December 1999, pp. 273–290.

32.   Zahna Caillat and Barbara Mueller, "Observations: The Influence of Culture on American and British Advertising: An Exploratory Comparison of Beer Advertising," *Journal of Advertising Research*, Vol. 36, No. 3, May/June 1996, pp. 79–88.

33.   Nicolaos E. Synodinos, Charles F. Keown, and Lawrence W. Jacobs, "Transnational Advertising Practices: A Survey of Leading Brand Advertisers in Fifteen Countries," *Journal of Advertising Research*, Vol. 29, No. 2, April/May 1989, pp. 43–50.

34.   Ibid.

35.   Craig Endicott, "P&G Leads All Marketers; China Pushes Up Gains," *Advertising Age*, November 20, 2006, p. 2.

Case 13-1

Selling the Donnelly Brand in Romania

Donnelly's Cigarettes of Martinsville, Virginia, is planning its international expansion into a rapidly growing market, Central and Eastern Europe. The company sells the popular, low-priced Donnelly brand in select Southern states, but it is currently looking for other venues for selling its brand. Encumbered with tight regulations in the United States, Donnelly is actively seeking markets that offer a higher profit potential than the home market.

Donnelly started out 7 decades ago as a tobacco farm that initially sold its products to cigarette manufacturers, such as Philip Morris. It started developing its own brand of tobacco in the 1980s, providing substantial competition to the lower-priced Philip Morris brands. To the Southern U.S. market, Donnelly offers filter cigarettes, light cigarettes, menthol and menthol lights, as well as ultra lights and menthol ultra lights. The company romanticizes the Donnelly brand's indigenous origins, and it pursues profits aggressively by stressing its homegrown quality. In its advertisements, it stresses the Virginia origins of the tobacco, and its point-of-purchase advertising displays the brand's homegrown characteristics—even though Donnelly imports most of the tobacco from Asia. In its advertising for the U.S. market, Donnelly claims that it uses a large percentage of U.S.-grown tobacco, higher than that of all the Philip Morris' brands.

The family patriarch, John Donnelly, a third generation tobacco farmer with an impressive business acumen, is presently investigating modes of expansion that are likely to increase company profits. Cigarettes are under scrutiny in the United States, and Donnelly is dealing with lawsuits by individuals claiming that smoking the brand led to health problems. Moreover, in the United States, state governments and localities have started to ban smoking from public buildings, leading many consumers to quit and many others to decide against smoking.

In its plans to expand in Central and Eastern Europe—as with its business in the United States—Donnelly will maintain a hands-on approach to marketing the brand. Research of the business literature revealed that cigarettes are especially popular in Romania, where they are in a profitable growth stage. John Donnelly found this market especially attractive after examining this research.

Romanians have had a long-running love affair with Western cigarettes. Kent cigarettes constituted important commodity money in this market for many decades during the communist rule. Western cigarettes in general were coveted status symbols for Romanian smokers.

Today, about 31.3 percent of individuals over 15 years of age smoke, in a country with a population of 22 million, with the highest prevalence in the 25-34 age group. The average age for starting to smoke is just under 19 years old. And 47.1 percent of all smokers smoke between 10 and 20 cigarettes daily. About 34.5 percent of men smoke daily, most in the 25-44 year-old group, whereas 21.9 percent of women smoke daily, with those between 15 and 24 years of age being the heaviest smokers.

As income increases across the board, premium brands are taking an increasingly larger share of the cigarette market, with the highest sales made in the upper mid-price brands, such as Pall Mall, Winston, Lucky Strike—especially mid-tar versions. In response to the growing health awareness of Romanian consumers, both because of improvements to standards of living and public campaigns against smoking, cigarette manufacturers launched new, "reduced harm" varieties of their products.

Excise duty on tobacco is continually rising to reach a level acceptable to the EU; Romanian authorities continue to raise taxes three times a year and will continue to do so more frequently, with higher increases. As a result, the selling of contraband cigarettes has intensified. Contraband cigarettes are usually imported from the Republic of Moldova and the Ukraine, countries where taxes are three times lower than in Romania.

Research also revealed that leading Western cigarette manufacturers have set up factories to take advantage of this market. The British tobacco giant B.A.T. Industries PLC built a $70 million factory in Romania in the mid-1990s, designed to produce more than 4 billion cigarettes a year; the company has a market share of just under 10 percent. R.J. Reynolds Tobacco International, a U.S. firm, opened a large plant there as well. R.J.R. has a 15 percent share of the market. Philip Morris holds an 18 percent share of the Romanian market. The company dominates the Central and Eastern European market for American blend cigarettes, with 70 percent of the market share. It has cigarette plants in the Czech Republic, Kazakhstan, Poland, Hungary, the Ukraine, and Russia, but not in Romania. Another company manufacturing cigarettes in Romania is Papastratos Cigarette Manufacturing Company of Greece.

A main competitor for Donnelly is the Romanian tobacco company, Galaxy Tobacco, that is currently reinventing itself to appeal to Romanian consumers' nostalgia for traditional Romanian brands, such as Snagov and Carpati. The company holds 50 percent of the market share in Romania. Donnelly believes that this important market segment prefers foreign cigarettes but cannot afford them; once Donnelly sells its affordable U.S. brand to the Romanian market, many consumers smoking Romanian brands are likely to switch to the Donnelly brand.

Donnelly planned to ship the products to Romania from the port of Norfolk, Virginia, and pick them up at the Romanian port of Constanta, on the Black Sea. Even with transportation costs and with the excise duties placed on both local producers and importers and an added tax of 20 percent, the Donnelly brand would still be much cheaper than its other Western competitors. The company is planning to sell its products directly to convenience stores—mom-and-pop types that would agree to lower gross margins, which would keep prices low for Romanian consumers. The major decision that remains for the company is how to advertise in this market. Donnelly presently does all its advertising in-house in the Martinsville office complex. However, John Donnelly believes that it would be risky to use materials produced in-house in a market that is so different from its Southern U.S. market. John Donnelly and his family are now contemplating the choice of an advertising company.

Many of the large multinational ad firms are present in Romania. Among them are Graffiti/BBDO, a division of BBDO Worldwide, among the first international firms to come to Romania; Grey Business Room, a division of Grey Worldwide; Olympic DDB; and Ogilvy Romania. John Donnelly believes that these companies have substantial expertise and capability, but their high costs are likely to infringe on company profits. Their ads would be exceptional in quality and impact, nevertheless.

The alternative would be to hire a local firm. Among prominent local firms are Ager Press S.A., a large formerly state-owned company; Andrei Advertising; Artmedia Group, a full-service advertising agency; advertigo, a full-service independent agency; and B&C Consulting, a full-service public relations and advertising agency. After examining the capabilities of the different local firms, Donnelly has found that two of them might be a better fit in terms of capability and expertise.

The first company, advertigo, is a full-service independent agency founded in 1998, serving a number of Romanian firms and a few prominent international firms and brands. Among them are 121 Marketing, Atlanta (a clothing company with brands such as Wampum Jeans, ATL, and Atlanta), Atlas Trading, Avanti Furs, Corporate Office Solutions, Corona Cosmetics, Creative Paving, and Johnson & Johnson—specifically, the company's baby care products, Carefree, o.b,, and Neutrogena brands. The company has experts in media strategies, media planning, copywriting, design, and research, as well as various business specialists. Its services span all media available in Romania.

B&C Consulting is a public relations and advertising strategy offering full service in communications and image consulting. Among its clients are the Romanian government, promoting Romania's image abroad with the B&C Consulting slogan "the strength beside you"; SNP PETROM, the large gas company, promoting its image with the slogan "the essence of movement"; and the popular Supermarket pop-rock group with its slogan "Pop-Rock Made in Supermarket." This young group creates edgy advertisements and memorable slogans in both Romanian and English.

John Donnelly must decide whether to use a multinational firm or a local firm. His family in Martinsville, the only other individuals with ownership in the company, has difficulty in offering advice. John must decide on the advertising agency before his trip to Romania in two months.

Sources: Euromonitor, "Tobacco in Romania," June 14, 2011; Anastasia Warpinski, "Tobacco Firms Look to Pocket Romania as Push in Central Europe Intensifies," *Wall Street Journal,* September 19, 1997, C1; http://www.advertigo.ro/; http://www.bcconsulting.ro/Portofoliu.html.

Analysis Suggestions

1.   Should Donnelly use in-house produced advertising in the Romanian market? Why or why not?

2.   What advantages would Donnelly have if it decided to use a U.S. advertising agency present in Romania? What would be the disadvantages of using a U.S. agency?

3.   Which advertising agency should Donnelly choose for advertising the Donnelly brand in Romania? Explain.

Chapter 14: International Publicity, Public Relations, and Sales Promotion Strategies

Learning Objectives

After studying this chapter, you should be able to:

- Provide an overview of international publicity and the different international public relations activities that can be used to influence it.

- Describe the different approaches to international consumer sales promotion and the activities involved.

- Describe the different approaches to international trade promotion and the different activities involved.

In the past, multinational firms hired advertising agencies and placed them in charge of advertising, and they handled publicity and most sales promotion in-house. Multinational companies today hire agencies to coordinate globally all aspects of their integrated marketing communications, including their public relations activities. Agencies' public relations machines stand ready to defend their client firms against any negative publicity. Consequently, they are more likely to leave all public relations activities, local and international, to firms with public relations expertise. This fact is readily evident especially in developed countries. The public relations machine stands ready to avert any negative doubts cast on multinationals.

Local firms and local governments in emerging markets, however, often appear to lag behind in their public relations actions, for example reacting too late or not at all to negative information. Chinese exports have encountered more than their fair share of negative publicity and, at first, they negated any responsibility, which has not served them well. Since then, the Chinese government has understood the importance of acting promptly and accepting responsibility, taking it to an extreme, even executing those responsible for manufacturing lethal Chinese products.

China's Export Products Scrutinized

China's exports to the rest of the world are soaring. But its reputation in manufacturing safe, high-quality products took a serious plunge a few years ago. China's goal is to sell cars to the West, but it is increasingly drawing the scrutiny of buyers and regulators alike. To date, only Jiangling Motors Corp. has cracked the Western European market. In 2005, its Landwind sport utility vehicle became the first Chinese car offered for sale in Europe. Selling for about $18,000, it appealed to cost-conscious consumers, but its safety quickly came under scrutiny as a result of a crash test by Germany's largest automobile club, ADAC, which gave the vehicle low marks. Jiangling quickly responded by recalling the automobile and addressing the ADAC concerns. However, the crash test prompted the European Commission to closely scrutinize the extent to which

Chinese automobiles meet EU safety standards.[1] This event did not deter Chinese automobile manufacturers from pursuing a large share of the European and North American market. In 2012, Great Wall Motor opened the first Chinese manufacturing plant in Europe (Bulgaria), with plans to make automobiles for the European market.

In other product safety breaches, China did not respond as effectively as it did in the Landwind case. One was melamine in pet food that killed 16 cats and dogs and made thousands of pets sick. Xuzhou Anying Biologic Technology Development, a small agricultural products trader that was the source of the melamine-contaminated wheat gluten, distributed to major pet food suppliers in North America. The gluten was adulterated with a toxic chemical that sickened or killed the animals. Another incident involved a Chinese toothpaste that contained diethylene glycol, a poison used in antifreeze, sold in the U.S. and elsewhere. Instead of promptly taking responsibility, Chinese officials conducted an investigation and found that the Chinese manufacturers, Goldcredit International Trading and the Jinmao Daily Chemicals Company, had done nothing wrong, and that small amounts of diethylene glycol can be safely used in toothpaste. What is especially concerning is that this same poison, made in China, contaminated 260,000 bottles of cold medicine in Panama, killing 100 people. In this case, Chinese regulators acknowledged that the two companies engaged in some misconduct in labeling and selling the diethylene glycol.[2]

In other incidents, tests found lead paint on expensive Thomas the Tank Engine toys manufactured in China. RC2 Corporation, the company that contracted with the Chinese manufacturer, promptly issued a recall on the toys. And imported Chinese seafood was contaminated with antimicrobial agents that are not approved for use in farm-raised seafood in the United States. More recently, in 2011, the U.S. Food and Drug Administration issued a caution against chicken jerky products used in dog treats, imported from China, that resulted in death or illness.[3]

Will consumers think twice when they purchase Chinese products? Does the brand name lessen consumer concerns about the safety of the product if that product is manufactured in China? With appropriate handling of the situation, which involves a prompt recall, or rectification, consumers' perceptions of Chinese products might not have suffered. Yet the Chinese have had to learn the importance of public relations. The first step for all the companies involved should have been to immediately rectify the situation. The second step should have been to hire a competent international public relations firm to further address consumer concerns. China's State Council eventually strengthened the oversight role of the local government in food safety, and increased fines for firms tampering with product safety, and shut down firms violating safety laws. It even executed a public official who took bribes for overlooking safety violations. However, a more systematic use of public relations in addressing this crisis would have limited the damage incurred in the international public opinion and, specifically, in international consumers' perceptions of Chinese products.

This chapter addresses the topics of international publicity, public relations, and sales promotion. Sales promotion is quickly catching on worldwide. Companies such as McDonald's and Burger King believe they are as much in the fast-food business as in the toy business, coming up with new promotions and generating excitement about the newest promotional event. The chapter looks at how competent international public relations activity can generate positive publicity for a firm. In the process, it discusses the different public relations tools that international marketing managers have at their disposal. The chapter also addresses the various international consumer sales promotion tools, the degree of sales promotion standardization worldwide, and the challenges presented by engaging in sales promotional activities in different countries. It also addresses international business-to-business sales promotion and offers examples of different international promotional activities of multinational companies.

14-1 Publicity and Public Relations

This chapter addresses three of a total of five components of the promotional mix: publicity and public relations, which are closely related, and sales promotion. The other components of the promotional mix are advertising and personal selling, covered in Chapter 13, "The International Promotional Mix and Advertising Strategies," and Chapter 15, "International Personal Selling and Personnel Management." Figure 14-1 (on the next page) illustrates the communication vehicles used by each component of the promotional mix addressed in this chapter.

14-1a Publicity

Publicity is *a communication about a company and/or the company's products that the company does not pay for.* In this category falls any type of print article, broadcast message, or word-of-mouth communication about the company and its products. The message may be positive, negative, or a mix of both.

> **publicity**
> Any communication about a company and the company's products that the company does not pay for; may be positive or negative.

Multinational corporations, in particular, frequently experience negative publicity. In general, there is a negative perception of multinational firm dominance and globalization. Brands that are especially vulnerable are those closely associated in consumers' mind with the country of origin. For example, McDonald's greatest appeal is the image it projects, that of the American way of life. However, its franchises are mostly locally owned, and the franchisees have consciously tried to present a local face. Nevertheless, the company has been the target of anti-American sentiment. In response to Europe's decision to ban hormone-treated beef, the U.S. government imposed high import tariffs on French Roquefort cheese, Dijon mustard, and foie gras. The French retaliated by vandalizing McDonald's restaurants. In their eyes, the company was a symbol of U.S. hegemony, globalization, multinationals, the power of the marketplace, and industrially produced food, all at the expense of individuals' health and French peasants' livelihood.[4] This event, although not McDonald's fault, created a strong sentiment at that time against the company.

In other examples, driven by anger over U.S. support for Israel, an anti-U.S. boycott started in Egypt and spread to other Arab countries. Local McDonald's franchisees countered, engaging in public relations that portrayed the company as a local company, and tailoring menus to local tastes, introducing the McFalafel sandwich, which was launched with the help of an ad jingle by a famous Egyptian singer, Sha' aban Ab-

Figure 14-1: *The publicity, public relations, and sales promotion components of the promotional mix.*

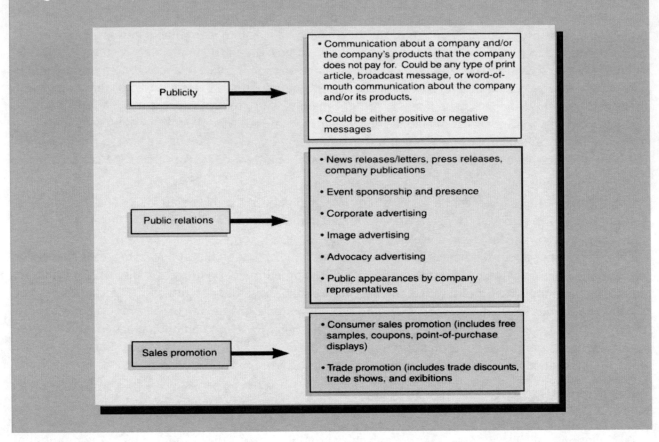

dul Raheem, best known for his nationalistic songs. McDonald's franchisees have also contributed to local charities: In Saudi Arabia and Jordan, a portion of sales for a given period was donated to charity. In other public relations efforts, in Indonesia, photos of local franchise owners, wearing traditional Islamic clothing, were posted at the entrance of the restaurant. In Argentina, when antiwar demonstrators blocked the entrances of a number of McDonald's restaurants, the company launched a campaign for the chain with the "Made in Argentina" theme.[5]

Entire industries can also come under public scrutiny. The diamond industry is still suffering from the impact of the negative publicity generated by the Warner Bros. action thriller, *Blood Diamond*. The movie moved audiences worldwide with bloody images of diamond smuggling from sub-Saharan Africa during the diamond business' heaviest selling season, in the month of December. The film was set in 1999 during Sierra Leone's civil war, and it portrayed a soldier turned smuggler chasing a rare pink diamond. The movie portrays smugglers of conflict diamonds, or blood diamonds—the name implies that sales of these diamonds are used to fund wars against legitimate governments. The industry pleaded with Warner Bros. to add disclaimers that voluntary industry reforms have eliminated conflict diamonds from the trade, but the film's producer, Ed Zwick, refused on the basis that the film was set during a time when conflict diamonds were common. In response, the World Diamond Council trade group fought an expensive fight. It launched a $15 million public relations and education campaign to disassociate the images of conflict diamonds from the diamonds the industry sells to wealthy buyers. It claims that conflict diamonds constitute less than one percent of all diamonds sold, and that it uses the Kimberly Process Certification System, backed by the United Nations, to guarantee that the diamonds sold are not conflict diamonds.[6]

Positive publicity, although difficult to come by, is valuable. Due to its independent nature, it is more credible than advertising. Companies use public relations, supporting their local community and community events to create positive publicity for their brands. They also use the other promotional tools—advertising, sales promotions, and personal selling—to create a positive buzz for the company and the brand.

Marketing practitioners believe that publicity is a must in international marketing. Table 14-1 illustrates strategies that international companies should use to maximize the benefits of publicity in a foreign market.

Table 14-1: *Strategies for Maximizing Benefits of Publicity in a Foreign Market*

General Strategies	Actions and Outcomes
Supplement ad campaigns with publicity campaigns.	The international company should establish third-party editorial credibility for products.
	The company should convey more information in greater detail about products.
Translate and be careful about translations.	Publishers are more likely to pick up a story if they have a good translation of the information.
Inform the managers in the home country about publicity.	This strategy can be helpful in securing funds for new campaign efforts.
Use publicity to secure a distributor or a distribution network.	The right distributor may approach if the company indicates it is looking for distributors.
Use publicity as a sales lead.	The company may obtain sales leads if it includes detailed information, including contact information, in the press release.

Source: Adapted from Hank T. Walshak, "Publicity Is a 'Must' for International Marketers," *Marketing News,* Vol. 24, No. 14, July 9, 1990, p. 14.

14-1b Public Relations

International public relations is defined as *a concerted effort on the part of a company to generate goodwill among international publics (community, government, consumers, employees, among others) that are essential to the company.* Its main purpose is to generate positive publicity about the company.

International public relations is big business. The leading public relations firms are primarily U.S.- and U.K.-based multinationals, as shown in Table 14-2 .

> **international public relations**
> A concerted effort on the part of a company to generate goodwill among international publics that are essential to the company; its main purpose is to generate positive publicity about the company.

Table 14-2: *The Top 10 Public Relations Firms (Ranked Based on 2011 Worldwide Net Fees)*

Rank	Firm Name	2011 Net Fees ($)	Rank	Firm Name	2011 Net Fees ($)
1.	Edelman	604,740,732	6.	W2O Group	47,577,000
2.	APCO Worldwide	120,701,000	7.	MWW Group	38,626,000
3.	Waggener Edstrom Worldwide	115,832,000	8.	ICR	32,030,483
4.	Ruder Finn	81,281,000	9.	Qorvis Communications	29,500,000
5.	.Text 100 Global PR	50,425,771	10.	DKC	26,800,000

Source: O'Dwyer, "Worldwide Fees of Top Independent PR Firms With Major U.S. Operations," www.odwyerpr.com/pr_firm_rankings/independents.htm (accessed June 1, 2012).

Much of the growth in public relations expenditures takes place in emerging markets, especially in large emerging markets such as China and India. Many new developments are taking place in the transition economies of Central and Eastern Europe as well, as illustrated in International Marketing Illustration 14-1.

International Marketing Illustration 14-1
Central and Eastern Europe: A Growing Market for Public Relations

Public relations firms are growing rapidly in numbers and in revenue in Central and Eastern Europe, overcoming some of the growing pains and environmental obstacles. Among some of the obstacles the companies continue to face are the overly close relationships between magazines and public relations companies. Often, companies pay journalists to write stories about them. Public relations agencies control the media, especially the popular lifestyle magazines where ads for the holidays and food are portrayed as editorial articles. Sponsoring companies pay for much of the travel for journalists. And publishers do not permit the journalists in their employ to write negative stories about the firms that advertise in their magazines and newspapers (i.e., to author negative publicity about their advertising clients).

The reverse situation also presents problems. Media, and newspapers in general, tend to be suspicious of public relations agencies. In fact, media owners are wary of corporations and often view any type of positive publicity as something they should be paid for. Hungarian and Czech newspapers even go as far as to place barriers against public relations companies and prevent journalists from having contact with them. When a company executive shares an important tip, he or she is quoted as the representative of an unnamed firm, rather than the representative of an identified firm.

Adding to the difficulties of the public relations firms in Central and Eastern Europe is the fact that most of their senior executives are younger than 30. They are perceived as inexperienced, and clients barely agree to pay them a fee of 15 percent on top of expenses. It is difficult to justify to clients that public relations involves important work that helps companies remain competitive. Yet, in spite of all the challenges, the public relations industry is growing by leaps and bounds, with firms increasing in number and suc-

cessfully competing with leading international firms. This is encouraging development because firms and their products are only strengthened by competent public relations.

Alternatively, negative publicity can be countered and its impact lessened by expert PR. Euro 2012, the European soccer tournament that took place in the Ukraine, could have benefitted from PR expertise. The Ukraine worked for two years to prepare for the tournament, built two stadiums and opened four airports at a cost of over $14.5 billion – quite a lot for a former Soviet state. However, just before the games, a former prominent British player stated that it was wrong to hold the Euro 2012 games in Poland and the Ukraine because of the racist attitudes there and the risk of coming back home in a coffin. The British Foreign Office followed up and advised fans of African or Asian descent to be careful if attending the games.

The Ukraine only has itself to blame for failing to sell itself. Kiev is a fabulous European capital, Ukrainian fans drink a lot of beer, and the country has an illustrious literary history (Bulgakov was born there, Chekhov wrote some of his famous work on the Crimean Peninsula), and much pride in its soccer history, with Dynamo Kiev winning twice the European cup. The Ukraine, much like the other countries in Central and Eastern Europe, needs good PR.

Sources: *The Guardian,* "Euro 2012 turning into PR disaster for Ukraine as racism fears scare off fans," 28 May, 2012, www.guardian.co.uk/football/2012/may/28/euro-2012-ukraine-sol-campbell; Maria Vornovitsky, "Advertising Changes in Post-Soviet Russia: Content Analysis," working paper; Katka Krosnar, "Hope for PR in Eastern Europe," *Marketing Magazine,* Vol. 106, No. 2, January 15, 2001, p. 6; Katka Krosnar, "PR Struggles in Eastern Europe," *Marketing Magazine,* Vol. 106, No. 1, January 1/8 2001, p. 6.

Public relations efforts fall into the following categories:

- News releases/letters, press releases, company publications
- Event sponsorship and presence
- Corporate advertising
- Image advertising
- Advocacy advertising
- Public appearances by company representatives

News Releases/Letters, Press Releases, and Company Publications

Multinational firms must, on a regular basis, communicate with their different publics (home-country, local, and international customers; trade; stockholders; government; and community). When new products are introduced in local markets, company representatives are likely to offer **news releases, press releases,** or **company publications** touting the advantages of the new products or services. Companies also use their websites to promote the brand and create excitement about events organized around their brand. In its news and press releases, Mexican Corona beer is touting its European campaign, announcing the Movida Corona parties. These parties revolve around live Latin music and are held at celebrated music venues throughout Europe—in Italy, at Rimini's Bahia Imperial; in Spain, at Madrid's Teatro Kapital; or in the United Kingdom, at London's Ministry of Sound. Corona also announced a campaign including a giant American truck and a mind-blowing laser and video show enhanced by a powerful sound system, which was targeted at Spain, Croatia, Denmark, France, Italy, the United Kingdom, Austria, Switzerland, Sweden, and Germany.[7]

news releases
Statements issued to the public to introduce a new product, touting its advantages; any other information shared with the media.

press releases
Statements issued to the press to communicate news about a company and its products.

company publications
Public relations publications that describe the products of a company to potential customers and summarize financial achievements.

event sponsorship
The financial support of cultural or sports-related events; companies use these events to get positive publicity.

Event Sponsorship and Presence

Event sponsorship is a growing venue for international marketing communication. Nearly every important international cultural or sports-related event has the backing of multinational corporations. Brands such as Adidas, MasterCard, Visa, Rolex, Coca-Cola, Pepsi, and Heineken, sponsor events ranging from World Cup Soccer to World Cup Cricket to the Davis Cup for tennis. And multinational and local Chinese companies fought for a prime spot at the Beijing 2008 Olympics, whereas British and other multinationals held this spot at the 2012 Olympics.

The Olympics Showcase of Sponsors

UPS was the official logistics and express delivery sponsor of the 2008 Olympic Games in China. Previously based in Hong Kong, the UPS regional marketing communications team relocated to Beijing in 2007 to oversee the project. For UPS, the Olympics offered a prime opportunity: After a decade in which it lagged rivals FedEx and DHL in China, the company bought out its local partner Sinotrans in 2004, and, given its market position, it was only fitting for the company to sponsor the 2008 Olympics.[8]

Lenovo, the most aggressive Olympic marketer, viewed the 2008 Games as an opportunity to showcase that they were truly China's global company. Lenovo invested an estimated $80 million in marketing at the Olympic Games. Adidas, the only brand-licensee partner for the Games, meaning it was the only company allowed to sell products co-branded with the Olympic logo, paid more than $80 million in cash and services and invested millions more in Games-related marketing and business development. Coca-Cola's Olympic sponsorship helped the company take on Pepsi in China, where Pepsi appeared to connect better with Chinese youth through Asian pop stars such as Jay Chou. The Coca-Cola 2008 Olympic pin program allowed consumers to design and trade Olympic-themed pins and to participate in a design contest. For Visa, the Olympics were a once-in-a-lifetime opportunity to lead the credit card market as it opened in China.[9]

The London Olympics of 2012 were also sponsored by several multinational companies. The top sponsors were Coca-Cola, Dow, GE, McDonald's, Omega, Panasonic, Procter & Gamble, Samsung, Visa, Acer, and Atos Origin, each sponsoring the Games to the tune of $100 million. Surprisingly, most people had no idea who the sponsor was – 16 percent of individuals surveyed indicated erroneously that Tesco was the sponsor. Also Cannon, Carlsberg, Sky and the mobile phone company Orange were erroneously cited as sponsors. Coca-Cola has been a continuous sponsor of the Olympics since the 1928 Olympic Games in Amsterdam and the partnership will extend for 12 more years, through 2024.[10] See Figure 14-2.

Figure 14-2: *Coca-Cola was yet again one of the top sponsors of the London Olympics in 2012.*

Across continents, cultural manifestations are supported by major international brands. For years now, Makedonski Telekom, the Macedonian subsidiary of the German company, Deutsche Telekom, has sponsored festivals in emerging markets. For example, it sponsors the International Arts Festival AKTO in Bitola, the Ohrid Summer Festival, and the Skopje Jazz Festival, in the capital, Skopje, bringing prominent jazz musicians from all over the world.[11]

LG, Pepsi, Maruti Suzuki, Nokia, Philips, Sony, Reliance Mobile, Future Group, Reebok and Emirates Airlines sponsored World Cup Cricket 2012.[12] Tata, the venerable Indian multinational that owns, among so many others, Tata Steel, Land Rover, and Jaguar, is sponsoring numerous events in emerging markets and developed countries alike, from the Ferrari Formula 1 team to the Cardiff Bay 5 Marathon benefitting cystic fibrosis in the United Kingdom.[13]

International sponsorship is so prevalent that it has drawn the attention of artists. Near a bus stop in Kassel, Germany, a kiosk that would normally carry advertisements is actually a work by New York–based artist Hans Haacke displaying quotes from executives telling why they sponsor art shows. Hilmar Kopper, head of Deutsche Bank, says: "Whoever pays, controls." Alain Dominique Perrin, Cartier's head, says: "[Sponsorship] is a tool for shaping public opinion."[14]

Corporate Advertising

Corporate advertising is used to promote the company behind the different brands. One particularly memorable advertisement of this kind in advertising history was designed by Philip Morris for the Chinese market on the occasion of the Chinese New Year. This ad portrayed traditional Chinese dancers dancing on the Great Wall to the Marlboro theme song, which was still familiar to consumers despite the fact that Marlboro cigarettes are no longer advertised on television. At the end of the ad, the advertisement wished Chinese consumers a happy new year from the Philip Morris companies.

In another example, on the occasion of President Horst Kohler of Germany visiting China, a full-page Daimler ad in China's newspaper *China Daily*, avowed: "A German soul, with a heart for China. Embracing the spirit of our commitment to Sino-German relations, Mercedes-Benz wishes President Horst Kohler a pleasant, successful, and prosperous visit to China. With a long industrial heritage, grounded in German technology and expertise, Mercedes-Benz is widely recognized for its passion for innovation and constant pursuit for perfection. This is our heart and soul—and what drives our commitment to China."[15]

corporate advertising
A type of advertising that is used to promote the company behind the different brands.

The ad sounds much like modern Chinese poetry and it resonates well with Chinese consumers, who responded positively to a respectful communication from the prestigious German company.

In other corporate advertising examples, Bombardier Transportation, a Canadian company with a strong presence in Berlin, Germany, where it has more than 18,200 employees working with 115 companies, [16] partnered with the Berlin Transportation Authority and the German railway system, Deutsche Bahn, to build the Berlin train station, a work of art and ingenuous technology. The company is promoting its prominent brand in the heart of the train station (see Figure 14-3).

Figure 14-3: Corporate presence: Bombardier, the Canadian aircraft and rail systems manufacturer, advertises in a prime location at the Berlin state-of-the-art train station.

Image Advertising

Image advertising is used to enhance perceptions of a company in a given market. McDonald's used image advertising to combat the negative attitudes of consumers and farmers in France in the late 1990s, when José Bové, a farmer campaigning against globalization, protested against McDonald's by bulldozing down a restaurant. More recently, in 2005, in an event that echoed the McDonald's bulldozing, the police in northern Lille found a stolen plastic figure of Ronald McDonald, dangling beneath a city bridge with a ball and chain attached to one foot. McDonald's reacted promptly in both situations to change the company's image. It intensified advertising campaigns, informing customers more about McDonald's France, what ingredients it used, and what kind of people it employed. The company's strategy was to blur the lines about McDonald's nationality: all the buns, meat, and other ingredients are from France and virtually all the work force is French.[17]

McDonald's is also improving its image on the labor front. In a campaign entitled "McDo = McJob," the company announces that its restaurant directors are supported financially by the company in pursuing a management or business degree.[18]

> **image advertising**
> An advertising campaign that enhances perceptions of a company in a given market by creating a positive impression on the target consumers.

Advocacy Advertising

Advocacy advertising is used by a company to stress a particular point of view. Benetton has always been an advocate—for multiculturalism, for reflections on the death row, and, now, for reflections on climate change. In an advocacy ad featured in its magazine *Colors,* the company asks what might happen in the summer of 2057 if the planet keeps getting warmer: "Will we have to drink water from puddles, move to igloos in the North Pole, shave the fur off polar bears, or always carry a hurricane kit in our bags?" The company wonders if they could move the editorial team to Vörland, an island off the coast of Scandinavia, which used to be thought of as a freezing, inhospitable island. But now, in the year 2057, it has become one of the most popular tourist destinations in the world, with mild temperatures, lush vegetation, wide and sandy beaches, and temperatures that are a far cry from the torrid summers of southern Europe. Vörland's currency is karbons, one travels by air balloon, and the island has complete energy self-sufficiency. Or so the story goes . . . [19]

Advocacy advertising is effective, and multinationals like to be known for the causes they embrace and for which they actively advocate.

Public Appearances by Company Representatives

In addition to **public appearances** to speak on behalf of the international firm and its products, which are typical of this category, company representatives frequently attend important international events. There are many opportunities for company representatives to show up in force to voice their concerns and show their support for various causes.

One such event is the World Economic Forum. The 2012 Forum for Africa in Addis Ababa was particularly well attended. According to Ethiopia's Ministry of Foreign Affairs, prominent representatives of industry attended, among them, Microsoft Corp. co-founder Bill Gates, an ardent supporter of campaigns to bring vaccines to the African continent, and Gao Xiqing, President of the China Investment Corporation (CIC) ; Monhla Hlahla, Chairperson, Industrial Development Corporation of South Africa; Donald Kaberuka, President, African Development Bank; and Doug McMillon, President and Chief Executive Officer, Wal-Mart International, all co-chairs of the Forum.[20]

14-2 Consumer Sales Promotion

Aside from advertising, personal selling, public relations, and publicity, all other sponsored communications offered to the end consumer or to the trade that stimulate purchases or improve relationships to intermediaries and retailers in the short term fall into the category of **sales promotion.** Among examples of consumer sales promotion are point-of-purchase displays, free samples to initiate product trial or brand switching, other incentives (coupons, cents-off, gifts, product tie-ins) to initiate trial or brand switching, and sweepstakes and contests. Among examples of trade (business-to-business) promotion are trade discounts, sweepstakes and contests, and trade shows.

advocacy advertising
Advertising a particular position or point of view.

public appearances
Company representatives' public involvement, speaking on behalf of the international firm and its products.

sales promotion
Sponsored communications to the target consumer or trade segment that stimulate purchases or improve relationships with intermediaries.

Figure 14-4: *In this store, free samples are offered to customers to induce them to try and to purchase the hot chili.*

Sampling is used primarily by food and beverage manufacturers, but can also be used by almost any type of good or service (see Figure 14-4). Free samples are offered at busy intersections or at train stations. People arriving with suitcases at Berlin's main train station on a particular day were given packets of Haribo *Gummibären* candy, free newspapers, and fruit drinks.

Coupons are often used to stimulate sales, especially in the short term. Worldwide, most coupons are delivered via direct mail. Coupons are also handed out at events with product samples. North American companies prefer using inserts and print media to distribute coupons because consumers must make an effort to clip and save the coupon. In most other countries, membership in a loyalty program creates a consumer database that companies then use for mailing coupons and other promotions. In Europe, few companies offer coupons. It is primarily U.S. fast-food restaurants, such as McDonald's and Burger King, that offer coupons frequently to gain, and later to maintain, customer loyalty. Their couponing strategy for Europe is similar to that used in the United States. In the case of Burger King, one coupon offers two double-Whoppers and medium-sized fries for €6.49 (regularly priced at €9.88); another coupon offers buy one Big King, get one Big King for free; and a third coupon offers two Crispy Chicken with medium-sized fries for €4.49 (regularly priced at €7.48).

Companies in Asia and Europe rarely offer instant redemption coupons or bounce-back coupons that consumers can redeem at a later time. However, the practice of beaming electronic coupons to the cell phones of consumers has been around for years in Asia and Europe, whereas in the United States, it has only recently started, with McDonald's, Starbucks, and Dunkin' Donuts paving the way.[21]

Premiums offer consumers free merchandise for purchasing a product. In the United States, the value of the premium is usually great, often a major benefit. Particularly when purchasing cosmetics, premiums can be of high value, as high as that of the purchased product itself. In the rest of the world, such gifts are of low value. For example, a cereal box might carry with it a small "prize," such as race car. Or your cosmetics salesperson will offer you a miniature cream to entice you to buy from her again.

Contests and *sweepstakes* allow participants to win prizes. In a contest, the participant needs to perform an activity or make a purchase to be able to win. For example, IKEA in Europe has a contest where one can win €500 in IKEA merchandise if one fills out a form and answers correctly the day of the week when IKEA holds its contests (Fridays)—the contest is held weekly.

Bonus packs, with additional merchandise offered at the same price or slightly higher, such as four packs of gum for the price of two, or a bundle of complementary products, are increasingly found in supermarkets outside of North America (see Figure 14-5).

Figure 14-5: *In many of the countries of the former Soviet Union, the German company Henkel sells its Persil laundry detergent in bundles, along with its Silan fabric softner.*

Promotional tie-ins include two products or services within the same promotional offer and they can be intracompany or intercompany. A Toggo children's television channel promotion in Germany and Austria offers parents the opportunity to purchase a children's Toggo cell phone with a GPS function where one can track their children—and phone calls to the parent's phone are free. A city family pass in a European city offers reduced-price access to the zoo, museums, public swimming pools—and, if you can prove that you have low income, you also get a reduction for public transportation. The pass is something that every family can pick up every year.

Frequency programs, also called loyalty programs, are aimed at current customers and are designed to create repeat purchase and loyalty. Such programs abound worldwide. Airlines in every country have some type of frequency program (e.g., frequent flier miles), and hotel chains offer free rooms and free access to their executive suites for sustained loyalty. Food stores and gas stations offer discounts for members (see Figure 14-6).

Figure 14-6:*This card from Metro (Austria), the hypermarket chain, is both a membership card and a loyalty card.*

Price-offs are reductions in the listed retail price of a product. They are used to attract consumers, and have the greatest impact on price-sensitive shoppers. This is a strategy that is often used for store openings. In one example, a large electronics retailer, Saturn, had advertised the opening of a new store for weeks in a large city in Germany. In addition, consumers were mailed inserts advertising the grand event (see Figure 14-7). At the opening of the five-floor retail establishment, the business was practically mobbed. Women with baby carriages had no babies seated in them, only merchandise piled high. Men were overwhelmed by the large number of packages they carried all at once to the registers. At the entrance at the store, there was a tiny convertible automobile exposed to the rain, with a flat-panel-TV box standing tall and obstructing all rear visibility. The deals were only so-so, but the excitement created by the advance promotion was high.

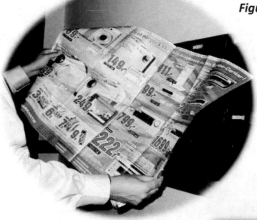

Figure 14-7: Saturn's direct mail piece, which advertise significant price-offs.

In the United States, firms also use *rebates* or *refunds*, which are cash reimbursements paid to consumers after they turn in a proof of purchase. These promotions are rarely used outside of North America.

Point-of-purchase displays are popular all over the world, if there is sufficient space for the display. Some could consist of valuable refrigerators with the company's brand name and various shelf structures with the manufacturer's brand name. Others could show the product in action as the train set pictured in Figure 14-8.

Figure 14-8: *This fast train point-of-purchase display was difficult to photograph. Children and parents were congregating around it at all times.*

14-2a Adaptation of Sales Promotion

International sales promotion campaigns fall into one of three strategies, paralleling international advertising and international product marketing strategies: global campaigns, modular campaigns, and local campaigns.

Global Campaigns

Global campaigns are rarely attempted in sales promotion. Even a company such as IBM, which wants consistent strategies worldwide, requires a priori feedback from local markets to ensure that the central strategy can be implemented.[22]

Certain types of sales promotion, such as point-of-purchase displays, lend themselves to a more standardized campaign. They do not rely on words, so different language versions are not necessary. They speak an international language by reinforcing logos and emphasizing brand image visually.[23] Yet, even point-of-purchase displays need some adaptation. Johnnie Walker Scotch whisky has a 200-square-foot point-of-purchase display for its Blue Label at Shanghai's Pudong Airport. In a dark, executive-suite-type setting, with deep blues everywhere, the display is a head turner. In glass cases, very, very special bottles lie next to their very special cases. In the front, at the desk, you can order engraving services for "your passport to luxury." Then, you can plop down a few thousand dollars for one of those pretty bottles, and it is all duty free.

Occasionally, the target market itself may encourage the use of a global, standardized approach. For example, in markets where multiple languages are spoken, and where English is one of the unifying languages, as in the case of India, using English for sales promotion may be appropriate. Even in countries where English is not a language used nationally, such as in Switzerland, using English as the language of the promotion may be a benefit. For example, promotions aimed at Swiss consumers often use English, rather than French, German, or Italian, because two groups of consumers would be offended if a campaign used only one of the three languages spoken in Switzerland.[24]

Modular Campaigns

Modular campaigns provide a template that can be varied from market to market. Even in the European market, different strategies are likely to be used in the United Kingdom than in continental Europe. In one example, McDonald's teamed up with the biggest children's TV network in Europe, Fox Kids, to run a Happy Meal push spanning 49 countries. The promotion was coordinated from London, but localized to suit individual countries. Its mission was to entertain, rather than educate, which fits with the objectives set by McDonald's for its Happy Meals. The Happy Meals have a spinning top that integrates a CD-ROM, decorated by either Power Rangers, Totally Spies, Gadgets & the Gadgetinis, and Medabots; there are eight premiums to collect—four are straightforward spinning tops and four contain the CD-ROM. McDonald's purpose is to get kids in front of computers and improving their information technology skills. However, in some targeted markets, such as Croatia, Estonia, Macedonia, Tahiti, and Romania, children may not have access to computers . . . but at least they are getting a spinner.[25]

Local Campaigns

Local campaigns are tailored to local needs, and retailer cooperation is of particular importance in ensuring that such sales promotion campaigns are successful. In the Netherlands, Albert Heijn appears to be favored as a grocery store where multinationals offer their new products and attempt to initiate consumer trials. The store, part of the Royal Ahold retail conglomerate, offers quality products aimed at the middle and upper-middle class. It was there that Procter & Gamble first introduced Bounty paper towels to Dutch consumers about 10 years ago. Albert Heijn displayed the product prominently using point-of-sale displays located near the cash registers and also offered the product in the paper products section of the stores. Simultaneously, the company mailed samples of Bounty in individual sheets, with different designs, in plastic bags, to selected homes. In another more recent exam-

global campaign
A worldwide standardized advertising campaign that is not adjusted to different target markets.

modular campaign
An advertising campaign that provides a template that is varied and customized from market to market.

local campaign
An advertising campaign that is tailored to local needs; especially used in markets that media cannot easily reach.

ple, Coca-Cola representatives offered free samples of Coke and Coke Light to consumers shopping at Albert Heijn. After sampling Coke in miniature cans, consumers were able to purchase the product with a two-for-the-price-of-one promotion.

14-2b The Online Venue for Sales Promotion

Online sales promotion is quickly becoming a pervasive mode of communication with prospective consumers. Whether the promotion involves sweepstakes, printed coupons, promotional pricing, or other strategies, companies find that consumers around the world respond well to aggressive online promotions. Most of the communications firms (the former traditional advertising firms) now serve their clients by providing to target consumers extensive interactive sales promotion that is in line with the company's other types of communications.

14-2c Legal and Ethical Issues in Consumer Sales Promotion

To a certain degree, adaptation to local markets is necessitated by legal requirements. Even in economically and politically integrated markets, such as the European Union, sales promotion–related legislation differs from one country to another. In Germany, for example, "buy one, get one free" offers are illegal; in France, premiums are restricted to seven percent of the product's value; and, in Belgium, retail sales can run for only a month and prices cannot be cut more than one third.[26]

In 2001, the European Union attempted to institute sales promotion regulations. However, its efforts were jettisoned by the European Commission after member states failed to reach a consensus. The idea was to create an internal market for sales promotion, allowing advertisers to run identical promotions across the EU. However, the members could not agree on a cap on prize funds and on regulations related to promoting to children. The regulation on sales promotions was designed to break down barriers to across-the-border sales promotions on discounts, premiums, gifts, competitions, and promotional games and to replace them with rules on transparency and information designed to ensure freedom of movement. The purpose of the regulation was to bring the countries with the most restrictive promotions laws—such as France and Belgium —into line with more liberal countries such as the United Kingdom.[27]

Sweepstakes based on pure chance are deemed illegal in Holland,[28] Canada, Sweden, and Belgium,[29] whereas, elsewhere in the world, additional legal requirements for sales promotion strategies diverge. Puerto Rican law, for instance, requires rules for all promotions to be printed in both English and Spanish, and both versions should be printed in a general circulation newspaper at least once a week for the duration of the campaign. Quebec requires sponsors to provide French translations, to pay a duty based on the total value of the prize pool, and to post a bond to run a promotion.[30] All paperwork regarding point-of-sale displays must be legalized by going through embassies in the Middle East, while displays going to Eastern Europe must be marked as not being for resale to avoid additional customs duties.[31]

Often the companies themselves are responsible for creating a bad reputation for sales promotion. Sales promotions aimed at emerging markets over time have been questionable. For example, local consumers wearing fur jackets and hats promoting luxury automobiles, investment funds, expensive cigarettes, and airlines—products and services they could not possibly afford—are common in developing countries in sub-Saharan Africa and Eastern Europe.

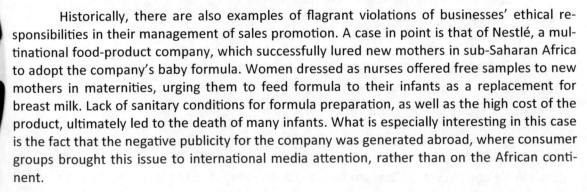

Historically, there are also examples of flagrant violations of businesses' ethical responsibilities in their management of sales promotion. A case in point is that of Nestlé, a multinational food-product company, which successfully lured new mothers in sub-Saharan Africa to adopt the company's baby formula. Women dressed as nurses offered free samples to new mothers in maternities, urging them to feed formula to their infants as a replacement for breast milk. Lack of sanitary conditions for formula preparation, as well as the high cost of the product, ultimately led to the death of many infants. What is especially interesting in this case is the fact that the negative publicity for the company was generated abroad, where consumer groups brought this issue to international media attention, rather than on the African continent.

14-3 International Trade Promotion (Trade Shows and Exhibitions)

Most sales promotion addressed in Section 14-2, "Consumer Sales Promotion," is primarily aimed at the final consumer—although sweepstakes and contests, as well as incentives such as price-off reductions, also may be aimed at the trade. **Trade shows and exhibitions** belong to the category of business-to-business promotion. They are also referred to as *international trade promotion*—sales promotion aimed at the trade. Trade shows and exhibitions are usually held annually in formats in which companies purchase exhibit space to display and demonstrate their offerings to the target market. There are numerous trade shows for most industries. To illustrate the extent to which companies have opportunities for exhibiting their work, view the different trade shows by searching by date, industry, location, at the U.S. Department of Trade website for the International Trade Administration (www.ita.doc.gov).

> **trade shows and exhibitions**
> Business-to-business promotions that usually are held annually in formats where companies purchase exhibit space to display and demonstrate their offerings to the target market.

Trade shows and exhibitions offer potential buyers and sellers a chance to meet face-to-face, as they bring many decision makers to a single location for a limited time, enabling firms to get their message to a large number of people at one time. In a typical promotional environment, the seller must pitch the product to the buyer. For trade shows and exhibits, however, the visitors are the ones who approach the seller, searching for new products and suppliers. Finally, trade shows and exhibits provide a neutral location for doing business and bring together managers from different departments in buyers' organizations, thus increasing the probability of meeting every decision maker who will influence the buying decision.[32]

Country and state governments are often involved in ensuring that national/local companies are represented at important fairs. In the United States, the Department of Commerce is actively involved in promoting U.S. companies abroad using trade shows as venues. Usually, the U.S. government shares the cost of the exhibits by sponsoring a national pavilion at the different fairs.

As mentioned, trade shows and exhibitions are organized annually or at set intervals and tend to be specialized in one domain. The Frankfurt Book Fair, for example, draws publishers and authors on all topics from around the world every fall to the city of Frankfurt, Germany. The *documenta,* takes place every five years, and the Venice Biennale takes place biannually. Both exhibits show art works of contemporary artists (see Figure 14-9). In other examples, DRUPA is an annual trade exhibition for the graphic arts industry, and Interkama is an international trade fair for industrial communication, automation, measurement, and analytics. Messe Dusseldorf, in Dusseldorf, Germany, for example, specializes in international trade shows for machinery, as well as for the medical, fashion, and services industries.

Figure 14-9: The Venice Biennale is one of the most important venues for showcasing contemporary art and artists. Among its sponsors were Fiat, AMB AMRO and illy coffee.

The World Exposition (the World's Fair) cuts across domains and is one of the most important venues for exhibiting new ideas, technology, and art in an environment where numerous countries are represented. Expo 2005 was organized in Seto, Japan, in the Aichi Prefecture, and Expo 2010 took place in Shanghai, China, with more than 70 million visitors in attendance. For Expo 2020, the bidding is in full swing, with Izmir, Turkey, Ayutthaya, Thailand, Yekaterinburg, Russia, São Paulo, Brazil, and Dubai, United Arab Emirates competing for the honor.[33]

Summary

Provide an overview of international publicity and the different international public relations activities that can be used to influence it. Publicity is a promotional tool that companies do not pay for; rather, publicity is a result of companies' performance and perception in world markets. For companies conducting business internationally, publicity in one country may have important repercussions on company perception in all the markets where the companies are present. Publicity can be positively influenced by using appropriate public relations tools, such as releasing relevant company publications, press releases, news releases; engaging in appropriate public appearances; and hiring agencies to design image advertising and corporate advertising that reflects company philosophies and strategies.

Describe the different approaches to international consumer sales promotion and the activities involved. International consumer promotions are becoming popular worldwide. Such activities include point-of-sale displays, free samples to initiate product trial or brand switching, and other incentives (coupons, cents-off, gifts, product tie-ins) designed with the purpose to initiate trial or brand switching. Promotional activities can be global in nature; modular, with some adaptation in select markets; and local, designed with local consumers in mind.

Describe the different approaches to international trade promotion and the different activities involved. International trade promotion, aimed at the business-to-business market, can involve trade shows and exhibitions, as well as trade discounts, sweepstakes, and contests. Trade shows provide a neutral environment where buyer and seller can meet face-to-face in a low-pressure situation in which the buyer is most likely to approach the seller, rather than vice versa.

Key Terms

advocacy advertising

company publications

corporate advertising

event sponsorship

global campaign

image advertising

international public relations

local campaign

modular campaign

news releases

press releases

public appearances

publicity

sales promotion

trade shows and exhibitions

Discussion Questions

1.   Describe the relationship between international public relations activities and international publicity.

2.   What are the different public relations tools that an international firm can use to fend off negative publicity?

3.   Describe some of the international consumer promotion activities that international firms currently engage in, while addressing ethical issues and international standards involved.

4.   How does international business-to-business sales promotion (trade promotion) benefit international companies and target consumers?

Chapter Quiz

True/False

1. Communication about a company that the company does not pay for is defined as publicity.

Answer: True

Rationale: Publicity is defined as a communication about a company and/or the company's products that the company does not pay for. The communication can be either positive or negative.

Section 14-1a, "Publicity"

2. The main purpose of public relations is to generate *positive* publicity about a company.

Answer: True

Rationale: Public relations is defined as a concerted effort on the part of a company to generate goodwill among its publics (community, government, consumers, employees, among others).

Section 14-1b, "Public Relations"

3. Companies must consider legal and ethical issues with consumer sales promotions. In Germany, "buy one, get one free" offers are illegal.

Answer: True

Rationale: Companies need to adapt their sales promotions to local markets to conform to legal requirements, which could vary from country to country even in markets where there is regional political and economic integration.

Section 14-2c, "Legal and Ethical Issues in Consumer Sales Promotion"

4. Trade shows are an example of consumer sales promotion.

Answer: False

Rationale: Trade shows and exhibitions belong to the category of business-to-business promotion. They are also referred to as international trade promotion—sales promotion aimed at the trade.

Section 14-3, "International Trade Promotion (Trade Shows and Exhibitions)"

Multiple Choice

1.   Marlboro was one of the official sponsors of Ferrari's Formula 1 team, endorsing Michael Schumacher. This is an example of

    a.   press release.

    b.   company publications.

    c.   event sponsorship.

    d.   advocacy advertising.

Answer: c is correct.

Rationale: Marlboro's sponsorship of the Ferrari team at Formula 1 is an example of event sponsorship public relations.

Section 14-1b, "Public Relations"

2.   According to the text, what international organization often uses advocacy advertising?

    a.   McDonald's

    b.   Benetton

    c.   Visa

    d.   Adidas

Answer: b is correct.

Rationale: Benetton's advertising is an example of advocacy advertising, used by a company to stress a particular point of view. Its current advocacy topic is global warming.

Section 14-1b, "Public Relations"

3.   Which of the following is an example of sales promotion?

    a.   product tie-ins

    b.   free samples

    c.   cents-off

    d.   all of the above

Answer: d is correct.

Rationale: These three promotions are offered to stimulate purchases or improve relationships to intermediaries and retailers in the short term. They fall in the category of sales promotion.

Section 14-2, "Consumer Sales Promotion"

4.   Which of the following types of sales promotion can be varied from one market to another?

    a.   Local campaigns

    b.   Modular campaigns

    c.   Global campaigns

    d.   None of the above

Answer: b is correct.

Rationale: Modular campaigns provide a template that can be varied from market to market. Multinational companies often launch worldwide a promotional campaign centered on one theme and then use advertising to customize the message for each individual market.

Section 14-2a, "Adaptation of Sales Promotion"

5.   What percent of Europeans and U.S. consumers make their purchase decision at the point of sale?

    a.   50

    b.   60

    c.   30

    d.   None of the above

Answer: a is correct.

Rationale: Half of consumers in Europe and the United States make their purchase decision at the point of sale.

Section 14-2d, "The Future of Consumer Sales Promotion"

6.   What city hosted the World Fair Expo 2010?

    a.   San Francisco

    b.   London

    c.   Shanghai

    d.   Munich

Answer: c is correct.

Rationale: Expo 2010 was held in Shanghai, China.

Section 14-3, "International Trade Promotion (Trade Shows and Exhibitions)"

Chapter 14 Endnotes

1   Stephen Power, "EU Lifts the Hood on Chinese Autos; Questions on Safety Abound As China Looks to Become a Major Player in the West," *Wall Street Journal*, October 7, 2005, 14.

2.   David Barboza, "Some Suspect Chemical Mix in Pet Food," *New York Times*, April 12, 2007, A1; Walt Bogdanich, "Toxic Toothpaste Made in China Is Found in the U.S., *New York Times*, June 2, 2007, A1.

3.   Food and Drug Administration, "Questions and Answers Regarding Chicken Jerky Treats from China," www.fda.gov/AnimalVeterinary/SafetyHealth/ProductSafetyInformation/ucm295445.htm (accessed on June 1, 2012).

4.   See Jon Henley, "Flip Flop, "*The New Republic,* Vol. 222, No. 1, January 3, 2000, p. 24.

5.   Examples adapted from Saleh AlShebil, Abdul A. Rasheed, and Hussam Al-Shammari, "Battling Boycotts: When a Company Is Targeted Simply Because of Its Nationality, What Can It Do?, *MIT Sloan Management Review*, April 27, 2007.

6.   *Sources:* T. L. Stanley, "Gem Sellers Launch Blitz Against "Blood Diamond,'" *Advertising Age*, December 11, 2006, 50 (12), p. 12; www. DiamondFacts.org.

7.   www.movidacorona.com; www.corona-extra.net.

8.   Arun Suhaman, "Tan Eyes First Place for UPS as Olympics Near," *Media*, November 3, 2006, p. 18.

9.   Normandy Madden, "Marketers Limber Up for 2008 Beijing Olympics," *Advertising Age*Vol. 77, No. 4, , October 30, 2006, p. 3

10.   Jacquelin Smith, "London 2012 Olympic Sponsorship Roundup," *Forbes*, July 18, 2012, www.forbes.com/sites/jacquelynsmith/2012/07/18/london-2012-olympic-sponsorship-round-up; Simon Rogers, London 2012 Olympic

sponsors list: who are they and what have they paid? www.guardian.co.uk/sport/datablog/2012/jul/19/london-2012 -olympic-sponsors-list.

11.   *Makedonski Telekom*, "Culture and Public Life," www.telekom.mk/en/?z=956 (accessed June 1, 2012).

12.   Meenakshi Verma Ambwani, Writankar Mukherjee, and Sreeradha D Basu, "Cricket World Cup: ESPN ropes in seven sponsors already," November 17, 2010. http://articles.economictimes.indiatimes.com/2010-11-17/ news/27629463_1_cricket-world-cup-icc-events-official-broadcaster-espn.

13.   *Autocar*, "Tata to Sponsor Ferrari," www.autocar.co.uk/car-news/industry/tata-sponsor-ferrari (accessed on June 1, 2012); *Cystic Fibrosis Trust*, "Tata Steel Cardiff Bay 5," May 6, 2012, http://www.cftrust.org.uk/help/events/ cb5.

14.   Thane Peterson and Sandra Dallas, "Tycoons on the Trail of the Next de Kooning," *BusinessWeek,* Vol. 3541, August 25, 1997, p. 16.

15.   *China Daily*, May 24, 2007, Special Advertising Insert.

16.   www.bombardier.com

17.   John Tagliabue, "A McDonald's Ally in Paris," *New York Times Online,* June 20, 2006.

18.   http://adsneeze.com/2007/03/01/mcdonalds-france-advert

19.   http://www.colorsmagazine.com/downloads/PDF/COLORS_71.pdf (accessed June 2, 2012).

20.   Ministry of Foreign Affairs of the Federal Democratic Republic of Ethiopia, "The World Economic Forum for Africa meets in Addis Ababa," 5 May, 2012, www.mfa.gov.et/weekHornAfrica/morewha.php?wi=364.

21.   Kathryn Williams, "Coupons Clip-Free," *Newsweek*, Vol. 145, No. 16, April 18, 2005, p. 11.

22.   "Pushing Back the Business Frontiers," *Marketing,* October 1997, pp. 49–50.

23.   Daney Parker, "Popular Choice," *Marketing Week,* Vol. 19, No. 10, May 31, 1996, pp. 39–40.

24.   Ibid.

25.   Suzy Bashford, "McDonald's and Fox Kids," *Promotions & Incentives*, February 2004, pp. 25–27.

26.   Ken Gofton, "How Euro Rules Will Change SP," *Marketing,* October 5, 2000, pp. 60–61.

27.   *Marketing Week*, "EC Abandons Plan for Sales Promotion Regulations," September 29, 2005, p. 6.

28.   Rob Furber, "Centre Shop," *Marketing Week*, Vol. 22, No. 38, October 21, 1999, pp. 51–54.

29.   Warner Bernhard, "Crossing the Border," *Brandweek,* Vol. 37, No. 48, December 16, 1996, pp. 37–38.

30.   Maxine Lans Retsky, "Global Promotions Are Subject to Local Laws," *Marketing News,* Vol. 31, No. 10, May 12, 1997, p. 8.

31.   Parker, "Popular Choice," pp. 39–40.

32.   Aviv Shoham, "Performance in Trade Shows and Exhibitions: A Synthesis and Directions for Future Research," *Journal of Global Marketing*, Vol. 12, No. 3, 1999, pp. 41–57.

33.   www.bie-paris.org/site/en/expos.html (accessed July 12, 2012).

Case 14-1

Promoting Coke in South Africa

Coca-Cola just moved its operating group headquarters from the United Kingdom to Johannesburg, South Africa, to be closer to target consumers. Coca-Cola is the largest consumer goods provider in Africa. To date, the company has grown through close collaboration with its bottling and retail partners. Company headquarters have an aggressive growth plan for the African continent and for South Africa in particular. With a large percentage of the population young and dynamic, this market should be carefully courted.

As part of its efforts to reach this population, Coke set up the Coca-Cola Africa Foundation, in which the company partners with other organizations to build sustainable communities on the continent. To reach young South Africans in particular, the company hired South African artists that would appeal to this segment of the population to participate in a remix of the "I'd Like to Buy the World a Coke" theme song as a musical montage of reggae, Kwaito, rap, hip-hop, and hard rock. The ad was part of the "Coke Side of Life" campaign, and the theme song was so popular that radio stations added it to their playlists.

South Africa was Coca-Cola's first stop on the African continent in 1928. The company set up the first bottling and distribution plant in Johannesburg and has expanded its business in the country ever since, employing more than 10,000 people. The company's presence in South Africa created many more jobs in the country. For every job created by the production and marketing of Coke products, 10 additional jobs, on average, were created in South Africa in related industries.

The Coca-Cola Company sells numerous nonalcoholic brands to South African consumers. Among them are Coca-Cola (with its Light and Vanilla Coke versions), Fanta (with its Orange, Grape, and Pineapple versions), Sprite, Tab, Sparletta, Lemon Twist, Schweppes, Mixers, Fresca, Minute Maid, Powerade, Bibo, Milo, Krest, Splash, Bonaqua, and Vitango. Its product mix in South Africa is more extensive than in the United States because, in South Africa, the company also bought out a number of popular regional competitors.

During its time in Africa, Coca-Cola ran a few successful promotions. First, in 2002, it hired Riverside Technologies in Wilton, Connecticut, to provide ideas on technologic modifications that would set the brand apart. Riverside came up with modules that could be inserted into the packaging; these modules would sing and announce the winner of a Coke promotion. Consumers who purchased the winning cans were instant winners of Panasonic stereo equipment. The winning cans were filled with carbon dioxide and water, to replicate the weight and feel of a real can, and were assembled into the Coke can by Schmalbach-Lubeca Continental Can in Bonn, Germany. Fifty talking cans were produced for the promotion and were distributed nationally. In just the first month of the promotion, sales of Coke cans rose by 3.2 percent, Diet Coke cans by 18.6 percent, and Fanta by 3.8 percent compared with the previous year. This was in line with the theme of the promotion, "This summer only Coca-Cola talks," literally—and figuratively, in terms of sales.

Since 2002, Coca-Cola hasn't had many promotions that delivered a similar impact. In the spring of 2004, for example, the company coordinated with its advertising agencies another promotion that was not as popular with South African consumers. The promotion asked them to nominate the most inspiring person they knew to carry the Olympic Flame in Cape Town. Distributors were unhappy that they were not involved in the promotion, and generally, it was felt that a more aggressive and creative approach was needed to resuscitate Coke sales again.

In early 2006, Coke hired Conceptualise, South Africa's leading promotional marketing specialist, whose area of expertise is the development and implementation of promotional competitions and games. The company developed the Coca-Cola Mega Millions game for the South African market, which has captivated South African consumers. Mega Millions had a game-show format, and it was broadcast live during prime time on one of South Africa's top network channels, SABC 1. In the game, contestants interacted live to win cars and large cash prizes. To enter the game, individuals had to purchase Coca-Cola carbonated drinks, check the label, and find out if they won a prize. Their number also qualified them to enter into a pool of candidates to become a contestant on the live show—a contestant was drawn during each show from the pool of potential contestants. The Mega Millions game was hugely successful, with 22 million entries over a 4-month period.

Another successful promotion was co-sponsored with the retailer Pick 'n Pay: the 2012 Olympics Pick 'n Pay promotion. Participants were required to purchase a Coke product from any of the retailer's stores and SMS the number at the bottom of their receipt to win as much as 20 million SA Rand in cash. This would cost the individual sending the SMS 1 Rand.

Sources:/www.cocacola.co.za/upload/documents/ competitions/20120703_OlympicPick_n_Pay_Promo_rules_03_July_2012_FINAL.pdf;   www.thecoca-colacompany.com/contactus/faq/africa.html; www.conceptualise.co.za; Andrew Kaplan, "Case Study: Drumming Up Sales," *Beverage World,* Vol. 122, No. 1724, March 15, 2003, p. 99; http://rsa.coca-cola.com; http://www.cocacola.co.za/.

Analysis Suggestions

1.   Evaluate Coke's market position in South Africa relative to other competitors and other businesses.

2.   Evaluate the different types of consumer promotions used in South Africa to increase sales for Coca-Cola South Africa. Are there any types of sales promotions that should not have been used in a country characterized by a wealth gap, with a substantial proportion of the population below the poverty line? Explain.

Chapter 15: International Personal Selling and Personnel Management

Learning Objectives

After studying this chapter, you should be able to:

- Examine companies' expatriate management strategies.

- Describe the different types of employees suited for a company's international operations.

- Address issues related to expatriate management, such as motivating international employees and ensuring successful assignment performance and repatriation.

International sales representatives are often the frontline personnel in a firm's relationship with an international target market. Their expertise, ability, demeanor, and appearance all convey information that is integral to the firm's product or service offering and help shape the firm's relationship with the target market, distributors, suppliers, and local government agencies overseeing the firm's operations. Frequently, sales representatives are expatriates, crossing cultural divides and bridging cultures on behalf of the firm, often in unfamiliar settings, where the culture and marketing practices differ from those in the sales representatives' home country. Expatriate sales representatives must survive the challenges posed by the new environment, continuously adapt to its changing demands, and play by the host-country rules while representing the company and selling its products and services in a foreign market.

Local sales representatives also have challenges as the company's frontline personnel. Although, as nationals of the host country, they understand the market and its intricacies, as representatives of the company, they also need to understand the company's home country and organizational culture, as well as its marketing practices.

This chapter addresses issues related to managing expatriate employees, motivating them for optimal performance, and ensuring their successful repatriation to the home country.

15-1 International Presence and Personnel Issues

From a company perspective, hiring expatriates or locals is a function of the company's involvement in the market. The company's presence in the market—entry mode—and its commitment to the market are important considerations in determining the size of the sales team and the types of sales representatives the company employs. Companies primarily involved in exporting are likely to engage in only minimal international sales activity. An example of such an activity might be sending representatives to an international trade show to exhibit the firm's products.

Companies using a home-country intermediary, such as an export trading company or an export management company, rely on the sales force of the intermediary for international sales and limit sales activity to the domestic market. The situation is similar if host-country intermediaries such as foreign-country brokers or agents are used. However, when using all the other types of host-country intermediaries, such as manufacturers' representatives and distributors, the company directly engages in some level of personal selling. When using host-country distributors, the respective company hires sales representatives who call on the distributors.

Personal selling is an important component of international marketing communications, especially for business-to-business transactions. Salespeople are the Chanel saleswoman selling the French brand in a leased department in a U.S. department store, the representative of the Coke bottler selling Fanta to a Burundi bottled drinks retailer, the Air India ticketing agent at JFK airport in New York, and the Polish manufacturer selling upholstery to the Fiat plant in Italy. Personal selling involves a face-to-face interaction between the seller and the buyer and, in industrial sales, their respective teams. As such, the interaction between the two parties will be affected by their national cultures.

order taker
An individual who processes routine sales orders from the customer.

In the international selling context, the **order taker,** the individual who processes routine orders from the customer, is likely to be a local employee who is familiar with the local customs and culture. Individuals working at the German/American Reformhaus are highly skilled in selling health foods and cosmetics free of preservatives. In Taiwan, these individuals would also have to be familiar with the local culture, and, in effect, act as a bridge between the German/Austrian and Taiwanese culture (see Figure 15-1).

Figure 15-1: *An order taker in this health food and organic cosmetics company would have to be highly skilled and familiar with the specifics of the products sold.*

Order getters, individuals who actively generate potential leads and persuade customers to purchase the firm's products, can be local or international staff who are highly skilled technically, as well as trained in conducting negotiations. In international marketing, most order getters work in the business-to-business area as field salespeople, going to customers to solicit business. Order getters selling to other businesses would go to their clients' places of business. Order getters selling to consumers directly would go to consumers' homes. For example, direct marketers such as Avon and multilevel marketers such as Amway hire salespeople to sell products to their network of friends.

In developed countries, telemarketing is also popular in selling products. For telemarketing campaigns to be successful, companies need to have access to a reliable telephone system and for the culture to accept telemarketing. In the United States and Canada, telemarketing is much more acceptable than in North Africa, the Middle East, or even Europe, for that matter. In these latter regions, even charity solicitations and opinion polling are not met with acceptance and do not generate a very good response.

After a sale is closed, companies sign contracts that address the terms of the transaction, costs involved, and the term of the relationship. In many countries, a written contract does not mean much: Sellers and buyers can readily choose to ignore the agreement without any penalty. The legal systems may endorse contracts but not defend them. In many cultures, a contract may have little value, while someone's word is fully reliable. In many countries outside the United States, trust relationships are expected, and company executives are insulted at the suggestion the agreement should be noted in a written contract.

At the next level of the buyer-seller relationship is the **electronic data interchange (EDI)** relationship, whereby buying and selling firms are able to share important data on production, inventory, shipping, and purchasing. EDI relationships are possible primarily if the firms have the appropriate resources and trust their local partner with the information. Such relationships entail a very high level of trust because the seller has access to all the buying firm's production information and the seller ships the products automatically. EDI relationships are typically single-source relationships, as sellers need to be assured that the buyer is not purchasing products from a competitor—at least as long as the contract is in place. In EDI relationships, switching vendors is a high-cost proposition. In many countries switching vendors is, in fact, difficult; consequently, one of the restrictions EDI imposes (i.e., the obstacle involved in switching vendors because of the high cost of linking with a new vendor) is, in some regards, a moot point. In others, it still presents problems. U.S. firms, such as Wal-Mart, expect full information from their suppliers. And, in many environments, there is a premium placed on company proprietary information. For example, firms in East Asia and Europe are less inclined to offer full inventory disclosure than firms in the United States.

Multinational firms are also increasingly using **extensible markup language (XML)** to efficiently manage their supply-chain relationships. XML is a system that encodes data on production, inventory, shipping, and purchasing and processes the content without human intervention, sharing it with the company's supply chain partners. It should be noted that XML and EDI exist primarily in developed countries. And, when they enter developing countries, they are often forced to revert to paper reports, which bring with them different inefficiencies —inaccuracies, inability to track shipments and to ensure timely delivery, lag time for inventory information, and so on. Frequently, large firms need to subcontract logistics operations with different companies to be able to ensure timely shipments. Logistics companies, such as Deutsche Post DHL, FedEx, and UPS, often rekey paper information from their clients' suppliers and factories and then offer their clients tracking information regarding manufacturing process, shipment, and delivery.

At the highest level of the buyer-seller dyad interaction is the **strategic partnership,** whereby buyers and sellers share information at the highest levels. The seller actively examines product improvements to better serve the needs of the buying firm.

order getter
Individual who actively generates potential leads and persuades customers to purchase the firm's products.

electronic data interchange (EDI)
Relationship whereby buying and selling firms are able to share important data on production, inventory, shipping, and purchasing.

extensible markup language (XML)
System that encodes data on production, inventory, shipping, and purchasing and processes the content without human intervention, sharing it with the company's supply chain partners.

strategic partnership
A partnership that represents the highest level of the buyer-seller dyad interaction, whereby buyers and sellers share information, and the seller actively examines product improvements to better serve the needs of the buying firm.

Depending on the tasks involved and the type of buyer-seller relationships the company establishes in the process of conducting its business in different international markets, the company needs to determine the types of salespeople it should hire for optimal performance. The foreign sales force of the multinational corporation could include *expatriates* (home-country nationals and third-country nationals) and *host-country nationals*.

15-1a Expatriates

expatriate
An employee working in a **foreign country.**

home-country national
A local employee who works in his or her home country for the international corporation.

Expatriates working in a particular foreign country belong to two categories: One category is the *home-country national,* an employee who was successful as a sales representative in the home country and has been assigned overseas. An example would be a Philip Morris International employee from the company's headquarters in New York City, engaging in sales in the company's Hong Kong operations. Representing the second category is the *third-country national,* a truly international salesperson, an expatriate who works in numerous countries. An example would be a Latin American salesperson who previously worked in sales in Italy and Spain calling on Colgate-Palmolive's trade accounts in Bulgaria.

Home-Country Nationals

Home-country nationals—known also as *parent-company nationals*—are preferred by companies whose products are at the forefront of technology, and when the selling function relies on extensive training and highly specialized information. In general, in situations in which a greater interdependence exists between an overseas unit and corporate headquarters, firms are more likely to dispatch home-country nationals. This is also true for situations in which complex operations are involved, there is a greater political risk, and there is a greater level of competition.[1]

A disadvantage of hiring home-country nationals for international operations is the high cost involved. In addition to the regular salary and commission the employee would have received in the home country, numerous incentives are considered standard for international assignment. A cost-of-living allowance, a housing allowance that often permits hiring household help, and a substantial education allowance for children, which pays for education at expensive international private schools, are standard. Other standard perks are an annual or biannual home-leave for the entire family or an annual visit from immediate family members living in the home country. In addition, the firm also is expected to pay for the costs of selling the employee's home in the home country, for storing furniture, and for moving household goods overseas, making it expensive for the firm to send the employee overseas.

Even sending an employee overseas for five months can be costly to the company. In one example, a Motorola employee working for a Siemens-Motorola joint venture in Dresden, Germany, was housed in a hotel for his entire stay, rented an automobile, and had a living allowance that even included a prepaid phone to keep in touch with family in the United States. In addition, the company paid for two business-class, round-trip tickets back to the United States, team-building exercises, and trips to London and Los Angeles. These costs were covered in addition to salary, bringing the overall company costs to more than $100,000 for the five months. Assignments in expensive world capitals, such as London, Paris (see Figure 15-2), or Tokyo will result in even higher costs.

Figure 15-2: *Sending a home-country national to a Paris assignment is going to be particularly costly – renting a two-room (one bedroom) apartment in the center will easily cost over 2,000 euros per month unfurnished and without utilities.*

Among other disadvantages of hiring home-country nationals are:

- The numerous cultural barriers faced by the home-country nationals in the country of assignment (see Figure 15-3);

- The expenses involved in training the home-country nationals in the culture (and, often, language) of the country of assignment;

- The lack of local personal connections to the important decision makers in the government and the local trade;

- The difficulty of finding quality employees willing to take on international assignments because they are reluctant to uproot their families or because they fear that they will lose visibility and status at the head office (international companies offer many incentives to overcome this impediment).

Figure 15-3: *Home country nationals from a U.S. firm might have difficulty adapting to Asian culture without understanding the local traditions and language.*

Using home-country nationals can also send the signal to the local target market that the company trusts only its own people to run the business. This backfired in the case of Wal-Mart Stores, which brought their own managers to manage its German operations, for example. Unlike Wal-Mart Stores, Tesco believes in being fully integrated in the local environment and hires mostly locals in the higher-profile, management jobs.

Third-Country Nationals

Third-country nationals are employees working temporarily in an assignment country, who are not nationals of that country or of the country in which the corporate headquarters of the company they work for are located.

Third-country nationals are "professional expatriates." They are accustomed to constantly adapting to new environments. They speak numerous languages, are familiar with customs and business practices in different environments, and have learned, through their vast international experience, to adapt optimally for international assignments. In certain countries, third-country nationals are more likely than home-country nationals and locals to be on international corporations' payrolls. Examples of such countries are the United Arab Emirates and Saudi Arabia, where international companies hire highly skilled employees from India, Pakistan, Egypt, and the Philippines, among others. One study found that expatriates working in Saudi Arabia typically save for future consumption and gear most of their purchases toward home-country consumption.[2] Third-country nationals are also less likely to return early from the foreign assignment due to difficulties in adapting to the local environment.

> **third-country national**
> An employee working in the country of assignment who is not a national of that country nor of the country in which the corporate headquarters of the company he or she works for are located.

Often, third-country nationals are competent company employees transferred from a subsidiary of the company operating in another country. Usually, third-country nationals cost less than home-country nationals (but more than locals) because they are not as likely to forgo the high salaries of the company's home country and expatriate allowances typical for home-country employees. There is at least one exception to this rule: hiring Emirati employees in the United Arab Emirates requires paying a premium. Most of the professional cadre in the UAE consists of third-country nationals, as local Emiratis constitute only 20 percent of the population.

In the Middle East, many countries have a large proportion of third-country nationals in their labor force. Take, for example, the following case of Oman.

Third-Country Nationals in Oman

In Oman, non-Omanis constitute almost 25 percent of the total population, and this is low compared with some other Gulf countries. Omanis make up more than 80 percent of the public-sector labor force, but constitute less than 20 percent of the private-sector workforce, with expatriates primarily from Asia filling most unskilled, low-paid jobs, as well as a large proportion of middle-management positions. In the past few years, the government pushed for the "Omanization" of the private sector, pressing for Omanis to replace expatriates.

Reducing the unemployment of Omanis is high on Oman's government's agenda. The country has a young population—with almost 55 percent younger than the age of 20, and 83 percent younger than 35—and many of Oman's young have moved to the cities in search of better job prospects. Today, 70 percent of the population is urban. Most Omanis are Muslim, but, as a result of its trading history, the country is a mixture of races, with a prominent trading family of Indian Hindu descent.[3] The country has a tradition of welcoming foreigners, and the perspective of "Omanization" is surprising to many expatriates.

In the case of both home-country nationals and third-country nationals, it should be noted that many governments, primarily in developing countries, dictate the number (usually a percentage) of foreign nationals that a foreign firm operating in the respective country is permitted to hire. In the case of third-country nationals, it is not uncommon for local governments to delay visas or otherwise complicate the hiring process. In all these situations, firms are forced to rely heavily on host-country nationals (locals) and may tap into international sales talent and expertise only to a limited extent.

15-1b Host-Country Nationals (Locals)

The local salesperson who works in his/her home country for an international corporation is a **host-country national.** An example would be the Hungarian brand manager schooled in a university in the United States, working for Procter & Gamble in Hungary. This individual understands the U.S. business environment, has been well trained technically at an accredited U.S. institution, and is willing to return to his/her home country to work for a U.S. multinational firm.

Increasingly, international firms appear to prefer local employees to expatriates. Cost is only one consideration. Frequently, locals with similar levels of education and training are available for employment at a fraction of the cost of expatriates. Host-country nationals also speak the local language and often have a well-developed network within the local industry and government. And, as mentioned in Section 15-1a, "Expatriates," some host governments restrict the number of foreign nationals working in the country. Thus, host-country nationals also fit with the country's employment policies.

host-country national
A local employee who works in his or her home country for the international corporation.

Many international firms compete for the types of individuals described here. Although the multinational company deems it appropriate to remunerate host-country nationals below the level of expatriates, not offering them the appropriate motivation to remain with the company increases their risk of flight to a competitor.

15-1c Another Alternative: Long-Distance International Selling

Multinationals are increasingly taking a more strategic view of international staffing, exploring a variety of supply-side issues, cost issues, demand-side issues, and career issues, and identifying a portfolio of alternatives to the traditional international assignment. Such alternatives are short-term assignments, commuter assignments, international business travel, and virtual assignments.[4]

Selling via the Internet or mail is an important venue for approaching new customers overseas. Costs of distance selling are lower—companies do not have to dispatch salespeople abroad and spend on cross-cultural training—allowing for greater market coverage. However, distance selling is difficult to coordinate internationally, often largely due to cultural differences.

15-2 Managing International Employees

15-2a Managing Relationships

Managing internationals—expatriates and host-country nationals—is no easy task for multinational corporations. Companies that attempt to transplant personnel policies that have proven successful in the home country run into obstacles in different international environments. Establishing quotas, assigning management responsibilities to employees within the firm, or even simply addressing employees by first names could prove to be challenges for the firm.

Issues related to culture, such as national character, could come into play. Rolling up one's sleeves and working on the assembly line results in an instant loss of status for the manager in Southeast Asia, Eastern Europe (see Figure 15-4), and South America.

Figure 15-4: *In Romania, even offering to brave the roads to go to the enterprise on foot, rather than being picked up by the company car, may lead to a loss of status.*

Problems related to social class or caste bring additional challenges. Placing a pariah (untouchable) in charge of a Brahman in India may be problematic, as would be placing someone of peasant origins in charge of someone from the intellectual class in Eastern Europe (even if training and education justify such an assignment).

15-2b Understanding the International Buyer-Seller Relationship

In a personal selling environment, challenges also arise in the **international buyer-seller relationship.** Certain approaches to selling work better than others. For example, a hard sell is not likely to be successful in most Asian countries, where modesty, a humble attitude, and respect are seen as valuable traits. Looking one's counterpart directly in the eye—a sign of honesty in the United States—is likely to be perceived as an aggressive stance in Asia. In one's first encounter with a Chinese counterpart, it is advised that business cards be exchanged. When one

> **international buyer-seller relationship**
> The distribution between the buyer and the individual involved in personal selling.

takes the Chinese manager's business card, one should do so with both hands and read it, as a sign of respect. The U.S. manager is advised to have business cards written in English and Chinese when dealing with the Chinese. It should be noted, however, that, increasingly, such pleasantries are cut short in the many dynamic business environments in Asia. In a busy work-life environment, sometimes the Chinese will surprise their U.S. counterparts and address bottom-line issues directly, but still gently.

In general, however, it is best to understand the difference between the Western and the Chinese approach to negotiations. While Western business cultures treat communication as an exchange of information—and the communication ends when the deal is over—the Chinese view the negotiation as an inseparable part of building and maintaining business relationships.[5] From the Chinese perspective, building relationships takes time and analysis. From the American perspective, time is money and they need to inform the headquarters that they have a done deal. Not taking into account these differences in approaches to negotiations will invariably lead to a breakdown in the dialogue, with American negotiators viewing the Chinese as inefficient, indirect, and even dishonest, while the Chinese view American negotiators as aggressive, impersonal, and excitable.[6]

In other negotiations examples, Italians typically enjoy engaging in the negotiation process and want to feel that they are special customers. They want to feel like they are getting a deal; offering them a bottom-line price at first is a strategy that will most likely meet with failure.[7] The strategy of focusing on closing the deal and aiming toward the next sale is unlikely to work in Latin America, where individuals prefer to take time to build a relationship with suppliers.[8] In this environment, it is best to first socialize, to build a relationship of friendship and trust, preferably involving the family. In the Middle East, this approach also works well, although it most often does not involve the family.

15-2c Understanding Cultural Values and the Relationship between Buyer and Seller

National Character, Organizational Culture, and Personality

The level of psychological overlap in communication between buyer and seller varies across three dimensions: **national character, organizational culture,** and **individual personality.**[9] A personal selling situation involves *content* and *style*. Content includes substantive aspects of the interaction, such as suggesting, offering, or negotiating product-specific utilities and expectations, whereas style refers to rituals, format, mannerisms, and ground rules of the buyer and seller during the course of their interaction.[10] An interaction between buyer and seller is satisfactory if the two parties are compatible on these two dimensions.[11] In cross-cultural sales interactions, style is shaped by national character, organizational culture, and the personality of the individuals involved in the interaction.[12]

national character
A set of behavior and personality characteristics shared by individuals of a certain country or region.

organizational culture
The shared norms and values that guide collective behavior in organizations and enduring traits that characterize individuals, motivating them to act or react to stimuli in the organization and in the environment in a particular manner.

individual personality
Enduring traits that characterize individuals, motivating them to act or react to external stimuli in a particular manner.

Chapter 5, "Cultural Influences on International Marketing," described national character in terms of personality traits shared at the national level. The dimensions identified as constituting national character are individualism, power distance, uncertainty avoidance, and masculinity/femininity.[13] To illustrate, in cross-cultural interactions, individuals from cultures low in power distance negotiating with counterparts from a high power distance environment have to adopt a more formal negotiation style, addressing these individuals by their last name and title, and following their hierarchy protocols.

Compatible organizational styles also contribute to creating a satisfactory interaction between buyer and seller. Organizational culture refers to shared norms and values that guide collective behavior in organizations. Here, too, a match in organizational styles will lead to a more successful relationship between buyers and sellers.

Personality refers to enduring traits that characterize individuals, motivating them to act or react to external stimuli in a particular manner. Congruency within the three dimensions between the buyer and seller is likely to result in the most successful transaction, whereas discrepancy is likely to result in a small chance for success. To have a better chance for success in international markets, a company could select a target market with a national character similar to that of its own home country, target companies with similar organizational culture, and hire international sales-people with the appropriate personality traits, as described in Section 15-3a, "Recruiting Expatriates."[14]

Low- and High-Context Cultures

As mentioned in Chapter 5, "Cultural Influences on International Marketing," individuals from cultures with a low context of communication use formal, direct communication that is verbally expressed, whereas individuals from cultures with a high context of communication use less verbal information to convey the message, relying instead on cues such as gestures and facial expressions. In the latter case, status of the speaker, individual background, values, associations, and so on are important in completing the message conveyed, thus linking the message to the context in which it was delivered.[15] Negotiators from high-context cultures, such as those of Latin America and Asia, are less programmatic and less rigid, especially in time management, contract signing, and closing deals, whereas negotiators from low-context cultures follow Western logic, with the negotiation terminating when an agreement is formally reached and in writing.[16] Furthermore, individuals from high-context cultures are less confrontational and place greater emphasis on interpersonal interaction than individuals from low-context cultures.[17]

15-3 Successfully Managing Expatriates

International management experts estimate that the cost of a failed expatriate assignment is in the millions of dollars and that more than 80 percent of companies experience expatriate failure, attributed primarily to candidate selection and the inability to adapt to host cultures.[18] The direct costs associated with each expatriate turnover are estimated to be in the hundreds of thousands of dollars. And indirect costs—such as reduced productivity and efficiency, lost sales, reduced market share, diminished competitive position, unstable corporate image, and tarnished corporate reputation—are even greater.[19]

Firms could attempt to minimize their early return rate by engaging in the appropriate training and development strategies for expatriates. Such strategies should involve the use of effective selection and screening criteria for recruiting expatriates, training them and preparing them for the international assignment, motivating them for peak performance, and ensuring their successful **repatriation**.

> **repatriation**
> The return of the expatriate employee to the home country.

15-3a Recruiting Expatriates

In the process of recruiting expatriates, companies should select those individuals who have traits such as[20]

- An openness and sensitivity to others, cultural sensitivity and awareness, awareness to relate across cultures, awareness of their own cultural values
- The ability to change their usual behavior in cross-national settings
- A high level of resiliency, as ascertained from the individuals' performance histories
- Extensive international knowledge or willingness to gain it
- A desire to go overseas and willingness to work in areas where there is political instability and a strong anti-American sentiment

Typically, potential recruits for international assignments—from within or outside the company—are given batteries of personality tests and are subjected to interviews to determine their motivation for an international assignment. Those prospects who are primarily interested in completing the assignments to earn promotions are not likely to be as successful as those who are eager to experience different environments.

culture shock
A pervasive feeling of anxiety resulting from one's presence in a new, unfamiliar culture.

15-3b Attenuating Culture Shock

Culture shock, which frequently accounts for early repatriation, is defined as *a pervasive feeling of anxiety resulting from one's presence in a new, unfamiliar culture* (see Figure 15-5). Culture shock could result in feelings of inadequacy, reluctance to experience the environment, and fear of failure. Cross-cultural communication experts advise companies that culture shock can be diminished when employees know what to expect in their new environment. Companies need to provide some familiarity with the physical and social environment (local customs, in particular) to the prospective expatriates to attenuate culture shock.

Figure 15-5: *Transplanting an expatriate's family from a quiet, suburban Midwestern town into the heart of Asia is likely to produce culture shock. The close, traditional, elaborately crafted homes here look nothing like the suburban lawns of the expatriate family's previous life.*

The family, in particular, must be prepared for the international assignment. Whereas the expatriate employee interacts within the company and has a company culture around him/her, the spouse and children often find themselves isolated, lacking support. They face different customs, lifestyles, and food (see Figure 15-6)

Figure 15-6: *Pretty restaurants in a bucolic traditional Chinese setting. Tour guides in China often impress foreigners with stories of restaurants serving live monkey brains. Would they go well with fries?*

Experts in culture shock suggest that expatriates who dealt with their culture shock effectively used what is called "stability zones" to which they would retreat when conditions in the host country became overly stressful to them, rather than becoming isolated, lonely, and falling into depression. These individuals could then deal successfully and productively with their stress.[21] Meditation, hobbies, or a place of worship all qualify as stability zones (see Figure 15-7).

Figure 15-7: *Stability zones are places to which individuals can retreat when conditions in the host country became overly stressful to them. It is always helpful when one has a stability zone that is everywhere in one's new city, and even wraps around local buses—as, in this case, Dunkin' Donuts.*

International Marketing Illustration 15-1 addresses issues related to the accompanying spouse and expatriate compensation.

International Marketing Illustration 15-1
The Financial and Legal Cost of the Expatriate Spouse

Expatriate employees often ask their employer to find their spouse a job in the country of assignment. The employer may agree to find the spouse a job either with the same subsidiary or with an affiliate company located within a reasonable geographic proximity.

From a legal perspective, finding employment for a spouse may be problematic for the employer. The marriage may end in divorce, and the company will be in a bind by continuing to accommodate the spouse. Or the spouse can claim that he/she is owed additional salary and compensation because, in fact, he/she is also an expatriate employee. Companies are covered if a written agreement makes clear that the request is, in fact, an accommodation for the accompanying spouse and that the spouse is not entitled to special benefits.

The company will also find that the costs of bringing the expatriate with an accompanying spouse are much higher than bringing the expatriate alone. Note that this amount does not include other costs, such as the cost of education in private school for the children or hardship allowances. And the cost of living varies greatly, worldwide. Transferring an employee from New York City to Moscow will increase the costs to the family by more than a third, based on the cost-of-living comparisons in Table 15-1.

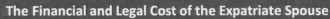

Table 15-1: *Cost-of-Living: Worldwide Rankings for Selected Cities in 2012*

Rank	City	Country		Rank	City	Country
1	TOKYO	JAPAN		25	LONDON	UNITED KINGDOM
2	LUANDA	ANGOLA		31	TEL AVIV	ISRAEL
3	OSAKA	JAPAN		31	GUANGZHOU	CHINA
4	MOSCOW	RUSSIA		*33*	*NEW YORK CITY, NY*	*UNITED STATES*
5	GENEVA	SWITZERLAND		34	NIAMEY	NIGER
11	SYDNEY	AUSTRALIA		37	PARIS	FRANCE
12	SÃO PAULO	BRAZIL		38	MILAN	ITALY
16	SHANGHAI	CHINA		39	LAGOS	NIGERIA
20	LIBREVILLE	GABON		44	DJIBOUTI	DJIBOUTI
21	COPENHAGEN	DENMARK		50	DAKAR	SENEGAL

(Base City: New York City, USA)

Source: Cost of Living Survey - Worldwide Ranking 2012, Mercer Human Resource Consulting, www.mercerhr.com.

15-3c Training for International Assignments

Companies use different strategies in training their employees for international assignments. The strategies range from short courses in cross-cultural communications to extensive cultural immersions. For example, Procter & Gamble, Motorola, Microsoft, and Hewlett-Packard require extensive cross-cultural training courses for their international salespeople, whereas other companies require employees to read books and other materials on the cultures before departure for the sales mission.[22] When the Abril Group, a diversified media company, sends its salespeople to Brazil, a country where it does much of its business, it requires them to participate in a 10-day Portuguese immersion program, studying the country's language, culture, and customs.[23]

In training expatriates for international assignments, a company must assess the fit between the individual salesperson and the client the person will call on. See International Marketing Illustration 15-2 for a number of important cultural elements that must influence the recruitment and selection of sales force personnel.

International Marketing Illustration 15-2
Hiring the Right Person for a Company's International Sales Force

A number of cultural elements are important to consider in the process of recruiting and selecting international sales force personnel. Among them are the ethnic composition of the sales force and the religious orientation and social class of the employees, as well as their gender:

- Ethnic composition—Managers should be aware of the ethnic composition in the country and match the salespeople with the customers appropriately; this is especially important in countries where there is cultural and ethnic diversity, such as India and Indonesia, and where the ethnic groups do not get along well.

- Religious orientation—Managers should match individuals with similar religious backgrounds to have the greatest impact.

- Social class—Countries with long social histories base social class on different criteria, such as seniority (Japan and other Asian countries), caste (India), or other criteria of which the marketer should be aware.

- Education—In many countries—Japan and most countries in Europe, for example—educational systems are more elitist and an appropriate match based on education is essential for optimal appeal to the target market.

- Gender status—Many countries keep women in the background and do not involve them in business. Consequently, it would be a mistake to have women in a sales force that sells products to male decision makers in countries such as Japan and most of the countries of North Africa and the Middle East.

After determining the cultural match, select only those expatriates evaluated as having the highest probability of cultural adaptation and prepare them with in-depth cross-cultural communication training. In addition, enhance their transition with additional support and host-country assistants and help integrate the expatriates into the host country.

Sources: Jean McFarland, "Culture Shock," Benefits Canada, Vol. 30, No. 1, January 2006, p. 31; Robert H. Sims and Mike Schraeder, "An Examination of Salient Factors Affecting Expatriate Culture Shock," Journal of Business and Management, Vol. 10, No. 1, Spring 2004, pp. 73–87; Jeffrey E. Lewin and Wesley J. Johnson, "International Salesforce Management: A Relationship Perspective," Journal of Business and Industrial Marketing, Vol. 12, No. 3/4, 1997, p. 236.

15-3d Motivating Expatriates

The success of an international assignment is predicated on a high degree of motivation. The intrinsic (internal) aspects of motivation for an international assignment are addressed in the recruiting process, which ensures that only those candidates who have the appropriate traits (see Section 15-3a, "Recruiting Expatriates") are deployed. The company controls the extrinsic aspects of motivation, such as compensation, leave and family policies, career incentives, and so on.

In terms of compensation, certain companies attempt to use uniform policies worldwide. More frequently, though, other companies offer numerous compensation incentives above those used for assignments in the home country, thus making the international assignment attractive. Some of the incentives are described next.

Cost-of-Living Adjustment/Post Adjustment

For many companies, the **cost-of-living adjustment** is above and beyond that justified by the local conditions. This type of compensation, also referred to as **post adjustment,** includes payment for household help, such as maids, cooks, gardeners, night watchmen, and so forth.

Housing Allowance

Often, companies cover part or the entire cost of housing for the expatriate employees while abroad (see Figure 15-8). The **housing allowance** will most likely also cover the cost of staying at a quality hotel until housing becomes available.

Figure 15-8: *This house is very similar to the typical expat houses in Bucharest. They tend to be large, have servants' quarters, and they might or might not look particularly well maintained.*

Education Allowance

The **education allowance** covers the cost of children's education at an international private school. U.S. companies pay the education allowance for their employees primarily so that they will be on par with employees working for European multinationals. Many European firms pay for high-quality education for their employees' children, regardless of whether they are in their home country or overseas, and for as long as they are attending school.

Home-Leave Allowance

The **home-leave allowance** pays for the family abroad to vacation in the home country. The company also may pay for the children remaining in the home country to attend school and to visit the family member or members posted abroad.

cost-of-living adjustment
A compensation incentive whereby the company adjusts expatriate salaries to reflect the cost of living in the new environment at standards in the expatriate's home country; also called post-adjustment.

post adjustment
A compensation incentive whereby the company adjusts expatriate salaries to reflect the cost of living in the new environment at standards in the expatriate's home country; also called cost-of-living adjustment.

housing allowance
A compensation incentive whereby the company covers part of or the entire cost of housing for the expatriate employee while abroad.

education allowance
A compensation incentive whereby the company agrees to cover the cost of children's education at an international private school in the country of assignment or at a boarding school in the expatriate's home country.

home-leave allowance
A compensation incentive that pays for the expatriate and his or her family to vacation in the home country.

moving allowance
A compensation incentive whereby the company pays for the household moving expenses to the country of assignment and, at the end of the assignment, back to the home country.

repatriation allowance
A compensation incentive whereby the company covers expenses involved in moving back to the home country, as well as a large sum paid for successfully completing the international assignment in some cases.

Moving Allowance

Household moving expenses to the country of assignment are usually covered. The **moving allowance** also may cover storage in the home country. Some companies also arrange for the sale of the expatriate's home, often incurring losses if the housing market is in a slump.

Repatriation Allowance

The **repatriation allowance** covers expenses for moving back to the home country. In addition, the repatriation allowance may consist of a considerable sum paid to the expatriate simply for returning from the international assignment.

Other Types of Allowances

Expatriates also can benefit from other types of allowances. Such allowances may, for example, cover family membership in a social or health club designed primarily for expatriates and for well-to-do locals.

Noncompensation incentives are important. Multinational corporations frequently offer as incentive to the expatriate a guaranteed promotion in the company ranks on his or her successful return from the country of assignment. Companies also must address career-related concerns of the accompanying spouse. In an effort to recruit the best candidates for international posting, companies often offer spouses positions in the companies congruent with their talents and objectives to ensure the continuity of their careers.

15-3e Obstacles to the International Sales Mission

Once in the country of assignment, expatriates must learn the culture quickly and not gravitate toward home-country expatriates.[24] When they are living in the expatriate community, however, such situations may be unavoidable. First, if the expatriates are assigned to a country where restrictions are imposed on interactions with foreigners, such as Saudi Arabia, China, and Cuba, the expatriate community is likely to be the only forum for social interaction.

Expatriates may be drawn toward their home-country expatriate community in other countries as well. For example, for U.S. expatriates, many home-country offices and representatives play an important part. Among them are the United States embassy, the various other offices present in a particular country in conjunction with the embassy (the Unites States Information Agency, the United States Agency for International Development, the Fulbright Office), as well as others associated with the embassy—the cultural, the military, and the commercial attaché. One responsibility of U.S. officers within these respective positions and structures is to organize activities that involve the participation of U.S. expatriates. Expatriates are invited to various functions, activities, and celebrations to participate and to represent the United States. Often, there are even American schools for expatriates' children and American clubs. The Marine House, which houses the marines stationed at the embassy, periodically shows American movies, accompanied by receptions. Most often, a recreation center is open to American expatriates so that they can play pool, watch American football games, and reminisce about life in America.

At the very least, one can find a website that unites expatriates in a particular region. Expat Forums is such an example, helping individuals cope with their foreign assignments and compare benefits, other company practices, and costs. Although the forum is open to any participants, most are U.S. expatriates. Other sites aimed at expatriates help them to "live abroad as they would in their home country," as expatries-france.com, a Web site aimed at French expatriates, claimed with its original slogan.

All these factors have the potential to impede expatriates' immersion in the local culture. An extreme outcome would be the expatriate who is isolated and lives primarily for his or her return to the home country. The only motivation for this individual's international presence is strictly monetary or is linked to the international assignment as a precondition for promotion. Individuals in this predicament are more likely to fail than those who actively participate in the life and culture of the host country.

Yet another extreme is the expatriate who has "gone native." In extreme cases, this individual may refuse to return to the home country, insisting on remaining abroad in the company's service, and in some situations even serving locals to the detriment of the company.

15-3f Repatriation Issues

On repatriation, expatriates often find themselves working in a company that has changed drastically during their absence. They find that their corner offices are occupied by their former underlings or by professionals new to the company and that they do not quite fit into their new work environment. They also suffer a loss of status in their home environment. Whereas, during their international assignment, expatriates and their families were involved in a close, elite social environment that was reserved for the local international community, on return, they often find themselves to be no more than average dwellers in nondescript suburbia. At this point, they may experience reverse culture shock, a feeling of anxiety associated with a longing for the international environment left behind or fear of not adapting in the new environment and losing one's job due to lack of fit.

Companies often try to soften the **reverse culture shock** experienced by expatriates—especially professional expatriates, who are often reluctant to return to their home country. An expat from a low-income country, spoiled by Western abundance and supermarkets and stores loaded with merchandise during his assignment abroad, will be shocked to go back home, where the infrastructure is in bad shape, and where Western-style merchandise of any kind is scarce and comes at a premium price. See Figure 15-9.

> **reverse culture shock**
> Anxiety experienced after returning to the home country, associated with a longing for the international environment left behind and with the difficulty of readjusting to the home country and to corporate life at one's firm.

Figure 15-9: *A low-income country expat used to a consumerist lifestyle in the West, being able to purchase products at low prices just about anywhere, may have difficulty repatriating to his homeland, where Western products and conveniences are scarce and come at a premium.*

Strategies used by companies to better prepare the expatriates for repatriation involve offering a substantial incentive package, such as a raise on return; guaranteeing a promotion; and providing a repatriation grant.

One of the most important actions of the company may be to keep the expatriates "in the loop" for the duration of their assignments.[25] This can be accomplished by flying them back to headquarters on a regular basis, preferably for extended stays, and keeping them on a regular mailing list for intra-office and intra-company communication. Expat Forums recommends ongoing communication to avoid the renegade syndrome and the "out-of-sight, out-of-mind" mind-set, and arranging for a mentor in upper management.

Summary

Examine companies' expatriate management strategies. Managing international employees requires using appropriate personnel management policies—a process complicated by obstacles presented by the international environment. Decisions such as assigning management responsibilities to employees, establishing quotas, or even simply addressing employees by their first names could prove to be a challenge. To further complicate matters, local culture and national character affects relationships between management at each tier of the organization, as does social class or caste.

Describe the different types of employees suited for a company's international operations. A company hires three types of employees for its international operations. Expatriates are home-country nationals groomed from within the firm's national operations. These employees are familiar with firm policy, operations, goals, and objectives and are likely to best represent company interests. Third-country nationals are professional expatriates who adapt easily regardless of the environment to which they were assigned. On the downside, they need to learn both about the local environment and the company's culture, procedures, and goals. Locals (host-country nationals) are familiar with the host-country operating environment and have relationships already established with the national government and other important agency representatives. They also are the employees most likely to sell out the company by creating a local competitor.

Address issues related to expatriate management, such as motivating international employees and ensuring successful assignment performance and repatriation. To ensure top performance, companies need to appropriately train and motivate expatriates. Training in the local language, however superficial, may benefit the expatriates, as does cultural training; both minimize culture shock. Appropriate motivation also improves performance. Some typical perks for expatriates are a housing allowance, moving allowance, education allowance, post-adjustment pay, and home-leave pay. In addition, the employees should be prepared for re-entry in the firm and home country at the end of the assignment to minimize reverse culture shock.

Key Terms

cost-of-living adjustment

culture shock

education allowance

electronic data interchange (EDI)

expatriate

extensible markup language (XML)

home-country national

home-leave allowance

host-country national

housing allowance

individual personality

international buyer-seller relationship

moving allowance

national and regional character

order getter

order taker

organizational culture

post adjustment

repatriation

repatriation allowance

reverse culture shock

third-country national

Discussion Questions

1.   Describe the three types of employees a company is likely to send to a foreign post. What are their strengths and weaknesses?

2.   Discuss some of the management and culture-related challenges involved in international sales force management. How do companies address those challenges?

3.   How do international companies select and train employees for international assignments?

4.   What are some of the methods that international firms use to motivate employees for international assignments, and how do these companies ensure that employees face minimal culture shock on repatriation?

Chapter Quiz

True/False

1. A third-country national is also known as a local.

Answer: False

Rationale: A third-country national is an expatriate working in a country other than his/her home country or the home country of the company.

Section 15-1a, "Expatriates"

2. An advantage of hiring home-country nationals for international operations is that they are less expensive for the company.

Answer: False

Rationale: Home-country nationals are the most expensive expatriates the company can send on an international assignment. They are preferred by companies whose products are at the forefront of technology and when the selling function relies on extensive training and highly specialized information.

Section 15-1a, "Expatriates"

3. Expatriates working in a particular foreign country are either home-country nationals or host-country nationals.

Answer: False

Rationale: Expatriates working in a particular foreign country belong to two categories: one category is the home-country national, and the other is the third-country national.

Section 15-1a, "Expatriates"

4. Organizational culture refers to personality traits shared at the national level.

Answer: False

Rationale: Organizational culture refers to shared norms and values that guide collective behavior in organizations.

Section 15-2c, "Understanding Cultural Values and the Relationship between Buyer and Seller"

5. Reverse culture shock is a feeling of anxiety experienced after returning to the home country.

Answer: True

Rationale: Reverse culture shock is a general feeling of anxiety associated with a longing for the international environment left behind or fear of not adapting in the new environment and losing one's job due to lack of fit.

Section 15-3f," Repatriation Issues"

6. In low-context cultures, what is said is precisely what is meant.

Answer: True

Rationale: In low-context cultures, what is said is precisely what is meant. In high-context cultures, the context of the message, including the characteristics and role of the sender, is equally meaningful.

Section 15-2c, "Understanding Cultural Values and the Relationship between Buyer and Seller"

Multiple Choice

1. In Asian countries, what approach to selling would work best?

   a.   Confident, persuasive

   b.   Modest, exhibiting a humble attitude

   c.   Serious, formal hard sell

   d.   None of the above

Answer: b is correct.

Rationale: A hard sell is not likely to be successful in most Asian countries, where modesty, a humble attitude, and respect are seen as valuable traits.

Section 15-2b, "Understanding the International Buyer-Seller Relationship"

2. What are some preferred traits of expatriates?

   a.   Sensitivity to others

   b.   Willingness to gain international knowledge

   c.   High level of resiliency

   d.   All of the above

Answer: d is correct.

Rationale: In the process of recruiting expatriates, companies should select individuals who have cultural sensitivity and awareness, the ability to change their behavior in cross-national settings, a high level of resiliency, extensive international knowledge or willingness to gain it, and a desire to go overseas.

Section 15-3a, "Recruiting Expatriates"

3. How do companies motivate expatriates?

   a.   Guaranteed promotion

b.   Travel and other allowances

c.   Finding spouses employment in the country of assignment

d.   All of the above

Answer: d is correct.

Rationale: The intrinsic aspects of motivation for an international assignment are addressed in the recruiting process, which ensures that only those candidates who have the appropriate traits are sent overseas. The company controls the extrinsic aspects of motivation, such as compensation, leave and family policies, and career incentives.

Section 15-3d, "Motivating Expatriates"

4.   To relieve reverse culture shock, companies can

a.   keep an employee updated with office e-mails.

b.   offer promotion on return to the home country.

c.   fly an expatriate back regularly for meetings.

d.   all of the above

Answer: d is correct.

Rationale: In addition to keeping in close contact with the expatriate throughout the assignment period, companies use certain strategies to prepare him/her for repatriation, such as updating the employee on changes in the organization, flying the expatriate back to the home country often, and offering a promotion on return.

Section 15-3f, "Repatriation Issues"

Chapter 15 Endnotes

1.   Nakiye Boyacigiller, "The Role of Expatriates in the Management of Interdependence, Complexity and Risk in Multinational Corporations," *Journal of International Business Studies,* Vol. 22, No. 3, Third Quarter 1991, pp. 357–381.

2.   Dana-Nicoleta Lascu, Lalita A. Manrai, and Sugandha Kamalapuri, "Purchase Behavior of Expatriate Consumers in Saudi Arabia: An Exploratory Study," in W. D. Herrington and R. Taylor (eds.), *Marketing Advances in Theory, Practice, and Education,* Mount Pleasant, MI: Society for Marketing Advances,1998, pp. 128–134.

3.   "Oman: Population," *EIU ViewsWire*, June 1, 2007.

4.   David G. Collings, Hugh Scullion, and Michael J. Morley, "Changing Patterns of Global Staffing in the Multinational Enterprise: Challenges to the Conventional Expatriate Assignment and Emerging Alternatives," *Journal of World Business*, Vol. 42, No. 2, June 2007, pp. 198–208.

5.   Clyde D. Stoltenberg, "Doing Business in China: Culture and Practice," *Thunderbird International Business Review*, Vol. 45, No. 2, March/April 2003, p. 245.

6.   John L. Graham and N. Mark Lam, "The Chinese Negotiation," *Harvard Business Review*, Vol. 81, No. 10, October 2003, p. 82.

7.   Cynthia Kemper, "Global Sales Success Depends on Cultural Insight," *World Trade,* Vol. 11, No. 5, May 1998, pp. S2–S4.

8.   Erika Rasmusson, "Can Your Reps Sell Overseas?" *Sales and Marketing Management,* Vol. 150, No. 2, February 1998, p. 110.

9.   Sudhir H. Kale and John Barnes, "Understanding the Domain of Cross-National Buyer-Seller Interactions," *Journal of International Business Studies,* Vol. 23, No. 1, First Quarter 1992, pp. 101–131.

10.   Jagdish N. Sheth, "Cross-Cultural Influences on the Buyer-Seller Interaction/Negotiation Process," *Asia Pacific Journal of Management,* Vol. 1, No. 1, 1983, pp. 46–55.

11.   Rosann L. Spiro and Barton A. Weitz, "Adaptive Selling: Conceptualization, Measurement, and Nomological Validity," *Journal of Marketing Research,* Vol. 16, No. 3, August 1990, pp. 355–369; Kale and Barnes, "Understanding the Domain," pp. 101–131.

12.   Kale and Barnes, "Understanding the Domain," pp. 101–131.

13.   Geert Hofstede, *Culture's Consequences: International Differences in Work-Related Values,* London: Sage Publications, 1980.

14.   Kale and Barnes, "Understanding the Domain," pp. 101–131.

15.   Alma Mintu-Wimsatt and Julie B. Gassenheimer, "The Moderating Effect of Cultural Context in Buyer-Seller Negotiation," *Journal of Personal Selling Sales Management,* Vol. 20, No. 1, Winter 1999, pp. 1–9.

16.   Ibid.

17.   See Edward Hall, *Beyond Culture,* Garden City: NY: Anchor Press/Double Day, 1976; and Mintu-Wimsatt and Gassenheimer, "The Moderating Effect," pp. 1–9.

18.   Jean McFarland, "Culture Shock," *Benefits Canada*, Vol. 30, No. 1, January 2006, p. 31.

19.   Earl Naumann, "A Conceptual Model of Expatriate Turnover," *Journal of International Business Studies,* Vol. 23, No. 3, Third Quarter 1992, pp. 499–531.

20.   See David M. Noer, *Multinational People Management,* Washington, D.C.: Bureau of National Affairs, 1975; Nancy J. Adler and John L. Graham, "Cross-Cultural Interaction: The International Comparison Fallacy?" *Journal of International Business Studies,* Vol. 20, No. 3, Third Quarter 1989, pp. 515–537; Stephen J. Simurda, "Finding an International Sales Manager," *Northeast International Business,* Vol. 1, No. 3, 1988, pp. 15–16; Rasmusson, "Can Your Reps," p. 110.

21.   Robert H. Sims and Mike Schraeder, "An Examination of Salient Factors Affecting Expatriate Culture Shock," *Journal of Business and Management*, Spring 2004, Vol. 10, No. 1, pp. 73–87.

22.   Kemper, "Global Sales Success," pp. S2–S4.

23.   Rasmusson, "Can Your Reps," p. 110.

24.   Ibid.

25.   Lambeth Hochwald, "Luring Execs Overseas," *Sales and Marketing Management,* Vol. 152, No. 2, February 2000, p. 101.

Case 15-1

Manufacturing in China: Information Technology Challenges

Each year, millions of GT, Mongoose, Pacific, Schwinn, and other bicycles traveled from Chinese factories to U.S. distribution centers owned by manufacturer Pacific Cycle LLC. Shipping the products was the easy part. The difficult part was moving the data and tracking the items as they moved from suppliers to manufacturing sites in China, and, from there, to Chinese ports. Today, Pacific has some help from Exel LLC, a third-party logistics company based in the United Kingdom, which gathers the data from the suppliers and factories, rekeys it into its own systems, and then uses EDI to transmit the data back to Pacific Cycle. Errors show up in 5 percent of the 4,000 documents Exel generates for Pacific Cycle, which can cause delays at U.S. customs if there are discrepancies between the shipments and the paperwork—and delays can translate into lost business.

For companies doing business in emerging markets, it often happens that the information technology infrastructure is considerably less sophisticated than the one they use—or the technology infrastructure might not even be there. But China is becoming the manufacturing giant serving the world, thanks to its competent, low-cost labor. Import and export volume is experiencing an explosion, at more than $1,000 billion yearly, and growing at more than 30 percent a year. However, the country has an immature information technology infrastructure, which, coupled with expensive inland transportation and the high price of land for building logistics hubs, increases the cost of doing business there. Compared with Europe, Japan, and the United States, the logistics cost per GDP is much higher —more than 50 percent higher.

One of the reasons for the high cost of logistics is that Chinese government mandates dictate everything from where companies can set up factories to the use of trucking and freight-forwarding companies, which are licensed by the government and permitted to transport goods in China. And companies cannot force these logistics providers, which have very low profit margins to begin with, to adopt expensive EDI connectivity. In fact, most do not even know what EDI is.

Multinationals would incur high costs setting up their own logistics operations—something China has allowed since 2004. For the moment, a model that works is that set up by large international logistics firms operating in China, such as DHL, FedEx, and UPS. They offer services similar to Exel's, rekeying paper-based data and using EDI to help companies track their orders and monitor warehousing and shipping information related to their Chinese operations.

Often, multinationals have to compensate for the lack of a seamless logistics infrastructure by pairing with more logistics firms. Celestica, a company manufacturing electronics equipment for Hewlett-Packard, IBM, and Nortel Networks, relies on Exel, Kuehne & Nagel, Menlo Worldwide, and Panalpina to help it stay connected to local suppliers and carriers via EDI or XML; these logistics firms run more than 10 vendor-managed inventory hubs for Celestica, all of them located right in its manufacturing facilities. This reduces their lead time for inventory, increases responsiveness, and reduces material liabilities.

GM has invested more than $1.6 billion in China in the past 10 years to build its own technology and physical infrastructure, and yet it continues to dispatch "milk runs," where supplier pickup and delivery instructions are given on paper to drivers of the local transportation companies GM employs, ensuring just-in-time delivery. The Chinese suppliers use GM's Internet portal to log on and check inventory status and to alert GM when orders have been picked up by local carriers.

Auto-parts supplier Delphi Inc., in China since 1993, has 11 factories in the country, and more than 200 Chinese and approximately 250 overseas suppliers support Delphi's operations in China. Some Chinese carriers are developing information technology capabilities that will improve documentation for customs and electronic invoicing, but the process is slow. The company installed software that helps partners efficiently navigate the congested roads and report on whereabouts—the software is also used by the company's suppliers in Europe, Mexico, and North America.

FedEx has built a supply-chain logistics service in Asia that ships a half-million pounds of goods daily from China to the United States and Europe. It has a logistics distribution center in Shanghai, among several others in Asia, that manages everything for customers from orders and inventory to the transport network, with EDI and XML technology systems. The FedEx EC-Inventory Visibility and FedEx EC-Warehouse Management, both Internet-based systems, update and validate orders placed against quantities in the distribution center, track and trace customer orders and shipments, maintain shipping and billing data, and detail purchase history. Their goal is to reduce costs for customers through sophisticated monitoring and reporting systems: They offer automatic notification of low-stock items and replace paperwork with online entries.

UPS had been the market leader in logistics in China until recently, when it was overtaken by the German Deutsche Post DHL, whose operations in China are worth $5.15 billion, and whose turnover in China is equal to the combined turnover of UPS, FedEx, and TNT. UPS has 33 large, wholly owned branch offices that serve more than 330 cities in China, and with plans for expansion and for building further connections between ground and air services, offering several flights a week connecting Shanghai and the United States, and other Asian flights from Shanghai to Japan and the Philippines, as well as to European cities. In 2009, the company opened its $20 million new hub at Shanghai Pudong International Airport. UPS flies Boeing MD-11s and 747s to China and plans to add more 747s—the hub is serviced by eight 747-400s. The new hub is designed to handle 17,000 items an hour by 2012, and it could employ more than 1,000 people by 2010. With these new capabilities, it will be able to offer more efficient information technology interfacing to its multinational clients manufacturing products in China.

Sources: China Times, "DHL, FedEx, UPS set to do battle in Chinese logistics market, July 19, 2012, www.wantchinatimes.com/news-subclass-cnt.aspx?MainCatID=0&cid=1502&id=20120719000049; Gareth Powell, "UPS Plans New Air Hub in China," *China Economic Review,* online edition, April 19, 2007; Robert Malone, "UPS Targets China," *Forbes.com,* October 2, 2006; Laurie Sullivan, "Road Work in China," *Information Week,* August 30, 2004, Vol. 1003, pp. 30–34.

Analysis Suggestions:

1. What efficiencies do Electronic Data Interchange systems provide in the relationship between buyers and sellers?

2. What are some of the logistics-related challenges and costs encountered by multinational firms manufacturing in China?

3. How does EDI lower the costs of manufacturing in China?

Case 15-2

The Expatriate Spouse: Managing Change

Geena Sorenson, a former Madison Avenue executive and spouse of a Kraft Foods expatriate from the company's New York headquarters assigned to Shanghai, found herself counting the hours until her first home leave scheduled in exactly nine months. She missed visiting her circle of friends and former classmates at New York University, spending her Saturday mornings visiting the Chelsea art galleries, buying her bagels hot at Tal Bagels, and experiencing the quiet trepidations of the city on a Sunday morning. Instead, she was counting the hours until her return, unable to fit into the local environment of an equally vivacious Shanghai. She felt much like the lonely characters of the movie *Lost in Translation,* unable to understand her environment, spending long hours in a high-rise apartment, and waiting on her busy husband, who was rarely home.

Reading the different journals and magazines for expatriates and looking at the readily available online literature, she found that the cost of sending a family to an international location is as high as $1 million. And yet companies are not as skillful in the selection and preparation procedure as one might think. A foreign assignment presents problems for the entire family—Geena could relate. The employee should be capable to cope, to learn how to lead, motivate, and work with staff from other cultures. The spouse, if female, may have to deal with living in a male-dominated culture. It is often likely that her world is limited to the local expatriate community. China, which is by far the most popular new destination for foreign assignments, is quite a problematic posting because expats face not only language and cultural barriers, but also challenges when it comes to housing, transportation, education, and medical care.

Geena also found that, in spite of China's status as an important destination for expatriates, the number of its expatriates is decreasing, primarily for two reasons. One, expatriates are increasingly hired on local terms, without the traditional expat package. Expatriates tend to have less pay and a shorter-term package and thus are less likely to accept the assignment. And, two, jobs are increasingly going to well-trained nationals.

In her search, Geena discovered a website, Expats in China, which offered an overview of the expatriate life in China, similar to the materials provided by her husband's company in the training materials for the assignment. Apparently, after South Koreans, U.S. citizens are the second largest group of nearly 600,000 foreigners living on the Chinese mainland. She also found useful referrals for various services she could potentially use in the future, a digest of the local and national news from various sources, but not much else. Other expatriate sites were also only marginally useful.

Using her entrepreneurial skills, Geena decided to create an agency that would address the needs of spouses like her, attempting to understand the local environment in spite of the culture shock, but also longing for her home country. The purpose of the agency would be to facilitate integration and dialogue about integration in a society that is culturally dissimilar.

Sources: Calum MacLeod, "U.S. expatriates pursue American dream in China," *USA Today*, July 12, 2011, www.usatoday.com/news/world/2011-07-12-Americans-China-dreams-transplants_n.htm; Rensia Melles, "Lost in Translation," *Canadian HR Reporter,* Vol. 17, No. 5, March 8, 2004, p. 14; "Hong Kong, A Classic Case of Expatriate Change," *International Money Marketing,* March 2004, p. 16; "Where Next for the Expat?" *International Money Marketing,* March 2004, p. 14; http://www.expatsinchina.com/.

Analysis Suggestions

1.   Is Geena experiencing culture shock? Explain. If the answer is yes, what can she do to lessen its impact?

 2.   What are the costs of bringing a spouse along for an assignment? Would the company be better off if the spouse remained in the home country? Explain.

 3.   How should Geena's agency help in addressing the needs of expatriate spouses? Offer ideas and activities that would benefit the large group of spouses accompanying expatriates in China.

Chapter 16: International Pricing Strategy

Learning Objectives

After studying this chapter,
you should be able to:

- Identify pricing-related internal challenges facing international firms.

- Identify pricing-related challenges imposed by competition on international firms.

- Identify pricing-related challenges imposed by the political and legal environment on international firms.

- Identify pricing-related challenges imposed by the economic and financial environment on international firms.

- Address international pricing decisions of international firms.

Pricing is especially important in international marketing strategy decisions because of its effect on product positioning, market segmentation, demand management, and market share dynamics.[1] The international pricing decision is complex. Variables internal to the firm, such as the location of production plants and factory utilization rates, as well as variables external to the firm, such as the economic climate, the price sensitivity of customers, and barriers to entry, must be evaluated before determining the final price of products and services. Pricing decisions are further affected by companies' experience in international markets, market share, exchange rates, tariffs, inflation, and government intervention in pricing.[2]

This chapter addresses challenges that international firms face internally when setting prices. It also addresses the impact of the international competitive, political and legal, and economic and financial environment on firm pricing decisions. Finally, it evaluates pricing policies of firms for different international markets.

16-1 Pricing Decisions and Procedures

Pricing decisions are determined by the location of production facilities and the companies' abilities to track costs.

16-1a Production Facilities

Production facilities are important *internal*—within the firm's control—decision-making factors in international pricing strategy. The location of production facilities determines the extent to which companies can control costs and price their products competitively. Multinationals usually can afford to shift production to take advantage of lower costs and exchange rates, whereas small to medium-sized firms are often limited to exporting as the only venue for product distribution.[3] Companies often price themselves out of the market in certain countries, especially if they do not shift production to a low-labor-cost, low-tax country. As an example, Marc Controls purchases raw materials in Korea, China, and India to lower the price of its products and ships them to the United States for manufacturing; its products are competitively priced when sold on the German market, but they are considered overpriced in most of Asia.[4]

Important aspects related to firms' production facilities are factory capacity utilization, internal cost structures, and the market contribution rate.[5]

Factory capacity utilization: Firms with factories operating at full capacity are able to spread fixed costs over more units, and thus have more flexibility in their pricing strategies. On the other hand, firms with factories operating at less-than-full capacity have high costs to contend with and do not have much price flexibility.

Internal cost structures: Some firms have more advantageous cost structures than others. For example, firms with production facilities in countries that have an abundance of cheap labor have an advantage over firms with production facilities in countries that have no excess labor. Also, firms that exploit technological advantages have cost advantages that ultimately have an impact on their pricing strategies.

Market contribution rate: This is the percentage of total firm profits from a particular product. This product will garner more attention than a less-lucrative product and thus affect pricing decisions.

16-1b Ability to Keep Track of Costs

Product components often are manufactured in different countries. Often, the final products are assembled in a particular country—which is usually not the company's home country—and then sold all over the world. It is consequently difficult for financial officers to keep track of product costs. However, with improvement in information technology and electronic data interchange (EDI) systems, which are increasingly coordinated throughout the supply chain, firms are better able to track product costs in emerging markets and even in lower-income countries.

16-2 Environment-Related Challenges and Pricing Decisions

Pricing decisions are affected by all the external elements in a company's international environment. An international company must react effectively to changes in the competitive environment, in the political and legal environment, and in the economic and financial environment. Figure 16-1 addresses examples of different challenges in the international firm's environment that affect the firm's pricing decisions.

Figure 16-1: Environmental factors affecting pricing decisions.

The Competitive Environment	• **Gray market/parallel imports** as a competitive threat • **Dumping** as a competitive threat
The Political and Legal Environment	• **Transfer pricing** • The price of protectionism
The Economic and Financial Environment	• Inflationary pressures on price • Fluctuating exchange rates • Shortage of hard currency and **countertrade**

16-2a The Competitive Environment

Competition

International and local competition often pose serious concerns to multinational firms. Competitors' offerings, as well as the price sensitivity of customers, influence the pricing decisions of the firm. Also, if there is a high cost for consumers to switch from one product to another, firms have to price their offering low enough to have the customers switch to their brand. On the other hand, if the firm is operating where barriers to entry—such as nontariff barriers, patents, or technological advantages—are high, they can retain relatively high prices without fear of competition.[6] Finally, if competition can keep product prices low by manufacturing in a low-labor-cost country, then the firm must meet this challenge and maintain a low price, potentially at a loss.

In retailing, and especially in service environments, companies often are challenged by local competitors offering legal copycat products at a much lower price. For example, Pizza Hut is challenged in every market in Poland by a local pizza chain that offers almost identical products, such as Neapolitan pizza, at a fraction of Pizza Hut's offering. Often, challenges at the retail level may be difficult to identify. Here's an example of such a challenge: firms operating in markets where retailers are likely to keep the price of their products under the even number of the banknote that would normally be used in purchasing those products so that the cashier can keep any change. For example, in Egypt and Romania, among others, retailers are unlikely to give back small change, or even any change at all, to customers. In such an environment, a company using an even-pricing strategy will be at a disadvantage because retailers will choose to sell competitors' products. This is the case even if the company's prices are below competitors' prices.

Grey Market/Parallel Imports as a Competitive Threat

A firm engaging in a differential pricing strategy could be vulnerable to competition from unauthorized channels. In fact, differential pricing (price discrimination) by the manufacturer has been identified as a main cause of parallel importing—diverting products purchased in a low-price market to other markets **(parallel imports)** by means of a distribution system not authorized by the manufacturer, otherwise known as a **grey market.**[7] (see Figure 16-2).

parallel imports
A distribution system not authorized by the manufacturer whereby the products purchased in a low-price market are diverted to other markets; also called gray market.

gray market
A distribution system not authorized by the manufacturer whereby the products purchased in a low-price market are diverted to other markets; also called parallel imports.

Figure 16-2: *This Mercedes A-170 crossover automobile could be brought to the United States, adapted according to the Department of Transportation requirements, and then resold at a small profit—a reasonable price would be $30,000. It would appeal to U.S. consumers who would like to pay much less than $60,000, the price of the smallest Mercedes station wagon or crossover available in the U.S. market. This automobile would be sold as a parallel import, through a channel that Mercedes did not authorize. Don't wear out any parts, though, because all the parts would have to be shipped from Stuttgart, Germany.*

A manufacturer may charge different prices in different markets for the same product:

- To meet the needs of target consumers who have a limited purchasing power.
- To keep the product price competitive in markets that are actively targeted by competition.
- Due to changes in the exchange rate in countries where the products are sold; the product is likely to be cheaper in the countries with the weakest currency.
- Due to the fact that it offers discounts to wholesalers buying higher quantities.
- Due to differences in wholesale prices in different markets; for example, wholesale prices for luxury goods are relatively high in the United States compared with wholesale prices in the rest of the world.

Grey markets or parallel imports are common in the United Kingdom and elsewhere in the world (see International Marketing Illustration 16-1).

International Marketing Illustration 16-1
Parallel Imports: A Perspective

In the United Kingdom, one can buy Coke produced for the Middle East, Russian Head & Shoulders shampoo, South African Colgate toothpaste, and Brazilian Dove soap.

Tesco even purchased Levi Strauss jeans in the United States to sell them at a discount in its U.K. stores. The stores sold about 15,000 pairs of Levi's jeans a week for half the price charged in specialty stores approved by Levi Strauss. Levi Strauss filed a lawsuit at the European Court of Justice, which was joined by Zino Davidoff, the perfume maker. The Court ruled that selling Levi's jeans meant for U.S. consumers was illegal. As a result of the Court's decision, Tesco and the public were outraged. Tesco was seen as attempting to level an uneven ground where jeans were sold as premium goods in Europe and as mass-merchandise in the United States, thus cheating U.K. consumers. Even attempts by Levi Strauss to explain that it is costly to sell jeans in the United Kingdom because of the limited availability of retail space were met with significant consumer skepticism. Levi Strauss subsequently agreed to introduce lower-priced jeans under the Signature brand name at Tesco, pricing it at about $40 a pair—a fraction of the price of its regular jeans.

In 2012, grey market cellphones constituted 13 percent of the global mobile handset business, at over 200 million units. These numbers were expected to increase despite the regional lockouts instituted by the manufacturer to prevent use in any market other than the one intended. In India, for example, an estimated eight mil-

lion handsets are imported in India every month, most through a grey market aimed at circumventing high import taxes of 25 to 30 percent. Cellphones are ideal grey market products, with their small size and high prices.

All in all, the international brand often speaks the wrong language in much of the world. Consumers may recognize that the brand looks somewhat different, but they are always glad to get a bargain: The brand name alone provides the guarantee. This debate will linger and, possibly, the only way to circumvent parallel imports is to closely control distribution. Gucci, the upscale Italian clothing manufacturer, was practically destroyed by loose licensing and overexposure in discount retailers. However, it was able to take charge of its situation, ending contracts with third-party suppliers, controlling its distribution, and opening its own stores. This strategy worked so well that it is difficult to find discounted Gucci products today.

Sources: IT Industry News Daily, "Grey Markets Boost Flash Memory," May 21, 2012, www.it-online.co.za/2012/05/21/grey-market-boosts-flash-memory (accessed June 17, 2012); *Green World Investor,* "India's massive illegal Grey Market for mobile phones raises concerns,"19 July, 2010, www.greenworldinvestor.com/2010/07/19/indias-massive-illegal-grey-market-for-mobile-phones-raises-concerns; "Market Report: Parallel Lines," *In-Store,* September 2003, p. 21; "Business: Trouser Suit; Parallel Imports," *The Economist,* Vol. 361, No. 8249, November 24, 2001, p. 76.

Dumping as a Competitive Threat

Firms also can face challenges from companies **dumping** products in their target market. Dumping is an important factor affecting pricing decisions. A typical example of dumping involves a foreign company that enjoys high prices and high profits at home as a result of trade barriers against imports. The company uses those profits to sell at much lower prices in foreign markets to build market share and suppress the profitability of competitors with open home markets. According to the World Trade Organization, dumping should be condemned if it threatens to cause injury to an established industry in a particular market and if it delays the establishment of a viable domestic industry.[8]

Antidumping policies differ somewhat from country to country. China, according to its Antidumping and Anti-Subsidy Regulations set forth by the State Council, defines dumping as the subsidization of exports resulting in substantial injury, or the threat of substantial injury, to an established domestic industry, or substantially impeding the establishment of a comparable domestic industry. According to Chinese law, dumping is involved if a product is sold at a price below its normal value, where normal value may be based on production costs plus reasonable expenses and profit or on the comparable price in the exporting country for an identical or like product. If there is no comparable price for the product in the exporting country, reference is made to the price at which the exporter sells a similar product in a third country.[9]

Similarly, the United States Department of Commerce, the government branch responsible for determining whether products are dumped on the U.S. market, considers that dumping takes place if products are priced only minimally above cost or at prices below those charged in the producing country. The European Commission, in charge of antidumping regulation in the European Union, has been particularly harsh on its trade partners: To obtain an antidumping penalty, an association of companies representing more than 25 percent of a sector must support an antidumping complaint and show that the alleged case of dumping has cut into their market share. However, the EU is planning to increase that percentage, perhaps to 40 percent. The EU is also planning to ask companies to publish changes in their market share to make the penalty cases more transparent.[10]

Dumping challenges and charges abound. China, Japan, and South Korea have often been challenged for dumping products in the United States and Europe. China has been accused of dumping everything from shrimp to household goods, from tissue paper to furniture and television sets. In 2011, seven American makers of solar panels filed a broad trade case in Washington against the Chinese solar industry, accusing it of using billions of dollars in government subsidies to help gain sales in the American market and dumping the solar panels in the United States for less than it costs to manufacture and ship them. The Commerce Department found several Chinese solar-panel companies guilty of dumping and slapped 31% tariffs on their products.[11]

As established by the World Trade Organization, after determining that price discrimination did indeed occur and that a particular local industry was injured by the dumping activity, governments are entitled to impose **antidumping duties** on the merchandise. Similar to these are **countervailing duties,** which are imposed on subsidized products imported into the country. Such subsidizing could, for example, take the form of government aid in the processes of production and distribution.

dumping
Selling products below cost to get rid of excess inventory and to undermine competition.

antidumping duties
Duties that must be paid by firms as a punishment for engaging in unfair price competition.

countervailing duties
Duties imposed on subsidized products imported into a country.

Enforcement of antidumping regulation is particularly intense when the economy is not faring well and when price competition is intense. In the recent past, the United States Department of Commerce and the International Trade Commission scrutinized numerous importers' pricing practices, using strict criteria to determine whether the importer had committed price discrimination and, if so, if it resulted in injury to a particular local industry. Electronics, textiles, and steel originating in countries from Japan and Russia to China and Mexico have been at the center of antidumping action in the past few decades. In the case of Mexico, the U.S. administration has imposed prohibitive and unreasonable antidumping duties on imports of cement, in spite of the shortage of cement in the United States. Instead, builders in the United States must rely on suppliers from Asia, who take on average 44 days to deliver the product at a U.S. port.[12]

In spite of more-strict enforcement, companies continue to be affected by pricing actions of importers taking advantage of loopholes in the antidumping legislation. To avoid price discrimination charges, the importers modify their products slightly so as not to permit them to be directly compared with products sold in other countries at higher prices.

16-2b The Political and Legal Environment

Governments regulate prices charged by multinational firms. Regulations and restrictions exist with regard to many pricing decisions, ranging from dumping to setting limits on wholesalers' gross margins and on the product's retail price. As mentioned in Chapter 12, "International Retailing," Walmart has been challenged in the European Union for charging prices that are too low (just above cost) and that drive competition out of business. Price promotions are severely restricted, limiting the manufacturers' ability to boost sales in the short term and to help retailers renew their inventories.

Multinational companies also are affected by local government subsidies to local manufacturers—in particular, to producers of agricultural products and to exporting firms. Subsidies lower the price charged in international markets for products and challenge the competitive position of firms operating in the same industry. Finally, governments can also impose tariffs and other duties on products in certain industries, especially if those industries are in infancy in the respective countries. Governments defend such action under the **infant industry argument,** which permits setting high tariffs on imports that challenge emerging local producers.

In general, governments use numerous strategies in their attempts to restrict the repatriation of profits by multinationals and to tax or to encourage the reinvestment of profits. One way that companies can bypass such restrictions is through the use of transfer pricing.

Transfer Pricing

Transfer pricing is a pricing strategy used in intra-firm sales: The pricing of products in the process of conducting transactions between units of the same corporation that are within or beyond the national borders of the parent company is known as transfer pricing and regarded as a legitimate business opportunity by transnational corporations.[13] Developing countries often bring the issue of transfer pricing to the attention of international trade bodies as a strategy that could help a multinational company under-report profits and decrease its tax burden in countries where it has foreign direct investment, thus evading taxation. Instead of pricing products at cost, products can be priced *at market level,* known as **market-based transfer pricing,** where the price reflects the price products sell for in a particular market; *at cost,* known as **cost-based transfer pricing,** where the cost reflects not the cost incurred by the company, but the estimated opportunity cost of the product; or products can be priced using a combination of the two strategies.

The Price of Protectionism

Protectionism adds to the final price paid by consumers. In spite of the Uruguay Round Agreement on trade liberalization and the strides made subsequently by

infant industry argument
A protectionist strategy aimed at protecting a national industry in its infancy from powerful international competitors.

transfer pricing
A pricing strategy used in intra-firm sales for commercial transactions between units of the same corporation, within or beyond the national borders of the parent company.

market-based transfer pricing
A pricing strategy used in intra-firm sales for commercial transactions between units of the same corporation, within or beyond the national borders of the parent company, whereby products are priced at market cost, rather than at the cost incurred by the company.

cost-based transfer pricing
A pricing strategy used in intra-firm sales for commercial transactions between units of the same corporation, within or beyond the national borders of the parent company, where the costs reflect the estimated opportunity costs of the product.

the World Trade Organization, protectionist actions continue to increase the costs of goods, and hence the price for the final consumer. Europe's economy, for example, is almost as protected as it was ten years ago, and its costs are as high as seven percent of the gross domestic product of the European Union—some $600 billion. To illustrate, the EU's banana-import restrictions cost European consumers up to $2 billion a year, or about 55 cents per kilogram of bananas. In other examples, European beef farmers receive large subsidies, while tariffs of up to 125 percent are imposed on beef imports; in addition, the EU has a ban on hormone-treated beef from the United States. The costs incurred by European beef consumers for subsidies, tariffs, and other restrictions amount to $14.6 billion a year in the form of higher prices and taxes, or around $1.60 per kilogram of beef.

These figures are high in the United States as well, especially in service industries such as shipping and banking.[14]

16-2c The Economic and Financial Environment

Inflationary Pressures on Price

An inflationary environment places strong pressures on companies to lower prices. Often, pricing competitively may mean that companies are not producing a profit. During inflationary periods, firms often find that they must decide between maintaining a competitive presence in a market and weathering the downside of the economic cycle or abandoning the market, which is a high-cost, high-risk proposition. Companies operating in Latin America in the 1980s and early 1990s often faced challenges posed by inflation. In the United States and Europe, inflationary fears emerged as a result of the rapid increase in gasoline prices in 2006 and 2007.

Fluctuating Exchange Rates

Fluctuating exchange rates provide both challenges and opportunities to firms trading in the global arena. Companies that do not pay attention to fluctuations in exchange rates could find that their profits are greatly eroded during the time lapsed between contract negotiations and the actual product delivery. Including a percentage that covers exchange rate fluctuations when specifying the product price is one strategy companies use to address the unpredictability of such fluctuations.

Traditionally, firms specified all transactions in a strong, stable, hard currency—usually the dollar. Since the dollar's ups and downs in the 1970s and 1980s, however, other currencies have emerged as standards for exchanges. Increasingly, pricing decisions are facilitated by the advent of successful venues for regional integration, such as the European Union and the Southern Cone Common Market (MERCOSUR). Member countries have adopted a single currency in the case of the European Union, or, in the case of MERCOSUR, they are attempting to peg the currency of member countries relative to each other. The advent of the euro in the European Union has greatly facilitated transactions in the region.

Shortage of Hard Currency and Countertrade

hard currency
Currency that is accepted for payment by any international seller.

soft currency
Currency that is kept at a high artificial exchange rate, overvalued, and controlled by the national central bank.

countertrade
A form of trade whereby a company sells a product to a buyer and agrees to accept, in return for payment, products from the buyer's firm or from the trade agency/institution of the buyer.

Developing countries face a significant shortage of hard currency reserves. **Hard currency** is currency that is accepted for payment by any international seller; **soft currency** is currency that is kept at a high artificial exchange rate, overvalued, and controlled by the national government. This situation, compounded by the inability to borrow from international banks or other sources such as the International Monetary Fund, has led developing countries to resort to **countertrade** to remain active in international trade and to address the needs of local consumers. Moreover, as global markets are growing competitive, increasingly, the balance of power is shifting from sellers to buyers. In the process, buyers require sellers to engage in reciprocal purchases, known as countertrade.[15]

Countertrade involves selling a product to a buyer and agreeing to accept, in return for payment, products from the buyer's firm or from the trade agency/institution of the buyer. Countertrade has been traditionally associated with companies from countries in the former Soviet Bloc and from other countries with a tightly controlled soft currency. The classic countertrade example is the one initiated by Pepsi with the former Soviet Union. In the late 1960s, Nikita Khruschev, then president of the Soviet Union, was impressed by the taste of Pepsi and agreed to an exchange of Pepsi syrup and bottling equipment in return for Stolichnaya vodka. This exchange was an example of successful countertrade conducted over decades. And countertrade is on the increase worldwide; it is estimated that the percentage of the total world trade financed through countertrade transactions is just more than 20 percent.[16] Many developing countries rely heavily on countertrade in their international trade activity. For example, as much as 70 percent of Russian industrial activity involves barter.[17]

It should be noted that countertrade is an important venue for firms in developed countries as well. For example, firms in the United States and Western Europe use countertrade exchanges routinely.[18]

The Position of the U.S. Government on Countertrade

The United States, in line with the mandates of the General Agreement on Tariffs and Trade (GATT) and the World Trade Organization (WTO), has a policy that opposes government-mandated countertrade. The U.S. government interferes only in the case of firms that operate with U.S.-government financing or firms that have contracts with the U.S. government. In this case, the U.S. government could compromise the competitive position of U.S. firms, which are at a disadvantage in developing countries compared with their Japanese and European competitors. However, the U.S. government does not deter firms from engaging in countertrade with private parties. Furthermore, the U.S. government supports countertrade for the sale of weapons and aircraft (countertrade constitutes the key form of trade internationally for defense equipment) and for agricultural surplus.[19]

Countertrade Brokers

Often, countertrade is conducted with the help of countertrade brokers because it is rare that a perfect match can exist for product exchanges and because the exchanges are complex. Exchanges could range from paying sausages to rock stars for their performances to bringing French high fashion to Russian consumers by selling quality Russian crystal to Saudi merchants. In the second example, the barter of French high fashion for Russian crystal is mediated by Saudi parties, who pay cash for the product to the French couturiers.

Numerous companies specialize in brokering barter deals. Located in many financial centers, such as London and New York, as well as in countries that have traditions of brokering barter agreements, such as Sweden, these brokers can put together intricate exchanges. Among the major U.S. corporate barter firms doing large-volume business are the firms of Argent Trading, Active International, Media Resources International, and Tradewell, Inc.[20]

Advantages of Countertrade

Countertrade offers substantial advantages to the involved parties. Countertrade allows firms from industrialized countries to sell their products in markets in the developing world that otherwise would not be accessible. Many countries that have a shortage of hard currency and that otherwise cannot secure bank loans to finance imports restrict the import of products considered nonessential by using foreign exchange controls and other barriers. Countertrade can help an exporting company bypass such restrictions.

In addition to offering an opportunity to many developing countries to participate in trade, countertrade also offers individuals from developing countries access to consumer products. Ministries of Foreign Trade in many developing countries tend to favor *heavy* industry imports and to restrict *light* industry imports, especially imports of soft consumer goods. For example, countertrade makes it possible for consumers in developing countries to have access to brand-name clothing and small appliances and to attend concerts of popular rock stars.

Disadvantages of Countertrade

Among the disadvantages of countertrade are the following:[21]

- Companies countertrading with an indebted nation may find that foreign lenders have prior claim on goods offered as part of the countertrading agreement.

- Countertrade arrangements often restrict profit margins, and during negotiations, price setting is difficult because not all cost factors are known in advance.

- Countertrade practices encourage economic inefficiency and are a cumbersome and time-consuming way of doing business.

- Prices are distorted as deliveries, which could take place over time, are made without reference to changes in technology, taste, quality, market structure, or competing products.

- Companies may receive inferior quality products as payment because rigorous quality control may not be a practice in the trading partner's enterprise.

- Exchange partners can, in the long term, become competitors.

- Countertrade agreements often require long and expensive negotiations.

Often, the goods firms receive as payment are unrelated to the products they sell, and the firms have no expertise in marketing these products. For example, Caterpillar Tractor received Algerian wine in exchange for its products but was unable to sell it in the U.S. market.

Types of Countertrade

The different types of countertrade usually involve monetary exchange to a certain degree. Barter is the only type of exchange that does not involve monetary exchange. At the next level are clearing agreements and switch trading, which involve the transfer of currency, usually a mutually agreed-on hard currency. All other types of countertrade are based on direct monetary exchange.

Barter

Barter can be traced back for centuries as a form of exchange. It involves a simple, nonmonetized exchange of goods or services between two parties. Although no money is involved in the exchange, the parties calculate the value of the goods in a particular currency and attempt to achieve value parity for the exchanged goods.

Clearing Agreement

A clearing agreement, also known as a **clearing account,** is a somewhat complex form of countertrade. Under this form of countertrade, a third party, usually a barter agent or some other type of broker, creates clearing accounts that represent trade credits for the respective parties, and companies trade in and out as necessary.[22] Under a clearing agreement, countries are likely to trade products up to a certain amount stated in a particular, mutually agreed-on hard currency and within a given time frame. When an imbalance occurs and one country owes money to the other, **swing credits** are paid in an agreed-on hard currency, known as the **clearing currency.**

Switch Trading

Switch trading involves buying a party's position in a countertrade in exchange for hard currency and selling it to another customer. Professional switch trading firms purchase products that are not accepted by the seller as payment for products and, for a commission, sell them on the market at a discount.

Compensation

Compensation involves payment in products and in cash, usually in a mutually agreed-on convertible currency. The firm compensated using this system is at

barter
A simple, nonmonetized exchange of goods and services between two parties.

clearing account
A complex form of countertrade whereby countries trade products up to a certain amount stated in a particular, mutually agreed-on hard currency and within a given time frame, and, when an imbalance occurs and one country owes money to the other, swing credits are paid in an agreed-on hard currency, known as the clearing currency; also called a clearing agreement.

swing credits
Amounts paid within the framework of a clearing agreement by the country that owes money to the other when an imbalance occurs.

clearing currency
The agreed-on currency used to pay swing credits in a clearing account or agreement.

switch trading
The process of buying a party's position in a countertrade in exchange for hard currency and selling it to another customer.

compensation
The payment in products and in cash, usually in a mutually agreed-on convertible currency.

lesser risk—especially if the proportion of cash is high—than the firm that is entirely dependent on the sale of the products it receives from the trading partner.

Counterpurchase

Counterpurchase involves two exchanges that are paid for in cash; as such, counterpurchase involves two parallel contracts—hence, its name of **parallel barter.** The seller agrees to purchase products that usually are unrelated to its business from the buyer and sell them on international markets. The purchase could be for the total sum of the products sold or for a fraction thereof. The exporter agrees to buy goods from a shopping list provided by the importer. The list typically consists of light manufactures and consumer goods. In a few historical examples, Volkswagen sold 10,000 cars to the former East Germany and agreed to purchase, over a period of two years, goods for the value of the automobiles, from a list of goods provided by the East German government. And, in another classic countertrade example whereby Pepsi sold its syrup to Russia in the late 1960s, the export agreement stated that Pepsi would subsequently import Stolichnaya vodka to be sold in the United States. [23]

The advantage of counterpurchase is that, typically, the seller is paid up front, in cash. The seller also has a specified, limited period (usually no more than a year) to sell the goods obtained through the exchange. Many governments of developing countries mandate counterpurchase as a requirement for firms exporting products to them.

Offset Purchase

Offset purchases involve large hard-currency purchases, such as the purchase of defense equipment, airplanes, telecommunications networks, railway or road building, and other expensive civil engineering projects, by a developing country. The seller agrees, in return for the sale of its offering, to purchase products that are valued at a certain percentage of the sale, ranging from 20 percent, which is quite typical, to as much as 100 percent for highly competitive deals. Among the advantages of offsets are reduced currency requirements, increased economic activity, and increased sales volume of both the product for the seller and of corresponding other products for the buyer and improved technology development throughout the country. And, in addition to the direct economic benefit to the buyer, offset purchases also provide indirect economic benefit to the country, as the offset provides a vehicle to increase a country's technology base, allowing the country to develop a competitive position in a well-established international market. [24] In one example of an offset transaction, the Taiwanese government is expected to spend roughly $16 billion for purchasing Patriot missiles, P-3 long-range antisubmarine planes, and diesel-engine submarines from the United States through the Foreign Military Sales (FMS) program, and the U.S. will, in turn, achieve offset credits. [25]

Buyback Agreements

In a **buyback agreement,** the seller builds and provides a turnkey plant, as well as the manufacturing know-how, the necessary equipment, patents, and licenses necessary for production and distribution of the product. The seller is paid up front part of the cost of the plant in an agreed-on convertible currency, which is typically obtained by borrowing from international banks or the International Monetary Fund. The seller agrees to purchase specific quantities of the plant's output over an extended period of time. An advantage of this type of countertrade to the seller is that it has the know-how in terms of marketing and distributing the products because the company operates in a similar business.

A buyback agreement that raised eyebrows was Royal Dutch Shell's Iranian deal. The company defied the U.S. government restrictions on trade with Iran and established a buyback agreement worth $10 billion with the National Iranian Oil Company to produce liquefied natural gas from the Iranian South Pars oil field. [26]

---

counterpurchase
A form of trade that involves two exchanges paid for in cash; it involves two parallel contracts whereby the seller agrees to purchase products that are usually unrelated to its business from the buyer and sell them on international markets; also called parallel barter.

parallel barter
A form of trade that involves two exchanges that are paid for in cash; it involves two parallel contracts whereby the seller agrees to purchase products that are usually unrelated to its business from the buyer and sell them on international markets; also called counterpurchase.

offset purchase
A large, hard-currency purchase, such as the purchase of defense equipment, airplanes, telecommunications networks, railway or road building, and other expensive civil engineering projects whereby the seller agrees, in return, to purchase products that are valued at a certain percentage of the sale.

buyback agreements
Agreements whereby the seller builds and provides a turnkey plant and is paid up front part of the cost of the plant in an agreed-on convertible currency; in return, the seller agrees to purchase specific quantities of the plant's output over an extended period of time.

16-3 International Pricing Decisions

16-3a Price Setting

Setting prices internationally tends to be intuition- and experience-driven and highly decentralized. The skill in pricing lies in exploiting differences in consumers' willingness to pay for products and services. Consequently, it is important for marketing managers to be familiar with the price elasticity of their products in a particular international market.[27]

Important determinants of the final price are currency fluctuations. Managers must decide what their reactions should be to currency fluctuations: Should they adjust their prices based on these fluctuations, or should they fix the prices on their home country currency or the currency in the country of production? Should they pass on price increases to customers or choose a lower profit? Due to the instability of currencies, many sales contracts have exchange rate clauses that address exchange rate fluctuations and exchange risk. Periodic examinations of exchange rate trends determine the adjustments necessary to align prices accordingly.

Additional important determinants of the final price are the prices paid down the chain of distribution, in business-to-business transactions. In these transactions, buyers and sellers need to agree to the terms of sale and on the terms of payment. The terms of sale determine what is and what is not included in the price quotation and when the seller takes possession of the goods. In a business-to-business environment, a buyer can correctly evaluate price deals on their face value only when fully taking into account the terms of sale and the terms of payment offered by the seller. Consequently, these considerations constitute important competitive tools when quoting prices: It is helpful to be aware not only of the prices that competitors set, but also the terms of sale and terms of payment quoted. Moreover, it is important to note that businesses in certain markets may have a preference for one type or category of quote over another, and that certain markets may not be well equipped to handle a higher level of risk, for instance.

Incoterms
Terms of sale used in transactions.

The terms of sale are stated using **Incoterms**—the International Commercial Terms, described in International Marketing Illustration 16-2. As a general trend, marketers tend to be more inclined to quote more inclusive terms—the D-terms described in the illustration.

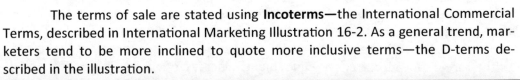

International Marketing Illustration 16-2

Terms of Sale

Incoterms apply both to domestic and to international transactions. They were first devised by the International Chamber of Commerce (ICC, based in Paris, France) in 1936 and, since then, have been updated a number of times, most recently in the year 2010. These terms of sale are also referred to as "Incoterms 2010."

The terms are further organized into E-terms, implying that the seller makes the goods available at the seller's plant, factory, or place of business. The E-term *EXW—Ex Works* (factory, warehouse, etc.)—states that the title and risk pass to the buyer from the seller's factory, plant, or warehouse. The seller's merchandise is not cleared for export, and the seller does not load merchandise on a vehicle. Ex Works is used for any mode of transportation, and it requires the minimum responsibility of the seller.

Prices are also quoted using F-terms, meaning that the seller delivers goods to the carrier that the buyer appoints. Among the F-terms are *FCA—Free Carrier* (a place after the origin point)—whereby the title and risk pass to the buyer at the point when the seller delivers goods that have been cleared for export to the carrier designated by the buyer. The seller loads the goods on the buyer's vehicle, and the buyer receives the seller's arriving vehicle unloaded. A product that is delivered *FAS—Free Alongside Ship* (at port, after all port charges)—requires the title and risk to pass to the buyer after the merchandise is delivered alongside the ship by the seller. This term is used for sea or inland waterway transportation. The seller is in charge of export clearance. *FOB—Free on Board* (port, after all port charges)—means that the title and risk pass to the buyer once delivered on board the ship by the seller—after the goods pass the ship's rail. This term is used for sea or inland waterway transportation. The seller is in charge of export clearance.

(Continued on next page.)

C-terms denote that the seller must arrange for transportation without assuming the risk of loss. *CFR—Cost and Freight* (destination port)—means that the title, risk, and insurance cost pass to the buyer when delivered on board the ship by the seller. The seller pays transportation costs to the destination port. *CIF—Cost, Insurance, and Freight* (destination port)—means that the title, risk, and insurance costs pass to the buyer when delivered on board the ship by the seller. The seller pays transportation and insurance costs to the destination port. CFR and CIF are used for sea or inland waterway transportation. *CPT—Carriage Paid To* (place at destination; includes all port charges)—means that the title, risk, and insurance costs pass to the buyer when delivered to the carrier or seller. The seller pays transportation and insurance costs to the destination port. A product delivered *CIP—Carriage and Insurance Paid To* (place at destination; includes all port charges)—means that title and risk pass to the buyer when delivered to the carrier or seller. The seller pays transportation and insurance costs to the destination port. Both CIP and CPT are used for any mode of transportation, and the seller is obligated to clear the goods for export.

D-terms imply that the seller bears all the costs and risks to bring the goods to a location agreed on by the buyers. *DAF—Delivered to Frontier* (border of country)—means that the title and risk pass to the buyer who is responsible for import clearance. This term is used for any mode of transportation. *DES—Delivered Ex Ship* (on board ship to destination port)—means that the title, risk, and responsibility for vessel unloading and import clearance pass to the buyer when the seller delivers goods on board the ship to the destination port. *DEQ—Delivered Ex Quay* (Wharf),

Duty Paid (destination port, includes duties and taxes but not destination charges and delivery)—means that the title and risk pass to the buyer when delivered on board the ship at the destination by the seller. The buyer clears the merchandise for import and pays for all formalities, duties, taxes, and other charges. The seller delivers goods on dock at the destination and clears merchandise for import. The terms *DES* and *DEQ* are used for sea or inland waterway transportation.

DDU—Delivered Duty Unpaid (destination; excludes all duties and taxes)—means that the title, risk, and responsibility for the vessel's discharge and import clearance pass to the buyer when delivered on board the ship at the destination point by the seller. Finally, *DDP—Delivered Duty Paid* (buyer's door; includes all charges)—means that the title and risk pass to the buyer when the seller delivers goods to the destination. The seller is responsible for import clearance. The terms *DDU* and *DDP* are used for any mode of transportation.

Now consider three identical shipments with identical prices for each shipment, quoted for EXW (Dieburg, Germany), CIF (Norfolk, Virginia), and DDP (Norfolk, Virginia) for Stihl merchandise shipped from Dieburg, Germany, to Norfolk, Virginia. The best deal for the buyer is the DDP (Norfolk).

Sources: http://www.iccwbo.org/incoterms; International Chamber of Commerce, *Incoterms 2000,* Paris: ICC Publishing, 2000; John Murray, Jr. "Risk, Title, and Incoterms," *Purchasing,* Vol. 132, No. 10, June 19, 2003, p. 26; John Shuman, "Incoterms 2000," *Business Credit,* Vol. 102, No. 7, July/August 2000, p. 50.

Other important determinants of the final price are the terms of payment offered by the seller. Handling the payment is often one of the last items to be considered in the international transaction and, as a result, it is sometimes given less weight. The methods of payment are typically determined by the company's reasons for going international, the company's strategy in the respective market, and its expected return. The company needs to find out what forms of payment are preferred in a particular market and are acceptable for the buyer; this information will also shed light on the partner's financial strength.[28] International Marketing Illustration 16-3 (on next page) examines the different terms of payment in international transactions.

In setting prices, companies need to examine existing competition, the labor market and materials costs, the buying power of consumers, and the goal of the company with regard to the respective target market. The company may price products higher or lower in the home market; it could engage in aggressive export pricing, skimming, or penetration pricing; or it could use standardized pricing worldwide or local pricing. These strategies are described next.

International Marketing Illustration 16-3
Terms of Payment

Buyers and sellers can agree to a number of methods of payment in international transactions:

Cash in Advance—This is the most advantageous payment option for the seller, but not for the buyer. It is used for sellers' markets primarily or for high-risk buyer environments.

Open Account—This method entails delivering goods or services without a guarantee of payment; the buyer and seller had conducted transactions in the past, and there is an expectation of continued business for both. The Basic Open Account entails payment reasonably soon after the shipment arrives or within an agreed-on period. This method is risky for the seller, who must choose buyers well.

Consignment with Open Account—Sellers can reduce risk with this type of Open Account because they still own the merchandise. However, the costs of recovering the goods are typically high in international transactions.

Documentary Collection—With this method, title and possession pass to the buyer when the documents attesting to the title and the shipping documents pass as well. These documents can be a bill of lading, a commercial invoice, an insurance certificate, or a certificate of origin. The payment document, known as a bill of exchange or draft, requiring the buy-

er to pay immediately (sight draft) or at a specified time (time draft), is sent through the seller's bank to the buyer's bank after the goods have been shipped. The buyer then pays the sight draft or accepts the time draft, the documents are released to the buyer, and the buyer can take possession of the goods.

Letter of Credit (L/C)—With this method, the letter is drawn by the buyer's bank, which guarantees to pay the seller for the merchandise upon the presentation of documents stipulated in the letter that provide evidence of shipment, adherence to the purchase order, and even inspection, if so stipulated. The bank releases the funds when all the conditions of the sale are met. Most L/Cs are irrevocable, in the sense that neither party can change it without the consent of the other parties.

It should be mentioned that the risk of selling to international buyers, especially using cash in advance or on open account, can be alleviated by purchasing insurance using the many different sources discussed in Chapter 2, "An Overview of the International Marketing Environment."

Source: Adapted from "Getting Paid or What's a Transaction For?" *World Trade*, Vol. 12, No. 9, 1999, pp. 42–48.

Prices Higher in the Home Market

Setting prices higher in the home market than in the international market is justified by one or a combination of the following reasons:

- A lower labor or raw material cost in the international market
- Strong local competition in the international market

- A lower buying power of host-country consumers relative to consumers in the company's home market

- A firm goal to increase market share by using a penetration pricing strategy in the international market, as is most likely in the example offered in Figure 16-3

Figure 16-3: Companies selling bottled water in the Czech Republic find that they have to price water at a lower price point in order to be able to compete with quality local competitors and gain market share.

Prices Lower in the Home Country

Setting prices lower in the home country, compared with company prices in the international market, is justified by one or a combination of the following reasons:

- There may be no cost advantages to producing overseas, such as economies of scale and labor to justify a lower price.

- There may be few or no challenges from competition in the international market.

- The market potential might be limited.

- Buyers in the international market can afford the higher price.

One strategy used by multinational firms to penetrate an attractive international market is aggressive export pricing.

16-3b Aggressive Export Pricing

To gain market share and to remain competitive in international markets, companies often engage in **aggressive export pricing.** One example of aggressive export pricing is **dynamic incremental pricing,** whereby a company assumes that it will have certain fixed costs whether or not it exports its products overseas. As such, the company does not factor in its international price marketing and promotion costs or its full overhead for domestic distribution. The price is based on variable international marketing and promotion costs, which allows the company to be more competitive.[29] The company allows for the product cost to reflect only the *variable cost* of taking the product abroad (thus using variable-cost pricing), rather than the *full cost* of the product (that is, full-cost pricing). Companies from Japan, Taiwan, and South Korea exporting semiconductor chips to the United States gained high market share rankings using aggressive export pricing.[30]

16-3c Standardized Pricing versus Local Pricing

Companies charge different prices for their products to meet the needs of consumers and to fit their purchase power and to account for differences in distribution systems, market position, and tax systems; this type of pricing is known as **local pricing.** In different markets, certain pricing traditions are followed. For example, in luxury markets in the United States, products are priced using even numbers—for example, $500 for a pair of Prada shoes. When those shoes go on sale, they are priced using odd pricing, such as $199. Alternatively, products in most discount outlets and in grocery stores are priced using odd pricing.

In Europe and Asia, odd/even pricing strategies are used increasingly, even though even pricing used to be preferred because it facilitated calculation. Strategies depend on the country, the currency, and even on the local price. To illustrate, in Japan, prices appear to be mostly even for non-luxury goods, as well as for luxury goods (see Figure 16-4), and this might have to do with the currency—there are 133 yen to the dollar.

aggressive export pricing
A pricing strategy that prices products below market price to penetrate new markets.

dynamic incremental pricing
A pricing strategy whereby a company assumes that it will have certain fixed costs whether or not it exports its products overseas and does not factor in its international price marketing and promotion costs or its full overhead for domestic distribution.

local pricing
A pricing strategy in which different prices are charged in different markets, reflecting differences in consumer purchase power, distribution costs, tax systems, or other market traits.

Figure 16-4: *Left: Even pricing for Japanese candy.*
Right: And even pricing for Japanese luxury goods, such as expensive alcohol.

Similarly, products in China are mostly priced evenly (see Figure 16-5), even though the currency there is on a closer parity to the dollar and the euro, at about seven yuan to the dollar. Consumer research shows that consumers in high context, non-Western cultures were found to be less prone to the illusion of cheapness or gain created by odd price endings, and more likely offended by perceived attempts to "fool" them. Thus, Western firms need to be cautious when attempting to replicate odd pricing practices in non-Western markets. Even pricing is thought to be a "safer" format for the Chinese and the Japanese.[31]

Figure 16-5: *Chinese products are priced using even pricing strategies.*

On the other hand, and contrary to the pricing theory discussed earlier, in Taiwan, odd prices appear to be predominant (see Figure 16-6). Even in luxury markets, sales signs abound and information on price-cutting is everywhere.

Finally, odd prices are becoming popular in the European Union. At first, just after the adoption of the euro, prices were pretty strange, with endings all over the place. European retailers wanted to prove to their consumers that they diligently transformed prices based on the original currency (franc, deutsche mark, lira) to the euro. Subsequently, odd-pricing strategies became prevalent. Figure 16-7 illustrates the strategy of a warehouse club—prices on top are wholesale prices, prices below are retail prices.

Figure 16-6: *In Taiwan, most prices advertised are odd prices.*

Figure 16-7: *Cheap wine, odd prices. Prices at a wholesale club: wholesale prices with corresponding retail prices below. Note that retail prices are primarily odd prices.*

16-3d Penetration Pricing and Skimming Strategies

Multinationals that have sales-based objectives, attempting to gain a high sales volume, are likely to use **penetration pricing.** Firms using this strategy price the product at first below the price of competitors to quickly penetrate the market at their competitors' expense. Compaq, which sells computers, was able to quickly capture the European market by using this strategy. In the Netherlands, for example, Compaq offered deals unmatched by any brand name competitor and coupled this pricing strategy with excellent warranties and support.

Alternatively, firms may have pricing objectives that are centered on generating a high profit and recovering the costs of product development quickly. Companies thus use a **skimming strategy,** pricing the product above that of competitors, when competition is minimal. In general, consumers responding to skimming strategies are more concerned with quality, uniqueness, and status, rather than price.

> **penetration pricing**
> A pricing strategy in which a product is first priced below the price of competitors' products to quickly penetrate the market at the competitors' expense and then raised to target levels.
>
> **skimming strategy**
> A pricing strategy in which a product is priced above that of competitors' products, when competition is minimal, to quickly recoup investments; consumers responding to skimming strategies are more concerned with quality, uniqueness, and status, rather than price.

Summary

Identify pricing-related internal challenges facing international firms. Product pricing is partially determined by the location of the production facilities; companies that do not move production to take advantage of low-cost labor are likely to price themselves out of the market. Because products are manufactured in one country, assembled in another, and then modified in yet another country, keeping track of product costs is difficult. Companies need to keep track of costs and ensure that the maximum profitability is achieved.

Identify pricing-related challenges imposed by competition on international firms. Products can face challenges from legitimate competitors; from grey markets, whereby a company's products from a low-priced market are sold through unauthorized channels in a high-priced market, competing with authorized distributors; and from dumping activities of competitors who price their products below cost to gain competitive advantage.

Identify pricing-related challenges imposed by the political and legal environment on international firms. Governments often regulate prices charged by multinationals, thus setting limits on wholesalers' gross margins and on the products' retail price and restricting price promotions. Governments can impose tariffs and other duties, thereby increasing the prices charged by the international firm.

Identify pricing-related challenges imposed by the economic and financial environment on international firms. Multinational companies are facing many challenges; among them are inflationary pressures on price, fluctuating exchange rates, and even the inability of governments to guarantee payment in hard currency. For the latter, a viable solution is countertrade, whereby a company accepts payment in kind, in product output of a company or in some other format, in return for the products it sells or for setting up operational factories in the respective country.

Address international pricing decisions of international firms. International firms use different pricing strategies in different markets. They may set prices higher in the home country if they want to penetrate new international markets or if the international markets cannot afford high prices. Or prices may be higher in international markets if those markets can afford it and pricing is in line with competitors' pricing, or if the international markets are not perceived as offering viable long-term opportunities. Companies need to make decisions such as determining whether aggressive export pricing is an appropriate strategy or whether they should use standardized prices throughout or local prices in their target markets.

Key Terms

aggressive export pricing

antidumping duties

barter

buyback agreements

clearing account

clearing currency

compensation

cost-based transfer pricing

counterpurchase

countertrade

countervailing duties

dumping

dynamic incremental pricing

grey market

hard currency

Incoterms

infant industry argument

local pricing

market-based transfer pricing

offset purchase

parallel barter

parallel imports

penetration pricing

skimming strategy

soft currency

standardized pricing

swing credits

switch trading

transfer pricing

Discussion Questions

1. What are grey markets? How do distributors using parallel imports affect a multinational firm's operations in the target market?

2. What is dumping? Why do international companies use dumping strategies in select target markets?

3. Countertrade helps a company do business in markets that otherwise would be inaccessible. What are the different approaches to countertrade that a manufacturer of telecommunications equipment could use to penetrate such markets?

4. What are the different motivations behind a company setting prices higher or lower in the home country?

Chapter Quiz

True/False

1. Dumping is defined as selling products at cost to get rid of excess inventory and to undermine competition.

Answer: True

Rationale: Dumping is defined as selling products below cost to get rid of excess inventory and to undermine competition.

Section 16-2a, "The Competitive Environment"

2. Dumping represents a problem if it threatens to cause injury to an established industry in a particular market and if it delays the establishment of a viable domestic industry.

Answer: True

Rationale: According to the World Trade Organization, dumping should be condemned if it threatens to cause injury to an established industry in a particular market and if it delays the establishment of a viable domestic industry.

Section 16-2a, "The Competitive Environment"

3. Hard currency is currency that is accepted for payment by any international seller.

Answer: True

Rationale: Hard currency is currency that is accepted for payment by any international seller, and soft currency is currency that is kept at a high artificial exchange rate, overvalued, and controlled by the national government.

Section 16-2c, "The Economic and Financial Environment"

4. Countries with a shortage of soft currency reserves are more likely to engage in countertrade.

Answer: False.

Rationale: Countries with a shortage of *hard* currency reserves are more likely to engage in countertrade.

Section 16-2c, "The Economic and Financial Environment"

5. Aggressive export pricing involves pricing products below market price to penetrate new markets.

Answer: True

Rationale: Aggressive export pricing is defined as pricing below market to penetrate new markets; a downside of exports priced well below fair market value is that they might place the company at risk for dumping challenges.

Section 16-3b, "Aggressive Export Pricing"

Multiple Choice

1.   Which of the following is NOT an external economic or financial factor affecting pricing decisions?

    a.   Inflation pressure on price

    b.   Shortage of hard currency

    c.   Transfer pricing

    d.   Fluctuating exchange rates

Answer: c is correct.

Rationale: Inflationary pressures, shortage of hard currency, and fluctuating exchange rates constitute external economic and financial factors that the company does not control. Transfer pricing is a pricing strategy that the firm can use for intra-firm sales.

Section 16-2c, "The Economic and Financial Environment"

2.   A manufacturer may charge different prices in different markets for the same product

    a.   to meet target market needs.

    b.   due to changes in the exchange rate.

    c.   due to differences in wholesale prices.

    d.   all of the above

Answer: d is correct.

Rationale: A manufacturer can charge different prices in different markets for the same product to meet the needs of target consumers who have a limited purchasing power, to keep the product price competitive in markets that are actively targeted by competition, to meet the needs of consumers in the countries with the weakest currency, and to address differences in wholesale prices in different markets.

Section 16-2a, "The Competitive Environment"

3.   What company was responsible for initiating a countertrade relationship with the Soviet Union in the late 1960s?

    a.   McDonald's

    b.   Pepsi

    c.   Philip Morris

    d.   None of the above

Answer: b is correct.

Rationale: Pepsi initiated countertrade with the Soviet Union, agreeing to an exchange of Pepsi syrup and bottling equipment in return for international distribution rights to Stolichnaya vodka.

Section 16-2c, "The Economic and Financial Environment"

4.   What type of countertrade involves buying a party's position in a countertrade in exchange for hard currency and selling it to another customer?

    a.   Compensation

    b.   Switch trading

    c.   Counter purchase

    d.   Offset purchase

Answer: b correct.

Rationale: Switch trading involves buying a party's position in a countertrade in exchange for hard currency and selling it to another customer. Professional switch trading firms typically purchase products that are not accepted by the seller as payment for products and, for a commission, sell them on the market at a discount.

Section 16-2c, "The Economic and Financial Environment"

5.   If a firm's objectives are centered on generating high profit and recovering product development costs quickly, it is likely to use which one of the following international pricing strategies?

  a.   Skimming

  b.   Penetration pricing

  c.   Standardized pricing

  d.   Competitive pricing

Answer: a is correct.

Rationale: A skimming strategy is used when competition is limited. This allows the firm to price the product higher than competitors, allowing for a higher profit margin.

Section 16-3d, "Penetration Pricing and Skimming Strategies"

Chapter 16 Endnotes

1.   Terry Clark, Masaaki Kotabe, and Dan Rajaratnam, "Exchange Rate Pass-Through and International Pricing Strategy: A Conceptual Framework and Research Propositions," *Journal of International Business Studies,* Vol. 30, No. 2, Second Quarter 1999, pp. 249–268.

2.   Howard Forman and James M. Hunt, "Pricing Issues in Industrial Marketing," *Industrial Marketing Management*, 34, 2, February 2005, 133-146.

3.   Virginia Citrano, "The Right Price," *CFO,* Vol. 8, No. 5, May 1992, pp. 71–72.

4.   Ibid.

5.   Discussion of internal factors adapted from Howard Forman and James M. Hunt, "Pricing Issues in Industrial Marketing," *Industrial Marketing Management*, Vol. 34, No. 2, February 2005, pp. 133–146.

6.   Ibid.

7.   For an additional discussion on parallel imports, see Chapter 11, "Managing International Distribution Options and Logistics."

8.   World Trade Organization, "Technical Information on Anti-Dumping," www.wto.org/english/tratop_e/adp_e/adp_info_e.htm (accessed May 21, 2012);

Greg Mastel, "The U.S. Steel Industry and Antidumping Law," *Challenge,* Vol. 42, No. 3, May/June 1999, pp. 84–94.

9.   Lester Ross and Susan Ning, "Modern Protectionism: China's Own Antidumping Regulations," *The China Business Review,* Vol. 27, No. 3, May/June 2000, pp. 30–33.

10.   John W. Miller, "Politics & Economics: EU to Revisit Trade Rule; Fines for Dumping May Have to Meet Higher Standard," *Wall Street Journal*, March 13, 2007, A8.

11.   Keith Johnson and Cassandra Sweet, "U.S. Imposes Tariffs on China Solar Panels, *The Wall Street Journal*, May 18, 2012, online.wsj.com; Philip Scott Andrews, "U.S. Solar Panel Makers Say China Violated Trade Rules, *The New York Times*, October 19, 2011, www.nytimes.com.

12.   "Housing Surge Threatened by a Shortage of Cement," *Wall Street Journal*, September 9, 2004, A17.

13.   Messaoud Mehafdi, "The Ethics of International Transfer Pricing," *Journal of Business Ethics,* Vol. 28, No. 4, December 2000, pp. 365–381.

14.   Examples from *The Economist,* "Finance and Economics: Europe's Burden," Vol. 351, No. 8120, May 22, 1999, p. 84.

15.   Dorothy A. Paun, Larry D. Compeau, and Dhruv Grewal, "A Model of the Influence of Marketing Objectives on Pricing Strategies in International Countertrade," *Journal of Public Policy & Marketing*, Vol. 16, No. 1, Spring 1997, pp. 69–82.

16.   Sam C. Okoroafo, "Determinants of LDC-Mandated Countertrade," *International Marketing Review,* Vol. 5, Winter 1988, pp. 16–24.

17.   David Woodruff, *Money Unmade: Barter and the Fate of Russian Capitalism,* Ithaca: NY: Cornell University Press, 1999.

18.   John P. Angelidis and Nabil A. Ibrahim, "Countertrading between United States and Western European Firms: An Empirical Analysis of the Benefits and Pitfalls," *International Journal of Management,* Vol. 18, No. 2, 2001, p. 252.

19.   Paun, Compeau, and Grewal, "A Model of the Influence of Marketing Objectives," pp. 69–82.

20.   Janet Aschkenasy, "Give and Take," *International Business,* Vol. 9, No. 8, September 1996, pp. 10–12.

21.   Nabil A. Ibrahim and John P. Angelidis, "Countertrading with Eastern Europe: A Comparative Analysis of the Benefits and Pitfalls," *International Journal of Commerce & Management,* Vol. 6, No. 3/4, 1996, pp. 22–40.

22.   Plank, Reid, and Bates, "Barter: An Alternative," p. 52.

23.   Jean F. Hennart, "Some Empirical Dimensions of Countertrade," *Journal of International Business Studies,"* Vol. 21, No. 2, Second Quarter 1990, pp. 243–270.

24.   Chyan Yang and Tsung-cheng Wang, "Multi-Criteria Analysis of Offset Execution Strategies in Defense Trade: A Case in Taiwan," *Journal of American Academy of Business*, September 2006, Vol. 10, No. 1, pp. 179-185.

25.   Ibid.

26.   Terry Macalister, "Shell Defies US Pressure and Signs £5bn Iranian Gas Deal,"

The Guardian Unlimited, online edition, January 29, 2007.

27.   Howard Forman and James M. Hunt, "Pricing Issues in Industrial Marketing," *Industrial Marketing Management*, Vol. 34, No. 2, February 2005, pp. 133–146.

28.   "Getting Paid or What's a Transaction For?" *World Trade,* Vol. 12, No. 9, 1999, pp. 42–48.

29.   Barbara Stottinger, "Strategic Export Pricing: A Long and Winding Road," *Journal of International Marketing*, Vol. 9, No. 1, 2001, pp. 40–63.

30.   Citrano, "The Right Price," pp. 71–72.

31.   Adam Nguyen, Roger M. Heeler, and Zinaida Taran, "High-Low Context Cultures and Price-Ending Practices," *Journal of Product and Brand Management*, Vol. 16, No. 3, 2007, p. 206.

Case 16-1

Travel Turkey: Pricing Decisions in a Changing Environment

Erdogan Eser, a former hotel sales manager with Hilton, decided to return to his home country, Turkey, to establish a travel agency called Travel Turkey. With an office in Taksim Square in the center of Istanbul, the travel agency is actually a broker between foreign tour operators and lodging operators in Turkey. Lodging operators—managers of hotels, bed and breakfasts, inns, and resorts—have voiced concerns about foreign tour operators, especially about the lack of guarantees when it came to occupancy. Similarly, foreign tour operators felt that their needs were not appropriately addressed by lodging operators. As a broker, Erdogan would be able to address concerns on each side and benefit each party by creating optimal matches. Travel Turkey will benefit from Erdogan's many years in the travel industry and from his extensive network of colleagues and friends in the travel business. Even though Turkey has experienced its own economic and political problems, the country remains quite attractive to tourists and is a preferred destination for many tourist groups.

Turkey's tourism has experienced an impressive boom since the early 1980s. The total number of tourists to the country approaches 10 million yearly. Turkey is an attractive destination, located at the crossroads of Asia and Europe, offering centuries-old cultural and historical sites. It is a dynamic destination of sun, sea (Aegean and Mediterranean), and archeological sites. The government has offered significant incentives to businesses to increase bed capacity, and it enacted Law 2634 to encourage the development of tourism in 1982; this support is still readily available.

One of the concerns in Turkey is the seasonality of tourism. Most tourists visit Turkey between the months of June and October. August is the high season, the hottest month, with temperatures hovering in the 90s, and with high humidity. The table below shows that this tendency is entrenched and there is little variation over time.

Month	2005	2006	2007	2008	2009	2010
Seasonality of Trips 2005-2010						
January	4.1	4.1	4.0	4.1	4.0	4.0
February	3.2	3.2	3.0	3.1	3.0	3.0
March	4.6	4.4	4.0	4.1	4.0	4.0
April	5.6	6.0	6.0	5.8	5.9	6.0
May	9.0	8.0	8.3	8.2	8.3	8.3
June	9.8	9.8	10.2	10.5	10.6	10.7
July	12.7	12.9	13.3	13.4	13.3	13.4
August	16.6	17.1	17.3	17.2	17.1	17.0
September	13.3	13.4	13.4	12.9	13.2	13.3
October	11.2	11.2	11.7	11.9	11.8	11.7
November	5.6	5.6	4.2	4.1	4.3	4.4
December	4.3	4.3	4.6	4.7	4.5	4.2
Total	100.0	100.0	100.0	100.0	100.0	100.0

The major players in Turkey's expanding tourism are Western European package tour operators, one of Erdogan's main target markets. These operators coordinate their activities with airlines and travel agencies in France, Germany, and the United Kingdom, in particular. The relationship between Turkish lodging operators and the European tour operators is not always smooth: A study of 200 Turkish lodging operators revealed the difficulties that are often encountered in their relationship with Western tour operators:

Types of Problems	Number of Times Cited
Cancellations	113
Delayed payments	126
Pressure to accept low prices	129
Artificial price competition	129
Reduced number of rooms blocked	118
Requests for complimentary rooms	65
Requests for last-minute reservations	116

Erdogan Eser will also target U.S. travel agencies, especially church groups visiting European capitals—a market that, in spite of safety concerns, remains relatively solid. There are still concerns and numerous reports that Americans are verbally attacked on the street in much of Europe by locals who oppose U.S. military policies around the world. Newspapers advise U.S. travelers: If you're heading overseas, be prepared to have discussions with people who think America is the devil. If the past 100 years were widely considered the "American Century," this new century is rapidly shaping up as the Anti-American Century. However, Erdogan feels that the right price would bring these tourists to the shores of the Bosphorus. After all, Greece and Turkey are among the hottest destinations for Christians: The ruins of Ephesus in Turkey, where Mary is said to have spent her last days, are especially popular. Travel Turkey could partner with Travel Dynamics International, which specializes in these types of tours.

Another important target market is the Eastern European travel operators who coordinate shopping trips to Istanbul. Eastern European consumers often take short trips to Istanbul to purchase quality leather products of Turkish provenance and knockoffs of top international brands. They may purchase products for their own and their family's use, or they may purchase for resale. Regardless, the buses always return to Russia, the Ukraine, and Romania full of merchandise.

Erdogan's plans are to assure lodging operators of large occupancy levels and obtain large discounts. He will then assure tour operators of rooms at reasonable rates that would meet their needs. For example, for a week in Istanbul, he would arrange with the Conrad hotel, the Ciragan Palace (a Kempinski Hotels property), and Swissôtel to book 100 rooms, each at 70 euros. For spending a week at one of these hotels, he would charge the tour operators as follows:

- Western European tour operators would pay 100 euros per room per night.
- Eastern European tour operators would pay 90 euros per room per night.
- U.S. tour operators would pay $130 per room per night.

One of the first to meet Erdogan in his capacity as travel agent, a U.S. tour operator, Jack Maloney, who heads a church travel agency in Cincinnati, Ohio, was concerned that the dollar price for the three hotels was rather high. His feeling was that because his Ukrainian colleague, another tour operator, was charged only 90 euros, his business should be charged the same amount. Moreover, even a tourist off the street would be able to book a room at the Conrad, for instance, for only $150 for a Conrad Saver rate—not much more than the deal he was getting. True, those are all premium properties and five-star hotels, but charging different prices for the East European operators seemed unfair, and Jack's travel agency would not be able to make a sufficient profit.

As a result of this meeting, Erdogan Eser decided to rethink his pricing strategy. Were there any international laws that did not allow him to charge different prices to different clients? This was never a concern in Turkey. And, at his previous job with the Hilton, charging different rates was customary. Was it ethical to give a break to the Eastern European tour operators? Was it unethical to charge the U.S. operators higher amounts, given that the dollar continues to lose in value relative to the euro?

Sources: Euromonitor International, "Travel and Tourism in Turkey," 8 April, 2011, Euromonitor.com; Marco R. della Cava, "Ugly Sentiments Sting American Tourists as Europeans Cite Frustrations with U.S. Policy," *USA Today,* March 4, 2003, 1–2; Gene Sloan, "Cruise Lines Are Forced to Bail Again," *USA Today,* March 4, 2003, 10b; Dan Reed, "American Wants to Get the Low-Fare Word Out," *USA Today,* March 4, 2003, 8A; Elizabeth Bernstein, "The Other Holy Lands—Spiritual Tourists Skip Israel for Sites in Cuba, Turkey; Keeping Kosher in China," *The Wall Street Journal,* December 6, 2002, W4; Kurtulus Karamustafa, "Marketing Channel Relationships: Turkey's Resort Purveyors' Interactions with International Tour Operators," *Cornell Hotel and Restaurant Administration Quarterly*, Vol. 41, No. 4, 2000, pp. 21–32.

Analysis Suggestions

1. Are there any legal or ethical concerns that might preclude Travel Turkey to charge different prices to different travel agents for the same room? Is it ethical or legal to charge different prices based on the home country of the tour operators and their respective tourists?

2. What can Erdogan do if the dollar continues to fall relative to the euro?

3. How can Travel Turkey ensure against foreign exchange risk and maintain its Eastern European and U.S. clients?

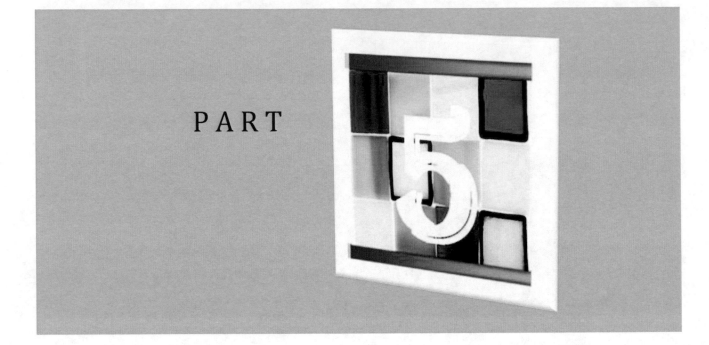

PART

International Marketing Strategy: Implementation

Chapter 17: Organizing and Controlling International Marketing Operations and Perspectives for the Future

Learning Objectives

After studying this chapter, you should be able to:

- Identify the factors in a firm's external and internal environment that determine the organizational design best suited for international operations.

- Describe different organizational designs and offer examples of designs that different international firms have adopted.

- Identify formal and informal controls necessary to ensure that company operations are in line with company goals and objectives as stated in the strategic plan.

    •

Multinational companies today are confronted with aggressive competition for markets world-wide. To meet the challenges of intensifying competition, multinationals have been forced to alter their organizational structures and to adapt their standards to the new environment, aligning executive compensation with the companies' new goals.

Ford, responding to rapid changes in the global economy, implemented a major reorganization, ending competing regional fiefdoms by consolidating engineering, design, and development within new global divisions. Motorola, faced with aggressive Asian competitors and falling profits, adopted a similar plan, replacing decentralized and competing businesses with three distinct global groups focusing on retail customers such as cell phone users, telecommunications companies, and government and industrial clients. Procter & Gamble initiated the broadest overhaul in its industry, transforming four business units based on geographic regions into seven global entities based on product lines such as baby care or food and beverage.[1]

As the international arena is becoming highly competitive, companies need to reorganize to more effectively meet challenges and communicate with key target consumers, as demonstrated in the following case of Borland.

Borland

Borland Software Corp., a leading application life cycle management vendor, is fully reorganizing its international operations. The company's goal is to become more customer focused and to accelerate its application life cycle management, or ALM, strategy, thus streamlining operations and better aligning its resources in the enterprise. In the "re-scoping of Borland's international operations," the company is engaging in geographic consolidation, thus achieving cost savings.

In this business, there is a need for collaboration between sales, presales, and services, and for a close collaboration with partners in the supply chain. Thus, Borland is also combining its customer service and research and development (R&D) functions, organizing them into an overall function that will respond more quickly to customer support requests.[2]

This chapter addresses the process of organizing for international marketing and controlling international operations, offering examples of organizational structures of firms worldwide. It also provides an overview of future developments in international marketing, with a focus on Internet-related trends.

17-1 Organizing for International Marketing Operations

Firms need to consider organizational designs that fit with their external environment and with company characteristics and goals. Organizational design is determined by numerous factors in the firms' operating environments. Among such factors are those in each firm's environment, such as competition, environmental stability, similarity with the home country, common regional traits and regional integration, and availability of qualified labor. Factors within the firm also affect organizational design—in particular, the priority given to internationalization. These factors are described in Sections 17-1a, "Factors in the Firm's Environment," and 17-1b, "Factors within the Firm."

17-1a Factors in the Firm's Environment

Competitive Environment

In environments characterized by intense competition, where decisions must be made quickly to counter competitive moves, a decentralized organization would allow for the most immediate reaction. In a decentralized organization, each subsidiary operates as a profit center and has full charge of its market. Such an organization permits direct offense on competition or immediate defensive action in reaction to competitive moves. High flexibility is essential to react to changes quickly. However, even in a highly competitive international environment, centralization helps firms avoid duplication and lower costs. Activities such as finance and research and development benefit from centralization. Even firms that have at one point adopted a decentralized model to compete effectively in the international market have rethought their strategies and opted for a centralized model. Section 17-2d, "The Matrix Structure," addresses changes at Philips, a multinational company that decided to move from a decentralized organization to a centralized organization to effectively compete internationally.

Environmental Stability

Countries characterized by unstable political environments or countries where government policies are unstable, countries that are characterized by high inflation and high unemployment, and countries with unstable currency require companies to adapt quickly to the changing environment. Such companies need to be able to take immediate action to adapt to the new environments and need an **organizational structure** that allows them to react quickly.

Environmental Similarity with the Home Country

Companies operating in countries that are similar to their home country are likely to use similar strategies. These companies would opt for an organization that integrates operations between the home and host countries.

Common Regional Traits and Regional Integration

Companies can organize their operations with a regional focus in countries that share language, religion, or other cultural similarities. Countries that share a border; or countries that are members of a regional alliance.

Availability of Local Qualified Labor

Companies operating in countries with ample educated and qualified labor delegate more control to local operations and have organizational structures that allow for more local control.

17-1b Factors within the Firm

Organizational design also is determined by company traits. A firm that considers internationalization a priority is likely to have an organizational structure with regional divisions in charge of particular countries. Other organizations involved in international business might have only an international division that oversees international operations. Companies that are only minimally involved in international business might have only a small international department.

Companies are likely to maintain their organizational structure when they go international. An organization that is hierarchical and centralized is likely to have a centralized international organization. An organization structured on the basis of product lines is also likely to maintain this structure for its international operations.

> **organizational designs**
> The organization of reporting and coordination within a company.
>
> **international division structure**
> An organizational structure whereby firms have separate domestic and international divisions.

17-2 Examining International Organizational Designs

Multinational companies use four types of formal structures in their international **organizational designs:** international divisions, worldwide regional divisions, product divisions, and the matrix structure.

17-2a The International Division Structure

Firms with an **international division structure** have two main divisions: the domestic division and the international division. When firms become involved in international business by exporting products overseas, they typically assign responsibility for all international operations to an export department. This is known as an export department structure. As their international involvement increases, they will most likely have an international division in charge of all their international operations. These firms are still primarily focused on domestic operations, but their international operations have an important standing, at the same level with all other divisions. In an international division structure, all foreign subsidiaries report directly to a single division responsible for international operations, which is separate from the one responsible for domestic operations.

17-2b The Worldwide Regional Division Structure

A **worldwide regional division structure** configures operations either by geographic region or by country. Under this model, subsidiaries report directly to the single division responsible for operations in the country or geographic region. Although this structure allows for some duplication of activities and thus might increase costs, managers consider this organization to be effective in creating competitive advantage for the firms.[3] A particular advantage of the worldwide regional division structure is that it is better equipped to immediately process and respond to country-specific information and conditions than other formal structures—at some cost to product-related information—because of its strong regional focus.[4]

Frito-Lay, which belongs to the Pepsi family of companies, has a worldwide regional division structure. The Frito-Lay Company, headquartered in the United States, oversees all the functional areas (i.e., marketing, manufacturing, research and development, finance, etc.). The regional divisions—Frito-Lay North America, headquartered in Plano, Texas; Frito-Lay Europe/Africa/Middle East, headquartered in Geneva, Switzerland; and Frito-Lay Latin America/Asia Pacific/Australia—oversee all regional operations, country subsidiaries, and offices (see Figure 17-1).

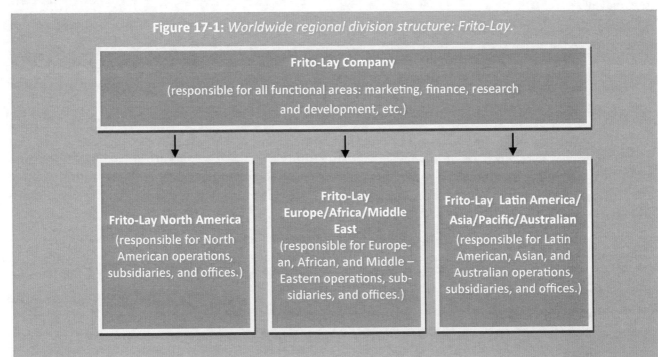

Figure 17-1: *Worldwide regional division structure: Frito-Lay.*

Frito-Lay Company

(responsible for all functional areas: marketing, finance, research and development, etc.)

Frito-Lay North America

(responsible for North American operations, subsidiaries, and offices.)

Frito-Lay Europe/Africa/Middle East

(responsible for European, African, and Middle-Eastern operations, subsidiaries, and offices.)

Frito-Lay Latin America/Asia/Pacific/Australian

(responsible for Latin American, Asian, and Australian operations, subsidiaries, and offices.)

worldwide regional division structure
An organizational structure whereby operations are organized by region or by country, and where subsidiaries report directly to the single division responsible for operations in the country or geographic region.

This type of structure is helpful for firms that have similar congruent product lines or services, such as Frito-Lay. The Guggenheim museum also has this type of structure, with the Guggenheim New York (the main museum and Guggenheim Soho); Guggenheim Venice (Italy); Guggenheim Bilbao (Spain); Guggenheim Berlin (Germany); and the Guggenheim Virtual Museum, an online museum for virtual exhibitions and artists' projects.

17-2c The Product Division Structure

In a regional or worldwide **product division structure,** subsidiaries report to the product division (strategic business unit) with responsibility for the particular products. In the past, this structure was common for high-tech companies or multinational companies with diversified portfolios. However, increasingly, this format is replaced by the matrix structure. Even companies that once were identified as typical examples of the product division structure, such as Sun Microsystems and Whirlpool, have adopted a matrix structure.

17-2d The Matrix Structure

The **matrix structure** takes into account the multiple dimensions involved in doing business internationally—functional areas, product, and region/country. In a matrix structure, two dimensions are integrated such that each operational unit reports to both region/country managers and product managers.

Many large multinationals have had a matrix structure for decades—among them Philips Electronics, Unilever, Electrolux, IBM, and Procter & Gamble. And, in recent years, many more multinationals have adopted this organizational structure—among them, BASF, Disney, and Rockwell International. This type of format works especially well for firms that have global brands as well as local brands; such companies need to coordinate marketing activities worldwide involving the global brands, and need to focus on the local market for the local brands.

Unilever's matrix structure is organized based on products (home and personal care products and Bestfoods products) and on regions around the world. Its divisions are Home & Personal Care, Africa, Middle East & Turkey; Home & Personal Care, Asia; Home & Personal Care, Europe; Home & Personal Care, North America/Latin America; Unilever Bestfoods Africa, Middle East & Turkey; Foodservice; Ice Cream and Frozen Foods; Latin America & SlimFast worldwide; Unilever Bestfoods, Asia; Unilever Bestfoods, Europe; and Unilever Bestfoods, North America.[5]

In another example of a matrix structure, Philips is organized into five divisions (see Figure 17-2), each run separately. The divisions are Philips Lighting, Philips DAP (Domestic Appliances & Personal Care), Philips Semiconductors, Philips Consumer Electronics, and Philips Medical Systems. The company initially ran its operations in different regions, with production, sales, and marketing coordinated separately for North America, Latin America, Asia, Africa, and Europe for each of the five divisions. In addition, the company had a separate division for research and development.

> **product division structure**
> An organizational structure whereby subsidiaries report to the product division (strategic business unit) with responsibility for the particular products.
>
> **matrix structure**
> An organizational structure whereby each operational unit reports to both region/ country managers and product managers.

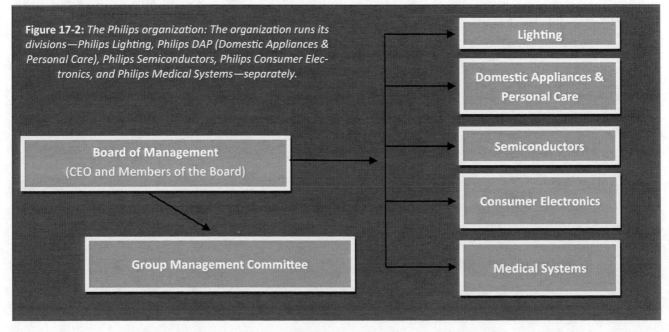

Figure 17-2: *The Philips organization: The organization runs its divisions—Philips Lighting, Philips DAP (Domestic Appliances & Personal Care), Philips Semiconductors, Philips Consumer Electronics, and Philips Medical Systems—separately.*

Board of Management (CEO and Members of the Board)

Group Management Committee

Lighting

Domestic Appliances & Personal Care

Semiconductors

Consumer Electronics

Medical Systems

Philips has been streamlining operations through a concerted effort to centralize its global operations. The company has reduced the number of business units and creation teams in each division and outsourced its customer service department. Table 17-1 illustrates the divisions of Philips. To illustrate, Philips Consumer Electronics, one of the company's five divisions, reduced the number of business units from seven to three, the number of creation teams from 21 to 12, and made other important changes, such as aligning research and development roadmaps and outsourcing and sharing service centers and consumer services.

Table 17-1: *A Comparison between the Organization for Consumer Electronics at Philips in 2003 and 2012*

2003 Organization for Consumer Electronics	2012 Organization for Consumer Electronics
Decentralized business planning, logistics, and accounting	Centralized business planning, logistics, and accounting
7 business units	3 business units
21 creation teams	12 creation teams
Individual R&D approach for each team	Aligned R&D roadmaps
Distinct regional marketing programs	Coherent global marketing approaches
Undifferentiated business models	Business model adapted to life cycle
In-house infrastructure	Outsourced, shared service centers
Large, company-owned consumer service organization	Outsourced consumer service

Source: www.philips.com

Philips Lighting, another Philips division and its principal business historically, reorganized around the different subdivisions: luminaries, lamps, lighting electronics, and automotive and special lighting (see Figure 17-3).

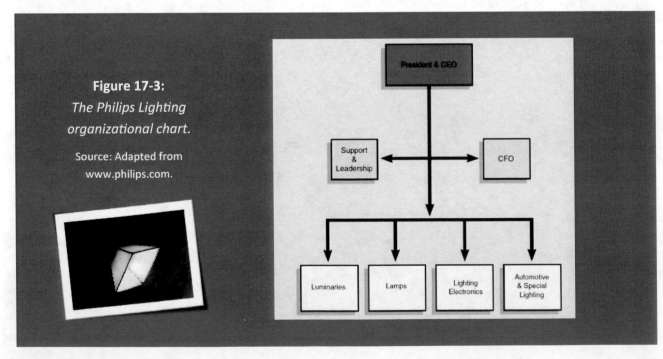

Figure 17-3:
The Philips Lighting organizational chart.

Source: Adapted from www.philips.com.

Likewise, Nokia recently adopted a matrix structure to keep up with competition from China and to maintain its market share. Although Nokia and Motorola have sold more cell phones to customers worldwide, Chinese brands are rapidly increasing in popularity and taking market share from both companies (see International Marketing Illustration 17-1).

International Marketing Illustration 17-1
Using the Matrix Structure as a Competitive Tool

Nokia engaged in a radical global restructuring, creating a new matrix structure in which four business lines—mobile phones, multimedia, networks, and enterprise solutions—are overlaid over three supporting groups—customer and market operations, technology platforms and research, and venturing and business infrastructure. The company found itself in a position in which its global market share, estimated to be between 15 and 20 percent, was going down from a leading position and getting close to that of Motorola. Hence, the company decided to restructure as a way to ensure that its reputation will be able to see off the challenge of cheaper and increasingly technologically advanced competition from Chinese manufacturers, with lower costs and profit targets. At the same time, China's Ningbo Bird and TLC, among others, are catching up fast in the highly competitive market.

The battle between cell phone makers is raging in every major international market. In China, for example, domestic cell phone manufacturers have more than 40 percent of the market. And Ningbo Bird, based in the central coastal city of Ningbo, China, ships more than 11 million cell phones per year. At the same time, China Mobile Communications Corp., the largest wireless operator in the country, just ordered phones from national manufacturers that it will sell bundled with service plans. This effort is likely to further boost sales of Chinese brands and increase their market share worldwide, at the expense of Nokia and Motorola. This picture is quite different from that of the 1990s, when Nokia commanded as much as 80 percent of the market share in China.

Nokia believes that a matrix structure will enable it to take into account the multiple dimensions involved in doing business internationally: functional areas, product, and region/country. In a matrix structure, these dimensions are integrated such that each operational unit reports to both region/country managers and product managers.

Sources: Daniel Thomas, "Nokia Faces Premium Challenge," *Financial Times,* 19 April, 2012, www.ft.com; Alfred Hille, "Nokia Faces Up to China's Challenges," *Media,* January 16, 2004, p. 1; and Evan Ramstad, "Two Tech Concerns in China Lose Luster," *Wall Street Journal,* March 2, 2004, A16.

17-3 Controlling International Marketing Operations

Controls are necessary to ensure that international company operations are in line with company goals and objectives, as stated in the company's strategic plan. Yet, controlling international operations and ensuring that performance standards are met throughout the company are complex tasks. Adding to the complexity are the following:

- Local units and a regional focus often add intermediate levels of management and staffing that further complicate the management, communication, and evaluation processes.

- Multinational companies are likely to have subsidiaries and branch offices in countries where the external environment is changing at different rates, having a different impact on company operations. Thus, standards and measures instituted for evaluation purposes are often not comparable across countries.

- Given the distance of subsidiaries from headquarters, there is a tendency to resist influence in both directions, such that subsidiaries often fight to retain autonomy in decision making and performance evaluation, while the headquarters may resist input from the subsidiaries in the planning and evaluation process.

Difficulties imposed by the complexity of the international management context can, to a certain extent, be offset by instituting the appropriate formal and informal controls.

17-3a Formal Controls

Instituting **formal controls** involves the following process:

- Establishing performance standards
- Measuring performance
- Addressing discrepancies

Establishing Performance Standards

The first step in establishing formal controls involves establishing **performance standards** in light of the company's projected market potential. Parameters must be developed in the strategic plan for evaluating dimensions of the external environment for the purpose of setting standards based on that potential. The evaluation must include a continuous assessment of competitive intensity (local and international competitors in the market), political stability, developments in the economy, regional and local trade, and other developments that directly affect company performance. In many emerging economies, currencies have fluctuated widely over the past few years, and many of these economies have seen major political overhauls. Hence, it is difficult to accurately measure outcomes and evaluate managerial performance. Moreover, postprivatization restructuring may take a long time to complete and may produce soft outcomes, so outcome measurability becomes problematic, thereby complicating management evaluation.[6]

Measuring Performance

Actual performance is measured based on established standards. At this point, measures such as sales, profit, and market share are assessed for the target market in a particular country or region and measured against previous performance or against competitors. These assessments are compared with company goals and objectives for the target market as expressed in the company plan.

Addressing Discrepancies

At the final stage of this process, discrepancies between standards and performance are corrected. If the standards were unreasonable or were not reached due to unanticipated changes in the external environment, they will be adjusted accordingly for the next assessment period. Lessons from the company's experience in other parts of the world and lessons learned from other companies' experiences are useful at this stage. For example, studies have found that the performance of European and Japanese multinationals is positively correlated with corporate policies emphasizing innovation and product designs that are standardized globally but adapted locally.[7] A company that may be keen on a standardized international product strategy may benefit from adapting its offer to suit local preferences. The company may also need to offer more innovative products to the target market. Both the local adaptation strategy and the focus on innovation need to be coordinated with company headquarters; in fact, for many firms, innovation takes place at the company's national headquarters.[8] For example, Procter & Gamble has 22 innovation centers in 12 countries worldwide.[9]

17-3b Informal Controls

In addition to the controls described in Section 17-3a, "Formal Controls," companies also can use **informal controls** to ensure that there is a fit between the standards and actual performance. The following are examples of informal controls a company can use:

> **formal controls**
> Systematic controls, such as performance standards and measurement, used in international marketing to ensure that international company operations are in line with company goals and objectives.
>
> **performance standards**
> A priori measures against which firm performance is evaluated.
>
> **informal controls**
> Systematic controls, such as dialogue between the headquarters and the international field operations, used in international marketing to ensure that international company operations are in line with company goals and objectives.

- Establishing frequent contact between the home-country headquarters and the regional or local office. Such contact serves as a means to better coordinate activities and ensure clear communication of expectations in both directions.

- Rotating managers to different assignments to obtain the maximum benefit from international experience. One often-used strategy is to hire third-country managers (from a country other than the home or the host country) to oversee new or problematic operations. These individuals have the flexibility and experience but not the biases created by an association with the home or host country of the company. In general, moving expatriates from one subsidiary to another offers valuable exchange in information to be used as input into the control function.

- Training the employees and inculcating a management culture that is consistent with company goals and objectives. Management development training can be used to share the mission and objectives of the company expressed in the relevant performance terms. For example, a company can focus on company growth or profitability objectives, innovation, the relationship with the target customer, or any other dimension that the company deems important.

17-4 International Marketing: Some Future Perspectives

The world economy has experienced revolutionary changes in the past few decades with the growth of the technology sector. The Internet and related technologies have expanded the realm of international marketing and dramatically increased access to new markets. World markets are expected to continue to benefit from the expansion in opportunities facilitated by e-commerce.

In 2012, almost 2.3 billion people worldwide used the Internet, with only 12 percent of those in North America. In comparison, in 2007, just 491 million people used the Internet, with almost one-third of those in the United States. Table 17-2 provides statistics on eight countries in terms of Internet penetration of the home market. The largest penetration of the population is in North America, at 78.6 percent, followed by Australia/Oceania, at 67.5 percent, and Europe, at 61.3 percent.[10]

Table 17-2: Internet Use in the Different World Regions

World Regions	Population	Internet Users	Penetration (% Population)	Users %
Africa	1,037,524,058	139,875,242	13.5 %	6.2 %
Asia	3,879,740,877	1,016,799,076	26.2 %	44.8 %
Europe	816,426,346	500,723,686	61.3 %	22.1 %
Middle East	216,258,843	77,020,995	35.6 %	3.4 %
North America	347,394,870	273,067,546	78.6 %	12.0 %
Latin America / Carib.	597,283,165	235,819,740	39.5 %	10.4 %
Oceania / Australia	35,426,995	23,927,457	67.5 %	1.1 %
WORLD TOTAL	6,930,055,154	2,267,233,742	32.7 %	100.0 %

www.internetworldstats.com, 2011

Differences exist with regard to Internet usage. For example, Americans are 8 percent more active on political news sites than Canadians. On the other hand, Canadians are 92 percent more likely to view entertainment news websites, 80 percent more active on humor websites, 27 percent more active on gaming sites, and 26 percent more active on sports sites. In addition, Canadians are 55 percent more active in online banking and 142 percent more involved with online trading.[11] The differences are even greater between American and Japanese consumers, who are used to handling many more transactions than their counterparts in the United States on the Internet, through high-tech vending machines and other interactive media. For example, Japanese travelers can select to purchase travelers' insurance from among different insurance companies from a vending machine situated right at the airport. There, they can select the terminal of their preferred insurance company and complete the transaction online. In the United States, such interaction requires the presence of a live salesperson.

It is expected that e-commerce will increase dramatically worldwide. The adoption of the Internet will continue to be the most rapid in highly industrialized countries, where it will achieve 100 percent penetration. It will be rapid in emerging markets and especially in those markets where English is widely spoken; and countries such as China, Brazil, India, and many countries in Latin America anticipate significant increases in usage.

The global online retail sector had total revenue of $434.6 billion in 2010, representing a compound annual growth rate of 16.3 percent between 2006 and 2010. The largest and most lucrative industry, accounting for 23.6 percent of the total revenue, was the electronics industry with total revenues of $102.4 billion. Online retailing is expected to exceed $800 billion by 2015.[12]

In the United States, the major Internet retailers include Lands' End, LL Bean, Amazon, Overstock, and Hanover Direct, and the industry is concentrated, with the top 50 companies accounting for about 70 percent of revenue. For most of these companies, the industry's revenue has shifted from catalog to Internet sales. Major international Internet retailers include Germany's Otto Group, the N Brown Group of the UK, and GS Home Shopping of South Korea.

The Internet has been a driver for internationalization because it offers companies the advantage of reaching customers worldwide. Yet, in spite of extensive Internet access worldwide, companies—even those with the best e-commerce capabilities—are not equipped to handle Internet sales and turn away many international orders because they do not have the processes in place to fill them or because language and cultural barriers hinder basic communications. Also, they may have difficulty handling the destination country's import and tax regulations or export controls in the home country. In addition, payment mechanisms are cumbersome, and there is a high rate of credit card theft, adding to the company's risk. Additional risk is posed by online security and data protection. Companies are increasingly partnering and releasing proprietary information for the benefit of the partnership. However, these relationships are sometimes jeopardized by lax data controls.

Many changes will take place in the product arena, where product life cycles will continue to manifest their current trend of acceleration. International firms must be prepared for rapid new product introductions simultaneously in world markets, regardless of the markets' levels of development. In Tibet, one of the most remote areas in China, separated by the mainland by often impassable mountain ranges, is undergoing rapid changes. In the past decade, train access has facilitated transportation to the region and planes land and take off continuously from Lhasa Airport. Moreover, access to Internet is both rapid and convenient, allowing consumers to purchase products that before were off limits. See Figure 17-4.

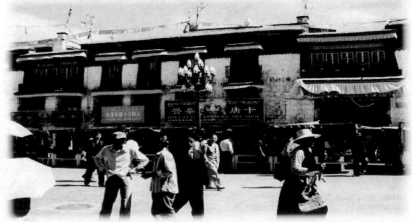

Figure 17-4: Lhasa, Tibet, has been off limits to marketers until recently.

In other developments, as seen in International Marketing Illustration 17-1, the battle for market share for market leaders often takes place in developing countries. The illustration portrayed Nokia as losing market share in China, negatively affecting its competitive stance worldwide. When new products such as smartphones are introduced, developing countries and emerging markets will be important battlegrounds.

As the world population grows, there will be significant changes in the consumption process. Environmental concerns will become critical, and pollution as well as the shortage of raw materials will place constraints on marketers. In the future, it is likely that substantial attention will be paid to environmental protection, and marketers will have to adapt their strategies to respond to consumers' and governments' environmental demands (see Figure 17-5).

Figure 17-5: China's cities are heavily polluted. To see the blue sky, one has to fly (high).

In terms of promotion, firms will compete on their ability to resonate themes that appeal to world consumers, and most efforts will be in the area of integrating their messages. Integrated marketing communications are becoming standard for both international consumer product companies and for business-to-business communications. Furthermore, consumers will expect extensive information on the websites of companies with which they do business.

With regard to distribution, companies will continue to pursue measures to reduce costs by adopting just-in-time inventory systems and creating product flows rather than stocks. They will also coordinate their inventory systems with suppliers and clients through improved versions of or alternatives to electronic data interchange.

Entertainment will be especially important when communicating with consumers in all retailing environments (see International Marketing Illustration 17-2 on the next page).

Finally, the future will be characterized by greater price competition and broader price alignment, as local businesses and multinationals compete over markets. This competitive surge is likely to be accompanied by increased governmental scrutiny.

International Marketing Illustration 17-2
Shoppertainment: The Future of Retailing

Brand experiences are thought to be the future of international marketing. Shoppertainment is the logical blend of retailing and leisure that increases the guests' length of stay and, importantly, the total spending on the retailer's premises. World retail brands and consumer product companies in the new millennium are aiming to create entertaining in-store environments that delight customers and increase the likelihood of repeat visits and spending.

Shoppertainment takes different forms. A factory outlet center in Livingston, Scotland, has one of the largest indoor Ferris wheels in the world. A large shopping center in Kent, England, has a nondenominational prayer "Quiet Room" with hair- and feet-washing facilities for Muslim guests. Girl Heaven has hot pink, glitter-flecked floors and training counters that teach teens the latest nightclub dance moves and makeup and hairstyle trends. Common are themed food courts, on-site jugglers and face painters, shuttle trains to parking lots, and onsite day-care centers. Large bookstores are partnering with Starbucks and other similar chains to attract shoppers who will drink coffee, leaf through a few magazines, and ultimately purchase a few books.

And Starbucks itself has reinvented itself as a brand that speaks to consumers in a way that is uniquely relevant to their stage of life, self-image, culture, or specific shopping motivation. Here, customers get more than coffee: They get great service and music and a comfortable upbeat meeting place where many peers show up. Together, these elements create a social club of consumption that is the unique Starbucks experience. And the Starbucks experience is continuously reinventing itself to appeal to its target market, with music and film and with new food, coffee, and tea offerings that are characterized by unique and innovative personalities, which allow Starbucks to appeal to a broad base.

Brick-and-mortar retailers worldwide are competing with online shopping and e-commerce, especially in developed countries. They are also competing for shoppers with limited time who expect a memorable and pleasant shopping experience. In the future, the competition will extend to emerging markets and developing countries, and marketers will need to devise global strategies for entertaining consumers as they engage in consumption: Experiential consumption will be the norm worldwide.

Source: 2007 Global Powers of Retailing, Deloitte, Touche, and Tohmatsu, www.stores.com; Allyson L. Stewart-Allen, "Europe Says 'That's Shoppertainment,'" *Marketing News,* Vol. 33, No. 17, August 16, 1999, p. 7.

Summary

Identify the factors in a firm's external and internal environment that determine the organizational design best suited for international operations. Organizational design is determined externally by the competitive environment: Intense competition requires a company to react quickly, and it can do so effectively if it has a decentralized structure. Companies operating in environments plagued by high inflation, unemployment, and political instability must be organized to be able to react quickly to changes. Multinational companies are likely to have similar operating structures to those in their home country if the countries where they operate are culturally similar to their own country. Companies that have competent, educated, local employees are likely to delegate more control to local operations. Companies that operate in a region with common traits, or within a regional bloc, will most likely organize the company with a regional focus. Firm traits such as degree of focus on international operations or its organization in the home country also have an impact on organizational structure.

Describe different organizational designs and offer examples of designs that different international firms have adopted. The four organizational designs for international operations are the international division structure, for firms with limited international involvement that are likely to have an export department; firms with a worldwide regional division structure, which operate either by region or by country; firms with a product division structure, where subsidiaries report to the product division with responsibility for the respective product; and firms with a matrix structure, which combine functional areas, product, and region in their organization.

Identify formal and informal controls necessary to ensure that company operations are in line with company goals and objectives as stated in the strategic plan. Formal controls involve establishing performance standards, measuring performance, and addressing discrepancies by either changing the standards to correct for differences in market traits or changing executive compensation to reflect firm priorities. Informal controls involve maintaining contact between headquarters and international operations, rotating managers to share experience with new operations, and appropriately indoctrinating new employees in the company's culture.

Key Terms

formal controls

informal controls

international division structure

matrix structure

organizational design

organizational structure

performance standards

product division structure

worldwide regional division structure

Discussion Questions

1. List the factors that influence organizational design. Describe how each factor influences the design.

2. Compare the international division structure and the regional division structure. What would make a company move from an international division structure to a regional division structure?

3. How does the matrix structure differ from the other three organizational structures? Explain.

4. Discuss the formal and informal controls used to ensure that international marketing operations are in line with company goals and objectives.

Chapter Quiz

True/False

1. Companies operating in countries characterized by unstable political environments or countries where government policies are unstable need an organizational structure that allows them to react quickly.

Answer: True

Rationale: Companies operating in politically unstable countries need an organizational structure that allows them to react quickly; they need to be able to take immediate action to adapt to the new environments.

Section 17-1a, "Factors in the Firm's Environment"

2. Companies operating in countries that have ample educated and qualified labor are more likely to be centralized.

Answer: False

Rationale: Companies operating in countries that have ample educated and qualified labor delegate more control to local operations and have organizational structures that allow for more local control.

Section 17-1a, "Factors in the Firm's Environment"

3. A worldwide regional division structure has two main divisions: the domestic division and the international division.

Answer: False

Rationale: A worldwide regional division structure configures operations either by geographic region or by country.

Section 17-2b, "The Worldwide Regional Division Structure"

4. An advantage of the worldwide regional division structure is that it is better equipped to immediately process and respond to country-specific information and conditions than other formal structures.

Answer: True

Rationale: A particular advantage of the worldwide regional division structure is that it is better equipped to immediately process and respond to country-specific information and conditions than other formal structures—at some cost to product-related information—because of its strong regional focus.

Section 17-2b, "The Worldwide Regional Division Structure"

5. In a regional or worldwide matrix division structure, subsidiaries report to the product division (strategic business unit) with responsibility for the particular products.

Answer: False

Rationale: In a regional or worldwide product division structure, subsidiaries report to the product division (strategic business unit) with responsibility for the particular products.

Section 17-2c, "The Product Division Structure"

6. Informal controls are used in international marketing to ensure that international company operations are in line with company goals and objectives.

Answer: True

Rationale: Informal controls, such as coordinating activities and ensuring clear communication of expectations, rotating managers to different assignments to obtain the maximum benefit from international experience, and training employees and inculcating a management culture that is consistent with company goals and objectives, are used in international marketing to ensure that international company operations are in line with company goals and objectives.

Section 17-3b, "Informal Controls"

Multiple Choice

1.   Which of the following companies has a worldwide regional division structure?

a.   Frito-Lay

b.   Coke

c.   Eli Lilly

d.   None of the above

Answer: a is correct.

Rationale: Frito-Lay has a worldwide regional division structure. The Frito-Lay Company, headquartered in the United States, oversees all the functional areas (i.e., marketing, manufacturing, research and development, finance, etc.). The regional divisions—Frito-Lay North America, headquartered in the United States; Frito-Lay Europe/Africa/Middle East, headquartered in Geneva, Switzerland; and Frito-Lay Latin America/Asia Pacific/Australia—oversee all regional operations, country subsidiaries, and offices.

Section 17-2b, "The Worldwide Regional Division Structure"

2.   Which of the following companies has a matrix structure?

a.   IBM

b.   Unilever

c.   Disney

d.   All of the above

Answer: d is correct.

Rationale: The matrix format works especially well for firms that have global brands as well as local brands; such companies need to coordinate marketing activities worldwide involving the global brands and need to focus on the local market for the local brands.

Section 17-2d, "The Matrix Structure"

3.   What is the process for instituting formal controls?

a.   Measuring performance, establishing standards, addressing discrepancies

b.   Establishing standards, measuring performance, addressing discrepancies

c.   Addressing discrepancies, establishing standards, measuring performance

d.   None of the above

Answer: b is correct.

Rationale: The first step in establishing formal controls involves establishing performance standards in light of the company's projected market potential. The next step involves measuring performance and comparing with the standards.

Section 17-3a, "Formal Controls"

4.   In spite of extensive Internet access worldwide, companies are not equipped to handle sales due to

a.   language and cultural barriers.

b.   difficulty handling the destination country's import and tax regulations.

c.   difficulty in handling export controls in the home country.

d.   all of the above

Answer: d is correct.

Rationale: Many potential transactions are turned away annually by companies doing business on the Internet due to language and cultural barriers, difficulties handling the destination country's import and tax regulations, or export controls in the home country. In addition, payment mechanisms are cumbersome, and there is a high rate of credit card theft.

Section 17-4, "International Marketing: Future Perspectives"

Chapter 17 Endnotes

1.   Jeffrey E. Garten, "Cutting Fat Won't Be Enough to Survive This Crisis," *BusinessWeek,* No. 3603, November 9, 1998, p. 26.

2.   Jason Stamper, "Borland Slashes Staff in Reorganization," Datamonitor, online edition, May 4, 2006.

3.   Allen J. Morrison, David A. Ricks, and Kendall Roth, "Globalization Versus Regionalization: Which Way for the Multinational?" *Organizational Dynamics,* Vol. 19, No. 3, Winter 1991, pp. 17–29.

4.   Bruce T. Lamont, V. Sambamurthy, Kimberly M. Ellis, and Paul G. Simmonds, "The Influence of Organizational Structure on the Information Received by Corporate Strategists of Multinational Enterprises," *Management International Review,* Vol. 40, No. 3, Third Quarter 2000, pp. 231–252.

5.   www.Unilever.com

6.   Ravi Dharwadkar, Gerard George, and Pamela Brandes, "Privatization in Emerging Economies: An Agency Theory Perspective," *Academy of Management: The Academy of Management Review,* Vol. 25, No. 3, July 2000, pp. 650–669.

7.   Masaaki Kotabe, *Global Sourcing Strategy: R&D, Manufacturing, and Marketing,* New York: Quoruom Books, 1992.

8.   *Annual Report, Procter & Gamble,* 2000.

9.   "R&D's Formula for Success," www.pg.com/science, September 24, 2004.

10.   Internet World Statistics, www.internetworldstats.com/stats.htm (accessed June 14, 2012); Nielsen Netratings, www.nielsen-netratings.com (accessed June 3, 2007).

11.   Rob Gerlsbeck, "Are Canadians and Americans Different Online Too?" *Marketing,* Vol. 112, No. 6, March 26, 2007, p. 10.

12.   Marketresearch.com, *Global Online Retail Report,* October 11, 2011, www.marketresearch.com/MarketLine-v3883/Global-Online-Retail-6652143.

13.   First Search Industry Profile, *Internet & Mail-Order Retail,* Hoover, Inc., June 25, 2012.

Case 17-1

iPhone: A Gem – But Not without Controversy

What is made in Taiwan, looks really cute, and left many leading European companies with their "nose out of joint" because they were initially rejected as its partners? Here is another hint: It combines a mobile phone, a widescreen iPod, and an Internet device into a handheld device, with full-screen web browsing, a multi-touch screen, and useful applications, such as GPS and wireless streaming of YouTube videos. It is the product that came with much buzz in 2007, when it was introduced, that bloggers called it the "Jesus Phone," a product that sold by the hundreds of thousands before it was even available on the market. It is, of course, the iPhone.

With the iPhone, Apple muscled its way into one of the world's most brutally competitive markets, rattling the cell phone industry's most dominant players by producing the number one must-have mobile phone on the market, a true innovation that changed consumer expectations about the capabilities of a smart phone.

The Service Provider Controversy

The first controversy that engaged the iPhone even before it was out on the market was its choice of providers during the first two years. In the United States, it limited its access to AT&T, America's largest wireless phone company. In Europe, multinational powerhouses Vodafone, France Telecom, Spain's Telefónica, and Germany's Deutsche Telekom's T-Mobile clamored for the honor to be the iPhone carriers. The stakes were high: The winner would sell more than six million iPhones over three years, and, most likely, half of that would be new service contracts. Speculations that Vodafone would get the deal sent its stock soaring. And then its stock took a dive when it was announced that Vodafone was off the list.

The European countries where the iPhone was launched are the same countries where Apple chose to launch its iTunes music stores: Germany, France, and the United Kingdom. And the winning service providers were Deutsche Telekom's T-Mobile in Germany, France Telecom's Orange network in France, and Spain's Telefónica's O2 network in the United Kingdom. Each provider is the largest in the three respective countries. However, industry experts believe that it would have been in Apple's best interest to have more than one operator distribute the phone because the European market is much more fragmented than the market in the United States. Moreover, T-Mobile has little or no presence in Italy, Spain, or France, whereas Vodafone is present in all European markets and beyond.

In the negotiations, one of the main concerns was that Apple's deals were much more onerous than previous agreements with other handset makers. For example, in the United States, the agreement between Apple and AT&T clearly put Apple in the driving seat, giving it a share of the customer revenue, which was substantial, as the iPhone was priced at $499 for the 4 GB model and $599 for the 8 GB model. In Europe, the iPhone is priced at €450 for the 8 GB model in the three countries. Moreover, for European customers, the iPhone ran on the same 2.5G data connection network as U.S. phones did in 2007, instead of on the faster 3G technology common in Europe at that time.

The provider controversy was eventually resolved and the product is now carried by the previously slighted providers, and by many carriers in emerging markets. In fact, the iPhone is performing phenomenally well even in markets where it was believed that consumers might not be able to afford it. In 2012, Apple's total revenue was $39.19 billion, up from $24.67 billion a year earlier. In China alone, it sold well over 100 million iPhones in 2011, with the Chinese market accounting for about 20 percent of Apple's revenues.

The Labor Controversy

Among the companies that benefited the most from iPhone's success were a handful of Taiwanese companies known only by a few consumers or investors. Apple does not manufacture most of its products—instead it hires manufacturing specialists: Taiwanese companies with extensive operations in China that assemble Apple's gadgets based on Apple's designs. They use parts from many suppliers throughout Asia who are running complex and labor-intensive production lines in China. Among these companies is Foxconn International Holdings Ltd., the Hong Kong unit of Hon Hai Precision Industry Co., the world's biggest electronics contract manufacturer by revenue. Hon Hai is in charge of handling the iPhone's assembly. Catcher Technology Co., which makes stainless-metal casing increasingly popular for cell phones and notebook personal computers, is supplying iPhone's casing. Other Taiwanese companies involved in the manufacturing of the iPhone are Primax Electronics Ltd., which makes digital camera modules for cell phones; Entery Industrial Co., a maker of connectors that join other components; and Unimicron Technology Corp., which makes printed circuit boards.

Manufacturing the iPhone in China and Taiwan allows Apple to reap immense profits and to keep prices relatively competitive. Apparently, however, this comes at a cost to the workers and to Apple's image. In China, workers assembling iPhones work in harsh conditions, facing daily hazards and deadly safety conditions. Employees, some of them under-age, are often forced to work excessive overtime, 7 days a week, and their legs swell until they can barely walk, and they live in dorms that are overcrowded at supplier's Foxconn's factories in Chengdu and Shenzhen. Suppliers in particular have falsified records and have improperly disposed of hazardous waste. In 2010, 137 workers working for a supplier in eastern China were injured after they were ordered to use a poisonous chemical to clean the phone's screens, and, in 2011, there were two explosions at iPad factories that killed four people and injured 77. At Foxconn's Chengdu factory, banners on the walls state "Work hard on the job today or work hard to find a job tomorrow." There, some workers worked as much as 12 hour days, or they worked back-to-back shifts to manufacture the iPhone. Apple claims it is strict with violators, terminating suppliers if they do not rectify the violations. In reality, fewer than 15 suppliers have been terminated for such violations since 2007.

And the Tax Controversy

Apple's earnings in 2012 were about $45.6 billion, but the taxes the company paid were minimal, compared to other companies. Apple's headquarters are in Cupertino, California, but it has an office in Reno Nevada to collect the company's profits, to take advantage of Nevada's tax rate, zero (compared with California's, at 8.84 percent). Apple similarly sidesteps income taxes on its worldwide gains by using subsidiaries in low-tax havens, such as Ireland, the Netherlands, Luxembourg and the British Virgin Islands – in some of these places, it has little more than a letterbox or a small office.

As a technology giant, Apple benefits from tax codes written for the industrial age which are not as well suited for the digital age: many of its profits are made from royalties on intellectual property, such as patents, software, apps, and downloaded songs and ringtones. Such profits are easier to move to low-tax states and countries.

Apple pioneered an accounting technique known as the "Double Irish With a Dutch Sandwich," which helped it lower its taxes by routing profits through Irish and Dutch subsidiaries and from there to the Caribbean, a tactic used by many other imitators today. If it had not used these tactics, Apple would have had to pay about $2.4 billion more in taxes in 2011. The company paid $3.3 billion in taxes on profits of $34.2 billion, at a tax rate of 9.8 percent. In comparison, Wal-Mart Stores paid $5.9 billion in taxes on profits of $24.4 billion, at a tax rate of 24 percent.

Sources: Nick Wingfield, "Apple Profit Rises on Higher iPhone and iPad Sales," *The New York Times*, April 24, 2012, www.nytimes.com; Charles Duhigg and David Barboza, "In China, Human Costs Are Built Into an iPad," January 25, 2012, www.nytimes.com; Charles Duhigg and David Kocieniewski, "How Apple Sidesteps Billions in Taxes," *The New York Times*, April 28, 2012, www.nytimes.com; Mark Halper, "Can Nokia Beat iPhone at Its Own Tunes?" *Fortune*, Vol. 156, No. 3, August 6, 2007, p. 12; Andrew Parker and Maija Palmer, "O2 Near iPhone Partnership," *FT.com*, July 5, 2007; *Financial Express*, "Genius Behind the iPhone Hype," July 2, 2007; *Marketing Week*, "T-Mobile Looks Set to Win Euro Distribution Rights for the iPhone," May 10, 2007, 8; Peter H. Lewis, "How Apple Kept Its iPhone Secrets, *CNN Money*, January 12, 2007; Jason Dean and Chiu Piling, "Taiwan Makers May Wring Big Profits from iPhone," *Wall Street Journal*, January 11, 2007, C1; Owen Thomas, "Apple: Hello, iPhone," *CNN Money*, January 9 2007.

Analysis Suggestions:

1. Describe iPhone's international presence. Discuss iPhone's entry modes during the introduction phase.

2. How is Apple leveraging its competitive advantage in each of the international markets discussed?

3. Firms' viability in international markets is predicated on offering a coveted product at a reasonable cost. How is Apple attempting to keep costs at a reasonable level and yet still provide staggering profits for investors? Comment on the strategies the company is using and on their long-term viability.

Appendix

The International Marketing Plan

OVERVIEW

The international marketing plan is an essential element of a company's strategic plan because it is an effort to maintain a fit between company objectives and capabilities and the continuously changing international environment. Students are advised to first focus on corporate planning and, subsequently, on the specific international marketing strategy.

The steps outlined in this blueprint are general and should be adapted based on the information available and based on the industry and on the country conditions at the time of the analysis.

STEP 1: ANALYZING THE COMPANY AND COUNTRY BACKGROUND

As a first step, the marketing plan should include a brief company background, with a focus on the product that will be marketed internationally and the country where the product will be introduced.

The company should rely on its mission statement to articulate its vision and principles for its international endeavors, underscoring the distinctive differentiating aspects of the business and the company's approach to its different stakeholders: consumers, employees, society. It should rely on its overall goals and objectives to create the specific goals and objectives for the international market. The company objectives may be to enter new international markets or to increase market share in its existing markets. Or they may involve focusing on research and development in order to bring leading-edge technology to the marketplace worldwide. Objectives can also be expressed in terms of societal outcomes, such as increasing literacy or reducing world hunger, depending on the focus of the business.

The ultimate organizational goal is creating profit for the company and wealth for its shareholders. Company goals could include increasing productivity and production volume; lowering labor costs by moving production to countries with low-cost labor; maximizing consumption of consumers worldwide; and, as a result, increasing sales.

In the process of achieving these organizational goals, companies compete to offer a wide variety of goods and services and a maximum number of choices for consumers. As they compete, they lower prices that consumers pay for their products to gain market share.

This step of the analysis could include the following information:

- Brief profile of the company

- Brief product profile

- Brief country background

- Rationale for introducing the product to the respective country

STEP 2: ANALYZING THE ENVIRONMENT

In the second step, the local and regional environment must be assessed to evaluate the country and target market attractiveness. At this stage, the local economy and the trade, political, and legal infrastructures are evaluated to determine the extent to which investing in the country constitutes a sound decision. The sociocultural environment also is assessed to identify the most viable marketing strategy to use in the respective country. Finally, the competitive environment is examined. Here, the competitive intensity (local and international) and the existing and potential barriers to entry imposed by the competition are evaluated to determine the resources needed for market penetration.

This step of the analysis could include the information on the following topics:

Economic and Trade Analysis

Population statistics and relevance of demographics to company plans

Economic development statistics (GNP, GDP, economic growth) and relevance to company plans

Overview of industrial and agricultural sectors, national resources, and labor

Analysis of transportation and telecommunication infrastructure

General analysis of the marketing support structure:

> Distribution and logistics
>
> Promotion infrastructure
>
> Marketing research suppliers

Trade trends:

> Membership in regional and international trade organizations
>
> Trade patterns (imports, exports, foreign direct investment) and rate of growth
>
> Barriers to trade

Political and Legal Analysis

Political stability:

> Legitimacy of political elite
>
> Diversity of ethnic groups with divergent interests
>
> Degree of political repression
>
> Nationalism
>
> Stability of government policies

Type of legal system

Transparency of the legal system

Degree of ambiguity of commercial laws

Degree to which laws are followed and enforced

Sociocultural Analysis

Languages and dialects and implications for marketing

Social institutions and implications for the company:

> Family
>
> Social class
>
> Social status
>
> Social groups and group dynamics

Religion, norms, and value systems and marketing implications

Target Market and Competitive Analysis

Target consumer analysis (product use, shopping behavior)

Existing distribution patterns for product category and availability of local distributors (wholesalers, retailers, logistics companies)

Existing promotion patterns for product category and availability of local promotion talent and media

Degree of competitive intensity

Competitor marketing strategies

Competitive barriers

STEP 3: EVALUATING THE INTERNATIONAL BUSINESS PORTFOLIO

The third step involves evaluating the different strategic business units of the international company. At this stage, the company must identify the products that have great promise in the marketplace and need additional resources, the products that are performing well in a mature market, and those that are not and must be divested. Establishing a strategic fit with the market is essential. Companies may have the resources to support a particular strategic business unit, but if the unit does not fit with the company's long-term goals, or if selling the unit would generate resources that could be invested to further the company's goals, the company may consider selling this particular business. Companies periodically review their different businesses and make decisions on whether to acquire new ones or divest those that might be unprofitable or that do not represent a good fit with the company.

Each business unit must develop its own mission statement, focusing on the strategic fit between resources and the company goals with regard to its international target markets. The mission statement of the business unit should be more specific than the corporate mission statement, focusing on the brand or product itself.

An important step in the analysis process involves identifying the company's strengths, weaknesses, opportunities, and threats (SWOT). Students should first examine the microenvironment of marketing, addressing its strengths and weaknesses; more specifically, students should examine strengths and weaknesses related to the company, consumers, suppliers, intermediaries, and other facilitators of marketing functions, as well as those of the competition. Next, students should examine threats and opportunities in the international sociodemographic and cultural environment, the economic and natural environment, the technological environment, and the political and legal environment. To facilitate the analysis, students can use Table A-1 and Table A-2 for each region or country.

Table A-1	Microenvironment, Country A	
	List of Strengths	**List of Weaknesses**
Company		
Consumers		
Suppliers		
Intermediaries		
Other facilitators		
Competition		

Table A-2	Macroenvironment, Country A	
	List of Threats	List of Opportunities
Sociodemographic and cultural environment		
Economic environment		
Natural environment		
Technological environment		
Political environment		
Legal environment		

STEP 4: DEVELOPING THE INTERNATIONAL MARKETING PLAN

The marketing plan focuses on the strategic business unit the company has selected: a product or service that the company has proposed to analyze. It involves the following topics:

Setting marketing objectives (express objectives in terms of sales, profit, and market share) based on corporate goals and objectives and market potential:

Product Decisions:

Decisions on standardization versus adaptation

Product mix decisions (short and long term) for the market

Promotion Decisions:

Advertising objectives

Media decisions

Message decisions

Distribution Decisions:

Decisions on whether to use existing channels or to build distribution

Decisions on wholesalers, retailers, warehousing, and logistics firms

Logistics decisions (intermodal transportation, freight forwarders, customs brokers, insurance agents, other facilitators)

Pricing Decisions:

Identifying local market traits and needs and product cost

Developing an international marketing budget based on cost

Identifying human and capital resources needed for local operations

Identifying International Marketing Objectives

Marketing objectives could be defined in terms of dollar sales or units sold, profit, or in terms of market share.

Defining the Marketing Strategy

The marketing strategy involves identifying international segments that are similar with regard to key traits and those who would respond well to a product and related marketing mix (market segmentation); selecting the segments that the company can serve most efficiently and developing products tailored to each (market targeting); and offering the products to the market, communicating, through the marketing mix, product traits and benefits that differentiate it in the consumer's mind (market positioning).

At this stage, students should identify the different international market segments, select the segments that represent the best fit with the company goals and objectives for the respective international market, and design the strategies aimed to serve these segments more effectively than competitors.

Developing the Marketing Mix for the International Market

At this stage, international marketing mix decisions address product, price, promotion, and distribution strategies that will be used for entering the international target market and the controls needed to evaluate marketing performance.

Product: Decide on design, features, brand name, packaging, and service components for a particular market. Refer to Chapter 9, "Products and Services: Branding Decisions in International Markets," and Chapter 10, "International Product and Service Strategies."

Place: Decide on the types of channels used, market coverage, assortment, transportation and logistics, and inventory management. Refer to Chapter 11, "Managing International Distribution Operations and Logistics," and Chapter 12, "International Retailing."

Price: Decide on the price, discounts, and credit terms. Refer to Chapter 16, "International Pricing Strategy."

Promotion: Decide on advertising, personal selling, sales promotion, public relations, and publicity that the company should pursue. Refer to Chapter 13, "The International Promotional Mix and Advertising Strategies," Chapter 14, "International Publicity, Public Relations, and Sales Promotion Strategies," and Chapter 15, "International Personal Selling and Personnel Management."

STEP 5: ESTABLISHING METHODS FOR IMPLEMENTATION AND CONTROL OF THE INTERNATIONAL OPERATION

Students should suggest how marketing plans can be turned into marketing action programs to accomplish the international marketing objectives.

The company will set performance standards and related controls to ensure that performance is in line with market potential given the country-specific operating environment.

This step of the analysis could include the following information:

- Standards for operation in light of market potential

- Proposed performance measures in light of goals and objectives

- Methods for addressing discrepancies

Appendix B

Glossary

A

accessibility: The ability to communicate with the international target market.

acculturation: The act of learning a new culture; encompasses intercultural interaction and adaptation.

actionability: The extent to which the target market segment is responsive to the marketing strategies used.

adaptation: The strategy of altering a product to better meet the needs of a local market.

adaptation of the advertising strategy: The act of changing a company's promotional mix to each country or market or creating local campaigns.

adiaphoras: The norms that refer to customs that a foreign national may engage in but is not necessarily expected to do so.

advertising effectiveness research: Studies conducted to examine the effectiveness and appropriateness of advertisements aimed at individual markets.

advocacy advertising: Advertising a particular position or point of view.

African Development Bank: A bank, headquartered in Abidjan, Ivory Coast, that has as a primary goal poverty reduction in Africa, providing support and expertise in agriculture, human resources, and health services, with an emphasis on small business. (See www.afdb.org.)

aggressive export pricing: A pricing strategy that prices products below market price to penetrate new markets.

all-purpose discount stores: General merchandise discount stores that offer a wide variety of merchandise and limited depth.

all-you-can-afford method: The process of allocating the maximum amount possible to advertising; this method is used by small and medium-sized corporations.

analogy method: A method for estimation that relies on developments and findings in similar markets or where the product is in the same life cycle stage.

Andean Common Market (AnCom): A trade group of the Andean countries that aspires to become a common market; it is currently in the process of agreeing on common external tariffs. (See www.comunidadandina.org.)

antidumping: Legislation designed to counter unfair price competition; lengthy antidumping investigations can also serve as an impediment to trade.

antidumping duties: Duties that must be paid by firms as a punishment for engaging in unfair price competition.

antitrust laws: Laws designed to prevent anticompetitive activities, such as the creation of monopolies and cartels.

appearances: An individual's physical attire and overall grooming.

applications positioning: The marketing of a precise product application that is differentiated in the consumers' minds from other products that have a more general use.

arbitration: Binding procedure for conflict resolution involving an independent third party; a faster and less costly procedure than a lawsuit.

ASEAN Free Trade Area (AFTA): A free trade agreement signed by members of the Association of Southeast Asian Nations (ASEAN). (See www.aseansec.org.)

Asian Development Bank: A bank, headquartered in Manila, the Philippines, that focuses on the private sector in Asia, sponsoring projects aimed at increasing access to technology and improving the functioning of government in the region. (See www.adb.org.)

Asia-Pacific Economic Cooperation (APEC): A trade group including all major economies of the Asia-Pacific region, it is a forum for economic cooperation and has as its goal the gradual reduction of barriers to trade and investment between member countries. (See www.apec.org.)

assimilation: The act of abandoning all home-country traditions while learning a new culture.

Association of Southeast Asian Nations (ASEAN): A successful example of integration in Asia, creating an environment that promotes mutual involvement in industrial development in the region and a free trade area composed of Brunei, Cambodia, Indonesia, Laos, Malaysia, Myanmar, the Philippines, Singapore, Thailand, and Vietnam. (See www.aseansec.org.)

attribute/benefit positioning: Positioning that communicates product attributes and benefits, differentiating each brand from the other company brands and from those of competitors.

automatic import license: A license granted freely to importing companies but may be used by government for the purpose of import surveillance, thus discouraging import surges, imposing administrative and financial burdens on importers, and delaying shipment.

B

back translation: The translation of translated text back into its original language, by a different individual, to ensure that the instrument has been translated as intended.

barter: A simple, nonmonetized exchange of goods and services between two parties.

benefit segmentation: The process of identifying international market segments based on important differences between the benefits sought by the target market from purchasing a particular product.

big emerging markets (BEMs): Large markets characterized by rapid economic development and high potential; big emerging markets set the pace for the economy in their geographic region.

bilateral agreement: Regional trade cooperation between two countries aimed at reducing or eliminating trade barriers for all or for selected products.

billboards: Advertisements in public areas appearing on large posters or electronic panels.

blocked currency: A strategy that does not allow importers to exchange local currency for the seller's currency or a currency that the seller is willing to accept as payment (hard currency).

bourgeoisie: A dominant social class, which, according to Marxist-Leninist theory, establishes lucrative means of production and achieves high productivity at the expense of exploited workers.

boycott: An action calling for a ban on consumption of all goods associated with a particular company or country.

brand awareness research: Research investigating how consumers' knowledge and recognition of a brand name affect their purchasing behavior.

brand name counterfeiting: Selling counterfeit products as brand name originals.

brand name generation and testing: The testing of brand names and logos; necessary when companies market their products internationally.

broadcast medium: A nonpersonal channel of communication such as television or radio.

brokers and agents: Intermediaries who bring international buyers and sellers together; they do not carry title to the product.

building channels: Creating new distribution channels, especially necessary in situations where there are no channels at all, or there are no channels that conform to the needs of the company.

buyback agreements: Agreements whereby the seller builds and provides a turnkey plant and is paid up front part of the cost of the plant in an agreed on convertible currency; in return, the seller agrees to purchase specific quantities of the plant's output over an extended period of time.

buyer behavior research: Research examining brand preferences and brand attitudes.

buying offices: Buyers representing different firms located abroad.

C

capitalism: A stage of economic and political development, which, according to Marxist-Leninist theory, is characterized, in its early stages, by an emerging bourgeoisie, the shift of production from the agrarian sector to the industrial sector, and, in its later stages, by imperialism, where capital loses its national identity by crossing borders and establishing monopolies.

catalog retailers: Retailers selling products through mail catalogs.

catalog showrooms: Showrooms displaying the products of catalog retailers, offering high turnover, brand name goods at discount prices.

category killers: Large general merchandise discount stores that carry a narrow variety of merchandise and a wide assortment; also called category specialists or stores with category dominance.

category specialists: Large general merchandise discount stores that carry a narrow variety of merchandise and a wide assortment; also called category killers.

causal research: Research that examines cause-and-effect relationships.

Central American Common Market (CACM): An economic agreement between Central American countries; this agreement includes plans for forming a regional economic union similar to the European Union and to advance regional and international trade.

channel of communication: The medium used to communicate a message about a product to the consumer.

channel performance and coverage studies: Studies investigating whether existing channels are appropriate for communication, if channels exist at all, or whether they are appropriate for international marketing communications.

chronemics: The timing of verbal exchanges.

clearing account: A complex form of countertrade whereby countries trade products up to a certain amount stated in a particular, mutually–agreed on hard currency and within a given time frame, and, when an imbalance occurs and one country owes money to the other, swing credits are paid in an agreed on hard currency, known as the clearing currency; also called a clearing agreement.

clearing currency: The agreed on currency used to pay swing credits in a clearing account or agreement.

code law: Comprehensive written laws that specify what constitutes legal behavior.

collectivism: The degree to which individuals prefer to act in the interest of the group, rather than in their own self-interest.

combination stores: Medium-sized retail stores that combine food and drug retailing.

common law: Laws that are based on prior court rulings (legal precedents).

common market: A market composed of member countries, characterized by the unrestricted movement of goods, labor, and capital.

Common Market for Eastern and Southern Africa (COMESA): An agreement between 20 member countries aimed at achieving economic integration; COMESA is currently eliminating all tariff and nontariff barriers to trade and is in the process of adopting common external tariffs.

Commonwealth of Independent States (CIS): A political agreement between the twelve non-Baltic countries of the former Soviet Union. (See www.cis.minsk.by.)

communism: A stage in economic and political development, which, according to Marxist-Leninist theory, is characterized by state and cooperative ownership of all means of production and property.

company publications: Public relations publications that describe the products of a company to potential customers and summarize financial achievements.

comparative advantage: The premise that countries benefit from specialization in an industry where they have comparative advantage and from trading with one another.

compensation: The payment in products and in cash, usually in a mutually –agreed on convertible currency.

competitive pricing analyses: Pricing studies that determine the price the market will bear for the respective product category.

competitive-parity method: The strategy of using competitors' level of advertising spending as a benchmark for the company's own advertising expenditures.

competitor positioning: The process of comparing the firm's brand with those of competitors, directly or indirectly.

complementary export agents: Firms that export other firms' products that are complementary to their offerings, along with their own products, for a fee/commission.

complementary export merchants: Distributors who take title to the complementary products distributed and are compensated in the form of a discount.

comprador: A foreign agent with an exclusive arrangement with a company, representing its operations in a particular country; also referred to as a managing agent.

concentrated targeting: The process of selecting only one market segment and targeting it with a single brand.

concept development and testing studies: Concept tests usually performed in developed countries evaluating the product/service offering and the related marketing mix in light of the different international target markets.

conceptual equivalence: The extent to which meanings remain the same in different cultural environments.

confiscation: The foreign government seizure of company assets and investors' assets without any compensation.

consortia: A company created with the participation of three or more companies; allowed in underserved markets or in domains where the government and the marketplace can control its monopolistic activity.

consumer segmentation studies: Research conducted to identify market segment profiles.

content analysis: Method that assesses the content of advertisements in a medium with verbal and visual content.

continuous innovation: Product innovation where there is no disruption in consumption patterns; such innovations involve product alterations such as new flavors or new products that are improvements over the old offerings.

contract manufacturing: A relationship between two companies wherein one company contracts with another to manufacture products according to the contracting company's specifications and for a specified period of time.

controlled test marketing: Test marketing that involves offering a new product to a group of stores and evaluating the market's reaction to it.

convenience stores: Small retailers located in residential areas, open long hours, and carrying limited lines of high-turnover necessities.

conventional supermarkets: Self-service food retailers with annual sales of more than $2 million and with an area less than 20,000 square feet.

cooperative export arrangements: Agreements that involve the use of a distribution system of exporters with established systems of selling abroad, who agree to handle the export function of a noncompeting (but not necessarily unrelated) company on a contractual basis; also called mother henning or piggybacking.

cooperative exporting: Using the distribution system of exporters with established systems of selling abroad who agree to handle the export function of a noncompeting (but not necessarily unrelated) company on a contractual basis; also called mother henning and piggybacking.

copyright: The rights to an original work of art (literature, music, film, design, and other works), enabling the owner to reproduce, sell, perform, or film the work.

core product strategy: The strategy of using the same standard core product/service worldwide, but varying certain aspects of the offering (product ingredients, advertising) from market to market.

corporate advertising: A type of advertising that is used to promote the company behind the different brands.

corruption laws: Laws designed to prevent multinational corporations from using unethical means to obtain competitive advantage in a particular market.

cost analyses: Methods used for projecting the cost of research.

cost-based transfer pricing: A pricing strategy used in intra-firm sales for commercial transactions between units of the same corporation, within or beyond the national borders of the parent company, where the costs reflect the estimated opportunity costs of the product.

cost-of-living adjustment: A compensation incentive whereby the company adjusts expatriate salaries to reflect the cost of living in the new environment at standards in the expatriate's home country; also called post-adjustment.

Council of Ministers: The decision-making body (the legislature) of the European Union, composed of one minister from each member country.

Council of Mutual Economic Assistance (CMEA): A trade agreement between the countries of the Soviet Bloc that disintegrated after the fall of communism. CMEA was an economic body similar in nature to a free trade area and approached what would be considered a political union.

Council of Nations: The constitutional council of the European Union consisting of representatives from parliaments of EU member states. (See www.europa.eu.int.)

counterpurchase: A form of trade that involves two exchanges paid for in cash; it involves two parallel contracts whereby the seller agrees to purchase products that are usually unrelated to its business from the buyer and sell them on international markets; also called parallel barter.

countertrade: A form of trade whereby a company sells a product to a buyer and agrees to accept, in return for payment, products from the buyer's firm or from the trade agency/institution of the buyer.

countervailing duties: Duties imposed on subsidized products imported into a country.

countervailing duty actions: Investigations initiated to determine whether imports are sold below fair prices as a result of foreign subsidies and the subsequent establishment of measures to offset subsidies.

country of manufacture: The country in which a particular product is manufactured.

country of origin: The country with which a particular product or service is associated.

creeping expropriation: A situation characterized by bureaucratic red tape and corruption, an unreliable judicial system, and shifting regulations, where foreign government actions discourage foreign investment, especially investment in nonessential sectors.

cross-border shopping: Purchasing products from a neighboring country where the consumers may be charged lower duties.

cultural variability: The classification of cultures on a number of dimensions, or continuums; Hofstede classified cultures on the dimensions of collectivism, masculinity, power distance, and uncertainty avoidance.

culture: The continuously evolving totality of learned and shared meanings, rituals, norms, and traditions among the members of an organization or society.

culture shock: A pervasive feeling of anxiety resulting from one's presence in a new, unfamiliar culture.

currency and capital flow controls: All protectionist activities involving the control of capital and hard currency flows in and out of a particular country.

customs union: A market composed of member countries imposing identical import duties and sharing import regulations.

D

data collection instrument: The instrument used to collect data, such as a printed questionnaire, a paper-and-pencil measure, or an electronic measurement device.

decentering: The successive translation (by different translators) of an instrument between the original language and the language of administration with the purpose of obtaining an instrument that is closest in meaning to the original.

decision support system: A coordinated collection of data, systems, tools, and techniques, complemented by supporting software and hardware designed for the gathering and interpretation of business and environmental data.

decline stage: The stage of the international product life cycle in which products are rapidly losing ground to new technologies or product alternatives, causing a decrease in sales and profits.

decoding: The process whereby the target consumer receives the message from the advertiser and translates it into meaningful information.

degree of product/service newness: The extent to which a product is new to the market in general or to a group of consumers.

Delphi method: A method of forecasting sales by asking a number of experts to estimate market performance, aggregating the results, and sharing this information with the said experts; the process is repeated several times, until a consensus is reached.

demographic segmentation: The process of identifying market segments based on age, gender, race, income, education, occupation, social class, life cycle stage, and household size.

department stores: General retailers that offer a broad variety of goods and wide assortments.

depth interview: A qualitative research method involving extensive interviews aimed at discovering consumer motivations, feelings, and attitudes toward an issue of concern to the sponsor using unstructured interrogation.

descriptive research: All research methods observing or describing phenomena.

design counterfeiting: Copying designs or scents of another company.

designing and developing the product: Developing product prototypes and giving the product a name, a brand identity, and a marketing mix; a step in the new product development process.

developed countries (also high-income countries): Highly industrialized countries with well-developed service sectors, mature markets, and intense competition; they are characterized by the World Bank as high-income, with a GNP per capita of US$9,266 and greater.

developing and evaluating concepts: Determining how consumers will perceive and use a new product; a step in the new product development process.

developing countries (also low-income countries): Countries that are primarily agrarian, often neglected or underserved by large multinationals, and characterized by the World Bank as low-income countries, with a GNP per capita of less than US$755.

differential exchange rate: The rate imposed by the local government to promote imports of desirable and necessary goods; it also can be the difference between the black market exchange rate and the official government rate.

differential response: The extent to which international market segments respond differently to marketing strategies.

differentiated targeting: A targeting strategy identifying market segments with different preferences for a particular product category and targeting each segment with different brands and different marketing strategies.

diffusion process: The process by which a product is adopted by consumers worldwide.

direct exporting: An export entry mode whereby a firm handles its own exports, usually with the help of an in-house exporting department.

direct mail retailing: Retailing using catalogs and other direct mail, instead of brick-and-mortar stores.

direct selling: Selling that involves a salesperson, typically an independent distributor, contacting a consumer at a convenient location—at his or her home or workplace, demonstrating product use and benefits, taking orders, and delivering the merchandise.

distribution alliance: A nonequity relationship between two firms, in which one firm handles the other's distribution or some aspect of the distribution process.

domestic marketing: Marketing that is focused solely on domestic consumers and on the home-country environment.

domestication: The process initiated by a foreign government leading to the gradual transfer of ownership and management to locals.

drive-to-maturity stage: A stage in economic development, described by Rostow, as characterized by the technological and entrepreneurial skill to produce anything society chooses to produce.

drivers in the business environment: Elements in the business environment, such as competition, technology, and labor costs, causing the firm to become involved internationally.

dumping: Selling products below cost to get rid of excess inventory and to undermine competition.

dynamic incremental pricing: A pricing strategy whereby a company assumes that it will have certain fixed costs whether or not it exports its products overseas and does not factor in its international price marketing and promotion costs or its full overhead for domestic distribution.

dynamically continuous innovation: Innovation that does not alter significantly consumer behavior but still entails a change in the consumption pattern.

E

early adopters: Consumers who purchase a product early in its product life cycle and who tend to be opinion leaders in their communities who take risks, but with greater discernment than innovators; they account for 13.5 percent of the total market.

early majority: Consumers who enjoy the status of being among the first in their peer group to purchase a popular product; they account for 34 percent of the total market.

ecology: The manner in which society adapts to its habitat (i.e., the distribution of resources within an industrialized country versus a developing country); the desire for efficiency, space-saving devices, or green products.

Economic Community of West African States (ECOWAS): A free trade agreement that strives to achieve economic integration in West Africa; domination by Nigeria, civil unrest, and regional conflict have served as impediments in the group's success. (See www.ecowas.int.)

education allowance: A compensation incentive whereby the company agrees to cover the cost of children's education at an international private school in the country of assignment or at a boarding school in the expatriate's home country.

electronic data interchange (EDI): Relationship whereby buying and selling firms are able to share important data on production, inventory, shipping, and purchasing.

electronic retailing: Selling through the Internet using websites to increase market penetration and market diversification; also called interactive home shopping and Internet retailing.

embargo: The prohibition of all business deals with the country that is the target of the embargo that is endorsed or initiated by the company's home country.

emerging markets (also middle-income countries): Countries that are developing rapidly and have great economic potential; the World Bank characterizes them as middle-income countries, with a GNP per capita of US$766 to US$9,265.

emic instrument: A data collection instrument constructed for each nationality to measure a particular factor; it is the best measure for culture-specific phenomena.

employment protection: Protection of local employment by not granting import licenses for products competing with similar locally produced goods.

encoding: The process whereby the advertiser puts the company's message about the product into words and images that are aimed at the target consumer.

enculturation: The process by which individuals learn the beliefs and behaviors endorsed by their own culture.

entry mode: The approach to international expansion a company chooses based on desired control and on the risk it can afford.

established channels: Distribution channels that already exist in a particular market.

ethnocentric orientation: Company strategies consistent with the belief that domestic strategies, techniques, and personnel are superior to foreign ones and therefore provide the most effective framework for the company's overseas involvement; companies adopting this perspective view international operations and customers as secondary to domestic operations and customers.

ethnocentrism: The belief that one's culture is superior to another and that strategies used in one's home country (presumably a developed country) will work just as well internationally.

etic instrument: A culture-free data collection instrument that can be used to measure the same phenomenon in different cultures.

Euroland: The nickname of the European Monetary Union. (See www.europa.eu.int.)

European Atomic Energy Community: A precursor to the European Union, it addressed issues related to the use and control of atomic energy.

European Bank for Reconstruction and Development: A bank headquartered in London, United Kingdom, which has as main goals reforming and strengthening markets in the transition economies of Central and Eastern Europe. (See www.ebrd.com.)

European Central Bank: The bank of the European Union charged with enacting monetary policy for the twelve countries that share a common currency, the euro. (See www.europa.eu.int.)

European Coal and Steel Community: An agreement that represents an early attempt at tariff reduction between members of the European Union.

European Commission: The body of the European Union in charge of initiating and supervising the execution of laws and policies. (See www.europa.eu.int.)

European Council: The highest policy-making body of the European Union. (See www.europa.eu.int.)

European Court of Justice: The Supreme Court–equivalent of the European Union. (See www.europa.eu.int.)

European Exchange Rate Mechanism (ERM): A precursor of the euro, a float that included the euro, the then-theoretical currency of the European Union; the float allowed for variability in each currency.

European Free Trade Association (EFTA): A free trade agreement between Iceland, Liechtenstein, Norway, and Switzerland; previously, Sweden, Austria, and Finland were also members, but they have since joined the European Union. (See www.efta.int.)

European Monetary Union (EMU): A union composed of the members of the European Union who adhere to the joint monetary policy enacted by the European Central Bank and who have adopted the euro as the single currency. (See www.europa.eu.int.)

European Parliament: The Parliament of the European Union, composed of members elected every 5 years by direct universal suffrage; seats in the Parliament are allocated among member states based on their population. (See www.europa.eu.int.)

European Union: An economic union consisting of most of the Western European countries; it is the only agreement that has achieved full economic integration and is now pursuing political integration. (See www.europa.eu.int.)

event sponsorship: The financial support of cultural or sports-related events; companies use these events to get positive publicity.

exclusives: The norms that refer to activities that are appropriate only for locals and from which individuals from a foreign country are excluded.

executive-judgment method: A budgeting process that allocates the company's advertising budget based on the opinions of executives.

expatriate: An employee working in a foreign country.

experimental research: Research that examines cause-and-effect relationships; it has the highest validity and reliability of all types of research.

exploratory research: Research conducted early in the research process that helps further define a problem or identify additional problems that need to be investigated.

export management companies: Companies specializing in the export function for client companies in a particular industry.

export marketing: Involvement in international marketing limited to the exporting function; although the firm actively seeks international clients, it considers the international market an extension of the domestic market and does not give it special consideration.

export merchants: Intermediaries who take title to and possession of the products they carry; they are responsible for shipping and marketing the products to the target market.

Export Trading Company Act: Legislation, passed in 1982, that encourages the formation of export trading companies by competing firms to promote U.S. exports without violating antitrust regulation.

expropriation: The foreign government seizure of company assets with partial reimbursement, usually not at market value.

extensible markup language (XML): System that encodes data on production, inventory, shipping, and purchasing and processes the content without human intervention, sharing it with the company's supply chain partners.

external secondary data: Data collected for purposes other than the problem at hand.

F

feedback: Information regarding the effectiveness of a company's message.

femininity: The degree to which a national culture is characterized by nurturing, rather than assertive, values.

feudalism: A stage in economic and political development, which, according to Marxist-Leninist theory, is characterized by the dominance of feudal lords, who own the land and its dwellers.

firm-specific drivers: Elements specific to the firm, such as product life cycle, causing the firm to become involved internationally.

focus group interview: A qualitative research approach investigating a research question using a moderator to guide discussion within a group of subjects recruited to meet certain characteristics.

food retailers: Retailers selling primarily food products.

foreign consumer culture positioning: The positioning of a particular brand as symbolic of a desired foreign culture.

Foreign Corrupt Practices Act: Legislation that makes it illegal for companies and their representatives to bribe government officials and other politicians or candidates to political office, either directly or through third parties.

foreign exchange permit: A permit that is generally provided by a country's Central Bank in conjunction with the Department of Trade (Ministry of Foreign Trade) and that gives priority to imports of goods considered to be in the national interest.

foreign trade zones: Tax-free areas in a country that are not considered part of the respective country in terms of import regulations and restrictions.

foreign-country intermediaries: Intermediaries who help distribute products in a target foreign market.

formal controls: Systematic controls, such as performance standards and measurement, used in international marketing to ensure that international company operations are in line with company goals and objectives.

franchisee: The recipient party to a franchise who pays royalties in return for the right to use the franchisor's brand name and related trademarks.

franchising: The main international entry mode for the service industry, whereby the franchisor gives the franchisee the right to use its brand name and all related trademarks in return for royalties.

franchisor: The owner of the franchise who gives the franchisee the right to use its brand name and all related trademarks and its business know-how, such as secret recipes and customer interfacing techniques, in return for royalties.

free trade agreement: An agreement whose goal is the reduction in, or even elimination of, customs duties and other trade barriers on all goods and services traded between member countries.

Free Trade Area of the Americas (FTAA): A plan to create a free trade association by 2005 that would comprise all member countries of the 34 democratic nations of North, Central, and South America. (See www.ftaa-alca.org.)

functional equivalence: The difference in the purposes for which products may be used in different country environments.

G

gender roles: The roles that women and men are expected to hold in a society.

General Agreement on Tariffs and Trade (GATT): The international trade agreement promoting trade and eliminating trade barriers, opening markets to international business, and creating a forum for resolving trade disputes; GATT issues are now addressed by the World Trade Organization. (See www.wto.org.)

general merchandise discount stores: Retailers that sell high volumes of merchandise, offer limited service, and charge lower prices.

generating new product ideas: Seeking ideas using different strategies as the first step in the new product development process.

geocentric orientation: Company strategies that are consistent with the belief that the entire world, without national and regional distinctions, constitutes a potential market with identifiable, homogeneous segments that need to be addressed differentially.

geographic segmentation: Market segmentation based on geographic location, such as country or region.

gift giving: The norms regarding the gifts that are appropriate to give to others.

global campaign: A worldwide standardized advertising campaign that is not adjusted to different target markets.

global consumer culture positioning: Marketing programs appealing to individuals who want to be part of a global consumer culture by purchasing a brand that is a symbol of that culture.

global consumers: The homogeneous consumer group worldwide sharing similar interests and product/brand preferences.

global elite: A psychodemographic group worldwide characterized by high income and desire for status brands and exclusive distribution.

global gay and lesbian segment: A psychodemographic group worldwide characterized by higher disposable income and high loyalty to brands positioned as gay-friendly.

global localization: The practice of global branding and localized marketing adaptation to differences in local culture, legislation, and even production capabilities.

global marketing: International marketing activities that do not have a country or region focus and that are possibly due to the emergence of global consumer segments and efficient global allocation of company talent and resources.

global standardization: The standardization of products across markets and, ultimately, to the standardization of the marketing mix worldwide; more commonly called glocalization.

global youth segment: A psychodemographic global group of teenagers considered to be astute consumers with precise desires for brand name clothing products and entertainment.

glocalization: The standardization of products across markets and, ultimately, the standardization of the marketing mix worldwide; also called global standardization.

grey market: A distribution system not authorized by the manufacturer whereby the products purchased in a low-price market are diverted to other markets; also called parallel imports.

greenfielding: Developing a brand new subsidiary.

growth stage: The stage of the international product life cycle characterized by increasing competition and rapid product adoption by the target market.

H

haptics: The use of touch while conversing.

hard currency: Currency that is accepted for payment by any International seller.

high mass consumption: A stage in economic development, described by Rostow, as characterized by leading sectors shifting toward durable goods.

high-context cultures: Cultures in which the context of a message—the message source, the source's standing in society or in a group, his or her expertise, tone of voice, and body language—are all meaningful parts of the message.

high-income countries: Highly industrialized countries with well-developed service sectors, mature markets, and intense competition, with a GNP per capita of US$10,726 and greater.

historical method: An approach to budgeting that is based on past expenditures, usually giving more weight to more recent expenditures.

home-country intermediaries: Intermediaries in the home country.

home-country laws: Laws of a company's home country that follow the international company all over the world.

home-country national: A local employee who works in his or her home country for the international corporation.

home-leave allowance: A compensation incentive that pays for the expatriate and his or her family to vacation in the home country.

host-country laws: Local laws; laws of the different countries where a company operates.

host-country national: A local employee who works in his or her home country for the international corporation.

housing allowance: A compensation incentive whereby the company covers part of or the entire cost of housing for the expatriate employee while abroad.

hypermarkets: Large retail stores that combine supermarket, discount, and warehouse retailing principles.

I

ideology: The manner in which individuals relate to their environment and to others, including their attitudes toward time, space, possessions, and referent others.

image advertising: An advertising campaign that enhances perceptions of a company in a given market by creating a positive impression on the target consumers.

imperatives: The norms referring to what individuals must or must not do in a certain culture.

imperialism: A stage of economic and political development, in which, according to Marxist-Leninist theory, capital loses its national identity by crossing borders.

import jobber: A merchant intermediary who purchases commodity goods from the manufacturer to sell to the trade (wholesaler, retailer, business-to-business client) in the target market.

import quota: The maximum quantity (unit limit) or value of a product that may be imported during a specified period.

import/export: Analysis research that aids companies in identifying the necessary logistics that serve their needs in a timely and cost-effective manner.

Incoterms (International Commercial Terms): Terms of sale used in transactions.

indirect exporting: An export entry mode whereby a company sells its products in the company's home country to intermediaries who, in turn, sell the product overseas.

individual personality: Enduring traits that characterize individuals, motivating them to act or react to external stimuli in a particular manner.

individualism: The degree to which people in a country prefer to act as individuals, in their self-interest.

infant industry argument: A protectionist strategy aimed at protecting a national industry in its infancy from powerful international competitors.

infomercials: Long television advertisements (one-half to 1 full hour in length) that are positioned as programming.

informal controls: Systematic controls, such as dialogue between the headquarters and the international field operations, used in international marketing to ensure that international company operations are in line with company goals and objectives.

innovation: A product new to the world.

innovators: Risk takers who can afford to pay the higher purchase price charged by companies during the introduction stage of a product; they account for 2.5 percent of the total market.

intellectual property rights: Laws protecting the rights of the inventor or of the firm employing the inventor to use and sell an invention for a specified period of time.

interactive home shopping: A venue for selling through the Internet using websites to increase market penetration and market diversification; also called electronic retailing and Internet retailing.

interactive medium: A nonpersonal channel of communication such as a Web page or a computer terminal on the retailer's premises.

Inter-American Development Bank: A bank headquartered in Washington, D.C., aiding companies in the Americas that do not ordinarily deal with the large development banks; this bank is involved in funding private sector projects, modernizing governments, strengthening institutions, and eliminating technology barriers. (See www.iadb.org.)

internal secondary data: Data collected by a company to address a problem not related to the current research question.

international buyer-seller relationship: The distribution between the buyer and the individual involved in personal selling.

international communication process: The communication process that takes place between the product sponsor and the international target market.

international division structure: An organizational structure whereby firms have separate domestic and international divisions.

international laws: Rules and regulations that countries agree to abide by, addressing agreements among countries with regard to trade, protection of property, and other issues in the political and economic sphere.

international market potential studies: Studies conducted to evaluate the potential that a particular country offers for a company.

international marketing: The processes involved in the creation, production, distribution, promotion, and pricing of products, services, ideas, and experiences for international markets; these processes require a substantial focus on international consumers in a particular country or countries.

international marketing research: The systematic design, collection, recording, analysis, interpretation, and reporting of information pertinent to a particular marketing decision facing a company operating internationally.

International Monetary Fund (IMF): Traditionally the lender of last resort; the IMF also has assumed the position of mediator between debtors and creditors, imposing stabilization programs; debt-reduction guidelines; ceilings for bank credit, budget deficit, borrowing, and international reserves; and development programs for borrowing countries. (See www.imf.org.)

international product life cycle (IPLC): A product life cycle theory, which states that firms from developed countries engage in domestic production in the early stage of the product life cycle, marketing the product to industrialized countries; as the product reaches maturity, product specifications and the manufacturing process stabilize, price competition becomes intense, and markets in developing countries become essential to the firm's success.

international promotional mix: The different modes of communication with international consumers about products and services, using international advertising, international sales force management, international sales promotion, public relations, and publicity.

international public relations: A concerted effort on the part of a company to generate goodwill among international publics that are essential to the company; its main purpose is to generate positive publicity about the company.

Internet retailing: Selling through the Internet using websites to increase market penetration and market diversification; also called interactive home shopping and electronic retailing.

introduction stage: The first stage of the international product life cycle when products are developed and marketed in industrialized countries.

Islamic law: A system of law based on the interpretation of the Koran, Islam's holy book, and on interpretations of the practices and sayings of the prophet Muhammad.

ISO 9000 certification: Certification that specifies that the organization must meet customer and regulatory requirements and follow its policies and procedures while advancing quality through continuous improvement.

ISO 14000 certification: Certification that a company follows guidelines that discourage firms from engaging in hazardous environmental practices, and ensures that corporate policies promoting environmentally sound, efficiency-embracing, innovative technologies and processes will contribute to establishing twenty-first century production and distribution systems that are far less environmentally degrading.

J

joint venture: A corporate entity created with the participation of two companies that share equity, capital, and labor.

jurisdiction: The country and legal body where a particular dispute should be adjudicated, according to the country's law, or according to the legal body's principles, respectively.

jury of expert opinion: An approach to sales forecasting based on the opinion of different experts.

K

keiretsu: A Japanese trading firm that consists of families of firms with interlocking stakes in one another.

kinesics: The movement of part of the body to communicate.

L

lag countries: Countries where a product or service is adopted after already being introduced in lead countries.

laggards: Consumers who are the last to adopt new products and do so only in late maturity because they are risk averse and conservative in their spending; they account for 16 percent of the total market.

language: The vehicle used for communication in a particular culture; includes spoken and written language and nonverbal communication.

late majority: Individuals of limited means who are likely to adopt products only if the products are widely popular and the risk associated with buying them is minimal; they account for 34 percent of the total market.

Latin American Free Trade Association (LAFTA): An attempt by Latin American countries to establish a free trade association; its demise is attributed to the economic disparity between member countries and to protectionist policies.

Latin American Integration Association (LAIA): Latin America's largest trade agreement striving to establish bilateral and multilateral agreements aimed at reducing tariff and nontariff barriers.

launching the product internationally: Introducing a new product to the international market as the last step in the new product development process.

lead countries: Countries where a product or service is first introduced and adopted.

licensee: The purchaser of the license who pays royalties to the licensor for the rights to use the licensor's technology, know-how, and brand name.

licensing: An international entry mode that involves a licensor, who shares the brand name, technology, and know-how with a licensee in return for royalties.

licensor: The owner of a product license who agrees to share know-how, technology, and brand name with the licensee in return for royalties.

local campaign: An advertising campaign that is tailored to local needs; especially used in markets that media cannot easily reach.

local consumer culture positioning: Positioning that associates the brand with local cultural meanings, reflecting the local culture, and portrayed as consumed by locals and depicted as locally produced for local people.

local content requirement: A protectionist measure requiring that a certain percentage of the products imported are locally produced.

local pricing: A pricing strategy in which different prices are charged in different markets, reflecting differences in consumer purchase power, distribution costs, tax systems, or other market traits.

logistics alliances: Distribution alliances between two firms involving product transportation and warehousing.

low-context cultures: Cultures in which what is said is precisely what is meant so that the verbal message carries the full meaning of the sentence.

low-income countries: Countries that are primarily agrarian, with a GNP per capita of less than US$875.

M

Maastricht Treaty: The treaty credited with establishing the European Union, eliminating all tariffs; establishing common external tariffs; allowing for the free movement of capital and labor within its territory; and setting regulations involving common trade policies, common agricultural and industrial policies, and common monetary and fiscal policies between member countries. (See www.europa.eu.int.)

managing agent: A foreign agent who has an exclusive arrangement with a company, representing its operations in a particular country.

mandatory adaptation: The adaptation of products to local requirements so that the products can legally and physically function in the specific country environment.

manufacturer's export agents: Agents in the firm's home country handling the exporting function of a certain manufacturer on a commission, per deal, basis.

manufacturer's representative: An agent who represents the manufacturer exclusively in the foreign target market.

manufacturing alliance: A nonequity relationship between two firms, in which one firm handles the other's manufacturing or some aspect of the manufacturing process.

maquiladora: Customs-privileged contract manufacturing facilities in Mexico that take advantage of low-cost labor.

market-based transfer pricing: A pricing strategy used in intra-firm sales for commercial transactions between units of the same corporation, within or beyond the national borders of the parent company, whereby products are priced at market cost, rather than at the cost incurred by the company.

marketing alliance: A nonequity relationship between two firms, in which one firm handles the other's marketing or some aspect of the marketing process.

Marxist-Leninist development model: A development model attributed to Karl Marx and Vladimir Lenin that maps the development of society from an agrarian, traditional society to a society characterized by shared ownership of the means and outcomes of production and an equitable resource allocation; advancement from one stage to another is based on class struggle and transfer of ownership from one class to another and, ultimately, to the state.

masculinity: The degree to which a national culture is characterized by assertiveness, rather than nurturing.

materialism: Individuals' degree of concern with material possessions.

matrix structure: An organizational structure whereby each operational unit reports to both region/country managers and product managers.

maturity stage: A stage of the international product life cycle characterized by a slowdown in sales growth as the product is adopted by most target consumers and by a leveling or decline in profits primarily due to intense price competition.

measurability: The ability to estimate the size of a market segment.

media availability: The extent to which media are available to communicate with target consumers.

media infrastructure: The media vehicles and their structure in an international target market.

media reliability: The probability of the media to air advertising messages on time, at an acceptable quality, and with the agreed on frequency.

media research: Studies that evaluate media availability and appropriateness of the medium for a company's message.

media restrictions: Legal or self-imposed restrictions on the types and the number of advertisements aired or published.

mediation: Nonbinding procedure for conflict resolution involving an independent third party.

medium/media: The channel(s) of communication that a company uses to send to the target consumer a message about its product or services.

merchant middlemen GL>Different intermediaries who carry the manufacturer's product line in a particular country; they both carry title to and have physical possession of the products they distribute.

middle-income countries: Countries with emerging markets and great potential, with a GNP per capita of US$875 to US$10,725.

Ministry of Foreign Affairs: The international institutional equivalent of the Department of State; it coordinates a country's involvement in international relations.

Ministry of Trade: The international institutional equivalent of the Department of Commerce; it coordinates a country's international trade relations.

modification: The alteration of an existing company product.

modular adaptation: The localization across markets of the product by offering parts (modules) that can be assembled worldwide in different configurations, depending on the needs of the market.

modular campaign: An advertising campaign that provides a template that is varied and customized from market to market.

monetary union: A form of economic integration characterized by the establishment of a common central bank enacting monetary policy for the group.

monochronic time: The interpretation of time as linear, such that individuals do one thing at a time, and in sequence.

monopolistic capitalism: A stage of economic and political development, in which, according to Marxist-Leninist theory, multinational companies establish monopolies and expand internationally with the goal of subjugating developing countries.

mother henning: Using the distribution system of exporters with established systems of selling abroad who agree to handle the export function of a noncompeting (but not necessarily unrelated) company on a contractual basis; also called piggybacking and cooperative exporting.

moving allowance: A compensation incentive whereby the company pays for the household moving expenses to the country of assignment and, at the end of the assignment, back to the home country.

multilateral forums and agreements: Agreements that involve multiple countries, have an informal structure, and do not necessarily have regional integration as their goal.

multilevel marketing: Using acquaintance networks through an alternative distribution structure for the purpose of distribution; also called network marketing.

multinational marketing: Marketing in different countries without coordinating across operations.

N

national and regional character: A set of behavior and personality characteristics shared by individuals of a certain country or region.

nationalism: An expression of fierce nationalist sentiment in a country where a company is operating, which poses an implicit threat to the company and its operations.

nationalization: The takeover of company assets by a foreign government with the aim of creating a government-run industry.

network marketing: Using acquaintance networks through an alternative distribution structure for the purpose of distribution; also called multilevel marketing.

new item in an existing product line: A new brand that the company offers to the market in an existing product line.

new line: A new product category offered by the company.

new product to existing company: A new product that the company offers to the market; the product competes with similar competitor offerings.

new product to existing market: A product never before offered to the market.

news releases: Statements issued to the public to introduce a new product, touting its advantages; any other information shared with the media.

noise: All the potential interference in the communication process.

nonautomatic import license: A license issued on a discretionary basis to restrict imports of a given product or from a particular country.

nonmandatory adaptation: The strategy of adapting a product to better meet the needs of the local market, without being required to do so.

nonpersonal medium: A channel of communication such as a print medium, a broadcast medium, or an interactive medium that does not involve contact between the seller and the consumer.

nontariff barriers: All measures, other than traditional tariffs, used to distort trade flows, used to increase prices of imports, and thus favor domestic over foreign products.

nonverbal communication: All communication that is not written or spoken; includes body language, gestures, facial expressions, eye contact, and silence.

Norazi agent: An export agent dealing in illegal and grey market products.

norms: Rules that dictate what is right or wrong, acceptable or unacceptable in a society.

North American Free Trade Agreement (NAFTA): An agreement between the United States, Canada, and Mexico, aiming to eliminate tariff and nontariff barriers between the countries. (See www.nafta-sec-alena.org.)

North Atlantic Treaty Organization (NATO): A military agreement between countries that were initially not part of the Soviet Bloc. (See www.nato.int.)

O

objective-and-task method: An advertising budgeting method in which the company first identifies advertising goals, conducts research to determine the cost of achieving the respective goals, and allocates the necessary sum for the purpose.

observational research: A research approach used frequently in international markets, whereby subjects are observed interacting with a product and the related components of the marketing mix.

obstacles to internationalization: Impediments that the firm may encounter in the process of internationalizing.

oculesics: The use or avoidance of eye contact during communication.

off-price retailers: Retailers who sell brand name products and designer merchandise below regular retail prices.

offset purchase: A large, hard-currency purchase, such as the purchase of defense equipment, airplanes, telecommunications networks, railway or road building and other expensive civil engineering projects whereby the seller agrees, in return to purchase products that are valued at a certain percentage of the sale.

offshore assembly plants: Plants located in customs-privileged bonded areas in countries with low labor costs, where products are manipulated and re-exported.

olfactions: The use of odors to convey messages.

open-ended questions: Questions with free-format responses that the respondent can address as he or she sees appropriate.

order getter: Individual who actively generates potential leads and persuades customers to purchase the firm's products.

order taker: An individual who processes routine sales orders from the customer.

orderly market arrangements: Protectionist measures involving intricate processes for establishing quotas in the textile and apparel industries.

Organization for Economic Co-operation and Development (OECD): An economic multilateral agreement. (See www.oecdobserver.org.)

Organization of the Petroleum Exporting Countries (OPEC): Industry-specific (oil) multilateral agreement aimed at managing the output and price of oil. (See www.opec.com.)

organizational culture: The shared norms and values that guide collective behavior in organizations and enduring traits that characterize individuals, motivating them to act or react to stimuli in the organization and in the environment in a particular manner.

organizational design: The organization of reporting and coordination within a company.

organizational structure: The outcome of the organization of reporting and coordination within a company.

orientations: Individuals' positioning relative to their counterparts during conversation.

outsourcing (also known as offshoring): The strategic use of outside resources to perform activities that are usually handled by internal staff and resources.

Overseas Private Investment Corporation (OPIC): U.S. government corporation that provides loans, guarantees, and insurance to U.S. corporations investing in countries that present high political risk.

P

paralinguistics: The nonverbal aspects of speech that include intonation, accents, and the quality of voice.

parallel barter: A form of trade that involves two exchanges that are paid for in cash; it involves two parallel contracts whereby the seller agrees to purchase products that are usually unrelated to its business from the buyer and sell them on international markets; also called counterpurchase.

parallel imports: A distribution system not authorized by the manufacturer whereby the products purchased in a low-price market are diverted to other markets; also called grey market.

parallel translation: The process of translating the original instrument by different translators and comparing the translations.

paratariff measures: Additional, nontariff fees that increase the costs of imports in a manner similar to tariffs.

patent: Protection of the rights of the inventor or of the firm employing the inventor to use and sell an invention for a specified period of time.

penetration pricing: A pricing strategy in which a product is first priced below the price of competitors' products to quickly penetrate the market at the competitors' expense and then raised to target levels.

percent-of-sales method: An advertising budgeting method that determines the total budget allocated to advertising on the basis of past or projected sales.

performance standards: A priori measures against which firm performance is evaluated.

performing a product business analysis: Calculating projected costs such as return on investment and cash flow and determining the fixed and variable costs for the long term.

Permanent-Normal-Trade-Relations status (PNTR): Trade status that grants equal tax treatment on imported products from most countries, with the exception of rogue nations.

personal medium: A communication channel that involves contact between the seller and the consumer.

piggybacking: Using the distribution system of exporters with established systems of selling abroad who agree to handle the export function of a noncompeting (but not necessarily unrelated) company on a contractual basis; also called mother henning and cooperative exporting.

plant/warehouse location studies: Studies that evaluate the appropriateness of plant or warehouse location to ensure that it is in accordance with the limitations of the national environment and with the needs of a company.

point-of-sale–based projections: Market share and other relevant market dimensions assessed by the use of store scanners in weekly and biweekly store audits.

political risk: The risk associated with actions of local, regional, and parastatal governing bodies affecting the international company, and with the overall economic and political stability within a particular country.

political union: The highest level of regional integration; it assumes a viable economic integration and involves the establishment of viable common governing bodies, legislative bodies, and enforcement powers.

polycentric orientation: Company strategies predicated on the assumption that each country's market is unique and should be addressed individually, with a country-specific marketing mix.

polychronic time: The interpretation of time as fluid, such that individuals can accomplish multiple tasks at once.

post-adjustment: A compensation incentive whereby the company adjusts expatriate salaries to reflect the cost of living in the new environment at standards in the expatriate's home country; also called cost-of-living adjustment.

postures: Individuals' physical postures during conversation.

power distance: The manner in which interpersonal relationships are formed when differences in power are perceived.

press releases: Statements issued to the press to communicate news about a company and its products.

price controls: Strategies requiring a product to sell for a particular price in the local market; price control strategies are typically used to increase the prices of imports to match the minimum prices of local competition.

price elasticity studies: Studies examining the extent to which a particular market is price sensitive.

price/quality positioning: A strategy whereby products and services are positioned as offering the best value for the money.

primary data: Data collected for the purpose of addressing the problem at hand.

primitive society: The first stage of economic and political development, characterized, according to Marxist-Leninist theory, by the joint tribal ownership of primitive means of production centered on agricultural tasks.

print medium: A nonpersonal channel of communication such as a newspaper, magazine, billboard, pamphlet, or point-of-purchase display.

private labels: Brands sold under the brand name of a retailer or some other distributor.

product class positioning: A strategy used to differentiate a company as a leader in a product category, as defined by the respective company.

product consistency: The extent to which a company's different product lines are related, use the same distribution channels, and have the same final consumers.

product depth: The number of different offerings for a particular brand.

product division structure: An organizational structure whereby subsidiaries report to the product division (strategic business unit) with responsibility for the particular products.

product length: The total number of brands in the product mix.

product line: All the brands the company offers in the same product category.

product mix: The complete assortment of products that a company offers to its target international consumers.

product packaging design studies: Studies that evaluate consumers' reaction to a package, the extent to which the package adequately communicates information to the consumer, and the distribution implications of the package.

product placement: The strategy of placing brands in movies with the purpose of promoting the products to viewers.

product testing: Studies that estimate product preference and performance in a given market.

product user positioning: A positioning strategy that focuses on the product user, rather than on the product.

product width: The total number of product lines that a company offers to its target international consumers.

product-country stereotypes: Product-specific stereotypes that associate the country of origin as a certification of quality.

profit analyses studies: Studies that estimate product profit in specific international markets.

protection of markets with excess labor: The erection of barriers to imports of products competing with local offerings in an effort to protect local jobs.

protection of markets with excess productive capacity: A protectionist measure used to prevent foreign buyouts, invoking the protection of local labor.

protectionism: All actions by national and local governments aimed at protecting local markets from foreign competitors.

proxemics: The amount of physical space individuals require to feel comfortable in the process of communication.

psychographic segmentation: The use of values, attitudes, interests, and other cultural variables to segment consumers.

public appearances: Company representatives' public involvement, speaking on behalf of the international firm and its products.

publicity: Any communication about a company and the company's products that the company does not pay for; may be positive or negative.

purchase behavior studies: Research aimed at evaluating consumers' reaction to and interaction with a company's products.

Q

qualitative research: Research that uses nonsystematic processes, such as nonrandom sampling and open-ended data, as well as involves the researcher as participant.

quantitative research: A structured type of research that involves either descriptive research approaches, such as survey research, or causal research approaches, such as experiments.

R

radical innovation: The creation of new industries or new standards of management, manufacturing, and servicing that represent fundamental changes for consumers, entailing departures from established consumption.

receiver: The target market that receives the advertising message from a sender.

regiocentric orientation: Company strategies that view world regions as distinct markets that share economic, political, and cultural traits that will respond to a regionwide marketing approach.

regional standardization: The use of a uniform marketing strategy within a particular region.

reliability: The extent to which data is likely to be free from random error and yield consistent results.

religion: A society's relationship to the supernatural.

repatriation: The return of the expatriate employee to the home country.

repatriation allowance: A compensation incentive whereby the company covers expenses involved in moving back to the home country, as well as a large sum paid for successfully completing the international assignment in some cases.

research approach: The method used to collect data.

reverse culture shock: Anxiety experienced after returning to the home country, associated with a longing for the international environment left behind and with the difficulty of readjusting to the home country and to corporate life at one's firm.

Rostow modernization model: An economic development model attributed to Rostow, according to which each stage of economic advance is a function of productivity, economic exchange, technological improvements, and income.

S

sales force compensation, quota, and territory studies: Different studies pertaining to personal selling activities; they are crucial in helping to determine the appropriate strategies for certain international markets.

sales force composite estimates: Research studies wherein sales forecasts are based on the personal observations and forecasts of the local sales force.

sales forecast: Projected sales for a particular territory.

sales potential studies: Studies forecasting optimal sales performance.

sales promotion: Sponsored communications to the target consumer or trade segment that stimulate purchases or improve relationships with intermediaries.

sample size: The number of study participants necessary to obtain a high study reliability.

sampling frame: The list from which sample units are selected.

sampling procedure: A decision involving the selection of sampling units.

sampling unit: The entity included in the study; it may be individuals or representatives belonging to particular groups.

sanctions: Punitive trade restrictions applied by a country or a group of countries against another country for noncompliance.

screening new product ideas: Eliminating product ideas that do not fit with the target consumers and the overall mission of the organization.

secondary data: Data collected to address a problem other than the problem at hand.

segmentation: The process of identifying consumers and international markets that are similar with regard to key traits, such as product-related needs and wants, and that would respond well to a product and related marketing mix.

self-reference criterion: Individuals' conscious and unconscious reference to their own national culture, to home-country norms and values, and to their knowledge and experience in the process of making decisions in the host country.

sender: The sponsor of an advertisement, usually represented by an advertising agency, who encodes the message into words and images and communicates it to the target market.

service barriers: Barriers encountered by services in different markets, such as requirements for local certification, local providers, and other requirements that favor local over international service providers.

simulated test marketing: Test marketing simulating purchase environments where samples of target consumers are observed in their product-related decision-making process.

skimming strategy: A pricing strategy in which a product is priced above that of competitors' products, when competition is minimal, to quickly recoup investments; consumers responding to skimming strategies are more concerned with quality, uniqueness, and status, rather than price.

slavery-based society: A stage of economic and political development, which, according to Marxist-Leninist theory, emerges as a result of tribes' dominance over other tribes: Dominant tribes claim ownership of conquered tribes and their property.

social structure: The organization of relationships in a society.

socialism: A transition stage of economic and political development, characterized, according to Marxist-Leninist theory, by the disappearance of private property and its replacement with collective, state property.

soft currency: Currency that is kept at a high artificial exchange rate, overvalued, and controlled by the national central bank.

sogo-shosha: A large Japanese trading company that specializes in providing intermediary services, risk reduction through extensive information channels, and significant financial assistance to manufacturing firms.

South African Customs Union (SACU): A customs union that includes Botswana, Swaziland, Lesotho, and Namibia. The group's main trading partner is South Africa, and member countries have partially or entirely tied their currencies to the South African rand.

Southern African Development Community (SADC): A free trade organization that promotes economic cooperation among a coalition of 14 of Africa's more affluent and developed nations, designed to foster increased economic and governmental stability through the use of collective peace-keeping forces.

Southern Cone Common Market (MERCOSUR): A free trade agreement in South America that has met with considerable success; MERCOSUR is presently in the process of becoming a viable customs union. (See www.mercosur.org.uy.)

special economic zones: Customs-privileged manufacturing facilities in China where multinational companies can take advantage of low-cost labor.

specialized markets: Markets that contain specialty stores specializing in a particular product category.

specialty stores: Retailers that offer a narrow product line and wide assortment.

spoken/written language: The language used in conversation/the language used in written communications.

stability over time: The extent to which preferences are stable, rather than changing, in a market segment.

standardization of the advertising strategy: The process of globalizing a company's promotional strategy so that it is uniform in all its target markets.

standardized pricing: A pricing strategy in which the same price is charged for a product regardless of local market conditions.

standards as barriers to trade: Trade barriers imposing performance, environmental, or other requirements that are primarily aimed at imports.

status concern: The value placed on symbols of status and on the attainment of high status in a society.

strategic alliance: Any type of relationship between one or more companies attempting to reach joint corporate and market-related goals; term used to refer to most nonequity alliances.

studies of premiums, coupons, and deals: Studies that help identify the practices in each target country where a promotion is planned by investigating the practice and legality of premiums, coupons, and special deals.

substantiality: The extent to which the market is large enough to warrant investment.

superstores: Large retailers such as combination stores or hypermarkets that sell food, drugs, and other products.

survey research: Descriptive research that involves the administration of personal, telephone, or mail questionnaires.

swing credits: Amounts paid within the framework of a clearing agreement by the country that owes money to the other when an imbalance occurs.

switch trading: The process of buying a party's position in a countertrade in exchange for hard currency and selling it to another customer.

T

take-off: A stage in economic development described by Rostow as one in which economic growth becomes the norm and improvements in production lead to the emergence of leading sectors.

target market: Consumers and international markets that are similar in aspects relevant to the company.

target marketing: The process of focusing on those segments that the company can serve most effectively and designing products, services, and marketing programs with these segments in mind.

tariffs: Taxes imposed on goods entering a country.

telemarketing: A personal channel of communication that involves a salesperson calling on consumers.

television home shopping: Retailing through cable channels selling to consumers in their homes, through infomercials, and through direct response advertising shown on broadcast and cable television.

television shopping networks: Cable channels that sell products to a television audience.

test marketing: Testing new-product performance in a limited area of a national or regional target market to estimate product performance in the respective country or region.

third-country national: An employee working in the country of assignment who is not a national of that country nor of the country in which the corporate headquarters of the company he or she works for are located.

time orientation: The manner in which individuals view time in relation to accomplishing tasks.

time series and econometric models: Models that use the data of past performance to predict future market demand.

trade secrets: Intellectual property such as know-how, formulas, special blends, and other elements that are not registered, and are thus not protected by law.

trade shows and exhibitions: Business-to-business promotions that usually are held annually in formats where companies purchase exhibit space to display and demonstrate their offerings to the target market.

trademark: A brand name, mark, symbol, motto, or slogan that identifies a particular manufacturer's brand and distinguishes it from the competitors' brands in the same product category.

Trade-Related Aspects of Intellectual Property Rights (TRIPS): An international agreement, under the World Trade Organization, that sets out minimum standards for the legal protection of intellectual property. (See www.wto.org.)

trading companies: Large companies that specialize in providing intermediary services, risk reduction through extensive information channels, and significant financial assistance to manufacturing firms.

traditional society: A stage in economic development defined by Rostow as one in which the economy is dominated by agriculture and relatively few exchange transactions occur.

transfer pricing: A pricing strategy used in intra-firm sales for commercial transactions between units of the same corporation, within or beyond the national borders of the parent company.

transitional society: A stage in the economic development process described by Rostow as characterized by increased productivity in agriculture and by the emergence of modern manufacturing.

trialability: The ability of the consumer to experience a product with minimal effort.

U

uncertainty avoidance: The extent to which individuals are threatened by uncertainty, risk, and ambiguous situations and thus adopt beliefs, behaviors, and institutions that help them to avoid the uncertainty.

undifferentiated targeting: A targeting strategy aiming the product at the market using a single strategy, regardless of the number of segments.

United Nations organizations: The totality of United Nations bodies created to maintain international peace and security; to develop relations among nations; to achieve international cooperation in solving international economic, social, cultural, or humanitarian problems; and to encourage respect for human rights and fundamental freedoms using the venues offered by the different UN organizations. (See www.un.org.)

United States Agency for International Development (USAID): An independent agency of the federal government that supports the economic development of and trade with developing countries aligned politically with the United States. (See www.usaid.gov.)

United States Department of Commerce: The U.S. governmental agency that oversees and promotes trade, offering export assistance and counseling to U.S. businesses involved in international trade, providing country information and country specialists, and bringing buyers and sellers together.

United States Department of State: The foreign affairs arm of the United States government, in charge of promoting relations with other governments. (See www.state.gov.)

usage segmentation: The process of segmenting markets based on the extent to which consumers are nonusers, occasional users, medium users, and heavy users of a product.

use positioning: The process of marketing a precise product application that differentiates it in the consumers' minds from other products that have a more general use.

user status segmentation: The process of determining the status as users of competitors' products, ex-users, potential users, first-time users, and regular users.

V

validity: The extent to which data collected is free from bias.

values: Enduring beliefs about a specific mode of conduct or desirable end-state that guide the selection or evaluation of behavior.

vending machines: Interactive modes of retailing convenience goods.

voluntary export restraints: A government's self-imposed export quotas to a particular country that are established to avoid more severe protectionist action by the respective importing country.

voluntary import expansion: A government's response to protectionist threats from another country whereby it agrees to open markets to imports and to increase foreign access to a domestic market to avoid more severe protectionist action.

W

warehouse clubs: Stores that require members to pay an annual fee operating in low-overhead, warehouse-type facilities, offering limited lines of brand name and dealer-brand groceries, apparel, appliances, and other goods at a substantial discount; also known as wholesale clubs.

Webb-Pomerene Associations: Associations of competing companies that are granted immunity from antitrust prosecution and that join resources and efforts to export internationally.

West African Economic and Monetary Union (WAEMU): One of the first attempts at economic integration in Africa. Although it is successful as a monetary union that has adopted a single currency, trade is quite modest within the WAEMU. (See www.dakarcom.com/EconReports/econ_waemu.htm.)

wholesale clubs: Stores that require members to pay an annual fee operating in low-overhead, warehouse-type facilities, offering limited lines of brand name and dealer-brand groceries, apparel, appliances, and other goods at a substantial discount; also known as warehouse clubs.

wholly owned subsidiary: The entry mode that affords the highest level of control and presents the highest level of risk to a company; it involves establishing a new company that is a citizen of the country where the subsidiary is established.

World Bank: The World Bank Group, headquartered in Washington, D.C., that is one of the largest sources of funds for development assistance aimed at the poorest countries worldwide. (See www.worldbank.org.)

World Trade Organization (WTO): The largest and most influential international trade organization whose primary goal is ensure the free flow of trade; WTO's agreements (negotiated and signed by member countries, ratified in their parliaments) represent trade rules and regulations and act as contracts guaranteeing countries trade rights and binding governments to trade policies. (See www.wto.org.)

Appendix

Index